From Networks to Netflix

Even as the television industry experiences significant transformation and disruption in the face of streaming and online delivery, the television channel itself persists. If anything, the television channel landscape has become more complex to navigate, as viewers can now choose between broadcast, cable, streaming, and premium services across a host of different platforms and devices. *From Networks to Netflix* provides an authoritative answer to that navigational need, helping students, instructors, and scholars understand these industrial changes through the lens of the channel. Through examination of emerging services like Hulu and Amazon Prime Video, investigation of YouTube channels and cable outlets like Freeform and Comedy Central, and critiques of broadcast giants like ABC and PBS, this book offers a concrete, tangible means of exploring the foundations of a changing industry.

Derek Johnson is Associate Professor of Media and Cultural Studies at the University of Wisconsin–Madison. He is the author of *Media Franchising: Creative License and Collaboration in the Culture Industries*, as well as the co-editor of *A Companion to Media Authorship, Making Media Work: Cultures of Management in the Entertainment Industries*, and the forthcoming *Point of Sale: Analyzing Media Retail*.

From Networks to Netflix

A Guide to Changing Channels

Edited by Derek Johnson

Routledge
Taylor & Francis Group

NEW YORK AND LONDON

First published 2018
by Routledge
711 Third Avenue, New York, NY 10017

and by Routledge
2 Park Square, Milton Park, Abingdon, Oxon OX14 4RN

Routledge is an imprint of the Taylor & Francis Group, an informa business

Library of Congress Cataloging-in-Publication Data
Names: Johnson, Derek, 1979– editor.
Title: From networks to Netflix : a guide to changing channels / [edited by] Derek Johnson.
Description: New York : Routledge, 2018. | Includes bibliographical references.
Identifiers: LCCN 2017038503 | ISBN 9781138998490 (hardback) | ISBN 9781138998513 (pbk.) | ISBN 9781315658643 (ebk.)
Subjects: LCSH: Television viewers—Effect of technological innovations on. | Television broadcasting—Technological innovations—United States. | Streaming technology (Telecommunications)
Classification: LCC HE8700.66.U6 F76 2018 | DDC 302.23/45—dc23
LC record available at https://lccn.loc.gov/2017038503

ISBN: 978-1-138-99849-0 (hbk)
ISBN: 978-1-138-99851-3 (pbk)
ISBN: 978-1-315-65864-3 (ebk)

Typeset in Warnock Pro
by Apex CoVantage, LLC

Channel Listings

Cable and Satellite Services

Introduction

Pop

Television Guides and Recommendations in a Changing Channel Landscape

Derek Johnson

In fall 2014, the US-based TV Guide Network announced it would abandon its name to become a new service called Pop. With ratings still "on the rise" for the existing channel, press releases described this shift not as a complete revolution so much as a "brand refresh"; carrying over interest in celebrity and celebration of television inherited from its predecessor, Pop would "focus on entertainment and the world of fandom." Channel president Brad Schwartz promised this embrace of pop culture would support quality programming "so good, it pops" ("Network" 2014). Yet one could also read a third kind of "pop" from this development: the bursting of linear models of television delivery in which many viewers relied upon print and electronic versions of *TV Guide* (or some other ordered list of channels and their scheduled program offerings) to navigate a complex channel environment.

When first published in 1953, *TV Guide* magazine featured in-color entertainment news stories about television stars and national network programming as well as black-and-white listings of the channels and programs scheduled for viewers throughout the day, with localized versions produced for over 100 different areas of the US. While *TV Guide* was the single most circulated national magazine in the 1960s (Farber and Bailey 2001, 397), the navigational need shared by television viewers supported similar efforts by *TV Choice* (United Kingdom), Figaro's *TV Magazine* (France), local newspapers, and many more publications across the world. Feature stories, spotlight reviews, and starred ratings all helped readers sort through their viewing choices—to which channels' curated programming lineups should they tune their televisions? This problem of choice would only exacerbate as new cable and satellite services joined terrestrial broadcast channels, beginning in the 1970s and expanding through the 1990s. Viewers required a guide in a crowded channel landscape.

The cable service TV Guide Network brought this navigational function to the television screen, experimenting with a mix of scrolling program listings and entertainment features. TV Guide Network was a channel about channels, providing viewers with a portal to the hundreds of choices available to them. As one of those choices, however, TV Guide faced pressure to thrive as an entertainment service in its own right; to attract carriage fees and advertising revenues, the channel needed to be more than a "waystation" for television viewing, but also a "destination" in and of itself (Motavalli 2004). Between 1999 and 2013, this pressure led to experimentation with new programming formats to run alongside—and eventually replace—its listings. The disappearance of TV Guide Network in favor of Pop, therefore, represents not just abandoned brand legacy, but more significantly the passage of an entire navigational apparatus for engaging with linear television. One might assume that viewers simply do not need this kind of guide anymore. Able to subscribe to, search for, and stream programs rather than relying on the linear programming schedules of broadcast and cable channels, the users of newer non-linear services like Netflix and Hulu have no need for program listings. Non-linear viewers can be their own guides.

However, as one of hundreds of channels fighting to sustain themselves in a mature television industry beset by challenges from digital upstarts, Pop's emergence from the vestiges of TV Guide reveals much about the forces currently transforming the experience and business of television. As much as the Pop story suggests the passage of linear guides from increasingly non-linear television screens, it also helps us see why channels—as well as guides for navigating them—remain useful and essential means of understanding, researching, and criticizing television, as much if not more than ever before. While their functions change, and new navigational guides provide new curated pathways and recommendations, channels still matter. This book shows its readers how and why, providing its own navigational guide that anyone interested in the television industries can use to make sense of the abundance of choices and changes that define the channel landscape.

CHANNELS AND CONJUNCTURES IN A NETWORKED ERA

Insistence on the continued relevance of channels and television guides is neither intuitive nor uncontroversial. In a "post-network" moment in which "viewers now increasingly select what, when, and where to view from abundant options," power has shifted considerably away from industry professionals who program specific channels and channel networks in uniform, scheduled ways (Lotz 2014, 28). The dominance of a few, bottlenecked broadcast services has given way to a "networked" era, as described by Aymar Jean Christian (2018), in which the more open and participatory affordances of the Internet enable audiences to make programming choices while independent modes of production and distribution thrive outside the control of traditional channel gatekeepers. If channels represent these older, passing industry models, some argue they should be of decreasing concern to those of us tracking this exciting post-network—but networked—state of affairs.

For example, *TechCrunch* writer Tom Goodwin (2016) argues that as streaming services like Netflix deliver television programming through the Internet, "two

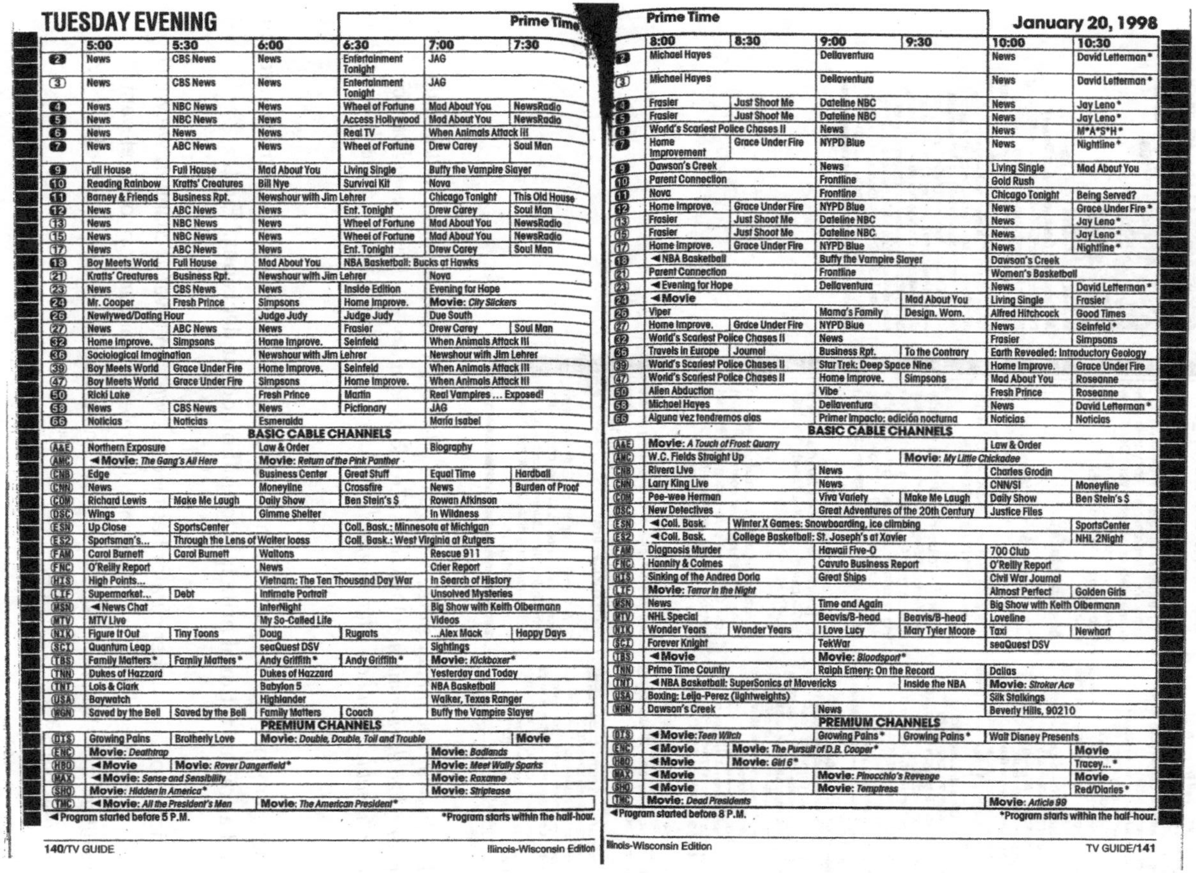

TUESDAY EVENING — Prime Time — January 20, 1998

Ch.	5:00	5:30	6:00	6:30	7:00	7:30	8:00	8:30	9:00	9:30	10:00	10:30
2	News	CBS News	News	Entertainment Tonight	JAG		Michael Hayes		Dellaventura		News	David Letterman*
3	News	CBS News	News	Entertainment Tonight	JAG		Michael Hayes		Dellaventura		News	David Letterman*
4	News	NBC News	News	Wheel of Fortune	Mad About You	NewsRadio	Frasier	Just Shoot Me	Dateline NBC		News	Jay Leno*
5	News	NBC News	News	Access Hollywood	Mad About You	NewsRadio	Frasier	Just Shoot Me	Dateline NBC		News	Jay Leno*
6	News	News	News	Real TV	When Animals Attack III		World's Scariest Police Chases II		News		News	M*A*S*H*
7	News	ABC News	News	Wheel of Fortune	Drew Carey	Soul Man	Home Improvement	Grace Under Fire	NYPD Blue		News	Nightline*
9	Full House	Full House	Mad About You	Living Single	Buffy the Vampire Slayer		Dawson's Creek		News		Living Single	Mad About You
10	Reading Rainbow	Kratts' Creatures	Bill Nye	Survival Kit	Nova		Parent Connection		Frontline		Gold Rush	
11	Barney & Friends	Business Rpt.	Newshour with Jim Lehrer		Chicago Tonight	This Old House	Nova		Frontline		Chicago Tonight	Being Served?
12	News	ABC News	News	Ent. Tonight	Drew Carey	Soul Man	Home Improve.	Grace Under Fire	NYPD Blue		News	Grace Under Fire*
13	News	NBC News	News	Wheel of Fortune	Mad About You	NewsRadio	Frasier	Just Shoot Me	Dateline NBC		News	Jay Leno*
15	News	NBC News	News	Wheel of Fortune	Mad About You	NewsRadio	Frasier	Just Shoot Me	Dateline NBC		News	Jay Leno*
17	News	ABC News	News	Ent. Tonight	Drew Carey	Soul Man	Home Improve.	Grace Under Fire	NYPD Blue		News	Nightline*
18	Boy Meets World	Full House	Mad About You	NBA Basketball: Bucks at Hawks			◄NBA Basketball		Buffy the Vampire Slayer		Dawson's Creek	
21	Kratts' Creatures	Business Rpt.	Newshour with Jim Lehrer		Nova		Parent Connection		Frontline		Women's Basketball	
23	News	CBS News	News	Inside Edition	Evening for Hope		◄Evening for Hope		Dellaventura		News	David Letterman*
24	Mr. Cooper	Fresh Prince	Simpsons	Home Improve.	Movie: *City Slickers*		◄Movie			Mad About You	Living Single	Frasier
26	Newlywed/Dating Hour		Judge Judy	Judge Judy	Due South		Viper		Mama's Family	Design. Wom.	Alfred Hitchcock	Good Times
27	News	ABC News	News	Frasier	Drew Carey	Soul Man	Home Improve.	Grace Under Fire	NYPD Blue		News	Seinfeld*
32	Home Improve.	Simpsons	Home Improve.	Seinfeld	When Animals Attack III		World's Scariest Police Chases II		News		Frasier	Simpsons
36	Sociological Imagination		Newshour with Jim Lehrer		Newshour with Jim Lehrer		Travels in Europe	Journal	Business Rpt.	To the Contrary	Earth Revealed: Introductory Geology	
39	Boy Meets World	Grace Under Fire	Home Improve.	Seinfeld	When Animals Attack III		World's Scariest Police Chases II		Star Trek: Deep Space Nine		Home Improve.	Grace Under Fire
47	Boy Meets World	Grace Under Fire	Simpsons	Home Improve.	When Animals Attack III		World's Scariest Police Chases II		Home Improve.	Simpsons	Mad About You	Roseanne
50	Ricki Lake		Fresh Prince	Martin	Real Vampires ... Exposed!		Alien Abduction		Vibe		Fresh Prince	Roseanne
58	News	CBS News	News	Pictionary	JAG		Michael Hayes		Dellaventura		News	David Letterman*
66	Noticias	Noticias	Esmeralda		Maria Isabel		Alguna vez tendremos alas		Primer impacto: edición nocturna		Noticias	Noticias
	BASIC CABLE CHANNELS											
A&E	Northern Exposure		Law & Order		Biography		Movie: *A Touch of Frost: Quarry*				Law & Order	
AMC	◄Movie: *The Gang's All Here*		Movie: *Return of the Pink Panther*				W.C. Fields Straight Up			Movie: *My Little Chickadee*		
CNB	Edge		Business Center	Great Stuff	Equal Time	Hardball	Rivera Live		News		Charles Grodin	
CNN	News		Moneyline	Crossfire	News	Burden of Proof	Larry King Live		News		CNN/SI	Moneyline
COM	Richard Lewis	Make Me Laugh	Daily Show	Ben Stein's $	Rowan Atkinson		Pee-wee Herman		Viva Variety	Make Me Laugh	Daily Show	Ben Stein's $
DSC	Wings		Gimme Shelter		In Wildness		New Detectives		Great Adventures of the 20th Century		Justice Files	
ESN	Up Close	SportsCenter		Coll. Bask.: Minnesota at Michigan			◄Coll. Bask.	Winter X Games: Snowboarding, ice climbing				SportsCenter
ES2	Sportsman's...	Through the Lens of Walter Iooss		Coll. Bask.: West Virginia at Rutgers			◄Coll. Bask.	College Basketball: St. Joseph's at Xavier				NHL 2Night
FAM	Carol Burnett	Carol Burnett	Waltons		Rescue 911		Diagnosis Murder		Hawaii Five-O		700 Club	
FNC	O'Reilly Report		News		Crier Report		Hannity & Colmes		Cavuto Business Report		O'Reilly Report	
HIS	High Points...		Vietnam: The Ten Thousand Day War		In Search of History		Sinking of the Andrea Doria		Great Ships		Civil War Journal	
LIF	Supermarket...	Debt	Intimate Portrait		Unsolved Mysteries		Movie: *Terror in the Night*				Almost Perfect	Golden Girls
MSN	◄News Chat		InterNight		Big Show with Keith Olbermann		News		Time and Again		Big Show with Keith Olbermann	
MTV	MTV Live		My So-Called Life		Videos		NHL Special		Beavis/B-head	Beavis/B-head	Loveline	
NIK	Figure It Out	Tiny Toons	Doug	Rugrats	...Alex Mack	Happy Days	Wonder Years	Wonder Years	I Love Lucy	Mary Tyler Moore	Taxi	Newhart
SCI	Quantum Leap		seaQuest DSV		Sightings		Forever Knight		TekWar		seaQuest DSV	
TBS	Family Matters*	Family Matters*	Andy Griffith*	Andy Griffith*	Movie: *Kickboxer**		◄Movie		Movie: *Bloodsport**			
TNN	Dukes of Hazzard		Dukes of Hazzard		Yesterday and Today		Prime Time Country		Ralph Emery: On the Record		Dallas	
TNT	Lois & Clark		Babylon 5		NBA Basketball		◄NBA Basketball: SuperSonics at Mavericks			Inside the NBA	Movie: *Stroker Ace*	
USA	Baywatch		Highlander		Walker, Texas Ranger		Boxing: Leija-Perez (lightweights)				Silk Stalkings	
WGN	Saved by the Bell	Saved by the Bell	Family Matters	Coach	Buffy the Vampire Slayer		Dawson's Creek		News		Beverly Hills, 90210	
	PREMIUM CHANNELS											
DIS	Growing Pains	Brotherly Love	Movie: *Double, Double, Toil and Trouble*			Movie	◄Movie: *Teen Witch*		Growing Pains*	Growing Pains*	Walt Disney Presents	
ENC	Movie: *Deathtrap*				Movie: *Badlands*		◄Movie	Movie: *The Pursuit of D.B. Cooper**				Movie
HBO	◄Movie	Movie: *Rover Dangerfield**			Movie: *Meet Wally Sparks*		◄Movie	Movie: *Girl 6**				Tracey...*
MAX	◄Movie: *Sense and Sensibility*				Movie: *Roxanne*		◄Movie		Movie: *Pinocchio's Revenge*			Movie
SHO	Movie: *Hidden in America**				Movie: *Striptease*		◄Movie		Movie: *Temptress*			Red/Diaries*
TMC	◄Movie: *All the President's Men*		Movie: *The American President**				Movie: *Dead Presidents*				Movie: *Article 99*	

◄Program started before 5 P.M. / ◄Program started before 8 P.M.

*Program starts within the half-hour.

140/TV GUIDE — Illinois-Wisconsin Edition — Illinois-Wisconsin Edition — TV GUIDE/141

FIGURE 1.1 *The program listing grid served a navigational utility, helping readers of publications like* TV Guide *to choose between numerous channel offerings (in this case, for prime-time offerings on the night of Tuesday, January 20, 1998).*

FIGURE 1.2 *In addition to full listings,* TV Guide *offered recommendations—which of the program options, like the premiere of* Dawson's Creek *on January 20, 1998, would be most worthwhile or "notable"? And on what channels could those recommended programs be found?*

foundational elements of TV choice architecture are wildly irrelevant for the future but are still used as organizational principle for billion dollar decisions." First,

> the old notion of a publisher curator has died . . . we don't watch channels we watch shows. . . . The role of TV channels is entirely irrelevant for curation, only relevant for the funding of shows we like. To take the entirely anachronistic device of the TV channel, and replicate it as an app, is stupid in the extreme.

Incredulous toward app-delivered television that extends channel logics of the past rather than embracing newer technological affordances, he continues, "Who wants to watch TV by selecting Apple TV, being paralyzed by 50 TV channel apps, then opening the CBS app, before selecting the show?" Rejecting the relevance of channels, he also questions the value of linear programming guides in a streaming environment. Services like Netflix have "freed" content from time: "this 'time shifting' for connected households is the predominant form of TV. Yet the centerpoint of TV remains the electronic programming guide and it's never changed. It shows irrelevant channels vertically and on a now irrelevant timescale." Frustrated with failed technological potential in favor of an "agonizingly complex" array of incompatible devices, services, and formats, he laments "I want all content to be linked . . . I want my remote to be my phone and control center for all content."

By these terms of analysis, this book would be doomed to the same stupidity and irrelevance in its interest in channels and its attempts to provide readers with a guide to their agonizingly complex landscape. However, if we temper techno-futurism with a critical understanding of media industries as contested, often contradictory systems of institutional meaning making and practice (Havens, Lotz, and Tinic 2009, 236–7), we might better see our continued need for guides to television channels. Television is not merely a set of technologies awaiting universal compatibility, but also a system of competing industrial forces in which human agents embedded in institutional structures manage and deploy those technologies in different ways. Goodwin's chimeric universal service would exist outside the competition and choice that in significant part define capitalistic television industries. A single service with the convenience of Netflix and an unrestricted content library would depend on all content owners agreeing to support it. Studios like 20th Century Fox, NBC-Universal, ABC-Disney, and CBS Studios would need to agree to collaborate in a single space, finding a way to share profits equally or acquiescing to the dominance of a single player (instead of offering competing proprietary streaming services like Hulu and CBS All Access). Streaming services like Amazon and Netflix would need to stop competing for exclusive access to content. Or, a single, monopolistic, vertically integrated service would need to own all program rights and choke off supply to any competition. Goodwin is correct that there is no good reason we simply must have television channels; they are not natural or inevitable, but products of how television technology has been historically organized as an industry. Yet channels persist as the expression of different companies attempting to organize television in economically advantageous ways, carving out distinct territories and brand identities in collaboration and opposition to one another.

Viewer relationships to television technologies have also depended on the logic of the channel. Television sets act as channels receivers, tuning in to over-the-air VHF, UHF, and now digital signals captured from the electromagnetic spectrum by antennas attuned to individual channel frequencies; but the expanded bandwidth allowed by coaxial wires added dozens then hundreds of additional channels that cable or satellite subscribers could feed to their television screens. Today's "smart," online-ready television sets, meanwhile, carry on-board app suites that receive services carried by Wi-Fi from our Internet routers. Other Wi-Fi enabled devices like Roku and Apple TV connected to our televisions by HDMI cable bring an even greater variety of apps to the menu of channels from which we can select. Apps and services like Netflix and Amazon Prime carried to our television are no mere channels, of course, but something different and more advanced. Yet these television apps use wired and wireless connectivity to modify, adapt, and reconfigure television to receive new channel inputs. While many no longer viewer television content on traditional television sets, opting instead for tablets, phones, and other personal devices, our ability to access specific programming services like Netflix over a Wi-Fi connection links these devices with the same tradition of receiving television signals channeled to us by the television industries.

In the face of disruption and new competition, moreover, legacy television industries hold dearly to channel logics. Local broadcast stations, national broadcast networks, and cable services devote serious energies to identifying and differentiating themselves as channels, all to cultivate viewer loyalty, affinity, or habit in choosing among an abundance of options. As relative newcomers like YouTube and Netflix intensify the fragmentation of the television audience into ever-smaller pieces, they too adopt some of these channel logics to position themselves in a crowded field. The creation of a channel, in this sense, results from branding practices (Arvidsson 2006; Lury 2004) that provide for product differentiation in competitive environments. In her landmark study of television branding, Catherine Johnson argues that the impetus to brand television services in both the US and the UK emerged as consumers gained access to a greater number of channels and services beyond the broadcast context (2012, 5). Yet as traditional television technology "becomes decentred as the primary means through which television programmes are watched," she asks if new digital services have "undermined the role of the channel brand in the US television industry" (38). Traditional television channels differentiated by their organization of specific content offerings lose ground in this digital environment to "service brands" like Hulu defined by the experience of "what you can do with television," she finds. Nevertheless, rather than a "death knell" for the television channel, this transformation drives "the development of the television channel as a global media brand that can be adapted and extended into new markets" (56–57). In other words, even as new digital services threaten legacy television channels, it is through channel brands that legacy media conglomerates negotiate this disruption. The channel is both at stake in the digital revolution and a means to survive it.

Rather than refer to Hulu as a "channel," Johnson refers to it as a "portal through which to engage in the extended experiences of television viewing that are enabled by the internet" (57). Amanda Lotz (2017) also embraces the language of "portals" for describing streaming television and its resistance to the time-specific viewing of linear television industries. Whereas broadcast and cable television programming relied upon a linear notion of time in its scheduling practices, distribution windows, program lengths, and episodic storytelling structures, online television need not adhere to that same timeliness. Instead, non-linear, online television portals support viewing experiences in which consumers choose what to watch when. It is thus worth considering the contemporary television industries as a struggle between legacy channels adapting to new conditions, on the one side, and the new portals that threaten to replace them, on the other. From that perspective, channels still matter as the persistent, not-yet-vanquished continuity in a story of media change.

Yet even if we distinguish services like Hulu or Netflix from legacy television channel brands like CBS or HBO, that difference need not be one of diametric opposition. While providing non-linear viewing experiences, streaming services may not fully transcend the linear limitations of television channels. Lotz (2017) contrasts the distributional model of portals to the "flow" and "publishing" models identified by cultural theorist

Bernard Miége (1989). The flow model of linear broadcast and cable television distributed scheduled media programming that could be integrated in the patterns of everyday life, while publishing logics allowed television to be marked, sold, and experienced at retail in the form of commodities like the DVD or iTunes downloads. Portals offer their own unique logic of distribution, however, providing users a menu of goods from which individualized media experiences can be constructed. Yet despite these distributional differences, Lotz shrewdly visualizes several ways in which portals carry forward channel strategies. Although portals are not so restricted in their "capacity constraint," offering more programming than could fit in a linear 24-hour-a-day schedule, they continue to engage in curatorial practices to select and organize content. Moreover, "the strategies of audience targeting—or channel branding—that have been characteristic of cable channels seem consistent here and applicable to the portal environment," especially as subscription services like Netflix target a multiplicity of specific taste cultures. So even as a new portal logic dominates the space of Internet-delivered television, its relationship to the television channel may not be one of opposition and obliteration so much as evolution and adaptation.

With that in mind, we can consider how television "flow" evolves even as new services operate outside of Miége's flow-based distributional logics. Raymond Williams developed his own theory of "flow" to describe, at the height of the network era, "the defining characteristic of broadcasting simultaneously as a technology and as a cultural form" (2003, 86). Analyzing the sequences in which programmers produced meaningful connections within television scheduling, Williams pushed his readers to think beyond individual television programs to consider the contexts of flow in which programming was delivered. Individual television shows shared generic and thematic links with the programs that preceded and followed them, as well as the ads aired during them. This flow concept also captured viewer relationships to the channel, where programmed sequences aimed to get us to "go with the flow" and be swept away in the resulting programming schedule, as Jostein Gripsrud (1998) once put it. The linear television channel programmer, in this sense, generated the current that could sweep up audiences and, above all, stop them from changing channels. Even then, changing the channel would prove to be less than an escape from flow, and more like navigation to another current in a greater programming stream.

Water metaphors abound in these attempts to understand how media industries organize television experiences: from channel to flow to streaming, all suggest the production of a current in which viewing occurs. They also imply movement, in that currents carry viewers forward in time, from the beginning of one program to the end and perhaps into another. Portals threaten this logic, as television industries surrender the power to sweep us away. From VCR to DVD to DVR and now streaming, new technologies have empowered viewers to remove themselves from linear currents and construct their own sequences of television, obliterating the idea of a single experience of flow. Moreover, in a digitally connected world, limitations once imposed upon television flows—such as the maintenance of global distribution territories—have been challenged by users who deliver television to one another across national boundaries. Instead of going with the flow, television viewers now create channels of flow. Within participatory media, it becomes harder to imagine channel flows that simply wash over us, where the undertow pulls us into the watery depths of industrially designed television experiences.

However, to proclaim flow as obsolete would miss its continued conceptual utility for thinking about industrial contexts of television creation, delivery, and experience. DVD and DVR did not eliminate flow so much as shift control over its "regime of repetition," where users not industry schedulers now determine when specific programs can be seen (Kompare 2005, 215). The same could be said of streaming services like Netflix: while no two users would likely have the same experience of flow, watching Netflix nevertheless produces a recognizable sense of flow, often fed by the platform's ability to gather data about viewing habits and generate personalized menus and recommendations. Users construct their own sequences of viewing, but the platform encourages particular pathways through the menu of options in its programming library. Netflix might grant one of its original series, like *House of Cards* (2013–) or *Orange is the New Black* (2013–), prominent placement on the home screen for some or even all of its subscribers. It can suggest one sample a library program like *Battlestar Galactica* (Sci-Fi, 2003–2009), perhaps, after receiving from the user five-star feedback for dramas like *House of Cards* and *The West Wing* (NBC, 1999–2006), based on the theme of presidential politics shared by all. Nothing can compel the viewer to follow that recommendation; but even in the era of network and cable dominance, viewers always had the option to change the channel. Thus, much like network programmers developed practices like "hot switching" to eliminate commercial breaks between programs in hopes of keeping viewers in the current, Netflix designs user experiences so one episode's conclusion automatically cues up and plays another. Encouraging us to "binge," Netflix hopes we will ride the current of the service it provides.

The menu of programs before us means that there is no universal, linear experience; yet Internet-delivered television is non-linear only in an abstract sense of quantum potentiality. Our social lives remain bounded by time: every episode we watch brings us ever closer to the next workday, appointment, or other obligation. Netflix can offer us unlimited programming resources for constructing our own television flows; but we as viewers remain limited in how many sequences we can string together within the linear passage of time. So more precisely, Netflix helps us to shape linear flows from the non-linear possibilities of its program offerings, privileging some quantum outcomes over others based on its economic and cultural priorities. Even if skeptical readers will not grant that Netflix *is* itself a channel in the traditional sense, it nevertheless *creates* multiple channels of individualized viewer experience.

The persistent significance of channels, then, does not depend on lumping all television services into a single category. As the organization of this book suggests, the television industry supports and maintains many different kinds of channels across the broadcast, cable, and streaming arenas. In different ways across these distinct sectors, industries use channels to create meaning out of and mediate experiences of watching television. Put another way, channels matter because they are sites at which media industries provide contexts and conjunctures for television to be produced and consumed. Reflecting on the intellectual project of cultural studies, Lawrence Grossberg describes

FIGURE 1.3 *Non-linear television services like Netflix encourage subscribers to construct particular programming flows out of the unlimited possibilities that they can build for themselves, foregrounding Netflix original series, new releases, and programs matched to users' tastes by recommendation algorithms.*

the conjuncture "as a way of constructing contexts," in which "the identity, significance, and effects of any practice or event (including cultural practices and events) are defined only by the complex set of relations that surround, interpenetrate, and shape it, and make it what it is" (2010, 20). The constantly changing nature of these relations, he adds, requires that cultural studies adopt a "radical contextualism" attuned to a continual process of articulation in which these relations are made, unmade, and remade. Analysis of channels, in this sense, produces insight into some of the specific contexts in which television programs, industry players, viewing practices, and hierarchies of value might become articulated to one another. At a second level, the changing significances of channels in an era of industry transformation encourage us to confront industry as a process of adaptation and rearticulation over time. Channels reveal currents that carry some content, ideas, and cultures while forcing others to swim upstream. Channels are tangible sites of industry practice where the agency and labor of cultural struggle can actually happen; while they may be sites of flow, they may also provide contexts for what Anna Tsing (2004) calls "friction"—clashes of culture as globalization brings media companies into new articulations with diverse audiences, tastes, and practices.

Examining channels means investigating currents, flows, and streams (and—beyond water metaphors—pathways, gateways, platforms, and portals) as contexts to be analyzed and deconstructed. This contextual analysis also contributes to burgeoning discussions about distribution and delivery in media studies (Curtin, Holt, and Sanson 2014; Perren 2013), revealing how television distributors of all kinds generate contexts and produce articulations in this sense. Every channel in the television landscape might therefore reveal industry efforts to shape television for viewers in specific historical and cultural contexts. From that perspective, this book embraces a case-study model in which a single channel like Pop can tell us something significant about the evolving television industries.

CHANNEL GUIDES GO POP

The origins of Pop from the TV Guide Network (and before that, the TV Guide Channel) reveal how the cable industry, as recently as the 1990s, leveraged the linearity of television as an asset, articulating viewer need for navigational assistance to new business models and channel brands. Prior to relaunching as Pop, TV Guide served two key industrial functions in the cable industry. The first was a "utility" function (Donaton 2000) through which the company provided listings and navigational guidance—a valuable service sought out by cable providers as scheduled channel offerings became more numerous. TV Guide functioned secondly as "entertainment"—a role that it occupied in an increasingly exclusive way as a less linear channel landscape meant less demand for the utility once offered.

To understand the utility of TV Guide, we can consider the longer history of the electronic program guide (EPG). As cable channel capacity grew, operators did not rely on publications like *TV Guide* (which initially lacked the same depth of cable listings as for broadcast), instead making navigation a part of the subscription service provided. In 1981, United Video Satellite Group began offering US cable system operators a service called the Electronic Program Guide that displayed a scrolling grid of program listings. Although not searchable and only projecting a couple hours into the future, early EPGs nevertheless challenged print guides as the dominant navigational utility. *TV Guide* thus developed a competing EPG service called TV Guide Onscreen, delivered to 3 million homes by 1996, compared to 40 million for United Video's EPG, by then called Prevue Guide (Flint 1996, 26). Parent company NewsCorp ultimately sold *TV Guide* and its cable interests to United Video in 1998, however; Prevue would be renamed in the merger to exploit the print publication's legacy brand ("TV Guide Deal" 1998).

Despite efforts to create a consolidated channel for cable listings from the merger, the new TV Guide Channel struggled to thrive as a utility in a cable industry otherwise organized around entertainment services. First, while carriage on major cable systems opened up the possibility of subscription and advertising revenue, sufficient funds proved difficult to secure. Even after the merger, advertisers were not particularly interested in the channel (Lafayette 2005). This was not due to low viewership, as TV Guide claimed 84 page views per television household a day (200 billion views a year) (Donaton 2000). However, because the program listing was omnipresent, advertisements shared screen space and viewer attention. Low advertiser interest fed other problems: believing that a utility channel would draw less viewer interest than entertainment programming, cable operators were not willing to pay TV Guide carriage fees of more than pennies per subscriber (Motavalli 2004; Farrell 2008). While generating revenue as a utility channel proved difficult, TV Guide enjoyed more success when it sidestepped its branded service, licensing new listing technology to cable operators who wanted their own proprietary program guides as part of the interface for digital set-top cable boxes (Lafayette 2004). These guides would no longer be "passive," but Interactive Program Guides (IPGs) allowing for searches, DVR, and other new functions ("TV Guide Channel Launches" 2004; "TV Guide Channel Selects" 2006). Throughout, viewers increasingly came to rely on search-enabled functions that TV Guide made available on its own website—billed as "America's No. 1 television entertainment Web site" in 2003 ("TV Guide Channel" 2003). Increasingly, it looked like that the television channel itself might best be used for other purposes.

After competing EPG provider Gemstar purchased TV Guide for $9.5 billion in 1999, the cable channel embraced a new programming format. Alongside scrolling program listings, TV Guide Channel began offering short-form programming centered around entertainment news, program previews, celebrity gossip, and more. Each programming hour would consist of ten three- to five-minute segments, with advertisements in between. This familiar arrangement of entertainment-embedded advertising (even if in split screen with channel listings) increased the channel's Nielsen ratings by 8% and overall ad revenues by 66% compared to the previous year (Friedman 2000). By 2003, the channel's self-described "signature" program was *What's On*, a ten-minute series airing every ten minutes to the hour throughout prime-time to preview the "most noteworthy programs in the next hour" and provide a guide to "primetime in real time" ("TV Guide Channel" 2003). Two years later, General Manager Tom Cosgrove announced his intent to build a "real schedule" relying on original series programmed at intervals of 30 and 60 minutes (Hibberd 2005).

Although these efforts maintained the channel's self-professed niche in "entertainment guidance" ("TV Guide Channel" 2006), they increasingly put TV Guide in competition with other entertainment channels to which it had once served more as a utility companion. By 2007, as the channel rebranded itself TV Guide Network, it veered harder into entertainment, deemphasizing navigation of other channels' offerings in favor of its own original programs. The 2007 TV Guide reality series *Making News: Texas Style*, for example, extended the channel's thematic interest in television by focusing on the production of a local television news program. In 2009, TV Guide Network began relying on second-run syndication to acquire scripted programs previously distributed by broadcast networks and other cable outlets, adding reruns of series like *Ugly Betty* (ABC, 2006–2010) and *Punk'd* (MTV, 2003–2012) to its schedule ("TV Guide Network" 2009). Crucially, this move to remake the channel in the image of more traditional, programmed cable outlets came as it dropped scrolling program listings altogether. Although *Advertising Age* reported that some 20 million basic cable subscribers without enhanced IPG service would lose on-screen navigational assistance (Learmonth 2009), the elimination of this broad-based utility followed the newfound pursuit of market segmentation. By 2010, the channel sought "entertainment-based original and acquired programming that appeals to the channel's core female viewers" (Umstead 2010, 11).

TV Guide Network now looked much like other cable channels: it offered a linear schedule of entertainment programming to attract specific consumer demographics it could package and sell to advertisers in the form of Nielsen ratings. Yet it now had to compete with those other services, too. When Macrovision purchased Gemstar in 2008, it immediately put the channel up for sale, hoping for $400 million or more; but perceptions of TV Guide Network as a losing investment led to a sale of only $255 million to Lionsgate in 2009. Ownership and control of the channel changed multiple times in succession, with Lionsgate selling a 49% stake to One Equity, which then sold to CBS Corporation in 2013 (Abrams and Littleton 2013). By the next year, CBS leveraged its partnership as a mean of reallocation, feeding encore presentations of *Amazing Race* (2001–) and *Survivor* (2000–) to TV Guide Network as a "secondary national platform" to build viewership for each new episode broadcast on CBS (Farrell 2013, 28).

So while the 2014 launch of Pop represented a significant change in brand name, it was only the most recent moment in a long transformation from viewing utility to entertainment service. Now competing on the same terms as most other channels, Pop offered a window into both the pressures facing television entertainment channels and the strategies imagined to negotiate those challenges. First, amid competition between cable channels for similar markets, Pop tried to articulate new, discrete audience segments to serve. Pop executives described their audience as the "modern grownup," a generation of viewers more "in touch with their youthful side" and more "engaged with culture" than the social expectations of marrying and having kids (Lafayette 2014). Pop also secondly communicated its commitment to original program production as a means of building viewership and justifying its individual channel value, promising 400 hours of original programming throughout 2015 (Lafayette 2014). Pop participated in a moment of "peak TV" in which desires to attract the attention of viewers who can choose what, when, and where to watch led to an abundance of original episodic television production—with insiders like FX Network President John Landgraf questioning its sustainability (Holloway and Littleton 2016). In other words, Pop helped drive a production "bubble" that might itself pop (Littleton 2017, 8). Even before the rebrand, industry analysts named TV Guide Network as one of many channels "hunting for prestige episodic series" (Goldstein 2014). Initial support by original production—as well as imports of original Canadian comedy series like *Schitt's Creek* (CBC, 2015–)— enabled Pop to sustain eight quarters of consecutive growth by 2016. This growth notably included a 30% increase in viewership by the 25- to 54-year-old women targeted by the channel, as well as carriage in eight million more new homes served by Cablevision, WideOpenWest, and AT&T Uverse (Umstead and Gibbons 2016, 8).

While just one case study, the transformation of TV Guide into Pop offers significant insight into how channels and channel logics operate amid disruption and change. TV Guide's efforts to leverage, manage, and ultimate abandon its utility functions underscore a fundamental industrial shift away from linear viewing experiences that required its particular navigational guidance and recommendations for scheduled programming. Instead of seeing this transformation as evidence that non-linear television has rendered utility functions obsolete, however, we might ask instead what interfaces or other industrial conjunctures are now providing these contexts for navigation and recommendation. This particular channel model may have passed, in other words, but its functions have not.

In the new forms and functions driving Pop as an entertainment service, meanwhile, we see the channel as the persistent foundation upon which legacy industries consolidate their power and try to adapt to change—even or perhaps especially if in retreat. Not all channels will survive this fragmented, disrupted environment: some will rebrand, like Pop; others will collapse. Finally, the Pop case study reminds us that the new world of online television is not one of universal experience. For some basic cable subscribers—millions of them, even if not those most valued by advertisers—the passage of TV Guide Network and its on-screen listings represented a loss of orientation in a linear channel landscape in which they were still very much embedded. While unsurprising that TV Guide and later Pop would ignore this less valuable consumer group, our own critical attention to a variety of channels should tune in to *all* the contexts, linear and non-linear alike, in which television is organized by industry and experienced by viewers.

LINEAR AND NON-LINEAR RECOMMENDATIONS

Each chapter that follows delivers on this promise by offering focused examination of a single television channel or service. These case studies show how their respective channels identify and distinguish themselves from competitors, how they reposition themselves in the face of disruption and change, and why they provide unique or fundamental insight into the history, present, and future of television. Digging into the logics of the television channel, and exploring a vast array of examples from different cultural, economic, regulatory, and infrastructural positions, this book provides a guide to help readers gain a critical understanding of the abundance of services and choices currently characterizing the medium. In its organization, the book even evokes the structure of channel listings—as a relative of sorts to *TV Guide*—laying out an ordered list of curated content and providing insight into a menu of channel offerings. This format encourages readers to turn their attention from channel to channel and, in the process, gain deeper understanding of the television industries and the logics by which they shape television culture. Yet while *TV Guide* and other popular channel listings help viewers decide what to watch from a channel menu, this book takes on the more critical mission of helping readers understand how and why those options have been constructed in the first place. Of additional note in the organization of the book is an attempt to integrate study of television channels as they operate and evolve on a global scale. By putting different channels from different national contexts in dialogue with one another, readers should gain a strong sense of how channel logics shape television as a transnational medium, how television services negotiate global boundaries, as well as how viewers situated in specific geographic and cultural relations across the globe engage with television through channels. Across all of these concerns, the channel listing serves as the metaphorical backdrop against which many different conversations in the critical study of television industries might be organized.

The first set of chapters focuses on traditional broadcast stations and networks whose over-the-air signals provide channel space for reaching large audiences while balancing tensions between the local and the national as well as between public obligations and commercial profits. Laying out a conceptual foundation for understanding network television as an industry, Kristen J. Warner explains how transitions in personnel and programming strategy at ABC extended from management of risk and crisis—where moves toward more racial equality in casting result from careful strategic calculation. Caryn Murphy emphasizes the importance of ownership in assessing network channels, finding that the relationship between The CW and CBS Corporation enables this broadcast service to target audiences on a smaller scale more common to the cable industry. In her chapter on Rede Globo, Courtney Brannon Donoghue shows how these relationships between channels and conglomerates unfold in both domestic and global dimensions, with Brazil's most powerful media company seeking to maintain local dominance as it contends with shifting media platforms and audience tastes worldwide. Turning investigation of broadcast networking to the realm of public television, Michele Hilmes identifies the US Public Broadcasting System as a crucial innovator of "crowdsourcing" models, illustrating how channels can serve the needs of local and national citizens alike. This tension in public broadcasting between the local and the national drives Allison Perlman's investigation of the Alabama Public Television Network, where she shows how local public television channels have served and will continue to serve as platforms for the construction of local identities and institutions within national televisions cultures. Looking beyond the US, Hanne Bruun considers the case of the Danish broadcaster DR to assess how public service changes in an era of digital technology, where channels continuing to receive public funds might challenge the interests of commercial services as they move to online platforms. Although his chapter on MeTV shifts focus back to US commercial broadcasting, Derek Kompare continues this investigation of what emerging media platforms mean for broadcasters, exploring how the small "diginet" uses digital subchannels to carve out a new space on broadcast television for syndicated programming and nostalgia-based marketing.

A second group of chapters shifts focus to channels that provide content to cable and satellite subscribers. Most often, these channels operate in the same commercial vein as many broadcast services—selling audiences to advertisers. However, a subscription economy in which channels supplement ad revenue with carriage fees paid for inclusion in subscription bundles, combined with an abundance of channel choices that fragments the overall television audience, means that these channels often carve out narrower niche markets compared to broadcasters. Instead of nations or publics they often serve specific demographics and tastes.

In her study of WGN America, Christine Becker bridges the gap between the broadcast economy and subscription television by tracing how a local television station transformed into a national cable service. Although sports channel ESPN has long served as an anchor for the bundles sold by cable and satellite providers, Travis Vogan explores how it responded to challenges from new streaming services by emphasizing prestige programming and the persistent value of liveness in an on-demand world. Meanwhile, Deborah L. Jaramillo argues that competitor NBC Sports Network differentiated itself by eschewing mass appeal and increasingly covering non-US events to give the domestic service a more elite sensibility. Focusing on the specific identities that channels construct to achieve this differentiation, Jon Kraszewski explains how The Weather Channel depended on a promise of trustworthiness—a valuable identity disrupted in struggles with cable and satellite operators who reframed its "docu-series" programming as "reality TV." Melissa Zimdars continues this investigation of the value of reality genres within channel programming and branding strategies by considering how TLC's focus on everyday spectacle depends upon compassionate discourses about food and fatness recognizable to viewers. Identifying these ways in which channels brand themselves as "prosocial," Laurie Ouellette examines MTV's self-promotional social outreach campaigns, arguing that the public service model of broadcast television has been reinvented in cause-oriented terms more lucrative for media companies.

The remaining chapters focused on cable and satellite channels explore how these services build and maintain programming appeals to specific audiences while potentially reorienting themselves around new target markets deemed more strategically or economically viable. David Craig and Derek Johnson characterize A&E in terms of a managed multiplicity, where the channel's initial investment in elite arts and entertainment grew to a more general entertainment focus incorporating multiple tastes, demographics, and ideological sensibilities, organized across subsidiary channel outlets. In her chapter on Spike TV, Amanda D. Lotz examines its aim to become the "first cable channel for men," revealing how and why attempts at constructing a gender-specific cable brand proved elusive. Similarly concerned with industry attempts to court young men, Nick Marx examines the seemingly progressive and feminist support that Comedy Central offered for female-led programming, arguing that promotional efforts nevertheless reaffirmed the power and privilege of men and masculinity amid these attempts at broadening appeal. Considering how Nick Jr. carved out a NickMom programming block within an otherwise child-oriented schedule, Erin Copple Smith illustrates the links between audience and dayparts as well as the challenges of balancing appeals to multiple markets. Kyra Hunting and Jonathan Gray build on this interest in marketing to children and parents by examining how Disney Junior uses a strategy of industrial intertextuality to create a network of connections between Disney properties (some new to the channel and some "classics" recognizable to parents), selling an entire "family" of products. Christopher Chávez, meanwhile, explores the limits of the cross-demographic marketing built into the Disney empire, arguing that the gender-specific service of a universal boyhood underlying Disney XD assumes whiteness and reveals how marketers' explicit interest in childhood gender neglects crucial intersections with race. Considering one last Disney-owned channel, Barbara Selnick examines the transformation of ABC Family into Freeform, a rebranding that articulated a new youth audience called "becomers" amid retreat from the idea of family viewing as a means of channel organization and identification. Finally, Alisa Perren investigates how El Rey, at launch, used the "indie" image of auteur filmmaker Robert Rodriguez to appeal equally to viewers relating to his Latino identity as well as his genre tastes—a match that struggled to cohere amid intense competition within the cable and satellite industries.

By contrast to these linear services, the third set of chapters focuses on new forms of television delivery enabled by online streaming platforms. In these cases, television channels based in open program development and participatory forms of engagement can emerge even as legacy logics of commercial advertising, merchandising, and public service persist.

Many of these new channels operate on digital and social media platforms like YouTube, Twitter, and Twitch. As argued by Avi Santo, AwesomenessTV supports itself not just as a multi-channel network on YouTube, but also as a fully branded and merchandised empire, leveraging a host of young social media celebrities across different genres, formats, markets, and licensing opportunities. While Santo traces a new strategic arrangement afforded by YouTube, Lori Kido Lopez focuses on its political potential: considering the channel ISAtv, she argues that the branding strategies afforded by platforms like YouTube can support Asian Americans and other communities that corporate media have previously ignored. Echoing these political possibilities for the public sphere, Subin Paul examines how East India Comedy's YouTube channel uses satire to carve out a space for citizen dialogue that broadcast institutions in India did not previously allow. Beyond YouTube, James Bennett and Niki Strange explore the ways in which social media platform Twitter has positioned itself in relation to the television industries, increasingly functioning as a television channel itself in the process. Building on this investigation of social media *as* television channel, Matthew Thomas Payne explores how Twitch.tv has applied a televisual framework to streaming of game play videos, creating a channel in which distribution of game footage and commentary becomes profitable and game spectatorship becomes accessible. Outside this profit-driven realm, Faye Woods considers the relaunch of BBC Three as an online-only, on-demand, platform-neutral public service broadcasting channel compelled to balance public interest obligations and the pursuit of popularity—all turning on efforts to connect with younger viewers. Using interest in new political possibilities as the foundation for launching an online television platform, Open TV founder Aymar Jean Christian explores how his web distribution channel enables development of television programming by independent producers—especially from communities long ignored by legacy television industries.

The final group of chapters in this volume explores the logic of "premium" television embraced by both upstart and legacy television channels as a means of generating revenue (as well as distinction) in an increasingly crowded marketplace for broadcast, cable and satellite, and streaming services alike. Premium channels depend on subscription revenues, using original, exclusive, or otherwise attractive programming to lure in those subscribers. As the global leader in this market, Netflix often denies interest in the branding strategies defining its cable and satellite progenitors; yet as Timothy Havens argues, Netflix relies on branding to differentiate itself from the competition while making general entertainment appeals to broad but diverse audiences around the world. Against these global aspirations, Evan Elkins identifies Hulu as uniquely American, maintaining a national focus in the digital era that respects "geoblocked" market territories and corresponds to the domestic priorities of the legacy networks (ABC, NBC, and Fox) that co-own it. Similarly interested in the persistence of the national amid globalization and digitization, Michael Curtin and Yongli Li examine China's most popular video streaming service, iQiyi, arguing that it represents a new moment in Chinese television where new conceptions of the audience, pushes toward commercialism, and continued state oversight support new kinds of programming. Attuned to the movement of non-media businesses into subscription television industries, Karen Petruska examines how Amazon Prime Video links television delivery to an economy of retail and free shipping, distinguishing itself from its competitors through a wider suite of technology-based services.

The remaining chapters consider how legacy television industries, too, navigate premium strategies in the face of channel disruption. Peter Alilunas highlights the case of Playboy TV, showing both how the channel embraced early premium cable models to establish a market for sexually explicit content and how those models face new challenges when online streaming platforms make the same kind of programming available for free. In the premium cable service Starz, Myles McNutt sees not just an attempt to compete with HBO and Showtime through claims to program quality, value, and distinctiveness, but also development of an affective marketing strategy geared toward cultivation of fandom suited to non-linear forms of distribution. Similarly, Cory Barker and Andrew Zolides track the transition of wrestling programming from a staple of broadcast and cable schedules to an over-the-top subscription service in its own right; as the WWE Network, the wrestling franchise can develop new production practices and industrial relationships, while protected by its established industry footholds from the risks facing many other new services. A final chapter brings this consideration of premium television—and channels more broadly—full circle by considering the case of CBS All Access, which uses exclusive content with built-in franchise appeal to encourage subscribers and broadcast affiliate stations alike to follow the broadcast network to the new subscription economy.

With any luck, the linear organization sketched out here coheres as an orderly, satisfying flow of content with a clear, curated identity. Nevertheless, readers are encouraged to read these chapters out of order as well, taking a hint from the television channel landscape under investigation. While traditional television channels present curated viewing schedules, we have long been free to change channels, moving from ABC to MTV—and now from YouTube to Netflix. Indeed, it is that long-standing freedom to choose for ourselves and build programming flows out of an abundance of channels that drives programmers' attempts to keep us tuned in and makes the enhanced freedom of choice provided by Netflix so desirable to many. As much as each linear channel might present a structured program, in the aggregate channels have offered choice and the possibility of movement between them. In that context, the reader of this book—whether a researcher, an instructor, or a student—should be encouraged to carve their own paths through the flow of the channel chapters.

Beyond reading within the four main sections elaborated here, therefore, readers are also recommended to read across them. Those interested in the role of executive and creative personnel in the management of television channels, for example, would benefit from reading the chapters about ABC, A&E, The Weather Channel, El Rey, and AwesomenessTV in combination. At the same time, those interested in conglomeration and/or the management of specific television companies can uncover a deeper story about how Disney operates across many channel holdings including ABC, Disney Junior, Disney XD, and Freeform.

Meanwhile, television's mediation of national and local identities can be read across commercial channels like Rede Globo, WGN America, East India Comedy, Hulu, iQiyi, and CBS All Access. In the public television sector, these same dynamics can be compared in the cases of PBS, DR, Alabama Public Television Network, and BBC Three.

Still other recommendations could be made. Coursing through several chapters is reflection on the particular value ascribed by the television industries to masculinity and male viewership, as seen in the case studies of Spike, Comedy Central, Disney XD, and Playboy. At the same time, one might explore the emergence of alternatives to those hegemonic valuations in the way that El Rey, ISAtv, and Open TV re-envision television channels as conduits for a greater variety of voices. Those interested in marketing and audiences might be intrigued by reading about the way channels like Pop, Freeform, and El Rey imagine new categories like "modern-ups," "becomers," and "strivers," respectively, into being. While Nick Jr, Disney Junior, and Disney XD obviously target children and families, MeTV, MTV, Freeform, AwesomenessTV, and BBC Three highlight issues of age and generation more broadly when read in concert. Those more intrigued by genre might enjoy reading the connections between The CW, The Weather Channel, Comedy Central, TLC, and WWE Network. Ruminations on the notions of quality, taste, and distinction in legitimating channel brands can be produced from reading about ESPN, NBC Sports Network, A&E, and Starz. And a theme on the value of liveness stretches across ESPN, Twitch.tv, and Twitter. All this is to say that the possibilities for reading this book and drawing out new perspectives on and arguments about television channels are fairly robust and non-linear. So just as one's use of Netflix helps generate new pathways and recommendations, this book too aims to produce value from having its linear content arranged and experienced in idiosyncratic ways. Perhaps the strongest recommendation that can be made to readers is this: consider using these chapters as templates to engage in your own investigation and analysis of the many more channels *not* featured in this volume, building your own conceptual connections along the way.

In sum, the following chapters hope to provide a critical guide to television channels by emulating them: providing the structured, curated presentation of legacy linear channels while also enabling unique pathways through a vast library of content as non-linear services can do. The chapters collectively recognize that as one channel logic pops, so to speak, another may pop up alongside it. By understanding the processes by which channels transform as well as the many different forms that they can take (whether that is the transformation of TV Guide Network into Pop, or the difference between Pop as a cable service and the non-linear channels that pushed programming guides to the industrial margins), the shape of changing television industries becomes easier to discern. With that perspective, our power and agency to impact that process— to change channels—may also more clearly pop into view.

REFERENCES

Abrams, Rachel and Cynthia Littleton. 2013. "TV Guide: Price Is Right for CBS." *Variety*, April 2. Accessed June 7, 2017. Proquest.

Arvidsson, Adam. 2006. *Brands: Meaning and Value in Media Culture*. London: Routledge.

Christian, Aymar Jean. 2018. *Open TV: Innovation Beyond Hollywood and the Rise of Web Television*. New York: New York University Press.

Curtin, Michael, Jennifer Holt and Kevin Sanson. 2014. *Distribution Revolution: Conversations about the Digital Future of Film and Television*. Oakland: University of California Press.

Donaton, Scott. 2000. "'TV Guide' Magazine Is Fading, and That's Fine with Joe Kiener." *Advertising Age*, September 4. Accessed June 7, 2017. Proquest.

Farber, David R. and Beth L. Bailey. 2001. *The Columbia Guide to America in the 1960s*. New York: Columbia University Press.

Farrell, Mike. 2008. "TV Guide Network a Tough Sell." *Multichannel News*, October 6.

Farrell, Mike. 2013. "CBS Spots Bargain in TVGN." *Multichannel News*, April 1.

Flint, Joe. 1996. "Merger to Create TV Guide Channel." *Variety*, July 1.

Friedman, Wayne. 2000. "TV Guide Channel Sees Sales Jump." *Advertising Age*, May 15. Accessed June 7, 2017. Proquest.

Goldstein, Gregg. 2014. "Can TV Save the Indies?" *Variety*, November 4. Accessed June 7, 2017.

Goodwin, Tom. 2016. "The Future of TV Isn't Apps." *TechCrunch*, December 18. Accessed December 19, 2016. https://techcrunch.com/2016/12/18/the-future-of-tv-isnt-apps/.

Gripsrud, Jostein. 1998. "Television, Broadcasting, Flow: Key Metaphors in Television Theory." In *The Television Studies Book*, edited by Christine Geraghty and David Lusted, 17–32. London: Arnold Publishers.

Grossberg, Lawrence. 2010. *Cultural Studies in the Future Tense*. Durham: Duke University Press.

Havens, Tim, Amanda Lotz and Serra Tinic. 2009. "Critical Media Industry Studies: A Research Approach." *Communication, Culture & Critique* 2: 234–53.

Hibberd, James. 2005. "TV Guide to Debut First Series Slate." *TelevisionWeek*, April 4. Accessed June 7, 2017. Proquest.

Holloway, Daniel and Cynthia Littleton. 2016. "FX's John Landgraf Sounds Alarm about Potential Netflix 'Monopoly,' Overall Series Growth." *Variety*, August 9. Accessed June 16, 2017. http://variety.com/2016/tv/news/fxs-john-landgraf-netflixs-massive-programming-output-has-pushed-peak-tv-1201833825/.

Johnson, Catherine. 2012. *Branding Television*. London: Routledge.

Kompare, Derek. 2005. *Rerun Nation: How Repeats Invented American Television*. New York: Routledge.

Lafayette, Jon. 2004. "TV Guide Channel Broadens Its Appeal." *TelevisionWeek*, January 26. Accessed June 7, 2017. Proquest.

Lafayette, Jon. 2005. "TV Guide Now Selling Ads." *TelevisionWeek*, May 2. Accessed June 7, 2017. Proquest.

Lafayette, Jon. 2014. "New Name's a Star to Make Network Pop." *Broadcasting & Cable*, September 22. Accessed June 7, 2017. Proquest.

Learmonth, Michael. 2009. "TV Guide Channel to Ditch the Scroll." *Advertising Age*, April 1. Accessed June 16, 2017. http://adage.com/article/media/tv-guide-channel-ditch-program-guide-scroll/135721/.

Littleton, Cynthia. 2017. "New Platforms, New Profits." *Variety Premier*, March 23.

Lotz, Amanda. 2014. *The Television Will Be Revolutionized*, 2nd edition. New York: New York University Press.

Lotz, Amanda. 2017. *Portals: A Treatise on Internet-Distributed Television*. Ann Arbor: University of Michigan Press. http://dx.doi.org/10.3998/mpub.9699689.

Lury, Celia. 2004. *Brands: The Logos of the Global Economy*. London: Routledge.

Miége, Bernard. 1989. *The Capitalization of Cultural Production*. New York: International General.

Motavalli, John. 2004. "Channeling Changes at TV Guide TV." *Television Week*, August 9. Accessed June 7, 2017. Proquest.

"Network Makeover: TVGN to Rebrand as POP." 2014. *Cablefax Daily*, September 19. Accessed June 7, 2017. Proquest.

Perren, Alisa. 2013. "Rethinking Distribution for the Future of Media Industry Studies." *Cinema Journal* 52 (3): 165–71.

Tsing, Anna. 2004. *Friction: An Ethnography of Global Connection*. Princeton: Princeton University Press.

"TV Guide Channel." 2003. *Advertising Age*, May 19. Accessed June 7, 2017. Proquest.

"TV Guide Channel." 2006. *Advertising Age*, April 24. Accessed June 7, 2017. Proquest.

"TV Guide Channel Launches on DISH Network, Bringing Its Distribution to Nearly 80 Million Homes." 2004. *Business Wire*, June 16. Accessed June 7, 2017. Proquest.

"TV Guide Channel Selects Ensequence to Offer Viewers New Interactive TV Programming Options." 2006. *PR Newswire*, April 10. Accessed June 7, 2017. Proquest.

"TV Guide Deal Sets Up Broadcast Opportunity." 1998. *Daily News*, June 12. Accessed June 9, 2017. www.highbeam.com/doc/1G1-83826997.html.

"TV Guide Network Acquires Rights to 'Punk'd.'" 2009. *Entertainment Close-Up*, September 9. Accessed June 7, 2017. Proquest.

Umstead, R. Thomas. 2010. " 'Re-Engineering' TV Guide." *Multichannel News*, May 31.

Umstead, R. Thomas and Kent Gibbons. 2016. "Pop Network Starts to Find Its Fans." *Multichannel News*, January 11.

Williams, Raymond. 2003. *Television: Technology and Cultural Form*. London: Routledge.

Broadcast Stations and Networks

 **ABC**

Crisis, Risk, and the Logics of Change
Kristen J. Warner

On May 22, 2017, ABC delivered on a promise nearly 14 years in the making when it launched a new season of its highly rated series *The Bachelorette* (2003–) with an African American woman in the lead. Attorney Rachel Lindsay of Dallas, Texas, had previously appeared as a contestant on Season 21 of *The Bachelor* (2002–), and after not being selected as one of the final two contestants by suitor Nick Viall yet remaining a fan favorite, viewers suspected a larger plan could be at work, hopeful that after 13 seasons ABC would finally cast an African American woman in the role. Indeed, when it was announced in March 2017 that Lindsay would be the next Bachelorette, many viewers celebrated this move toward greater diversity. However, the timing for such a casting move would follow industry strategy rather than broader social shifts or fan interests. After a US District Court judge ruled against two African American plaintiffs in 2012, deciding that casting decisions made by *The Bachelor* enjoyed First Amendment protections, it was clear that changes in the diversity of casting decisions would be determined by the internal choices of producers and influences of the network ("Judge" 2012). That impetus seemed to have arrived by August 2016, however, when newly appointed ABC Entertainment president Channing Dungey—the first African American to lead a major broadcast network—presented ABC's fall lineup at the summer Television Critics Association meeting. In response to the persistent lack of diversity among leads in the *Bachelor* franchise, Dungey asserted: "I would very much like to see some changes there" (de Moraes 2016). Because of the cyclical process whereby runners-up on one program might become leads on the next, Dungey signaled that lead diversity would not be achieved overnight but through "the need to increase the pool of diverse candidates in the beginning." Her remarks suggest a clear directive to the *Bachelor/Bachelorette* production team to widen the pool to improve the odds of diversity in this cyclical selection process.

Rachel Lindsay represented the fruit of that directive, not only strategically including her in a pool of women vying to become the next Bachelorette lead as much if not more than a match for Viall, but also within the pool of relatable, professional African American women assembled across many of ABC's programs. Lindsay's well put together yet approachable look and "super smart yet super fun girl" persona matched the needs of the network and deemed her worthy of investing time and marketing effort. As I argued elsewhere prior to her official selection, "in order for her to be the remotest possible suitor, I think she would need to be 10s across the board. Her socioeconomic class, her education, her looks—she needs to be above board in all those things" (Ricciardi 2017). While Lindsay's background and affect were familiar to fans of *The Bachelor*, they also resonated against other ABC scripted series that featured similarly intelligent, professional African American women such as Kerry Washington's Olivia Pope in *Scandal* (2012–) and Viola Davis's Annalise Keating in *How To Get Away With Murder* (2014–).

The precise placement of Lindsay as the first diversity hire in *Bachelor/Bachelorette* history crystallizes the efforts of ABC over the previous decade to specialize in multicultural casts and women of color leads—many of these spearheaded by African American showrunner Shonda Rhimes with support from Dungey in her previous role as executive vice president for drama development under her predecessor as ABC President Paul Lee. Yet ironically, Dungey's ascension to ABC leadership under Ben Sherwood, three years into his own role as president of the larger Disney/ABC Television Group, signaled as much the possibility for strategic transition as continuity with the priorities of a previous regime. While past network presidents helped ABC center diverse casting as part of its overall programming strategy for a time, shifts in network leadership introduce opportunities for strategies to be disrupted. As power changes hands, new regimes want their tastes and development instincts to be credited for successes while the missions of previous eras might become perceived as obsolete. This chapter explores how ABC's internal transitions of senior executive leadership, most often informed by the logics of risk and crisis, factor into its programming decisions and, ultimately, the demographic shifts that reveal the ever-changing mission and vision of the network.

CRISIS AND TRANSITION: UNDERSTANDING NETWORK LOGICS

Before exploring how network leadership transitions determine which audiences are targeted for programming, it is first useful to outline some of the logics that inform these decisions. These logics are paradoxical in that, on one hand, much decision-making follows an organized system of in-house market research that offers executives a range of choices and assessments of their potential to stimulate growth. On the other hand, this system depends on humans with biases, worldviews, and perspectives, which means its logics are far from ideologically neutral but instead very much informed by subjective experience and tastes. From that understanding, media industries researcher Joseph Turow provides a macro analysis of how networks act as cultural productions systems "characterized by a constant and pervasive tension between innovation and control" (1984, 151). In the course of producing television programming, innovation leans more toward the creative where media professionals think "outside the box" to develop new ideas or reconceptualize old ones. Meanwhile, control points toward the economics of keeping costs down while maximizing profit. Of course, innovation and control always sit in tension because failure is a near certainty in television; most series will not be hits. Thus, the goal with these two structuring forces is to reduce as much *risk* of failure as possible. Alleviating risk within television industries relies on predictable formulas and routines previously proven profitable and economically efficient. Turow outlines the behaviors that creators in these cultural production systems adopt to neutralize as much risk as possible:

> Greater the risk involved, greater the chance that creators will both (1) structure their activities toward highly predictable, highly patterned mass media content and (2) orient their routines toward certain administrative techniques not so obviously reflected in content itself. These administrative techniques of coping are routines designed to help creators seek out information or personnel that will maximize the chance of a particular product's success.
>
> (1984, 156–7)

The checks and balances assumed in this risk management model are predicated on routine and predictability. As Turow notes, continuity of personnel and leadership provides one a way to mitigate anxiety: working with the same above- and below-the-line laborers, promoting executives from in-house, selecting talent from familiar pools, and relying upon big ticket stars all become ways to eschew risk.

Nevertheless, despite their aversion to failure, television networks turn on significant moments of innovation, change, and disruption too. Turow describes two motivators that counter risk aversion: transition and crisis. In leadership transitions, newly promoted executives clear current production slates to make way for new strategic visions or adjust programming acquisitions to accommodate new brands and demographics that will differentiate them from their predecessors. However, even in the midst of leadership transitions, crises can emerge when networks face poor quarterly returns or declining Nielsen ratings compared to their competitors. Transition and crisis often function like safety valves, introducing change in case of an emergency. Leadership shakeups can be costly in terms of time, resources, labor, and severance compensation, leading to a preference for in-house promotion and extreme caution in general. In neither case where transition or crisis occurs is there any guarantee that risks taken will pay off; but, if the goal is to demonstrate change and innovation to put stakeholders at ease in a moment of crisis, transitions of leadership can be rationalized as serving the best interest of a network.

FOURTH PLACE CRISES: 2004 AND 2016

ABC offers a concrete case study of these dynamics between crisis, transition, and risk. In fact, looking at the network's efforts at innovation and control in both 2004 and 2016 we can see parallel tales of ratings crisis giving way to risky creative maneuvers resulting in different programming strategies and, ultimately, huge shakeups in executive personnel. In both these years, under ambitious entertainment presidents, ABC found itself in fourth place, last in a competition for viewers as measured by ratings with three other major US broadcast networks—NBC, CBS, and Fox—who, by 2016, all fought for market share in an oversaturated television industry increasingly fragmented by cable and online streaming platforms. Thus, last-place finishes fed internal resolutions that may have been worth the risk to make large-scale changes to leadership and programming.

Having failed to post a profit in seven years in addition to its fourth-place finish, ABC needed a win in 2004. Chairman of the Entertainment Group Lloyd Braun sought out successful *Alias* creator and showrunner J. J. Abrams to rewrite a series pilot outline that was pitched to Braun by previous writers but never quite hit the mark. Olga Craig details Braun's vision: "He envisaged the show as a cross between *Cast Away*, the 2000 film starring Tom Hanks, and *Survivor* (CBS, 2000–), the reality television show set on a desert island" (Craig 2005). According to Craig, Braun was so impressed with Abrams's outline for *Lost* (2004–2010) that he began to imagine how it could get ABC out of its current rut and into stronger competition with the other broadcast networks. Braun said of Abrams's outline: "It's the best piece of television I've ever read. I was out of my mind. I knew it would make noise that would be so big, so different, you couldn't avoid it" (Craig 2005). Braun greenlit the project and set the pilot episode budget at a reported $12 million—quite a fortune for a television series at that time, and quite a risk based on an outline with no official script yet approved. Perhaps what allayed Braun's anxiety about investing so much into an untested project of this scale was Abrams's status as a proven showrunner.

Nevertheless, Braun immediately faced scrutiny for this risk. Then Chairman and CEO of Disney Michael Eisner and his deputy Bog Iger both considered *Lost* to be an out of control passion project. Craig sets the scene:

> behind the scenes, while the pilot was being filmed in Hawaii, Braun's bosses were furious at the cost and had decided to pull the plug on him. Iger, insisting that it would never work as a series, saved the worst of his sarcasm for the fact that the writers still did not even know what the mysterious presence on the island was. Eisner was equally scathing, describing it as another "crazy" Abrams project.
>
> (Craig 2005)

Ultimately, what Eisner and Iger perceived as a runaway production exceeding the usual balance of innovation and control in favor of reckless spending on an untested property resulted in a leadership shakeup at ABC. Braun was out, replaced by Stephen McPherson. The shakeup also gave them cover to redistribute power, renaming McPherson's position as "chief programming executive" (no longer a "chairman") and making him report to Anne Sweeney, who became president of the Disney/ABC Television Group. Nevertheless, with regard to programming, *Lost* survived the pilot season despite its champion's departure, most likely because so much money was sunk into the series that Eisner and Iger could not justify killing it before its fall premiere. Of course, Braun's risky gamble paid off: supported by an effective advertising campaign under the new regime, *Lost* became a runaway success for ABC, earning the network its biggest ratings since 2000, garnering a host of critical acclaim and awards, and becoming ABC's fastest selling show internationally (Craig 2005). The story of *Lost* and Braun reveals a deeper understanding of the network logics through which risk is both cultivated—within reason—and also managed through moments of transition when those tolerances are exceeded.

While *Lost* showcases how a network like ABC navigates the pressure to deliver innovative success within relatively safe margins set by the Disney upper echelon, Braun had other series in development when he was fired that provided the network years of additional success. The same motivators that moved him to champion *Lost* influenced him and his second in command, ABC president Susan Lyne, to order pilots for *Desperate Housewives* (2004–2012), *Dancing with the Stars* (2005–), and *Grey's Anatomy* (2005–). Peter Lauria described what McPherson inherited from Braun:

> In 2004, the year McPherson took the reins, *Lost* made its debut, in lockstep with *Desperate Housewives*, *Dancing With the Stars*, and *Grey's Anatomy*. ABC Entertainment broadcast revenue, which includes the ABC network, television stations owned by its parent company, and other items, jumped from $5.4 billion to $6.6 billion two years later.
>
> (Lauria 2010)

Newsweek reinforced the network success story:

> The sexy suburbanites of ABC's *Desperate Housewives* are the darlings of the fall TV season, with more than 20 million viewers tuning in to each of the first two shows. And more than 18 million people are watching *Lost* to find out which castaway will be the next meal for the mysterious monster. Those two hits have given something ABC hasn't seen in a long time: solid berths in the Nielsen top 10. In addition to *Housewives* (No. 4) and *Lost* (No. 9), two other new shows, *Boston Legal* and *Wife Swap*, have been strong performers, providing ABC momentum to pull out of its fourth-place slump. The network is now in second place among the coveted 18- to 49-year-old audience, running ahead of NBC, whose once unbeatable Thursday lineup is no longer must-see TV.
>
> ("Desperate" 2004)

Although Braun may have focused on crafting the creative and mysterious *Lost* juggernaut, that series' diverse, ensemble cast as well as the prominence of women in leading roles on top programs like *Desperate Housewives* and *Grey's Anatomy* suggests that he and Lyne were cultivating both white women and women of color audiences for the network. Indeed, in 2004, trade journal Mediaweek reported that Lyne's strategy to return the network to its "roots" as a strong broadcast network meant "putting on more female-oriented family dramas like past ABC hit *thirtysomething*" (Consoli 2004, 7). While these moves paid off—ultimately, for Braun's predecessors—the network would soon return to more manageable, predictable norms without a crisis to motivate continued risk.

Although ABC may have been rated second in the coveted 18- to 49-year-old demographic in 2004, it had by 2016 returned to fourth-place status among the major broadcast networks. Of the series that had launched its successful 2004 run, only two were still on air: *Grey's* and *Dancing*. McPherson was put out to pasture in 2010 officially for failing to reproduce the success he inherited from Braun and Lyne and unofficially because of sexual harassment allegations. Coming from successful turns in charge of BBC America and, most recently, ABC Family, Braun's replacement Paul Lee opted to expand the production relationship between the network and *Grey's* showrunner Shonda Rhimes. By 2014, ABC began marketing a host of shows under her Shondaland production company banner that by 2014 contributed to a Thursday night programming block called "TGIT"—Thank God It's Thursday. Lee's risktaking centered around building out a diverse and inclusive brand with field tested and established talent such as Rhimes, ultimately branching out into comedies with Kenya Barris's *black-ish* (2014–) and Nahnatchka Khan's *Fresh Off the Boat* (2015–). Lee promised that programs incorporating inclusion and diversity would showcase an authenticity that resonated with audiences across all racial groups—a strategy that surely informed decisions to pursue greater diversity in casting the Bachelor franchise, too. However, although critics respected ABC's efforts, the gambits Lee pursued had not by 2016 translated into sufficient success to prevent another transition. With Ben Sherwood, president of the Disney/ABC Television Group, believing that major changes and personnel strategies could be justified after two years of pursuing this particular programming agenda had led to a new fourth-place crisis, Lee stepped down in February 2016.[1]

Initiating another leadership transition, Sherwood promoted Channing Dungey to entertainment president. Rising to senior leadership under Lee's regime, Dungey had overseen all of the Shondaland series in her previous role as executive vice president of drama development. Now the first African American to run a major broadcast network, Dungey offered Sherwood a promise of smooth transition (thanks to her 13-year tenure with ABC) as well as sign of corporate commitment to greater diversity. However, similarly to how Eisner and Iger redistributed power after Braun and Lyne, Sherwood utilized the leadership change to redefine the position as well, limiting Dungey's position to entertainment president for the network as opposed to also leading ABC Studios as her predecessors had. In this new model, the president of ABC Studios reported directly to Sherwood. Cynthia Littleton (2016) posited this as a logical change:

> The decision to break up the reporting structure of the network and studio was meant to provide more independence to the studio, which has become a bigger profit center than the network through the growth of the worldwide content licensing business.

Yet Sherwood's act of consolidating power over network and studio alike certainly lessened the degree of influence and agency to effect change past entertainment chiefs enjoyed. Sherwood rationalized this move as part of the "winds of change" fueling the leadership transition.

> Paul [Lee] oversaw the network and the studio, and when this change happened, it was a chance to let the winds of change blow through the organization and bring Channing to the table with all of her ideas and her energy and her collaborative spirit, and also to bring Patrick [Moran, president of ABC Studios] to the table with all his dynamism and his teamwork and all his ideas.
>
> (Birnbaum 2016)

Collaborative spirit may have abounded, but more people reporting to Sherwood also ensured fewer fiefdoms outside his control. Sherwood's gain could only be made in a time of crisis, when his winds of change allowed him to (re)set the agenda for the future of the network. Sherwood continued to play a game of risk but it primarily circulates around confidence in his own labor, his management of other executives, and his ability to get them on board with a new vision—one that recuperated ABC's appeals to white audiences.

ENDS ARE BEGINNINGS: FROM DIVERSITY TO THE HEARTLAND

The winds of change generated by ABC's 2016 fourth-place crisis did not just enable Sherwood to place his chosen personnel, but also determined what reorientations were in store for the network's programming. Prior to resigning, Lee helped orchestrate a brand designed around diversity and inclusion that better represented America. Much ABC programming attempted to target a variety of audience demographics including, but not limited to, people of color. As Stephen Battaglio writes,

> He [Lee] consistently picked shows that he felt exemplified ABC's brand—layered, often provocative and with a hint of mirth—and advocated for guilty pleasure serials that appeal to women, such as *Scandal* with plots that unfold over several weeks.
>
> (Battaglio 2016)

Lee banked on a slate of serialized, soapy, sexy shows that targeted men and women of color as well as white women. However, this strategy later conflicted with Sherwood's vision of what types of shows and audiences could, once again, lift ABC from their fourth place rut. Battaglio notes that Sherwood took stock of what CBS, the number one broadcast television network, was producing and suggested Lee consider carrying similar kinds of series. "Sherwood . . . encouraged Lee to take a page from CBS' book by developing more procedural shows, such as *NCIS*, that allow viewers to watch occasional episodes without feeling like they are missing out" (Battaglio 2016). Moving the needle from predominantly serialized series to more episodic fare would likely also shift the demographics of viewers—advantageous as ABC slipped to fourth place overall.

David Sims asserts that while episodic shows on CBS like *NCIS* (2003–) and *Criminal Minds* (2005–) are hugely successful and do allow new viewers to enter at any point, they also "tend to skew much older, while ABC does better in the youthful demographics favored by advertisers" (Sims 2016). While it may be counterintuitive to abandon a desirable demographic, Sherwood's strategy may have stemmed from desiring a consistent, loyal base of viewership as well as larger overall audience in an age of shrinking Nielsen ratings.

By the time Dungey became entertainment president, this move toward Sherwood's idea of crime procedurals was already taking shape. When asked what she would like to see from her future ABC programming, she posited,

> I would love to see more closed-ended procedurals on the network, particularly because we have to schedule 35 weeks of a year, and it's nice because, with a procedural, you can generally do 22 episodes, and they also repeat pretty well.
>
> (Villareal 2016)

Using similar language as Sherwood, Dungey's desire to embrace more procedural series to poach CBS's viewers made clear how tensions between innovation and control can privilege already successful, predictable routines over creative innovation, even in crisis.

Beyond this desire for CBS' procedural audience, Dungey and Sherwood publicly stated after the 2016 US presidential election an interest in targeting more programming to working class voters they perceived to have supported Donald Trump. At a media summit in December 2016, Dungey remarked:

> With our dramas, we have a lot of shows that feature very well-to-do well-educated people who are driving very nice cars and living in extremely nice places. There is definitely still room for that, and we absolutely want to continue to tell those stories because wish fulfillment is a critical part of what we do as entertainers. But in recent history we haven't paid enough attention to some of the true realities of what life is like for everyday Americans in our dramas.
>
> (Adalian 2016)

A network's programming mission can of course grow, but in this instance it seemed as if the mission was being redefined to cater to unnamed but heavily inferred rural white audiences in the Heartland who did not indulge in the wish fulfillment ABC had been offering in series set in and aimed at the so-called liberal coasts. While Dungey nominates markers of class difference, the wish fulfillment that ABC had offered turned as much on race, given that its Lee-era series of featured leads of color and diverse casts living in utopic worlds of equality. Thus, it seems like the network's new imagined future would increasingly involve programming for working class white viewers looking for a refuge from that vision—even as ABC maintained a balance of series appealing to viewers already invested in the network's previous offerings. That existing audience, moreover, was likely not as diverse as the characters offered on screen. In 2017, Nielsen reported that four of ABC's biggest series including *Scandal, black-ish, Secrets and Lies* (2015–2016), and *How to Get Away With Murder* featuring African American lead actors were watched by more than 60% non-black audiences ("For" 2017). While the report does not specify the specific percentage of white audience members, they likely constitute a significant amount. In short, the ABC mission could retain some measure of racial diversity as decoration and wish fulfillment for its refigured audiences, but series explicitly targeting white women and people of color had no guarantee of withstanding the new priorities of the Sherwood/Dungey regime.

Returning to *The Bachelorette*, we can now see how in her capacity as entertainment president, Dungey finally brought racial equity to a series that had so long resisted it, executing a strategy to deliver change. However, what if that story of "success" actually signaled the end of the Paul Lee mission to differentiate ABC from the competition, and the beginning of a new moment of crisis in which casting practices and demographic priorities were to be reoriented around new goalposts? For Ben Sherwood, ABC's recurring fourth-place crisis opened up a possibility to reimagine the network's audience, to capture a different kind of viewer while hoping to maintain the trust of the audience ABC already had. In sum, understanding how leadership changes impact programming and audience can reveal the often-paradoxical positions industrial stakeholders occupy in the course of developing program content while negotiating transition and crisis. Furthermore, considering the power of logics such as risk, innovation, and control forces our conversations about the television industries away from cliché axioms about programmers "giving the people what they want" and toward keener perception of the way audience interests are constructed alongside dramatic shifts in power and status among different networks and internally among decision-making personnel. Making cultivated gambles to effect innovation and change, networks like ABC operate in a perpetual cycle of success and crisis in which risks are taken to disrupt one status quo before ultimately installing another.

NOTE

1 According to Caroline Framke (2016), the terms for Lee's exit from ABC are unclear: "The ABC press release says he 'decided to step down,' while *Hollywood Reporter* claims he was 'forced out,' and *New York Times* says he 'resigned after losing a struggle over the network's direction.'"

REFERENCES

Adalian, Josef. 2016. "ABC Wants to Focus More of Its Programming on the Working Class in the Age of Trump." *Vulture*, December 1. www.vulture.com/2016/12/abc-changing-program ming-philosophy-due-to-trump.html.

Battaglio, Stephen. 2016. "New ABC President Channing Dungey Gained Respect Amid Rise to Top." *LA Times*, February 17. www.latimes.com/entertainment/envelope/cotown/la-et-ct-channing-dungey-abc-entertainment-20160217-story.html.

Birnbaum, Debra. 2016. "ABC Heads Ben Sherwood and Channing Dungey on Paul Lee's Exit, Making History and Live Programming." *Variety*, February 19. http://variety.com/2016/tv/news/abc-ben-sherwood-channing-dungey-paul-lee-changes-challenges-1201710443/.

Consoli, John. 2004. "ABC Turnaround Not That Simple." *Mediaweek*, March 8.

Craig, Olga. 2005. "The Man Who Discovered 'Lost'—and Found Himself Out of a Job." *Telegraph*, August 14. www.telegraph.co.uk/news/worldnews/northamerica/usa/1496199/The-man-who-discovered-Lost-and-found-himself-out-of-a-job.html.

de Moraes, Lisa. 2016. "'The Bachelor' Needs More Diverse 'Pool of Candidates,' Says Programming Chief Channing Dungey—TCA." *Deadline Hollywood*, August 4. http://deadline.com/2016/08/the-bachelor-diversity-pool-candidates-channing-dungey-unreal-tca-1201798469/.

"Desperate? Not ABC." 2004. *Newsweek*. www.newsweek.com/desperate-not-abc-129849.

"For Us by Us? The Mainstream Appeal of Black Content." 2017. *Nielsen.com*, February 8. www.nielsen.com/us/en/insights/news/2017/for-us-by-us-the-mainstream-appeal-of-black-content.html.

Framke, Caroline. 2016. "ABC's Channing Dungey Is Now the First Black President of a Major TV Network." *Vox*, February 17. www.vox.com/2016/2/17/11038430/abc-president-channing-dungey-paul-lee-shonda.

"Judge Dismisses 'Bachelor' Discrimination Lawsuit." 2012. *CNN*, October 16. www.cnn.com/2012/10/16/showbiz/bachelor-lawsuit/.

Lauria, Peter. 2010. "ABC's Stephen McPherson Resigns as Entertainment Chief." *The Daily Beast*, July 27. www.thedailybeast.com/abcs-stephen-mcpherson-resigns-as-entertainment-chief.

Littleton, Cynthia. 2016. "ABC Shakeup: Simmering Tensions Between Ben Sherwood, Paul Lee Come to a Boil." *Variety*, February 17. http://variety.com/2016/tv/news/abc-ben-sherwood-paul-lee-shakeup-1201708578/.

Ricciardi, Tiney. 2017. "Why Dallas' Rachel Lindsay Makes All-Too-White 'Bachelor' and 'Bachelorette' Better." *Guidelive*, March 6. www.guidelive.com/reality-tv/2017/03/06/dallas-rachel-lindsay-makes-all-too-white-bachelor-bachelorette-better.

Sims, David. 2016. "Is Creative Television Bad for Business?" *The Atlantic*, February 17. www.theatlantic.com/entertainment/archive/2016/02/paul-lee-abc-network-television-channing-dungey/463290/.

Turow, Joseph. 1984. *Media Industries: The Production of News and Entertainment*. New York: Longman.

Villarreal, Yvonne. 2016. "New ABC President Looks Forward, Talks 'Bachelor's' Diversity Problem, and Bringing 'Star Wars' to TV in First TCA Appearance." *LA Times*, August 4. www.latimes.com/entertainment/envelope/cotown/la-et-ct-abc-dungey-tca-20160804-snap-story.html

The CW

Media Conglomerates in Partnership
Caryn Murphy

The CW is both the smallest and the youngest of the national broadcast networks, by several measures. The CW draws the lowest viewership, it only programs ten hours of prime-time each week, and it has contract agreements with fewer affiliates than the broadcast competition (NBC, ABC, FOX, and in principle, CBS). It was formed in 2006, when CBS Corporation and Warner Bros. agreed to shut down their competing networks, UPN and the WB, and join forces on a new venture that would exploit the most popular programming and retain the strongest affiliate stations from those outlets. The CW also has the youngest audience target demographic of any of the broadcast networks; as a result, the actual audience skews younger than that of the competition.[1] The business of broadcasting has historically been focused on reaching the largest possible audiences; as a broadcast network, the CW's continued existence would seem to confound this expectation. In terms of Nielsen ratings, the network has never launched a show that has cracked the top 20. The smallest network has cultivated a particular kind of value, however, by serving the interests of its corporate parents. The industrial practices of the CW are of interest because they represent cooperation rather than competition between two of the largest global media conglomerates, CBS Corporation and Warner Bros. (a division of Time Warner). This chapter examines three case studies in scripted programming to analyze how the CW operates as a hybrid of a traditional broadcast network and a cable channel that serves more specific audiences. Since 2011, the network has refined its practices related to program ownership and distribution in order to derive maximum benefit for its parent companies.

"THE ECONOMICS OF THE CW": *RINGER* (2011–2012)

CBS, the "most-watched U.S. television network," ordered a pilot episode of *Ringer* in early 2011 (Serjeant 2011). This hour-long drama starring Sarah Michelle Gellar was co-produced by CBS Television Studios (CTS) and ABC Studios. Many series typically fail at this early stage, when a pilot might be rejected by its intended network. In this case, however, when CBS decided not to order *Ringer* to series, the CW stepped in and added the program to its fall schedule. The shift from CBS to the CW was publicized as a canny business decision because *Ringer* centered on a young woman who poses as her wealthy twin. Its female protagonist and subject matter marked it as a better fit for the CW because young female audiences were the network's primary demographic target. *Gossip Girl* (2007–2012), a serialized drama about wealthy teenagers, was the network's first breakout success, and its popularity among young women had a definitive impact on CW programming in the network's early years as it sought to replicate its success by adding similar series. *Ringer* was closer in tone and content to the prime-time offerings on the CW than the rest of the dramas at CBS, which were primarily episodic procedurals, and this affinity was cited in the announcement that the former outlet had picked up the series.

ABC Studios abandoned the project when CBS rejected it, however, reportedly balking at "the economics of the CW" (Andreeva 2011). If the series had aired on CBS, ABC Studios would have commanded a higher license fee per episode, on the basis of the network's impressive viewership and substantial advertising rates. CTS found a new production partner in Warner Bros Television (WBTV); the two companies co-produced *Ringer* for distribution on the CW, the network co-owned by their parent companies. Although the CW operates on a smaller scale than CBS, the smaller network's "economics" changed substantially when *Ringer* premiered in the fall of 2011.

Ringer received a full season order in October, just days before the CW signed a groundbreaking licensing deal with Netflix (Goldberg and Ng 2011). Netflix secured the rights to stream the CW's scripted programming for a four-year period, in a deal that held a potential valuation of one billion dollars (McMillan 2011). Netflix purchased the right to air previous seasons of series that were currently airing, and the streaming service would add current seasons once they had completed first-run on the broadcast network. In the event of a series cancellation, the deal allowed Netflix to stream all of the episodes for a four-year period. This licensing deal did not prevent the CW from negotiating other sales, including the sale of international rights. At the time it was announced, WBTV president Bruce Rosenblum told the trade press that "the terms won't be repeated" because "other networks don't own (as much of) their own content" (Lieberman 2011b). *Ringer*, for example, could be included in this lucrative licensing deal because it was co-produced by companies that CBS Corporation and Warner Bros controlled.

As of 2011, the CW's new business strategy necessitated owning as much of its programming as possible. Immediately following the deal with Netflix, the CW signed a licensing deal with Hulu that made current episodes of its series available via the over-the-top service (Lieberman 2011a). These agreements enabled the CW to break even as a network, and for CTS and WBTV to profit; both companies received licensing fees from Netflix and Hulu for *Ringer*, for example, even though the series' cancellation after a single season made a traditional broadcast or cable syndication sale impossible. Leslie Moonves, CEO of CBS Corporation, explained that the Netflix deal "creates a brand-new window for CBS and Warner Bros. to be paid for the content we supply the network" (McMillan 2011).

These licensing agreements primarily benefit the companies that produced the programming, and have therefore increased the incentive for CBS and Warner Bros. to hold a financial interest in all of the programming that airs on the CW. In 2011, the network aired some prime-time programming produced by independent production companies. By 2015, programming owned in whole or in part by one (or both) of the network's parent companies made up 100% of the prime-time schedule. In the present day, the basic "economics" of the CW are as follows: the network pays a per episode license fee to air programming produced by CTS, WBTV, or the two companies in partnership; the CW sells commercial time to advertisers who seek to reach the broadcast network's target audiences; CW programming generates further revenue through licensing deals with Netflix and Hulu.[2] CBS Corporation and Warner Bros. benefit from revenues generated by the network *and* from revenues generated by the programming that they produce.

A BROADCAST NETWORK THAT ACTS LIKE A CABLE CHANNEL: *CRAZY EX-GIRLFRIEND* (2015–)

Television journalists often note a similarity between the CW as a broadcast network and the programming and practices of cable channels. Josef Adalian, for example, has termed the CW a "hybrid network," claiming that "It's an old-school broadcast network with the heart and soul of a niche cable channel" (2016). The CW undoubtedly participates in the broadcast business because it distributes programming free, over the air, via a network of local affiliate stations. As a broadcaster, it is also regulated by the FCC's ownership and content standards. The network has to carefully manage resources in order to provide affiliates a substantial number of program hours each season, while serving the broadcast network goal of selling audiences to advertisers. The CW has historically targeted a more specific audience than its broadcast competition, but this is not the sole basis for comparison to cable outlets. A typical season of a broadcast network series includes at least 22 episodes, but the CW has frequently ordered fewer episodes, a strategy more characteristic of a cable channel.[3] The network offers fewer hours of original programming than its broadcast network competitors, and it also relies substantially on producers with a proven track record at the network. Julie Plec produced three weekly hours of prime-time programming for the CW in 2015, for example, and Greg Berlanti was responsible for five weekly hours of the 2016 television season.[4] The CW is also slower to cancel low-rated shows, and has a reputation for allowing programming time to develop. This trait is the result of the network's economics, discussed earlier, but is further driven by a desire to measure program success as a cable channel might in terms other than Nielsen ratings. Although a number of CW series languished at the bottom of the ratings during the fall of 2015, CW president Mark Pedowitz renewed all of the scripted series that the network had on the air in March of 2016 (Lynch 2016b). *Crazy Ex-Girlfriend* maintained the lowest ratings of all of these series; its development process highlights key distinctions between the CW and cable outlets.

In 2015, CTS developed a half-hour pilot for a musical comedy series they planned to sell to Showtime, a premium cable channel that is also a division of CBS Corporation. When Showtime declined to move forward with the series, CTS worked with the series' creators, Rachel Bloom and Aline Brosh McKenna, to redesign it for the CW. This process necessitated significant structural changes; the original pilot was a commercial-free half hour, but the CW required hour-long episodes that would be built to accommodate commercial breaks. The Showtime project also incorporated adult language and sexuality, as is typical of original content developed for that type of outlet. These elements had to be toned down or excised for air on broadcast television in order to meet FCC content standards and generate interest from advertisers. A typical season order at Showtime would consist of 10 to 12 episodes, whereas Bloom and Brosh McKenna produced 18 episodes for the series' first season at the CW. Despite the significant hurdles involved in making a cable program into a broadcast network property, executives at CBS Corporation felt there was particular value in *Crazy Ex-Girlfriend*, which they scheduled to air on the CW as a complement to *Jane the Virgin* (CW, 2014–), presuming that the irreverent tone of both series might indicate an overlap in their viewership. As the trade press reported in their coverage of the deal, "CBS Studios, CW and Showtime are all part of the CBS family" (Andreeva 2015). CBS Corporation benefited from its corporate parentage of the CW in the development of this series, because the broadcast network provided a space for a project that otherwise would have failed at the pilot stage. The development process for a premium cable series is often costly, and although Showtime turned down *Crazy Ex-Girlfriend*, press coverage of the CW deal noted that the channel would likely recoup the production costs incurred (Andreeva 2015).

The first season of *Crazy Ex-Girlfriend* ranked 91st out of 91 broadcast network series, with a .4 rating among 18- to 49-year-old viewers (Porter 2016), which raises the question of why the show was granted a renewal for a second season.[5] This question returns us to consideration of how the CW might be similar to a cable channel. The CW's support of critically beloved but low-rated programming helps to brand it as a distribution outlet for "quality" content. *Crazy Ex-Girlfriend* did not make a significant mark in traditional ratings measures, but it was one of the most acclaimed shows of the 2015 season. Critics praised the series for being "fresh," "distinctive," and "experimental," which are not typically characteristics for which broadcast programming is lauded (Poniewozik 2016). The series was nominated for four Emmys in 2016, setting a record for the CW, and star Rachel Bloom won a Golden Globe award for best actress in a comedy series. Notably, *Jane the Virgin* was also a favorite of television critics in its first season and series' star Gina Rodriguez also received the Golden Globe. In its second season, *Jane the Virgin* had only a slightly larger audience than *Crazy Ex-Girlfriend*; the series ranked 86th out of 91 broadcast network shows, with a .7 rating among 18- to 49-year-olds (Porter 2016). Although *Jane the Virgin* attracted critical acclaim and social media buzz, this did not translate into significant viewership, and its continued ratings struggles cast doubt on the ability of *Crazy Ex-Girlfriend* to grow its audience.

The CW could have justified a renewal for *Crazy Ex-Girlfriend* if the series substantially increased its viewership through digital distribution, including Hulu, Amazon, iTunes, or the CW's own website, CWTV.com. Indeed, networks acknowledge that it's difficult to measure the success of programming in an environment where viewership is so dispersed. In a presentation to the Television Critics Association, Mark Pedowitz noted the lack of "optimistic statistics or measurements" to support the continuation of *Crazy Ex-Girlfriend*, but insisted regardless, "We're going to give it a chance to get seen" (Koblin 2016). The network's financial interest in its programming plays a key role in justifying this mantra. As industry analyst John Koblin notes,

> In recent years, as ratings began to decline, many of the networks tried to develop their shows in-house using a studio team owned by the parent company. If a network has an ownership stake in a show, it is more likely to give a show a chance to work.
>
> (2015)

Glenn Geller, president of CBS Entertainment, explains,

> If we get these shows to a good place and let them find solid viewership and we get to sell them into syndication, they go into streaming, they go everywhere and suddenly it's good for the corporation. And we get paid on both sides.
>
> (Koblin 2015)

This ability to generate revenue for the network and its parent companies is thus the defining element of the CW's position in the contemporary broadcast landscape.

"GENRE SHOWS WITH A SERIALIZED ELEMENT": *SUPERGIRL* (CBS, 2015–2016; CW, 2016–)

At the May 2016 upfront presentation to advertisers, Mark Pedowitz claimed that the deal to move *Supergirl* from CBS to the CW came together in less than two weeks because "our parent companies recognized that this was the right place for it" (Lynch 2016a). Although the network president stated this with certainty in 2016, the CW had passed on *Supergirl* just one year earlier. An examination of how *Supergirl* eventually landed at the CW further illuminates the network's relationship to its partnered corporate entities, as well as its target audiences.

When the CW initially passed on the pitch for *Supergirl*, the cost of the series' production at WBTV would have been a major factor. The trade press reported that *Supergirl* was the most expensive new series airing on CBS in 2015 (Goldberg 2016). Series creators Greg Berlanti and Andrew Kreisberg had already launched adaptations of DC Comics' *Arrow* and *The Flash* on the CW, but Berlanti emphasized the "scope and epicness" of *Supergirl* at the time of its premiere on CBS, which suggests that the series required a higher budget than the CW could support (Itzkoff 2015, 21). The series' season two transition to the CW therefore required cuts to the production budget. Even before the renewal deal was struck, WBTV had announced plans to move production from Los Angeles to Vancouver (Goldberg 2016).

Supergirl may also have lacked appeal for the CW because of concerns about the network's saturation with DC properties. The *New York Daily News* reported that when he was asked why the show went to CBS, Pedowitz said, "We're still a broadcast network," which the reporter interpreted as an acknowledgement of the responsibility to "offer programming to a wider range of viewers" (Hinckley 2015, 4). In the 2015 television season, the CW aired three series based on DC comics: *Arrow, The Flash*, and *Legends of Tomorrow*.[6] When *Supergirl* was added to the fall 2016 schedule, a full 40% of CW prime-time consisted of programming based on DC Comics. DC Entertainment is a unit of Warner Bros., and although it produces programming for other outlets, the CW distributes most of its television output.

The CW has utilized comic book adaptations to fundamentally shift its audience composition. When the CW added *Ringer* in 2011, the network's target audience was 18- to 34-year-old women, and 70% of the actual audience was female (Morabito 2011, 4). The majority of the network's series had female protagonists or demonstrated appeal for female viewership. The specificity of the demographic target presented problems for the broadcast network's relationship with advertisers and affiliate stations, and these concerns spurred a shift in priorities. New programming was developed under a directive to maintain core viewership while growing appeal in underrepresented demographics (Steel 2015). The introduction of *Arrow* in 2013 helped to draw in more male viewers. When *The Flash* launched during the next season, it became the most popular series that the CW had ever aired. As the 2015 television season concluded, the CW's audience composition was almost evenly split between male and female viewers (Lynch 2016a). Viewership was up by 27% (from 2011), even as the number of other programming options available to viewers (especially online) had significantly expanded (Ryan 2015).

The DC-based series exemplify the CW's programming strength, which television critic Maureen Ryan (2015) has described as "genre shows with a serialized element." The network specializes in scripted programming that encourages long-term viewer engagement with story and character. Each series encourages loyal viewership by telling a continuing story. In the same way that CBS' success is tied to episodic, procedural dramas like *NCIS*, the CW is identified with series that encourage investment in a specific narrative universe or mythology. *Supergirl*, then, should have seemed like a perfect fit from its inception.

However, the CBS network wanted *Supergirl* to help it reach a younger audience that would skew more heavily female, although the show itself did not neatly align with the rest of the network's offerings. In direct contrast, the CW may have initially avoided the series because its focus on a white female heroine in a comic-book adaptation would align too closely with the network's former image. Pedowitz has claimed that relations with advertisers and affiliates improved as the CW worked to shift its emphasis away from young female viewers (Holloway 2014, 13). According to the executives involved, at the time of the second season's renewal, *Supergirl*'s ideal distribution outlet had become a matter of internal debate within CBS Corporation. The series' first season was far from disappointing; it was the highest-rated new CBS drama with an average of ten million viewers, and the fourth-highest rated new broadcast series (Holloway 2016). Leslie Moonves claimed that CBS might have been willing to renew the series if a deal had not been struck with the CW, explaining, "It's great to own two networks. *Supergirl* fits better on the CW" (Andreeva 2016). Even with a precipitous decline in viewership, the show could be considered a hit for the CW, where it shares a narrative universe with the network's established DC series.

CONCLUSION

As recently as 2011, the trade press had regularly predicted the CW's imminent demise. The network's focus on selling young female viewers to advertisers, as exemplified by its distribution of *Ringer*, had resulted in limited viewership and strained relations with affiliate stations. The shift toward stability was driven by lucrative licensing deals that provided the network with cash infusions and a clarified sense of purpose. In the end, the CW does not function like a traditional broadcast network, as its long-running series are viewed by smaller, more specific audiences. Nor can it reasonably be considered to follow the same programming models as cable channels, because it produces up to 300 hours of scripted programming each year to provide to its network of affiliate stations. Since 2011, the CW has worked to increase its value to affiliates by increasing its appeal to a broader audience base. This goal complements the network's larger industrial strategy of providing value to its corporate parents. Recent years have seen the CW focus on its role as a platform for programming owned by corporate parents CBS Corporation and Warner Bros. The smallest network may never attain the viewership numbers that characterize major broadcasters, but as television distribution continues to evolve, those larger outlets may increasingly imitate the CW's business model.

When the financial interest and syndication rules expired in 1995, industry analysts predicted that broadcast networks would immediately revert to producing their own programming, and independent television production would fail to thrive. While the shift toward vertical integration between studios and networks has taken hold more slowly, this examination of the CW makes clear that broadcast industry economics no longer favor independent production. In the present day, a broadcast network is more likely to develop and support a series in which it maintains an ownership interest. The CW is unlikely to air any series that is not produced by CTS or WBTV, and if it did, the current financial logics of the industry would encourage the network to quickly cancel an independent that failed to generate substantial viewership. The larger national broadcast networks may increasingly emulate the CW as audience fragmentation continues, and this will certainly have implications for the future of both independent and vertically integrated television production.

NOTES

1 The median age of the CW viewer rose from 36.8 to 41.7 between 2011 and 2014, but this remains the youngest audience among the broadcast networks (Holloway 2014, 12).
2 In 2016, the CW announced a new licensing deal with Netflix to replace the 2011 agreement. The new agreement ensures that CW programming will air on Netflix more quickly and like the previous agreement, it holds a potential valuation of more than one billion dollars. The CW and Hulu were unable to come to new terms, and so the network's licensing deal with the streaming service ended (Littleton 2016).

3 In the 2015 television season, for example: *Reign* (CW, 2013–2017) aired 18 episodes, *iZombie* (CW, 2015–) aired 19 episodes, and *The 100* (CW, 2014–) aired 16. Significantly, in the era of "peak TV," other broadcast networks are also experimenting with airing shorter seasons of series.

4 Plec produced *Vampire Diaries* (CW, 2009–2017), *The Originals* (CW, 2013–), and *Containment* (CW, 2016). Berlanti produced *Supergirl* (CBS, 2015–2016, CW, 2016–), *Arrow* (CW, 2013–), *The Flash* (CW, 2014–), *Legends of Tomorrow* (CW, 2016–), and *Riverdale* (CW, 2017–). Greg Berlanti began a long-term development contract at WBTV in 2011 that extends through 2018.

5 A .4 rating indicates an audience of less than 600,000 viewers (Koblin 2015).

6 *iZombie* is also based on a comic book published by Vertigo, an imprint of DC. As of this writing, it does not share a narrative universe with these three series.

REFERENCES

Adalian, Josef. 2016. "The CW Is One of the Bigger TV Success Stories of the Decade." *Vulture*, May 19. Accessed May 31, 2016. www.vulture.com/2016/05/cw-is-a-tv-success-story.html.

Andreeva, Nellie. 2011. "Sarah Michelle Gellar's 'Ringer' to Get Picked Up by CW; Disney Pulls Out." *Deadline*, May 13. Accessed February 1, 2016. http://deadline.com/2011/05/surprise-sarah-michelle-gellars-the-ringer-to-get-picked-up-by-cw-131684/.

Andreeva, Nellie. 2015. "'Crazy Ex-Girlfriend': How Did Racy Showtime Comedy Land at CW." *Deadline*, May 14. Accessed March 27, 2016. http://deadline.com/2015/05/crazy-ex-girlfriend-showtime-comedy-the-cw-changes-cast-1201426315/.

Andreeva, Nellie. 2016. "'Supergirl' Could Have Continued at CBS If Not Picked Up by the CW." *Deadline*, May 18. Accessed May 31, 2016. http://deadline.com/2016/05/supergirl-stay-cbs-picked-up-the-cw-1201758715/

Goldberg, Lesley. 2016. "'Supergirl' Renewed for Second Season—at the CW." *Hollywood Reporter*, May 12. Accessed May 31, 2016. www.hollywoodreporter.com/live-feed/supergirl-season-two-cw-892629.

Goldberg, Lesley and Philiana Ng. 2011. "CW's 'Ringer' Gets Full Season Order." *Hollywood Reporter*, October 12. Accessed February 1, 2016. www.hollywoodreporter.com/live-feed/ringer-sarah-michelle-gellar-cw-245246.

Hinckley, David. 2015. "CW Passes on 'Supergirl,' But It Goes to CBS." *New York Daily News*, August 16.

Holloway, Daniel. 2014. "The CW's Male-Pattern Boldness." *Broadcasting & Cable*, October 27.

Holloway, Daniel. 2016. "'Empire,' 'Sunday Night Football' Top List of Highest Rated TV Shows for 2015–16." *Variety*, May 27. Accessed May 31, 2016.

Itzkoff, Dave. 2015. "She's More than Ready to Right Wrongs." *New York Times*, October 18.

Koblin, John. 2015. "With TV Viewing Changing, Networks Take Longer to Drop Shows." *New York Times*, November 18. Accessed May 31, 2016. www.nytimes.com/2015/11/19/business/media/with-tv-viewing-changing-networks-take-longer-to-drop-shows.html.

Koblin, John. 2016. "TV's Self-Reflection: Ratings May Be Down, But Choices Are Many." *New York Times*, January 18. Accessed May 31, 2016. www.nytimes.com/2016/01/19/business/media/tvs-self-reflection-ratings-may-be-down-but-the-choices-are-many.html.

Lieberman, David. 2011a. "CW Strikes 5-Year Licensing Deal with Hulu." *Deadline*, October 28. Accessed February 1, 2016. http://deadline.com/2011/10/cw-strikes-5-year-licensing-deal-with-hulu-188321/.

Lieberman, David. 2011b. "Update: CW Could See $1B from 4-Year Licensing Deal with Netflix." *Deadline*, October 13. Accessed May 31, 2016. http://deadline.com/2011/10/netflix-signs-4-year-licensing-deal-with-the-cw-182444/.

Littleton, Cynthia. 2016. "Netflix, CW Output Deal Reflects Changing Priorities for Key Players." *Variety*, July 12. Accessed September 8, 2016. http://variety.com/2016/tv/columns/the-cw-netflix-the-flash-jane-the-virgin-streaming-output-deal-1201812607/.

Lynch, Jason. 2016a. "After Snagging Supergirl, the CW Will Devote 40% of Its Fall Schedule to Superhero Shows." *Adweek*, May 19. Accessed May 31, 2016. www.adweek.com/news/television/after-snagging-supergirl-cw-will-devote-40-its-fall-schedule-superhero-shows-171570.

Lynch, Jason. 2016b. "The CW Renews All 11 Series It Currently Airs for Next Season." *Adweek*, March 11. Accessed May 1, 2016. www.adweek.com/news/television/cw-renews-all-11-series-it-currently-airs-next-season-170152.

McMillan, Graeme. 2011. "The CW Signs Potential Billion-Dollar Netflix Streaming Deal." *Time*, October 14. Accessed February 1, 2016. http://techland.time.com/2011/10/14/the-cw-signs-potential-billion-dollar-netflix-streaming-deal/.

Morabito, Andrea. 2011. "Inside the CW's Launch Plan: Trying to Slay a Broader Audience." *Broadcasting & Cable*, August 22.

Poniewozik, James. 2016. " 'Crazy Ex-Girlfriend': Everything It Promised and Then Some." *New York Times*, April 18. Accessed May 31, 2016. www.nytimes.com/2016/04/18/arts/television/crazy-ex-girlfriend-season-1-finale.html.

Porter, Rick. 2016. "Fall 2015's Lowest-Rated Network Shows: Not Everything Can Be a Hit." *TV by the Numbers*, January 2. Accessed May 31, 2016. http://tvbythenumbers.zap2it.com/2016/01/02/fall-2015s-lowest-rated-network-shows-not-everything-can-be-a-hit/.

Ryan, Maureen. 2015. "The Man Behind the Heroes: Mark Pedowitz Breaks the CW Out of Its Niche." *Variety*, October 14. Accessed May 31, 2016. https://variety.com/2015/tv/features/mark-pedowitz-the-cw-the-flash-arrow-1201617084/.

Serjeant, Jill. 2011. "CBS Most Watched TV Network; Fox First in 18–49s." *Reuters*, May 24. Accessed February 1, 2016. www.reuters.com/article/us-ratings-idUSTRE74N7UN20110524.

Steel, Emily. 2015. "Virgin Conceives; Network Profits." *New York Times*, January 2. Accessed February 7, 2016. www.nytimes.com/2015/01/03/arts/jane-the-virgin-helps-raise-cws-profile.html?_r=0.

Rede Globo

Global Expansions and Cross-Media Extensions in the Digital Era

Courtney Brannon Donoghue

The 2014 telenovela *Geração Brasil* (*Now Generation*) features a Brazilian Steve Jobs–like mogul Jonas Marra (Murilio Benicio) who invents an inexpensive personal computer that revolutionizes the computing industry. He announces his Silicon Valley-based Marra Corporation will move to Brazil where he will search for a successor from his country of origin. Rede Globo, or TV Globo, the nation's historically dominant television network, produced and distributed *Geração Brasil*. The Portuguese-language ensemble drama is a conventional "*novela das sete*" (7 p.m. novela) exploring storylines from business endeavors and romantic intrigue to lighter family dynamics and humor intended for a broad prime-time audience. The show is optimistic about the powerful potential of digital technology within contemporary society, particularly within the Global South. The first episode opens with one of Marra's Jobs-esque presentations in which a dizzying montage shows how state-of-the-art tech devices—gaming, robotics, smartphones—can lead to productivity, connectivity, and globality in users' daily lives. In this world, Brazil is the land of future innovation and promise where access to technology and information promises mobility.

The series emerges at a pivotal moment not only for the communication and media industries but also Brazil at large. On a broad level, the show's digital optimism juxtaposes a rapidly shifting national climate. Brazil entered the twenty-first century driven by a similarly optimistic view of socioeconomic mobility and a quickly growing middle class only to face disappointment and turmoil due to pivotal public health, governmental, and financial crises a decade later (Lewis and Jelmayer 2016). Amid the promise of hosting the 2014 World Cup and 2016 Summer Olympics, high inflation, unemployment, looming presidential impeachment, and the Zika crisis shook the nation on a global stage. While *Geração Brasil* could not anticipate the political, economic, and cultural climate to unfold in the following years, the telenovela represents the strategy of TV Globo and its parent company Grupo Globo at a transformative institutional and industrial moment. The show's celebration of digital platforms and cross-media convergence parallels a shift in Globo's television business model to address the increasingly digitized and globalized media industries.

This chapter offers a window into contemporary TV Globo institutional structures and strategies, particularly as a network relying on increased global audiences and digital platforms for expansion in a fragmented television landscape. A brief historical overview of Globo illustrates the importance of telenovela production cultures to its role in the national mediascape, specifically how this product must operate simultaneously as locally specific and globally expandable. From here, I discuss two key areas of growth for Globo's business model at home and abroad: (1) cross-media convergence and (2) globalized production, digital content, and online delivery systems. Even as Brazil's most powerful media conglomerate, Globo faces the same kind of challenges as its domestic and global competitiors, contending as a channel with shifting new media platforms and audience habits in an age of convergence and globalization.

REDE GLOBO: INTO THE TWENTY-FIRST CENTURY

Roberto Marinho inherited the daily newspaper *O Globo* in 1925. Over the next century, Marinho and his family grew the business into one of the most powerful media conglomerates worldwide. The company expanded into radio by the 1940s and launched its first television network, TV Globo, in 1965. In addition to its supportive and cozy, albeit highly controversial, relationship with the Brazilian military dictatorship (1964–1985) via various news outlets, Rede Globo built a sizable domestic audience on prime-time telenovelas, variety shows, news programming, and so on. A telenovela—an hour-long serial ensemble drama—typically runs every night from Monday to Friday or Saturday and lasts from four to six months. The Latin American format is the central commercial production model across Spanish- and Portuguese-language television networks. Globo distinguished its telenovela style early by investing in bigger budgets and higher production values along with developing an in-house star system characterized as a "Brazilian Hollywood" (Straubhaar 2017).

Today high-profile stars, prominent writers, expansive studio infrastructure, and commercial production values represent the Globo corporate brand. Industry professionals and audiences characterize the network's production aesthetic and prominent position through the company's *"padrão de qualidade"* (standard of quality). As Globo grew in the 1970s, it also launched the music label Som Livre to sell telenovela soundtracks. Globo's expansion into various media sectors reflected a larger trend of conglomeration and convergence occurring simultaneously across US, Latin American, and other regional industries since the 1980s. With a neoliberal policy turn across Latin America, ownership rules relaxed and Grupo Globo continued to expand and diversify by launching satellite and cable networks as well as a film division by the 1990s.

As of 2016, Grupo Globo's divisions span radio, print, broadcast and online news, magazines, streaming platforms, free TV, pay TV, and film. Corporate headquarters is located in Rio de Janeiro and includes Projac (Projeto Jacarepaguá)—Globo's studio facilities for producing prime-time telenovelas, news shows, children's programming, and variety shows. A massive studio spanning over one million square meters, Projac produces over 800 hours of telenovela programming per year.

Rede Globo has long been an illustrative case in understanding transnational media flows and audience reception. On a global level, some media and communication scholars bemoan Hollywood's hegemonic grasp worldwide, seeing culture and information circulate in an uneven, one-way flow from the West to the rest of the world (Schiller 1979; Tomlinson 1991), while maintaining that smaller industries like Brazil with fewer economic resources and cultural impact cannot compete with American media giants. However, John Sinclair (2000), Joseph Straubhaar (2007), Daya Kishan Thussu (2007), and others counter arguments about an all-powerful Hollywood by looking at media industries in the Global South, particularly their distribution and reception. Globo's vast domestic market share and international export power offer examples of reverse flow and cultural proximity in which local television audiences prefer culturally specific programming. A significant area of global media studies explores the importance of media production and circulation in key cultural-linguistic regions—Hispanophone, Lusophone, Francophone, and so on—in which institutions like Globo continue to disrupt or challenge Anglophone media power.

On a domestic level, while TV Globo is the fourth-largest commercial television network in the world, it can also capture between 60% and 80% market share in major Brazilian cities (Simpson 2003; Straubhaar 2007). Ana Lopez calls Globo the "national agenda setter" serving as the "national cement or glue" for an imagined televisual community and public discourse (Lopez 2015). Globo historically portrayed the nation and *brasilidade* (Brazilianness) from a narrow ideological perspective, whether telenovela representations of heteronormative family life, gender and sexuality, and patterns of consumption or conservative national news coverage on shows like *Jornal Nacional* (La Pastina, Rêgo, and Straubhaar 2003; La Pastina and Straubhaar 2005; Porto 2012). In fact, Rede Globo continues to have a controversial hand in Brazilian politics, most recently its harsh criticism of the PT (Partido dos Trabalhadores/Worker's Party) and impeached President Dilma Rousseff. As one Brazilian journalist remarks: "Globo today is an economic power without parallel in Brazilian communications. There has never been a media group with as much political and economic power" (Gindre 2015).

GLOBO'S CONVERGENCE

Despite this legacy of cultural and economic power both domestically and internationally, TV Globo and its parent company must adapt to an increasingly fragmented global television landscape in the twenty-first century. Convergence—a process of interaction between media technologies, industries, content, and audiences that feeds availability, interconnectivity, and concentration of ownership by a few transnational companies—characterizes global competition across growing digital platforms in the current industry climate (Jenkins 2004, 34). With media properties developed for the longer life spans made possible by wider international markets, production and distribution logic relies heavily on serialization, extension, and replication to connect these various delivery channels. For Globo, its production of scripted content—specifically telenovelas—and its delivery of this programming parallels larger industrial trends of economic and technological convergence favoring interconnectivity and availability of content. However, institutional power and media property development varies depending upon sociocultural and industrial contexts. While larger industrial forces reshaping the global media industries favor strategies of developing content that can move across boundaries of media and nation, Globo imagines cross-media content for global audiences quite differently than an American film studio or European television network.

Cross-Media Practices

Grupo Globo (then Globo Organizações) launched Globo Filmes during a transformative moment in 1998. A series of audiovisual policies restructured a Brazilian film industry historically dependent on direct state subsidies into a market-driven, tax incentive supported system. Thanks to the introduction of Audiovisual Law, specifically Article 3, foreign companies (i.e. Hollywood studios) with local operations were encouraged to partner with local media companies to invest taxed income into Brazilian filmmaking. The audiovisual laws stimulated a production boom (the 1994–1998 *retomada*/rebirth) and a financing system, reviving commercial filmmaking and making Globo a key player in Brazilian cinema by the 2000s (Rêgo 2005; Brannon Donoghue 2014).

Globo Filmes mobilized the conglomerate's brand and television properties to establish the new venture. The film division established a production model still used in the mid-2010s by developing films with an eye to serving as platforms for their telenovela stars as well as supporting potential extension into film series or sequels. The film division, led by Carlos Eduardo Rodrigues until 2013, initially co-produced films starring their popular television personalities, such as former model turned children's television host Xuxa, who starred in seven children's films between 2001 and 2009 (Cajueiro 2002; Simpson 2003). Globo Filmes also relied on network content by adapting miniseries for theatrical release. After airing Guel Arraes's miniseries, *O Auto da Compadecida* (*The Dog's Will*), in four parts on TV Globo in early 1999 to high ratings and critical acclaim, Daniel Filho, the artistic director of Globo Filmes, gave Arraes the greenlight to cut the series from its original 2 hours and 40 minutes to a more theater friendly 104-minute version. Based on a beloved play and featuring Globo stars Matheus Nachtergaele and Selton Mello, the satire follows two young, poor *nordestinos* (men of the Northeast) in the impoverished 1930s *sertão* (semiarid region known as the country's backlands) (Cannito 2000; Cajueiro 2001). The film drew a local audience of over two million, earning around R$11.5 million (US$6 million). *O Auto da Compadecida* opened the doors for other "hybrid films" to move from television to film, including *Caramuru—A Invenção do Brasil* (2001).

Globo Filmes is not the majority film producer on an individual project, nor the distributor. Globo Filmes often partners with prominent local production houses (O2, Conspiração, Diler, Lereby, Total), local distributors (Paris, Downtown), and local divisions of transnational studios (Warner Bros., Sony, Fox, and Paramount), whereas the division's central involvement in a film project is promotion and marketing. Due to the conglomerate's holdings spanning television, radio, news, and online platforms, Globo

Filmes utilizes cross-media strategies to promote film projects. To promote an upcoming biopic (*Gonzaga—de Pai pra Filho/Gonzaga: From Father to Son*, 2012) about father and son *Nordeste* musicians, Globo Filmes targeted a specific audience through television programming and prime-time advertising. This strategy included featuring the cast on a talk show, television spots on the prime-time news program *Jornal Nacional*, advertisements during live soccer broadcasts, and so on. Additionally, beyond the theatrical release, a film will have an extended lifespan through Globo's various free and pay-TV networks. As explained by a Globo Filmes executive, representatives from sibling divisions—entertainment, programming, journalism, pay TV—must all review and approve the potential project along with the film division (Director of Production 2014). Significantly, a central consideration by Globo Filmes when deciding whether or not to greenlight a film production is its creative and financial potential as well as its ability for cross-media expansion across Globo's platforms.

As an equity investor, Globo does not typically invest directly into a production budget. Instead, they provide marketing across various parent company media platforms by giving the films an 85% discount on TV spots as well as promotional exposure across talk shows, telenovelas, etc. (Saturnino 2010). According to the general manager of a local Hollywood office, at certain times of the fiscal year Globo's advertising clients buy fewer commercial spots. In turn, Globo offers this surplus unsellable or less valuable airtime to Fox, Warner Bros., Paramount, or Sony at an 85% discount in exchange for a percentage of the film distribution fee (Managing Director 2014). This Brazilian studio manager credited Globo's business model of offering unsellable commercial slots to its film partners as reflecting its continued market power.

Globalization and Digitization

Even as Rede Globo built its business and market share from domestic programming and audiences, the network moved into international sales by the mid-1970s. In addition to its telenovelas, Rede Globo sold a variety of television programming including variety shows, miniseries, and so on to over 50 markets in 1979 and more than 130 markets by 1991 (Sinclair and Straubhaar 2013, 81). In addition to distributing television programming internationally, the Globo parent company moved into international ownership by buying networks in key markets including SIC in Portugal in 1992 and launching the satellite network TV Globo International in 1999. Joseph Straubhaar argues that Globo's televisual presence and dominance worldwide operates as "a source of soft power for Brazil" (Straubhaar 2017). It is through the successful circulation of Brazilian telenovelas not only within Latin America and the Lusophone region but also internationally that made Globo a cultural powerhouse in the television industry. Globo's historically dominant domestic presence is interdependent with its global position and revenue stream in many ways. In turn, the Globo telenovela simultaneously must be a broadly global and specifically local product.

Since the 2000s, TV Globo has continued to expand its presence in the global marketplace through international co-production partnerships and format sales. Timothy Havens sees the changes in international production and circulation as part of a larger post-Fordist shift in the global television industry including "just-in-time production, consumer segmentation, and customized products" (2006, 35). Globo has increasingly globalized the storylines and production cultures of its premiere telenovelas to differentiate their programming and appeal to broader international audiences (Rêgo and La Pastina 2007). A handful of its premiere telenovelas shoot on-site in locations including the US (*América*, 2005; *Geração Brasil*, 2014), Morocco (*O Clone/The Clone*, 2001), and India (*Caminho das Índias/India: A Love Story*, 2009). *América* centers on a Brazilian woman's undocumented immigration and trafficking to the United States, whereas *O Clone* explores issues of cloning, drug abuse, and controversial portrayals of women in Muslim societies.

Beyond Globo's brand dependency on commercial genres, stars, and high production values, the new era of globalized telenovelas relies upon a blockbuster mentality with an extensive production scale and wide global scope. In the case of *Caminho das Índias*, TV Globo International utilized a behind-the-scenes approach to promote the large-scale production as part of its international sales strategy. A trailer for buyers in international territories boasts the series' expansive production history, locations, and facilities:

> For the first time, Brazil and India team up for an unprecedented TV production available in HD. An investment of $50 million, 10 week shooting in India: Agra, Varansi, Bombay, Jaipur, Jodhpur, Dubai, Rio de Janeiro: 140,000 square feet of backlot, 75,000 square feet of set, 35 million viewers in Brazil. A love story that unites two cultures and that will capture hearts and minds around the world.
>
> ("India" n.d.)

Caminho das Índias was a commercial hit domestically and distributed to 89 territories (Rai and Straubhaar 2016). The series exemplifies Globo's aims to situate the locally specific Brazilian telenovela format focusing on multitiered class storylines (*Clase* A to C, Brazil's upper class to working class classifications) about family, work, and love alongside broader social and political issues and culturally "exotic" characters and locations (Rêgo and La Pastina 2007). Globo's production model in the 2000s thus reflects a moment in the global television industry. The telenovela format depends on the appeal of cultural difference and universal values for both domestic and international viewers. Even as Timothy Havens (2014) traces a shift in industry lore and international TV sales from "universal themes" to "cultural journeys," Globo's biggest telenovelas exist somewhere in between. The company's power operates simultaneously on a domestic level and a transnational level, and is dependent on a markedly Brazilian product of a regionally specific format that can travel internationally.

In addition to increasingly globalized production and international sales, Globo evolves traditional television broadcast models to offer new content delivery systems for domestic and international audiences. Rede Globo works to rebrand itself in the digital era through platform upgrades and exclusive content. The Brazilian broadcaster expanded its Globo TV+ app and introduced a new multiplatform video on demand (VOD) service in 2015. Compatible with smartphones, tablets, and computers, Globo

Play offers new content, live streaming events, and a library of older programming including its most popular telenovelas. Whereas Amazon and Netflix led the earliest wave of subscription platforms to offer 4K HDR content, Rede Globo became one of the first free broadcasters to upgrade their content in 2016. The network released the first episode of its miniseries *Dangerous Liaisons* in 4K HDR via Globo Play prior to its broadcast on its open network (Hopewell 2016a).

Globo's VOD service, with both free and subscription options, also offers exclusive content stemming from its prime-time telenovelas. For the 2016 telenovela *Totalmente Demais* (*Total Dreamer*), about a young woman's Cinderella romance and upward mobility, Globo produced and launched "Episode Zero" exclusively online prior to the series premiere on Rede Globo. Furthermore, the network created a spin-off series extending character backstories. The ten-episode series was only available to the subscription video on demand (SVOD) accounts and garnered over three million views. While TV Globo experimented with exclusive web content in the past, the SVOD service provided a multilayered experience that leveraged digital access and availability. In a *Variety* interview, Globo CEO Carlos Henrique Schroder identifies the challenge of traditional broadcasters moving into online streaming as seeking:

> to find economic models of relevant content in which linear and nonlinear TV complement each other, while exploiting the full potential of each one. Not only should linear and nonlinear TV be fully explored, but also a combination of the two.
>
> (Hopewell 2016b)

While Rede Globo built a broadcast audience based on accessibility and programming aimed at a broad, general audience, the VOD strategy inevitably targets a more exclusive audience: one that can afford 4K television, fast broadband service, and a subscription fee. Globo built its media empire on open TV, and later pay TV audiences in the twentieth century, and the company hopes the twenty-first-century expansion into streaming services and exclusive content will appeal to a more privileged consumer class. Yet, Globo Play exists more as a complementary extension of Rede Globo and its programming because it remains dependent upon its prime-time content and broadcast legacy brand to be competitive in increasingly crowded online sector. It is less about expanding an individual media property and more about extending the Globo brand into other media sectors without cannibalizing its core business—television.

CONCLUSION

TV Globo's production of scripted content and delivery of this programming parallels larger industrial trends of structural and technological convergence, globalization, and digitization. Since the 1990s, Globo has built new partnerships and launched new film and web content; yet these ventures firmly take root in cross-media collaborations and international strategies dependent on established television production cultures and properties in order to extend their global footprint through three central areas—cross-media content, transnational production, and digital delivery systems. Globo's continued reliance upon television as its flagship in order to compete in a changing global landscape results in a dilemma. With the entry of new content providers like Netflix and Amazon as well as competing free and pay TV networks, Globo is vying for an increasingly smaller share of domestic and international audiences.

On the one hand, Globo has adapted a "total entertainment" model where content is produced and circulated through exploiting commercial media properties and connected storyworlds, where branded media flows strategically across Globo's corporate divisions and platforms. A telenovela can be spun-off into a web series or a miniseries can transform in a theatrical film. Fluidity and flexibility characterize the contemporary Globo media product. On the other hand, despite the expansion and diversification into sectors like film production and digital distribution, television remains the core business for Grupo Globo's entertainment divisions. Even as the company works to adapt to the twenty-first-century media landscape, an interdependence to and interconnectivity with the flagship broadcast division Rede Globo remains. Globo capitalizes upon its wide array of broadcast and digital channels to cross promote and market content and extend their life spans across ancillary markets as the company struggles to compete with a new generation of networks and channels. Many of the new ventures into film and web content rely upon an established star system and/or media properties. In turn, Globo is not diversifying across media sectors so much as reimagining television across a variety of production and distribution spaces in an increasingly competitive landscape.

REFERENCES

Brannon Donoghue, Courtney. 2014. "The Rise of the Brazilian Blockbuster: How Ideas of Exceptionality and Scale Shape a Booming Cinema." *Media, Culture & Society* 36 (4): 1–15.

Cajueiro, Marcelo. 2001. "Globo *Auto* in High Gear to Top B.O." *Variety*, January 3.

Cajueiro, Marcelo. 2002. "*Xuxa* Dwarfs B.O.: 'Latest Franchise Installment Is Hot in Brazil.'" *Variety*, February 23.

Cannito, Newton. 2000. "A TV Encontra o Cinema em *O Auto da Compadecida*." In *Revista de Cinema*, pp. 32–3.

Director of Production, Globo Filmes. 2014. Interview by author, August 5. Rio de Janeiro, Brazil.

Gindre, Gustavo. 2015. "Os Protestos de Domingo e a Estratégia da Globo." *Carta Capital*, August 17. www.cartacapital.com.br/blogs/intervozes/os-protestos-de-domingo-e-a-estrategia-da-globo-8793.html.

Havens, Timothy. 2006. *Global Television Marketplace*. London: BFI.

Havens, Timothy. 2014. "Towards a Structuration Theory of Media Intermediaries." In *Making Media Work: Cultures of Management in the Entertainment Industries*, edited by Derek Johnson, Derek Kompare and Avi Santo, 39–62. New York: New York University Press.

Hopewell, John. 2016a. "Brazilian Giant Globo Reveals First Results, Strategies of New VOD Service Globo Play." *Variety*, February 23. http://variety.com/2016/tv/news/globo-vod-globo-play-1201712749/.

Hopewell, John. 2016b. "Brazil's Globo Bows Multi-Platform Novelas." *Variety*, October 17. http://variety.com/2016/tv/global/globo-brazil-mipcom-innovates-traditional-telenovela-format-1201891145/.

"India—a Love Story." n.d. *TV Globo International*. www.globotvinternational.com/prodDet. asp?prodId=115&catId=1.

Jenkins, Henry. 2004. "The Cultural Logic of Media Convergence." *The International Journal of Cultural Studies* 7 (1): 33–43.

La Pastina, Antonio C., Cacilda M. Rêgo and Joseph D. Straubhaar. 2003. "The Centrality of Telenovelas in Latin America's Everyday Life: Past Tendencies, Current Knowledge, and Future Research." *Global Media Journal* 2 (2). www.globalmediajournal.com/open-access/the-centrality-of-telenovelas-in-latin-americas-everyday-lifepast-tendencies-current-knowledge-and-future-research.php?aid=35095.

La Pastina, Antonio C. and Joseph D. Straubhaar. 2005. "Multiple Proximities between Television Genres and Audiences." *Gazette: International Journal for Communication Studies* 67 (3): 271–88.

Lewis, Jeffrey T. and Rogerio Jelmayer. 2016. "Brazil's Economy Shrinks Again." *Wall Street Journal*, August 31. www.wsj.com/articles/brazils-economy-shrinks-again-1472648269.

Lopez, Ana. 2015. "Domestic Service, Transmediality, and the Contemporary Brazilian Telenovela." *Society for Cinema and Media Studies Conference*, Montreal, Canada.

Managing Director, Local Hollywood Studio Office. 2014. Interview by author, August 10. Rio de Janeiro, Brazil.

Porto, Mauro. 2012. *Media Power and Democratization in Brazil: TV Globo and the Dilemmas of Political Accountability*. New York: Routledge.

Rai, Swapnil and Joseph Straubhaar. 2016. "Road to India—a Brazilian Love Story: BRICS, Migration, and Cultural Flows in Brazil's *Caminho das Índias*." *International Journal of Communication* 10: 3124–40.

Rêgo, Cacilda M. 2005. "Brazilian Cinema: Its Fall, Rise and Renewal (1990–2003)." *New Cinemas: Journal of Contemporary Film* 3: 85–100.

Rêgo, Cacilda M. and Antonio C. La Pastina. 2007. "Brazil and the Globalization of Telenovelas." In *Media on the Move: Global Flow and Contra-Flow*, edited by Daya Kishan Thussu, 99–115. New York: Routledge.

Saturnino Braga, Rodrigo. 2010. Interview by author, September 15. São Paulo, Brazil.

Schiller, Herbert. 1979. "Transnational Media and National Development." In *National Sovereignty and International Communication*, edited by Kaarle Nordenstreng and Herbert I. Schiller, 21–32. Norwood: Ablex.

Simpson, Amelia S. 2003. *Xuxa: The Mega-Marketing of Gender, Race and Modernity*. Philadelphia: Temple University Press.

Sinclair, John. 2000. "Geolinguistic Region as a Global Space: The Case of Latin America." In *The New Communications Landscape: Demystifying Globalization*, edited by Georgette Wang, Anura Goonasekera and Jan Servae, 19–32. London: Routledge.

Sinclair, John and Joseph Straubhaar. 2013. *Latin American Television Industries*. London: BFI.

Straubhaar, Joseph. 2007. *World Television: From Global to Local*. Los Angeles: Sage.

Straubhaar, Joseph. 2017. "Grupo Globo." In *Globo Media Giants*, edited by Benjamin J. Birkinbine, Rodrigo Gomez and Janet Wasko, 226–38. New York: Routledge.

Thussu, Daya Kishan (ed.). 2007. *Media on the Move: Global Flow and Contra-Flow*. New York: Routledge.

Tomlinson, John. 1991. *Cultural Imperialism: An Introduction*. London: Continuum.

PBS

Crowdsourcing Culture Since 1969
Michele Hilmes

As the sole national public[1] television network in a media market as prominent as the United States, the Public Broadcasting Service (PBS) has flown remarkably under the radar as far as media scholarship goes. While some of its programs, most notably the children's franchise *Sesame Street*, have been widely studied in educational circles, rarely have media scholars devoted extended attention to the channel's deep roots, participatory audiences, innovative programs, and role in mediating and shaping US arts, science, politics, and culture.[2] For most of its history, its reliable 1%–3% share of the US television audience relegated it to the status of a highbrow niche channel, a "market failure" outlet for types of programming not likely to succeed commercially but with redeeming social value. In addition, its dispersed institutional structure and complex financial model make it very difficult to discern a "there" there (to paraphrase Gertrude Stein): by design, PBS lacks a powerful central administration with control over creative decisions, as Congress intended when it founded the service in 1967—about 40 years after most nations had instituted powerful centralized public broadcasters.

Yet in the 2000s PBS' profile in the US television spectrum has risen considerably, as its market share, "crowdsourced" infrastructures, and niche programming strategy have become the norm, or even the leading edge, of the new digital media environment. Occasionally, as with the breakout hit series *Downton Abbey* (2010–2015), PBS' viewership figures have outshone the major commercial networks, and it regularly attracts larger audiences than high-profile pay channels like HBO and Showtime, ranking fifth among all US TV networks. Its online strategies have led the field. So why does it still remain something of a dark horse in American public consciousness?

The United States has always had a strong resistance to government-supported media, and the elitist, good-for-you, educational roots of public television make some viewers, as well as academics with a more populist agenda, shy away from its "quality programming" emphasis. Demographics might have something to do with it as well:

PBS' strongest audience categories are the under-12s and over-40s, never perceived as cutting-edge.[3] But which national network's nightly news program was the first to be co-anchored by two seasoned female journalists, one of them African American?[4] Which one carries the longest-running prime-time drama program in the history of US television?[5] Which one has produced the most award-winning children's television show ever, the staple of millions of childhoods, with local versions now spread across the globe to 140 countries in 20 different languages?[6] That would be PBS. Its story is worth telling. Furthermore, as the rest of the US television universe adapts to new digital realities, PBS' funding strategies, relationship with audiences, and flexible programming patterns may point towards the television of the future.

HISTORY

PBS grew out of the educational broadcasting movement that began in the 1920s as radio spread across the nation. Many US universities were early developers of radio technology whose experiments with tubes and transmitters evolved into educational stations still on the air today (Blakeley 1979; Slotten 2009). Yet commercial stations had public service obligations under FCC regulations as well; the big commercial networks NBC and CBS pioneered many of the leading educational programs of the period (Goodman 2011) as non-commercial stations struggled. With federal encouragement, the educational radio movement grew in strength and organization in the 1930s and '40s; in 1945 a few FM radio frequencies were set aside for educational broadcasting (88 to 93 MHz) and the field began to flourish. By the early 1950s emphasis shifted towards television, and with the help of the Ford Foundation and the continued commitment of universities and other public institutions, educational television found a foothold. In the emergence of the National Educational Television network (NET) in the early 1960s, linking educational stations across the country, we see a prototype for PBS.

Yet NET lacked stable funding, and as the Cold War intensified and the US took on a heightened role on the world stage, the absence of a national public broadcaster—one that could highlight the best of American culture and support the other performing and creative arts—began to seem a serious lack. Under President Lyndon Johnson's "Great Society" program in the 1960s a host of new cultural agencies were created, most notably the National Endowment for the Humanities (NEH) and the National Endowment for the Arts (NEA), the first time the United States had attempted federal cultural funding on such a large scale. To provide a global showcase for the fruits of these efforts, and to provide "serious" public affairs and educational programs to the entire nation, the Public Broadcasting Act of 1967 created the Corporation for Public Broadcasting (CPB), tasked with establishing national public networks for both radio and television.[7] As a later report puts it:

> Recognizing the sheer power of media in the lives of citizens, there was strong consensus that there should be at least one place in the media landscape where the ownership, production and distribution of content would be shielded from both political crossfire and the commercial marketplace. Public broadcasting would be free of

government control and the pressure to turn a profit by the promotion of products and thus enabled to pursue the mission of informing and educating our citizens.

(Corporation 2012, 5)

CPB is a private, non-profit corporation that accepts both government and private funds and allocates them to the hundreds of public radio and television stations scattered across the country, as well as to PBS and National Public Radio (NPR), launched in 1969 and 1971, respectively.

Yet the rules set in place by the Public Broadcasting Act limited the autonomy of American public broadcasting in two significant ways. Rather than the "insulated funding" that the system's proponents had recommended through a tax on television set sales that would go automatically to funding public broadcasting and thus protect it from political interference (Carnegie Commission 1979), the Act stipulated that CPB would have to appeal to Congress for reauthorization of its budget every two years. This regularly places PBS in the political crossfire, often facing threats to repeal its funding altogether, most notoriously under Presidents Nixon and Reagan and again in the 1990s under Newt Gingrich's congressional leadership. Public broadcasting evaded this fate by developing alternative revenue streams, many of which seem particularly well-suited to the digital era, as will be discussed below.

Another way that Congress limited the power of its first national public broadcaster was to make sure it could not develop into a centralized public production monopoly, like the BBC in Britain. It expressly forbade CPB and PBS (though not NPR) from producing programs; instead, the bulk of CPB's funding goes directly to individual public broadcasting stations, which in turn produce the programs that are distributed over PBS and NPR. About two-thirds of CPB's annual budget goes to television (the remainder to radio), and of that about two-thirds goes directly to local stations (the remainder to support station-led program initiatives and to network administration). Stations themselves have to come up with the rest of their operational budgets, again mostly from local sources, as will be discussed below. Thus programming on the PBS network, by design, is "crowdsourced" from the ground up, with individual local stations creating programs that may be picked up by PBS or by other local stations; they are known as "presenting stations" in PBS jargon because they take the lead in proposing and producing programs.

HOW IT WORKS

American public television is built on the primacy of its 350 local stations and the audiences that not only view but support them through membership contributions: resistant to congressional interference, crankily independent, sometimes stodgy, always underfunded, but vitally involved in their communities. A few key presenting stations serve as the network's creative powerhouses, producing the majority of the programs distributed across its schedule nationwide, most notably WETA-Washington, DC (*PBS NewsHour, Washington Week*, Ken Burns's documentaries like *The Civil War, Baseball, The Roosevelts*, and more), WGBH-Boston (*Masterpiece, Nova, American Experience, Frontline, Arthur*, and many more), and WNET-New York (*American Masters, Great*

Performances, Nature, Sesame Street). Yet almost every station produces some programs, either for its own local audience or for wider circulation across the PBS network. One example of the latter is *Sewing With Nancy*, produced by Wisconsin Public Television since 1982—never a prime-time hit, but aired during daytime hours on more than 300 PBS stations, avidly followed by its audience of do-it-yourselfers. Another is WBPT2-Miami's five-minute "naked eye astronomy" show *Star Gazers*, carried on virtually all PBS affiliates.

A few efforts from smaller stations have become key features of PBS' schedule, such as *Mr. Rogers' Neighborhood* from WQED-Pittsburgh, *Austin City Limits* from KRLU-Austin, and *The McLaughlin Group* from WTTW-Chicago. One recent report highlights this crowdsourced creative structure by quoting Andrew Walworth, head of an independent production company:

> The wonderful thing for producers about public television is that there is no single gatekeeper—there are all these points of entry, perhaps 50 to 100 program managers who will decide whether your program is broadcast-ready. It is the most democratic (small "d") of media institutions where independent producers can create news and public affairs programs.
>
> (Bowers 2015)[8]

Typically, public television producers also retain their ownership rights over material broadcast and thus can release their work through other distribution channels once the contract period has passed.

Individual PBS stations also acquire programs from syndicators and independent producers to fill out their local schedules. Before cable television emerged as a national medium in the 1980s, PBS stations were often the only place on the dial where classic Hollywood cinema, foreign films, and reruns of classic television series could be seen (many of them British). In 1975, it was station KERA-Dallas that introduced *Monty Python's Flying Circus* to American audiences, buying it directly from its distributor, Time-Life Films, a decision soon followed by 130 other local stations ("Return" 2005). Today this practice is particularly prevalent in the area of children's programs, which fill up much of public television stations' morning and afternoon schedules.

The PBS network is the prominent face of public television nationally and its main distributor of programs as well as a major production partner for presenting stations. A private, non-profit member organization, its members are the 350 public television stations built and sustained by CPB funding across the nation.[9] PBS receives funds from the CPB and other sources, but its main revenue comes from station membership fees, an amount calibrated by audience share and a few other factors; membership entitles stations to broadcast the programs distributed by PBS. During prime-time "common carrier" hours, member stations are strongly urged to take the main PBS schedule in order to create national cohesion.[10] Other dayparts can be programmed as the stations choose, and schedules at all times tend to differ from station to station far more than commercial outlets. This can create confusion and a lack of network coherence, especially because many local stations have added secondary or even tertiary outlets in recent years, thanks to cable carriage and digital multiplexing. Wisconsin Public Television, for instance, not only broadcasts its flagship channel WHA-TV but also provides The Wisconsin Channel (in-depth Wisconsin news and university-based programs) and WPT Create, which streams the Create channel produced by American Public Television (discussed later in this chapter), featuring lifestyle and instructional programming.

PBS is not the only national public television program provider, however. It competes with CPB-funded program initiatives like the Independent Television Service (ITVS), founded by an Act of Congress in 1988 and primarily known for its *Independent Lens* series, a showcase for innovative independent filmmaking, both drama and documentary, which public stations might carry instead or in addition to PBS fare. *POV* is a similar long-standing offering, produced by American Documentary, a "catalyst for public culture" that partners with stations to bring original documentaries to public TV audiences ("Overview" n.d.). Another competitor is American Public Television (APT), older than PBS itself because its origins lie in the former Eastern Educational Network, founded in 1961 as a program-sharing cooperative. Today APT claims to offer over 4,000 hours of television programming to public TV stations, much of it older programs in syndication, including classics like *The French Chef* with Julia Child and the *This Old House* franchise. APT, working with PBS and key public program producers, also directly funds or acquires new programs that it provides either to stations through syndication or directly to viewers through its two digital web channels, CreateTV and WORLD. Most of its original offerings, however, do have at least one station as primary presenter, thus preserving American public television's basic bottom-up structure.

Though PBS mainly works with stations to produce and distribute programs, it does occasionally fund or acquire programs directly, without a station partner. This practice has increased in recent years as a result, some claim, of the *Downton Abbey* "windfall" from DVD and streaming sales that put unexpected money into PBS' pockets. In an effort to give PBS "more influence in shaping programs" and to maintain high production values, the network purchased and scheduled a number of independently produced series in recent years without a partner presenting station, including *Call the Midwife* (BBC), *Last Tango in Halifax* (BBC), *The Bletchley Circle* (ITV), and *Genealogy Roadshow* (Krasnow Productions) ("Stations" 2013).[11] Some argue that this practice violates PBS' basic charter as a distributor, not a producer, and threatens to undermine the station-based system that has been the mainstay of public television operations. Increasingly, digital media platforms have threatened to wreak havoc with the station-based structure as well, insofar as they allow viewers to access programs from sources other than their local station. However, PBS has worked hard to make de-localization difficult; access to the PBS website, especially to information about specific programs and any streaming opportunities, requires specifying one's local station and constantly reinforces the local broadcaster connection ("Stations" 2013).

CROWDFUNDING

CPB allocations were never sufficient to fund a nationwide, high quality public television network. From the beginning, PBS and its member stations relied on grants from private foundations; other public funding sources like universities and state and local governments; and, primarily, contributions from audiences who themselves become "members" of their local PBS station community. Increasingly, donations from private corporations in exchange for ever-longer in-program acknowledgments—known as "corporate underwriting"—factor as a highly significant source of funds, a trend that for some critics undermines the whole concept of public broadcasting (Hoynes 1994; Ledbetter 1997). According to a 2012 CPB report, approximately 18% of public television funding overall comes from federal allocations; another 18% flows from state or local governments to their local stations. Universities provide 8% of the budget, often through the provision of facilities and salaries for campus-based employees, because many public stations are still run by universities. Thirteen percent comes from corporate underwriting and 7% from private foundations. However, these proportions can vary greatly depending on the size of the station; for smaller stations federal funding might make up more than 30% of their overall budget, while in the largest stations it may amount to no more than 10% (Corporation 2012, 17).

The single largest source of funding, however, continues to be contributions from individuals to their local stations: 22% of the overall budget on average but, again, often much larger for more powerful stations. But even more importantly, it is this close, contributory relationship with local communities that inspires further funding from local, state, and foundation sources. It is also a force that has held proposed federal cuts at bay: Republican as well as Democratic voters love their local public television stations, as their state representatives well know, creating a built-in bipartisan resistance to recurrent federal-level threats to defund PBS.

In terms of larger-scale individual donations, a new concept has emerged in the era of *Downton Abbey*: the program-specific trust. The Masterpiece Trust, initiated in 2011, is "a collaborative initiative between MASTERPIECE'S producing station WGBH Boston and PBS stations nationwide" that "provides the opportunity for individual donors and families who care deeply about the series to help provide for its future in a substantial way while also supporting their local PBS stations." A lengthy list of major donors follows this description on the website, led by the names and photos of a few especially prominent individuals who also appear in a video endorsement during the program's on-screen credits ("Masterpiece" n.d.). Its success—over $10 million in donations since 2011—has sparked several other such initiatives, including Friends of the NewsHour, "a group of dedicated individuals who are committed to helping secure the NewsHour's future by enabling the best journalism to thrive, grow, and adapt" ("Friends" n.d.) as well as the Better Angels Society (supporting documentary producer Ken Burns) and The Frontline Journalism Fund.

From the beginning private foundations have played a key role in the development of educational and public broadcasting. Starting with the Ford Foundation in the 1950s, a number of large foundations figure significantly in PBS history up to the present time, including the MacArthur Foundation, the Markle Foundation, and the Mellon Foundation. Most of these grants have traditionally gone to individual stations, with the largest presenting stations receiving the bulk of the funding. In 2004 PBS formed its own foundation, to attract donors "at the national level" ("Who We Are" n.d.). By 2016

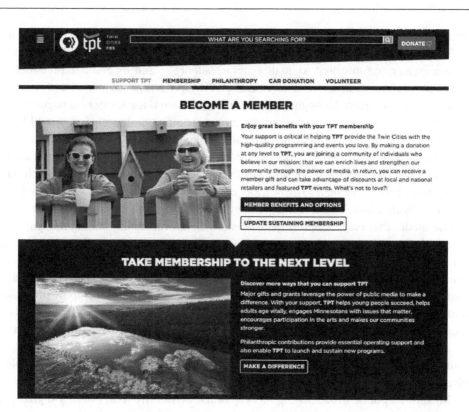

FIGURE 5.1 *Online membership campaigns from Twin Cities station TPT represent the PBS "crowdsourcing" model.*

it had acquired a lengthy list of contributors featuring all the traditional supporters along with new ones drawn from more recently created fortunes: the Bill and Melissa Gates Foundation, the George Lucas Family Foundation, the Adobe Foundation, Newman's Own Foundation, and many more. Such funding often reflects the specific giving emphasis of individual foundations, and because education is a prominent emphasis in the philanthropic world, PBS' classroom-oriented initiatives are an ever-expanding part of its public service that goes unnoticed by most viewers.

Most controversial, however, is the practice of corporate underwriting, amounting in 2012 to about 13% of public television system revenues as a whole (Corporation 2012, 17). Originally, it operated much as the sponsor system did in early radio, with relatively muted and infrequent mentions of corporate donors' names, products, and services interrupting the programs in discreet places. Over the last two decades the corporate messages punctuating most programs have become longer, better crafted, more frequent and more overt, with "brand name" ads predominating: Viking cruises, Ralph Lauren fashions, Audible audiobooks. PBS has recently stepped up its efforts in this area, again along lines prominent in the digital media universe. The Sponsorship Group for Public Television, founded in 1997 but consolidated and strengthened in 2005, offers "a full-service sales, marketing and client services team that secures national corporate sponsors for signature PBS programs" ("Why Sponsor" n.d.). Here, PBS strategically exploits its "halo effect"—the fact that "viewers believe PBS sponsors have a greater commitment to quality and excellence"—and its demographic niche of "affluent, educated, influential consumers" ("Why Sponsor" n.d.).

Critics of PBS from the beginning worried that, even if the service managed to fend off Republican attempts to repeal its funding, creeping commercialism would be the death of public broadcasting's role in meaningful political debate and social commentary (Engelman 1996; Hoynes 1994; Starr 2001). Recently such criticism has faded. It seems that in the digital era not only has the range of outlets for political speech taken pressure off PBS, allowing it to grow more comfortably mainstream, but also that it now blends in with a host of other independent, highly political, diverse, and contentious online media that have adopted the PBS style of crowdfunding: memberships, donations, grants, and in-text ads for commercial products and services. These are precisely the strategies that have proven successful across a range of digital media offerings over the last decade, including "membership" by subscription to services like Netflix, HBO, and specialists like Sundance; cultivation of a "community" relationship by podcasters and YouTube celebrities; and fund raising by independent filmmakers and artists on sites like Kickstarter and Indiegogo. What PBS achieved by focusing on local communities, digital media expanded to national and global levels—as have PBS' own digital efforts, including the launch of PBS America on the Sky service in 2011, available in Great Britain and Ireland.

Meantime, public broadcasting has expanded across the web, offering digital platforms and enhancements that have far outstripped most commercial competitors. As long as viewers continue willingly to contribute to their local public stations in the belief that they are receiving higher quality, more trustworthy and insightful programs than commercial networks provide, public broadcasting's semiprivate, semipublic structure seems likely to keep it afloat and growing. While commercial network audience figures have declined drastically over the last two decades, PBS has held relatively firm, leading to its upward mobility in network rankings.

MISSION ACCOMPLISHED?

Does PBS deliver what it promises to the American public? PBS has often updated its mission statement over the years; its current version reads:

> PBS offers programming that expands the minds of children, documentaries that open up new worlds, non-commercialized news programs that keep citizens informed on world events and cultures, and programs that expose America to the worlds of music, theater, dance and art.
>
> ("About " n.d.)

Notable here is the omission of "entertainment," a goal featured prominently in other national public broadcasters' mission statements. Yet in the eyes of PBS, entertainment is what commercial media provides, all too well.[12] No mention is made of the production of original drama or comedy, despite the fact that high quality drama is what the active and engaged audience of PBS most wants (hence the 40+ year run of *Masterpiece Theatre* and its offshoots). Also, in contrast to the stated missions of most national public broadcasters, we see no overt mandate to promote and support national culture. The Canadian Broadcasting Corporation (CBC), for example, is specifically required to provide programming that is "predominantly and distinctively Canadian" and that "reflects Canada and its regions to national and regional audiences" (Government of Canada 1991). Clearly visible, however, are PBS' deep roots in *educational* broadcasting; education plays a far stronger role in America's public broadcasting mission than in Canada's, which must only "include" educational programs.

Despite the popularity of prime-time drama on PBS as elsewhere, PBS has produced very little of its own drama over the years, drawing heavily on its long-standing co-production relationship with British television in particular (Hilmes 2012). Most of its local stations' daytime schedules are taken up with educational programs for children, instructional and "how-to" shows, and discussion of local culture, history, and politics. Prime-time schedules heavily feature news and documentary programs, along with arts and performance, some of them among the longest-running in US television history: *Wall Street Week* (1970–), *Firing Line* (1971–), *Great Performances* (1972–), *Nova* (1974–), *Austin City Limits* (1975–), *Live from Lincoln Center* (1976–), *Live from the Met* (1977–), *Frontline* (1983–), and *Nature* (1982–). All of these, of course, reflect and enhance aspects of American culture, as do more specifically named programs like *The American Experience* (1988–) and *American Masters* (1985–), along with the many historical documentaries series produced by Ken Burns, a filmmaker whose career has been built on public television almost exclusively. Yet, for many decades it was the one place on the dial where Americans could view programs produced in other nations, primarily Britain and Canada, and where music, art, theater, film, and documentary from a wide range of national origins found an outlet. Though today other television options have expanded to include much more international material than before, along with other types of programs long the specialization of PBS, public television's prominent local role and free-to-air service, as well as its long-standing reputation for quality, give it a higher profile and a more loyal audience base than ever before.

What is the future of public broadcasting? In 2015, the Sesame Workshop announced a five-year collaboration with HBO to produce the beloved children's program, with HBO getting first-run distribution rights for a nine-month window, followed by broadcast as usual on PBS. The deal raised many of the old fears about commercialization of public broadcasting. However, as defenders pointed out, only 10% of *Sesame Street*'s funding in recent years came from public funds; the rest derived from licensing fees. When licensing income declined sharply in 2008, the program's survival was threatened; HBO's offer promises to keep it alive. Unlike other private/public collaborations in previous years, the deal prompted soul-searching but few furious denunciations. Many wondered if it was the sign of things to come, the "canary in the coal mine." After all, as one PBS advisor put it, "We've never answered the question of how we want to fund public programming" (Sefton 2015). Yet fund it we do, from the grassroots as well as the corporate suite: messy, but durable, the PBS model has gone viral in myriad ways across the digital media universe and may well provide the model for future development, as commercial television faces declining advertising revenues and alternatives remain scattered and de-centralized. From a struggling "market failure" network to a "quality" media brand with nearly 50 years of national prominence, PBS seems poised to continue riding the tide of crowdsourced culture.

NOTES

1 In this context, "public" means that PBS is a non-profit private corporation, supported by taxpayer funds as well as grants from both public and private sources. It contrasts with other national broadcasters like the BBC in Britain, known as "public service" broadcasters due to their public ownership, stricter accountability to governments, and more dominant national roles.

2 Studies of public television have focused primarily on its political battles and its news and public affairs programs; see Engelman 1996, Hoynes 1994, Ledbetter 1997, and Starr 2001.

3 Though today they are ranked 20th in age 15–34 viewership, ahead of many commercial cable competitors.

4 Gwen Ifill and Judy Woodruff hosted and managed *PBS NewsHour* until Ifill's untimely death in November 2016.

5 Rebecca Eaton has executive produced *Masterpiece*, formerly *Masterpiece Theatre*, since 1985.

6 *Sesame Street*, of course, created in 1969 by Joan Ganz Cooney and Lloyd Morrisette.

7 See Mitchell (2005) for an account of radio's last-minute inclusion.

8 Others, however, describe it as "super uber difficult" because of the confusing complex of stations and distributors (Bowers 2015).

9 Not all public television stations are PBS members; some are too small and struggling to qualify, or can't afford the membership fees. Most famously, station KCET-Los Angeles withdrew from PBS in 2010 after programming and financial disputes with the network and now describes itself as America's largest non-commercial educational independent station.

10 Though this is a loose arrangement; fewer than 70% of stations reliably carry PBS' prime-time lineup (Corporation 2012, 61).

11 The first three of these shows draw on well-established partnerships between PBS and British production companies; the last, *Genealogy Roadshow*, was underwritten by Ancestry.com.

12 See Ouellette (2002) for a convincing cultural studies critique of PBS' approach to entertainment.

REFERENCES

"About." n.d. *PBS*. Accessed July 1, 2016. www.pbs.org/about/about-pbs/mission-statement/.

Blakeley, Robert J. 1979. *To Serve the Public Interest: Educational Broadcasting in the United States*. Syracuse: Syracuse University Press.

Bowers, Lisa. 2015. "Public Television Distribution for Documentaries: A Roadmap Through the Maze." *Cultural Weekly*, August 27. Accessed July 1, 2016. www.culturalweekly.com/.

Carnegie Commission. 1979. *A Public Trust: The Landmark Report of the Carnegie Commission on the Future of Public Broadcasting*. New York: Bantam Books.

Corporation for Public Broadcasting. 2012. "Alternative Sources of Funding for Public Television Stations." June 20. Accessed July 1, 2016. www.cpb.org/files/aboutcpb/Alternative_Sources_of_Funding_for_Public_Broadcasting_Stations.pdf.

Engelman, Ralph. 1996. *Public Broadcasting in America*. New York: Sage.

"Friends of the NewsHour." n.d. *PBS NewsHour*. Accessed July 1, 2016. www.pbs.org/newshour/friendsofnewshour/.

Goodman, David. 2011. *Radio's Civic Ambition: American Broadcasting and Democracy in the 1930s*. New York: Oxford.

Government of Canada. 1991. "Broadcasting Act—Broadcasting Policy for Canada." Accessed July 1, 2016. http://laws-lois.justice.gc.ca/eng/acts/B-9.01/page-1.html#h-4.

Hilmes, Michele. 2012. *Network Nations: A Transnational History of British and American Broadcasting*. New York: Routledge.

Hoynes, William. 1994. *Public Television for Sale*. Boulder: Westview Press.

Ledbetter, James. 1997. *Made Possible by . . . : The Death of Public Broadcasting in the United States*. London and New York: Verso.

"Masterpiece Trust." n.d. *Masterpiece*. Accessed July 1, 2016. www.pbs.org/wgbh/masterpiece/about-masterpiece/masterpiece-trust/.

Mitchell, Jack. 2005. *Listener Supported: The Culture and History of Public Radio*. New York: Praeger.

Ouellette, Laurie. 2002. *Viewers Like You: How Public TV Failed the People*. New York: Columbia University Press.

"Overview." n.d. *American Documentary*. Accessed July 1, 2016. www.amdoc.org/aboutus.php.

"Return of the Pythons." 2005. *Current*, December 19. Accessed July 1, 2016. http://current.org/2005/12/return-of-the-pythons-their-pbs-premiere/.

Sefton, Dru. 2015. "Sesame Workshop—HBO Deal Sparks Soul-Searching Among Public Broadcasters." *Current*, August 24. Accessed July 3, 2016. http://current.org/2015/08/sesame-workshop-hbo-deal-sparks-soul-searching-among-public-broadcasters/.

Slotten, Hugh. 2009. *Radio's Hidden Voice: The Origin of Public Broadcasting in the United States*. Champaign: University of Illinois Press.

Starr, Jerold M. 2001. *Air Wars: The Fight to Reclaim Public Broadcasting*. Philadelphia: Temple University Press.

"Stations Fear Exclusion from Show Production as PBS Shifts Strategy." *Current*, June 13. Accessed 1 July 2016. http://current.org/2013/06/shift-in-strategy-at-pbs/.

"Who We Are—What Is the PBS Foundation?" n.d. *PBS Foundation*. Accessed July 1, 2016. www.pbs.org/foundation/who-we-are/.

"Why Sponsor PBS?" n.d. *Sponsors Group for Public Television*. Accessed July 1, 2016. www.sgptv.org/.

Alabama Public Television Network

Local Stations and Struggles Over Collective Identity

Allison Perlman

In the summer of 2012, controversy befell the public television system in Alabama as the Alabama Public Television Network's (APTN) executive director was fired by the Alabama Educational Television Commission (AETC). Created in the 1950s by the Alabama state legislature to develop noncommercial television in the state, the AETC had been the entity licensed to operate public television stations in Alabama. In 2012, members of the AETC wanted the network to telecast a series that argued that the US had been, since its founding, a Christian nation, as well as other programming that discussed creationism. When Allan Pizzato, the executive director, refused, he and his deputy Pauline Howard lost their jobs. In response, over 100,000 people signed two petitions protesting the firings and the ombudsman for the Corporation for Public Broadcasting (CPB) published a detailed report of the incident, describing the actions of the Commission as "improper, unethical, and outrageous" (Sefton 2012a; Fry 2012; "Alabama" 2012; Seitz-Wald 2012).

This scandal was one more chapter of a longer story in which the decisions of the AETC became a site of public contention. By analyzing three controversies to beset public television in Alabama, this chapter examines how Alabama public television long has been a political battleground, one in which contesting views of the political function of public television, the composition of the civic body to be served by it, and the respective rights of broadcasters and their audiences have been fought. If commercial network television, especially in the classical network era, was imagined to be the locus of a national culture—its inclusions and exclusions constituting the parameters of national belonging—then, as Alabama's history illuminates, local public television channels frequently have been seen as spaces in which definitions of the local—of its citizens and its values—have taken shape. As a result, fights over local public television channels have been, and continue to be, battles over competing understandings of local identity.

Such fights have taken on special significance in places like Alabama, where public television channels are controlled by a government agency. Since it was created by the Alabama legislature in 1953, the AETC was charged with creating the first statewide educational television network: a group of interconnected broadcast stations that would serve the entire state of Alabama. With Alabama's structure as their model, a number of other states formed similar statewide educational television networks, likewise run by state commissions appointed by state governors. While, as this chapter discusses, this arrangement has raised critical legal questions about the speech rights of public telecasters, it also has intensified the tendency to see local public television channels as synedoches of the states themselves, their programming decisions reflective of the states' social and political culture.

To examine the APTN is additionally to see how the public broadcasting sector has been, and continues to be, composed of local channels whose programming priorities, and whose vision of what public media should be, have diverged from one another and importantly from the national organizations that serve them. Since the passage of the 1967 Public Broadcasting Act, which allocated federal tax dollars to support public television, by design and by law public television in the US was to avoid the affiliate-network structure that governed commercial broadcasting and instead operate as a constellation of local channels with whom lay the authority over programming priorities, both local and national. In contrast to the British Broadcasting Corporation (BBC), US public television was not envisioned as a technology of nation building, but rather was to be a profoundly decentralized system of local channels that tended to local needs. As Michele Hilmes so well documents in this volume, local public television stations operate as presenting stations (stations that produce programming that circulates nationally), producers of local content, and schedulers who determine which and when the majority of programming reaches local audiences. Yet the public television sector also has been served by national organizations that have faced the difficult task of providing programming and support (financial and technical) to a diverse range of local channels. The story of Alabama public television thus also illuminates this tension between the local and the national, a tension that frequently has spoken to internal fights within Alabama over its own collective identity.

THE DEVELOPMENT OF PUBLIC TELEVISION IN ALABAMA

From the very beginning, the US noncommercial television sector was heterogeneous. In the late 1940s and early 1950s, many people fought for a space in the US television sector for educational channels. Building on the uneven history of educational radio stations, which for decades had committed to using the airwaves to provide educational and cultural programs, advocates of educational TV saw television as a technology that could democratize access to both educational materials and ennobling forms of culture. When in 1952 the Federal Communications Commission (FCC) reserved 242 channels for noncommercial educational television stations, it provided a tremendous opportunity to make good on these visions of the sociopolitical potential of the new medium (Perlman 2016, 18–32).

In the following decade, a range of experiments with educational television took hold in communities across the country. They differed with respect to their communities of service (local, statewide, regional) and locus of control (statewide commissions, universities, school boards of education, nonprofit organizations). Importantly, the mission of the stations also varied. Some, especially coastal stations like KQED (San Francisco) and WGBH (Boston) sought to provide cultural and public affairs programming; others, notably a number of Midwestern stations, emphasized adult education and programming that addressed the local concerns; still others, in a number of regions but especially in the South, utilized television as an instructional technology—in both classrooms and at home—that was to ameliorate the uneven distribution of resources across educational institutions in their communities. It was this latter use of educational television that inspired political leaders in Alabama to start a statewide educational television network.

Early in 1953, Alabama Governor Gordon Persons investigated the feasibility of educational television in his state. The state of education in Alabama in the early 1950s was dire. Alabama public schools had a dearth of qualified teachers, its teachers were paid substantially less than their counterparts in other states, and its facilities were subpar (Permaloff and Grafton 1995, 28–9). A statewide television network could allow a singular expert teacher to provide instructional lessons to thousands of students and thus was imagined to be an economical and efficient way to address the state's education crisis; in this, television in the 1950s was imagined in similar terms to online education in the twenty-first century: as a technological fix to address deficiencies in underresourced educational systems. In addition, educational television would have the additional benefit of forestalling school integration. In the years leading up to and following the 1954 *Brown v. Board of Education* ruling, which ruled segregated schools unconstitutional, Alabama and other southern states looked to ways to "equalize" educational resources across white and black schools. Educational television would allow both white and black students to receive identical instructional materials without requiring them to sit in the same physical space (Perlman 2016, 39–40).

The state legislature created the Alabama Educational Television Commission (AETC), a five-person body appointed by the governor, and confirmed by the state legislature, to be the licensee for and oversee the operation of the network. The Alabama network's educational mission was multifaceted. Its programming was to instruct school children and to bring cultural works (ballet, opera, theater) to the homes of people who otherwise would be deprived of these experiences. The network telecast lectures, allowing it to become a "space age Chautauqua" for "the discriminating viewer" (Perlman 2016, 40). The Alabama Educational Television Network (AETN) also prioritized materials of civic import, from the governor's inaugural address to tax advice. The AETC contracted with three universities in Alabama, which would produce local programming for the network.

The AETN was a state-run network designed to address state needs, defined in accord with the political views of state officials. In its formative years, the AETC and the network it ran were therefore deeply intertwined with the system of racial supremacy in its state. In its first 15 years of operation, it not only sought to maintain school segregation, but omitted the state's substantial African American population from its leadership, its programming, and its perception of its public. The AETC's desire to cordon off Alabama from the social and political transformations that engulfed the nation in the 1960s, especially surrounding African American civil rights, led to the first major controversy to beset the local television network.

CONTROVERSY 1: STATES' RIGHTS, PUBLIC TELEVISION, AND RACIAL DISCRIMINATION

Throughout the 1960s, states like Alabama imagined educational television as a technology to ameliorate social inequalities while simultaneously shoring up existing power relations in the state; it could at once equalize access to educational and cultural programming without requiring the redistribution of resources, both material and political. By contrast, National Educational Television (NET), a Ford Foundation–supported organization that produced and distributed programming across educational television stations nationally, pursued educational television as a tool to disrupt, rather than affirm, the status quo. Throughout the 1960s, NET circulated a wide range of public affairs and cultural affairs programs, addressing hot-button topics like African American civil rights (Brooks 1994).

The AETC, like many other educational telecasters, refused to air much of this controversial programming. Throughout the 1960s, virtually none of the national programming circulated by NET on racial inequality was aired on the Alabama state network. The network, furthermore, did not replace national programs on civil rights with other programs that addressed this exigent topic from a local perspective. Thus, in a state in which a third of its citizens were African American, it became increasingly untenable to many of its residents that virtually no African Americans worked for its state-run television network, served on the commission that controlled its licenses, or appeared within its programming. In 1969, residents of Alabama filed a petition to deny the AETC's licenses on racial discrimination grounds (Perlman 2016, 57).

All broadcast stations, both commercial and noncommercial, at this time were granted broadcast licenses for three years, after which they had to submit applications for renewal with the Federal Communications Commission (FCC), who was to determine if renewal was in the public interest. At the heart of the challenge to the AETC's licenses were two intertwined questions over the definition of the Alabama "public" and over what it meant to serve it. The petitioners asserted that to whitewash the network's programming, and to refuse to air any shows addressing—or even meaningfully featuring—African Americans, not only denied audiences access to important perspectives, but transformed Alabama educational television into "media for White Supremacy" (Richey 1970). The AETC, in turn, refused to concede that diverse publics required a diversity of programming, insisting that to presume that all publics could not be served by high quality programming *itself* constituted racism; in this, the AETC charged that recognition of racial difference as meaningful was itself a form of racial discrimination. In addition, the Commission stated that its refusal to air the NET shows was an exercise in taste and judgment, not racial animus, and that its decisions were within its editorial discretion. In 1974, the FCC ultimately sided with the petitioners, citing the AETC's racially discriminatory practices as in violation of its public interest obligations (Perlman 2016, 59–60). All eight of the public television stations in the state simultaneously had their licenses revoked.

Though an historical anomaly—only one other television station (the commercial station WLBT in Jackson, Mississippi) had lost a license on racial discrimination grounds, and the AETC the following year successfully filed for and was awarded the licenses for Alabama's public television stations—the revocation of the AETC's licenses was a big deal at the time. The fight over public television in Alabama exposed the deep cleavages between the imagined national public sought by NET, the limiting parameters of the Alabama public as constituted by the AETC, and the inclusive local public fought for by the petitioners. It illuminated the fissures between the national and the local as well as within the local itself, exposed disparate understandings of the mission of public television, and revealed the power dynamics between national institutions and local channels. If NET and local Alabamians saw the AETC's decisions to omit national civil rights programming as expression of state-sanctioned racism, the AETC viewed NET as recklessly and insultingly dismissive of the mores and concerns of local channels in its programming priorities.

The license challenge, which took over six years to resolve, coincided with substantial changes in the noncommercial television sector. The 1967 Public Broadcasting Act, which redubbed *educational* television as *public* television, had created the Corporation for Public Broadcasting (CPB) to disburse federal monies and further develop the public television sector. The CPB, in 1969, decided to create a new organization, the Public Broadcasting System, to be the primary distributor of national programming to local public television stations, displacing NET in that role. NET merged with WNDT, the New York public television station, to form WNET, which would be one of the primary presenting stations for PBS. The balance of power of the public television sector was to shift with the creation of PBS, which by design was to be far more deferential to local stations than NET had been. The apotheosis of this emphasis was the 1974 formation of the Station Program Cooperative (SPC), which put the decision-making power for nationally distributed programs in the hands of local public television stations (Avery and Pepper 1980, 131). These changes resulted in part to ameliorate the tensions between local stations and the national organizations that served them. And yet, as the next major controversy to surround the AETC indicates, these changes did not end the frictions between the local and the national nor the very live debates within Alabama over the role of its public television channels.

CONTROVERSY 2: SPEECH RIGHTS AND STATE-RUN PUBLIC TELEVISION

The next big controversy for Alabama public television originated in the AETC's decision not to air a docudrama, *Death of a Princess*, in 1980.[1] The film told the story of the execution of a Saudi princess and her commoner lover. Based on interviews conducted by journalist Antony Thomas, the film at once uncovered what had happened to Princess Misha'al and exposed the religious and cultural mores of elite Saudi society. *Death of a Princess* had been co-produced by Boston station WGBH and Britain's Associated Television Corporation, was scheduled as part of WGBH's *World* series, and had been funded partially through the SPC members, including the AETC (Hershey 1980; Keneas 1980).

The firestorm in the US in the weeks leading up to the scheduled May 12 broadcast of *Princess* was intense. The film's airing in Britain in April 1980 had outraged the Saudi government, which objected to its representation of Saudi royal women as "repressed, uneducated, wallowing in luxurious boredom and generally adulterous" (Keneas 1980). Saudi Arabia retaliated by removing its ambassador from London and ousting the British ambassador from Jeddah (Ibrahim 1980). The Saudis also pressured US officials to block PBS from distributing the program. Acting Secretary of State Warren Christopher sent a letter to PBS President Lawrence Grossman asking PBS to give consideration to Saudi concerns over the film. Two members of Congress urged that the show be shelved, and Mobil Oil ran an ad in newspapers in major cities that suggested that the film "raises some very serious issues" ("State" 1980; Singleton 1980). To advocates of the film, its opponents seemed willing to sacrifice freedom of expression in order to placate a foreign government and secure the economic interests of major oil companies in the Middle East; to its detractors, *Princess*'s telecast would unnecessarily anger an American ally in the Middle East. PBS was steadfast in its decision to air the film, but added to the telecast a panel discussion of differing views on the film's legitimacy and accuracy (Nash and Matthews 1981).

Even so, a number of local stations decided not to air it. The South Carolina Educational Television Network, out of loyalty to the state's former governor and current ambassador to Saudi Arabia, John West, did not telecast the program across its five stations. KLCS-TV in Los Angeles and KUHT-TV in Houston deemed the film not in the national interest. And the Alabama Public Television Network, for ostensible fear the telecast would endanger the lives of Alabamians working in the Middle East, two days before the film's scheduled broadcast decided not to air it (Kelly 1980; Mitchell 1980). In advance of the scheduled telecast, business leaders with contracts in the Middle East contacted the AETC to express concern over the film (*Muir* 1982, 1054). In response, Alabama residents filed a lawsuit against the AETC, seeking to compel the film's telecast and desiring a permanent injunction against the Commission from making "political" decisions with regard to programming. A similar lawsuit was filed in Houston against KUHT (*Muir* 1982). In addition, the petitioners argued that the AETC's decision not to air the film violated their First and Fourteenth Amendment rights (*Muir* 1981).

The legal question considered by the courts was whether stations licensed to state agencies were afforded the same First Amendment protections as privately controlled stations. For the petitioners, the AETC had engaged as a government agency in an unconstitutional act of censorship by refusing to air the film; for the AETC, this decision was part and parcel of the editorial discretion the courts had historically afforded broadcasters. The Fifth Circuit Court of Appeals determined that commercial and noncommercial stations are generally subject to the same regulatory requirements, but stations that operate as "state instrumentalities" are "without the protection of the First

Amendment." While all parties in the case allowed for state-run public television stations to have some editorial discretion, the question was whether this discretion must be "carefully neutral as to which speakers or viewpoints are to prevail in the marketplace of ideas" (*Muir* 1982, 1041). The court ultimately rejected the idea that to cancel the program was to censor it—it could be shown in other venues in the state—and affirmed the editorial discretion of public telecasters, even those run by state governments, to make determinations about their programming schedule, guided by the public interest requirements of federal communications law. In a withering dissent (one of three filed in this case), Judge Frank Johnson Jr. determined that the decision by broadcasters in Alabama and Houston to cancel the telecast because of the viewpoints expressed within it was a textbook case of illegitimate state censorship (*Muir* 1982, 1053).

While the case turned on questions of legal rights—the rights of the petitioners to hear viewpoints, the rights of the AETC to determine what to broadcast over its channels—it also spoke to core disagreements over Alabama's values. If the petitioners fought for a state that valued the circulation of diverse ideas, the AETC privileged the safety of Alabamians working abroad—and, perhaps, the business interests of Alabama companies—over the speech rights of the broader public. If the license challenge in 1969 spoke to the relationship between local public television and the state's racial diversity, this court challenge considered how Alabamians would balance the marketplace of ideas with other state priorities; like the license challenge, it was a battle over the collective identity of the state, its public television channels imagined as a critical space where that identity would be defined.

CONTROVERSY 3: CHURCH/STATE AND LOCAL PROGRAMMING

Alabama public television's 2012 controversy placed the state's channels in a modern culture wars debate. It was, from one perspective, a clash over the role of religion in the public sphere. Members of the AETC wanted the public television network to telecast lay evangelical historian David Barton's ten-part series, *The American Heritage Series*; they also wanted public television channels in Alabama to program shows about creationism. In addition, the AETC disapproved of the APTN's inclusion of "sexual orientation" in its diversity statement. After firing executive director Allan Pizzato and his deputy Pauline Howland for refusing these requests, the AETC subsequently jettisoned the network's diversity statement altogether (Sefton 2012a; Fry 2012; "Alabama" 2012). Howland would be reinstated two days after she was fired, and by November 2012 Pizzato had been hired as president and general manager of the WYES-TV public television station in New Orleans (Sefton 2012b).

Yet the AETC's actions were greeted with outrage both within and outside of Alabama. Seven members of the Alabama Public Television Foundation's Board resigned in protest,[2] as did three members of the Alabama Educational Television Foundation Authority.[3] Charles Grantham, the APTN's chief operating officer resigned as well and wrote an open letter to Alabama Governor Robert Bentley decrying Pizzato's dismissal over "ideological differences" between him and the Commission. Bentley referred to the

AETC's meddling as a "destructive spiral" that could precipitate the "untimely death" of public television in Alabama. In addition, thousands of people voiced their opposition to the AETC's actions (Carlton 2012; Seitz-Wald 2012). While no legal actions followed, this most recent debate over the AETC took place in the court of public opinion.

As with the previous controversies, this 2012 incident centered on conflicting understandings of Alabama's identity, refracted through the programming of its local public television channels. Barton—and the approach to history he endorsed on his website, in his books, and in this film series—was a contentious figure. He argued that the US has always been an explicitly Christian nation; he also insisted that the doctrine of church/state separation, often interpreted as key to the religious freedom protections of the First Amendment, was a falsehood propagated by a mistaken Supreme Court that, like professional historians, erroneously diminished the centrality of Christianity to American nationhood. Professional historians reject Barton's views, seeing them as a projection of "contemporary political and religious notions back onto the eighteenth century, distorting the Founders by making them into twenty-first century born-again Christians" (Stephens and Giberson 2011, 65–6). In desiring Barton's work on the APTN, and in advocating for programming that endorsed creationism, the AETC not only sought to propagate concepts rejected as false by field experts, but to use a state instrument— public television—to promote religious ideas. The AETC's opposition to including the LGBTQ community in the network's diversity similarly spoke to the Commission's desire to ground public television in Alabama in the mores of evangelical Christianity.

The outrage over the AETC's demands, and its retaliatory actions against Pizzato and Howard, responded most directly to the Commission's desire to use the APTN as an instrument to propagate religious beliefs presented in the guise of legitimate history. To these critics, promotion of religious views by a state agency would directly violate the First Amendment protection of religious liberty and its prohibition of state religion. It was to impose the political and religious values of the commissioners themselves on all Alabamians.

But, as had been the case historically, this controversy was also over the mores and values of Alabama itself, and the relationship between its public television channels and its collective identity. The actions of the AETC raised questions over Alabama's conception of its body politic, its respect for established sites of expertise, and its embrace or rejection of its diverse publics. This struggle generated public debate, as had the previous controversies, over what sort of state Alabama was, a question in the public mind deeply intertwined with the programming commitments of its public television channels.

Ultimately, the history of Alabama public television channels offers an alternate window to the politics of noncommercial US television. It disrupts the notion of a monolithic public media sector and flags the importance, past and present, of local channels in determining what can be said, and who can be seen, on public TV. And, as the 2012 controversy attests, it signals the continued salience of local channels in our contemporary mediascape to local communities, who see in them a reflection—sometimes contested—of their own collective identity.

NOTES

1 The texts referenced relating to *Death of a Princess* (Hershey 1980; Ibrahim 1980; Kelly 1980; Keneas 1980; Mitchell 1980; Nash and Matthews 1981; "State" 1980; Singleton 1980) are all found in the James Day Collection, Box 27, Folder 18, National Public Broadcasting Archives, College Park, Maryland.

2 The Alabama Public Television Foundation Board is a private group that helps raise money for the network.

3 The Alabama Educational Television Foundation Authority is a board that consists of the seven commissioners and five people appointed by the Commission. It is given the authority to raise funds for the stations.

REFERENCES

"Alabama Public Television Board Members Quit after Executives Fired." 2012. *The Associated Press*, June 16. Accessed September 13, 2013. http://blog.al.com/businessnews//print.html?entry=/2012/06/alabama_public_television_boar.html.

Avery, Robert K. and Robert Pepper. 1980. "An Institutional History of Public Broadcasting." *Journal of Communication* 30 (3): 126–38.

Brooks, Carolyn N. 1994. "Documentary Programming and the Emergence of the National Educational Television Center as a Network, 1958–1972." Unpublished Dissertation, University of Wisconsin, Madison.

Carlton, Bob. 2012. "Birmingham Pastors Present Petitions to Alabama Public Television Objecting to History Series." *Al.com*, July 26.

Fry, Erika. 2012. "Firings Raise Questions at Alabama Public Television." *Columbia Journalism Review*, June 27. Accessed September 13, 2013. www.cjr.org/behind_the_news/firings_raise_questions_at_ala.php?page=all&print=true

Hershey Jr., Robert D. 1980. "Film about Executed Princess Upsets British-Saudi Relations." *New York Times*, April 11.

Ibrahim, Youssef M. 1980. "Saudis Tell London to Pull Out Envoy." *New York Times*, April 24.

Kelly, J. B. 1980. "'Death of a Princess' Requires No Apology." *The New Republic*, May 17.

Keneas, Alex. 1980. "Death of a Princess." *Newsday*, May 12.

Mitchell, Alison. 1980. "'Death of a Princess' Airs in U.S. Despite Protests." *Newsday*, May 13.

Muir v. AETC. 1981. 656 F.2d 1012.

Muir v. AETC. 1982. 982. 688 F.2d 1033.

Nash, Laura L. and John B. Matthews. 1981. *Death of a Princess*. Cambridge: Harvard Business School.

Perlman, Allison. 2016. *Public Interests: Media Advocacy and Struggles over U.S. Television*. New Brunswick: Rutgers University Press.

Permaloff, Ann and Carl Grafton. 1995. *Political Power in Alabama: The More Things Change. . . .* Athens: University of Georgia Press.

Richey, B. J. 1970. "Alabama ETV Under Fire for Racism, 'Censorship.'" *Mobile Register*, June 18. Birmingham Public Library, 23.1.7.11.1.

Sefton, Dru. 2012a. "Alabama Firings Expose Rift over PTV Mission, Editorial Standards." *Current.org*, June 25. Accessed September 13, 2013. http://current.org/2012/06/alabama-firings-expose-rift-over-ptv-mission-editorial-standards/.

Sefton, Dru. 2012b. "Veteran Pubcaster Allan Pizzato to Lead WYES-TV in New Orleans." *Current.org*, November 14. Accessed March 15, 2014. www.current.org/2012/11/veteran-pubcaster-allan-pizzato-to-lead-wyes-tv-in-new-orleans/.

Seitz-Wald, Alex. 2012. "Tea Party Takes over Alabama Public TV." *Salon*, August 9. Accessed July 7, 2016. www.salon.com/2012/08/09/tea_party_takes_over_alabama_public_tv/.

Singleton, Donald. 1980. "Seas of Protest over Saudi Film Flood Ch. 13." *Daily News*, May 10.

"State, Hill and Mobil Put Heat on PBS over 'Death of a Princess.'" 1980. *Broadcasting*, May 12.

Stephens, Randall J. and Karl W. Giberson. 2011. *The Anointed: Evangelical Truth in Secular Age*. Cambridge: Harvard University Press.

DR

License Fees, Platform Neutrality, and Public Service Obligation

Hanne Bruun

The Danish radio and television corporation, DR, is the oldest and biggest radio and television provider in Denmark. The company was established as a publicly owned national monopoly in 1925, and this status lasted until 1988. In 1951, television became a part of the company's activities, while in 1996 DR added a website to its platforms (www.dr.dk), and in 2012 launched a video on demand (VOD) and streaming service (DRTV). Throughout its history, DR has had public service obligations and the privilege of having all its activities funded by a license fee. In Denmark, households have to pay a license fee to own a television set or a device with access to the Internet. The license fee is paid directly by the citizens to the media corporations that are required to provide public service content. The Minister of Culture decides on the amount of the license fee supported by the finance committee in the Danish parliament (presently 353 dollars a year). A four-year media agreement (presently *Mediepolitisk aftale 2015–18*) between the sitting government and a number of political parties regulates how the license revenue will be distributed and what obligations that need to be met in order to get that license fee support. Presently, DR gets 67% of this revenue. It is therefore important for the political survival of DR to establish the public service legitimacy of its activities and performance in the eyes of both citizens and their representatives in parliament.

In Denmark, as many other developed nations, the use of traditional, linear, flow-organized television declines, whereas streaming television content live or on demand is on the increase. However, the interpretation of what "public service" means, as well as how it should be organized and pursued in Denmark, is also challenged by the disruptive influence of the Internet to legacy media institutions. As a consequence, the activities and performance of DR prove to be an important battleground between the supporters of a strong public media sector, and the supporters of a strong private media sector. In order to frame the challenges DR faces—as well as the advantages that its funding by the license fee might provide in negotiating those challenges—the chapter begins with a short introduction to the Danish television market with its mixture of public and private television broadcasters. From there, DR's public service obligations are secondly examined in order to explain why DR's activities and performance presently create conflicts, and why the ideals of public service create contested advantages for the company. Finally, the chapter discusses present challenges to DR and political projects aimed at redefining its public service obligations in the digital era. These efforts could result in news limitations on DR's scope of activities in the future.

DR'S POSITION IN THE DANISH TELEVISION MARKET

With a population of only 5.6 million, Denmark is a very small country in which the political system supports what Syvertsen et al. (2014) term a "media welfare state." This model allows television to be conceptualized as a public good, leading to a history of (pro)active cultural politics that includes a tradition of heavy state subsidies. These support private media companies (in sectors such as journalism, print media, and film production) as well as public media corporations (in radio and television). A key goal of this model is to secure a production of written and audio-visual content in Danish in support of a political and cultural democracy.

There are four important television companies in this Danish market: DR, TV 2/ Danmark, MTG TV, and Discovery. DR and TV 2 are over-the-air broadcasters, while MTG TV and Discovery are satellite-based. All four have large portfolios of five to six television channels each. They also offer one or more streaming services each to provide on-demand and live access to the content they produce. All these companies have elaborate websites, and they are all eager users of social network media. Furthermore, they all use mobile phones and social network media in connection with the production and distribution of television content. This focus on producing cross-media television content is driven by the fact that Danes are frequent users of social network media— especially Facebook, which supports 3.9 million Danish profiles. Instagram and Snapchat are also very popular. There are, however, important differences between the four major television providers. In terms of ownership, DR is an independent and publicly owned institution, and TV 2/Danmark is a publicly owned limited company; MTG TV and Discovery are the Danish branches of multinational corporations operating across many other countries, too. Both broadcast to Denmark from the UK in order to avoid Danish television advertising laws, which are stricter than those formulated by British (or European Union) regulations. TV 2/Danmark, MTG TV, and Discovery are all funded by commercial advertising and subscriptions. However, TV 2/Danmark is only allowed to place commercials *between* programs (not within) according to Danish law. While this limitation stems from the public service obligation of TV 2/Danmark's main channel and eight regional news affiliates, DR's scope of obligations is much larger by comparison. This includes mandates for programming aimed at special target groups but also extends beyond media content; for example, DR has obligations to run choirs, orchestras, and a concert hall.

In terms of traditional, linear, flow-based television broadcasting, TV 2/Danmark and DR have a combined audience share of 70%. Of this, DR's share is 34%, while TV 2/

Danmark's public service oriented main channel has a share of 24%. In short, with these channels capturing a combined share of 58%, it seems the Danes actually prefer public service television to commercial television. The two commercial corporations have a combined share of 21% by comparison, and MTG TV's share is 11%. In 2016, Danes spent 2 hours and 52 minutes a day on average watching traditional flow-based television, dwindling since 2010 from an all-time high of 3 hours and 10 minutes. The reason for this decline is that on-demand viewing and streaming continues to grow in popularity (*Mediernes udvikling i Danmark* 2017, 26). The streaming services provided by public service broadcasters are popular among the Danes, with access to DR's streaming service DRTV included in the same license fee that provides access to traditional television. Starting in 2017, the daily viewing measurements provided by Kantar Gallup include the use of television *regardless of* platform, leading broadcasters to expect these reports of overall decline in television viewership to cease. However, new transnational over-the-top competitors are also increasingly popular in Denmark. Netflix was introduced on the Danish market in 2012 and has a 30% share of subscribers on the subscription video on demand (SVOD) market, and 28% of the Danes use Netflix every week (*Medieudviklingen 2016* 2017, 21). All in all, even if public service television—including DR—has a strong position on the Danish television market, the competition for the attention of the audience has increased.

THE OBLIGATIONS OF A PUBLIC SERVICE PROVIDER

The strong position of DR is the result of a long tradition for media policies and regulations supporting the ideal of television as a public service. In recent years, DR has been given a key role in the conceptual transformation from public service *broadcasting* to public service *media* (Lowe and Bardoel 2007). In Danish media regulation, "public service" must provide citizens with "a variety of content and services including news services, information and education, art and entertainment" (*Bekendtgørelse* 2014). Diversity, pluralism, quality and impartiality are the core values guiding these broad content categories. These obligations also require public service television to secure content produced in Danish about Danish culture (in both a broad anthropological understanding of the term "culture" and a narrower sense connected to highbrow culture and art). These ideological formulations invite interpretation, meaningfully negotiated in specific historical and technological contexts by politicians, media corporations in their own public communication, and in the actual production of content for citizens. There are many possibilities for political and cultural taste-related conflicts, discussions, and discrepancies in these interpretive processes, and Danish television history is ripe with examples of cultural struggle over the idea of public service.

To narrow the interpretative playing field a bit, the four-year media agreements clarify more specific obligations for each period in question. Finally, the Minister of Culture and DR agree on a specific four-year contract based on the media agreement. The present four-year contract (*Mediepolitisk aftale* 2014) emphasizes DR's obligation to organize service for all Danes around four goals or pillars: first, to strengthen the democratic capacity of the citizens; second, to unite Danes in communities both small and large as well as to mirror the diversity of Danish society; third, to stimulate Danish culture and language as well as the Christian cultural heritage; and finally, to promote knowledge and insight. In addition, the idea of platform neutrality informs the current contract, giving DR "the right and the obligation to offer public service content on all relevant platforms" (*DR's public service-kontrakt* 2015, 2). This means content has to be universally accessible to all citizens who pay the license fee. If, for example, young adults use VOD, a tablet or a smartphone, and social network media instead of television, DR's content should—at least in principle—be made accessible on all these platforms and media.

According to the obligations and the remit of DR spelled out in this contract, DR has to offer content that will appeal to the mainstream as well as to special taste segments and age target groups among the audience, and thus achieve the goal of uniting Danes in different ways. The public service contracts for DR that describe this content obligation mandate a portfolio of six linear television channels that are also accessible online on the streaming service DRTV:

- DR1, with a mainstream oriented profile and mixed programing model including news and entertainment, current affairs and documentaries, factual entertainment, and fiction.
- DR2, with a profile of highbrow current affairs and political talk shows, documentaries, art house films, and satire.
- DRK, with a profile of highbrow art and culture, art house films, and classical music.
- Two children's channels: DR Ramasjang for 3- to 6-year-olds and DR Ultra for 7- to 12-year-olds.
- Finally, DR offers the channel DR3 targeted at 19- to 39-year-olds with a programming mix of documentaries, factual entertainment, films, and television fiction.

Within this portfolio, the broad appeal of DR1 plays a key role in securing the political legitimacy of the license fee across the whole population. Furthermore, the obligation to cater to the mainstream audience with a schedule of mixed programming has forced the organization to develop popular yet high quality content in the Danish language. This emphasis on popular quality programming has also led to the national and international success of Danish television drama series, especially those broadcasted by the mainstream DR1 channel on Sunday nights at 8 p.m. Many of these series have since 2002 been exported to around 150 countries inside and outside of Scandinavia as part of the transnational industry trade in "Nordic Noir" ("DR hjembringer" 2016). The products exported include series like *The Killing* and *The Bridge*, which have both been circulated in their Danish context as well as formatted in original, localized reproduction for the American market. DR was given an International Emmy Directorate Award in November 2016 for these achievements.

Today, the obligation to unite the Danes in large and small communities is explicitly mentioned in the present contract framing DR's activities. However, the obligation can be said to have led DR to practice a culturally broad interpretation of the public ser-vice remit for many years. During DR's monopoly on national television for 37 years, DR often looked to American television as well as British for inspiration in the popular programming it aimed to produce (Bruun 2005). A current example of this still very liberal and all-inclusive interpretation of what counts as public service programming is DR's continued broadcasting of its Danish adaptation of the reality talent show *X-Factor* since 2008. DR also has a track record of producing high quality television journalism and documentaries in Danish that are able to attract large audiences in prime-time. All in all, DR has survived for many years by embracing popular genres and trends in the international television industry, then adapting them to its public service profile. This is no doubt one reason for DR's continued success in the market for viewer attention in the digital era.

However, DR arguably enjoys in other ways a privileged position to sustain its role as a "cultural forum" (Newcomb and Hirsch 1994; Lotz 2014) in the digital era. The license fee provides the organization with a secure and long-term economic foundation outside of the commercial media market that is stable and reliable even if it is based on political processes and agreements as well as changing governments. Echoing one of DR's 2016 branding slogans, the platform neutrality principle additionally leaves DR free to make its content available "whenever you want it, wherever you want it." In short, DR has the privilege and the obligation to be a public service content *provider* instead of a broad-caster linked explicitly to television in a more limited way. This is a huge advantage in regards to DR's ability to secure an audience in the digital era.

CHALLENGING THE PLATFORM NEUTRAL PUBLIC SERVICE REMIT

Even if DR's position in the digital era can be regarded as favorable, a number of con-cerns can be raised. As described earlier, DR's position in the Danish television market is relatively strong, but declining viewership for traditional television flow—especially among older children (tweens) and young adults—has measurable impact on specific channels in the portfolio. Since its launch in 2013, DR Ultra has experienced significant difficulties in attracting its target audience of 7- to 12-year-olds. This means that DR's obligation towards this target group of future license fee payers is considered unmet. Especially among 7- to 12-year-olds, YouTube is the preferred channel, not public service television (*Medieudviklingen 2015* 2016, 54). In the light of these difficulties, DR has decided that DR Ultra will become an online service only in 2020 and the tradi-tional linear broadcast television channel will be closed.

DR3 has similar problems with its target group appeal and is up for evaluation and assessment by policymakers in 2018. DR3 will perhaps become an online service too, following BBC's example when the youth channel BBC3 was moved online in 2015. However, the new audience measurements that count television viewership regardless of platform will in the coming years show whether DR's problems with these target groups are only a question of distribution methods and platforms. The problems with the specific target groups might also be a question of content and the challenges of an on-demand digital economy that supports much more segmented audiences and specific genre interests while giving audiences agency to seek out content in other types of cultural fora (Lotz 2014, 47–9).

The on-demand television economy holds additional challenges as well, particularly for DR's mandate to provide and cater to specific kinds of taste cultures. As mentioned above, DR's obligation by law, media agreement, and contract is to offer schedules of mixed programming carried out by the six channels regardless of platform, in Danish, and with an emphasis on Danish culture. This implies a citizen/a viewer equally interested in a well-rounded, prescribed menu of mixed viewing including news, sports and current affairs, as well as fiction and entertainment, all organized around a political and cultural interest in Danish language content. Even in a nonlinear environment, the streaming service DRTV tries to hold on to and to encourage mixed viewing by curating a mixed schedule of genres and programs for viewers to choose from. However, audiences' enhanced control over what to watch, when and where to watch it might challenge this conceptualization of the public television viewer in the years to come. Choosing your own schedule of television content is becoming easier, for example by subscribing to over-the-top services like Netflix and HBO. These providers specialize in fiction (films and television series) and a limited number of American and British documentaries and entertainment programs. Younger segments of the audience especially prefer what these new companies have to offer compared to DRTV's public service (*Mediernes udvikling* 2017, 21). Even if Danes prefer Danish language television content, DR will likely have to work much harder to attract an audience for traditionally less popular television genres in order to meet its obligations. In recent years, ratings for television news, current affairs, and documentaries are already in decline.

A third challenge demands that DR provides public service media that will be considered worthwhile to select and use on a regular basis regardless of its viewers' class, gender, or education. This makes a recognizable and identifiable "brand" more important to the survival of DR as a public service as a means of supporting this new provider-viewer relationship (Johnson 2012). The traditional national boundaries for audio visual content set by spectrum scarcity and broadcasting technologies are increasingly porous. DR addresses this new competitive situation with a profile of content that can command the viewer attention, interest, and loyalty necessary to fulfill its obligation to unite the Danes in big and small viewer communities. The biggest challenge for DR's continued political legitimacy will be to sustain its ability to cater to the mainstream regardless of platform. DR is currently doing well among the well-educated and wealthy segments of the Danish audience, especially on niche channels DR2 and DRK that rely on a more traditional and limited interpretation of public service content.

Most significantly, perhaps, the continuing management of DR's public service obligations—and especially the content produced—will depend on political discussion of what public service television is or should be in the digital era. For example: what is the point of public service television distribution in a media environment where citizens have a multitude of national and international channels, providers, and content from which to choose? Does this context make license fee–funded public service television distribution regardless of platform more important than ever to secure public service content? Or is it redundant, and part of an old-fashioned way of regulating the media system? Presently, political negotiations and public debates are taking place to settle the next four-year media agreement beginning June 2019. The principle of platform neutrality underwriting DR's right and obligation to be present on all relevant platforms is creating dilemmas. Private media companies seek to curb DR's perceived expansion across every digital platform. The association of newspaper publishers in Denmark, Danske Medier, argues that DR is using the financial support of the public license fee to produce written news journalism on its website, and in this way DR is a de facto online newspaper. This is viewed as harmful competition because it makes the Danes uninterested in subscribing to a physical and/or online newspaper in the commercial sector (Danske Medier 2016). Another complaint raised by the private media sector is that DR jeopardizes or dilutes its unique public service position outside of the commercial media market when it places content on commercial platforms like Facebook and YouTube. By doing this, DR asks license fee payers to create a user profile in order to access this content, and DR helps these external commercial media to capitalize personal data.

The right-wing parties and, as of 2017, the sitting right-wing government in the Danish parliament seek to help private media compete with DR as well as growing transnational competition from over-the-top-providers and social media. These forces suggest cutting back on the license fee revenue given to DR in the future, and limiting DR's scope of activities. The argument is that in order to have a clearer role to play in the television market of the digital era, public service should be defined to a much larger degree by what the private market cannot or will not deliver. In this view, DR should concentrate much more on producing political and culturally important but also less popular genres, and focus on content for commercially non-profitable target groups (for example: old citizens, young children, the disabled, and minorities). This approach, they believe, will make what is and what is not public service content much clearer to the viewers. This political interest in redefining DR's public service obligations extends from an overall ambition to reduce the size of public television sector in Denmark. The sitting 2017 government aims to sell TV 2 to a private owner, putting its continued public service obligations to political negotiation and debate. A government committee report published in November 2016, imagining five different scenarios for the future, will be a major factor in these political negotiations.

To conclude, the ongoing changes that define the television industry in the digital era will affect the way public service is understood and how DR will respond to meet these expectations. Whatever the future, DR has proven its ability to adapt to changes in the media environment and remains a cornerstone of the television system in Denmark. The current position of DR, however, depends on the privilege and advantages of the license fee it enjoys as well as the platform neutral mandate to go where the audience is in order to secure a public service that meets political and cultural obligations as currently defined. The present political trends are pointing in the direction of a much narrower interpretation of what those obligations of public service television are both in terms of what platforms are allowed, and in terms of content and target groups. If this interpretation is implemented DR will perhaps sidestep its current dilemmas but will also run the risk of losing its ability to attract an audience of scale on the digital media platforms the Danes actually use. This might lead to a kind of "heroic suicide," as Søndergaard has termed it (1995, 91), where the ideals of public service will be preserved, but DR will face difficulties meeting many of its public service obligations, putting the political legitimacy of license fee–funded public service television in danger.

REFERENCES

Bekendtgørelse af lov om radio- og fjernsynsvirksomhed [The Radio and Television Law]. 2014. Kulturministeriet.

Bruun, Hanne. 2005. "Public Service and Entertainment: A Case Study of Danish Television 1951–2003." In *Cultural Dilemmas in Public Service Broadcasting*, edited by Gregory Ferrell Lowe and Per Jauert, 143–63. Göteborg: Nordicom.

Danske Medier. 2016. "Rapport om DR og de regionale TV 2-stationer I konkurrence med de private medier" [Report on DR and the Regional TV 2-Channels in Competition with the Private Media]. København.

"DR hjembringer Emmy for drama i verdensklasse" [DR Brings Home an Emmy for World Class Drama]. 2016. *DR Ajour* Newsletter, November 21.

DR's public service-kontrakt for 2015–2018 [DR's Public Service Contract 2015–2018]. 2015. Kulturministeriet.

Johnson, Catherine. 2012. *Branding Television*. London: Routledge.

Lotz, Amanda D. 2014. *The Television Will Be Revolutionized*. New York: New York University Press.

Lowe, Gregory Ferrell and Jo Bardoel (eds.). 2007. *From Public Service Broadcasting to Public Service Media*. Göteborg: Nordicom.

Mediepolitisk aftale 2015–2018 [Media Agreement 2015–2018]. 2014. Kulturministreret.

Mediernes udvikling i Danmark 2016 [Development of the Media in Denmark 2016]. 2017. Kulturministeriet.

Medieudviklingen 2015. [The Media Development 2015]. 2016. DR.

Medieudviklingen 2016. [The Media Development 2016]. 2017. DR.

Newcomb, Horace and Paul M. Hirsch. 1994. "Television as a Cultural Forum." In *Television the Critical View*, 5th edition, edited by Horace Newcomb, 561–73. New York: Oxford University Press.

Søndergaard, Henrik. 1995. "Public Service i Dansk Fjernsyn: Begreber, Status og Scenarier" [Public Service in Danish Television: Concepts, State of the Art and Scenarios]. Rapport til Statsministeriets medieudvalg, København.

Syvertsen, Trine, Gunn Enli, Ole J. Mjøs and Hallvard Moe. 2014. *The Media Welfare State: Nordic Media in the Digital Era*. Ann Arbor: The University of Michigan Press.

☐ MeTV

Old-Time TV's Last Stand?

Derek Kompare

As digital media platforms proliferated in the first decades of the twenty-first century, they continued to be filled with the residual media texts of the twentieth century: images, sounds, books, films, and television programs. The central argument of my 2005 book *Rerun Nation* was that the redistribution of past programming (film and television libraries, book publisher and record label back catalogues, etc.) has been one of the American media industries' primary functions (Kompare 2005). Over a dozen years later, and well into the "post-network" era of online streaming media platforms like Hulu, Netflix, and Spotify, much (though certainly not all) of the technological development, business strategy, and creative and cultural energy of media remains focused on the issue of reselling access to old media texts. Even while these services put enormous resources into the development and marketing of their own original programming, older music, films, and TV shows continue to be their "bread and butter": basic fare that fills out their offerings and fosters a steadier stream of interest in more familiar material. Indeed, the interest in reruns on these platforms has even prompted the revival of long-cancelled programs, as seen in Netflix's revivals of *Full House* (ABC, 1987–1995) and *Gilmore Girls* (WB/CW, 2000–2007).

Throughout television history, new platforms and technologies ostensibly developed to expand the diversity of programming have been adapted instead for the commercial redistribution of existing (i.e., "library") programming. An important, if surprisingly little noticed, example of this phenomenon has been the multiplexed digital broadcast channel allotment of the Advanced Television Systems Committee system (ATSC), initially proposed in US telecommunication policy in the 1990s as a replacement of the decades-old analog NTSC system and rolled out with the closing off of analog television broadcasting in 2009. Under this system, television stations are now licensed to broadcast multiple simultaneous digital signals carrying video programming (and other data streams). Broadcasters may choose from an array of signal resolutions at the SD

(Standard Definition, 480 or 576 horizontal lines) or HD (High Definition, 720 or 1080 horizontal lines) standards. A broadcast license holder now typically opts to transmit a "primary" signal as a higher bandwidth HD signal (i.e., as channel x.1), and two or more secondary signals at a lower bandwidth SD resolution (often leased out to other distributors, and located on tuners as channels x.2, x.3, x.4, etc.). This continued availability of lower resolution video not only allows for a greater number of multicast signals; it also extends the potential life span of twentieth-century pre-HD video, the vast majority of which has not been upgraded to higher resolutions.[1]

The combination of a new, accessible media platform and a vast library of existing programming propelled the development of MeTV (Memorable Entertainment Television): a national network distributed on multiplexed digital subchannels that is mostly reliant on SD reruns of programming originally from the 1950s through 1990s. MeTV's rapid growth and influence on the digital frontier has been somewhat paradoxically propelled by its adoption of "old-school" programming and marketing techniques meant to appeal to a 40-years-old-plus audience of Baby Boomers and Gen Xers. It thrives by offering these viewers more of the shows of their youth, while providing advertisers affordable access to a large group of lucrative, yet neglected, consumers. However, its position is also fairly precarious, as it resides in a marginal corner of a still-fragmenting media universe, and has little room for growth as its target demographic ages.

The multiplexing system, which takes advantage of both digital compression and a reallocation of the broadcast spectrum, was designed to boost both the commercial and public service potential of terrestrial broadcasters. In practice, however, and not unlike the path taken by cable television since the 1970s, the result has been yet another platform for new, nationally oriented TV networks. These multiplexed subchannel networks, known in the industry as "diginets," became available for cultivation just as the market for new cable networks had effectively peaked. Cable networks had thrived as cable capacity (both technological and economic) had expanded, growing in two spurts: in the late 1970s through early 1980s, and again in the early to mid-1990s. The first period brought us channels like CNN, ESPN, A&E, and Nickelodeon; the second brought us Fox News, ESPN2, HGTV, and TV Land. By the 2000s, however, cable systems were saturated with multiplexed networks of established brands (for example, all the HBO channels including HBO2, HBO Comedy, HBO Family, HBO Signature, etc.), as well as the cable companies' dozens of new VOD (video on demand) channels, which typically provided access to recent movies and live sports. At a time of increasing anxiety over audience fragmentation and the nascent possibilities of online streaming, there was relatively little space, interest, or capital (ca. 2009, at least) to develop new brands in cable distribution. By contrast, multiplexed digital broadcasting opened up opportunities to develop new channel networks across the country on stations with a lot of space to fill, and without the ordeal of negotiated carriage on cable systems. They could also potentially recapture a neglected but nevertheless significant audience of viewers who did not subscribe to cable and only received TV over the air. In addition, a new television receiver policy ensured that all new TV sets sold in the US had to include the ATSC tuner used to receive these channels. At a similar juncture in the 1960s, the All-Channel Receiver Act (1962) required all US-distributed sets to receive channels 2–13 (in the VHF range) and 14–83 (in the UHF range), and was critical to the development of UHF television stations in the second half of that decade. In the late 2000s and early 2010s, the sales of digital television tuners and sets necessary for the new ATSC broadcasting system increased, meaning increasing number of viewers now had access to the new subchannels.

MeTV was one of the first of these diginets to develop a national profile. It started locally in 2005 in Chicago as a branded block of syndicated reruns programmed by Weigel Broadcasting's independent station WMME—although this block also included the original local program *Svengoolie*, a continuation of the long-running (1970–1973, 1979–1986, 1994–) homage to the hosted late-night horror movies of the first decades of TV. In 2008, this format then expanded to Milwaukee station WBME, one of several stations Weigel owned in the Midwest. Seeing the opportunity for expansion on the new frontier of digital subchannels that opened up in 2009, Weigel decided to offer the programming format to other station owners at a national level, and launched MeTV as a diginet on December 15, 2010.

Its business plan has been effective on several fronts. First, MeTV has partnered with station owners eager to develop the subchannel tier with familiar programming and a marketable brand, gaining access to audiences in key markets and attracting advertisers. Second, it has gained the distribution rights to large but relatively inexpensive rerun programming libraries (initially from CBS and Twentieth Television), maximizing the ability to fill their schedule at a minimal cost. And finally, it has targeted a relatively neglected TV audience: people over 40 who fondly remember "old" TV and the pop culture of the second half of the twentieth century. This strategy has allowed MeTV to structure its entire network brand around playful cultural nostalgia in familiar trappings (of both original programs and newer paratexts).

The opportunity to develop a new market for older television fare emerged as syndicated reruns had otherwise started to otherwise disappear from television by the late 2000s. Cable networks had increasingly turned to original production in reality series and prestige drama, while cable and broadcast channels increasingly narrowed the scope of their interests in syndication, competing with one another for the rerun rights to more recent or ongoing sitcoms with broad appeal (*The Simpsons* [FOX, 1989–], *The Big Bang Theory* [CBS, 2007–], *Two and a Half Men* [CBS, 2003–2015), etc.). Meanwhile, DVD boxsets of old TV shows, though plentiful, did not necessarily appeal to casual viewers who did not want to amass bulky collections or deal with renting and returning physical media. Finally, another factor leading to the diminution of the traditional broadcast rerun syndication market emerged as new streaming video on-demand (SVOD) platforms gave viewers more direct control over the scheduling of TV reruns. As distributors of programming and viewers of older TV shows have increasingly looked to non-linear SVOD services like Hulu and Amazon, traditional broadcasters began to question the value of licensing older programming from syndicators in order to program it for audiences to watch it at specific, scheduled times. For all these reasons, syndicated reruns of old programming appeared to be in decline.

Yet that decline was also an opportunity for a new broadcast service to take advantage of the lowered costs to acquire older programming (given the decline in demand) as well as the potential to develop appeals to an underserved audience with these undervalued reruns. Accordingly, a channel dedicated to maintaining access to older TV history, while reviving programs ranging chronologically from *Our Miss Brooks* (CBS, 1952–1956) to *CHiPs* (NBC, 1977–1983), seemed like a relatively low-risk bet. MeTV's costs to acquire older programs were low, and the audience relatively small; but amortized across dozens of markets (covering 96% of US television households), they added up. By 2015, MeTV had managed to attract an audience larger than most cable networks, averaging over a half million viewers in the daytime, and almost 700,000 in prime-time ("Companies" 2015).

MeTV's model has since become the dominant approach for the commercial development of the digital subchannel tier, and older reruns have again become big business on broadcast TV. In MeTV's wake, several more national rerun-based diginets have gone on the air, like Antenna TV, RetroTV, HOT TV, and big media ventures like Comcast's Cozi, Sony's GetTV, and CBS' Decades, which pull from their respective parent corporation's deep programming libraries. In addition, taking the trend a step further, several audience and/or genre-specific rerun-centered networks have entered the fray, including Heroes & Icons (action-adventure), LaffTV (sitcoms), Buzzr (game shows), GritTV (westerns), Comet (sci-fi, fantasy, and horror), Bounce (African American series and films), and Escape (action and mystery). This influx of new channels, and thus new buyers, has also reinvigorated the syndication market for older fare. While some series are not exclusive to any particular channel, and might be found on multiple channels, as well as on streaming sites like Netflix or Hulu (e.g., the original *Star Trek* [NBC, 1966–1969]), other featured series on diginets are more obscure and not as well remembered. This reflects less an expansive and conscientious archival sensibility and more commercial necessity: if a diginet has hours to fill, and cannot afford the license for *I Love Lucy* (CBS, 1951–1957), perhaps it can get away with its much cheaper and largely forgotten (though quite entertaining) contemporary *I Married Joan* (NBC, 1952–1955). A 2014 blanket agreement on residuals between distributors and the major production guilds—usually a major issue limiting the affordability of redistribution rights—opened the doors to further mining of television's past (Barnes 2014). Along the way, some particularly unlikely material has been unearthed. Antenna TV, for example, shows entire episodes of *The Tonight Show Starring Johnny Carson* (NBC, 1962–1992), unseen since the 1970s and 1980s, while GetTV has aired several one-off TV specials from the 1960s, featuring performers like Judy Garland, Johnny Cash, Carol Channing, and Smokey Robinson, as well as long-buried rarities like *The Sonny and Cher Comedy Hour* (CBS 1971–1974) and *Yancy Derringer* (CBS 1958–1959). In addition, although certainly fueled by nostalgia rather than historiography, these diginets are all arguably as "archival" a caretaker of their vintage programming as is commercially practical today. MeTV, for example, usually presents its series in their original 4:3 aspect ratios, provides original airdates and other details about each episode, and leaves opening and closing credits intact.

However, as these decades-old program titles indicate, the diginet channels that rely upon them will never be at the forefront of viewers' and advertisers' minds. These diginets are explicitly marginal: existing in the shadow of their primary channel allocation, and often not available at all to viewers of cable and satellite systems, which are not obligated to carry multiplexed subchannels. That said, even in the low viewership margins of multiplexed television, advertising markets can flourish. Overhead costs are low, with cheap programming libraries, few new production expenses (beyond cutting some promos and graphics packages), and minimal permanent staff. Accordingly, with national coverage, even low-end ad rates can be profitable. Advertising on MeTV aims towards a broad Gen X and Baby Boomer swath, and includes appropriately sedate "adult" products like car insurance, fast food, and low-end, low-profile consumer products. Still, the channel actually outpaces most cable networks, and, by 2015, sat comfortably in the top ten of all channels, broadcast or cable, in the 35- to 64-year-old demographic (Stilson 2015).

Even on these margins, MeTV's brand is significant in the TV landscape in its embrace of "old-school" programming and marketing strategies. As many television scholars have noted, the mid-2000s marked an industrial shift away from the linear, network-oriented strategies of the 1980s and 1990s, and towards what Amanda Lotz has referred to as the "post-network" era, when online distribution, time-shifting, and dispersed audiences have challenged the dominance of established linear broadcasting brands (2014, 28–32). In this environment, MeTV deliberately adopted a contrarian branding strategy, harking back strategically to 1980s–1990s cable networks, with programming that evokes the 1950s–1970s. As Catherine Johnson notes, "the use value of a brand . . . lies in what people do with the brand" (53). At a time when traditional linear distributors work to learn how to become interactive digital services, MeTV branded itself as an "old-school" linear distributor, owning its status as a traditional broadcaster. Its use value is the identity it encourages in its viewers to embrace "Me": the simple allure of the nostalgia of "memorable entertainment television" of the 1950s–1980s found on both its schedule and its website. The use of "Me" throughout their branding encourages viewer identification with its series and stars, as they tune in for "The Summer of Me," a "Love Me" Valentine's Day marathon, and similar events, complete with the jingle "it's memorable, it's Me!"

While fueled by this nostalgic ethos, MeTV still must function as a twenty-first-century media brand. Accordingly, its broadcast profile and television ad revenues are only part of an overall audience cultivation strategy, which also includes an extensive website and social media presence. The MeTV website features a constant stream of clickbait articles and quizzes centered on television and pop culture nostalgia, with titles like "21 Things That Happen on Every Episode of *Gilligan's Island*," "Whatever Happened to Louise Lasser?," and "Did These Events Happen in 1982 or Not?" In addition, it has a small library of sample episodes from about a dozen different series, as well as promo spots (embedded from its YouTube account) for its series, featuring new appearances from actors like Lou Ferrigno (*The Incredible Hulk* [CBS, 1977–1982]), Vicki Lawrence (*Mama's Family* [NBC/syndication, 1983–1990]), and Dawn Wells (*Gilligan's Island* [CBS, 1964–1967]). More intriguingly, it has an ad-supported streaming music player that offers up pop songs from the 1960s–1980s, and a shop full of nostalgic TV merchandise. The site's structure of ad-saturated articles, videos, and games is common today, particularly similar to online culture hubs like Buzzfeed. As with all such sites, this enables MeTV to capture and sell its users' attention and data many times over, with everywhere they look and click.

However, MeTV's website is also very *unlike* mainstream, increasingly non-linear television network websites today, which function almost solely as streaming portals to programming, with minimalist, app-centered interfaces. On their websites, the major broadcast and cable networks, including MeTV's spiritual ancestor TV Land, have left busy click-centric design principles far behind, and no longer rely on quizzes, listicles, or even banner ads. MeTV, with no critical attention, no original programming (bar segments of *Svengoolie*), and no desirable demographics, doesn't aspire to join that elite circle on TV or on the web, and instead cultivates an active, clicking user base. Much like its TV ad model, however, even this seemingly low-end activity of a few tens of thousands of users can add up.

As Amy Holdsworth argues about television's engagement with its own history,

> what is central to the textual re-encounters with past television is not the recovery of the original broadcast or viewing experience but its positioning within new frames and contexts that hold the past at a distance and reframe it in relation to the present.
>
> (2011, 98)

Whether online or on the air, MeTV viewers are assembled through a mode of address that builds upon a knowing model of nostalgic TV viewership pioneered by Nick at Nite in the 1980s and 1990s, where the past is not recreated as much as framed as a distinct and engaging sensibility to visit. At that time, Nickelodeon, building off the same tools and styles used to great effect at sibling network MTV, built an approach to the television past that acknowledged an ironic distance but encouraged a playful appreciation. As I've previously described about Nick at Nite, past TV shows were mined for moments that could be repurposed in promotional paratexts and celebrated in order to draw new attention to them (from both old and new viewers), and promulgate a self-aware, media-savvy sensibility (Kompare 2005, 179–84). Decades later, while Nick at Nite (and its spin-off, TV Land) now only offers a slimmed-down array of more recent late–Gen X and early Millennial–skewing programs from the 1990s (including *The Fresh Prince of Bel-Air* [NBC, 1990–1996], *Friends* [NBC, 1994–2004], *Everybody Loves Raymond* [CBS, 1996–2005], and *The King of Queens* [1998–2007]), MeTV has reclaimed the original nostalgic strategy and audience demographic. For example, MeTV promotes its "Super Sci-Fi Saturday Night" block of superhero, science fiction, and horror shows with an appropriately retro logo and playful tone, incorporating brief moments of action or dialogue (from four or more different programs). In one spot, actor Lou Ferrigno (who played the titular character of *The Incredible Hulk* from 1977 to 1982) gets green-screened into *Star Trek*, *Wonder Woman* (ABC/CBS, 1976–1979), *Batman* (ABC, 1966–1968) and *Svengoolie*. In another series of spots, called "Find Me on MeTV," retired actors like Clu Gulager and Robbie Rist invite viewers to spot their appearances across several of the channel's series. An intriguing spot inspired by the opening credits to Netflix's popular horror series *Stranger Things* (2016–) used no images, but only the original audio from classic lines of dialogue (e.g., "To serve man . . .

FIGURE 8.1 *MeTV's website features dozens of clickable articles, quizzes, games, and videos, as well as a stream of 1960s–80s pop songs.*

it's a cookbook!") to promise that its nightly reruns of *The Twilight Zone* featured the "Strangest Things."

While national clearance on multiplexed subchannels, acquisition of rights to popular programs, and marketing and brand-building prove critical to the success of MeTV, at the core of the enterprise are the broadcast schedule and the programs themselves. MeTV's schedule shifts every few months, but it generally draws from many genres and periods from the mid 1950s through early 1990s, straddling the likeliest range of tastes and interests for its target Baby Boom and Gen X audience. In the time-honored broadcast fashion that only this target demo would understand, it builds dayparts of sitcoms in the early morning; hour-long procedural dramas in the later morning and afternoon; popular sitcoms in the early evening; and crime, action and supernatural shows in the later evening. On Saturdays, it offers several hours of westerns in the daytime followed by several hours of science fiction at night, shrewdly bridged by the genre-straddling, vaguely steampunkish *The Wild Wild West* (CBS, 1965–1969). On Sunday mornings, it skews "young"—that is, to the slightly under-40 crowd—with a block of 1990s kids' favorites including *Beakman's World* (syndicated, 1992–1997), *Bill Nye the Science Guy* (PBS, 1994–1999), and *Saved by the Bell* (NBC, 1989–1993). Throughout its schedule, MeTV invites viewers not as much to particular programs as to particular genres and nostalgic experiences, asking them to settle in and leave it on the channel to evoke favorite TV memories. As noted earlier, its website has a similar logic, and functions as an endless game of "remember when" with TV, music, and other pop culture trivia.

However, given that its target demographic has already aged out of the traditional 18- to 49-year-old range most desirable to advertisers, these distinctions will be appreciated by a continually shrinking audience. Indeed, rerun diginets like MeTV, Antenna TV, GetTV, and similar channels are likely the last broadcast gasp of linear, twentieth-century rerun programming. Few people born after 1980 will have the necessary affective attachment to TV (or films, for that matter) made decades before they were born. This is not to cast aspersions on Millennials' cultural values, but rather to acknowledge a stark outcome of shifting television viewing practices. In their lifetimes, most younger people in the US, and in most other countries with advanced media systems, have always experienced a media system built on catering to specific audiences and accessibility of programming, whether through dedicated cable networks like MTV and Disney, cheap VHS tapes and DVDs, or now online, on-demand streamers like YouTube and Netflix. While there certainly still remain significant gaps in the representation of different identities and sensibilities in television programming, since the 1990s there has never been a shortage of new programming aimed at children and teens. In contrast, the rerun culture of the 1960s–1980s that MeTV is built upon was cultivated out of the necessity of broad, accessible programming in an era of linear schedules and relative scarcity. Boomers and Gen Xers watched many of these shows in reruns as children at that time primarily because *there was nothing else on*, and certainly nothing aimed exclusively at them in prime-time. Their resultant affection for (or at least recognition of) these shows, and the era from whence they came, emerged from this kind of ubiquitous repetition of a limited range of programs. While interest in past television may persist (at least among media historians), it is unlikely that endeavors like MeTV will be commercially viable without that connection. Given the fragmentation of audiences and viewing practices, it's unlikely that they could eventually "move on" to the TV of the 1990s–2010s to capture Millennial and younger viewers, particularly because so much programming from that era has already long been available on cable networks and streaming services. But for now at least, in the decade or two left while it is still feasible to target Boomers and Gen Xers based on their memories of the broadcast era, MeTV and its compatriot rerun-based diginets have successfully offered yet another after-market for film and television libraries, a lucrative media venture for broadcast license holders, and a comfortable and familiar source of television culture for an appreciative audience that is itself past prime-time.

NOTE

1 "Video" in this particular context refers to moving images formatted for television distribution. If the original material is film, it may be rescanned and redistributed at HD or higher resolutions (as has been done with many classic feature films and film-based TV series on Blu-ray and/or HD streaming). If it was originally produced and/or distributed on analog SD video—typically with up to 480 lines of resolution—it cannot be easily upgraded to HD without considerable trouble and expense. Hence, most legacy material is still most frequently broadcast in SD, rather than HD.

REFERENCES

Barnes, Brooks. 2014. "Studio Deals Unlock a Trove of Reruns." *New York Times*, August 25. Accessed May 2, 2017. www.nytimes.com/2014/08/26/business/media/studio-deals-unlock-a-trove-of-reruns-from-shows-like-breaking-bad-and-sons-of-anarchy.html.

"Companies Turn to Classic TV as a Low-Cost Solution." 2015. *The Buffalo News* (New York), April 4.

Holdsworth, Amy. 2011. *Television, Memory and Nostalgia*. New York: Palgrave-McMillan.

Johnson, Catherine. 2012. *Branding Television*. New York: Routledge.

Kompare, Derek. 2005. *Rerun Nation: How Repeats Invented American Television*. New York: Routledge.

Lotz, Amanda D. 2014. *The Television Will Be Revolutionized*, 2nd edition. New York: New York University Press.

Stilson, Janet. 2015. "Why Leave It to Beaver Has Stations Seeing Green." *Adweek*, February 16. Accessed May 2, 2017. www.adweek.com/tv-video/why-leave-it-beaver-has-stations-seeing-green-162972/.

Cable and Satellite Services

WGN America

From Chicago to Cable's Very Own

Christine Becker

When the *Chicago Tribune* took command of a local radio station in the early 1920s, the company also acquired the call letters WGN as an acronym for its longtime slogan, World's Greatest Newspaper. Since then, those same three letters have also represented an independent television station, a network affiliate, a superstation, and a cable channel. WGN's evolution across these stages offers a handy guide to the evolution of television itself, as the medium moved from limited channels in the broadcast network era to the multi-channel expansion of the cable era and now is in the fiercely competitive landscape of the post-network era. The story of how WGN, a local television station, eventually begat WGN America, a national cable channel, with a superstation stage along the way, helps to illuminate US commercial television's economic, technological, and regulatory infrastructures in each of those eras and thereby illustrate the principle that television channel configuration and content inevitably change as those infrastructures evolve.

A decades-long plan by Tribune publisher Robert McCormick to bring WGN to television was realized in April 1948 when the station flickered to life on Channel 9 on Chicago's TV sets (Fink 1961, 79). After a period of affiliation with the pioneering commercial network DuMont that lasted until the network's 1956 demise, WGN-TV would stand as an independent television station targeting the Chicago market for the next two decades, filling each daypart with programming of its own choosing, rather than anything dictated by a network custodian. The station's deep broadcasting roots helped provide the framework for a significant volume of local productions, including standout news, lifestyle and talk shows, children's shows, and sports coverage. WGN also established a model for effective counter-programming of network fare in prime-time, featuring a substantial library of movies and the airing of local news at 9 p.m., one hour earlier than its network affiliate counterparts, which helped WGN become one of the rare independent stations that could frequently build bigger ratings than its network competition (Haley 2004a).

WGN subsequently had its local status parlayed into national reach via the super-station model. Since the early 1960s, WGN-TV's signal had been carried on a handful of rural cable television systems across the Midwest via microwave transmission, but government regulations had limited wider importation into bigger markets in order to protect nascent broadcasters from distant competition and audience fragmentation (Mullen 2003, 37). The Federal Communications Commission (FCC) began to relax those restrictions in the 1970s to encourage wider economic development of cable tele-vision, while satellite technology simultaneously emerged as a more efficient means of distributing television signals to cable system operators across the nation. The first inde-pendent station to take advantage of these new conditions was Ted Turner's Atlanta-based WTCG, soon to be renamed WTBS. In 1976, Turner uplinked WTCG's signal to a communications satellite and offered it to distant cable systems around the US, mak-ing it the first superstation. Megan Mullen explains the term:

> A superstation is an independent broadcast station whose signal is picked up and redistributed by satellite to local cable television systems. Within its originating market, the station can be received off the air using a home antenna. Once uplinked to a satellite, however, the station functions as a cable program service or cable "network."
>
> (2004, 2224)

Mullen notes that WTBS was an "active" superstation, in that Turner voluntarily dis-tributed his local station across the country, targeting programming toward the nation-wide market and seeking national advertising. WGN would soon become part of the superstation revolution but via an involuntary or "passive" model by which the local signal was uplinked to a satellite by a common carrier, or a company that transmits communications services, without formal consent from WGN (Mullen 2003, 113–15). This was legal under the period's FCC regulations overseeing satellite resale common carriers, and it meant that WGN's superstation channel was not borne initially from WGN's own corporate self-determination; it was created by another company's initia-tive as sanctioned by the FCC's regulatory governance.[1]

Not many independent stations had built up enough distinction during the net-work era to be worthy of national distribution once cable arrived, but WGN certainly had. Beginning in 1978, WGN-TV's signal was retransmitted to cable systems by an Oklahoma-based common carrier called United Video Satellite Group. United Video's president said WGN, the highest-rated independent station in the country, was their top retransmission choice out of all stations in the US (Haley 2004a). Importantly, FCC regulations enabled United Video to receive the retransmission fees paid by cable oper-ators for the rights to carry WGN; neither the station nor the Tribune Company saw any of this revenue. WGN gained benefits elsewhere, though, primarily in advertising revenues and brand exposure, as the extended distribution helped the station's national reach leap from fewer than 100,000 cable subscribers in 1970 to over three million by 1982 (Mullen 2003, 135). WGN's general manager Shelley Cooper described his company's reaction to United Video's retransmission of the station's signal: "We were not glad. We were opposed, but it was a little like the comedian who holds one hand up as if to say 'don't applaud anymore' while using the other hand to signal that he'd like more applause" (Haley 2004a). Fitting with the passive superstation model, the local market was still WGN's top priority, reflected in the slogan the station introduced in 1983, "Chicago's Very Own." But many of its most valuable assets appealed nationally in the early cable era, as WGN featured a deep library of Hollywood films, unique programs like the children's show *Bozo's Circus* (1960–2001), popular network reruns, and a bevy of live Chicago sports, including over 130 Chicago Cubs games every year.

WGN's superstation and independent status would evolve subsequently due to the further expansion of both broadcast and cable television. As superstations spread on cable systems across the 1980s, local stations and syndicated programming owners found it problematic that a superstation could duplicate the programs already airing in a local market, thus lessening their potential economic value. Therefore, in 1990 the FCC instituted the syndicated exclusivity rules, which required cable operators to black out any superstation programming that duplicated a local station's offerings (Mullen 2003, 136–7). WGN responded by providing a separate transmission signal for the superstation that replaced locally exclusive programs with other fare (Haley 2004a). That feed was renamed WGN Superstation in 2001, and the amount of programming shared between WGN-TV and the superstation feed by then amounted to about 40% (Haley 2004c).

WGN-TV itself underwent a major change in the 1990s, which began with the Tribune Company's further expansion into broadcast ownership. Thanks to the FCC's loosening of television station ownership restrictions, the Tribune expanded its station group by buying up numerous TV stations across the country, and it also purchased a minority stake in a new broadcast network, The WB. The WB launched with a single night of programming in January 1995 with ten Tribune-owned stations as affiliates, including WGN-TV. WGN Superstation also affiliated with The WB initially, but the partnership was always intended to be short term. Because of the superstation's national reach on cable systems, it would potentially duplicate The WB programming already airing via local station affiliates, but it would take a number of years for The WB to garner enough affiliates and build up enough nights of programming for that to be an issue. In the meantime, the superstation partnership granted The WB crucial early national reach and exposure (Flint 1993). By the time The WB was on the verge of launching its sixth and final night of programming in 1999, the network and Tribune mutually agreed to end the affiliation (Moss 1999).[2]

The Tribune's interest in WGN Superstation's prospects turned from passive to active in the 2000s, as it took greater command of the financial potential that the superstation held. Rather than continue to allow a separate common carrier to benefit from retransmission fees, in 2001 the Tribune Company took over distribution of the superstation feed and started collecting those fees itself (Haley 2004a). Another small yet meaningful name change came the following year, with the newly christened Superstation WGN illustrating the priority of national distribution over local orientation. Also, "Get It All" became Superstation WGN's new slogan, intended to connote the range of general entertainment programming carried by the superstation, rather than "Chicago's

Very Own" programming on WGN-TV (Haley 2004b). However, Superstation WGN's lineup was filled mostly with reruns and movies of the sort that could now be seen all over the expanded cable television landscape; the quaint *Bozo Show* couldn't compete with trendy Nickelodeon and Disney Channel programs and was cancelled in 2001; and a *Tribune* journalist mocked the superstation for airing vacuous programs like *Funniest Pets & People* in prime-time (Rosenthal 2008).

In fact, Superstation WGN was holding on to an outdated business model by that point. As early as 1996, a media analyst had proclaimed that "the heyday of the super-station seems to be past" (McConville 1996), and by the early 2000s, WGN was the lone remaining nationally distributed superstation. Superstation pioneer TBS had converted to a national cable channel in the late 1990s due to the greater financial incentives available (Mifflin 1997). Converting to a national cable channel meant severing all ties to the local station, removing the channel from regulatory status as a superstation. Retransmission fees paid to the common carrier would therefore convert to carriage fees paid to the channel owner. Superstation signals came to cable operators retransmitted in whole, whereas cable channels were offered to pay TV operators with a few minutes of each hour available for the operator to sell ad space. This made cable channels higher revenue earners for cable operators, thus encouraging a higher carriage fee than a superstation's retransmission fee (Petrozzello 1997). Additionally, superstation carriers were required to pay copyright fees to a federal royalty tribunal for redistribution to owners of programming that aired on superstations in order to account for the fact that programming licensed for distribution to a local area would be airing nationally without compensation otherwise (Porter 2004, 595–6). Conversion to a national cable channel meant the cable operator would no longer have to pay these fees, offering another advantage over super-stations. For these reasons, plus the branding advantages of targeting content toward national audiences exclusively as opposed to a fractured combination of the local and the national, TBS saw conversion as the optimal way forward.

Before the Tribune Company could do the same with Superstation WGN, it had larger financial challenges to sort out. The volatility of the newspaper business in the digital era came home to roost, as the company filed for bankruptcy in 2008 following a leveraged buyout by billionaire investor Sam Zell. It emerged from bankruptcy in 2013 with a new structure, as the Tribune separated its publishing division from its broadcasting assets by creating two discrete companies. Control of the broadcast stations and the superstation would rest with the Tribune Media Company, while the newspaper holdings became part of the Tribune Publishing Company (Szalai 2013). The World's Greatest Newspaper would no longer own WGN.

Digital technologies had brought similar upheaval to television. While a concern of the cable era had been superstations duplicating local programming, now in the post-network era, the Internet potentially made television channels themselves obsolete. *Chicago Tribune* reporter Phil Rosenthal described Superstation WGN's challenge accordingly:

> For those outside the immediate Chicago area, there was a time when the only place to get this city's news, sports and Bozo the Clown was through Superstation WGN. But Bozo has thrown his last pie, you can get a report and video of any Chicago news story

you want on the Internet, and sports is practically everywhere you look these days. Which means the superstation must reinvent itself if it wants to be truly super again.

(2008)

The Tribune Company began this reinvention in 2008 by renaming the superstation yet again. It would henceforth be called WGN America, a clear sign that the channel's status as a superstation would soon expire and that the national, not the local, was now the chief focus (Pursell & Lafayette 2008). The *Chicago Tribune* referred to WGN America in 2012 as a "sleeping giant" with lucrative prospects if it could convert to a national cable channel and start receiving the wider distribution, more lucrative carriage fees, and higher advertising revenue that status could offer (Channick 2012). In that year, WGN America ranked 40th among cable channels in viewership and reached only 75 million households, whereas more successful cable channels were available in over 100 million; it drew in less than 10 cents a month per subscriber from cable operator fees, while TBS was garnering around 50 cents; and TBS could tout $823 million in advertising revenue to WGN America's mere $176 million (Channick 2012; Jannarone 2014). But demanding higher fees and ad rates would require more distinctive programming. The content that had once helped an independent WGN beat the networks at their own game and Superstation WGN stand out when cable piped in only 50 channels was now ubiquitous across hundreds of cable channels and the Internet. Going forward, the aspirational model would now be less TBS and more FX and AMC, which had leapt to prominence with buzz-generating original dramas like *The Shield* (2002–08) and *Mad Men* (2007–15).

Accordingly, the job of running Tribune Media and awakening the sleeping giant was handed to CEO Peter Liguori, who had previously run FX (Lieberman 2013). Liguori first had to oversee the structural conversion of WGN America into a national cable channel, which meant renegotiating all of WGN America's existing distribution contracts with pay TV operators to account for this new status. This process would take a number of years to fully play out, but national cable channel status for WGN America officially began in late 2014 with a new Comcast carriage agreement covering five markets, including Chicago (Gibbons 2014). In negotiating those new deals, Tribune Media's representatives had to convince pay TV outlets that the new version of WGN America was worth paying much more for than the superstation version. Liguori explained this challenge:

> WGNA was just kind of a nonexistent brand telecasting some Cub games and some Chicago news. It was our thinking that there was zero doubt that we were going to go into affiliate renewals and lose WGNA. We were going to lose an asset that had 70 million homes. That is something you don't fritter away. So we made the decision to invest in it.

(Feder 2014)

A key move toward investment in WGN America's future involved the elimination of one holding, the Chicago Cubs. The Tribune had purchased the Cubs franchise in 1981 to capitalize further on WGN's game broadcasts, but the team was sold in 2009 as part of the bankruptcy restructuring. With the synergistic benefit gone, Liguori decided in

FIGURE 9.1 *From top to bottom, the local WGN station logo followed by logos for the 2001–02 superstation, the 2002–08 superstation, and the 2014 cable channel, representing the shift from Chicago-identified broadcasting to national reach.*

2014 to drop Cubs games from the WGN America lineup. Though the Cubs were WGN's most nationally recognizable asset, Liguori believed the high fees required to license the national rights to games would well exceed the advertising revenue they could generate and that original scripted programming held much greater revenue potential (Marek 2014). Original programming would also mark WGN America as distinctive within the cluttered cable lineup. Liguori described, "Originals are important because they brand your network. There is no tagline, there is no marketing campaign that will ever work for a network that is as good as showing your performance" (Steel 2016).

To foster this performance, Liguori hired Matt Cherniss as president and general manager of WGN America (Andreeva 2013). Cherniss had previously helped to develop successful dramas like *Nip/Tuck* (2003–10) and *Sons of Anarchy* (2008–14) as Senior Vice President of Original Programming at FX. *Variety* described Cherniss's goal as establishing "WGN America as the next FX or AMC, with original shows that can attract a loyal fanbase, generate strong word-of-mouth and ratings for a channel now known for airing reruns of sitcoms and syndicated talkshows" (Graser 2013). All the talk of moving WGN America away from its superstation and Chicago identities might have heralded a full rebranding and yet another name change to remove any prior associations, but Cherniss felt that would be a mistake. He explained to *Variety*:

> [T]he truth is, we've spent so much time and effort finally getting people to be aware of WGN America as a home for our programming that to then change the name and then

have to recommunicate to all those people what our name is? I think your shows brand and define you much more than your call letters. FX is Fox without the "o," right? But that's not what defines it. The shows that are on it define it. I don't know how many people can tell you what AMC stands for, but they *can* tell you *The Walking Dead* is on that network.

(Adalian 2016)

Cherniss therefore turned his attention to program development, and four original scripted programs put WGN America on the prestige drama map. The first was *Salem*, an historical drama about the Salem witch trials that premiered in April 2014 and aired three seasons. *Manhattan*, a period drama about the Manhattan Project, began airing a few months after *Salem*'s premiere, but was cancelled after two critically acclaimed yet low-rated seasons. January 2016 brought the arrival of *Outsiders*, a contemporary drama about a mountain family fighting against a mining company in Appalachia. Two months later came the premiere of *Underground*, an historical drama that tells the story of men and women escaping slavery via the Underground Railroad. The latter two were ratings and critical successes from the start, earning them season renewals. Across the board, the early results were impressive. WGN America's overall audience shot up by 51% in the first quarter of 2016 compared to the year before, and the channel saw a 900% improvement in the coveted 18-to-49 demographic in its new programming time slots (Adalian 2016). Of course, the significance of such percentage leaps can be deceiving when the starting point is low, but they seemed to augur well for WGN America's future. Matt Cherniss correspondingly said the ultimate goal was to have one original scripted series airing in any given week (Adalian 2016).

However, like many others, Cherniss probably didn't foresee the US presidential victory of Donald Trump, which ushered in conservative leadership at the FCC and a subsequent loosening of broadcast ownership limits. With those regulatory barriers diminished, Sinclair Broadcast Group announced a deal in May 2017 to purchase Tribune Media, which in addition to numerous local stations would add WGN America to its portfolio. Sinclair CEO Chris Ripley immediately declared that WGN America would shift away from high-end original scripted dramas, arguing that the ratings they earned weren't sufficient to justify their budgets (Lieberman 2017). Ripley explained, "The channel could be run much more profitably on a fraction of what they spend on programming" (Littleton 2017). *Hollywood Reporter* critic Tim Goodman accordingly predicted "a retreat into perhaps a cheaper world of reality programming" at WGN America, as it and like-minded cable channels drop out of the expensive prestige drama race (2017). The deal will require federal regulatory approval first, however, and there is even talk that Sinclair might aim to convert WGN America into a conservative news channel to compete with Fox News (Littleton 2017).

Regardless of whether WGN America's future lies in reality television, news, or scripted programming, it's prudent to reflect upon Matt Cherniss's comment that content defines channels now, not call letters. After all, viewers today have no idea that WGN once stood for World's Greatest Newspaper, and they don't seem to particularly care whether a program originates from a broadcast network, cable channel, or website. As Cherniss describes, "There's more content than ever out there, and more demand for people's eyeballs, but the audience is more willing to find entertainment wherever it may come from. Compelling content is your best security against changing platforms" (Graser 2013). To some extent, this has always been true. The Chicago Cubs were part of WGN-TV's security in competing against national networks in Chicago, just as their games were Superstation WGN's security in competing early on in the cable era. But as platforms change, security strategies change, and because the post-network era is overflowing with platforms, change seems to be the only consistent strategy.

NOTES

1 For more on the FCC regulations that enabled superstation retransmission, see Amy J. Cassedy, "As the World Turns: Copyright Liability of Satellite Resale Carriers," *Columbia Journal of Law and the Arts* 9 (1984): 89–119.
2 WGN-TV ended its affiliation with The WB when the network was shut down in 2006; the station then signed a ten-year contract to affiliate with The WB's replacement, The CW. That affiliation ended in 2016, and WGN-TV went back to being an independent station once again. The superstation never affiliated with The CW. For more detail, see Caryn Murphy's chapter in this collection.

REFERENCES

Adalian, Josef. 2016. "How Did WGN America So Quickly Become a Formidable Player in the Scripted TV Game?" *Vulture*, April 6. Accessed June 25, 2016. www.vulture.com/2016/04/wgn-america-scripted-tv-underground-outsiders-salem.html.

Andreeva, Nellie. 2013. "Matt Cherniss Joins Tribune as President/GM of WGN, Newly Formed Tribune Studios." *Deadline Hollywood*, March 19. Accessed June 25, 2016. http://deadline.com/2013/03/matt-cherniss-joins-tribune-as-president-gm-of-wgn-newly-formed-tribune-studios-456899.

Channick, Robert. 2012. "WGN America May Be Channel of Change for Tribune Co." *Chicago Tribune*, December 9. Accessed June 23, 2016. http://articles.chicagotribune.com/2012-12-09/business/ct-biz-1209-tribune-wgn-20121209_1_wgn-america-snl-kagan-peter-liguori.

Feder, Robert. 2014. "WGN America Comes Home to Chicago." *Robert Feder*. December 15. Accessed June 26, 2016. www.robertfeder.com/2014/12/15/wgn-america-comes-home-to-chicago.

Fink, John. 1961. *WGN: A Pictorial History*. Chicago: WGN, Inc.

Flint, Joe. 1993. "WB Network Signs WGN-TV." *Broadcasting & Cable*, December 6. Accessed June 23, 2016. Expanded Academic ASAP.

Gibbons, Kent. 2014. "WGN America Converts to Cable in Five Markets." *Broadcasting & Cable*, December 16. Accessed June 26, 2016. www.broadcastingcable.com/news/programming/wgn-america-converts-cable-five-markets/136444.

Goodman, Tim. "Critic's Notebook: The Peak TV Bubble Hasn't Burst, But It's Leaking." *Hollywood Reporter*, May 10. Accessed May 11, 2017. www.hollywoodreporter.com/bastard-machine/tim-goodman-peak-tv-bubble-hasnt-burst-but-leaking-1002250.

Graser, Matt. 2013. "How Matt Cherniss Is Building Provocative New Worlds for WGN America." *Variety*, November 29. Accessed June 26, 2016. http://variety.com/2013/biz/news/wgn-manhattan-project-salem-1200888723.

Haley, Kathy. 2004a. "Birth of a Nation's Superstation." *Multichannel News*, April 5. Accessed June 21, 2016. Expanded Academic ASAP.

Haley, Kathy. 2004b. "Defining a Brand." *Multichannel News*, April 5. Accessed June 21, 2016. Expanded Academic ASAP.

Haley, Kathy. 2004c. "Swinging for the Fences." *Multichannel News*, April 5. Accessed June 21, 2016. Expanded Academic ASAP.

Jannarone, John. 2014. "Tribune: A Comeback Story Hot Off the Press." *CNBC*, May 14. Accessed June 23. www.cnbc.com/2014/05/14/tribune-a-comeback-story-hot-off-the-press.html.

Lieberman, David. 2013. "Tribune Taps Peter Liguori to Be CEO, Eddy Hartenstein to Run LA Times, as Expected." *Deadline Hollywood*, January 17. Accessed June 24, 2016. http://deadline.com/2013/01/tribune-peter-liguori-eddy-hartenstein-406955.

Lieberman, David. 2017. "WGNA to Focus on 'Cost Effective' Originals and Reruns, Sinclair CEO Says." *Deadline Hollywood*, May 8. Accessed May 11, 2017. http://deadline.com/2017/05/wgn-america-focus-cost-effective-originals-reruns-sinclair-ceo-1202086763/.

Littleton, Cynthia. 2017. "Sinclair Plans Big Changes for WGN America, Eyes MVPD Offering with Tribune Media Deal." *Variety*, May 8. Accessed May 11, 2017. http://variety.com/2017/tv/news/wgn-america-underground-sinclair-tribune-media-1202418701/

Marek, Lynne. 2014. "WGN America to Drop Chicago Sports." *Crain's Chicago Business*, May 30. Accessed June 26, 2016. www.chicagobusiness.com/article/20140530/NEWS01/140539978/wgn-america-to-drop-chicago-sports.

McConville, Jim. 1996. "TCI Move Not So Super for Superstations." *Broadcasting & Cable*, December 9. Accessed June 27, 2016. Expanded Academic ASAP.

Mifflin, Lawrie. 1997. "Turner Superstation to Collect Cable TV Fees." *New York Times*, August 1. Accessed June 26, 2016. www.nytimes.com/1997/08/01/business/turner-superstation-to-collect-cable-tv-fees.html.

Moss, Linda. 1999. "WGN Drops WB, Adds Movies, Sitcoms." *Multichannel News*, September 20. Accessed June 23, 2016. Expanded Academic ASAP.

Mullen, Megan. 2003. *The Rise of Cable Programming in the United States: Revolution or Evolution?* Austin: University of Texas Press.

Mullen, Megan. 2004. "Superstation." In *Encyclopedia of Television*, edited by Horace Newcomb, 2224–6. New York: Fitzroy Dearborn.

Petrozzello, Donna. 1997. "Conversion Factors Fall into Place for WTBS." *Broadcasting & Cable*, August 4. Accessed June 30, 2016. Expanded Academic ASAP.

Porter, Vincent. 2004. "Copyright Law and Television." In *Encyclopedia of Television*, edited by Horace Newcomb, 593–8. New York: Fitzroy Dearborn.

Pursell, Chris and Jon Lafayette. 2008. "Tribune Plans Safety Net for Stations." *Television Week*, June 16. Accessed June 28, 2016. LexisNexis Academic.

Rosenthal, Phil. 2008. "Exec May Try to Soup Up Superstation." *Chicago Tribune*, February 6. Accessed June 24, 2016. ProQuest Historical Newspapers.

Steel, Emily. 2016. "Tribune Chief Discusses Transforming a Mature Media Company." *New York Times*, March 25. Accessed June 26, 2016. www.nytimes.com/2016/03/26/business/media/tribune-chief-discusses-transforming-a-mature-media-company.html

Szalai, Georg. 2013. "Tribune Co. to Spin Off Newspaper Unit." *Chicago Tribune*, July 10. Accessed June 28, 2016. LexisNexis Academic.

ESPN

Live Sports, Documentary Prestige, and On-Demand Culture

Travis Vogan

In 2010, News Corp. CEO Rupert Murdoch proclaimed "[c]ontent is not king, it is the emperor of all things digital" (Szalai 2010). And as content goes, live sports television proves particularly powerful: "Sports absolutely overpowers film and everything else in the entertainment genre," Murdoch remarked (Milliken 1996). Live sports remain a scarce commodity within a plentiful digital media ecosystem (Hutchins and Rowe 2009). Sporting event broadcasts are sold on an exclusive basis, garner predictable ratings, and maintain status as appointment viewing in an industry increasingly organized around on-demand content. They continue to be one of the few types of programming consumers expect to view in real time—an exceptional status in on-demand culture that boosts sports' value to media outlets and advertisers.

In this light, no entity in contemporary sports media is more imperial than the Walt Disney Company's ESPN, which *Forbes* rates as the world's most valuable media property (Badenhausen 2014). The organization based in Bristol, Connecticut, holds rights to carry marquee sports content across television, radio, print, and digital platforms. It also owns at least part of 26 TV networks outside of the United States, which provide 61 countries with programming tailored to their sporting preferences. As former ESPN chairperson Steve Bornstein gloated, "The sun never sets on the ESPN empire" (Hiestand 1997). Bornstein's successor George Bodenheimer (2005) added that the company works to "deliver a fully branded experience at every touch point."

ESPN's power, however, cannot be reduced to a function of its content, platforms, and expansive reach. The organization carefully brands itself as an industrial and cultural authority—an effort that crystallized with its 1998 implementation of the motto "The Worldwide Leader in Sports." ESPN reinforces this self-aggrandizing slogan by participating in a variety of activities that bill it as an exceptionally artful site of sports media—a context otherwise identified more with transmitting event coverage than creating content that educates or inspires. To that end, ESPN produces documentaries, curates film festivals, publishes books, and employs Pulitzer Prize-winning journalists. Though none of these activities generates anywhere near the revenue its live event programming gathers, they drive "a shrewd effort to distinguish ESPN from other sports media outlets, compete for market share, expand its demographic reach, promote its content, and even cut costs" (Vogan 2015, 4).

The deregulated media industry's amenability to corporate media conglomerates like Disney further aids ESPN's status and value. As of 2016, Disney leveraged ESPN's popularity to charge cable operators $6.55 monthly per subscriber to carry the channel. TNT was the next most costly channel at $1.58 per month. Moreover, Disney uses ESPN as the centerpiece of its cable bundle of channels, which constrains operators to carry less popular Disney properties like Freeform in order to have ESPN. Faced with the alternative of not carrying cable TV's most popular channel, operators pay the exorbitant fees for ESPN and pass the rising costs along to subscribers.

But ESPN's dominance is being threatened by the swelling number of consumers opting to abandon the traditional cable subscriptions that furnish the bulk of its income for smaller packages or digital streaming services. ESPN has adjusted to this new environment by developing its own streaming service for existing subscribers in 2010, WatchESPN, which expanded into a mobile application the following year. Beyond adapting to these industrial and technological transformations, ESPN reasserts its self-styled "Worldwide Leader" status in on-demand culture by stressing the singular value of the live sports it carries across platforms and by accompanying this event coverage with acclaimed documentaries geared toward the "binge-able" consumption that characterizes digital streaming services.

BECOMING "THE WORLDWIDE LEADER IN SPORTS"

ESPN was the first all-sports cable network when it launched on September 9, 1979. The company began as Bill Rasmussen's effort to provide a cable service focusing on Connecticut-area sports. While developing the idea, Rasmussen and his partners reserved space on RCA's SATCOM1 satellite for distribution and quickly realized it would be just as easy to transmit content nationwide as it would to serve Connecticut— a feature that made the venture enticing to sports organizations, advertisers, and investors. As a result, Getty Oil's division of diversified operations purchased an 85% interest in the fledgling outlet and financed ESPN's development.

Getty rightly wagered that cable operators would view ESPN as a "major lift" network that would draw subscribers to the still-nascent medium and help to sell more lucrative premium channels like HBO. In particular, it promised to attract moneyed men, a traditionally elusive demographic that advertisers would pay a premium to reach. Budweiser recognized this potential and signed a $1.38 million deal—the largest contract in the history of cable TV up to that point—to become ESPN's exclusive beer (Vogan 2015, 17–18).

ESPN steadily established partnerships with well-known sports organizations and used its live event and news coverage to grow a loyal audience of sports junkies. By 1983 it surpassed TBS as the United States' most popular cable network. Cable operators no longer dared sell their packages without including the all sports channel. Despite its rising prominence, however, ESPN lost money. The advertising it sold could not keep pace with the rights fees necessary to acquire popular sports. The cable channel audaciously leveraged its renown by demanding that cable operators pay it 10 cents monthly per subscriber. ESPN was the first outlet to adopt the arrangement, which gave it an additional revenue stream and became standard practice throughout the industry (26).

ESPN's rising prominence motivated ABC—then the dominant voice in network sports television—to purchase a majority stake in the cable channel in 1984. ESPN's relationship to ABC gave it the resources and credibility to secure rights to telecast higher profile sports. Most notably, ESPN became the first cable network to which the NFL awarded a contract in 1987. Its bulging portfolio of partnerships helped ESPN become the first cable network to achieve 50% penetration in television households. When Disney purchased ABC's parent company Capital Cities Communications in 1996—the second largest corporate media takeover ever—CEO Michael Eisner called ESPN "the crown jewel" of the $19 billion acquisition and identified it as a "magic name" with brand recognition comparable to Coca-Cola (Carter and Sandomir 1995). The new Disney property placed greater emphasis on manicuring this "magic" brand and expanding it into offshoot channels, radio, print, and even a chain of ESPN Sport-Zone sports bars (most of which have shuttered).

ESPN paired these far-reaching brand extensions with an investment in practices meant to enhance its respectability. It began to produce documentaries, for example, to borrow the genre's reputation as an edifying variety of television (Curtin 1995). The media outlet earned each of its Peabody Awards—accolades not limited to sports TV that demonstrate the media outlet's ability to garner acclaim beyond it—for its documentaries. ESPN permanently invested in the symbolically powerful genre by creating ESPN Films in 2008. The subsidiary markets its documentaries as uniquely cinematic TV productions driven by the artistic visions of the participating filmmakers it recruits—common strategies network and cable TV outlets use to bill content as exceptional (Caldwell 1995; Newman and Levine 2011; Vogan 2015). Beyond the prestige they cultivate, ESPN Films' documentaries cost less than live sports, can be scheduled flexibly to promote event coverage, and remain "evergreen" productions that can be used in perpetuity across ESPN's steadily expanding slate of channels. They work to secure ESPN's industrial authority and cultural prominence in sports media while complementing the live content that draws its biggest audiences and largest advertising rates.

As ESPN solidified its industrial dominance, the United States' major networks launched their own sports-themed cable channels: a group that includes CBS Sports Network (2011), NBC Sports Network (2012), and Fox Sports 1 (2013). Scrambling to maintain its splintering market share, ESPN began spending wildly to lock down long-term contracts. Between 2011 and 2012, it pledged $15 billion to the NFL, $12.6 billion to the National Basketball Association, $5.6 billion to Major League Baseball, $5.6 billion to the NCAA for its College Football Playoffs, $1.5 billion to the NCAA's PAC-12 Conference, and $480 million to the Wimbledon tennis tournament (Ourand 2011). ESPN planned to absorb these colossal expenses by relying on its tried and true strategy of increasing subscriber fees, which it raised by nearly 40% between 2011 and

2015—from $4.69 to $6.55. The rapid escalation in the amount ESPN paid to secure rights and the prices it demanded from cable operators provoked *SportsBusiness Journal*'s John Ourand (2011) to ponder whether a perilous bubble in the sports media market was emerging.

This bubble did not exactly burst, but mounting numbers of consumers—dissatisfied with the rising fees—began opting out of traditional cable packages in favor of less expensive streaming services and smaller, "skinny" cable packages that did not include ESPN. In a January 2012 discussion at the Citigroup Global Entertainment, Media and Telecommunications Conference, Disney CFO Jay Rasulo dismissed these shifts as passing fads. "I can't imagine that any of them," Rasulo said of cable operators, "are going to want to move their business model towards a series of skinnied-down packages. It doesn't make sense economically for them and the response to these skinnied-down packages has been historically extremely limited" (2012). But ESPN lost 7% of its subscribers between 2011 and 2015, a decline company president John Skipper eventually attributed to such smaller packages (Sharma and Ramachandran 2016). He maintained, however, that those subscribers ESPN lost did not watch sports and that the network's overall viewership and ad rates remained unaffected.

Despite Skipper's hopeful prognosis, a January 2016 poll conducted by BTIG Research found that 56% of cable subscribers would rather eliminate ESPN and ESPN2 from their cable packages than pay $8 per month for the channels. It also revealed that only 6% of those consumers would pay $20 a month for a standalone over-the-top (OTT) package that consisted of ESPN and ESPN2 (Wilcox 2016). The results bluntly suggested that ESPN's traditional business model is passé and that its powerful status as an anchor driving cable subscriptions has waned.

ESPN made a variety of modifications to compensate for its sustained and projected losses, which ranged from closing down the boutique website Grantland.com in October 2015 to laying off 300 employees that same month. In a memo he penned to ESPN employees after the layoffs, Skipper (2015) suggested ESPN was planning to adapt to the industrial and technological developments that threatened to leave it behind:

> These ongoing initiatives include: Constant and relentless innovation, including integrating emerging technology into all aspects of our business; Enhancing our sales and marketing efforts with new tools and techniques that generate greater data, personalization and customization for our advertisers; Integrating our distribution efforts to better serve current and future distribution partners with our industry leading networks and services.

ESPN placed greater emphasis on WatchESPN's streaming and mobile capabilities and joined the OTT online service Sling TV in early 2015, which bundles the sports network with a small handful of other channels. Sling charges subscribers lower monthly rates than traditional cable packages while gathering ESPN similarly disproportionate fees compared to other cable channels. Yet ESPN lacked the distinction in this new environment that it enjoyed in traditional cable TV and, as Skipper's dispatch suggests, the channel clamored to reassert its diminishing supremacy. It did so in part by emphasizing the different but complementary qualities of liveness and prestige that its sports coverage and documentaries furnish.

"QUEUE"

ESPN emphasized the extraordinary value of its live content amid these changes with a promotional spot titled "Queue" that debuted on May 5, 2016. The promo begins with a woman sitting on a couch listlessly surfing through the menu of a streaming service as the passage "Movies can wait, because movies aren't real" appears in the foreground. "So your streaming algorithm thinks you'll like this film about a diamond heist," the woman says in an irritated voiceover as she continues searching with little faith that the service will recommend items relevant to her preferences. In her boredom, she glances outside to see a group of children playing basketball. The scene sparks an epiphany that brings her apathetic surfing to a halt. "But unlike you," she continues, "it [the algorithm] didn't just think, 'Duh, the [Golden State] Warriors game is on.'" She promptly flips to ESPN's live NBA coverage. "Maybe my diamonds can wait," she says. "After all, they're safe in a vault." The promo ends with her chuckling "silly algorithm" as she pulls on a blanket with the likeness of Warriors coach Steve Kerr on it and contentedly nestles into the couch to watch the game. Her frustrated search for fulfilling content, "Queue" suggests, is over.

The heavy-handed promotion indicates that ESPN possesses something that most streaming services do not: live sports. Unlike the diamond heist film—which can be consumed whenever—ESPN's live event coverage will severely diminish in value after the game concludes. It harbors an ephemeral vitality that cannot be entombed within a streaming service's vault. "Queue" indicates that ESPN's live event coverage is impervious to and stands apart from the on-demand culture to which streaming services cater. It reinforces the long-standing myth of liveness as television's ontological essence to brand ESPN's coverage as uniquely authentic TV during a moment when the medium is in flux (Feuer 1982).

FIGURE 10.1 *ESPN's "Queue" campaign emphasizes the value of its live content.*

Along these lines, "Queue" also distinguishes ESPN's live coverage as more human than the content that streaming algorithms recommend. The Warriors game has a clear connection to the woman's identity. It connects to facets of her interests that exceed the algorithm's "silly" attempts to predict who she is and what she will enjoy.

As the promo fades to black, a row of icons depicting a mobile phone, television, computer, and headphones emerges and then melds into ESPN's logo to highlight the media outlet's multiplatform identity. But "Queue" makes clear that live television coverage of major sports like the NBA remains ESPN's key point of distinction. Moreover, the promo's decision to feature a woman demonstrates ESPN's efforts to expand its demographic range beyond the male sports fans it traditionally courts as its subscriber base shrinks.

O. J.: Made in America

Though "Queue" works to differentiate ESPN within on-demand culture through underscoring its live sports, the network's competitors in the sports genre all offer similar content and delivery options for subscribers. ESPN extended its efforts to assert its exceptional status one month after "Queue" with the debut of ESPN Films' 7.5-hour, five-part documentary, *O. J.: Made in America*. Directed by Ezra Edelman and marketed as a "documentary event," the production chronicles the rise and fall of football player O. J. Simpson through examining his playing career, celebrity status, murder trial, controversial acquittal, and eventual conviction and incarceration for a 2007 robbery. *Made in America* eschews the format of a straightforward biographical profile in favor of exploring the links between Simpson's role as one of the United States' first crossover African American athletes and the history of race relations in Los Angeles, where he played college football during the late 1960s at University of Southern California, lived after his career in the NFL, and stood trial for murder. Edelman probes Simpson's complex status as an African American celebrity whose success resulted in part from his willingness to divorce himself from the African American community and appease mainstream white culture. "I'm not black, I'm O. J.," Simpson would reportedly say when asked about his racial identity. *Made in America* highlights how Los Angeles' African American community suffered poverty, racism, and rampant police brutality as Simpson enjoyed fame and wealth in the same city. It then investigates the irony of how Simpson's identity—as black, not O. J.—informed the racially polarized public reaction to his murder charges and acquittal.

ESPN Films executive producer Connor Schell trumpeted *Made in America* as "the most ambitious undertaking ESPN Films has embarked upon" (Montgomery 2016). Edelman claims the documentary's unusual length was necessary given his wide-ranging approach. "I was interested in the 30 years before the murders, the city, race and identity, and the juxtaposition with O. J.'s story. This is a big American studies paper," he remarked. "This touches on everything in our culture" (Roston 2016). The documentary, Edelman asserts, approaches Simpson's story as an interdisciplinary research project that tends to the multifarious nexus of culture and power. For instance, the first installment combines footage of Simpson's triumphs while at USC with images of the racial and political turmoil occurring within and beyond Los Angeles at the time. The scene underscores USC's and Simpson's distance from and even indifference to this unrest. By extension, it critiques mainstream sport culture's frequent lack of social consciousness.

Edelman explains that *Made in America* was inspired by Ken Burns's sweeping historical documentaries and the 2004 French series *The Staircase*, which explores the case of a North Carolina novelist accused of murdering his wife (Roston 2016). The production also premiered shortly after HBO's *The Jinx: The Life and Deaths of Robert Durst* (2015) and Netflix's *Making a Murderer* (2015)—popular and acclaimed long-form documentary projects that explore mysterious and controversial murder cases. Like these documentaries, *Made in America* garnered nearly universal praise after its debut—often from arts and culture commentators who seldom pay attention to ESPN's programming. *Rolling Stone* called it a "major cultural event," *Wired* dubbed it "infinitely absorbing," and *New York Times* film critic A. O. Scott claimed the documentary "has the grandeur and authority of the best long-form nonfiction. If it were a book, it could sit on the shelf alongside *The Executioner's Song* by Norman Mailer and the great biographical works of Robert Caro" (Sheffield 2016; Raferty 2016; Scott 2016). These practices and discourses separate *Made in America* from run-of-the-mill sports TV and assert ESPN's membership in the diverse but respectable cultural traditions Ken Burns, HBO, and Norman Mailer represent.

ESPN further constructed *Made in America*'s outstanding artfulness by premiering it at the Sundance Film Festival—a practice it has adopted with other ESPN Films documentaries to build buzz before their television debut and expose them to audiences who might not typically watch sports TV (Vogan 2015, 124–5). It also gave *Made in America* a one-week theatrical run in Los Angeles and New York to satisfy the Academy of Motion Picture Arts and Sciences' minimum requirements for Academy Award consideration in hopes that the documentary would be nominated for an Oscar. Ultimately, the film was not just nominated but also won the best documentary feature award—a first for ESPN that took its efforts to build respectability to new heights.

But aside from cultivating prestige, ESPN designed *Made in America* to be watched on-demand through WatchESPN. "As we were thinking about the compelling nature of this content, it became more and more clear that there might be people who may want to sit down and watch the whole thing," explained ESPN senior vice president Lori LeBas. After debuting the first segment on ABC in prime-time, ESPN simultaneously released the subsequent four parts online through WatchESPN before they aired on TV. "This is about helping people understand that, yes [WatchESPN is] about being able to see games in a portable way if you're not at home," LeBas remarked. "But it's also a way to sit back and consume content in a more binge-able fashion the way you might with other services" (Battaglio 2016). In particular, ESPN adopted the binge-able model Netflix and Amazon use for their original series. It advertises WatchESPN as a service that both offers access to the live event coverage that cannot wait and includes a vault of original content that can be consumed anytime. However, *Made in America*'s premier at Sundance and Academy Award prestige situate the production as a more artful and cinematic documentary than the binge-worthy television series it otherwise resembles. With *Made in America* and its other documentaries, then, ESPN participates in on-demand culture while positioning its content as exceptional in that context. The documentaries augment ESPN's live content and suggest the media outlet harbors a degree of quality that competing sports media streaming services—which do not invest in binge-able and renowned documentaries like *Made in America*—lack.

CONCLUSION

As sports media scholar Raymond Boyle (2014, 747) points out, "TV remains a remarkably resilient cultural form and is the one still central to sporting popular culture." Nearly 40 years after its launch, ESPN is also quite durable. While live sports remain ESPN's cornerstone, the media outlet participates in and even drives television's reinvention beyond the medium's traditional barriers. It does so in ways that reinforce its industrial and cultural primacy amid this change and persuade consumers that it is worth the relatively steep—and continually increasing—subscriber fees required to access it. As "Queue" markets ESPN's live event programming as more immediate and exciting than typical on-demand content, *Made in America* situates ESPN's original documentaries as uniquely artful on-demand viewing. These practices illustrate the self-named Worldwide Leader's recent efforts to stabilize and even grow its imperial status within a rapidly shifting sports media landscape. They also demonstrate the complementary cultural and industrial roles live sports and documentary play in this setting.

REFERENCES

Badenhausen, Kurt. 2014. "The Value of ESPN Surpasses $50 Billion." *Forbes.com*, April 29. Accessed July 8, 2016. www.forbes.com/sites/kurtbadenhausen/2014/04/29/the-value-of-espn-surpasses-50-billion/#34ef1665b69b.

Battaglio, Stephen. 2016. "ESPN Wants Viewers to Binge on Its O. J. Simpson Series." *Los Angeles Times*, June 9. Accessed July 8, 2016. www.latimes.com/entertainment/envelope/cotown/la-et-ct-oj-espn-marketing-20160608-snap-story.html.

Bodenheimer, George. 2005. "Keynote Speech." *UBS 33rd Annual Conference*, December 5.

Boyle, Raymond. 2014. "Television Sport in the Age of Screens and Content." *Television & New Media* 15: 746–51.

Caldwell, John T. 1995. *Televisuality: Style, Crisis, and Authority in American Television*. New Brunswick: Rutgers University Press.

Carter, Bill and Richard Sandomir. 1995. "The Trophy in Eisner's Big Deal." *New York Times*, August 6.

Curtin, Michael. 1995. *Redeeming the Wasteland: Television Documentary and Cold War Politics*. New Brunswick: Rutgers University Press.

Feuer, Jane. 1982. "The Concept of Live Television: Ontology as Ideology." In *Regarding Television*, edited by E. Ann Kaplan, 12–22. Frederick: University Publications of America.

Hiestand, Michael. 1997. "Pioneer Steers ABC, ESPN to Top of Game." *USA Today*, December 10.

Hutchins, Brett and David Rowe. 2009. "From Broadcast Scarcity to Digital Plentitude." *Television & New Media* 10: 354–70.

Milliken, Robert. 1996. "Sport Is Murdoch's 'Battering Ram' for Pay TV." *The Independent*, October 15. Accessed July 8, 2016. www.independent.co.uk/sport/sport-is-murdochs-battering-ram-for-pay-tv-1358686.html.

Montgomery, James. 2016. "Inside ESPN's Definitive Simpson Doc." *Rollingstone.com*, June 2. Accessed July 8, 2016. www.rollingstone.com/movies/news/o-j-made-in-america-inside-espns-definitive-simpson-doc-20160602.

Newman, Michael Z. and Elana Levine. 2011. *Legitimating Television: Media Convergence and Cultural Status*. New York: Routledge.

Ourand, John. 2011. "How High Can Rights Fees Go?" *SportsBusiness Journal*, June 6. Accessed July 8, 2016. www.sportsbusinessdaily.com/Journal/Issues/2011/06/06/In-Depth/Rights-Fees.aspx.

Raferty, Brian. 2016. "*O. J.: Made in America* is a Rigorous, Infinitely Absorbing Documentary." *Wired*, June 7. Accessed July 8, 2016. www.wired.com/2016/06/inside-o-j-made-in-america.

Rasulo, Jay. 2012. "Q & A." Presentation at *Citigroup 22nd Annual Global Entertainment, Media and Telecommunications Conference*, January 2. Accessed July 8, 2016. http://cdn.media.ir.thewaltdisneycompany.com/2012/events/jar-citi-2012-0105-transcript.pdf.

Roston, Tom. 2016. "It's a Long Story: *O. J.: Made in America* Seeks Your Time." *New York Times*, May 19. Accessed July 8, 2016. www.nytimes.com/2016/05/22/movies/its-a-long-story-oj-made-in-america-seeks-your-time.html?_r=0.

Scott, A. O. 2016. "Review: *O. J.: Made in America*." *New York Times*, May 20.

Sharma, Amol and Shalini Ramachandran. 2016. "ESPN's John Skipper Plays Offense on Cord-Cutting." *Wall Street Journal*, January 19. Accessed on July 8, 2016. www.wsj.com/articles/espns-john-skipper-plays-offense-on-cord-cutting-1453228543.

Sheffield, Rob. 2016. "What *O. J.: Made in America* Says about America Right Now." *Rollingstone.com*, June 29. Accessed on July 8, 2016. www.rollingstone.com/tv/features/what-o-j-made-in-america-says-about-america- right-now-20160629.

Skipper, John. 2015. "Message from John Skipper." *ESPN MediaZone*, October 20. Accessed July 8, 2016. http://espnmediazone.com/us/174517-2/.

Szalai, Georg. 2010. "Content Is Emperor, Not King." *Hollywood Reporter*, February 2. Accessed July 8, 2016. www.hollywoodreporter.com/news/murdoch-content-emperor-not-king-20199.

Vogan, Travis. 2015. *ESPN: The Making of a Sports Media Empire*. Urbana: University of Illinois Press.

Wilcox, James K. 2016. "Most Cable Subscribers Would Dump ESPN to Save $8 a Month." *Consumer Reports*, January 16. Accessed July 8, 2016. www.consumerreports.org/streaming-media-players-services/most-cable- subscribers-would-dump-espn-to-save—8-a-month/

NBC Sports Network

Building Elite Audiences
From Broadcast Rights

Deborah L. Jaramillo

NBC Sports Network (NBCSN) entered the cable landscape in 2012, so its story is brief—in fact, it is still a toddler finding its footing within an extended family of cable channels. Its DNA bears the imprints of the National Broadcasting Company, NBC's former parent company General Electric, as well as its current parent company, Comcast. Its heritage is rich and complicated, shaped by the market for sports rights, the waning dominance of broadcast television, and the conglomeration of media companies. The density of NBCSN's family tree and the deft matchmaking that led to its conception are perhaps best understood by following the timeline of a close relative called NBC Sports. NBC Sports was an enterprise enabled by General Electric and enacted by network executive Dick Ebersol, a brand made more industrially feasible by the NBC-Universal merger, and a multi-channel, multiplatform assortment of upmarket niches supported by the infrastructure of cable company Comcast. It was first and foremost a broadcast venture ultimately limited by that fact, unable to funnel its ambition and its accumulation of programming through the singular channel of the NBC network. As it became a feeder for content-hungry cable channels, however, NBC Sports had the means to sustain Ebersol's legacy while cultivating the niche, "quality" audiences that cable television so often prefers to serve. In the story of NBCSN, we see how regulatory, technological, and corporate transformations have resulted in televised sports venues that put the mass appeal of sports programming in tension with a strategic push toward smaller audiences differentiated by narrow, niche tastes. While NBC Sports proved able to gather profitable broadcast rights in the network era to support experimentation with niche sports programming, it was only with access to a greater number of cable outlets—and ultimately the creation of NBCSN—that these efforts became viable. The realization of that promise, however, has encouraged a focus on the same socially stratified logics and preferences for elite audiences that defines so much of the cable landscape.

NBC SPORTS, DICK EBERSOL, AND THE HUNT
FOR BROADCAST RIGHTS

Hired by NBC in 1989 to run its sports division, Dick Ebersol steered NBC through the increasingly complex and expensive pursuit of sports programming (Chad 1989). As the 1980s drew to a close, NBC Sports was on the cusp of transitioning from a mass appeal sports broadcaster to a curated slate of more prestige programs for cable and beyond. Legislation passed almost three decades prior to Ebersol's leadership was central to his positioning of NBC within the sports world. The Sports Broadcasting Act of 1961 exempted sports teams from prosecution for "pooling" their broadcast rights (Horowitz 1978, 415). The Sherman Antitrust Act forbids anti-competitive behavior among two or more parties, but the 1961 Act made it legal for many different football teams/parties, acting as one league, to circumvent the prohibition (Griffith 2003, 20). Overturning a 1960 court ruling that restricted the National Football League's (NFL) ability to control its teams' individual attempts to sell their own games, the 1961 Act freed up the NFL to create a national market for league games. The fact that there were only three buyers at the time—the three national networks: NBC, CBS, and ABC—meant that the competition for sports rights was fierce and any victory would be expensive.

Ebersol was simultaneously frugal and outsized as he sought out sports compatible with his network. Ebersol's predecessor, Art Watson, saw Major League Baseball (MLB) leave NBC and ABC for CBS Sports, which paid $1.06 billion for four years of the coverage (Chad 1989). NBC would begin spring 1990 without baseball, so Ebersol immediately turned to the National Basketball Association (NBA) in 1989, assembling a four-year $600 million deal that would take the NBA from CBS. Ebersol justified the $600 million figure by arguing that the network's ability to broadcast more games would yield more advertising dollars (Chad 1989).

Despite his confidence in the profitability of basketball, the rising price of sports rights pushed NBC to adopt a risk-averse strategy. The network eschewed both the MLB and NFL when talk of new contracts began in 1992. NBC president Robert Wright did not see the benefit of being the number one network if that title came with substantial losses as well as job cuts, and Ebersol agreed (Carter 1992). Sports still had a home at NBC; the task was to find the right sports. For example, in 1992 NBC clinched the college football audience with the Cotton Bowl, the Fiesta Bowl, and the Orange Bowl (Martzke 1992). And by 1993 NBC had seen its relationship with the NBA pay off, so it extended that relationship by four years with a $750 million deal (Sandomir 1993a). The NBA had become such a solid investment for NBC that the two bodies agreed to share revenue once NBC reached just over $1 billion in advertising sales (Rogers 1993). The NBA's sizeable young audience also prompted Miller Brewing Company, which Ebersol called "the fuel for the NBC Sports engine," to extend its own deal with NBC to be "the exclusive beer advertiser" of the NBA games (Rogers 1993).

For all its talk of dumping the MLB and NFL, NBC paid $40 million for the 1994 Super Bowl and began a six-year deal (along with ABC) for the MLB in 1994 (Sandomir 1993a). These two deals, while not risk-free, aligned with both Ebersol's priorities and NBC's overall strategies. Ebersol was attracted to spectacles, and NBC was not above splitting rights fees to share risk. The swift way in which NBC launched and rekindled relationships with basketball, baseball, and football was hailed in the press as "one of the great television comebacks of the 1990s" (Antonucci 1994). Ultimately support of the initial NBA deal by parent company GE saved NBC Sports, at least in Ebersol's estimation. In an interview with *The New York Times*, he remarked, "With the loss of baseball, if we hadn't gotten the NBA, very possibly NBC Sports, as people knew it, might have gone away" (Sandomir 1995). Profits from the NBA deals created opportunities for NBC to pursue sports with both broad and niche appeal and gave the network the flexibility to opt out of both baseball and football in the late 1990s (Sandomir 1998). However, NBC's relationship with sports had to change as new competitors crowded the market for sports.

THE CABLE PROBLEM

The big three US sports commanded the largest financial investments, but NBC wanted a diversified programming slate. Tennis, for example, was a mainstay of NBC Sports; NBC's relationship with Wimbledon reached back to 1968, a deal the network extended by five additional years in 1994 ("French Open" 1997; Sandomir 1994). NBC shared these rights with HBO, however. The premium cable network, built on live sporting events such as boxing, had also televised Wimbledon since 1974. NBC and HBO's shared interest in tennis points to the broadcast network's willingness to pursue a small yet upscale audience and desire to maintain a brand association with a prestigious (read: European) event.

The Wimbledon deal also underscores a shift in the distribution of sports programming: the three broadcast networks were no longer the only competitors for sports. Megan Mullen writes that "a rapidly shifting regulatory terrain" transformed cable television from a highly restricted technology in the 1960s to a liberated delivery system in the 1970s (2003, 65). As a result, sports leagues' value increased substantially when ESPN began bidding for rights (Cave and Crandall 2001, F10). Although NBC belonged to GE, the transindustrial conglomerate had no cable holdings. This rapidly became a problem.

NBC's cable problem revealed itself when the network experimented with the Barcelona Olympics in 1992 (Turner 1991). Without solidifying their plans with cable providers around the country, NBC and Cablevision joined forces to provide a three-channel pay-per-view option for viewers. Called the "TripleCast," the scheme needed cooperative cable companies to free up three channels to allow viewers to subscribe to up to three streams of Olympic coverage. Whether unwilling or unable to participate, subscribers did not flock to this added pay-per-view service, so the plan to outsource cable distribution to multiple providers had failed. NBC and Cablevision lost $100 million.

Unfazed by the pay-per-view debacle, Ebersol believed the Olympics were essential to the NBC brand and doggedly chased them. ABC and CBS entered bids for the 1996 Atlanta Olympics with the intent to partner with cable outlets like ESPN and TNT, but NBC, which won the games for $456 million, had no such partner arranged (Turner 1993; Sandomir 1993b). GE's lack of diversification within the television industry compromised the possibility of cross-tier Olympic coverage within the same corporate family. In 1995, NBC confirmed its long-term investment in the Olympics, paying $1.27 billion for the rights to the 2000 Sydney Olympics and the 2002 Winter Olympics in Salt Lake City. More important than the enormity of the offer was NBC President Robert Wright's justification for assembling such a package. Wright wanted to ensure that his broadcast network would be a destination for viewers increasingly bombarded by "new navigational systems," or new ways to access TV (Carter 1995). Central to NBC's attempts to differentiate itself amid these television choices were "big events" that, while accentuating the appeal of broadcast, filling the coffers of network affiliates, and boosting retransmission fees from cable providers, could potentially extend the NBC-Olympics association across the newly formed cable channels CNBC (launched in 1989) and America's Talking (launched in 1993) as well as NBC's new cable arm in Europe, Super Channel (Carter 1995).

While NBC was set to make $70 million from the Atlanta Olympics, the network was already plotting the distribution of the 2000 Olympics coverage across broadcast, CNBC, and MSNBC (formed in 1996) (Farhi 1996; Hiestand 1996). Eager to exploit new cable holdings, NBC still reserved the "marquee events" for broadcast (Hiestand 1996). The enormity of televising the 2000 Olympics prompted NBC to create a separate Olympics division, of which Ebersol became CEO and chairman (Diuguid 1997).

DIVERSIFICATION

The value of the Olympics to the NBC Sports brand and to NBC's vitality across television tiers was paramount. NBC's first experiment with a diversified basic cable platform came with the 2000 Sydney Olympics. Intended as a corrective to the neglect of women's sports in the 1996 Games, the plan to build a more diverse viewership and spread coverage across MSNBC and CNBC nevertheless failed to improve upon the previous Olympics' ratings.[1] The 2006 Torino Winter Olympics—held two years after the NBC-Universal merger—were the first to be distributed across the NBCU "cable tonnage" that newly combined MSNBC and CNBC with USA (Hiestand 2006). By 2008, NBC was able to tap even more cable holdings for its coverage, with its additional reach extending to Telemundo, Universal HD, and Oxygen (Sandomir 2008). While the NBC-Universal merger enhanced NBC Sports' reach, which now included Spanish-speaking audiences, the major turning point in the division's future came with cable operator Comcast's purchase of 51% of NBCU in 2011. Comcast's entrance prompted the exit of Dick Ebersol, who resigned reportedly because of "a difference in philosophies between [his] free-spending ways for sports rights and Comcast's priority that sports should not be a deep loss leader" (Powers and Guthrie 2011).

With Ebersol gone, uncertainty about NBC's relationship with the International Olympic Committee followed (Sandomir 2011a). But Comcast's $4.38 billion bid for the Summer and Winter Games through 2020 opened up the coverage to even greater distribution possibilities, including Comcast's national sports outlets Versus and the Golf Channel, as well as its regional sports channels (Sandomir 2011a). Mark Lazarus replaced Ebersol, and Lazarus would get the credit for developing a fully branded sports channel that eventually aligned itself with niche sports originating outside of the US.

Comcast owned two sports channels well before the merger: the Outdoor Life Network and the Golf Channel. The Outdoor Life Network was rebranded first as OLN and then as Versus in 2006, but it never assumed a coherent identity. The *New York Times* called it a "second-tier network whose highest-profile sports, the NHL and the Tour de France, aren't blockbusters" (Sandomir 2009b). The *Times* further asserted that Comcast needed to "turn Versus into a more viable competitor to ESPN" (Sandomir 2009a). Doing so meant that NBC's new owner would have to invest in "big acquisitions" and not just "sports that ESPN [did not] want" (Sandomir 2009b). Comcast held the rights to a slew of low-end sports; its most promising asset was IndyCar, an open-wheel auto racing series closer in spirit, technology, and expense to Formula One than to NASCAR. Comcast's least promising assets were bull riding and mixed martial arts. While making sure to keep "marquee sporting events" on over-the-air television, Comcast needed to sharpen its cable sports operations (Fernandez 2010).

Arguably the most important sporting event on Versus was hockey, for which Versus paid $70 million per year (Sandomir 2011b). The cable channel needed to retain those rights when the contract expired in June 2011, particularly because strikes threatened to disrupt NFL and NBA programming ("NBCU Warms" 2011). The resulting $2 billion, ten-year deal between NBC Sports and the NHL, which included digital rights, marked a departure from previous revenue-sharing deals between NBC and the NHL and was figured to be "the cornerstone in the rebranding of Versus" (Guthrie 2011).

REBRANDING

Versus became NBC Sports Network in January 2012, signaling a "complete repositioning of the brand" that would, for Mark Lazarus, exemplify and finally realize the "NBC Sports brand promise" (Szalai 2011). That brand promise meant eliminating hangovers from the OLN days—continuing coverage of sports and leagues that NBC Sports head of programming John Miller euphemistically referred to as too "niche" (Hiestand 2011). Opting for a "higher quality" niche, NBCSN dropped almost half of Versus' offerings, but in the process it also lost overall viewership numbers (Atkinson 2012).

Three programming developments—all occurring in 2012–2013—created a more fully realized identity for NBCSN based less on mass market popularity and more on an elite, increasingly European sensibility. In October 2012, NBCU looked to Europe for two major rights acquisitions: Formula One (F1) and English Premier League (EPL) soccer. An open-wheel racing series known for its technological innovations, upscale manufacturers (Ferrari, Mercedes), and cosmopolitanism (races in Monaco, Singapore, and Abu Dhabi mark the pinnacle of luxury), F1 previously aired on News Corporation's Speed channel and suffered from poor promotion and distribution. Bernie Ecclestone, then head of the company that controls F1's rights, was understandably pleased with the potential multiplatform presence for the sport, which has struggled to gain a foothold in a NASCAR-dominated country (McDonald 2012).

FIGURE 11.1 *November 29, 2015 NBCSN telecast of the Abu Dhabi Grand Prix using split screens to promote an upcoming Premier League soccer game, demonstrating the channel's investment in sports with an elite, global sensibility.*

Also in October 2012 NBCU entered into a three-year, $80 million per year soccer deal with EPL.[2] EPL's previous US home was at Fox Soccer; its NBC deal promised increased visibility via NBCSN, its attendant streaming platform, CNBC, and USA, as well as Telemundo and mun2 (NBCU's two cable channels targeting Hispanic audiences) (Sandomir 2012; Sandomir 2013). While NBCSN's launch had yielded low ratings, the EPL debut gave the channel its largest viewership outside of the London Olympics (Roxborough 2013). John Miller applauded NBSCN for not "Americanizing" the coverage, and he noted that soccer audiences were younger and "a much better educated demo" (Roxborough 2013). The audience turned out to be so valuable that in 2015 NBC entered into a $1 billion, six-year deal to keep EPL, which had become, according to the *New York Times*, "one of the pillars of NBCSN, along with the NHL, NASCAR, F1 and IndyCar" (Sandomir 2015). Ironically, the tone of the 2015 deal is less in keeping with Comcast's statements about belt tightening and more in line with Dick Ebersol's original vision for the Olympics on NBC Sports. According to Mark Lazarus, while the EPL deal was not and would not be profitable in its own right, "it add[ed] to the profitability" of NBCU in terms of "advertising, affiliate deals, [and] digital monetization" (Sandomir 2015). EPL was a loss leader, which contradicted Comcast's original stance but dovetailed perfectly with the branding aspirations of most cable channels. NBCSN also extended EPL's presence with the comedic EPL recap show/talk show *Men in Blazers*. *MIB* promotes NBCSN's EPL programming and, via its interview segment, other NBCU personalities who may or may not have a connection to English soccer teams.

A third development in 2013 has nothing to do with sports rights or even with programming developed by NBCSN, but nevertheless points to a rupture between NBCSN's past and future. In October 2013, NBCSN cancelled *Under Wild Skies*, a program sponsored by the National Rifle Association and one of the few remaining outdoor programs on the channel. In a September episode, program host and "NRA strategist" Tony Makris killed an elephant. In response to the backlash he encountered, NBCSN subsequently cancelled the show (Spangler 2013). In a seemingly unrelated development, NBC Sports withdrew its sponsorship from the Shooting, Hunting, and Outdoor Trade Show. Regardless, in a very short time, the cable channel visibly severed ties with a politically problematic and financially undesirable demographic compared to its more elite audience of European sports fans.

Less than a decade old, NBCSN has already fostered an identity considerably dependent on sports attractive to followers of European sports and sports like hockey and polo assumed to be more popular with educated and wealthier viewers. When NBCSN distanced itself from the NRA and from gun-related programs in general, it excised an audience segment often perceived to be lower income, lower class, and more significantly rural. While that stereotype extends to NASCAR audiences as well, which NBCSN continues to court, NASCAR retains a large audience that, like football and basketball, helps bankroll NBC Sports' interest in developing narrower niche appeals. Moreover, despite accommodations for fans of soccer and other sports niches, NBCSN has excluded some demographics entirely from its narrowcast appeals. When NBCU invested in EPL rights—rather than the rights to Confederation of North, Central American, and Caribbean Association Football (CONCACAF) games or South American Football Confederation (CONMEBOL) games—it overlooked the sizeable audience for Latin American soccer that lives in the US and watches Telemundo or mun2. Fox Deportes and Univision hold most of the rights for these games in the US, and it remains to be seen if NBCU would attempt to move NBCSN into a soccer market two of its channels already appear to covet.

Even as it lies outside its interests in more elite or European sports genres, NBCSN's continued embrace of NASCAR as a profit center allows the channel to showcase sports like EPL that mean more to the brand than to the practical matter of advertising revenue. Like other cable channels, sports-related or not, NBCSN can afford to cater to niche tastes because of dual revenue streams and synergies facilitated by conglomerate ownership. Of course, threats to those synergistic imperatives can emerge with unexpected ownership changes. In January 2017 Liberty Media bought Formula One and promptly looked to Millennial-friendly platforms to broaden the sport's reach digitally (Ramchandani 2017). NBC Sports viewed Liberty's strategy as direct competition with the channel and its "distribution partners" and elected not to continue carrying F1 (Steinberg 2017). ESPN and Formula One subsequently entered into an extended "linear and digital partnership" ("ESPN Secures" 2017). In this case, then, the prerogatives of the rights holder disrupted the continuation of what Ebersol began with his repeated acquisition of programming like Wimbledon and the Olympic Games. Nevertheless, changing industrial conditions have enabled NBC to expand its Olympic coverage and televise non-marquee sporting events on cable, and in keeping with Ebersol's original strategy, NBCSN has exploited audiences beyond those for the NFL, NBA, and MLB. Predictably, though, the commercial logics of cable television have encouraged the channel to gravitate in socially stratified ways toward the more valuable "quality" audiences that it seems many other cable services pursue.

NOTES

1 Ratings were 36% lower than in 1996, and NBC had to compensate advertisers as a result (Christie 2001).
2 The top soccer clubs in the UK's Football Association formed EPL in 1992 to profit from rights fees (Cave and Crandell 2001, F7).

REFERENCES

Antonucci, Mike. 1994. "NBC Makes a Comeback with Sports." *Philadelphia Inquirer*, January 30. Accessed May 1, 2016. LexisNexis Academic.

Atkinson, Claire. 2012. "What the Puck? Lazarus' NBC Sports Net Ratings Flop in Quarter." *New York Post*, March 31. Accessed May 1, 2016. LexisNexis Academic.

Carter, Bill. 1992. "NBC Thinks Being No. 1 Is Too Costly." *New York Times*, January 20. Accessed May 1, 2016. LexisNexis Academic.

Carter, Bill. 1995. "With Its Olympics Megadeal, NBC Sees Itself as the Network of Big-Time Sports." *New York Times*, August 14. Accessed May 1, 2016. LexisNexis Academic.

Cave, Martin and Robert W. Crandall. 2001. "Sports Rights and the Broadcast Industry." *The Economic Journal* 111: F4–F26.

Chad, Norman. 1989. "The Name Is the Game at NBC Sports." *Washington Post*, August 12. Accessed May 1, 2016. LexisNexis Academic.

Christie, James. 2001. "IOC Won't Play Games, Pound Says." *Globe and Mail*, February 24. Accessed May 1, 2016. LexisNexis Academic.

Diuguid, Carol. 1997. "NBC Launches Olympics-Only Arm." *Daily Variety*, December 18. Accessed May 1, 2016. LexisNexis Academic.

"ESPN Secures US Formula One Rights from 2018." 2017. *ESPN.com*, October 4. Accessed October 4, 2017. www.espn.com/f1/story/_/id/20912083/espn-secures-us-formula-one-rights-2018.

Farhi, Paul. 1996. "For NBC, Olympics Are the Golden Days." *Washington Post*, August 3. Accessed May 1, 2016. LexisNexis Academic.

Fernandez, Bob. 2010. "Comcast Reaches Deal to Keep Sports Events on Free TV." *Philadelphia Inquirer*, June 20. Accessed May 1, 2016. LexisNexis Academic.

"French Open to Remain on NBC." 1997. *Atlanta Journal and Constitution*, December 19. Accessed May 1, 2016. LexisNexis Academic.

Griffith, Clark C. 2003. "Sports Licensing." *The Licensing Journal* 23 (2): 29–30.

Guthrie, Marisa. 2011. "NBC Sports Chief Says Network Will Make Money on $2 Billion NHL Deal." *Hollywood Reporter*, April 19. Accessed May 1, 2016. www.hollywoodreporter.com/news/nbc-sports-chief-says-network-179903.

Hiestand, Michael. 1996. "For 2000, NBC Show Stories, Cable Gets Sports." *USA Today*, August 5. Accessed May 1, 2016. LexisNexis Academic.

Hiestand, Michael. 2006. "NBC Has Cable-Hold on Torino." *USA Today*, January 11. Accessed May 1, 2016. LexisNexis Academic.

Hiestand, Michael. 2011. "NBC Sports Network Gets into Game." *USA Today*, December 30. Accessed May 1, 2016. LexisNexis Academic.

Horowitz, Ira. 1978. "Market Entrenchment and the Sports Broadcasting Act." *The American Behavioral Scientist* 21 (3): 415–30.

Martzke, Rudy. 1992. "NBC Adds Cotton Bowl, Sets 'New Tone' for Fees." *USA Today*, April 16. Accessed May 1, 2016. LexisNexis Academic.

McDonald, Norris. 2012. "How NASCAR Will Fight F1." *Toronto Star*, October 20. Accessed May 1, 2016. LexisNexis Academic.

Mullen, Megan. 2003. *The Rise of Cable Programming in the United States: Revolution or Evolution?* Austin: University of Texas Press.

"NBCU Warms to Puck Pact." 2011. *Daily Variety*, April 5. Accessed May 1, 2016. LexisNexis Academic.

Powers, Lindsay and Marisa Guthrie. 2011. "Dick Ebersol Resigns from NBC Sports." *Hollywood Reporter*, May 19. Accessed May 1, 2016. www.hollywoodreporter.com/news/dick-ebersol-resigns-nbc-sports-190278.

Ramchandani, Nisha. 2017. "F1 Turning to Tech to Thrill Fans, Millennials." *The Business Times Singapore*, September 18. Accessed October 5, 2017. Lexis Nexis Academic.

Rogers, Prentis. 1993. "NBA Scoring Big Ratings and Revenue." *Atlanta Journal and Constitution*, June 15.

Roxborough, Scott. 2013. "Has NBC Sports Found the Secret of Selling Soccer to US TV Viewers?" *Hollywood Reporter*, August 30. Accessed May 1, 2016. www.hollywoodreporter.com/news/has-nbc-sports-found-secret-618389.

Sandomir, Richard. 1993a. "NBC and NBA Agree to $750 Million Pact." *New York Times*, April 29. Accessed May 1, 2016. LexisNexis Academic.

Sandomir, Richard. 1993b. "NBC Wins TV Rights to 1996 Atlanta Games." *New York Times*, July 28. Accessed May 1, 2016. LexisNexis Academic.

Sandomir, Richard. 1994. "NBC and HBO Outbid Fox, Renewing Wimbledon Pact." *New York Times*, December 22. Accessed May 1, 2016. LexisNexis Academic.

Sandomir, Richard. 1995. "$2.3 Billion Deal to Give NBC Rights to Future Olympics." *New York Times*, December 13. Accessed May 1, 2016. LexisNexis Academic.

Sandomir, Richard. 1998. "When NBC's Millions Counted for Something." *New York Times*, January 23. Accessed May 1, 2016. LexisNexis Academic.

Sandomir, Richard. 2008. "With 2,200 Hours of Live Video, NBC Embraces Online Coverage." *New York Times*, August 4. Accessed May 1, 2016. LexisNexis Academic.

Sandomir, Richard. 2009a. "A Possible Glimpse of Ebersol's Future." *New York Times*, November 13. Accessed May 1, 2016. LexisNexis Academic.

Sandomir, Richard. 2009b. "With NBC, Comcast Zeros in on ESPN." *New York Times*, December 2. Accessed May 1, 2016. LexisNexis Academic.

Sandomir, Richard. 2011a. "NBC Wins U.S. Television Rights to Four More Olympics." *New York Times*, June 8. Accessed May 1, 2016. LexisNexis Academic.

Sandomir, Richard. 2011b. "Networks Secure Deal with NHL." *New York Times*, April 20. Accessed May 1, 2016. LexisNexis Academic.

Sandomir, Richard. 2012. "NBC Setting Plans for Premier League." *New York Times*, October 29. Accessed May 1, 2016. LexisNexis Academic.

Sandomir, Richard. 2013. "NBC Is Set to Showcase Elite Soccer." *New York Times*, August 16. Accessed May 1, 2016. LexisNexis Academic.

Sandomir, Richard. 2015. "In NBC Deal, English Soccer Proves a Force in America." *New York Times*, August 11. Accessed May 1, 2016. LexisNexis Academic.

Spangler, Todd. 2013. "NBC Sports Will Not Sponsor Gun Trade Show Next Year." *Variety*, October 7.

Steinberg, Brian. 2017. "Formula One Racing to Return to ESPN." *Variety*, October 4. Accessed October 5, 2017. http://variety.com/2017/tv/news/espn-formula-one-racing-nbc-sports-1202580435/.

Szalai, Georg. 2011. "Versus to Be Rebranded as NBC Sports Network." *Hollywood Reporter*, August 1. Accessed May 1, 2016. www.hollywoodreporter.com/news/be-rebranded-as-nbc-sports-217640.

Turner, Melissa. 1991. "Pay-Per-View and the Future of Sports." *Atlanta Journal and* Constitution, December 8. Accessed May 1, 2016. LexisNexis Academic.

Turner, Melissa. 1993. "The Olympic TV Deal." *Atlanta Journal and Constitution*, July 28. Accessed May 1, 2016. LexisNexis Academic.

The Weather Channel

Genre, Trust, and Unscripted Television in an Age of Apps

Jon Kraszewski

The launch of The Weather Channel's IOS app in 2007 and its Android app in 2008 quickly rendered the station's prime-time television programming obsolete. *The Evening Edition* (2001–2009) had conveyed meteorological information to viewers through three segments: the local on the 8s (which gave local conditions, local radar, and a weekly forecast), regional weather (where on-site meteorologists reported significant weather patterns in different parts of the country), and national weather (told from studio meteorologists analyzing radar, weather maps, and forecasts). *The Evening Edition* allowed viewers to learn their local forecast and place it in the context of regional and national weather, but the new app offered The Weather Channel viewers access to information normally available on the local on the 8s at any time, with just the touch of a finger. Thus, within four months of the Android app's debut, executives cancelled *The Evening Edition*. Over the next 20 months, The Weather Channel executives rebranded the channel so that unscripted television programs were its defining prime-time feature. In 2011, *Coast Guard Alaska* (2011–2015) premiered. The following year included the debuts of *Coast Guard Florida* (2012) and *Lifeguard* (2012). Mid-decade programs such as *Coast Guard Cape Disappointment/Pacific Northwest* (2014) and *Fat Guys in the Woods* (2014–2015) made the everyday lives of professionals who worked in extreme weather conditions central to evening lineups.

This chapter focuses on the way different players in the television industry constructed the generic identity of these unscripted programs on The Weather Channel. When the shows premiered on The Weather Channel, station executives billed them as "docu-series" in an attempt to brand them as serious entertainment. However, by 2014 the cable companies DirecTV and Verizon Fios denigrated these same programs as "reality TV" and claimed that fledging weather stations such as AccuWeather and Weather Nation offered viewers valuable meteorology information while The Weather Channel aired trashy reality television series. How and why could channel executives and cable companies have different classifications for the unscripted shows and different value assessments of The Weather Channel itself?

Two industrial issues guide my examination of this battle over the generic identity of these programs. First, how do these unscripted shows emerge from a history of The Weather Channel's efforts to reconstitute trust as new technologies render obsolete old formats (i.e., key textual features that mark a program or group of programs of a station as unique)? Trust is a foundational value at The Weather Channel, as executives have always wanted viewers to trust the information offered. It might seem obvious that executives would ask viewers to believe scientific data about weather on the station, but the construction of trust at The Weather Channel is a complex issue. Media scholar Roger Silverstone argues that trust is an essential quality of media. Trust allows media to "invite us to believe in the authenticity and authority of the electronic image" (1999, 123). Television garners trust in institutions and the knowledge they provide for our daily living. But this trust is manufactured. The trust that institutions offer becomes a product that we consume. Sarah Banet-Weiser (2012) extends this line of inquiry into branding cultures, arguing that companies manufacture feelings of authenticity central to the identities and politics of consumers. We consume brands because of the way they package their authenticity and trustworthiness. Following Silverstone's and Banet-Weiser's leads, I investigate how station executives packaged the weather in formats meant to convey trust and how The Weather Channel's emerging programming strategies reimagined trust as new technologies took over the channel's prior role in disseminating older forms of trustworthy material.

Second, how do battles over defining the generic identity of unscripted programs on The Weather Channel reveal the discursive terrain of genre that makes it a site of industrial struggle over channel value, status, and trust/authenticity? The way that two companies in the cable industry had contrasting generic definitions for these unscripted programs underscores how genres operate not as sets of textual properties but as discursive categories spoken by various users. While all of these unscripted programs on The Weather Channel share textual features that give them a distinct format, the struggle to label them as either docu-series or reality television has more to do with the assumptions of cultural value of those genres than with matching the right textual features to the right generic category. Television genre theorist Jason Mittell argues that "by regarding genre as a property and function of discourse, we can examine the various ways in which various forms of communication work to constitute generic definitions, meanings, and values within a particular historical context" (2004, 12). Susan Murray (2009) has used Mittell's theory of genre to analyze the differences between documentary series and reality television, arguing that many programs have liminal textual features that could fall within either category. For Murray, a proper analysis explores how users bestow those categories onto unscripted series in an effort to value or devalue them, for documentary series are assumed to be high-minded, artistic, and objective, whereas reality shows are viewed as sensationalistic, lowbrow, and subjective. I agree with Murray's assessment of the cultural weight those categories have, but I am interested in seeing how those generic designations assign value to the channel itself, not merely to the texts. Executives can build prestige into a cable brand by promoting it as a center for docu-series production. Likewise to build a station brand around reality television might articulate a lower cultural status to a channel within these dominant genre discourses.

The battle over classifying The Weather Channel's unscripted television programs was a battle over the value of the station itself. The Weather Channel executives originally billed their unscripted programs as docu-series in an effort to promote the value of the television station as offering a type of programming that encouraged viewers to continue to tune in, despite the fact that they could retrieve meteorological data from the app. By associating The Weather Channel with docu-series production, executives envisioned the station as continuing to deliver trustworthy material to viewers through serious television programming. Meanwhile, cable companies later classified the unscripted shows as reality television while renegotiating carrier fees with the channel. Carrier fees are part of customers' monthly cable bills, in which a certain portion of each subscriber payment goes to each television station that the cable provider carries. Some fees are relatively high, with ESPN charging $5.06 a month per customer. The Weather Channel's fee, $0.13, is cheap by comparison. Still, during carrier fee renegotiations in 2014, DirecTV and Verizon Fios attempted to devalue The Weather Channel and secure a lower carrying fee by arguing that the station's focus on reality television programming made it less relevant than upstart weather channels such as AccuWeather and Weather Nation, which focused on forecasts and not unscripted programming. The resolution to this genre war has less to do with one company winning and more to do with a continuing need to reimagine trust to fit the changing commercial needs of the industry.

When The Weather Channel premiered on May 2, 1982, executives viewed trust as both a central tenet of the channel's brand and as a way to unite disparate branding practices under a common goal. Executives partly built trust into the brand through a no-frills presentation that prioritized meteorology over entertainment. Frank Batten, chairman and CEO of Landmark Communications Inc., The Weather Channel's founding company, said that "although our product was rough and ready, people trusted it. Because we gave good information, and because we presented it in a low-key, non-flashy way, we earned our viewers' trust" (Batten and Cruikshank 2002, 166). Executives constructed trust in the 1980s and early 1990s by employing talented meteorologists and making them on-screen reporters. They lacked on-screen dynamism but were promoted as the most qualified people to explain weather to the public. Moreover, The Weather Channel founder John Coleman insisted that his meteorologists resist weather hyping and infotainment in order to provide reliable information. The no-frills logo and graphics for the channel also conveyed trust. Executives knew that their blue box logo with white letters spelling out the channel's name was retro. Yet this aesthetic implied that the scientists at the channel cared more about their work than design (166–7). In this way, the channel's brand was a sort of anti-brand. Batten claims that "during The Weather Channel's first twelve years, we never gave a lot of thought to developing our brand. We had other things on our mind" (166). To focus on polished professionalism takes time away from conveying trustworthy information.

Executives grouped two other aspects of the channel's accidental/anti-brand with trust. First, The Weather Channel was always "there." Whenever viewers needed to know how changing weather and major weather events would affect their lives, The Weather Channel had meteorologists on the scene. Batten claims, "Whenever they [viewers] needed to know how their lives would be affected by one of the most changeable forces of nature, we were there to tell them" (166). Viewers could trust The Weather Channel to cover major weather events. Second, the channel expanded into new markets—most notably new media markets. While executives found their adventures in creating channels in other countries typically failed, they recognized the importance of meeting American consumers in different platforms beyond television. This occurred first with the launch of Weather.com in April of 1995. Viewers could trust that they could find The Weather Channel in various media, wherever they needed it.

The astonishing success of The Weather Channel's website in the late 1990s and early 2000s, however, required that executives reimagine trust on the television channel in interpersonal, not scientific, terms. By late 1998 the website received 150 million hits per month and was ranked 19th on Relevant Knowledge's world ranking of websites. By 2002 the site averaged 3.5 billion page views per year (192). The Weather Channel's website succeeded because it could do what the television channel did in the 1980s and early 1990s: deliver weather data in a no-frills, impersonal manner. The website eliminated the on-screen personality of the weather person in favor of numbers, forecasts, and radars. With ratings declining on the television station, executives wanted viewers to think of the channel as a "trusted and caring friend instead of just a box of meteorological data" (Kempner 2002). Patrick Scott, president of The Weather Channel networks, said, "Up until now, the weather has been the star, not the people. Weather is still the star, but we can add more personality" (Kempner 2002). Scott hired on-camera talent who were trained television personalities, not meteorologists. Although The Weather Channel meteorologists in the 1980s were mostly white men, executives now wanted on-air talent to show gender, racial, and ethnic diversity (Kempner 2002). These engaging, multicultural personalities invited viewers to trust them as friends, not scientists. To stress the interpersonal connections between viewers and on-screen personalities, the shows increasingly ignored technical aspects of weather deemed irrelevant to the average viewer (Kempner 2002).

The Evening Edition was created in 2001 as an effort to place these new engaging station personalities in programming blocks instead of round-the-clock formats focusing on weather information. To build on this initiative, The Weather Channel premiered *Storm Stories* (2003–2007) two years later; it was an hour-long weather disaster show that ran at 8 p.m. Episodes mixed personal recordings, surveillance footage, and first-person accounts of the way people survived weather disasters. On *Storm Stories*, weather threatened the fabric of communities, and it placed our trust in humanity to triumph over nature. *Storm Stories* boosted the channel's ratings 81% in the 8–9 p.m. hour (Pursell 2007).

Hit hardly by the recession of 2008, Landmark Communications looked to sell most of its media companies, including over 50 daily newspapers. Selling The Weather Channel was a tall order, though; its value was high due to its successful website and apps.

Ad Age ranked Weather.com as the eighth best web brand that year; it was also the most trafficked website for a television channel (Hampp 2008). Additionally The Weather Channel launched its IOS app and neared completion on its Android app. Put up for sale at $5 billion, The Weather Channel's only potential buyers were NBC Universal and Time Warner. Ultimately, NBC Universal paid $3.5 billion. Company President Jeff Zucker said The Weather Channel "really gives us a suite of unparalleled assets, and it gives us a real push ahead in digital. This is where we see the strength of our company in the coming years—cable and digital" (Littleton 2008). While digital potential drew NBC Universal to The Weather Channel, the company invested significant energies to boost the ratings and expand the audience for the television channel. Furthermore, such a move to redefine The Weather Channel's television station was imperative given the success of The Weather Channel app. As of 2013, the app had been downloaded over 100 million times. The app receives, on average, 38 million users on phones and 6 million users on tablets per month (Butcher 2013). To put it bluntly, the television channel risked becoming irrelevant because users found what they needed just on the apps.

NBC Universal attempted to bolster The Weather Channel's television ratings by filling its evening schedules with docu-series; the use of that genre moniker—as opposed to reality television—shows the continuing importance and the evolving nature of trust and authenticity on the channel. Al Roker, the long-standing weather person on NBC's *The Today Show* (1952–), emerged as a major player at The Weather Channel. He became a station personality with the premiere of *Wake Up With Al* (2009–2015), a weekday morning show co-hosted with Stephanie Abrams that included news from MSNBC rolling at the bottom of the screen and celebrity interviews from *The Today Show*. Roker then started producing series for The Weather Channel. News stories written about Roker's first series, *Coast Guard Alaska*, in *Hollywood Reporter, New York Daily News, New York Post, Daily Variety*, and *Pittsburgh Post-Gazette* defined the program as a docu-series. The assumptions of the genre's objectivity, educational nature, and commitment to enlightenment reinforced The Weather Channel's commitment to public safety, trust, and authenticity. Turning The Weather Channel into a docu-series channel added prestige to the television station in an effort to bring back viewers.

News stories promoting *Coast Guard Alaska*, for example, lent the trustworthiness of channel meteorologists to the cast members of the docu-series. In a July 28, 2011, article "Meteorologists Explain Why They Weather The Storm," The Weather Channel executive vice president Bob Walker says one of the channel's main goals is to "make sure we keep people safe." Walker then outlines how both on-location meteorologists and docu-series cast members help to achieve this goal: both take "people and immers[e] them in the actual weather experience themselves." Meteorologist Stephanie Abrams says, "I can tell people how to prepare better because I've lived it." Likewise, the cast members of *Coast Guard Alaska* help people deal with the grueling weather on the perilous waters off the Alaska shores. Walker claims both types of programs build trust because "severe coverage for us is about helping people understand what is going on, helping people understand why it is going on" (Owen 2011).

This emphasis on the trustworthiness of Coast Guard members and meteorologists shaped the rather narrow ways in which the unscripted shows represent what the

FIGURE 12.1 *Screenshot of The Weather Channel's attempts to place promotional emphasis on* Coast Guard Alaska *as a docu-series.*

Coast Guard actually does. The US Coast Guard is one of the five branches of the US Armed Forces and is the only branch that operates under the Department of Homeland Security. According to its government webpage, its mission is to "ensure our Nation's maritime safety, security, and stewardship" ("Missions" n.d.). For the Department of Homeland Security, the Coast Guard enforces port, waterway, and coastal security; drug interdiction; defense readiness; and other law enforcement. These items rarely appear in The Weather Channel programs. The series instead focus primarily on the missions that are outside of the jurisdiction of Homeland Security, items such as marine safety, search and rescue, and ice operations. The programs mediate relevant aspects of the Coast Guard's duties by focusing on the ones that involve braving the elements and ignoring the ones that entail broader law enforcement and security measures.

For example, *Coast Guard Alaska* shows Coast Guard members responding to medical emergencies—both job-induced injuries and general health emergencies—on commercial fishing boats. Because of the extreme climate of Alaska, rescuers on the series stress the dangerous nature of the rescue itself: how rescues are done via helicopters because the rough waters prohibit boat rescues, how long the Coast Guard members can be in the water during a rescue because of its cold temperature, and how winds can affect the lowering of a Coast Guard member from the helicopter to the boat or ocean.

Coast Guard Florida emphasizes the trustworthiness of the Coast Guard to rescue vacationers, novice water enthusiasts, and experienced water sports athletes from the risks of the seemingly inviting Atlantic and Gulf waters. One episode focuses on a vacationer snorkeling. He doesn't understand the power of a boat motor and suffers lacerations when he gets sucked into it. Other episodes follow the Coast Guard helping vacationers who get the bends while scuba diving. In one episode the Coast Guard rescues a senior citizen with Alzheimer's disease who mistakenly walks into the Gulf waters and gets carried away by the current. When *Coast Guard Florida* does acknowledge the Homeland Security agency's drug prevention mission, many such episodes ask viewers to trust that the Coast Guard will keep Americans safe from drug smugglers moving drugs from other countries to Miami's ports.

Trust also surfaces on these series by assuring viewers that only the most qualified people serve in the Coast Guard. Episodes convey this theme through two different narrative arcs. First, each episode follows the training of new recruits. Episodes emphasize that only the fittest—physically and mentally—are cut out for this prestigious institution. Each episode has two new recruits report to the commanding officer in charge of training. The episode intersperses a series of physical tests (long-distance running, long-distance swimming, swimming across a pool while pulling a rescued swimmer, etc.) between rescue missions. Recruits are also not heroes. A majority of them either fail to pass the admissions test or drop out of the program because it is too physically challenging, even though they are in stellar shape. Second, each episode devotes time to regular cast members. In part these segments make the repeatable cast members as familiar as the meteorologists who previously worked for and represented the channel. They become trustworthy people who reappear on television screens to show how to negotiate extreme weather safely. Another way that regular cast members convey trust on these shows is through vignettes that show their lives with spouses and children away from the job. Cast members are loving family members, and spouses talk about each guard's commitment to public safety. Segments then show the family's favorite leisure activities, such as camping, walking on the beach, and going to wildlife sanctuaries. These vignettes build viewer trust in the Coast Guard by demonstrating that the people who work in this institution are moral and grounded in their commitment to traditional ideological structures such as the family.

Despite these efforts to produce trusted docu-series, a different value judgment of The Weather Channel's unscripted programs came as cable companies tried to renegotiate carrier fees in the mid-2010s and claimed the channel aired nothing but reality television. The first and most publicized dispute materialized with DirecTV in January

FIGURE 12.2 *Scene from* Coast Guard Florida *demonstrating the importance of training as a means of evoking trust.*

of 2014. The Weather Channel requested a modest increase from its 13-cent fee during a carrier renewal. DirecTV demanded a lower fee, given that the company had its own weather station, Weather Nation, which provided only meteorological information and no unscripted programming (Atkinson 2014b). Additionally, AccuWeather planned to launch its own competing cable weather station in 2015. While The Weather Channel's app still cornered the market for the consumption of meteorological data on mobile devices, The Weather Channel's television station appeared not to be as valuable because of this increasing competition. DirecTV dropped The Weather Channel from its lineup for three months, claiming in articles in popular newspapers such as the *New York Post* that The Weather Channel no longer provided the public with important weather information (Atkinson 2014a). The circulation of these claims in newspapers as opposed to industry trades suggests DirecTV was trying to court television viewers/subscribers to support its position in the battle and not merely announce its position to industry insiders. In 2015 Verizon Fios followed DirecTV's path and permanently dropped The Weather Channel because AccuWeather's new station offered weather at a cheaper carriage fee and didn't show reality television (Daily 2015).

After a three-month feud with DirecTV that often continued to take place in the popular press, The Weather Channel executives felt as if their image as a trustworthy channel had indeed been tarnished by the efforts of cable companies to reclassify its unscripted shows as reality TV. Once again, therefore, executives reimagined the channel's claim to public trust in response to the changing media landscape (in this case, the rise of competing cable weather stations). The Weather Channel abruptly cancelled all of the unscripted shows that had been frequently classified as reality television shows in exchange for a 1-cent increase in its carrier fee from DirecTV customers. To further entice DirecTV to increase the carrier fee, The Blackstone Group, a minority owner of both The Weather Channel and Hilton Hotels, agreed to make DirecTV the cable provider in Hilton Hotels if the company continued to carry The Weather Channel. The Weather Channel did not drop unscripted prime-time programs altogether, however. While it cancelled all of its continuing character shows such as *Coast Guard Alaska* and *Fat Guys in the Woods*, it retained unscripted science shows such as *Strangest Weather on Earth* (2013–), which use a narrator and scientists to explain unique weather phenomena. The Weather Channel's new image of trustworthiness stemmed from a return to weather and science, and the channel promised DirecTV that it would offer more weather reporting.

The tale of The Weather Channel's unscripted programs focusing on professionals who brave extreme weather conditions—and the generic classification of them—is a fascinating look into the way genre functions as a key discourse in the battle over the value and status of a channel's brand identity. Initially The Weather Channel executives promoted these programs as docu-series in an effort to win back viewers to the station through prestige shows during a moment when The Weather Channel apps became a ubiquitous part of American digital culture. Years later, DirecTV and Verizon Fios devalued The Weather Channel's brand by claiming it prioritized the perceived trash of reality television more than meteorological information and public safety. DirecTV did not win this classification battle; yet they set the terms for The Weather Channel executives to reimagine trust in a television channel once more.

REFERENCES

Atkinson, Claire. 2014a. "DirecTV Doesn't Like Reality TV, Weather Channel Relents." *The New York Post*, April 9.

Atkinson, Claire. 2014b. "Not a Penny More: DirecTV Drops Weather Channel over 1 Cent." *The New York Post*, January 15.

Banet-Weiser, Sarah. 2012. *Authentic: The Politics of Ambivalence in a Brand Culture*. New York: New York University Press.

Batten, Frank and Jeffrey L. Cruikshank. 2002. *The Weather Channel: The Improbable Rise of a Media Phenomenon*. Boston: Harvard Business School Press.

Butcher, Mike. 2013. "Weather Channel App Passes 100 Million Downloads as Weather Stays . . . Unpredictable." *techcrunch.com*, January 15.

Daily, Sean. 2015. "Fios Cuts Weather Channel." *Tampa Bay Times*, March 12.

Hampp, Andrew. 2008. "Weather Channel on Sales Block; Landmark Wants $5 Billion for Network, Website." *Television Week*, January 7.

Kempner, Matt. 2002. "Change in the Air at the Weather Channel." *The Atlanta Journal-Constitution*, April 28.

Littleton, Cynthia. 2008. "Clear Skies at NBC U." *Variety*, July 7.

"Missions." n.d. United States Coast Guard/Department of Homeland Security. www.overview.uscg.mil/Missions/.

Mittell, Jason. 2004. *Genre and Television: From Cop Shows to Cartoons in American Culture*. New York: Routledge.

Murray, Susan. 2009. "'I Think We Need a New Name for It': The Meeting of Documentary and Reality TV." In *Reality TV: Remaking Television Culture*, 2nd edition, edited by Susan Murray and Laurie Ouellette, 65–81. New York: New York University Press.

Owen, Rob. 2011. "Meteorologists Explain Why They Weather the Storm." *Pittsburgh Post-Gazette*, July 28.

Pursell, Chris. 2007. "Off-Network Hours Clearing for 2008: *Storm Stories, Boston Legal* Land Stations." *Television Week*, November 12.

Silverstone, Roger. 1999. *Why Study the Media?* London: Sage.

TLC

Food, Fatness, and Spectacular Relatability

Melissa Zimdars

In an episode of TLC's *Freaky Eating* (2010–2011) entitled "Addicted to Cheesy Potatoes," a woman eats only potatoes slathered in cheese for all of her meals—and has since childhood—resulting in her consuming almost 3,000 pounds of potatoes each year and being medically categorized as obese. "It's definitely more than food, it's like crack to me," she says. Her uncontrollable eating of potatoes inspires feelings of shame and causes her to eat her "ooey gooey" food in secret, paralleling the reported behavior of those addicted to drugs like cocaine or heroin. Kelly is not alone in her experience, as each episode of *Freaky Eating* follows a different, self-described "Junk-Food Addict" with the same problem: a compulsion to eat specific foods, whether pizza, cheeseburgers, maple syrup, or corn starch.

Freaky Eating exists as part of a larger trend in food television programming, which has grown from the Food Network's 1993 debut, plus a smattering of instructional cooking shows on PBS, to dozens of programs across NBC, CBS, FOX, SyFy, Bravo, IFC, OWN, Travel Channel, Lifetime, WE, Discover, Cooking Channel, and of course, TLC. The proliferation of food television can be partially explained by the fact that it is inexpensive to produce, ripe for product placement, and supported by a $12 billion food advertising market (Weprin 2010). Food has also taken on greater importance culturally and socially (though this may be partly thanks to television), whether we are foodies, aspiring amateur chefs, or just everyday eaters. Beyond thinking about what we eat in a given day, many of us express concern about the dominance of highly processed foods and our contemporary foodways, or how our food cultures, traditions, and histories contribute to our current obesogenic environment.

Food television on TLC alone reflects these different foci with programming taking a variety of forms, from instructional programming like *Inedible to Incredible* (2010); cooking competitions like *Ultimate Cake Off* (2009) or *Next Great Baker* (2010–); explorations of meals, chefs, and restaurants through series like *Man vs. Food* (2008–),

Little Chocolatiers (2009–2010), or *DC Cupcakes* (2010–); stories about food consumption and food addiction like *Freaky Eating*, and series merging explorations of food and fatness, including *One Big Happy Family* (2009–2010), *My 600 Pound Life* (2012–), and *My Big Fat Fabulous Life* (2015–). TLC's large quantity and diversity of food programming position the channel as a major player in food television and "strengthen TLC's middle finger to the Food Network" (Hahnefeld 2010).

Furthermore, TLC is unique in the way it tells stories about food and fatness in the context of the obesity epidemic. Like most TLC programming, whether about weddings, polygamy, or little people, series at the thematic intersections of food and fatness work to combine the spectacular into the everyday. The relatable enjoyment of eating combines with the addictive or problematic potentials of our highly processed food environment, and the focus on embodiment plays off the difficulties of navigating the world in large body. TLC's combination of ordinary stories of the spectacular, and spectacular stories of the ordinary, also resist some of the worst elements of other fat television programs—the weigh-ins, extreme close-ups, and dramatic change for "maximum emotional effect" (Palmer 2014, 299). By focusing on lived experiences, personal stories, and everyday life, rather than on shrinking body parts or on the "shameful" food put into bodies, TLC instead explores the complexities and banalities of food and fatness.

However, this kind of programming strategy—combining the spectacular and the relatable—is actually less unique and far from new. Raymond Loewy, an industrial designer working in the early 1900s, argued that the key for making all kinds of "things" appealing to people is to take something surprising and make it familiar, or take something familiar and make it surprising (Thompson 2017). For example, lots of people use coupons when they grocery shop, but how many *extreme coupon* their bills down to zero or a negative amount like on *Extreme Couponing* (2010–)? Most Americans are categorized as overweight or obese, and may overeat when tempted by their favorite foods or choose a drive-thru for dinner after a long day, but how many know what it's like to weigh 600 pounds and struggle with food addiction or physical impairment like on *My 600 Pound Life*? This combination of familiarizing the spectacular, or spectacularizing the familiar, is thus a reliable throwback to our earliest understandings of consumer preferences. Yet what is significant about considering this strategy, and understanding it in relation to TLC, is how its deployment to develop relatable content for audiences in this specific industrial context works to support—and maybe even bring about—alternative and more compassionate discourses connecting food and fatness.

TLC AS EVERYDAY TV

Owned by Discovery Communications, TLC reaches an estimated 307 million international subscribers across 29 television markets throughout Europe, Asia, and Latin America, and boasts about 95 million subscribers just in the US. TLC ranks in the top 10 of US cable networks for women (Discovery 2015), and its series *My Big Fat Fabulous Life* frequently ranks as the most watched program during its Tuesday night time slot among 18- to 49-year-old women. Like most broadcast networks and cable channels,

TLC has employed different programming styles and taglines since its 1980 launch, from "A Place for Learning Minds" (1980–1998), which was used when TLC was still an acronym for The Learning Channel, to its shift toward lifestyle content under the more vague banners of "Life Unscripted" (1998–2006), "Live and Learn" (2006–2008) and "Life Surprises" (2008–). Currently, the channel uses "Everyone Needs a Little TLC" (2014–), embracing the colloquial phrase "Tender Loving Care." Each tweak in strategy necessarily corresponds with shifts in content, with TLC moving from educational series about dinosaurs, such as *Paleoworld* (1994–1997), into home makeover programs such as *Trading Spaces* (2000–2008), and then other documentary-style shows featuring personally extraordinary yet socially common life events, including *A Wedding Story* (1996–2005) and *A Baby Story* (1998–2011). According to channel President Eileen O'Neill, TLC's current strategy is to tell relatable stories about people because "there's nothing more fascinating than real life" (Levin 2010). In fact, most TLC press releases and executive quotes in industry trade publications echo the same message: TLC is the home of programming "everybody can relate to," where programming emphasizes "universal themes" (Hendrickson 2010). TLC explores these universal themes according to its "brand promise," which is to tell stories from an "inclusive, non-judgmental perspective" while being "the best destination to find the extraordinary in the everyday" (Discovery 2014).

Despite channel executives framing their programming as relatable and non-judgmental, TLC has a reputation among TV critics for exhibiting the sensational and "serving up a steady diet of junk food" (Lowry 2012) through series focusing on pregnant women in prison, families with 19 children, gypsy weddings, funerals, and extreme coupon users. These external assessments suggest a tension between what producers say they are doing and what TLC series actually convey to some audiences. For example, a producer for *Toddlers and Tiaras* (2009–) says the show merely "documents what's happening in the field," but Kristen Pike (2014) argues the show instead creates a problematic and retrograde reality. In a review of *My Big Fat American Gypsy Wedding* (2010–2015), critic Neil Genzlinger (2012) writes, "[TLC] is hardly a place to turn to for serious enlightenment. It's a place to turn to for sideshows." One short-lived TLC show, *Best Funeral Ever* (2012), is even described as running reality TV "into the ground" due to TLC hitting "new depths" with its programming decisions (Kenneally 2012). To others, shows like TLC's *Hoarding: Buried Alive* (2010–2014) are just "TV Spectacles" (Abrams 2012), where participants in TLC's programming are only "being made to look like freaks" (Owens 2015).

Yet even these spectacular tales serve important social functions when grounded in the ordinary and everyday. For example, many of the stylistic choices and manufactured narrative elements in TLC's *Here Comes Honey Boo Boo* (2012–2014) frame the family as a "redneck" spectacle, but the Thompsons remain, in many ways, a typical and rarely represented working class family (Zimdars and Hawley 2012). According to communication scholar Shaheed Nick Mohammed (2015), TLC's *All-American Muslim* represents the everyday lives of American Muslims and resists discourses of difference and othering. Additional academic analyses of TLC programming find that shows like *Sister Wives* (2010–2016) queer heterosexuality (Bailey 2015) and challenge traditional family constructs (Jorgenson 2014), while shows like *Police Women of Broward County* (2009–2011) negotiate gendered stereotypes (Cox 2012). My own analysis of TLC's *Big Sexy* (2013) identifies a productive, body positive space for the copresence of obesity epidemic and fat acceptance discourses (Zimdars 2015). According to Grace Wang, reality TV has a general tendency to "package difference into comfortingly stock characters and stereotypes" (2010, 405), yet TLC programs about food and fatness highlight differences to make them relatable, complicating and negotiating stereotypes of fat individuals through discussions of food. By combining spectacular tales with depictions of the relatable, and suggesting unique individuals and families are "just like us," TLC produces content "everyone can relate to" while playing with the very notion of "ordinary" and creating space for alternative discourses of food and fatness.

FOOD & FATNESS

TLC began positioning itself as a "destination for food lovers" (Levine 2009) by adding "food" as one of their "tent pole genres" (Schneider 2010a) alongside stories about families, such as *Little People, Big World* (2006–2015), and weddings, such as *Say Yes to the Dress* (2007–). TLC President O'Neill contends that food programs fit the desires of TLC's core audience because of their relatability, with the general logic being that "nothing brings people together better than food" (Malone 2016). The success of TLC's *Cake Boss* (2009–2015), which averaged almost 2 million viewers per week at its peak (Levine 2010), led to spin-offs like *Ultimate Cake Off* (2009) and additional series including *Little Chocolatiers* (2009–2010), *BBQ Pitmasters* (2009), *Food Buddha* (2010), *Mega Bites* (2010), *Best Food Ever* (2010–), and *Craving Comfort* (2010).

Many of the programs occupying these "tent pole genres" of food, families, and weddings coalesce around particular channel themes, especially fatness, which create connective strands between programming in ways that TLC's typically vague taglines do not make explicit. In addition to *Freaky Eating*, TLC aired *Honey, We're Killing the Kids* (2006), *I Eat 33,000 Calories a Day* (2007), *650 Pound Virgin* (2009), *Say Yes to the Dress: Big Bliss* (2012), *Big Brooklyn Style* (2012), *Curvy Brides* (2014), *Obese and Expecting* (2012), and *Fat Chance* (2016), among other specials and short series, all of which featured fat individuals. The industrial lore seems to be that television's increased interest in fatness actually goes "hand-in-hand" with the trend in food television (Schneider 2010b), premised on the idea that fatness results from overeating (Warner 2009). As Michael Schneider notes for *Variety*, "As American waistlines continue to grow, so does reality TV's fascination with fat. Showcasing more realistically sized people on reality TV would seem to be a no-brainer" (Schneider 2009). Following TLC's channel logics, series that combine stories of food consumption and experiences of fatness are imagined as possessing relatability. One TV reviewer for *Variety* explains, "So many Americans are wrestling with their weight that it's easy to identify with . . . struggles when it comes to eating better and exercising more" (Lowry 2009). In fact, two thirds of people in the US are considered to be overweight or obese, according to the problematic yet widely used Body Mass Index, reinforcing the idea that fat is nearly as relatable as food.

SPECTACULARLY RELATABLE

Much of the weight-loss programming across the television landscape, particularly *The Biggest Loser*, mocks fat individuals as "symbols of indulgence" (Palmer 2014, 303), or represents them as "raw and untutored in their food choices and therefore in need of sustainable training, adjustment, and realignment" (300). These weight-loss programs thus reinforce dominant discourses of the obesity epidemic by positioning fatness as shameful and undesirable (Zimdars 2015). In contrast, TLC Vice President for Development Rita Mullins explains TLC's different and televisually unique approach to representing fatness:

> You can't ignore how successful *The Biggest Loser* has been. But more important than that, society is looking at the issue in a different way now. The kind of programming we're doing on cable reflects that. We're putting a human face to what had been, before, a punch line. When you watch a show like *650 Pound Virgin* or *Ruby*, suddenly you realize, "I can identify with this person."
>
> (Schneider 2009)

By balancing the spectacular and the ordinary, TLC programs about fatness and food instead represent people as knowing they have problematic relationships with food and thus wanting help, whether from medical experts or from family members, to alter those relationships. Rather than "lifestyle television simplifying obesity for effect" (Palmer 2014, 302), many TLC programs present fuller, more complex, and often compassionate understandings of how fatness is differently experienced, and how individuals manage or fail to manage their relationships with food, creating a televisual alternative to typical weight-loss series. Furthermore, the programs operating at this thematic food/fat intersection deliver upon TLC's relatable yet extraordinary non-judgmental "brand promise."

For example, *One Big Happy Family* follows Tameka and Norris Cole of North Carolina, and their kids Amber and Shane, who each weigh around 350 pounds. Viewers join the family as they indulge in a dinner of their favorite comfort foods, including lasagna and fried chicken wings, while discussing the need to change their eating and exercise habits, as Shane risks developing diabetes. Most of the first episode details what the Coles family eats, showing Norris putting butter inside of his pancake batter and the family enjoying funnel cakes, slushies, and cheesecake to console themselves after being on display at a waterpark. The pilot episode elicited several accusations that TLC had exploited the Coles and made light of their body sizes (France 2010), arguing that food buffets and their large, swimsuited bodies worked to create a visual spectacle. Yet the episode also works to make the family relatable to viewers. Tameka explains, "Food for me is comfort. It makes us feel good. Eating keeps our family close. I'm willing to go to the ends of the world to make them happy."

The remainder of the series primarily focuses on the positive steps the family takes to avoid "junk foods" and lose weight, including ridding the house of processed foods and exercising together as a family. At first, the family complains about eating plain, broiled, skinless chicken breasts, but they eventually learn how to make enjoyable and flavorful healthy meals. Each episode features ups and downs in their weight-loss journeys, but there are no dramatic setbacks, starvation diets, or marathon exercising sessions. And the secondary focus is somehow more banal: the Coles's daily lives. The show follows Amber as she joins the high school's color guard, Tameka as she goes to work, Norris picking out a re-engagement ring for his wife, and casual activities like shopping for clothes, making friends, and going on a family camping trip. Steadily, the spectacular elements of the series give way to these more mundane aspects of everyday life. Nancy Daniels, a senior vice president of production and development for TLC, tells CNN: "What appealed to us about the Coles is that they are a very real and relatable family going through a very real and relatable issues that many American families face" (France 2010). The series concludes with each of the Coles losing a moderate amount of weight; they weigh themselves in the family kitchen, avoiding the tearful, public weigh-ins of *The Biggest Loser* (2003–) and *Extreme Weight-Loss* (2011–) while allowing for a different kind of television narrative about fatness and food to unfold.

My 600 Pound Life also balances the spectacular with the ordinary. Through hour-long episodes, *My 600 Pound Life* follows individuals for a year as they qualify for, undergo, and recover from weight-loss surgery. While televised depictions of surgery may indeed be spectacular, weight-loss surgery itself is far more commonplace, with hundreds of thousands of people undergoing bariatric procedures every year (American Society for Metabolic and Bariatric Surgery 2016). Each episode begins by visually depicting participants as they struggle to shower or bathe, or as being confined to beds and recliners. Simultaneously, each participant explains difficulties in their daily lives, why and how they believe they gained weight, and their problematic relationships with food. One participant, Milla, explains, "Food equals love, food equals appreciation. Food is everything to me. It's the last thing I think about before bed and the first thing I think about when I get up in the morning" (Season 4, Episode 10). Another participant, Lupe, elaborates, "Food is my comfort. I'm an emotional eater. When I eat food, I feel happy. Food is how we celebrate, how we have a good time. It's happiness, but it's also killing me. I just have to eat something that tastes good because my legs are so swollen" (Season 4, Episode 12). Although extreme, these stories echo everyday experiences of yo-yo dieting and tales of emotional or stressful eating (Björntorp 2001). Like *One Big Happy Family*, the beginning of each episode includes numerous close-ups of the fat body and scenes where participants eat large amounts of unhealthy foods. Yet as each episode progresses, the spectacular images and behaviors again give way to far more mundane depictions. Participants are shown grocery shopping, watching television, arguing with their loved ones, or making food with their families. Often times these everyday activities appear difficult because of each participant's large size; however, these activities humanize and make subjects relatable in their focus on everyday lives rather than just the bodies they inhabit.

Spectacular imagery does come back into play as each participant undergoes bariatric surgery. Cameras capture footage from inside each participant's body and zoom in on removed parts of the stomach on the operating table. Yet like *One Big Happy Family*, each episode concludes in rather unexciting ways. Participants lose varying amounts of weight, but there are, again, no sensational final weigh-ins or lavish monetary prizes. Instead, we see participants getting in and out of cars with greater ease, having a picnic in the park, or going to a restaurant for the first time in years. Despite "extraordinary" tales of weight gain and the spectacular images of weight-loss surgery, participants are represented as having relatively ordinary, if not boring, lives.

Finally, *My Big Fat Fabulous Life* features Whitney Way Thore, a dancer who became famous through her viral "Fat Girl Dancing" videos on YouTube. The series follows her as she struggles with polycystic ovarian syndrome, which caused her to gain almost 200 pounds in college. Like *One Big Happy Family* and *My 600 Pound Life*, early episodes of the series focuses on the physical difficulties of being fat (her mother helps her apply baby powder to her chafed legs, for example) as well as complicated relationships with food (Thore indulges in a large pizza with her friend, Buddy, and laments, "A life without pasta is not a life I want to lead"). As the series progresses, however, Thore discusses her preference for being fat, fit, and healthy—through her No Body Shame Campaign—given the realities of her underlying medical condition, which make it incredibly difficult for her to lose weight, and the realities of weight-loss in general, which pose challenges for a majority of people in the imagined audience.

Throughout each episode, Thore discusses the obstacles she experiences because of her weight, such as finding clothes to wear or finding a partner who is not attracted to her solely because she is BBW (a big beautiful woman); but episodes primarily revolve around her everyday life: moving into a new home, getting a new job, teaching her Big Girl dance classes, exercising with her trainer, and online dating. While the story of Thore dealing with elevated blood sugar levels and that situation's impact on her food consumption remains a theme throughout season two, like the medical issues detailed in other TLC series, it becomes a backdrop for the sharing of otherwise relatable life moments.

Across all of these show examples, viewers may see people who likely do not look or act quite like them, but yet the everyday experiences of individuals on screen can resonate nonetheless. This combining of the relatable and the spectacular generates viewer interest and encourages different kinds of identification, namely that fat individuals on screen need to be understood beyond what numbers appear on a scale. Further, these alternative narratives provide greater support to compassionate and complex ways of thinking about food and fatness in comparison to the stereotyping and shaming representations found across so many series looking at *either* fatness *or* the role of food, fast food, and food industries.

CONCLUSION

None of these programs culminates in a big reveal of an "after body," and generally feature minimal "success" in terms of achieving normative body sizes, which mirrors the lack of sustained, "real world" success that most people experience. Like TLC, food and bodies straddle the ordinary and the spectacular: we eat to fuel our bodies, but we also associate food with celebration and comfort. Our bodies have numerous mundane processes, but they can also do extraordinary things and be sources of both scorn and pleasure. Of course not all TLC programming can successfully defend against accusations of exploitation or its embrace of the "freaky," nor should we accept TLC's own discourses of "relatability" and "non-judgmental" brand values as automatically true. However, through this programming strategy and thematic intersection, TLC creates a discursive space for alternative, compassionate, and sometimes light-hearted explorations of situations otherwise framed as a dire in the context of obesity epidemic.

REFERENCES

Abrams, Lindsay. 2012. "*Hoarders:* From a TV Spectacle to a Newly Defined Psychiatric Condition." *The Atlantic*, August 10. Accessed December 26, 2016. http://www.theatlantic.com/health/archive/2012/08/hoarders-from-a-tv-spectacle-to-a-newly-defined-psychiatric-condition/260997/.

American Academy of Metabolic and Bariatric Surgery. 2016. "Estimate of Bariatric Surgery Numbers, 2011–2015." July. Accessed February 14, 2017. https://asmbs.org/resources/estimate-of-bariatric-surgery-numbers.

Bailey, Courtney. 2015. "Love Multiplied: *Sister Wives*, Polygamy, and Queering Heterosexuality." *Quarterly Review of Film & Video* 32 (1): 38–57.

Björntorp, P. 2001. "Do Stress Reactions Cause Abdominal Obesity and Comorbidities?" *The International Association for the Study of Obesity, Obesity Reviews* 2 (2): 73–86.

Cox, Nicole. 2012. "Kicking Ass . . . with Lip Gloss: Mediating Gender on TLC's *Police Women of Broward County*." *Critical Studies in Media Communication* 29 (2): 149–63.

Discovery Communications Inc. 2014. "TLC Unveils New Brand Campaign and Tagline." July 22. https://corporate.discovery.com/discovery-newsroom/tlc-unveils-new-brand-campaign-and-tagline/.

Discovery Communications Inc. 2015. "30 Years of Bringing You the World: 2014 Annual Report." https://corporate.discovery.com/wpcontent/uploads/2015/07/disca2014_download.pdf.

France, Lisa Respers. 2010. "'Big' Concerns Surround New Reality Show." *CNN.com*, January 12. Accessed November 17, 2016. www.cnn.com/2010/SHOWBIZ/TV/01/12/one.big.happy.family/.

Genzlinger, Neil. 2012. "'Gypsy Wedding' Another Spectacle on Reality TV." *Telegram.com*, April 30. Accessed December 26, 2016. www.telegram.com/article/20120430/NEWS/104309975.

Hahnefeld, Laura. 2010. "TLC Launches *Best Food Ever* (or Yabba-Dabba-Done-to-Death)." *Phoenix New Times*, May 3. Accessed December 14, 2016. www.phoenixnewtimes.com/restaurants/tlc-launches-best-food-ever-or-yabba-dabba-done-to-death-6513133.

Hendrickson, Paula. 2010. "Food, Wedding Among Reality Hot Topics." *Variety*, June 6. Accessed November 29, 2016. http://variety.com/2010/tv/awards/food-wedding-among-reality-hot-topics-1118020282/.

Jorgenson, Derek A. 2014. "Media and Polygamy: A Critical Analysis of *Sister Wives*." *Communication Studies* 65 (1): 24–38.

Kenneally, Tim. 2012. "TLC's 'Best Funeral Ever' Runs Reality TV into the Ground." *The Wrap*, December 13. Accessed December 26, 2016. http://www.thewrap.com/tlcs-best-funeral-ever-special-promises-real-dead-mans-party-69206/.

Levin, Gary. 2010. "TLC Banking on 'Genuine' People; Reality-Driven Lineup Focuses on Families, Food and Feuds." *USA Today*, April 8.

Levine, Stuart. 2009. "TLC Heating Up 'BBQ Pit.'" *Variety*, September 28. Accessed November 17, 2016. http://variety.com/2009/scene/markets-festivals/tlc-heating-up-bbq-pit-1118009274/.

Levine, Stuart. 2010. "Cable Nets Are Comfy in the Kitchen." *Variety*, February 21.

Lowry, Brian. 2009. "Review: 'One Big Happy Family.'" *Variety*, December 27. Accessed November 29, 2016. http://variety.com/2009/tv/reviews/one-big-happy-family-1200477785/.

Lowry, Brian. 2012. "'Extreme Cougar Wives' & 'Along for the Bride': Thanksgiving Can't Stop the Junk Food on TLC." *Variety*, November 20. Accessed November 16, 2016. http://variety.com/2012/voices/opinion/extreme-cougar-wives-along-for-the-bride-thanksgiving-cant-stop-the-junk-food-on-tlc-1200572036/.

Malone, Michael. 2016. "'Cake Boss' Back for Seasons Eight and Nine." *Broadcasting and Cable*, June 1. Accessed November 29, 2016. www.broadcastingcable.com/news/programming/cake-boss-back-seasons-eight-and-nine/156958.

Mohammed, Shaheed Nick. 2015. "The Muslims Next Door: Transgressive Hybridity in TLC's *All-American Muslim*." *Mass Communication and Society* 18: 97–118.

Owens, Chante. 2015. "TLC Takes an Inside Look at the Lives of Tall Women in 'My Giant Life.'" *The San Francisco Globe*, July 17. Accessed December 26, 2016. http://sfglobe.com/2015/07/15/tlc-takes-an-inside-look-at-the-lives-of-tall-women-in-my-giant-life/.

Palmer, Gareth. 2014. "Legitimate Targets: Reality Television and Large People." In *Reality Gendervision: Sexuality and Gender on Transatlantic Reality Television*, edited by Brenda Weber, 299–315. Durham: Duke University Press.

Pike, Kristen. 2014. "Freaky Five Year Olds and Mental Mommies: Narratives of Gender, Race, and Class in *Toddlers & Tiaras*." In *Reality Gendervision: Sexuality and Gender on Transatlantic Reality Television*, edited by Brenda Weber, 282–98. Durham: Duke University Press.

Schneider, Michael. 2009. "Reality TV Continues Fascination with Fat." *Variety*, July 25. Accessed November 29, 2016. http://variety.com/2009/tv/features/reality-tv-continues-fascination-with-fat-1118006475/.

Schneider, Michael. 2010a. "Another Tasty TLC Entree." *Variety*, April 22. Accessed November 29, 2016. http://variety.com/2010/scene/markets-festivals/another-tasty-tlc-entree-1118018141/.

Schneider, Michael. 2010b. "TLC and John Goodman Search for the 'Best Food Ever.'" *Variety*, April 22. Accessed November 29, 2016. http://variety.com/2010/tv/news/tlc-and-john-goodman-search-for-the-best-food-ever-16026/.

Thompson, Derek. 2017. *Hit Makers: The Science of Popularity in the Age of Distraction*. New York: Penguin Press.

Wagner, Leonie. 2015. "Big, Fat and Happy with Life." *The Times* (South Africa), November 20.

Wang, Grace. 2010. "A Shot at Half-Exposure: Asian Americans in Reality TV Shows." *Television & New Media* 11 (5): 404–27.

Warner, Jennifer. 2009. "Obesity Epidemic: Overeating Alone to Blame." *WebMD.com*, May 11. Accessed February 1, 2017. www.webmd.com/diet/news/20090511/obesity-epidemic-overeating-alone-to-blame#1.

Weprin, Alex. 2010. "Cable Nets Hungry for Food Ads." *Broadcasting and Cable*, April 5. Accessed November 16, 2016. www.broadcastingcable.com/news/programming/cable-nets-hungry-food-ads/36282.

Zimdars, Melissa. 2015. "Fat Acceptance TV? Rethinking Reality Television with TLC's *Big Sexy* and the Carnivalesque." *Popular Communication* 13 (3): 232–46.

Zimdars, Melissa and Alexander Hawley. 2012. "The Tube: Go-Go Juiced." *Little Village*, September 26. Accessed December 27, 2016. http://littlevillagemag.com/the-tube-go-go-juiced/.

MTV

#Prosocial Television

Laurie Ouellette

In April 2014, MTV launched a "prosocial" initiative to combat racial, gender, and LGBTQ bias. Sandwiched between steamy teen romances, pop culture and celebrity news, and provocative reality shows, the Look Different campaign connected the MTV brand to a mission of tolerance and social equality. "Even though we may think we're open to diversity, almost all of us have hidden, subconscious biases," explained a series of public service announcements that called on MTV viewers to address their own prejudices and put an end to "microaggressions" based on gender, race, and sexual orientation. To open the minds and change the behaviors of its Millennial audience, MTV aired special programming across MTV, MTV2, and the college network MTVU, developed digital content (including interactive "bias cleanses"), launched Twitter and Facebook campaigns, and enlisted actors, musicians and social media influencers to promote the cause. According to MTV, the "results" have been demonstrable: besides "driving a meaningful conversation on bias," more than two million young people "have taken action nationwide" because of the Look Different campaign, claims the network ("MTV's" 2016).

Look Different is only the latest example of MTV's commitment to corporate social responsibility. Launched in 1981 as a cable channel devoted to music videos, MTV was branded as a space on the dial for youth culture as well as the sensibilities and values associated with rock music. In the early 1990s, the channel diversified and began to air other types of television programming, including the first-person documentary series *True Life* and the hybrid reality series *The Real World*, both of which addressed "hot button" issues from AIDS/HIV to racial tension. In 1992, MTV launched "Choose or Lose," a campaign to bolster voter turnout that has been revamped for each subsequent presidential election. In 1998, MTV's long-standing promotion of sexual health, ethical treatment of animals, global famine relief, and other progressive causes was expanded and formalized under the rubric of its Strategic Communication and Public Affairs

Division, otherwise known as the Prosocial Department. Since then, MTV has devoted resources and airtime to pinpointing and solving what are deemed the "most pressing" problems of its core 14- to 24-year-old demographic, from teenage pregnancy to rising student debt to cyberbullying. Conceived as collaborations between MTV executives, researchers, TV producers, marketers, nonprofit agencies, and philanthropies, prosocial campaigns attempt to "nudge" young people's thinking and behavior toward desired outcomes (Thaler and Sunstein 2009). At the same time, they establish MTV as an ethical and "responsible" media brand.

This chapter takes MTV as a case study for considering how television "governs at a distance" (Foucault 1991) in an increasingly deregulated, branded, and interactive mediascape. Situating prosocial TV within the broader ascension of neoliberalism, I argue that the concept of the public interest in US broadcasting has been reinvented in cause-oriented terms that are lucrative for media corporations. Campaigns like Look Different offer compatibility with the free market rationalities of the neoliberal era in which state oversight of public life (including television) has given way to privatization, competition, and intensified self-regulation and self-care (Rose 1996). At the same time, they problematize and attempt to correct the injurious tendencies (Brown 1995) and consequences of this historical transition. Prosocial television is an ambivalent response to the decline of the public sector as the guardian of welfare, fairness, and equality—as well as a mechanism to differentiate channels in a cluttered marketplace and generate "ethical value" for brands (Arvidsson 2005). As a niche channel that has long stitched the "conduct of conduct" (Foucault 1991) into its business operations and identity, MTV provides much more than a "distraction factory," as earlier scholars suggested (Goodwin 1992). Instead, MTV operates as a technology of citizenship that guides and shapes "ethical" subjects within the boundaries of its targeted youth market and global brand.

"I WANT MY MTV"

When broadcasting developed in the United States in the 1920s, federal legislators approved commercial ownership but mandated radio and later television to serve the "public interest, convenience and necessity," much like a public utility. Beyond universal access to broadcast signals, the public interest was dominantly interpreted as the expectation that broadcasters provide cultural resources (information, culture, education) for citizenship on a national scale. Rooted in the liberal welfare stage of capitalism, this conception of the public interest generally invoked a need for "serious" news and public affairs programming and aligned closely with the legitimated tastes and habits of white, educated opinion leaders (Ouellette 2002). At a time when three television networks addressed the largest audience possible, commercial broadcasters resisted this responsibility, claiming that "mass taste" would not support such fare. Public broadcasting emerged in the late 1960s to temper this mounting tension between commerce and citizenship (see essays by Hilmes and Perlman in this volume).

The social and political upheavals of the late 1960s and 1970s, the fragmentation of the mass market, and the expansion of cable television informed a new way of thinking about television's public interest responsibilities. With channel scarcity blamed for lowest-common denominator appeal, the expanding cultural marketplace promised greater diversity—including greater opportunities for news and educational programming. While not required to serve a general public interest by the FCC, the new cable industry did voluntarily promise to cater to the needs and interests underrepresented consumers defined by specialized demographics, tastes, interests, values, and ideological preferences. In this sense, it aligned itself with a reinvention of the public interest in corporate terms. MTV was the first US cable channel to encourage a new form of consumer citizenship (Turow 1997; Banet-Weiser 2007) rooted in shared lifestyle, taste, self-actualization, and brand membership. As Andrew Goodwin (1992) pointed out, teenagers were encouraged to see MTV as an integral dimension of their unique identities and lifestyle, encouraged to "fight" for their right to consume differently under the marketing slogan "I Want My MTV." This slogan pitched MTV as a quasi-political representative of youthful consumers—and was used as a rallying cry to force cable operators to carry the new cable channel. By claiming to reflect the voices, experiences, and aspirations of youth, MTV in turn promised to serve the "public interest" in a different way. The top-down public interest rationales of the broadcast era appeared incompatible with this promise of consumer partnership, their somber, educational aesthetics at odds with MTV's irony, rebellious sensibilities, and fast-paced visual style. Within this shifting cultural context, television's operation as a technology of governing subjects would necessarily take a different form.

In the 1980s, deregulation put the nail in the coffin of the public interest as a regulatory principle. FCC chairperson Mark Fowler described television as a "toaster with pictures," a business like any other, and the free market was posited as the best regulatory framework. Public oversight was no longer necessary, according to this logic, because if consumers wanted uplift, civic education, educational programming, serious news, or anything else, the post-scarcity television marketplace would provide. In retrospect, however, it is clear that the impetus to guide and shape citizen subjects that undergirded liberal understandings of the public interest was not eradicated. Instead, these shifts reinvented television as a technology of citizenship in ways that connected governmentality to new forms of niche marketing and post-industrial profitmaking. As corporate social responsibility (CSR) and cause marketing (in which corporate and nonprofit sectors promote action on issues from recycling to cancer research) have expanded in recent decades, television has been remodeled as both a mover of merchandise and a platform for "doing good" within branded environments. This often includes an interactive component, with television conceived as a focal point or interface (Lury 2004) for socially responsible ventures that engage and mobilize viewers through digital platforms and social media. With its long history of prosocial campaigns, MTV pioneered this tendency.

Why would MTV mobilize young people to vote, promote sexual health, or attempt to combat prejudice and bias in the absence of any formal requirement to do so? Why would a network owned by Viacom, one of the world's largest media conglomerates, bother to address its viewers as ethical subjects-in-training as well as consumers of youthful entertainment and goods? According to Andrew Barry, the corporate sector's embrace of social issues and ethical problems in recent decades is closely connected to "neoliberal" policies and reforms. As state responsibility for citizens has declined, corporations (including media conglomerates) are called upon to fill the gaps and "perform the job of government at a distance" (2004, 202). What Barry calls "ethical capitalism" has reshaped the US television industry, as television networks (and their corporate owners) take up dispersed forms of societal problem-solving and citizenship training voluntarily. Unlike abstract notions of public enlightenment, this move to shape ethical subjects is affective, behaviorist, and cause-oriented (curing breast cancer, protecting the environment, getting people to the polls, encouraging volunteerism). Still, CSR provides a platform for buttressing age-old tensions identified by Toby Miller (1993) between the demands of the consumer economy and the needs of the political order. What has changed is that good citizenship has come to hinge on measurable actions and outcomes carried out within the boundaries of the brand (Ouellette 2012). This assumes a powerful role for media corporations as arbiters of social life, as suggested by MTV's oft-repeated claim to use its "superpowers for good." However, it also presumes that TV viewers choose to constitute themselves as ethical subjects in partnership with MTV as a dimension of their identity and agency. These efforts invite young people to play an active role in prosocial campaigns (and their desired outcome) by watching specially themed MTV programs, interacting online, utilizing the resources offered, participating in contests, and following the projects on social media. In the process, they are called upon to join an ethical community of consumer citizens organized through and around MTV.

CSR is not at odds with a free market approach to broadcasting, but it is integral to it. "Never before has the claim that corporate virtue can and should be profitable enjoyed so much currency or influence," observe business analysts of the uptake of CSR as a contemporary profitmaking strategy (Vogel 2006, 25). Like corporations from Apple to Dove, MTV embraces ethical capitalism to differentiate itself as a channel committed to "making a difference." According to MTV research, 80% of "millennials prefer brands that have social engagement and do good in the world" (Dishman 2013); prosocial campaigns establish MTV as a brand of television that cares. This ethical sensibility also places the network within a "new spirit of capitalism" in which, according to Luc Boltanski and Eve Chiapello (2007), many of the countercultural sensibilities of the 1960s—including resistance to capitalism—become enfolded into corporate logic. The desire to make a meaningful contribution to society through one's work, for example, along with demands for greater flexibility and creativity on the job, have been embraced by corporations to manage employees and increase their productivity. According to MTV executives, a commitment to corporate social responsibility attracts "top talent" to the network and bolsters morale at every rung on the corporate ladder because it allows staffers to see their purpose as contributing to social change, rather than just generating dollars (Dishman 2013). Campaigns like Look Different likewise encourage MTV viewers to see themselves as active and ethical subjects, rather than merely passive TV consumers.

As branding has become more central to the TV industry, attempts to address TV viewers in this way can be monetized as a type of "ethical surplus." In a post-industrial capitalist economy, profit derives not only or even primarily from the manufacture and sale of goods, but also from the meanings, associations, feelings, and communicative practices that consumers experience in their daily engagement with brands (Arvidsson 2005). At a time when neoliberal citizens are called upon to donate, volunteer, take private action, and practice self-care as an alternative to "big government," corporations channel these expectations into socially responsible brand identities. MTV viewers, in other words, perform their duties as neoliberal citizens and *simultaneously* create the ethical value of the MTV brand when they watch "special" programs, tweet, take quizzes, enroll in contests, as well as think about, discuss, and perform suggested prosocial actions. This alignment of "good citizenship" and branding is what makes corporate social responsibility profitable.

GOVERNING BY MTV

MTV's commitment to social responsibility also eschews the discourse of sobriety typically associated with news, documentary, and other classic public interest forms. While MTV does produce versions of these genres, it replaces "boring" talking heads with youth-centered topics told in a snappy, celebrity-studded, rapid-paced style (Ouellette 2015). Just as often, however, the network uses entertainment (including teen melodrama and reality shows) to advance prosocial agendas. MTV conceives its audience both as a consumer market to "win" for advertisers and shareholders, and as a population to be governed, guided, and reformed through pedagogy. In this sense, MTV combines and reworks the bifurcated (but equally controlling) approach to the audience associated with earlier stages of commercial and public broadcasting (Ang 1987, 1991). Because these consumerist and governmental aims are sometimes at odds, prosocial campaigns highlight contradictions within the socially responsible MTV brand.

MTV conducts extensive research to "capture" an audience for advertisers and shareholders, as well as to monitor youth so that problems and risks can be identified and addressed. These agendas fuse and contradict. In the *Frontline* documentary "Merchants of Cool" (2001), Douglas Rushkoff traces the construction of the puerile male "mook" and the oversexualized female "midriff" (both assumed to be white and middle class) across MTV audience research, marketing, and programming. While MTV has capitalized on these constructions of MTV viewers with hits like *Beavis and Butthead, Jackass, Jersey Shore*, and newer productions like *Ridiculousness* and *Ex on the Beach*, these character types also invoke the imagined subjects of prosocial campaigns designed to reduce unprotected sex, promote sexual consent, and curb gender discrimination. This dual imagination of audiences as both consumers and subjects of reform is especially clear in MTVU's 2008 Indebted campaign, which promoted fiscal prudence as a solution to the student loan crisis. MTV has long promoted consumerism as an integral aspect of youth identity and self-realization, and its programs carry plentiful ads (and product placements) for clothes, cars, phones, beauty products, and other goods. Blaming financial distress and ballooning loan balances on students themselves (rather than on structural causes like the decline of public funding for college), the Indebted campaign advised MTVU viewers to give up their fancy lattes and luxurious spring break packages to take responsibility for their financial futures. Music videos previously circulated as part of an aspirational consumer culture were recaptioned with pop-up graphics that criticized the excessive consumption and "irresponsible" spending habits of artists like 50 Cent and Britney Spears. With prosocial campaigns like these, MTV establishes itself an ethical platform for addressing "problems" the network simultaneously defines and perpetuates.

MTV's prosocial initiatives campaigns pursue an instrumental approach to social change, from using a condom during sex to showing up at the polls to avoiding sexualized stereotypes and prejudicial slurs. To promote these desired outcomes, the network and its partners take cues from the entertainment-education tradition developed by social scientists. Entertainment-education refers to coordinated efforts by nonprofit agencies, researchers, and governments to promote biopolitical agendas related frequently to health, family planning, and population control (Greene and Breshears 2010). Popular entertainment conventions and appeals are deployed as "bait" for educational messages hoped to induce attitudinal and behavioral changes in targeted audiences. MTV similarly uses its television series, webisodes, YouTube videos, and celebrity performances to promote a range of objectives related to the body, sexuality, mental health, and social relationships. It does not assume that the audience will passively absorb the educational messages that circulate within and around entertainment, however. What might otherwise be perceived as top-down social management is joined and tempered by the forms of recognition, agency, and belonging that come with consumer citizenship. Likewise, the self-work and self-care required of MTV's prosocial campaigns—and the use of interactive technologies that enable input and participation—transform the objectives of authorities into the desires and capacities of subjects.

Social marketing, a behaviorist approach to social change that has gained currency in recent decades, also aligns with the reinvention of the public interest as a matter of corporate social responsibility and prosocial activity. Like entertainment-education and cause marketing, social marketing attempts to reform subjects in specific and measurable ways, such as getting them to exercise more or quit smoking. These "nudges" drive market-based forms of governmentality that guide and shape populations at a distance from direct state control. Applying the techniques of advertising and promotion to the regulation of conduct, social marketing campaigns serve as technologies of subjectification, in that "targeted populations, who are simultaneously audiences, can be expected, if the campaign is successful, to diffuse, multiply and facilitate the take up of the behavioral norms and values being promoted" (Balnaves and O'Regan 2002, 19). Such technologies operate particularly effectively in cultural contexts that invite audiences to become the "co-creators" of their objectives (19). MTV's prosocial campaigns, which ask young people to play an active role in social agendas that connect behavioral change to youth empowerment, exemplify this trend. For example, the enormously successful *16 and Pregnant* and *Teen Mom* franchises revolve around the everyday lives of young women who are said to have made the "wrong choices." To attract audiences, teasers and promotions promise interpersonal conflict, melodrama, and gossip, playing up the "ordinary" celebrity of the young mothers. At the same time, the series deliver advice about reproductive choices, family planning, and delayed parenting. In partnership with nonprofit agencies, MTV circulates public service announcements, after shows, study guides, quizzes, and other pedagogical resources to reinforce these prosocial aims. These paratexts present the avoidance of pregnancy as a type of self-empowerment for young women who can no longer rely on state assistance, reinforcing neoliberal norms of personal responsibility and self-sufficiency. While profoundly contradictory, MTV's attempt to market delayed parenting succeeds in presenting this goal as a desire for autonomy and empowerment to be shared by female audiences.

LOOK DIFFERENT?

At a juncture when affirmative action policies are contested, the work of social movements is claimed to be already accomplished, and the state has retreated from public life, MTV's Look Different campaign calls out racism, sexism and homophobia, and calls on the MTV brand community to address these problems. As with all prosocial initiatives, nonprofit agencies and advocacy organizations—including the Gay and Lesbian Association Against Defamation (GLAAD) and the Southern Poverty Law Center—lend ethical legitimacy and guidance as formal partners. While the campaign has many progressive dimensions, it tends to downplay the structural causes of inequality and discrimination (including neoliberal policies), promoting change as a matter of increased personal awareness and behavior modification. For example, tie-in episodes of *Girl Code*, *True Life*, and other series and special programming like the documentary *White People* expose everyday gender, sexual, and racial privileges as well as bias. But these one-off, singular interventions constitute only a small percentage of the network's programming. MTV's designated YouTube channel features a series of short videos on critical concepts like intersectionality—but this material is relegated to digital sphere. MTV also directs viewers to the Look Different website, where they can learn more about discrimination and take interactive, seven-day "cleanses" via a series of email prompts that provide daily tasks, exercises and tools to "chip away at your biases." These prompts direct the possibility for political change inward, asking users to recognize hidden racial, gender, and LGBT bias in themselves, without making structural demands on society (such as a redistribution of resources or policy changes). On Day 3, for example, the cleanse attempts to reduce sexist ideas about women and science, advising cleansers to set an image of a black female scientist as their phone background to "reprogram our minds to build new associations that are different from stereotypes we may automatically hold." While following the anti-bias cleanse (and tweeting about it as MTV suggests) may be valuable, it casts sexism, racism, and heterosexism as personal problems that can be solved at the individual level, rather than structural inequalities and systemically uneven power dynamics in which corporations like MTV are implicated (Kraszewski 2009).

While MTV encourages respect for women, people of color, and LGBTQ communities through its Look Different campaign, its "regular" programming remains disproportionately white and saturated with sexual objectification, class othering, and racial disrespect. From *Buckwild*, a reality show about the antics of redneck hillbillies, to the bikini-clad hot tub culture featured on *The Real World*, MTV tries to have it both ways in service of its commercial purposes. Writing in the *Washington Post*, journalist Soraya

FIGURE 14.1 *MTV's Look Different campaign and its support for "bias cleanses" underwrite the channel's claims to social responsibility.*

Nadia McDonald (2015) juxtaposed the Look Different campaign's claim to "educate people about bias based on race, gender, and sexuality" as a way to eradicate it, and the persistent cultural privileges and inequalities underpinning the 2015 Video Music Awards—MTV's signature annual production. At the VMAs, Miley Cyrus "tumbled from one . . . unnecessary racialized gambit to the next," including referring to Snoop Dogg as her "mammy," appropriating aspects of black culture, and using black men as "props" in ways that played into stereotypes. If MTV wants "so badly for the world to Look Different, shouldn't it start with its own show?" McDonald questioned. If prosocial campaigns lend ethical value to MTV as a brand of television, they have not yet overridden tried-and-true approaches to profit maximization that trade on the commodification of stereotypes. In fact, they work in concert, with prosocial campaigns providing individual solutions to the structural inequalities in which MTV participates at an industrial level.

Look Different raises questions about branded governance and the limits of private action as a solution to inequality. When the public interest gives way to cause-oriented, ethical campaigns carried out by "responsible" corporations, the role of the polity is subsumed by private authority, and citizenship is constituted as self-regulation within a profit-generating brand community. Prosocial television is not a cynical corporate ruse, but a consequence of the wider conflation of the market and society under neoliberalism. MTV operates at the forefront of this transformation.

REFERENCES

Ang, Ien. 1987. "The Viccitudes of Progressive Television." *New Formations* 2: 91–106.

Ang, Ien. 1991. *Desperately Seeking the Audience.* New York: Routledge.

Arvidsson, Adam. 2005. *Brands: Meaning and Value in Media Culture*. New York: Routledge.

Balnaves, Mark and Tom O'Regan. 2002. "Governing Audiences." In *Mobilising the Audience*, edited by Mark Balnaves, Tom O'Regan and Jason Sternberg, 10–28. Queensland: University of Queensland Press.

Banet-Weiser, Sarah. 2007. *Kids Rule! Nickelodeon and Consumer Citizenship*. Durham: Duke University Press.

Barry, Andrew. 2004. "Ethical Capitalism." In *Global Governmentality: Governing International Spaces*, edited by Wendy Larner and William Walters, 195–211. London: Sage.

Boltanski, Luc and Eve Chiapello. 2007. *The New Spirit of Capitalism*. London: Verso.

Brown, Wendy. 1995. *States of Injury: Power and Freedom in Late Modernity*. Princeton: Princeton University Press.

Dishman, Lydia. 2013. "Before and After: How MTV Gave One Nonprofit a Makeover and Got Schooled in Social Storytelling." *Fast Company*, May 23. www.fastcompany.com/1683031/before-and-after-how-mtv-gave-one-nonprofit-a-makeover-and-got-schooled-in-social-storytelli.

Foucault, Michel. 1991. "Governmentality." In *The Foucault Effect: Studies in Governmentality*, edited by Graham Burchell, Colin Gordon and Peter Miller, 87–104. Chicago: University of Chicago Press.

Goodwin, Andrew. 1992. *Dancing in the Distraction Factory: Music Television and Popular Culture*. Minneapolis: University of Minnesota Press.

Green, Ronald Walter and David Breshears. 2010. "Biopolitical Media: Population, Communications International, and the Governing of Reproductive Health." In *Governing the Female Body: Gender, Health and Networks of Power*, edited by Lori Reed and Paula Saukko, 186–205. Buffalo: SUNY Press.

Kraszewski, Jon. 2009. "Country Hicks and Urban Cliques: Mediating Race, Reality, and Liberalism on MTV's the Real World." In *Reality TV: Remaking Television Culture*, edited by Susan Murray and Laurie Ouellette, 205–22. New York: New York University Press.

Lury, Celia. 2004. *Brands: The Logos of the Global Economy*. London: Routledge.

McDonald, Soraya Nadia. 2015. "MTV, Racial Consciousness, and the Limits of Corporate Social Responsibility." *Washington Post*, August 31. www.washingtonpost.com/news/arts-and-entertainment/wp/2015/08/31/mtv-racial-consciousness-and-the-limits-of-corporate-social-responsibility/?utm_term=.dbd7c376b462.

"Merchants of Cool." 2001. *Frontline*. Boston: WGBH-TV.

Miller, Toby. 1993. *The Well-Tempered Self: Citizenship, Culture and the Postmodern Subject*. Baltimore: Johns Hopkins University Press.

"MTV's Look Different Campaign." 2016. *Shorty Awards*. http://shortyawards.com/1st-social good/mtvs-look-different.

Ouellette, Laurie. 2002. *Viewers Like You? How Public TV Failed the People*. New York: Columbia University Press.

Ouellette, Laurie. 2012. "Citizen Brand: ABC and the Do Good Turn in US Television." In *Commodity Activism: Cultural Resistance in Neoliberal Times*, edited by Roopali Mukherjee and Sarah Banet-Weiser, 57–75. New York: New York University Press.

Ouellette, Laurie. 2015. "True Life: The Voice of Television Documentary." In *Contemporary Documentary*, edited by Daniel Marcus and Selmin Kara, 107–23. New York: Routledge.

Rose, Nikolas. 1996. "Governing 'Advanced' Liberal Democracies." In *Foucault and Political Reason: Liberalism, Neoliberalism and Rationalities of Government*, edited by Andrew Berry, Thomas Osbourne and Nikolas Rose, 37–64. Chicago: University of Chicago Press.

Thaler, Richard and Cass R. Sunstein. 2009. *Nudge: Improving Decisions about Health, Wealth and Happiness.* New York: Penguin.

Turow, Joseph. 1997. *Breaking Up America: Advertisers and the New Media World.* Chicago: University of Chicago Press.

Vogel, David. 2006. *The Market for Virtue: The Potential and Limits of Corporate Social Responsibility.* Washington, DC: Brookings Institute Press.

A&E

From Art to Vice in the Managed Channel Portfolio

David Craig and Derek Johnson

In the wake of Donald Trump's victory in the 2016 US presidential election, media trade paper *The Hollywood Reporter* inquired whether television programming too would pivot towards the conservative, embracing the irresistible pun to ask "Are We Telling the Right Stories?" (Rose 2016). If the nation's politics had shifted to the right, with conservatives succeeding in part from appeals to white male voters in more rural areas, perhaps this signaled too the market potential in catering to viewer tastes outside of the more socially liberal urban-minded professional audience (Becker 2006) long perceived to dominate industry marketing priorities. Not all television services were behind the curve, however, in thinking about the value of these appeals, and in this moment channels that might have been previously considered lowbrow could offer new guidance and wisdom. Asked to reflect on her channel's long-standing effort to program to rural, white, uneducated male demographics, A&E CEO Nancy Dubuc claimed,

> people in the entertainment community have put their noses up at the kind of programming that we do. Maybe they would be better served by paying a little more attention to actually watching and understanding the stories that we're telling.
>
> (Rose 2016)

Perhaps no other series affirms this better than A&E's highly rated reality series *Duck Dynasty* (2012–2017). The series features a family of backwoods, Louisiana-based, camouflage wearing, Bible-toting entrepreneurs who made their fortune selling duck calling and hunting paraphernalia. The series has also come under criticism for the patriarch's homophobic and transphobic (France 2016; Ford 2013) comments in affirmation of the family's conservative and evangelical beliefs. Described by *Rolling Stone* as "the worst television series of all time" (Sheffield 2016), the series distances A&E from the discourses of "quality" sought by many other cable outlets. Still airing consistently in reruns on the channel even after its series conclusion, *Duck Dynasty* is only one of several rural and/or working-class reality series that A&E has recently offered, including *American Hoggers* (2011–13), *Cajun Justice* (2012), *Country Bucks* (2014–2015), *Hoarders* (2009–2013, 2016–), and *Live PD* (2016–). In a television industry reconsidering the value of rural, conservative viewers, A&E offered a potential model for other channels to emulate.

Ironically, such accounts of A&E's programming strategies and its credibility outside of the more liberal worldviews typically associated with the entertainment industry operate in some contrast to the channel's initial audience composition and core programming. When the cable channel launched in 1984, it adopted the label the "Arts and Entertainment" Network. As the merger of two early failed cable arts networks, the network's programming featured high arts (dance, painting, opera, symphonies) and acquired documentary, mostly historical, programming. This programming included a decade-long partnership with the BBC and posed direct competition for PBS' acquisitions and co-productions with UK public broadcasters. Within a few years, the network was producing original documentary series and specials, most notably the critically acclaimed series *Biography* (1987–2006), as well as crime-themed documentary series like *City Confidential* (1998–2005). In this light, A&E's recent notoriety as a cable channel more concerned with populist reality television genres and conservative tastes represents not just a market distinction, but also a transformation in channel identity over several decades.

It may be tempting to read this shift in the terms suggested by *Hollywood Reporter*—as a push-and-pull between different demographics, a zero-sum game where television channels switch focus dramatically to pursue the "right" audience with more value. However, the complex history of A&E reveals a creative and strategic process of media management characterized less by major breaks and more an expansion via growing multiplicity of tastes, demographics, and ideologies across a range of subsidiary channel outlets and services. These management practices help us account for the network's seemingly bipolar and highly iterative programming evolution, while also speaking to its polymorphous evolution into multiple networks across multiple platforms.

Although A&E may have started as a single channel on the cable systems that carried it, the channel has since morphed into A+E Television Networks, a multinetwork and multiplatform media brand including channels like History, Lifetime, and, most recently, Viceland. In addition, the company has partnered aggressively with networks and/or partners in 85 countries across more than 90 global channels while also launching a vertically integrated program production system with the launch of A&E Studios. So while the flagship A&E channel may currently prioritize lucrative reality TV entertainment and the ideologies of white rural conservatism, it has never truly abandoned its initial investment in highbrow claims to arts, history, and culture that it fostered along the way. Instead, it repurposes them across its channel portfolio. In this evolution from channel to multi-channel, A&E has invested in a multiplicity of ideologies and taste cultures simultaneously. A&E's recent interest in rural, conservative viewers is not evidence of the primacy of that market so much as its inclusion in a wider, multi-ideological strategy of media channel management.

MANAGING A&E

In the entertainment industries, the idea of management can encompass many different labor roles and types of practices. Johnson, Kompare, and Santo discuss media management broadly in terms of "a culture of shifting discourses, dispositions, and tactics that create meaning, generate value, organize, or otherwise shape media work throughout each moment of production and consumption" (2014, 2). In this chapter, we focus on how the management of A&E as a channel depends on larger structural and cultural conditions that rework and delimit its identities, programming priorities, as well as articulations to specific audiences and taste cultures. As with many other cable networks, the management of A&E has unfolded in pursuit of maximizing the channel's ability to weather persistent disruption from digitization in a multi-channel, post-network era. For A&E, as we will see, the management of that industrial transformation has required the channel to adapt and evolve beyond a single service or market into something that can generate value across a range of different brands, platforms, and experiences. Management, in this sense, is the process of imagining and driving change in what A&E is and how it is perceived to have value at any one point in time.

Thinking about management means considering the human agents behind this process of building, maintaining, and rebuilding value. This can involve attention to specific network executives and other agents of management, analyzing the "roles, opportunities, and constraints" that such creative industry managers face in the course of their work, as Amanda Lotz (2014, 38) suggests. At the same time, an interest in management demands that we consider the priorities, strategies, and interactions of the corporations for which these managers work. It is typical for cable channels to be managed in service of the needs of major media conglomerates that launch and acquire them to provide programming for their cable delivery services, with ownership sometimes changing hands frequently. Across most of its long history, however, A&E could be distinguished by a relatively stable and highly profitable joint ownership across the Disney-ABC, Comcast-NBC-Universal, and Hearst media empires. Only relatively recently in 2012 did the Comcast-NBC-Universal television group sell its stake back to its partners for $3 billion (Andreeva 2012). Each of these three conglomerates has, in their respective histories, experienced volatile shifts in ownership and management, including an emphasis towards vertical and horizontal integration across multiple media industries. However, the nature of the joint venture has inured the network from the same kind of volatile changes in personnel and strategy witnessed by each conglomerate's wholly owned television outlets. Given the need for coordination, communication, and consensus across the strategic interests of multiple stakeholders, the network has been led by only three CEOs and a handful of programming executives across more than three decades. Depending on perspective, the network's management practices either affirm a multilateral culture of leadership or reflect a more irrational approach that places a premium on interpersonal relationships and collaborative dispositions.

Nevertheless, despite this continuity of managerial labor, A&E's evolution as a channel has been more dramatic, perhaps, than another other cable service. Across programming content, audience demographics, and the ideological values ascribed to both, the management of A&E has depended on an embrace of multiplicity as a means of adapting to industry change. Whether in its attempts to launch spin-off channels or its willingness to match its original emphasis on "arts and entertainment" with more lowbrow appeals, A&E has positioned itself to take advantage of multiple and diverse emerging media markets.

BALANCING ARTS AND ENTERTAINMENT

Launched in February 1984, The Arts and Entertainment Channel was a joint venture compiled from the detritus of two arts-themed cable networks, Hearst/ABC-owned Alpha Repertory Television Service and the RCA/NBC-owned Entertainment Channel. Building on what Newman and Levine (2011) refer to as discourses of distinction and legitimacy, RCA executive Herbert Schlosser claimed that "the newly launched Arts & Entertainment Network is basic cable's last shot at gaining a niche culture and high quality specialized programming" (Crook 1984, 156). The network's management strategy, however, centered on "an expansion of the service's concept from a narrow definition of 'highbrow' fare—restricted largely to the performing and visual arts—to a broad program mix with the emphasis on entertainment" (Knoll 1984, H26). This new framing juxtaposed arts to the value of entertainment in ensuring greater sustainability. In addition to guaranteed placement on major cable systems, the inheritance A&E received from the previous Hearst and RCA channels included an archive of inexpensive arts content plus an exclusive deal for programming from British Broadcasting Corporation (BBC). The latter strategy would position the network as a direct competitor against underfunded PBS, not only for programming but also managerial expertise. A&E's first head of programming, Curtis Davis, had spent a decade at public TV's old NET production center in New York (O'Connor 1985, H25).

In its first few years, A&E avoided the failure of earlier arts networks by quickly diffusing arts with entertainment. By 1985, the channel had secured syndication deals for former broadcast network programming, including NBC sitcoms *The United States* (1980) and *Buffalo Bill* (1983–1984), as well as a ten-part CBS miniseries about Ben Franklin. Industry analysts read these acquisitions against prior reliance on BBC programming as "a way for A&E to Americanize its line-up and broaden its concept of quality alternative programming" (DiMatteo 1985, 26). Expanding into more populist genres, A&E's first forays into original content production included stand-up comedy series like *Evening at the Improv* (1982–1996) and crime series like *Investigative Reports* (1991–2011) (Goldman 1988, 15). Marketing and branding strategies in trade publications further telegraphed A&E's ambitions to the industry. "A&E only shows opera, ballet and theatrical performances, right?" one three-page advertisement in the trade paper *CableVision* asked. "Wrong . . . A&E brings home more premiers than HBO . . . carries a tune better than MTV . . . entertains the family better than CBN, 'The Family Entertainer'" ("A&E" 1986, 24–7).

This dual arts/entertainment identity presented challenges and even schism within the management of the channel. By the late 1980s, programming chief Peter Hansen mused that despite interest in building higher ratings, "we're not going to become total slaves to numbers. If we were, we would abandon performing arts altogether. This is a part of what we are" (Taylor 1987, Calendar 6.1). Even as entertainment was used to manage the commercial value of arts programming, A&E tried to quantify its arts commitment, claiming that 45% of the network was "cultural" based on its anthropological, historical, and performing arts programs (Walley 1993a).

Throughout the 1990s, then, A&E continued to seek a balance in its dual high-low programming strategy. A&E renewed its partnerships with the BBC, claiming that "BBC co-productions have served as the 'cornerstone' of programming with the network" (Toumarkine 1991). In 1996, this continuity of strategy would deliver impressive ratings, critical praise, and industry recognition for *Pride and Prejudice*, sold to audiences and Emmy voters as an A&E co-production with the BBC. Along with British cultural heritage programming, a mythic, culturally authorized past would remain a fixture of the channel's programming strategy with its successful *Biography* series, tracing the life stories of historical figures every Monday through Friday at 8 p.m. Yet the most populist and profitable strategy was A&E's acquisition of the off-network rights to the NBC procedural *Law & Order* (1990–2010). A&E paid $180,000 per episode to syndicator MCA-TV (modest in syndication terms but three times more than A&E had ever paid before), and the series would become a massive ratings hit on cable (while also helping to increase the ongoing ratings on NBC). According to MCA's Shelly Schwab, "This puts A&E on a new plateau. The message is that they are now at the same level as several other cable networks in bidding for mainline product" (Walley and Tyrer 1994, 3).

CANNIBALIZATION IN THE MULTI-CHANNEL PORTFOLIO

Throughout the 1990s, A&E faced increasing competition from channels like Bravo that offered their own performing arts programming, which called into question the value of trying to keep a foot on base in that genre even as it pursued mainline entertainment. The multiplication of A&E from a single channel into a portfolio of distinct channels thus helped resolve its dual identity while maintaining its multiple investments across different markets and taste cultures. In 1994, A&E launched the History Channel (then HTV), capitalizing on its existing library of historic and military-themed documentary programming (Walley 1993b, 36). In 1999, A&E launched two additional services: The Biography Channel carved out a dedicated space for the vast *Biography* library (and similar acquired programming) while History Channel International offered a uniquely global spin on historical programming. While *Biography* remained a staple of the original A&E schedule for some time, this multiplication of services allowed the A&E flagship to surrender to other parts of the channel portfolio the genres that did not fit with its continued evolution toward entertainment. In other words, building from a single channel into a portfolio was part of a cannibalistic process of generic management that provided new channel space for programming in which the multi-channel network maintained long-term investment, even as non-"entertainment" genres fell by the wayside on A&E.

Yet by the early 2000s, growth in ratings and returns to investors took a dramatic downturn. A decade of efforts to carve out managed spaces of specialization across the channel portfolio had the unintended effect of exacerbating the audience fragmentation that had already made for fierce competition in cable television. Further weakening the channel's claim to mainline entertainment was its refusal to renew its *Law & Order* deal at significantly higher costs. By October of 2002, A&E ratings dropped almost 30% from their 2000 peak, with many of those lost viewers following *Law & Order* to cable competitor TNT. These losses led to rare upheaval in the executive ranks, with the replacement of the network's general manager, head of programming, and head of marketing (Umstead and Forkan 2002, 1).

In response, A&E made one last effort to reinvest in its potential as a highbrow cultural destination, hiring veteran network and cable programmer Allen Sabinson (Higgins 2000). Having helped Showtime and TNT become destination viewing in the cable market, Sabinson had a reputation for supporting critically acclaimed and highly rated programming, particularly in original television movies. Consequently, A&E's programming shifted to tony original dramas, including filmmaker Sidney Lumet's return to television after a half century. Legal drama *100 Centre Street* (2001–2002) was hailed for giving A&E "instant prestige" (Pennington 2001). The network also launched the period detective drama *A Nero Wolfe Mystery* (2001–2002), based on the classic series by Rex Stout. Within two years, however, both series were cancelled and Sabinson was out. Acknowledging the challenges of balancing high/low appeals in this multi-channel moment, CEO Nick Davatzes acknowledged "we cannibalized ourselves" before retiring and handing control over to Abbe Raven (Dempsey 2002).

FROM ART TO VICE

While Raven had impressively risen the ranks from Davatzes's secretary to general manager, her long history with the network did not determine her programming strategies. Raven quickly installed a team of executives expert in tapping into audiences' interest in reality programming. As head of "alternative programming." Senior Vice President Nancy Dubuc launched series about bounty hunters (*Dog the Bounty Hunter*, 2004–2012), mafia families (*Growing Up Gotti*, 2004–2005), rock star families (*Gene Simmons Family Jewels*, 2006–2012), goth magicians (*Criss Angel: Mindfreak*, 2005–2010), tattoo artists (*Inked*, 2005–2006), and addicts (*Intervention*, 2005–)—converting the network from arts and entertainment into the entertainment of everyday life, often in ways perceived as voyeuristic and salacious. By 2008, Dubuc took charge of programming for History, too, where she equally applied these strategies. As industry veteran J.M. Pressley lamented,

> History Channel abandons history in favor of ratings. . . . Under her watch, A&E went from featuring a mix of fine arts, documentaries, and original literary screen adaptations to a pastiche of reality series shamelessly pandering to the lowest common denominator . . . A&E by the end of Ms. Dubuc's tenure had utterly devolved into a jaded reality freak show on parade. . . . History will be another A&E within the next few years.
>
> (Pressley 2008)

While perhaps overstating A&E's prior focus on the highbrow, this critique identifies other channels like History as a long-time means of preserving some legacy cultural programing on the margins of the channel portfolio. Yet against the diversity of this channel multiplicity loomed fear about entertainment creep and the end of arts, history, and the like.

This shift in A&E's programming formats and content was accompanied by growing appeals to the socially and culturally conservative market that had been underserved by prior determination to use "quality" programming as a means of securing younger, upscale, urban viewers. The top-rated A&E series *Duck Dynasty* illustrates this dynamic—particularly in the controversy surrounding remarks that on-screen patriarch Phil Robertson made about the "sin" of "homosexual behavior" in a December 2013 *GQ* interview prior to the fifth season premiere. When these remarks went public, A&E suspended Robertson from the series, declaring the incompatibility of his words with the network's corporate commitment to "unity, tolerance and acceptance among all people" (Ford 2013). Yet for media analysts like Porter Bibb, this controversy represented a "win-win" scenario for A&E: while the channel could distance itself from Robertson and claim prosocial corporate enlightenment, the temporary nature of the suspension would allow continued production of a valuable reality franchise and affirm the industrial value of socially conservative politics (Fixmer 2013). With the series attracting 14.6 million viewers per episode and generating $480 million in combined advertising and merchandising revenue for A&E, the channel could hardly afford to keep Robertson sidelined (particularly if it meant non-cooperation from the rest of his co-starring family members). Moreover, the inevitable end of the suspension permitted a moral victory of sorts for religious groups who used the controversy as an opportunity to express support for Robertson's socially conservative values in opposition to the presumed corporate liberalism of A&E. Faith2Action, an Ohio-based family values advocacy group, organized a website called MailtheDuck.com to send rubber ducks to A&E in protest. The win-win of the controversy, then, emerges from A&E's opportunity to disavow one ideological premise while seeming to capitulate to consumer demands devoted to another.

A&E has similarly courted regressive political ideologies in its development of *Generation KKK* (2016), a docu-series exploring everyday participants in white supremacist movements. The channel notably worked to disavow any endorsement of the politics being represented. Disclaimers promised that "The following program explores how hatred and prejudice are born and bred in our country." Meanwhile, A&E general manager Rob Sharenow clarified, "We certainly didn't want the show to be seen as a platform for the views of the KKK." He continues, "The only political agency is that we really do stand against hate" (Shattuck 2016). Yet as critic Nick Shrager (2016) countered, the series

> does something worse than just provide a platform for the KKK. It employs the formal format and devices of the channel's other hits (*Hoarders, Intervention*) to transform its bigots into colorful characters, thereby placing them on the same plane as the rest of cable TV's freaky reality stars.

In other words, *Generation KKK* worked to normalize and legitimize white supremacy, making it just another troubling but entertaining and sympathetic part of everyday life.

Duck Dynasty and *Generation KKK* represent extremes in which racist and homophobic ideologies serve a role in the management of A&E's market appeals, where new space is carved out for cultural and ideological sensibilities beyond the highbrow content A&E once promised. Yet while these shifts suggested a reorganization of identity for A&E, the management of the channel portfolio sustained simultaneous interest in the upscale markets, tastes, and ideologies that might seem to be abandoned. By 2017, the network's programming featured critically-acclaimed series about children with Down's Syndrome (*Born This Way*) and former members of Scientology (*Leah Remini: Scientology and the Aftermath*). Nonetheless, after a decade of failed, low performing efforts, the network abandoned its scripted drama series strategy, including planned remakes of mini-series *Roots*, to "return to its roots" in non-fiction programming (Andreeva 2017). These roots, however, referred not to arts or history programming; rather the network refocused on crime-themed programming like *60 Days In* and *Live P.D.*, which, in turn, would compliment another cable channel in the A+E umbrella, Crime and Investigation.

A+E's diverse, if seemingly contradictory, ideological management strategy is reflected in their investment in Viceland. Founded in Montreal in 1994 as a "punk" publication focused on arts, culture, and entertainment, then becoming a cross-platform journalism, film, recording, and publishing imprint, Vice Media entered a deal with A+E Networks in 2015 to create a new Vice television channel (replacing H2, the former History Channel International, in cable lineups). According to the *New York Times*, the deal represented effort to "diversify" the A+E portfolio and help it attract more male viewers as well as younger Millennials while giving Vice better advertising inroads (Ember 2015). Young and urbane, the joint cable venture named Viceland represents, at least on its surface, an antithesis to the worlds of homophobic duck hunting and racist hatemongering that might define the flagship A&E channel in the same cultural and industrial moment. In sum, while A&E specializes in one niche in the television market, A+E has developed a strategy of managed multiplicity across a portfolio of channels to hedge its bets across numerous genres, markets, tastes, and ideologies.

CONCLUSION

A&E continues to pivot, reaching backwards to relaunch venerable and acclaimed series like *Biography* while leaping sideways to make deals with social media platform Snapchat. Meanwhile, it had disavowed decades of efforts in scripted programming to focus more exclusively on "non-fiction series." The shifts have been described as "returning to its roots" (Andreeva 2017), although, as described here, the network's history is one of rhizomatic, managed multiplicity without a singular, unitary form. A&E's volatile management practices and dramatic shifts in programmatic could be seen as strategic attempts to resecure value in a shifting field of competition. Or, they could reveal management in a state of panic in response to ongoing industrial disruption. Or these practices could simply be habitual, like a gambler compulsively placing chips on every number at the roulette table.

While A&E has pursued many markets, tastes, and politics at once, not every one of these has proven to be a perennial focus; in the shuffling of focus across so many different eras and sister channels, some genres like performing arts and history programming have been hybridized, cannibalized, or weeded out in favor of other possibilities with more value to those charged with stewarding the strategic orientation of the channel. One might consider that a process of evolution in which only the strongest programming survives. However, it may be more instructive to consider it as a process of management in which corporate decision makers seek to negotiate shifting industrial conditions and, throughout that practice, shape and reshape the perceived value of the channel and its offerings. As the case of A&E shows, that value is one that can be managed through articulation (Hall and Grossberg 1996, 141)—a process of linking, delinking, and relinking the channel to different cultural formations of genre, taste, and ideology. Articulating art to vice and everything in between, A&E represents the potential for channels to be multiple in their values, unfixed over time and across the portfolios in which they are embedded.

REFERENCES

"A&E Advertisement." 1986. *CableVision*, March 3.

Andreeva, Nellie. 2012. "Comcast-NBCU Selling A&E Networks Stake." *Deadline Hollywood*, May 4. http://deadline.com/2012/05/nbcuniversal-to-sell-stake-in-ae-networks-267150/.

Andreeva, Nellie. 2017. "A&E Doubles Down on Nonfiction, Exits Scripted in Programming Strategy Shift." *Deadline Hollywood*, April 27. http://deadline.com/2017/04/ae-nonfiction-exits-scripted-programming-strategy-shift-1202077488/.

Becker, Ron. 2006. "Gay-Themed Television and the Slumpy Class: The Affordable, Multicultural Politics of the Gay Nineties." *Television & New Media* 7 (2): 184–215.

Crook, David. 1984. "Channels Merge for Cable Arts." *Los Angeles Times*, January 31.

Dempsey, John. 2002. "Raven Flies to Top A&E Post." *Variety*, Oct 22.

DiMatteo, Robert. 1985. "A&E's *United States* an Austere Sitcom." *CableVision*, September 9.

Ember, Sydney. 2015. "Vice Gets Cable Channel in Deal with A&E Networks." *New York Times*, November 3. www.nytimes.com/2015/11/04/business/media/vice-is-said-to-near-cable-channel-deal-with-ae-networks.html.

Fixmer, Andy. 2013. "A&E Ends 'Duck Dynasty' Patriarch Suspension." *Bloomberg News*, December 28. www.wbai.org/articles.php?article=1645.

Ford, Dana. 2013. "'Duck Dynasty' Star Suspended for Anti-Gay Remarks." *CNN*, December 18. www.cnn.com/2013/12/18/showbiz/duck-dynasty-suspension/.

France, Lisa Respers. 2016. "'Duck Dynasty' Star Phil Robertson Faces Transgender Bathroom Backlash." *CNN*, May 10. http://edition.cnn.com/2016/05/10/entertainment/phil-robertson-duck-dynasty-transgender/index.html.

Goldman, Kevin. 1988. "ABC News Making Shows for Cable." *Newsday*, August 16.

Hall, Stuart and Lawrence Grossberg. 1996. "On Postmodernism and Articulation: An Interview with Stuart Hall." In *Stuart Hall: Critical Dialogues in Cultural Studies*, edited by David Morley and Kuan-Hsing Chen, 131–50. New York: Routledge.

Higgins, John M. 2000. "Sabinson Joins A&E." *Broadcasting & Cable*, April 10.

Johnson, Derek, Derek Kompare, and Avi Santo. 2014. "Introduction: Discourses, Dispositions, Tactics: Reconceiving Management in Critical Media Industry Studies." In *Making Media Work: Cultures of Management in the Media Industries*, edited by Derek Johnson, Derek Kompare, and Avi Santo, 1–21. New York: New York University Press.

Knoll, Steve. 1984. "Culture Struggles for Survival." *New York Times*, June 10.

Lotz, Amanda D. 2014. "Building Theories of Creative Industry Managers: Challenges, Perspectives, and Future Directions." In *Making Media Work: Cultures of Management in the Media Industries*, edited by Derek Johnson, Derek Kompare, and Avi Santo, 25–38. New York: New York University Press.

Newman, Michael and Elana Levine. 2011. *Legitimating Television: Media Convergence and Cultural Status*. New York: Routledge.

O'Connor, John J. 1985. "Freud, Warts and All, Sits for the Camera." *New York Times*, January 20.

Pennington, Gail. 2001. "Legendary Director Sidney Lumet Gives New A&E Series Instant Prestige." *St. Louis Post-Dispatch*, January 10.

Pressley, J. M. 2008. "History Channel Abandons History in Favor of Ratings." *JM Pressley*, September 9. www.jmpressley.net/articles/arts/dubuc1.html.

Rose, Lacey. 2016. "TV Networks, Studios Shifting Program Strategies in the Trump Age: 'Are We Telling the Right Stories.'" *Hollywood Reporter*, December 16. www.hollywoodreporter.com/news/tv-networks-studios-shifting-program-strategies-trump-age-are-we-telling-right-stories-956768.

Shattuck, Kathryn. 2016. "Inside the Ku Klux Klan, with an A&E Documentary Series." *New York Times*, December 18. www.nytimes.com/2016/12/18/arts/television/inside-the-ku-klux-klan-with-an-ae-documentary-series.html.

Sheffield, Rob. 2016. "12 Worst TV Shows of All Time." *Rolling Stone*, September 26. www.rollingstone.com/tv/news/12-worst-tv-shows-of-all-time-w441775.

Shrager, Nick. 2016. "'Generation KKK' Is a Disgrace: How A&E's New Reality Show Normalizes White Supremacists." *Daily Beast*, December 21. www.thedailybeast.com/generation-kkk-is-a-disgrace-how-aandes-new-reality-show-normalizes-white-supremacists.

Taylor, Clarke. 1987. "Arts & Entertainment Network in a Party Mood." *Los Angeles Times*, February 6.

Toumarkine, Doris. 1991. "A&E, BBC Ink New 5-Year Accord." *Hollywood Reporter*, September 17.

Umstead, R. Thomas and Jim Forkan. 2002. "A&E, History Swap GMs; Critics Carp: Not Enough." *Multichannel News*, October 28.

Walley, Wayne. 1993a. "Eye on the Ball: A&E's Davatzes Stays Focused on Success." *Electronic Media*, April 19.

Walley, Wayne. 1993b. "Two New History Channels in Works for Cable." *Electronic Media*, April 12.

Walley, Wayne and Thomas Tyrer. 1994. "'Order' Skips Syndication for A&E." *Electronic Media*, January 17.

Spike TV

The Impossibility of Television for Men

Amanda D. Lotz

What does it tell us about men, masculinity, and television in the new millennium that a dominant media conglomerate—arguably one with the most successful record of targeting particular demographic segments with precisely branded content—launched a channel for men in the early years of the twenty-first century, but the targeted "men" didn't show up? Or even more curious and indicative of tension in gender norms, social scripts, and the status of television in culture, what does it tell us that this channel, advertised explicitly as the "first network for men," succeeded in markedly growing its female audience? This was the case of Viacom's rebranding of its vaguely defined existing channel, TNN, as Spike in 2003.

This case study of Viacom's efforts to transform The Nashville Network into The National Network and then into Spike reveals several challenges related to rebranding, specificity in brand creation, and targeted branding "for men." Despite promoting a more focused brand identity, Spike—like many cable channels—filled much of its schedule with programming acquired after it aired on and was designed for a more generally targeted broadcaster. Sometimes this was because of costly and long-term acquisition deals made before a rebranding; sometimes it was just a function of available programming. The challenge of this acquired programming was that it could dilute and even contradict the brand identity the channel sought. Spike also encountered specific problems related to branding itself as a network for men—because men are not monolithic and women are a significant component of the television audience.

Spike "officially" launched in August 2003 after a few months of anticipation following Viacom's announcement that it would rebrand its TNN channel that January. The origin of TNN can be traced back to a March 1983 debut as The Nashville Network, a channel then owned by Opryland USA that began by offering six hours of new country music–focused programming nightly that it then repeated twice more daily ("Buyouts Shuffle" 1986). The channel gradually expanded into what was described as a country "lifestyle channel" throughout the late 1980s, meaning it provided "country" versions of traditional genres such as game shows, sports, and news, but often with a particular focus on service programming (typically programs that provide a lesson of some sort, such as cooking or talk). In an effort to dominate the country niche, The Nashville Network's owner (Opryland/Gaylord) bought a controlling stake and subsequently took over emerging competitor CMT (Country Music Television) in January 1991 and programmed the two networks to complement each other throughout the 1990s. Westinghouse Electric (owner of CBS at the time) purchased The Nashville Network and CMT from Opryland/Gaylord in February 1997, shortly before renaming itself as the CBS Corporation. The Nashville Network was already well established as a cable service by this point and had the eighth most expansive distribution, with over 70 million subscribers ("Gaylord Sells" 1997).

The Nashville Network began changing in late 1999 shortly after the announcement of the intended sale of CBS to Viacom. The channel moved away from its country roots, first dropping the extended name of The Nashville Network to be simply TNN (Rice 2000). Viacom then renamed it The National Network in September 2000. At this point, much of TNN's remaining country programming shifted to CMT so that The National Network could become more of a general entertainment destination. The channel featured the recent Viacom acquisition of WWF wrestling—which had long been the highest-rated weekly basic cable series when airing on general entertainment competitor USA—and the channel sought "to create a balanced programming schedule that will appeal to adults 18 to 49" (Dempsey 2000). In late 2001, The National Network developed a branding strategy featuring the tagline "We Got Pop" to advance its perception as a general entertainment channel, and it added *Baywatch, Star Trek: The Next Generation*, and *MadTV* to its lineup.

Although its country roots were not central to Spike's branding, this industrial history is important. Spike was not a new channel, but emerged from the rebranding of one of the earliest established cable channels, making it broadly available on the most basic tier of most cable services, often with a fairly low channel number.[1] Placing a new channel on cable systems nationwide was difficult in some periods of cable history and such channels were often numbered far from the most watched channels.

In January 2003, Viacom announced Albie Hecht as the new president of TNN and that TNN would become "television's first entertainment network for men" (Dempsey 2003). Hecht pronounced that TNN planned "to do for men what Lifetime has done for women." In reality though, the new name and rebranding campaign simply promoted a gradual evolution that had been developing since the Viacom purchase and the introduction of wrestling.

In between the January announcement of Spike as an "entertainment network for men" and its late summer debut, it evolved—at least it seems in Hecht's mind—into more of a *lifestyle* network for men. Hecht reportedly dumped a pile of men's magazines such as *Maxim* and *FHM* on the desk of his boss, Herb Scannell, in the planning of Spike and proclaimed, "We're going to own this" (Swanson 2003). Significantly, magazines such as these are primarily lifestyle in nature, and while *Maxim* was surging in popularity at the time, the economics of magazines are quite different than cable channels. The lifestyle versus entertainment focus is also significant from an economic perspective because lifestyle fare, with its emphasis on talk and easy incorporation of product placement, tends to be a much cheaper source of content than creating new scripted series or even purchasing previously aired series.

In identifying these magazines as models, Hecht effectively narrowed the target of Spike as a channel for a specific set of men who conformed to the "new lad" masculinity. The construct of the "new lad" emerged in the British magazine market in the mid to late 1990s as titles such as *Loaded, Maxim*, and *FHM* surprised the industry by proving the men's style subgenre was far more profitable than expected. As Imelda Whelehan explains, the new lad was "self-centred, male-identified, leering and obsessed by sport" (2000, 5). But the new lad wasn't simply a reversion to a pre-second-wave masculinity; he was more complicated, often featuring fundamentally sexist perspectives, but "under the shield of irony," which was used to deflect feminist criticism (Whelehan 2000, 5).

But despite these aims, it was difficult to identify Spike as a network for men, let alone new lads. Spike's history is full of complicated negotiations and contradictions that indicate a fair amount of slippage between what the channel claimed to be and what it actually was. Sound bites from the channel's top executives—such as Hecht's desire to be the television version of *Maxim*—suggested a clear sense of what they thought "men" wanted and how Spike should reach them, but for viewers, there seemed little correlation between these branding statements and the channel's actual programming. Regardless of the advisability of designing a channel targeting new lads, the difficulty of finding or affording programming consistent with this brand make it difficult to assert Spike was ever really a network for men.

An average day just after its launch in September 2003 featured syndicated episodes of familiar programs *Baywatch, Miami Vice, The A-Team, Real TV Renewal, Seven Days, Star Trek: The Next Generation, Highlander*, and *Blind Date*. None of this programming was original to Spike and was created to compete in a competitive environment of male and female viewers. At most, Spike aggregated a collection of shows that skewed to male audiences on a single channel. Even in terms of original programming—which is often what channels use to cement their brand identity—Spike initially featured programs purchased before Viacom relaunched as a channel for men. The initial program lineup for Spike consequently was not all that different than it might have been if the channel had stayed branded as TNN.

The most successful new original content during its first year was the reality series *The Joe Schmo Show*, which twisted the then still emerging reality genre by featuring one "contestant" who thought he was part of an unscripted reality competition show while the rest of the cast was populated by actors following a loose script. While clever and innovative, *Joe Schmo* was not particularly consistent with "the first network for men" brand. It wouldn't have been out of place on any generally branded channel, except for constructing misogynistic versions of standard reality show contests, such as "Hands on a High-Priced Hooker," in which the last contestant with a hand on a female stripper earned "immunity" from that episode's voting.[2] Otherwise, Spike was best known during its first year for its wrestling program *WWE: Raw*, which it had aired since 2000 and the channel's days as TNN. In the cases of both *The Joe Schmo Show* and *WWE:*

Raw, the programming that brought most viewers to Spike was not particularly related to its newfound identity as a network for men.

Spike's incumbent programming from its TNN days—mostly series created for broadcast networks—was "successful" in drawing audiences; however, many of these shows contributed little to the rebranding because they weren't particularly identifiable as television for men. The dilemma of having its most successful programming reach an audience not in sync with its brand identity emerged clearly a year after Spike's launch when it began airing daily episodes of the CBS crime drama *CSI*. TNN purchased the series at a pricey $1.6 million per episode in April 2002, well before the rebranding announcement in January 2003, as such sales are typically made two to three years before the programming will begin airing.[3] Spike began airing back-to-back episodes between 7:00 p.m. and 9:00 p.m. Monday through Friday in September 2004, and the program ranked first among all basic cable channels in both adults and males ages 18 to 49 on its first night (Reynolds 2004).

Spike did achieve audience growth and expanded awareness in its first year with the new brand; it increased its prime-time audience by 61% by October 2004 from a year earlier. The problem was what programming and which audience groups accounted for that growth (Vasquez 2004). Year-to-year, Spike achieved a 3% gain in males ages 18–34 and 21% among men ages 18–49. However, the network also achieved a 63% increase in women ages 18–34 and 81% gain among women ages 18–49. Consequently, the channel went from men composing 68% of its audience at launch in August 2003 to 58% by the end of 2004 (Hempel 2005). Low previous viewership among women may have been part of the spectacular jump, but the growth among 18- to 49-year-old women was now enough to rank Spike sixth in prime-time *women's* viewership overall (Vasquez 2004). Unsurprisingly, women weren't tuning in for "television for men" but for *CSI*.

Adding to Spike's challenges was that it tried to build a channel on a particularly narrow subgroup of the male population and one that was widely perceived to be fleeing television at the time. Industry journalist Kevin Downey summed up the situation of Spike as a "bold experiment" for "relaunching as a cable network targeting the very young men who then appeared to be leaving network TV" (2005). According to Downey and the media buyers interviewed for his story on Spike's early stumbles, Spike failed because targeting this narrow demographic of young men required more substantial programming budgets than the channel had available and because—and related—it failed to develop a program that was distinctively emblematic of Spike TV. John Spiropoulos, associate research director of MindShare, explained that

> Strategically, it makes sense to target men within the cable realm. However, tactically it's a nightmare. Cable networks that have been successful attracting men have done so with small programming blocks, like Cartoon Network's Adult Swim and Discovery's Monster Mondays.

Spiropoulos acknowledges the complexity and variation of the male audience relative to the economics of cable programming and advertising. The subgroup of men who support Adult Swim—a block of mature cartoons airing from 11:00 p.m. through

5:00 a.m.—was not a big enough demographic to support an entire channel—much like the case of the new lads Spike sought. However, it also didn't work to combine various blocks of programming targeting different types of men or so-called men's interests into a men's channel, because any particular man still had the unrewarding experience of coming to the channel and, more often than not, finding something that appeals to a different type of man or—in the case of much of Spike—programming that remained from TNN and didn't particularly target men at all.

While the "new lad" focus was a strategic miscalculation, many of Spike's other struggles were familiar to many cable channels. Most channels did not have budgets that could afford the scale of original production that would create programming that matched the brand. Content available for acquisition—the bulk of cable schedules—was designed for the broader target of the original licensors.

Spike consequently quietly pivoted its brand focus from new lads to action programming. Spike lost the contract for its most popular programming World Wrestling Entertainment (WWE) in September 2005 and replaced it with mixed-martial arts competitions (MMA) through a contract with Ultimate Fight Championship (UFC) (Martin 2005). The deal included *The Ultimate Fighter*—a reality competition featuring 16 athletes who compete to win a contract to fight UFC pros, including a UFC event during its finale (Lafayette 2005). Described by one journalist as a "roid-ragin' version of *America's Next Top Model*," *The Ultimate Fighter* series introduced MMA to a more mainstream audience, and the Spike/UFC relationship proved valuable for both entities—bringing Spike its biggest audiences and providing an initial foray for UFC into non-pay television (Press 2006).

After the UFC announcement in early 2005, there was little change at Spike until early 2006 as the channel left most existing programming in place and did not establish much new programming. The core of the schedule remained heavily reliant on old episodes of *CSI*, *Star Trek: The Next Generation*, and *Star Trek: Deep Space Nine*. The *Ultimate Fighter* was the marquee original offering on the channel, which otherwise continued low-budget unscripted fare (both original and acquired) grouped in blocks, such as the "PowerBlock" weekend lineup of shows about vehicles (*Xtreme 4x4, Trucks!, Car and Driver, Horsepower TV*) and "real" video (*Real TV, World's Most Amazing Video, Disorderly Conduct*).

By March 2006, an evolution into Spike 2.0 had transpired. The cursive logo that critics had long noted as incongruent with its intended brand was replaced with tough block letters in chrome. The "first network for men" tagline had disappeared shortly after Spike's launch, but now the network clarified what viewers could expect from the network with a tagline call of "Get More Action." Despite allowances for construing this as a double entendre resonant with the new lad of Spike 1.0, in terms of programming, the network's interpretation seemed decidedly literal. The channel's focus evolved from aiming to be a men's lifestyle channel into a men's action entertainment channel; a "men's" channel at least to the degree that action programming skews toward male audiences and features male protagonists. Spike President Doug Herzog explained, "The network is about testosterone, action and unpretentiousness. And we're unapologetic about all of it. Spike is a place where a guy can be a guy and not feel bad about it" (Martin 2006). But in a strategic shift, such gendered claims were no longer part of promotion. Although a preference for action programming may correlate with gender and certain constructions of masculinity, branding the channel as the place for viewers seeking a particular genre made the channel's identity clearer and eliminated the sense that accomplishments such as increasing women viewers should be considered a failure of branding.

As a site for action, Spike attempted different programming strategies related to this genre and tried to developing original programming rather than relying on acquired series. Most of this programming was themed around sports, adrenaline, or service topics. In terms of sports, Spike stayed clear of the mainstream sports that were the domain of broadcast networks and ESPN, instead continuing to build its lucrative relationship with UFC and adding the non-WWE wrestling program *TNA Impact*. The series *Deadliest Warrior* also debuted strongly for the channel in 2009 and reinforced its action identity with episodes that pit "history's greatest warriors"—such as Gladiator vs. Apache—against each other using contemporary science, experts, and CGI technology. By 2009, Spike's action guy had developed morbid interests—seen most clearly in

FIGURE 16.1 *Transition from the first cursive logo of Spike 1.0 and the new, more generic "action" identity of Spike 2.0.*

the program *1000 Ways to Die* (which reenacted horrific yet unusual deaths, in ways the series' tone suggested were comical), while *Jesse James Is a Deadman* similarly capitalized on adrenaline in its offering of daredevil feats.

Even in the Spike 2.0 era, the center of the channel's scripted programming continued to be airings of *CSI*, which was eventually joined by *CSI: New York*. Spike 2.0 significantly diminished the diversity of its acquired series; in 2008, the channel began a five-year run of *Married . . . With Children* (a series that had completed production over a decade earlier) and *Unsolved Mysteries* (curiously, most recently found on Lifetime, which had been "Television for Women"), and Spike drew attention by purchasing television rights to the *Star Wars* and *Rambo* franchises. Each of these programming acquisitions made some sense on its own: *Unsolved Mysteries* paired well with *CSI*; *Married . . . With Children* offered more of the crass and irreverent aspects of Spike 1.0; and *Star Wars* and *Rambo* broadened beyond the Bond films that were Spike's primary theatrical fare. Nevertheless, only *Rambo* fit the action brand well.

The scheduling strategy Spike developed also helped contain the incongruence of its acquired series. By summer 2009, the channel sometimes aired as many as *nine episodes a day* of the *CSI* series, although seven episodes following a two-hour morning block of *Married . . . With Children* was fairly common Monday through Friday. Although not promoted this way, this effectively made the channel the *CSI* network by weekday, while retaining its identity as Spike at night and during the weekend.[4] Spike strategically emphasized its most brand-relevant programming in the hours it was most likely to reach its audience. Its *CSI*-packed daytime did little to advance its action guy brand, but it proved lucrative by pulling in a broad audience during the hours in which its target audience was less likely to view. Despite Spike's brand struggles, NBCUniversal decided to launch a channel targeted to men as the Esquire Channel in 2013. Drawing on *Esquire*'s magazine brand, it was designed as a men's lifestyle channel aimed at the "modern man," thus far removed from the versions of a men's network that Spike offered.

Spike also emphasized its identity through its Spike.com site during the era before YouTube, Hulu, and Netflix came to dominate Internet-distributed video. The site featured a combination of professional video and amateur postings and came closer to illustrating the breadth of material a "men's network" would require (Mahmud 2008). The site expanded beyond the genre parameters of Spike 2.0's action guy and created a space augmented with an array of "men's" interests. Because users just go to the parts of a website that interest them—instead of the way a channel programs particular content at particular times—Spike.com could simultaneously address a heterogeneity of men. Once YouTube and multi-channel networks began dominating online video aggregation, Spike.com morphed into a more conventional website built around the channel's schedule and content.

Despite its struggles in establishing itself as men's network, Spike was a very successful channel throughout the first decade of the twenty-first century. In April 2008, it was the fourth most-watched cable network among 18- to 49-year-olds (Crupi 2008). The channel's viewer composition was "most male" during *The Ultimate Fighter*, when its gender skew was 75% male (Grayman 2008). That a quarter of its audience was still female suggests the value of a brand that does not exclude audience members with like tastes through demographically specific branding. Its responses of adjusting to a genre-based brand, segmenting its program schedule, and using its web platform to address a range of men's interests significantly assuaged Spike's earlier challenges.

The situation of Spike can also be read in comparison to the situation of the multiple channels for women that developed in the early 2000s. During this time, Lifetime, Oxygen, and WE each built a program identity around a distinctive femininity while proclaiming itself a destination for women (Lotz 2006). Spike's 2.0 action guy isn't all that different from what could be called Lifetime's "melodrama mama" in the sense that the channels targeted a subpopulation of a demographic with a particular aesthetic taste. In the gender-segmented sector, this appeal through genre proved more successful than demo/psychographic appeals—such as Spike's early efforts to reach new lads or the "thinking woman's" fare programmed by Oxygen at its launch.

Spike's story illustrates the distinctive competitive conditions of the first decade of the twenty-first-century US television industry. Before the late 1990s, cable programming was mostly a backwater of series acquired from broadcast networks and old movies, and by 2010 Internet-distributed television radically readjusted industrial norms and introduced yet additional competing program services that utilized the different affordances of Internet distribution. Spike 1.0 might have been more viable if it had emerged as an Internet-distributed service. Without a linear schedule to fill, Internet portals can develop content for more precise tastes—for example, for a monthly fee of $9.99, the WWE Network offers wrestling and programs targeted at audiences interested in wrestling. It doesn't have to buy content to "fill out its schedule," and subscriber funding encourages precise rather than broad content appeal. Spike was certainly not alone in being better suited for the affordances of Internet-distributed television. Just as cable had recalibrated broadcast's mass appeal, by 2016 Internet-distributed services introduced yet new strategies and business models that likewise shifted the programming possibilities of television.

In January 2017, NBCUniversal gave up its attempt at television for men and announced it would shut down the Esquire Network. Less than a month later, Viacom announced the end of Spike, which would be rebranded as the Paramount Network—drawing on the film brand also owned by the Viacom conglomerate. News of Spike's rebranding arrived just a week after NBCUniversal made official the rebranding of female-targeted Oxygen as a crime-focused channel.

In a matter of weeks, three of five gender-branded cable channels left the cable ecosystem. Spike was the most successful of the shuttered channels in terms of number of viewers. All channels—and their few owners—were challenged by the shifting competitive dynamics of television introduced by the arrival of internet-distributed television that allowed on demand access to programs, often supported by subscriber fee rather than advertising. Substantive adjustments in the television marketplace only expanded as content creators shifted to innovating for this new distribution technology. Notably, with the exception of the Lifetime Movie Club—arguably about genre as much as gender—no gender-branded portal had launched by the end of 2017.

NOTES

1 While channel number may seem unimportant today, this was long a very important feature. When audiences faced fewer channels and could reasonably scan through them all, a low number was considered valuable.
2 The game was a variation on the "Hands on a Hardbody" competition common at the time that required contestants to maintain one hand on a vehicle that the last remaining competitor won.
3 Notably, this deal, which involved a series half owned by Viacom-owned CBS, was completed in early 2002 and predated any public announcement of the rebranding of TNN.
4 Spike's prime-time block also typically offered original programming until 1:00 a.m. to capitalize on the heavier viewing of its target demographic in the late-night fringe hours.

REFERENCES

"Buyouts Shuffle 1985 Media Rankings." 1986. *Advertising Age*, June 30.

Crupi, Anthony. 2008. "Spike Rolls Out Tough-Guy Reality Pilots." *Mediaweek*, May 8.

Dempsey, John. 2000. "TNN Goes National: MTV Plans Overhaul for Country Cabler." *Daily Variety*, September 19.

Dempsey, John. 2003. "Hecht Leads TNN's Shift to Dude TV." *Daily Variety*, January 10.

Downey, Kevin. 2005. "For Spike TV, a Bit Less Testosterone." *Media Life*, February 1.

"Gaylord Sells CMT and TNN to Westinghouse." 1997. *Music & Copyright*, February 26.

Grayman, Thomas. 2008. Personal communication. New York, June.

Hempel, Jessi. 2005. "Spike TV's Feminine Side?" *Business Week*, February 21.

Lafayette, Jon. 2005. "Spike TV Still Full of Fight." *Television Week*, March 14.

Lotz, Amanda D. 2006. *Redesigning Women: Television after the Network Era*. Urbana: University of Illinois Press.

Mahmud, Shahnaz. 2008. "Spike.com Relaunches." *Adweek*, May 29.

Martin, Denise. 2005. "Spike TV Smacks WWE." *Daily Variety*, March 11.

Martin, Denise. 2006. "Spike Unveils Macho Makeover." *Variety*, March 14.

Press, Joy. 2006. "Girls vs. Boys: Two Gender-Specific Cable Networks Undergo Extreme Hormone Therapy." *Village Voice*, April 25.

Reynolds, Mike. 2004. "*CSI* Leads Spike TV Surge." *Multichannel News*, September 13.

Rice, Jerry. 2000. "TNN Strengthens Action Muscle, New Action Image?" *Daily Variety*, May 5.

Swanson, Carl. 2003. "Babes, Yes Please: Female Viewers, No." *The New York Times*, June 15.

Vasquez, Diego. 2004. "Macho Spike TV's Quite the Lady's Thing." *Media Life*, November 3.

Whelehan, Imelda. 2000. *Overloaded: Popular Culture and the Future of Feminism*. London: Women's Press Limited.

Comedy Central

Transgressive Femininities and Reaffirmed Masculinities

Nick Marx

"Everyone's talking about feminism. People are getting together, and they're addressing discrimination. Black Lives Matter, transgender activists," laments an angry middle-aged man played by Carrie Brownstein (in drag) in a 2017 episode of *Portlandia*. "What I hate about it is that none of it's about us, none of these movements are about us. I mean, where's our movement?" replies a friend played by Fred Armisen before the duo launch into a song called "What About Men?" On one level, the sketch lampoons responses by men's rights movements and the alt-right to various identity-based political struggles in the 2010s. The song critiques the notion that although men—particularly straight white men—have long held cultural, political, and economic power in the United States, they now feel threatened. The fact that identity-based movements are gaining visibility does little to diminish men's power—certainly not enough to ask for a falsely equivalent "our movement," as Armisen's character ironically implores.

On another level, the *Portlandia* scene gestures to broader shifts in the relationship between gender and comedy for the television industry. It is no accident that the program's network, IFC, ditched its long-time brand (the "Independent Film Channel") in 2010 in order to program hipster comedies like *Portlandia*. In that light, "What About Men" might thus be read as a jab at competitors like Comedy Central with its core viewership of straight white men. Indeed, comedy has long been assumed to be a male/masculine genre, as evidenced by that network's history of male-oriented programs like *South Park*, *Tosh.0*, and of course, *The Man Show*. Comedy Central even commissioned research for advertisers looking to target desirable male viewers which found "[m]ore than music, more than sports, more than 'personal style,' comedy has become essential to how young men view themselves and others" (Carter 2012).

Although it has long exploited (and contributed to) a presumed link between men and comedy—as well as all the social, political, and economic consequences of that link—Comedy Central has recently taken a different tack. With programs like *Inside*

Amy Schumer and *Broad City*, Comedy Central is courting more "diverse" audiences, or at least ones that include female viewers. What's more, it is doing so without alienating the core viewership of straight young white men so important to its brand. We might call Comedy Central's new strategy, as well as its echoes elsewhere on television, a "post-politics" approach to gender and comedy. "Politics" in this sense, then, refers not to party affiliations but to broader discourses that construct and circulate identities such as gender (and also race, class, sexuality, age, and more).

By calling these shows "post" politics, I do not mean to say that gendered discourses no longer matter in assessing the strategies of a channel like Comedy Central—quite the opposite, in fact. Instead, I hope to highlight how gender inequality persists despite the critical power of these programs' humor. In other words, *Inside Amy Schumer* and *Broad City*, among others, strive to satirize televisual representations of gender without positioning any one gendered identity as dominant over another. The progressive and feminist meanings of these shows shift, however, when considering them in the context of Comedy Central's highly gendered distribution and publicity practices. As I explore in this chapter, these practices include an emphasis on multiscreen and mobile media viewing (behaviors the channel associates with male audiences), as well as discursive strategies from executives and journalists that reinscribe gendered hierarchies. Despite the progressive, feminist representational impulses of Comedy Central shows, the industrial practices surrounding them still have the effect of reaffirming the power of its already powerful core audience: men.

COMEDY CENTRAL AND THE COMPETITION FOR COMEDY ON CABLE

After Time Warner and Viacom merged their competing comedy outlets and relaunched as Comedy Central in 1991, the fledgling network—like many of its cable contemporaries—relied on inexpensive syndicated fare while experimenting with a strange brew of clip shows, stand-up specials, game shows, and formally adventurous originals (Boone 2012; Mullen 2003). Although it would have modestly successful multiseason runs with some of these programs, Comedy Central's major hits arrived later that decade with *The Daily Show* and *South Park*, the two flagship shows that prop up the network's brand identity to this day. Over the following two decades, these programs bolstered Comedy Central's brand identity as a home for contentious comedy about everything from gender roles to presidential elections.

The most significant industrial function of these early shows for Comedy Central, though, was their ability to court and foster intense loyalty in young, tech-savvy male viewers. Comedy Central has used the regular viewership of *The Daily Show* and *South Park* as a promotional mechanism in launching and scheduling new programs. After the taxing production schedule of *South Park* drove creators Trey Parker and Matt Stone to half season orders every fall and spring, for instance, Comedy Central filled its vacated Wednesday timeslot with the second season of *Tosh.0* in 2010. The program has become the network's new flagship for the contemporary moment of convergence between television and digital media. Moreover, *Tosh.0* regularly rates highest for its telecast night among cable viewers 18-to-49 and excels at attracting men aged 18-to-24 (Gelt 2013). In 2011 Comedy Central, in order to celebrate its twentieth birthday, began what it hoped would be an annual Comedy Awards show. One profile of the event notes both the legacy of *South Park* and *The Daily Show* and quotes a Viacom executive describing *Tosh.0* as "the template for future success stories" due to its multiplatform engagement with young men (Stelter 2011).

Both The Comedy Awards and *Tosh.0*'s emergence as Comedy Central's top program came on the heels of a 2011 rebrand for the network. Publicity discourses for the rebrand reiterated the importance of multiplatform content to be viewed, shared, and commented on by viewers who were either explicitly depicted or implicitly constructed as straight young men. One promotional video, for instance, highlights Comedy Central's new logo and design by depicting men swiping and clicking Comedy Central content on smartphones, computer screens, and tablets (Keegan n.d.; Sloan 2011). These male viewers access clips focused on bawdy bodily humor: *South Park*'s Randy Marsh microwaving his genitals, Jon Stewart mockingly exclaiming "sex with ladies in their vaginas!," and rapidly scrolling text beside the new logo declaring, somewhat perplexingly, "SHIT. BALLS. COMEDY." In addition to these depictions of male viewers and male-oriented humor, commentary from network and advertising executives about the rebrand reiterated the importance of television content being "screen agnostic," able to be accessed and shared across media platforms (Sloan 2011). These publicity discourses construct a presumed young male viewer of television comedy, one whose attention channels in the post-network era seek to seize and retain in multiscreen viewing environments through the use of provocative sexual and/or racial humor (Sienkiewicz and Marx 2014). Of course, Comedy Central had implemented this strategy long before the contemporary convergence era through incendiary characters such as *South Park*'s Eric Cartman. But by early 2011, Comedy Central had (re)declared itself a television and online home for young male consumers of humor, one evolving both in programming and distribution to align with the ribald and high-tech habitus of this demographic perceived to hold high value.

By the end of 2011, Comedy Central routinely promoted itself as the top non-sports cable network among men 18–34 and 18–24 (Gorman 2011). At around the same time, though, Comedy Central saw a surge in competition from cable networks looking to court young men by programming contentious comedy and bolstering their digital presences. These strategies were part of a broader move among many cable networks in the early 2010s away from "content" (fact-based programming like documentaries) toward "entertainment" programming to compete for young male viewers (Hamilton 2011). History, for instance, rebranded in order to move away from historical documentaries toward blue-collar reality shows like *Pawn Stars* and *American Pickers*. In the comedy realm, TBS increased its original comedic programming by building around *Conan* in 2010, IFC shifted its focus to "alternative" comedy programming that same year, and FXX launched in 2013 as a comedy-focused addition to the FOX family of cable outlets. By 2014, even the prestige drama network AMC and the general interest website Yahoo! developed or added comedies, with the latter resurrecting *Community*, the canceled NBC sitcom with an intensely loyal online following. As the cable and digital landscapes became more cluttered in the early 2010s, then, networks increasingly viewed comedy as a way both to stand out from the pack and to attract young male viewers.

By the end of 2012, Comedy Central's corner on the comedy market was under siege from multiple cable competitors. The nightly average of the network's total prime-time audience had fallen more than 25% from 2008 (Chozik 2013), a trend that prompted parent company Viacom to increase the amount of ad time on Comedy Central by 9% (Vranica and Jannarone 2012). Despite ongoing efforts to extend its presence into off-screen ventures like merchandising and live tours, Comedy Central also struggled to develop new programming for its linear cable channel. Comedic talent began bringing television projects to competitors like *Adult Swim*, bypassing Comedy Central due to its growing "reputation as perhaps the most professionally thoughtless and creatively obtuse operation in the business" (Morgan 2012). In the midst of this malaise, Comedy Central made two management changes that highlight the relationship between gendered identities and multiplatform viewing as ongoing foci for comedy outlets in the post-network era.

The network first brought in Brooke Posch, the female executive who would develop *Inside Amy Schumer* and take *Broad City* from web series to television hit. Second, Comedy Central consolidated both digital and television program development under Kent Alterman, then elevated the creatively-inclined executive to network president in 2016. Although press coverage indicates no direct correlation between Comedy Central's early 2010s stagnation and the management changes, it is rife with what John Caldwell, in his study of television production culture, calls "aesthetic status metaphors," or canned responses designed to highlight executives' abilities and trigger "favored cultural and psychological associations" among industry brethren (2007, 205).

In a deft bit of industrial maneuvering, Alterman routinely "performs" his executive role comedically for press, but always in a way that effaces his authority in an effort to subvert gender expectations. Of Posch's promotion as his second-in-command in 2014, for instance, Alterman quips that he's "just grateful [Posch]'s letting me be her boss" (Andreeva 2014). Of Allison Kingsley's promotion to head of the digital studio, Alterman wryly concedes, "Allison uses techy words I don't understand, so I know she's the right person for the job" (O'Connell 2013). Profiles of the executive repeatedly emphasize his sense of humor, implicitly legitimating his decisions both on-screen and off: "Spend time with Kent Alterman, and one can forget that he is not a comedian who appears on Comedy Central shows but rather the executive who programs them" (Rose 2013). These managerial moves, and the press discourses about them, also highlight how executive personnel at Comedy Central are involved in the construction of gendered discourses seeking to differentiate the network from all its male-oriented competitors. Clearly, Alterman's deflection of authority is meant to assign creative and managerial agency to the women working beneath him. However, it does so in a way that draws attention to his comedic and, in some regard, more important executive voice than the managerial moves on which he is commenting. It is meant to be funny, for instance, that Brooke Posch would be Alterman's boss, and that Allison Kingsley "uses techy words," because both are unexpected inversions of gender norms in the television industry. Despite his progressive intentions, Alterman's lauding of his female colleagues underscores the extent to which men remain the presumed norm both as executives and as on-screen talent in the world of television comedy.

Aesthetic status metaphors centered on gender pervade press about *Inside Amy Schumer* and *Broad City*, too. As I explore in this chapter, incendiary humor from the perspective of women provide the basis for much of the programs' comedy. Although I do not wish to suggest that these shows' stars consciously follow a mandate from executives to engage debates about representation in a post-politics way, I do wish to highlight how the programs' reflexive humor serves Comedy Central's expanded brand identity without alienating its core audience. The channel touts the many transgressions of its contentious comedies, as well as the diversity of its talent and audience, to contrast itself with the predominantly male makeup of cable competitors. Comedy Central's promotion and distribution strategies, however, ultimately constrain those transgressions, tethering them to the tastes of young men.

"A SORT OF FEMINIST BENT ON A MALE-SKEWING NETWORK"

In order to address the implications of Comedy Central's promotion and distribution of humor from female comedians, a formal analysis of its programming must be integrated with a deeper understanding of the industrial discourses described earlier. Such dialogue between television economics and textual representations avoids characterizations of comedic programs as unified, coherent commodities, and accounts for their processual, polysemic meanings. In other words, the key to understanding Comedy Central's move to a post-politics treatment of gender is to analyze closely both its programs and their industrial contexts. Reading *Broad City* and *Inside Amy Schumer* solely as products of the network's rebrand neglects their potential for transgressive meanings that might undermine Comedy Central's economic strategy. In the same way, celebrating the programs as transgressive purely based on their comedic critiques ignores the extent to which *Broad City* and *Inside Amy Schumer* circulate as profit-seeking consumer products. The clearest picture of the significance of Comedy Central and its programs emerges only when we see their cultural and industrial contexts as mutually constitutive.

In this way, we can see how Comedy Central shows function as "programme brands" that "invite multiplicity, not just in their formal construction (for example, being made up of multiple segments that can be unbundled and/or transferred onto other products), but also in their address to viewers" (Johnson 2012, 165). One way in which many of the programs discussed below "invite multiplicity," for instance, is their use of the sketch format, structuring their humor around short vignettes with myriad cultural and industrial functions. Sketch comedy's modularity not only allows comedians to take up myriad performative identities but also provides Comedy Central with "unbundled" content able to travel quickly and easily across platforms. This relationship between form and function puts Comedy Central and its talent in a tricky bind. On the one hand, the network develops shows with segments and sketches that can be easily excerpted from episodes and circulated beyond television. This content is often centered on incendiary humor about race, gender, or other edgy topics that can be empowering to marginalized comedians and viewers. On the other hand, Comedy Central's attempts to court young men via multiscreen viewing and its jokingly gendered press discourses ensure that the transgressions of its edgy content remain limited. Although many Comedy Central shows satirize television's politics of representation, their critique is constrained by the hegemonic meanings encoded by the network's promotional and distribution strategies.

One recent example of this tension between Comedy Central's programs and economic imperatives is the 2014 *Inside Amy Schumer* sketch "Focus Group." It begins with a nondescript boardroom full of young men giving feedback to a fictional Comedy Central executive about the show while its eponymous star looks on from behind a one-way mirror. The executive asks routine questions ("What do you think about the balance between sketches and stand-up?"), and various participants respond with crass remarks about Schumer's physique or their willingness to sleep with her. After several iterations of the gag, one participant interjects, "I like the routines where she was on the street talking to people, and I appreciated how it had a sort of feminist bent on a male-skewing network. But I must say I would enjoy the routines more if she had a ten percent better 'dumper,'" referring to Schumer's posterior. The focus group ends with the participants being paid in beef jerky and energy drinks, but not before we see Schumer behind the mirror with a look of incredulous delight that "a couple of them said they would 'bang' [her]."

The sketch satirizes the notion that Schumer's humor "works" for Comedy Central only insofar as the network's male audience finds her attractive, a recurrent critique across much of the show. Many *Inside* sketches like "Focus Group" similarly invert sexist assumptions about women in comedy—male comedians are rarely, if ever, judged first by their appearance the way female comedians are. Men are often the target of satire throughout the show, and gendered jokes function reflexively to critique Comedy Central's predominantly male audience. The focus group member who briefly breaks from salivating over Schumer to note the "feminist bent" of the interview segments, for instance, highlights the gendered pleasures of television talk (Fiske 1987, 183; Shattuc 1997). Similarly, in the case of *Broad City*, idiosyncratic patter between co-creators and series stars Abbi Jacobson and Ilana Glazer underscores the blurry boundary between homosocial friendship and homosexual romance between the two. The duo often appropriates masculine slang like "dude" in creating comedic moments grounded in women's everyday lives. Jacobson and Glazer's characters also explicitly decry and deconstruct the sexual or professional shortcomings of male characters, reasserting their homosocial relationship as the series' driving narrative force.

In contrast with *Inside* and *Broad*'s comedic critiques, Comedy Central publicity and promotion discourses construct femininity in a way that positions masculinity as a presumed norm for comedic performers and consumers, implicitly reaffirming patriarchal presumptions about comedy in the process. The home page for *Inside Amy Schumer* on the Comedy Central website, for instance, features photos of a fully made-up Schumer dressed to accentuate her curvy physique. Thumbnails for episodes available to stream

FIGURE 17.1 *Promotional images for Inside Amy Schumer position masculinity as a presumed norm for comedic performers and consumers.*

sample salacious sexual material, such as a lineup of bulbous female buttocks for the 2015 sketch "Milk Milk Lemonade," rather than other sight gags. Elsewhere, one profile of Schumer notes as a matter of course in detailing her ascendance, "Bookers and producers quickly took notice of her long, blonde hair and all-American look" (Seabaugh 2014). One common opinion among many reviewers is that Comedy Central's comediennes are "not gendered necessarily in their comedy, they're just funny" (Greenwald 2014), an observation that only serves to highlight the already-highly gendered nature of what we presume to be funny. In a similar vein, a *New Yorker* profile of Jacobson and Glazer suggests that their popularity "seems to arise not only from the calibre of the comedy but also from the apparent authenticity of the women's affection for each other," positioning their gendered affection as extrinsic to high "calibre" comedy (Paumgarten 2014). Ultimately, this tension between *Inside* and *Broad's* textual representations and extratextual publicity functions hegemonically, constructing appeals to female viewers in ways that affirm comedy's male biases.

One important context of Comedy Central's ambivalent approach to gender is that of "post second-wave" feminism on contemporary cable television. Amanda Lotz's study of "contested" masculinities in cable programs like *Breaking Bad*, *Dexter*, and *Men of a Certain Age* suggests "it is cable's ability to derive commercial success by narrowcasting to smaller and specific audience niches that allowed these unconventional characters" (Lotz 2014, 32). The contested femininities *of Inside Amy Schumer* and *Broad City*, however, indicate that narrowcasting to small audience niches may not be enough as competition for that same niche—young men—intensifies.

Comedy Central's post-politics turn represents an unconventional tweak to the type of narrowcasting described by Lotz and embraced by so many cable competitors increasingly programming comedy. In some ways, it is taking the opposite tack of narrowcasting in its attempt to supplement young male viewers with female ones. In the hypercompetitive cable environment, Comedy Central is attempting to expand its young male audience without alienating it, a dynamic borne out by ratings data and comments from executives. Alterman notes of Jacobson and Glazer, for instance, that he "saw with them an opportunity to expand our audience . . . but never at the expense of our core audience" (Greenwald 2014). Posch highlights a similar balancing act, noting that "[o]ur ad buys are for men, so we can't lose them," but also touts Schumer's femininity: "Amy celebrates being a girl and being girly. Amy gets 50–50 male-female demos" (Zinoman 2013). Stories lauding *Broad City*'s Internet-to-television success (Berkowitz 2014) or touting the streaming numbers of *Inside Amy Schumer* via the network's app (Petski 2016) bolster the same tech-savvy viewing behaviors depicted in Comedy Central's rebrand efforts. This preference for content amenable to cross-platform movement implicitly constructs a tech-savvy male audience whose attention can be seized and retained with incendiary sexual humor.

While the hypercompetitive cable environment has fostered shows featuring contested, post-politics gender constructions, so too has it enabled programs "targeting audiences desiring unreconstructed, patriarchal masculinities" (Lotz 2014, 32). Indeed, Comedy Central's prime-time schedule has long showcased heteronormative masculinities; but in attempting to broaden its appeal with female-skewing shows, Comedy Central is essentially trying to have it both ways—that is, showing both men and women in a position of comedic, cultural power. This is why it remains crucial to consider the industrial context of comedic programming, particularly as this context becomes more and more cluttered with competition. Seen from this broader perspective, *Inside Amy Schumer* and *Broad City* lampoon the network's tradition of targeting men, but through their industrial circulation, the shows revalue that very demographic.

REFERENCES

Andreeva, Nellie. 2014. "Brooke Posch Upped to SVP Original Programming at Comedy Central." *Deadline Hollywood*, February 27. www.deadline.com/2014/02/brooke-posch-upped-to-svp-original-programming-at-comedy-central/.

Berkowitz, Joe. 2014. "How the Creators of *Broad City* Turned Their Web Series into a TV Show." *Fast Company*, February 5. www.fastcompany.com/3025672/how-the-creators-of-broad-city-turned-their-web-series-into-a-tv-show.

Boone, Brian. 2012. "The Origin and Early Programs of Comedy Central." *Splitsider*, January 11. http://splitsider.com/2012/01/the-origin-and-early-programs-of-comedy-central/.

Caldwell, John Thornton. 2007. *Production Culture: Industrial Reflexivity and Critical Practice in Film and Television*. Durham: Duke University Press.

Carter, Bill. 2012. "In the Tastes of Young Men, Humor Is Most Prized, a Survey Finds." *New York Times*, February 19. www.nytimes.com/2012/02/20/business/media/comedy-central-survey-says-young-men-see-humor-as-essential.html.

Chozik, Amy. 2013. "A Comedy Show That Comes via a Hashtag." *New York Times*, April 21. www.nytimes.com/2013/04/22/business/comedy-central-to-host-comedy-festival-on-twitter.html?pagewanted=all.

Fiske, John. 1987. *Television Culture*. London: Routledge.

Gelt, Jessica. 2013. "Comedy Central Renews 'Tosh.0' for Three Seasons." *Los Angeles Times*, December 13. http://articles.latimes.com/2013/dec/10/entertainment/la-et-st-comedy-central-renews-tosh0-for-three-seasons-20131210.

Gorman, Bill. 2011. "Comedy Central Ends 2011 as the #1 Entertainment Network in Cable Among Men 18–34 and 18–24." *TV by the Numbers*, December 21. http://tvbythenumbers.

zap2it.com/2011/12/21/comedy-central-ends-2011-as-the-1-entertainment-network-in-cable-among-men-18–34-and-men-18–24/114431/.

Greenwald, Andy. 2014. "The Andy Greenwald Podcast: Comedy Central Programming Head Kent Alterman." *Grantland*, April 23. http://grantland.com/hollywood-prospectus/the-andy-greenwald-podcast-comedy-central-president-kent-alterman/.

Hamilton, Peter. 2011. "U.S. Cable Networks: What Do Males Want? Content? or Entertainment? Who's Delivering Which?" *Documentary Television*, October 26. www.documentarytelevision.com/commissioning-process/u-s-cable-networks-what-do-males-want-content-or-entertainment-whos-giving-what/.

Johnson, Catherine. 2012. *Branding Television*. London: Routledge.

Keegan, Kiffer. n.d. "Comedy Central Rebrand." *KifferKeegan.com*. www.kifferkeegan.com/Comedy-Central-Rebrand.

Lotz, Amanda. 2014. *Cable Guys: Television and Masculinities in the 21st Century*. New York: New York University Press.

Morgan, Richard. 2012. "What's Wrong with Comedy Central?" *Splitsider*, March 19. http://splitsider.com/2012/03/whats-wrong-with-comedy-central/.

Mullen, Megan. 2003. *The Rise of Cable Programming in the United States: Revolution or Evolution?* Austin: University of Texas Press.

O'Connell, Michael. 2013. "Comedy Central Launches Digital Production Studio, Taps Allison Kingsley as VP." *Hollywood Reporter*, January 31. www.hollywoodreporter.com/news/comedy-central-launches-digital-production-417123.

Paumgarten, Nick. 2014. "Id Girls." *The New Yorker*, June 23. www.newyorker.com/magazine/2014/06/23/id-girls.

Petski, Denise. 2016. "*Inside Amy Schumer* Renewed for Fifth Season on Comedy Central—TCA." *Deadline Hollywood*, January 6. http://deadline.com/2016/01/inside-amy-schumer-renewed-fifth-season-comedy-central-amy-schumer-1201676749/.

Rose, Lacey. 2013. "Comedy Central's Kent Alterman on Leno, Rape Jokes and a Jon Stewart-Free 'Daily Show.'" *The Hollywood Reporter*, May 1. www.hollywoodreporter.com/news/comedy-centrals-kent-alterman-leno-448317.

Seabaugh, Julie. 2014. "Variety's 2014 Breakthrough in Comedy Winner: Amy Schumer." *Variety*, January 6. http://variety.com/2014/tv/news/amy-schumer-a-year-for-living-dangerously-1201029531/.

Shattuc, Jane M. 1997. *The Talking Cure: TV Talk Shows and Women*. New York: Routledge.

Sienkiewicz, Matt and Nick Marx. 2014. "Click Culture: The Perils and Possibilities of *Family Guy* and Convergence-Era Television." *Communication and Critical/Cultural Studies* 11 (2): 103–19.

Sloan, Jaeger. 2011. "In-Depth: Comedy Central Re-Brand." *Motionographer*, January 5. http://motionographer.com/2011/01/05/in-depth-comedy-central-re-brand/.

Stelter, Brian. 2011. "Comedy Central Still Strong at 20." *New York Times*, April 11. www.nytimes.com/2011/04/11/business/media/11comedy.html.

Vranica, Suzanne and John Jannarone. 2012. "Viacom Loads More Ads on Channels." *Wall Street Journal*, August 12. http://online.wsj.com/news/articles/SB10000872396390444082904577609893517491070

Zinoman, Jason. 2013. "Amy Schumer, Funny Girl." *New York Times*, April 18. www.nytimes.com/2013/04/21/arts/television/amy-schumers-comedy-central-show-from-the-inside.html?pagewanted=all.

Nick Jr.

Co-viewing and the Limits of Dayparts
Erin Copple Smith

"Mom, you've entertained the kids all day. Now it's time we entertain you."

Juxtaposing the image of a bowl of mac & cheese with a glass of red wine, this evening sign-off from cable channel Nick Jr.'s preschooler-friendly content saluted moms for completing a day of hard work and ultimately heralded Nickelodeon's move to leverage their primary audience of preschoolers and their parents into a new nighttime programming block aimed at parents alone. Since its debut under the name Noggin in 1999, the Nick Jr. channel had aired preschooler-friendly content 24 hours a day, but in October 2012 it turned over its overnight hours (10 p.m. to 2 a.m. Eastern) to a new block called NickMom. With its tagline, "motherfunny," the branded block took an irreverent view on motherhood, offering comedic reality series and syndicated comedies. The logic behind the development of NickMom was clear: turn a slow daypart into a moneymaker by appealing to the viewers who are already part your audience but not explicitly targeted with programming suiting their own interests. Demand for preschooler programming goes down after kids are in bed, after all, so it made sense to give those parents who might already have their TV tuned to Nick Jr. some "adult" programming to enjoy. Yet in spite of these logics, the strategy met with resistance from audiences who were frustrated with the unsuitability of NickMom content to a channel persistently aimed at a preschool audience, demonstrating the power of audiences' expectations to set limitations for niche cable channels in the post-network era. The block never really took off, even after the loudest oppositional voices died down, and NickMom faded slowly from the airwaves, ending officially in November 2015.

In the post-network era, cable channels have worked to find new ways of growing their audience base without alienating their original niche viewership. One strategy channels have employed to manage this balance is the development of daypart programming blocks that expand viewership but manage to fit within an overall brand. Cartoon Network's Adult Swim block, launched in 2001, is one example of a block intended to move the cable channel from its kid-oriented daytime content toward more adult-themed content aired in the overnight hours when children were expected to be sleeping. As Evan Elkins notes, Cartoon Network has consistently used Adult Swim to discursively reinforce the characteristics of its imagined audience—namely "young, white, heterosexual masculinity" (2013, 596). The Adult Swim block did this "by selling its programs to young, white men and investing heavily in cross-platform expansion and promotion," all in an effort to leverage not just the adult viewers who had long been loyal to the channel's animated programming but also the potential to hold on to their young male viewers as they aged into adulthood (597). In other words, Cartoon Network used Adult Swim as a way to "graduate" its younger viewers into more adult-themed programming in an effort to keep them loyal to the brand. This strategy has been employed by kid-targeted cable channels for a long time—including Nickelodeon's own very successful experiments with its Nick at Nite programming block in prime-time hours—but often with those channels funneling their audiences into a different channel altogether (Pecora 2002). For example, Nick Jr. moves preschoolers toward Nickelodeon, which in turn moves its tweens toward TeenNick. Nick Jr.'s launch of NickMom was a move more similar to Adult Swim's, aimed at keeping the audience on the same channel. The key difference, of course, is that the moms targeted by Nick Mom aren't "graduating" from *Dora the Explorer*—they are only on the channel because their kids are.

Nickelodeon's origins as an irreverent place for kids (Banet-Weiser 2007) focused on defining the channel's brand as something distinct, but by 2012, the channel was losing ground to their competitors. Going back to the Nick at Nite strategy by developing NickMom made sense from multiple perspectives: the ubiquity and popularity of Nick Jr. meant that many parents had already tuned their TVs to the channel, the "irreverence" of the Nickelodeon brand was consistent with the tone of NickMom's "motherfunny" content, and the use of programming dayparts was a strategy Nickelodeon itself pioneered in the 1980s. Nonetheless, the strategy ultimately chaffed against increasingly expectations in an on-demand channel landscape that Nick Jr. might offer 24-hour preschooler-appropriate content.

My analysis of NickMom as a programming block illustrates the logics behind developing dayparts, particularly the difficulty of balancing appeals to new and distinct audiences in one daypart without abandoning or alienating existing audiences. Moreover, the launch of NickMom (and its predecessor, Nick at Nite) demonstrates the changing role of "flow" in the post-network era. Whereas cable channels in the multi-channel transition (beginning in the 1980s and lasting until the early 2000s) were able to rely on inertia to maintain their audience throughout the day, audiences in the post-network era (early 2000s–) are more likely to seek programming that suits their needs outside the strictures of the television schedule through timeshifting or streaming, both of which render "flow" vastly less reliable (Lotz 2014). Thus, though Nick at Nite was able to leverage its daytime audience into a nighttime audience in the 1980s, viewers in 2012 were less interested in simply staying tuned into the channel because their kids went to bed.

NickMom illustrates this disconnect between established industry strategies (that audiences can be converted across dayparts due to the inertia of "flow") and audience expectations (that specific channels serve specific purposes and viewers, with Nick Jr. intended for preschoolers not adults). Whereas Nickelodeon expected audiences to operate as they did in the 1980s, they were surprised to find a small but vocal group of protesters complaining that the block was too far afield of their expectations for Nick Jr., offering grown-up themes that ran counter to parents' view of the channel as an ever-ready tool in their parenting arsenal. To demonstrate these shifts in channel logic and reception from the multi-channel transition to the post-network era, this chapter offers an historical overview of the development of Nick at Nite in order to compare the strategies deployed in launching NickMom, as well as an exploration of why these same strategies failed 30 years later.

FROM NICK AT NITE TO NICK JR.

Dayparts are perhaps the most crucial element of the story of Nickelodeon, a channel that managed to expand its brand by segmenting its programming into blocks targeting specific subcategories of its primary audience. By considering the emergence of programming blocks at Nickelodeon throughout its history, a sense of the institutional logics behind the strategies emerges—one that illustrates the difficulty of balancing audiences' expectations for a channel with efforts to expand content offerings and grow the audience.

Nick at Nite was developed at Nickelodeon as the channel began airing content 24 hours per day in 1984, a move that presented opportunities and challenges. In moving to a 24-hour cycle, Nickelodeon began to break up the day into different parts targeted at different audiences (in the same way a broadcast TV station does, with morning news shows, midday talk and game shows, evening news, prime-time network content, and late-night talk shows). As Norma Pecora (2004) describes, beginning in the mid-1980s, Nickelodeon worked to carve the daily schedule into dedicated dayparts, with preschooler-targeted programming during school hours (eventually referred to as the "Nick Jr." block), elementary-targeted content in the afternoons and evenings, and eventually Nick at Nite beginning at 8 p.m. Eastern. By strategically blocking out the day to target audiences most likely to be home and watching TV, Nickelodeon sought to maximize viewership within each block by providing content specifically targeted to the available audience. Offering programming for adults in prime-time and overnight hours made sense—kids were in bed at this time, but adults were awake.

Yet in the cases of both Nick at Nite and NickMom, efforts were made to find content that would work well enough within the existing brand so as not to alienate the existing audience. At Nick at Nite, though the programming shifted significantly from kid-friendly cartoons and irreverent series like *Double Dare* and *You Can't Do That on Television* to "classic" TV series, Nickelodeon executives thought hard about how to make that shift work for viewers. Then Nickelodeon President Geraldine Laybourne explains, "We were primarily concerned with not closing the door on kids as we opened the door to adults" (Jenkins 2004, 150). As Derek Kompare writes, Nick at Nite was intended "to attract the baby boomer parents of its daytime viewers, with slightly older-skewing but still child-friendly series" (2005, 181). By securing content consistent with

Nickelodeon's existing brand identity, executives were able to carefully and precisely manage this doorway between dayparts. Moreover, Nickelodeon worked to tie the kid-friendly "irreverence" that functioned as the channel's hallmark to parental nostalgia, reminding Baby Boomer audiences of the "classic" TV of their own childhoods (Murray 2004). Laybourne points out that several early ad campaigns for Nick at Nite were "trying to get the audience to feel that they owned the network, the way we were getting the kids to feel about Nickelodeon" (Jenkins 2004, 151).

As each Nickelodeon daypart succeeded in finding its targeted audiences, it was spun off into its own channel—TV Land first in 1996, followed by several others including Noggin, the channel that eventually became Nick Jr. Launched in 1999, Noggin was developed as a key arm of the broadly kid-focused Nickelodeon. The strategy behind Noggin was to target preschool-aged children, drawing them into the Nickelodeon "universe" in such a way that these preschoolers would eventually "graduate" to Nickelodeon. With all this in mind, we can understand Nick Jr. in close relationship to each of these Nickelodeon enterprises, where the channel itself need not necessarily be profitable in its own right. Channels like Nick Jr. can serve as loss leaders for media industries; their primary function is not to generate revenue (through ratings and ad sales), but rather to generate audiences who will then be made profitable through various later transactions and relationships: by purchasing content in secondary markets (via DVD or online video), by buying branded merchandise, and by becoming loyal fans and audience members of the parent channel and its other subsidiaries. Even more importantly, the channel can generate content that could be syndicated and sold in other markets. As a loss leader, Nick Jr. can also provide a point of entry for audiences to the entirety of parent company Viacom's digital cable network suite, so that consumers who subscribed to a "family package" through their cable provider would find themselves with several Nickelodeon offshoots, including Nickelodeon, Nick Jr., TV Land, TeenNick, and others. Furthermore, this loss leader status requires Nick Jr. to air very little advertising during the day; though there is some outside advertising, promotion focuses primarily on keeping kids interested in Nick Jr. by hyping other Nick Jr. series or branded toys.

FAILING TO REPEAT NICK AT NITE'S SUCCESS

By 2012, however, viewership was down for Nickelodeon and many of its subsidiary channels (Bond 2012). A high-profile dispute with DirecTV highlighted these faltering ratings. As reported in June, "Nickelodeon's viewership [was] down almost 30 percent in the past several months," leading analyst Todd Juenger to speculate that the channel might no longer be a good buy for cable and satellite carriers (Gardner 2012). Juenger's prediction proved accurate in July, when DirecTV dropped 17 Viacom-owned channels (including Nickelodeon and Nick Jr.) from its offerings (Nordyke 2012). The dispute centered on Viacom's request for an increase in DirecTV's carriage fees (the amount DirecTV pays Viacom to carry the channels) of more than 30% over the previous year, despite falling ratings. DirecTV saw the ratings decline as an indication of diminished consumer demand for Viacom's channels, thus lowering its value for the satellite company. Amid this turmoil, however, Nick Jr. continued to perform admirably for Viacom. In March 2012, Viacom announced that the preschooler arm of the company boasted 74 million subscribers and year-to-year growth, improving its ratings by 4% in the previous year (Reynolds 2012). In fact, not only was Nick Jr. a success with its kid audiences, it was also performing well with parents who often "co-viewed" with their children. A 2012 *Multichannel News* article notes that in the fourth quarter of 2011, Nick Jr. had a "53.3% [parent and child] co-viewing ratio . . . the highest of all kids networks" and on that basis of that strength would soon debut the NickMom programming block to target those parents already watching Nick Jr. during the day (Reynolds 2012). In short: as ratings faltered at Viacom, Nick Jr. remained strong, offering the parent company a way to leverage co-viewing strength into new viewership during an otherwise slow daypart.

Thus, NickMom and Nick at Nite share similar origins as prime-time and overnight content designed to appeal to the parents of their channel's primary audiences. Rather than rely solely on syndicated content, however, NickMom did include original programming in its October 2012 debut, but those originals were very low budget. The flagship talk show *Parental Discretion with Stefanie Wilder-Taylor* was filmed on a single soundstage with a live audience; unscripted series *Mom Friends Forever* adopted a vlogging style to follow a couple of mom pals from St. Louis; and *NickMom Night Out* featured stand-up comics doing routines in front of a live audience in a very basic studio. In addition to these three original series was *What Was Carol Brady Thinking?*, a pop-up video version of *Brady Bunch* episodes with comedic insights into Carol's mind during the family's hijinks. In each case, the series was inexpensive to produce, and aired in repeated blocks overnight, enabling Nick Jr. to fill otherwise little-watched hours with cheap content designed to appeal to the "modern mom." Eventually, NickMom evolved to include syndicated series including *The New Adventures of Old Christine*, *That '70s Show*, and *Yes, Dear*, along with movies like *Riding in Cars With Boys*, *Lifesize*, and *Eat Pray Love*.

But unlike Nickelodeon in the 1980s, Nick Jr. was not structured according to dayparts prior to introduction of NickMom. Whereas the flagship channel divided its day according to audience, the intensified narrowcasting of the post-network era that led to the development of Nick Jr. required the channel to cater to only one audience: preschoolers. Thus the Nick Jr. schedule is broken into blocks by program (two episodes of *Team Umizoomi* back-to-back followed by two episodes of *Peppa Pig*, for example), not by anticipated audience. So whereas marking one of Nickelodeon's dayparts as more adult-oriented with Nick at Nite made sense in the 1980s and 1990s, the same strategy deployed at the even more narrowcast Nick Jr. prompted a more fundamental shift in the channel's overall scheduling logics.

Indeed, that attempt backfired on multiple fronts: new reliance on dayparts failed because many parents now expected 24-hour preschooler-appropriate content. The development of a 24-hour-a-day, 7-day-a-week channel devoted to airing content appropriate for preschoolers had come to suit the needs of many families. In addition to simply having content available for kids when they wanted it, Nick Jr. came to be relied upon by second- and third-shift parents whose families operated on an adjusted schedule, families in the Pacific time zone as well as Alaska and Hawaii whose children stayed awake three or more hours later than those on the East Coast, as well as parents of sick or insomniac children. In response to this perceived loss of service, some viewers found the NickMom content so offensive and problematic they launched the Cancel NickMom movement shortly after the block's premiere, citing the unsuitability of the NickMom series on a channel otherwise aimed at a preschool audience. The Cancel Nick Mom on Nick Jr. petition on MoveOn.org has only 45 of its necessary 50 signatures, but declares

> We as concerned parents/care givers don't feel that it is appropriate to have a rated R television serious [sic] on a "Jr" network television regardless what time it is. There are children that are up at that time of all ages weather [sic] they are sick or fighting bedtime. Its [sic] is wrong and false advertising. Nick jr is and always has been for young children. We need Blues Clues, Wonder Pets, or Yo Gabba Gabba on not rated R innaprorate [sic] shows on.
>
> ("Cancel Nick Mom on Nick Jr." n.d.)

A comment on the homepage of CancelNickMom.com in December 2012 read:

> Why have you put garbage such as NickMom on a PRESCHOOL channel??? Sometimes, I do allow my child to stay up past 10 pm, and sometimes, she does wake up in the middle of the night. Used to [sic], I was able to let her watch nickjr [sic] until she went back to sleep. Nick jr [sic] is the biggest reason I have kept the satellite plan I have. But if I have to tolerate this nonsense, she won't be watching the channel at all."[1]

FIGURE 18.1 *Some audiences resisted the presence adult-oriented content on a channel they saw as the province of their preschoolers, pressuring Viacom to remove NickMom from Nick Jr.*

As these comments suggest, some audiences in 2012 were not interested in finding adult-oriented content on a channel they saw as the province of their preschoolers. Rather, their expectations for Nick Jr. focused solely on the constant availability of content their children enjoyed and they themselves found safe and appropriate—and many of them felt strongly that NickMom was far too adult.

The block's slogan, "motherfunny," highlights the kind of vaguely blue humor at the heart of both the new brand and the controversy surrounding it. *What Was Carol Brady Thinking?* made gently sexual references to Mike Brady, for example, and comedians at *Parental Discretion* roundtables would talk about being hungover. A 2012 *New York Times* review criticized the block as "a collection of shows both aggressively lowbrow and narrowly focused on a few areas of interest to the female audience, namely sex and children" (Genzlinger C1). Similarly, London's *Daily Telegraph Magazine* called Nick-Mom "a 'girls' night out from the comfort of your own couch' that is 'designed especially for moms'—which is TV lingo for 'offensively low-brow bilge'" (Walden 2012, 13). It's not that NickMom programming was overly blue in tone, but it was certainly more adult than would be suitable for a toddler.

Despite the fact that Cancel NickMom failed to cohere significant support (failing to collect enough petition signatures, for example) and thus did see their demands immediately met (the block wasn't canceled until 2015), NickMom did face blowback from advertisers in the wake of the outcry. Cancel NickMom successfully lobbied some advertisers to withdraw from the channel, including preschooler staples Fisher Price and General Mills (including the Cheerios and Green Giant brands in particular).[2] Moreover, though NickMom was intended as a way for Nick Jr. to leverage existing audience into improved overnight ratings, it had the opposite impact. A 2012 *Wall Street Journal* article reports "In the week of its Oct. 1 debut, NickMom averaged just 131,000 viewers, down 74% from the same time slot a year earlier. On some nights, certain programs in the block didn't draw enough viewers to have their audience measured" (Jannarone 2012). By November 2015, Viacom pulled the plug on this failing NickMom initiative. Ultimately, although the small but vocal CancelNickMom movement did not appear to have a huge or immediate impact on the block's existence, adult audiences were clearly disinterested in the programming on offer at Nick Jr., likely because they could easily find content more suited to their individual tastes elsewhere.

CONCLUSION

Ultimately, Viacom missed the mark by misunderstanding their audience's expectations in 2012. Whereas adults could find suitable programming for their needs across the cable landscape, preschooler programming is still a relatively small subset of the cable market. An angry online commenter in 2012 notes,

> I am far from a prude and I find Nickmom to be offensive and this channel would be the last one I would view for mommy relief! there are many other channels that can do that, but there are few for preschoolers!

> (Copple Smith 2012)

A columnist for the *Tampa Bay Times* sums up the problem neatly:

> Can Nick Jr. ever get it through their heads that what moms loved most about Noggin was it aired quality shows from PBS and Nickelodeon all day and night without commercials and was a nice way to calm night terrors or soothe a sick child at odd hours? We don't need another adult show.
>
> (Wynne 2012, 5)

By any measure—press coverage, ratings, longevity—NickMom was a failure for Viacom. Nonetheless, its failure can be educative in demonstrating why strategies successful in previous industrial contexts (in this case, the Nick at Nite formula during the multi-channel transition) cannot be easily or reliably transposed to the needs of the post-network era. In borrowing a strategy developed in the era of 1980s cable, Nickelodeon forgot to account for the changing expectations of audiences in the intervening 30 years. No longer were audiences looking for variety *within* a specific channel because there is now plenty of variety *among* cable channels. Audiences seeking out adult-oriented content overnight could surely find it among other cable offerings (not to mention via streaming services like Netflix and Hulu) with which they already have ongoing relationships and brand affinities. Whereas Nick at Nite offered content audiences couldn't find elsewhere in 1985, NickMom offered adult-oriented reruns in lieu of kid-appropriate content audiences expected in 2012. Despite Nick Jr.'s exhortation, voiced in the daily sign-off, "You made it! The playdates are over! The kids are tucked in bed and finally it's your time—the one being catered to, the center of attention, the only one in charge," the company soon learned that parents were not really interested in using their "me time" on the channel's "motherfunny" content.

NOTES

1 CancelNickMom.com is now defunct, thus the original comment is irretrievable.
2 General Mills returned to the channel once some of the racier NickMom content was eventually canceled.

REFERENCES

Banet-Weiser, Sarah. 2007. *Kids Rule! Nickelodeon and Consumer Citizenship*. Durham: Duke University Press.

Bond, Paul. 2012. "Analyst: Nickelodeon Isn't Pulling Its Weight at Viacom." *The Hollywood Reporter*, September 10.

"Cancel Nick Mom on Nick Jr." n.d. *Move On.org*. http://petitions.moveon.org/sign/cancel-nick-mom-on-nick.

Copple Smith, Erin. 2012. "Nick Moms vs. NickMom." *Antenna*, December 14. http://blog.com marts.wisc.edu/2012/12/14/nick-moms-vs-nickmom/.

Elkins, Evan. 2013. "Cultural Identity and Subcultural Forums: The Post-Network Politics of Adult Swim." *Television & New Media* 15: 595–610.

Gardner, Eriq. 2012. "Analyst: Nickelodeon Might Be in Danger of Being Dropped by Some TV Distributors." *The Hollywood Reporter*, June 12.

Genzlinger, Neil. 2012. "Women's TV Block with 2-Track Mind." *The New York Times*, November 9.

Jannarone, John. 2012. "Mom Shows Hurt Nick Jr." *The Wall Street Journal*, October 12. www.wsj.com/articles/SB10000872396390443749204578052881834903510.

Jenkins, Henry. 2004. "Interview with Geraldine Laybourne." In *Nickelodeon Nation: The History, Politics, and Economics of America's Only TV Channel for Kids*, edited by Heather Hendershot, 134–52. New York: New York University Press.

Kompare, Derek. 2005. *Rerun Nation: How Repeats Invented American Television*. New York: Routledge.

Lotz, Amanda D. 2014. *The Television Will Be Revolutionized*, 2nd edition. New York: New York University Press.

Murray, Susan. 2004. "'TV Satisfaction Guaranteed!' Nick at Nite and TV Land's 'Adult' Attractions." In *Nickelodeon Nation: The History, Politics, and Economics of America's Only TV Channel for Kids*, edited by Heather Hendershot, 69–84. New York: New York University Press.

Nordyke, Kimberly. 2012. "Viacom Networks Go Dark on DirecTV." *The Hollywood Reporter*, July 11.

Pecora, Norma. 2002. *The Business of Children's Entertainment*. New York: Guilford Press.

Pecora, Norma. 2004. "Nickelodeon Grows Up: The Economic Evolution of a Network." In *Nickelodeon Nation: The History, Politics, and Economics of America's Only TV Channel for Kids*, edited by Heather Hendershot, 15–44. New York: New York University Press.

Reynolds, Mike. 2012. "Nick Jr. Says: Do the Math." *Multichannel News*, March 19.

Walden, Celia. 2012. "Celia Walden Has Nothing in Common with the Dummy Mummies." *The Daily Telegraph Magazine*, December 1.

Wynne, Sharon. 2012. "Whoa Momma!" *Tampa Bay Times*, October 12.

Disney Junior

Imagining Industrial Intertextuality

Kyra Hunting and Jonathan Gray

At the 2008 International Radio and Television Society and Disney Digital Media Summit in Burbank, California—an event that allowed academics a rare peak under Disney's hood—various Disney staffers repeated Chairman and CEO Bob Iger's declaration that the company was now in the business of selling not shows, not films, but three key commodities: Disney, ABC, and ESPN. The rationale offered by some staffers was that in an era of ever-increasing competition for viewer attention and of bittorrenting, selling brands not texts would be a more reliable method of holding onto viewers, of ensuring that they watched in Disney's preferred (i.e.: fully monetized) settings, and of swatting away competitors who could only fight them one text at a time. Certainly, in the last decade, much has been said in both the media industries and media studies about the power and importance of branding (Johnson 2012). In this chapter, we contend that Disney Junior provides a relatively new form of programming, one that aims as much at selling the channel itself and indeed the entire Disney name/brand and "family" of texts as at selling any particular program or character on that channel.

The chapter also argues that Disney Junior represents a rich example of intertextuality being used as an economic strategy. Intertextuality is more regularly discussed in the realm of textual analysis, or is used to explain more linear models of extension and adaptation of a single intellectual property in modes of industrialized intertextuality such as spin-offs, franchises, sequels, remakes, and ripoffs. But in exploring Disney Junior's more ambitious experiment in connecting a wider network of disparate programs and characters textually, generically, and technologically, we see something more intricately interlaced and multidirectional that has received less academic discussion to date. Given that Disney Junior takes minimal "sponsorships," no traditional advertising, and receives carriage fees reported as low as 14 cents per subscriber (Fritz 2014), much of the channel's economic value to the parent company may be indirect, lying in its ability to create and promote brands. Towards this end, the channel offers a tightly woven net of Disney intertexts. In doing so, it provides an example of how intricately channels can be constructed, so that texts constantly feed back into one another and connect viewers to the sprawling corporate network that is Disney, selling not just texts but a family of them. Disney Junior is all the more important, for aiming to be a child's entry point to the larger intertextual kingdom of Disney—it is, as the channel's slogan states, "where the magic begins"—while simultaneously using intertextuality to leverage parental nostalgia and good will.

WHERE THE INTERTEXTUAL MAGIC BEGINS... AND CONTINUES

Not all of Disney Junior's characters and shows feed directly into a larger Disney franchise, for cross-promotion takes a great deal of time, energy, and often capital (Copple Smith 2012) that cannot be expended on every show in a programming lineup. Nevertheless, Disney Junior's executives have not been coy about the role they hope they will play in introducing young viewers to the Disney brand. A year after the channel's introduction, a *New York Times* article described then Disney-ABC Television Group President Anne Sweeney as devising "her fast-growing TV portfolio to retain children as they grow," and quoted her as saying that "these children are the Walt Disney Company's most important audience [. . .] they're the future, and this is their first introduction to our brand" (Barnes and Chozick 2013). Meanwhile, Gary Marsh, president and chief creative officer for Disney Channels Worldwide, described Disney Junior prior to its launch as "an entry point into the world of Disney for young kids, creating a world [. . .] that captures the magic of Disney and its classic heartfelt storytelling and timeless characters beloved by generations" (Morabito 2011).

Consequently, the ties between the channel's programming and the Disney family are plentiful. For instance, *Mickey and the Roadster Racers* follows new adventures of Mickey, Minnie, Donald, Daisy, Pluto, Goofy, and Pete. *The Lion Guard* spins off from famed Disney film *The Lion King*; centered on Kion—Prince of The Pride Lands, and child to *The Lion King*'s Simba and Nala—and his friends, while bringing back many of the film's original characters, even if only briefly. In each case, the shows introduce Disney Junior's target audience of under-eight-year-olds to some of Disney's most iconic characters while also aiming to capitalize upon parents' nostalgic relationships to Mickey, Simba, and friends, luring them in to the channel with the promise of familiarity and reliability. The intertextuality, in other words, works both to introduce Disney to children and to entice parents to deliver a whole new generation of viewers.

But of course Disney is not just talking mice and lions. Thus *Sofia the First* follows a young girl "from the village" whose mother married a king, rocketing her into life as a (Disney) princess. She is aided by the magical Amulet of Avalor that allows her to communicate with animals and summon other Disney princesses in times of need. Quite practically, then, the amulet acts as a portal for Disney princesses to appear to Sofia and the viewer, building audience familiarity with the characters. However, beyond the occasional Disney princess visit to the show, the strongest service performed by *Sofia* for the Disney family is arguably to introduce "princess culture" more generally.

As the opening theme song explains, Sofia attends a princess school (alongside teachers Flora, Fauna, and Merryweather, the Three Good Fairies from Disney's *Sleeping Beauty*) where she's "gotta figure out how to do it right" and where she's "finding out what being royal's all about." Sofia is a handy device, therefore, to "teach" child viewers what it means to be a (Disney) princess and to provide a venue to update this definition. The inclusion of Flora, Fauna, and Merryweather and, occasionally, other princesses introduces a small cast of Disney characters to child viewers, thereby directing them to the larger Disney universe while, in savvy fashion, also seeding the narrative with characters to whom parents may have nostalgic, fond attachments, thereby directing the Disney universe into *Sofia*.

Similarly, *Jake and the Neverland Pirates* is situated within the realm of Peter Pan, following child pirates Jake, Izzy, Cubby, and their parrot Skully in a quest for gold doubloons and adventure in Neverland. Many of the markings of the Peter Pan franchise are present: the titular setting, forever-antagonist Captain Hook, Mr. Smee, and Tick-Tock the Crocodile, flying fairy dust, and Peter himself has appeared. More broadly, the central characters are siblings, and their status as children serves as no impediment in their continual battles with Captain Hook—indeed, it is framed as a boon. The world is, predictably, tamed somewhat for the younger age group, as Hook has "challenges" with the protagonists, rather than trying to kill them, and the melancholic absence of parent figures in *Peter Pan* is not broached in *Jake*. But once again the show works simultaneously to familiarize child viewers with one of Disney's key franchises, and to co-opt parents' nostalgic relationships with Neverland.

The degree to which *Mickey and the Roadster Racers*, *The Lion Guard*, *Sofia*, and *Jake* draw heavily from and feed into existing Disney characters and worlds is admittedly unmatched by Disney Junior's other regular shows; however, loose intertextual ties, echoes, and shadows abound elsewhere. Invoking the Disney-trademarked Tomorrowland in its title, for example, *Miles from Tomorrowland* follows a family of space explorers. The show began in 2015, the same year as the theatrical release of *Tomorrowland*—contributing, therefore, to a coordinated revival of the Disney-trademarked amusement park venue Tomorrowland—and the same year as the much-anticipated re-entry of now-Disney-owned *Star Wars* to the popular cultural orbit. The fact that *Miles* was picked up when, according to Nancy Kanter, executive vice president of original programming and general manager of Disney Junior Worldwide, the channel was looking specifically for a "space adventure" (Owen 2015) suggests that this looser form of intertextuality, in this case related to genre, may be strategic. Mark Hamill's highly publicized appearance as a voice actor in early episodes of *Miles* and the circulation of a short on Disney Junior teaching kids the "Chopper Dance" with a character from DisneyXD's *Star Wars Rebels* further encouraged viewers, at least parents, to make connections between these texts and sister channels.

Similarly, though *Henry Hugglemonster* was based on a best-selling book, the series about a world of adorable monsters launched in April 2013, two months before the theatrical release of Disney/Pixar's *Monsters, Inc.* sequel, *Monsters University*. *Goldie & Bear*, too, is situated in a fairy tale world that officially originates in Hans Christian Anderson and other folk tales, but that Disney colonized as its own through *Sleeping*

Beauty, Cinderella, and other famous retellings and have continued to claim ownership over with the ABC series *Once Upon a Time* and live-action remakes of its animated classics. Kanter has bluntly described *Goldie & Bear* as designed to "keep these classic stories, and classic characters, in kids' minds" (Steinberg 2015a). Even *Doc McStuffins*, while not connected *directly* to any other Disney property, alludes to Disney's *Toy Story* franchise with the combination of talking toys and animation that is reminiscent of Pixar's visual style. "Loose" intertextual ties such as these may, of course, not activate for many viewers, yet we should not underestimate their relative importance to Disney, as they ensure that Disney Junior constantly grows seamlessly into and out of other Disney properties, characters, and stories.

THE WONDERFUL WORLD OF CHARACTER-BASED CHANNEL BRANDING

Recognizable characters were essential to the early success not only of Disney Junior's programming but its construction of an identity for the channel as a whole. While among several series imported from a previous preschool programming block on the Disney Channel, Playhouse Disney, *Mickey Mouse Clubhouse* represented a first real success (Grosz 2011) and proved instrumental in early branding efforts for the new channel (Weisman 2010) by flagging Disney Junior's strong connection to the Disney brand and its classic characters. The logos and idents developed for Disney Junior visualized this connection, reworking the letters in "Junior" to resemble new and classic Disney characters, with the first and most basic version transforming the "i" into a variation of Mickey himself.

In later years, Disney Junior's use of idents would continue to demonstrate the channel's dual function of introducing new character brands specific to its youngest viewers while incorporating classic Disney. For instance, during a single afternoon's viewing in 2016, one could see the transforming logo highlight Disney Junior originals from *Miles from Tomorrowland*, to continuing hits like *Frozen*, to familiar and classic Disney favorites like *Dumbo* or *Lilo and Stitch* (see Figure 19.1). The *Frozen* ident hangs Anna's signature burgundy cape around the N in Junior, while offering Elsa's braid to the dot of its I, and a huge pair of Sven's antlers to its R; meanwhile a *Dumbo* ident turns the U into a big-top tent, puts huge Dumbo ears and yellow cap on the I's dot, and dresses the R in the red coat of Timothy Q. Mouse. These shifting idents propose to parents that even the newest offerings of Disney Junior are securely part of a Disney tradition.

Disney Junior's evocation of well-known Disney characters clearly connects it to the larger Disney brand and makes its potential for inculcating "future brand loyalty" (Barnes and Chozick 2013) immediately evident. However, Disney Junior has also aimed to stay competitive by rapidly responding to changes in the children's television market. In 2011, Paige Albiniak identified "co-viewing, live-action, and digital platforms" as hot areas for children's television, and Disney Junior has, indeed, emphasized co-viewing (the watching of children's programming by parents alongside their children) and digital platforms extensively by drawing on the Disney brand. Many other channels are experimenting with co-viewing too, of course, but Disney Junior's relatively innovative strategy has been to focus on corporate brands, not specific franchises alone. By using

FIGURE 19.1 *Channel idents introducing Disney Junior audiences to characters and iconography from classic Disney properties.*

characters from legacy Disney properties, Disney Junior aims to leverage parents' nostalgia not just to encourage them to put on the channel while they exit the room, but also to entice them to watch alongside their children. Co-viewing may deepen the relationship a child has to a show—s/he is not just watching television, but watching with a parent—but it is also economically important for Disney Junior, given that the channel has no traditional advertising and instead focuses on limited "sponsorships." Many of these sponsorships are targeted at parents (advertising diapers, cleaning supplies, and learning websites, for instance) and hence are based on the expectation of parents' presence while the channel is being watched. More broadly, of course, parents may be more likely to buy toys and other merchandise not only from shows they feel positively towards but from shows set in worlds to which they, as parents, have strong nostalgic ties. Consequently, the use of recognizable characters and genres can do double duty for Disney from a co-viewing and advertising perspective.

This combination of discovery, nostalgia, and continuity can be seen elsewhere in Disney Junior's advertising and programming. While the channel touts its lack of traditional advertising to parent viewers, it does, in fact, have lengthy breaks between shows that include one or two outside "sponsorships" but consist mostly of ads for Disney Junior series and products as well as promotional "shorts." For example, the "Unlock the Adventure" shorts features children describing classic Disney princess films. "Muppet Moments," introduced five months before ABC's *The Muppets* premiered, depict Kermit and friends in playful segments talking to preschoolers. Disney Junior also airs classic Disney films in a series called *The Magical World of Disney Junior*, encouraging family viewing while promoting other Disney texts. In each case, the nostalgic value of these characters exists alongside the possibilities of the discovery of new characters in which younger kids may become interested.

These shorts were used to great effect to prepare viewers for the channel's 2016 series *The Lion Guard*, a show that in many ways is emblematic of Disney's multifaceted approach to intertextuality, co-promotion, and co-viewing. As early as August (three months before *The Lion Guard*'s premiere), Disney Junior began airing a "Night Light" short telling the basic story of *The Lion King* using finger puppets and a child's voice-over. These shorts aired three to four times a month starting in October and provided the necessary backstory for children who had never seen *The Lion King*, while simultaneously appealing to parents by reminding them of the pleasures of a well-known film as experienced through the eyes of a child. Meanwhile, Disney Junior worked hard to reinforce continuity with *The Lion King* via an attempt to "preserve 'The Lion King's' hand-drawn appearance" (Galas 2015) and the casting of James Earl Jones (Mufasa) and Ernie Sabella (Pumbaa) to reprise their roles. Nancy Kanter, executive vice president of original programming and general manager of Disney Junior Worldwide, said of the series that "we look forward to introducing a whole new generation of kids to both the Disney legacy characters and to new friends and heroes" (Baysinger 2014), but the preservation of the original's "look," songs, and scenes make clear an interest in pleasing those already familiar with *The Lion King* as well. Disney appears to have been successful in appealing to both sides of its dual-audience: *The Lion Guard* garnered 33% of its premiere's high ratings from adults 18-to-49 (Kissell 2015). Adults are an expected part of the children's television viewing audience, exemplified in the concept of co-viewing, but nostalgia appears to have garnered *The Lion Guard* an unusually strong adult audience. By contrast, Disney Junior's next premiere, *Elena of Avalor*, ranked number one in total viewers of a series broadcast on a kid's television channel in 2016 but received only 26% of its audience from the 18-to-49 demographic (Milligan 2016).

So far, we have illustrated how Disney Junior's various characters and worlds connect to other texts, worlds, and genres in the wider Disney family. At first glance, then, its intertextual unity may be seen as directed *outward* from the channel—from *Sofia* to Disney Princesses, from *The Lion Guard* to *The Lion King*, or so forth—and *inward* from the Disney universe inasmuch as it aims to entice parents to deliver their children unto Disney, but not *laterally* between shows. Crossover episodes are made slightly less likely by the different styles and worlds that make up Disney Junior's shows, but they would not be impossible: Doc McStuffins could easily be given a branded Disney toy such as Sheriff Callie, or Miles could visit a planet of Hugglemonsters. This lateral intertextual unity, however, exists in abundance in the shows' paratextual iterations, where it is common to see the characters travel together. Indeed, as any observer of Disney should know, its texts are only one small part of an industrial strategy that always includes its toys, merchandise, and other paratexts too. Disney Junior's toy licenses were among the fastest growing in 2013 (Fritz 2014) and its character brands have also been hits when translated to books (Raugust 2013) and apps (Kissell 2014).

At all these paratextual sites, Disney Junior's characters and shows regularly "hang out" together: one can buy Disney Junior storybooks that collect tales from across the channel's shows: (see Figure 19.2) *Disney Junior Magazine* similarly unites them; the Disney Junior Guess Who? game is one of many that places characters alongside each other; the Disney Junior DJ Shuffle and Get Up and Dance series offer music from across the shows; one could buy the Disney Junior Valentines and Lollipop Kit to unite Sofia, Mickey, Minnie, and Jake; pencil or pen sets regularly bring together various Disney Junior characters; the Disney Junior Wall Calendar rotates between characters; Huggies diapers unite several Disney characters in one pack; and so forth. Meanwhile, quite apart from specific merchandise uniting the characters, they are regularly juxtaposed as paratexts in retail spaces. Disney's online store has a specific Disney Junior page, and offline one also finds Disney Junior sections in Toys 'R' Us, Target, and other major retail outlets, where a plush Henry Hugglemonster is likely to sit on the shelf next to a plush Lambie or Kion. As such, the shows no doubt benefit from impulse buying "add-ons" or supplements, when parents go looking for a specific item from a specific show, yet relent to buy more or are forced to find something else instead. In such situations, moreover, we might expect a certain degree of reinforcive familiarity, wherein children and parents alike come to know the entire Disney Junior family well, even if one show or character is especially beloved.

Here, it is worth stopping to contemplate how rare such groupings are within the media universe, at least at the level of merchandise: where, for instance, does one find a CBS book that collects stories about *Big Bang Theory, NCIS*, and *The Good Wife*? Or where is the AMC *Risk* game that has zombie hoards battling for global supremacy with meth dealers and 1960s admen? Significant paratextual extensions have long been part of children's franchises, but Disney's particular paratextual articulations unite characters from within the same channel—not just from within the same franchise or narrative world.

Intertextuality as an industrial strategy is also present in Disney Junior's utilization of digital media extensions through its TV Everywhere strategy and its extensive array

FIGURE 19.2 *Licensed storybooks collecting tales from across the channel's programs.*

of digital transmedia brand extensions. The use of apps for distribution of Disney Junior programming is described as a way for Disney to "keep up with its tiniest viewers" (Barnes 2013) who increasingly have access to mobile devices and a desire to stream content (Steinberg 2015b), but Disney Junior's use of apps for both viewing and interactive content is more complex both economically and in relationship to the way their content is presented along intertextual lines. Disney's act of releasing some series like *Sheriff Callie's Wild West* on its *Watch Disney Junior* app before cable (Steinberg 2015b) demonstrates its willingness to embrace digital streaming, indicating that promoting the visibility of its new brands and characters was prioritized over traditional premiere strategies. Once driven to the *Watch Disney Junior* app by streaming first strategies, families can see exemplified the channel's dual investment in character brands and the coherent Disney family of brands. The *Watch Disney Junior* app simultaneously reinforces each of Disney Junior's individual brands by promoting "character pages" with full episodes, digital shorts, and interactive games while also creating a sense of a Disney Junior family—and indeed of a broader Disney family—by creating sections around themes like "Winter Wonderland" that include videos from multiple Disney Junior shows as well as short videos that include characters from across Disney Junior's programming.

Looking at Disney Junior's apps, we can see how interactive digital strategies have evolved to increasingly promote interaction and play with characters from both its own stable and the larger Disney library. While initially Disney Junior and Disney apps were kept separate, newer apps like *Disney Color and Play* combine interactive coloring playrooms for Disney Junior characters with coloring activities for classic Disney characters and Pixar characters. Similarly, *Disney Story Theater* provides options for kids to create puppet shows with *Sofia*, *Sheriff Callie*, and *Frozen* characters. In each case, users who are drawn to images from either Disney or Disney Junior when choosing the app are given opportunities to discover more Disney character brands (see Figure 19.3). Moreover, these apps and games often emphasize distinctive genre elements and iconography associated with famous Disney characters or films, providing viewers with a visual media vocabulary that is then echoed in Disney programming and merchandising. Young viewers may first encounter the iconic wizard's cap in a *Sofia the First* coloring book based on the episode "Cedric's Apprentice" but will encounter it again in the film *Fantasia*, on top of a Sorcerer Mickey plush set a few feet away from a Sofia doll in a local Disney Store, and as the centerpiece of their visit to Hollywood Studios at Disney World.

Iconographic intertextuality can also be seen throughout Disney Junior's apps. The *Sofia the First: The Secret Library* in the *Watch Disney Junior* app is structured as a hidden object game with many of the hidden objects specifically evoking classic Disney princesses, while the *Miles from Tomorrowland* hidden object game relied so thoroughly on science fiction iconography that it could be confused at first glance with a *Star Wars* game. Discussing Disney Junior's interactive app-based episodes, called appisodes, Lauren DeVillier, the vice president of digital media for Disney Channels Worldwide, described the advantage of the format as allowing kids to "take an active role in the story" while giving "our shows a whole new life on another platform" (Winslow

FIGURE 19.3 *Disney Junior app content uniting the channel's characters around "puzzle" activities.*

2013). While, undoubtedly this is an appeal of the unique appisode experience, this statement downplays the extent to which both elements are already key parts of Disney Junior's programming and brands, whose complex intertextuality and use of strongly genre-identified content encourages viewers to make active connections between texts in a rich (Disney-centered) media ecosystem that crosses platforms both through digital viewing platforms and extensive multimedia and merchandising brands.

CONCLUSION

Whether children's and parents' first encounter with Disney Junior comes via app, the cable channel, or even a storybook, they will likely find not only a character or show but also an integrated channel brand. From its earliest branding efforts, Disney Junior employed intertextuality as an industrial strategy—an evolution of Disney's ongoing experiments with television intertextuality since *Disneyland* in 1955 (Anderson 1994, 134). Ranging from breakout hits incorporating well-known Disney characters to looser intertextual relationships, Disney Junior uses its platform to usher children into the Wonderful World of Disney while encouraging parental good will and co-viewing through appeals to nostalgia. Disney Junior's earliest ident reminded viewers that it "all started with a mouse," yet its strategy of industrial intertextuality shows that the mouse is now just one member of an interconnected Disney family of which even and especially the youngest viewers are invited to become a part.

REFERENCES

Albiniak, Paige. 2011. "Kids Programming More Competitive than Ever." *Variety*, March 12. http://variety.com/2011/tv/features/kids-programming-more-competitive-than-ever-1118033474/.

Anderson, Christopher. 1994. *Hollywood TV: The Studio System in the Fifties*. Austin: University of Texas Press.

Barnes, Brooks. 2013. "Disney Show Will Appear First on App for Tablets." *New York Times*, October 27. www.nytimes.com/2013/10/28/business/media/disney-show-will-appear-first-on-app-for-tablets.html.

Barnes, Brooks and Amy Chozick. 2013. "Disney Characters Make It Big in TV's Preschool Playground." *New York Times*, March 31. www.nytimes.com/2013/04/01/business/media/disney-junior-challenges-nick-jr-in-preschool-tv.html?_r=0.

Baysinger, Tim. 2014. "Disney Junior Sets 'Lion King' Sequel Movie & TV Series." *Broadcasting & Cable*, June 10. www.broadcastingcable.com/news/programming/disney-junior-sets-lion-king-sequel-movie-tv-series/131670.

Copple Smith, Erin. 2012. "'Affluencers' by Bravo: Defining an Audience Through Cross-Promotion." *Popular Communication: The International Journal of Media and Culture* 10 (4): 286–301.

Fritz, Ben. 2014. "For Disney Junior, Toys Above TV." *The Wall Street Journal*, June 9. www.wsj.com/articles/for-disney-junior-toys-above-tv-1402353750.

Galas, Marj. 2015. "Animation Veteran Ford Riley Gives Eco-Spin to Disney Channel's 'Lion Guard.'" *Variety*, November 19. http://variety.com/2015/artisans/production/disney-channel-puts-ecological-spin-on-new-series-lion-guard-1201643903/.

Grosz, Christy. 2011. "Disney Junior Acing Frosh Year." *Variety*, September 26. http://variety.com/2011/digital/news/disney-junior-acing-frosh-year-1118043061/.

Johnson, Catherine. 2012. *Branding Television*. New York: Routledge.

Kissell, Rick. 2014. "Disney Junior No. 1 with Kids in First Quarter, Boosts Company Overall." *Variety*, April 4. http://variety.com/2014/tv/news/disney-junior-no-1-with-kids-in-first-quarter-boosts-company-overall-1201152344/.

Kissell, Rick. 2015. "'The Lion Guard' Off to Roaring Ratings Start for Disney Channel." *Variety*, November 30. http://variety.com/2015/tv/news/disney-channel-ratings-the-lion-guard-1201650325/.

Milligan, Mercedes. 2016. "'Elena of Avalor' Premiere Rules Ratings." *Animation Magazine*, July 29. www.animationmagazine.net/tv/elena-of-avalor-premiere-rules-ratings/.

Morabito, Andrea. 2011. "TCA: Disney Junior to Launch February 14." *Broadcasting & Cable*, January 10. www.broadcastingcable.com/news/programming/tca-disney-junior-launch-feb-14/37270.

Owen, Rob. 2015. "TV Preview: Disney Junior Introduces 'Miles from Tomorrowland.'" *Pittsburgh Post-Gazette*, February 9. www.post-gazette.com/ae/tv-radio/2015/02/09/TV-Preview-Disney-Junior-introduces-Miles-From-Tomorrowland/stories/201502070010.

Raugust, Karen. 2013. "From 'Doc McStuffins' to 'Sofia the First,' Disney Junior Drives Book Sales." *Publishers' Weekly*, December 13. www.publishersweekly.com/pw/by-topic/childrens/childrens-industry-news/article/60357-from-doc-mcstuffins-to-sofia-the-first-disney-junior-drives-book-sales.html.

Steinberg, Brian. 2015a. "Disney's 'Goldie & Bear' Mixes Fairy Tales with Digital Distribution." *Variety*, August 20. http://variety.com/2015/tv/news/disney-goldie-bear-kids-tv-fairy-tales-1201574581/.

Steinberg, Brian. 2015b. "How Kids' TV Networks Are Fighting Off Their Frightening Decline." *Variety*, September 2. http://variety.com/2015/tv/features/ kids-tv-strategy-nickelodeon-disney-digital-1201582874/.

Weisman, Jon. 2010. "Disney Junior Branding Effort Launches." *Variety*, October 7. http://variety.com/2010/tv/news/disney-junior-branding-effort-launches-1118025328/.

Winslow, George. 2013. "Disney Junior Appisode App Launches." *Multichannel*, April 4. www.multichannel.com/news/content/disney-junior-appisode-app-launches/358873.

Disney XD

Boyhood and the Racial Politics of Market Segmentation

Christopher Chávez

> You may already have noticed that girls are quite different from you. By this, we do not mean the physical differences, more the fact that they remain unimpressed by your mastery of a game involving wizards, or your understanding of Morse code. Some will be impressed, of course, but as a general rule, girls do not get quite as excited by the use of urine as a secret ink as boys do.
>
> —*The Dangerous Book for Boys* (2007)

Within popular imagination, there exist many normative assumptions about what constitutes the intrinsic nature of boyhood. On one hand, boys are said to be analytical: good at science, math, and engineering. Yet boys are also said to be creative beings, immersing themselves in the world of fantasy and science fiction. They are predisposed to sports, adventure, and discovery, but are also believed to be less mature than girls, engaging in gross humor and pranks. Boys, it is said, are simply different beings from girls.

Such claims, of course, connect to dominant narratives about gender differences, but they are also based on the presumption that there is indeed a universal boyhood experience, regardless of one's class, ethnicity, religious background, and so forth. It is no surprise, then, that when the Walt Disney Company launched Disney XD in 2009, they purported to have created a media destination that would appeal to all boys. In their annual report to investors (Walt Disney Company 2009) the year the channel launched, the company described the network this way: "Disney XD has a mix of live-action and animated programming for kids ages 6–14, targeting boys and their quest for discovery, accomplishment, sports, adventure and humor." Rich Ross, president of Disney Channels Worldwide, put it more simply: Disney wanted to "create a destination for boys" (Chimielewski 2008). This begs the question: Whose boyhood is Disney capturing? For that matter, how does this construction of boyhood turn on characters, themes, and activities that these boys are presumed to like?

In this chapter I argue that Disney's decision to launch a boy-centric cable channel reflects the overall logic by which the children's television marketplace has begun to organize itself. Here it is important to think of children's television as a maturing market in which a growing number of channels are competing for more narrow slices of the children's audience. Disney's decision to target children based on gender while simultaneously obscuring differences in that boyhood experience—including children's racial identities—provides significant insights into which kinds of cultural differences television industries deem appropriate to acknowledge in children and which they do not.

CHILDREN'S TELEVISION AS A MATURING MARKETPLACE

Like the audience itself, childhood may be considered a construct that reflects the social, cultural, and economic conditions of its time (Ariès 1962; Mintz 2004). However, over the course of the twentieth century, this stage in the lifecycle began to take on new economic exchange values, what Cook (2004) calls the "commodification of childhood." During this time, marketers routinely began to appeal directly to children as individual subjects with consumer desire and, as early as 1917, dedicated media began to emerge targeting children as a matter of business strategy.

The advent of television increased marketers' capacity to reach children on a mass scale. Early on, television networks developed programming designed for children, whether in the form of family-oriented programs or dedicated programming blocks on weekend mornings. However, dedicated networks began to emerge shortly after the advent of cable. In 1977, Nickelodeon launched the first-ever dedicated children television's network and was later acquired by the global media giant Viacom. Disney entered the market shortly after, launching The Disney Channel in 1983. At first, the network utilized its massive catalog of content, but later developed programs exclusively intended for its cable properties. Time Warner's Cartoon Network launched in 1992 too, focusing on animated programming.

Given the limited number of broadcast television channels, early children's television was a shared space, designed to appeal to children in general. Programs were designed to reach an idealized, prototypical audience, what Sammond (2005) describes as "the generic child." According to Sammond, while that "generic child" presupposed a set of universal qualities, it was a construction based firmly in white, middle-class sensibilities, thus erasing significant social differences. In recent years, however, the proliferation of channels in the post-network era has complicated the practice of targeting a single, generic child. With the advent of new technologies, including cable and satellite television as well as streaming services, the amount of dedicated children's programming has increased, compelling media companies to pursue smaller niche markets.

This, in turn, has motivated media companies to engage more fully in the practice of audience segmentation, or dividing the overall market into subsets based on the perception of shared characteristics such as age, gender, income, geographical area, and so forth. While audience segmentation is often described in scientific terms, Sender (2005) argues that the decision to target a particular audience reflects both economic and cultural considerations. Choices about what programs are considered to be relevant to the targeted consumer, who gets to be included in the target audience, and how resources will be allocated, all reflect preexisting ideological biases about viewers, their identities, and their values. In his discussion of video games, Jenkins (1998) argued that video-game producers reified gender-specific play strategies, essentially adopting the preconceptions of an earlier generation of cultural producers. Children's literature too began as undifferentiated according to gender, but soon evolved to clearly distinguish between "boys' culture" and "girls' culture," in ways that associated boys with adventure, daring, exploration, while relegating girls to the familiar and the domestic (Segal 1986). In similar ways, children's television began as a shared space with the potential for crossover experiences of childhood. However, the separation of male and females into distinct audiences, further encouraged the gender-specific viewing strategies that defined the enterprise of Disney XD.

GENDERING CHILDREN'S TELEVISION

Disney has long been criticized for its stark gender politics, but the formation of a dedicated boys' network institutionalizes its presumption of essential distinctions between boys and girls. By pursuing this strategy, Disney XD follows in the tradition of other kinds of cable networks, such as Spike TV for men and Lifetime for women that have deployed gender differences as a means of market differentiation. The fact that Disney can easily pivot in this direction suggests that gender segmentation has become an equally acceptable strategy in children's television.

At face value, the launch of a boys' network is driven by economic motives. Disney XD competes directly with other children's television channels in an increasingly crowded marketplace. While independent players such as Sprout and Qubo have made inroads, much of the growth has come from dominant players that launch additional channel services to expand their product portfolios. A byproduct of this growth has been to further segment the marketplace based on gender. For example, Viacom's Nickelodeon, notable for developing programs that featured strong female leads (Banet-Weiser 2007), launched NickToons in an effort to capture an audience of boys with exclusively animated programming.

In the same way, the launch of Disney XD responds to Disney's prior failure to win over boys in this increasingly gender-specific marketplace. When The Disney Channel first launched in 1983, the vision was to develop programming that would build on Disney's overall success with the generic child. However, due to its reliance on the various Disney "princess" franchises as well as the later success of such properties as *Hannah Montana* and *High School Musical*, the network had skewed decidedly female. As a result, prospective advertisers for video games and action figures did not see Disney Channel as a viable option for marketing products that were themselves gendered. Greg Kahn, senior vice president of strategic insights for media buying firm Optimedia International USA Inc., put it this way:

> You're fighting the brand perception, the very, very strong brand equity that's been in the marketplace for many, many years. . . . It would almost require a completely

separate effort to reach tween boys, with a completely different name somehow associated with the Disney property, to reach these tween males.

(Chimielewski 2008)

And that's exactly what Disney did. They took an existing asset, DisneyToons, and recreated it from the ground up. In practice, this launch of an all boys' network involved the ideological to clearly demarcate gender differences and preferences. This kind of "borderwork" (Thorne 1993) is made manifest in the very practical decisions concerning programming and branding. To establish itself as a "boys network," XD's branding includes all the appropriate signifiers of boyhood. The name XD, short for "Extreme Digital," evokes the notion of extreme sports as well as a technological mastery. Furthermore, the XD is stylized with heavy, block letters, which helps to offset the softer, rounded nature of the traditional Disney logo. Finally, the brand's color palette includes black, silver, and neon green, all colors that fall safely within normative standards of masculinity.

While establishing the visual style for the network was a relatively easy task, finding a programming mix that would appeal to their target audience has been an evolving process. Initially, Disney's goal was to move beyond animation and develop programming that would represent a more complex perspective on boyhood. As Disney Channels Worldwide President Rich Ross (Rose 2009) described the new platform's audience appeal:

> While they liked animation, they were looking for more. They were looking for live-action series, which exist in a couple of places, but not in plentiful amounts. They wanted them to be in a range of comedies and dramas, which is what we're producing. They loved movies, so the network is going to have a movie block. Sports are very important to them, and we're able to work out a relationship inside of our company with our brother network ESPN.

During an interview with the *Los Angeles Times*, Ross put it differently:

> They want a place, essentially a headquarters for them where their favorite content exists, that has this broad array of shapes and sizes and tenors and complexities, and treats them with the respect that Disney Channel treats all kids.

(Chimielewski 2008)

Ross' comments suggest that the original vision for the network was to present a version of boyhood that would be more inclusive and multifaceted. The execution of this vision, however, was much more narrow. Early XD programming was essentially modeled on the basic format of its sister network Disney Channel, only reimagined for boys. For example, the channel launched with *Aaron Stone*, a live-action series about Charlie Landers, a teenager who leads a double life as a government agent. This storyline is similar to *Hannah Montana*, a show about Miley Stewart, precocious teenager who also leads a double life as Hannah Montana, a famous pop star. Similarly, following

Disney Channel's success with original films, Disney XD launched *Skyrunners*, a made-for cable film about a boy who acquires supernatural powers after encountering an alien life form.

While Disney XD found additional success with animated programs such as *Phineas and Ferb*, the channel initially failed to attract a loyal following. In response, Disney executives made two key adjustments. First, instead of targeting tweens, Disney narrowed their target to younger boys ages six to eight. Second, they embraced animation, reversing their original programming strategy of providing more live-action and drama. XD's change in programming strategy coincided with two major purchases on behalf of the company. In 2009, the company's purchased comic book giant Marvel for $4.2 billion and in 2012, they purchased *Star Wars* for $4 billion. Today, both assets account for a majority of Disney XD's current programming. Marvel delivers *Guardians of the Galaxy, Ultimate Spiderman, and Marvel Avengers Assemble* while the Star Wars franchise delivers *Star Wars Rebels, LEGO Star Wars*, and *The Freemaker Adventures*.

These properties have also helped Disney cultivate business partnerships with desired advertisers—especially in the realm of digital games. With *LEGO*, Disney has produced *LEGO Star Wars*, which is both a television and video game series set in the *Star Wars* universe, but in which the main characters are animated in the form of the distinct minifigures from the *LEGO* toy sets. Similarly, Disney has cultivated a partnership with Electronic Arts. In 2009, the video game publisher boosted its advertising spending with Disney by close to 30% (Norman 2009) and in 2013, it signed an exclusive ten-year deal with Disney to design its own games based on the *Star Wars* universe (Cai and Fritz 2013). In 2015, Disney XD produced *Clash of Karts: Mario Kart 8*, in collaboration with Nintendo, a show that featured a battle between four two-person teams who were coached by YouTube stars. Nintendo and Disney XD also teamed up for a one-hour special based on the Nintendo World Championships 2015. This focus on video games defines much of Disney XD's programming, representing the significance of digital play to contemporary constructions of boyhood (Jenkins 1998) compared to previous iterations based in athletic play. In their original positioning of the network, Disney executives had signaled an interest in making greater use ESPN, the company's lucrative cable asset, but this strategy has never fully been realized. During its lifetime, XD has only developed a handful of programs with ESPN including *Sports Center Kids* (2009), *Disney XD ESPN Sports Science* (2016), and *Becoming* (2016), produced by NBA star LeBron James.

THE COLORBLIND BOY

While Disney has actively segmented the children's audience based on gender, the network has on the other hand avoided segmentation based on racial difference. Many other cable channels, including ASPiRE, BET, El Rey, and MTV Tr3s all utilize race and ethnicity as their primary form of segmentation; meanwhile Disney-owned Freeform builds explicitly multiculturalist themes into its attempts to target Millennial cable viewers. By contrast, Disney XD adopts a colorblind approach, in which children are presumed to operate in a world in which racial difference simply does not exist.

Disney's strategy of showcasing video game culture, for example, is often embodied in the figure of the white gamer, a recurring trope within XD's programming. Disney XD launched with *Aaron Stone*, a series featuring a white protagonist who assumes the role of his online avatar. Yet in her analysis of The Disney Channel, Turner (2014) found that even nonwhite characters are often written in ways in which their race and racialized experiences are negligible. In a similar way, Disney XD *The Gamer's Guide to Pretty Much Everything* depicts a boyhood that while not always white is nevertheless color-blind. In the role of Conner, who is attempting to balance life as a normal teenager with that of a professional video game player, lead actor Cameron Boyce is African American but phenotypically white. His casting in this role illustrates Warner's (2015) point that, in a colorblind world, actors who have the capacity operate in multiple cultural registers are at an advantage because they can invoke race without isolating a white, mainstream audience. In the show, Boyce's character sits comfortably within white, middle class America, but Disney has also utilized Boyce's blackness in a 2016 public service announcement celebrating Black History Month, in which he acknowledged his grandmother's role in school integration. Disney's PSA is effective at placing racial discrimination comfortably in the past, however. Boyce's role as an exemplar of progressive colorblindness is remarkable because, in the present, gaming has often become a racially charged cultural space (Gray 2012).

Therein lies the problem with a colorblind approach on television. It depicts race without the racial politics. This dynamic can also be seen in *Lab Rats*, a live-action series about a family that includes three bionic teenagers. The show's protagonist is Leo Dooley, an African American boy whose mother Tasha has recently married the wealthy, high-tech genius Donald Davenport, who is white. Unbeknownst to Leo and Tasha, Donald has been secretly training three bionic siblings: Adam, Bree, and Chase. Once Leo discovers the trio, they become the siblings he never had and he helps them to integrate into the social world of high school. The fact that Tasha, a black woman, is mother to three visibly white teenagers, goes undiscussed in the series. Furthermore, outsider status belongs neither to Leo and Tasha, but rather to Adam, Bree, and Chase, who have difficulty with social life because of their bionic abilities.

A heavy reliance on animated programming only exacerbates this issue. Unlike The Disney Channel, in which animated girls adhere to a strict body type (small and thin with large, wide-set eyes, high foreheads and small, button noses), boys' bodies on XD can assume many more forms. In the *Star Wars* and Marvel franchises male bodies tend to be hypermasculine with well-defined musculature, but in other instances like *Phineas and Ferb*, boys' bodies assume more geometric shapes. Animation may also abstract bodies altogether. *Pickle and Peanut*, is an animated series about two friends and their misadventures, in which case boys are literally embodied as a peanut and a pickle. Disney's heavy rotation of Marvel and *Star Wars* properties amplifies these issues by presenting worlds in which typical human signifiers of race and ethnicity such as surname, skin color, and linguistic style are less recognizable, and identities are hidden behind masks, cowls, and full-bodied costumes. In science fiction, characters may take on both human and non-human forms. Phenotypically, they can be green, red, or blue.

Despite efforts to ignore race, however, racial politics inevitably manifest themselves. At its worst, Disney XD animated characters reify stereotypical treatments of race. This can be found in the character of Soos (short for Jesús), a buffoonish handyman on the network's widely popular *Gravity Falls*, or in the character of Baljeet Tjinder on *Phineas and Ferb*, a side character who speaks English with a vague South Asian accent and perpetuates the stereotype of the intellectually gifted but socially awkward Asian. In most cases, however, race and ethnicity are simply rendered invisible. Most of Disney XD programming is a sort of post-racial fantasy, in which nonwhite characters are included, but unencumbered by their outsider status, including class and linguistic differences. In the animated show, *Star vs. Forces of Evil*, for example, the Princess Star Butterfly arrives in our universe and befriends Marco Diaz. While Marco's surname designates him as Spanish or Latino, there are no other signifiers of race. Voiced by Anglo actor Adam MacArthur, Diaz speaks English with no trace of a Latino accent. Race is both present and obscured through these creative practices.

FRAGMENTING THE "GENERIC CHILD"

As television has become more and more fragmented, cable channels have explored infinite ways of categorizing the audience, including segments based on gender (Oxygen), race (Black Entertainment Television), linguistic preference (Univision), Lifestyle (Food Network), and so forth. When it comes to children's television, however, age and gender have become the dominant forms of segmentation while segmentation based on children's race and ethnicity has been conspicuously absent. The conspicuous absence of racial acknowledgement may be grounded in what Mintz (2004) calls a romantic view of childhood, in which it is believed that children must be shielded from the realities of adult life, including sexuality, and, of course, racial politics. However, the categorization of the children's television market only serves to reify gender and racial hierarchies, only in different ways. Both strategies ensure the privileged status of a heteronormative, white boyhood.

While these practices are not enacted by Disney alone, the network does seem particularly conservative relative to other children's networks. For example, Banet-Weiser's (2007) research on Nickelodeon suggests that, while problematic in its own ways, the network has found some success creating a shared space for both boys and girls. Furthermore, Nickelodeon is more apt to acknowledge the racial identities of children. What truly makes Disney unique from its competitors, however, is the scale in which it can enact ideologies around race and gender. Disney's business is not limited to television, but extends to radio and film, as well as a range of auxiliary products such as video games, children's apparel, toys, and theme parks. In short, Disney is one of the most prolific producers of childhood culture and has the unique capacity to shape childhood itself in profound ways.

Compelled by the logic of capitalism, Disney will continue to expand its television portfolio. In the process, it has begun to abandon historical strategies for pursuing the generic child while beginning a new process of cultivating different kinds of children (markets) with different viewing strategies. Fragmenting the generic child into more divisible segments, however, does not necessarily equate to a more nuanced understanding of the childhood experience. Market segmentation is still based on the assumption of order and uniformity and does not allow for diverse, complex range of lived experience.

By contrast, we know that identities intersect in meaningful ways. We know, for example, that black boys are stigmatized in a different way than black girls, and experience oppression unknown to white boys. Yet Disney's stubborn insistence on representing children of color without any of the politics surrounding their bodies can seem drastically out of touch with the actual lives that many boys live. After all, the same year that *Lab Rats* debuted with Leo living an upscale existence with a white father, Trayvon Martin was killed, sparking a sobering, nationwide discussion regarding the way in which society deals with black boys. Disney XD does not account for this reality, but in order for the channel to achieve its mandate of delivering younger boys to advertisers, the construction of boyhood must not be complicated with the messy, racialized realties of everyday life.

REFERENCES

Ariès, Philippe. 1962. *Centuries of Childhood: A Social History of Family Life*. New York: Random House.

Banet-Weiser, Sarah. 2007. *Kids Rule! Nickelodeon and Consumer Citizenship*. Durham: Duke University Press.

Cai, Debbie and Ben Fritz. 2013. "EA to Make 'Star Wars' Games for Disney." *Wall Street Journal*, May 6. www.wsj.com/articles/SB10001424127887323372504578467333843380880.

Chimielewski, Dawn. 2008. "Enough with the Girls, Tween Boys Get Their Own Brand of Disney Love." *Los Angeles Times*, August 7. http://articles.latimes.com/2008/aug/07/business/fi-disney7.

Cook, Daniel Thomas. 2004. *The Commodification of Childhood: The Children's Clothing Industry and the Rise of the Child Consumer*. Durham: Duke University Press.

Gray, Kishonna. 2012. "Intersecting Oppressions and Online Communities." *Information, Communication & Society* 15 (3): 411–28.

Iggulden, Con and Hal Iggulden. 2007. *The Dangerous Book for Boys*. New York: Harper Collins.

Jenkins, Henry. 1998. "'Complete Freedom of Movement': Video Games as Gendered Play Spaces." In *From Barbie to Mortal Combat: Gender and Computer Games*, edited by Justine Cassell and Henry Jenkins, 262–97. Cambridge: MIT Press.

Mintz, Steven. 2004. *Huck's Raft: A History of American Childhood*. Cambridge: Harvard University Press.

Norman, Michael. 2009. "Cable-Channel Shift Reflects Disney's Boy Trouble." *Cleveland.com*, September 2. www.cleveland.com/tv/index.ssf/2009/09/cable_channel_shift_reflects_d.html

Rose, Lacey. 2009. "Disney Goes Where (It Hopes) the Boys Are." *Forbes*, February 12. www.forbes.com/2009/02/12/disney-rich-ross-business-media_0212_disney_xd.html.

Sammond, Nicholas. 2005. *Babes in Tomorrowland: Walt Disney and the Making of the American Child (1930–1960)*. Durham: Duke University Press.

Segal, Elizabeth. 1986. "'As the Twig Is Bent. . . .': Gender and Childhood Reading." In *Gender and Reading: Essays on Readers, Texts, and Contexts*, edited by Elizabeth A. Flynn and Patrocinio P. Schweickart, 165–86. Baltimore: John Hopkins University Press.

Sender, Katherine. 2005. *Business, Not Politics: The Making of the Gay Market*. New York: Columbia University Press.

Thorne, Barrie. 1993. *Gender Play: Girls and Boys in School*. New Brunswick: Rutgers University Press.

Turner, Sarah E. 2014. "BBFFs: Interracial Friendships in a Post-Racial World." In *The Colorblind Screen: Television in Post-Racial America*, edited by Sarah Nilson and Sarah E. Turner, 237–60. New York: New York University Press.

Walt Disney Company. 2009. "Fiscal Year 2009: Annual Financial Report and Shareholder Letter." https://ditm-twdc-us.storage.googleapis.com/2015/10/2009-Annual-Report.pdf.

Warner, Kristen. 2015. *The Cultural Politics of Colorblind TV Casting*. New York: Routledge.

Freeform

Shaking off the Family Brand within a Conglomerate Family

Barbara Selznick

In 2016, ABC Family changed its name to Freeform as part of a long rebranding process informed by industrial imperatives faced by the network's owner, the Walt Disney Company. The new name underscores the goal to ground the brand position of this network in relation to Disney's other broadcast and cable outlets, and solidify a clear but fluid target audience that will not "age out" of the network and its programming. Similar to the way that Disney Channel appeals to children at a particular stage of life (tweens),[1] Freeform targets what Disney labeled "becomers," young people who are becoming who they are going to be. Or, as Freeform president Tom Ascheim explains, it's the age range that falls "from your first kiss to your first kid" (Barnes 2015). The name change to Freeform and the identification of a new target audience is part of a long process of branding that reveals a great deal about the importance of particular audiences to advertisers and media companies in the face of contemporary sociocultural and technological shifts as well as new viewing practices.

The shift from ABC Family to Freeform specifically highlights fluctuating ideas about family viewing in contemporary times. The Walt Disney Co. took over the family network in the midst of social, economic, and technological circumstances that potentially weakened the value of a "family" network. Was it still possible to create programming that a family would watch together but that also spoke to the identity and values of the viewers that advertisers sought? As will be discussed, ABC Family pursued the teen and young adult Millennial viewers who were born roughly between the early 1980s and early 2000s. These viewers could be encouraged to develop fierce loyalty to brands that helped them shape their emerging identities. In terms of television watching, Millennials were imagined to be close to their families but also solitary television viewers who used various platforms to consume media. In addition to being an advertiser-friendly target demographic, this teen/young adult audience might allow ABC Family to fit into the already layered structure of the Disney/ABC conglomerate—if the connection to "family" could be successfully negotiated.

Throughout its existence, the network that is now Freeform went by several names as it changed corporate owners. The network began in the 1970s as part of the Christian Broadcast Network owned by Pat Robertson. The network's most famous show, *The 700 Club*, still airs on Freeform. The religious program's continuation on the network in perpetuity was part of the contract when the network was sold to News Corp. in 1997 (when it became Fox Family) and again when News Corp. sold the network to Disney/ABC in 2001.[2] Throughout its time as The Family Channel, Fox Family, and ABC Family, the network chased different audiences with a range of programming. In 2001, the Walt Disney Company bought Fox Worldwide, which included Fox Family, for approximately $3 billion along with the assumption of approximately $2 billion in debt ("Disney Buys Fox Family" 2001). This purchase was considered by some to be a questionable decision by CEO Michael Eisner (Ayres 2001); however, the Walt Disney Co. would eventually grow the network to be the fourth most watched cable network by the 18- to 24-year-old demographic ("ABC Family, MTV Miss Their Targets" 2015).

Renamed ABC Family, the network scaled back its children's programming to avoid competition with Disney Channel. ABC executives initially developed plans to change the name of the network to XYZ and transition programming to focus on teens and college-age students (Shine 2015). Although revisited every few years, the renaming idea was continuously dropped, presumably in part because of an assumed contractual requirement to keep "family" in the network's name (Shine 2015). Over time, however, ABC Family shifted its programming away from families towards teens and young adults, demonstrating an effort to complement the audiences already being targeted by the various Disney-owned networks.

INDUSTRIAL CONTEXT: FRAGMENTED AUDIENCES, CONGLOMERATES, AND THE FAMILY BRAND

ABC Family was created within the complex media industries culture shaped by 1990s trends of audience fragmentation and conglomeration. As I have discussed elsewhere, these dual factors are contradictory in that fragmentation requires narrowcasting to particular audiences through a clear brand, while conglomerates often expect networks to grow audiences and broaden the loyal viewer base of the conglomerate (Selznick 2009). These pressures influenced ABC Family in multiple ways that led the network away from its family focus, creating confusion around the network's name.

Audience fragmentation, although generally associated with the rise of new media technologies, stemmed also from sociocultural changes. The rise of the "postmodern family" changed the dynamics of family life (Allen 1999, 114–15). Throughout the 1990s and into the 2000s the number of single-parent families, blended families, families with same-sex parents, and families of choice continued to grow. Additionally, families with two working parents became increasingly common (Tapscott 2009, 224). The aging of Baby Boomers, as well as a tendency to marry and have children later in life, increased time demands on parents who worked while caring for parents and young children alike. Research found that children increasingly spent time alone (Andreasen 2000, 14).

Concurrently, parents of Millennials worried about their children's emotional development as well as their safety, leading to an increased emphasis on media in family life. Children were encouraged to develop their individual interests and tastes outside of family through activities, hobbies, and media use (Livingstone 2007, 307). Media, in fact, became a "safe" alternative for children who were discouraged from spending time outside in the world in unsupervised activities, such as hanging out at malls, skating rinks, or just around neighborhoods—all of which could be seen as potentially dangerous (304–305). With parents busy at work, children and teens relied on in-home media—often consumed alone—to help develop their identities and relationships (317).

The growth of digital technologies amplified this fragmentation and individualization of audiences. In 1989, researchers found that 70% of television viewing was done by an adult with a child; however, that number declined when there were more television sets in the household (Fabes, Wilson, and Christopher 1989, 338). Simply having the means to watch television on different sets within the home increased audience fragmentation. The development of cable channels through the 1980s and into the 1990s further segmented the audience. The growing number of personal devices for viewing developed in the 2000s, such as iPods, iPads, and personal computers, only increased this trend toward fragmentation, as the "ability to watch television on other smaller more personal screens has acted as a centrifugal force" pulling people away from communal/family viewing (Brown and Barkhuus 2011, 109). By the late 1990s, many upper-middle-class teens had "media rich" bedrooms used to escape their families and support their developing identities (Livingstone 2007, 309, 317). The concept of "family viewing," while certainly not eliminated, was suspected to be even more rare.

Furthermore, increased media channels and technology both enabled the growing sociocultural trend toward audience fragmentation and increased the connection of media brands with viewer values and identity. Because identity is in flux for younger viewers, they are considered more likely to be influenced by these brand connections and channeled toward an emotional connection with a commercial brand that speaks to them (Serazio 2013, 609). Teenagers and tweens increasingly attracted the attention of marketers and, therefore, television networks, who saw great potential in using television to connect younger viewers to products (Sutherland and Thompson 2003, 79–88).

While becoming part of Disney/ABC influenced ABC Family in very obvious respects (changes in programming, executives, network name), conglomeration also shaped the network in more complex ways. ABC Family was purchased at a time when media corporations recognized the benefits of repurposing television content. Programs created for one network could be reused and shown on another. Such repurposing did not simply fill time on broadcast and cable outlets, but also allowed media companies to create strong (often high-budget) content that appealed to audiences across media platforms (Vukanovic 2009, 82). The goal, then, was to create content that could move across several (corporate-owned) distribution platforms. Corporate executives clearly recognized the potential for using ABC Family as a second cycle outlet for family-friendly Disney content. CEO Michael Eisner described the purchase of ABC Family as "a kind of safety net to be able to continue high-end, well-written, well-produced, high-talented filmed entertainment" (Carter 2001). In other words, the ability to repurpose content on another network would allow ABC to continue to fund and distribute expensive programming.

Extensive repurposing between ABC and ABC Family did not last long, however. Using large amounts of repurposed programs, including *The Bachelor* (2002–) and *Whose Line Is It Anyway?* (1998–2007) led to low ratings and made cable operators unhappy (Schneider 2008, 19). The network found more success with syndicated programs, primarily from the WB, such as *Gilmore Girls* (2000–2007), *7th Heaven* (1996–2007) and *Smallville* (2001–2011), as well as some older sitcoms from ABC's TGIF line up such as *Boy Meets World* (1993–2000) and *Sabrina the Teenage Witch* (1996–2003) (Murphy 2014, 19). These programs helped to define an audience for ABC Family, and in 2004, the network acknowledged their target audience of 14- to 28-year-old viewers, primarily women (Giges 2008). This audience was "an age bracket that Disney hadn't really targeted until recently—too old for Disney's more saccharine youth fare (they've outgrown 'Hannah Montana'), but too young for the company's more adult programming like 'Grey's Anatomy'" (Schneider 2008, 16). ABC Family found a way to navigate the pressures of both fragmentation and conglomeration by tapping into an advantageous audience that Disney, as a conglomerate, was not already exploiting and, thus, contributing to corporate growth.

This target audience for ABC Family—Millennial teens and young adults—could still be courted within the confines of the "family" brand of the network (Weprin 2008, 30). These teens, raised by late Baby Boomers and early Gen Xers, were often showered with attention (Howe and Strauss 2000, 43), developing strong family ties. The Millennials' love of their families contested images of teenagers sitting alone in their rooms watching television. Some researchers suggested that, due to their "high regard" for their parents (Keeling 2003, 32), Millennials might respond well to family-friendly marketing approaches. Additionally, the increased availability of mobile devices allowed marketers to imagine that families would continue to watch television together while simultaneously using their personal media devices (Lee 2013). Family viewing, therefore, remained a possibility in targeting this new generation.

Paul Lee, ABC Family president from 2004–2010, recirculated these accepted beliefs about Millennials, saying they are

> optimistic, they make decision by consensus, and they're diverse—but most importantly they love family, which is great for our name and for the brand. . . . They may define family differently—it's not Ozzie and Harriet, but rather a much messier, more passionate, more fun, more real family.
>
> (Umstead 2009, 18)

ABC Family thus created programs that depicted the postmodern families experienced by many Millennials, adopting the tag line "A Different Kind of Family" in 2006.

With shows such as *Greek* (2007–2011), *Kyle XY* (2006–2009), *The Secret Life of the American Teenager* (2008–2013), and *Make It or Break It* (2009–2012), ABC Family targeted its core 14- to 28-year-old audience, but also offered programs that could be watched by parents as well. This "family" approach made the network advertiser friendly. One media buyer explained, "You can get millennials other places, but ABC Family offers a nice, warm environment. It's been good for our advertisers and good for the marketplace" (Schneider 2008, 19). Unlike MTV, which appealed to a similar target audience, ABC Family avoided controversy, and offered advertisers a "safe" place to promote products while still attracting coveted consumers.

THE RISE OF FREEFORM: PERCEPTION GAPS, AGING MILLENNIALS AND BECOMERS

On the surface, ABC Family appeared to have found a successful formula that balanced the demands of Millennial viewers and their families, becoming one of the most watched networks on cable television with its target audience (ABC Family 2015a). Industry analysts and viewers were surprised, therefore, when ABC Family announced a name change on October 6, 2015, noting that networks with ABC Family's level of success rarely change their names (Barnes 2015). The shift, however, was seen as a continuation and solidification of the brand position created by the network since the early 2000s, and particularly since the success of its social media phenomenon *Pretty Little Liars* (2010–2017), which *Mediaweek* described as "at once spooky and steamy, but chaste enough for its 8pm time slot. It's like *Gossip Girl* with a curfew" (Crupi 2010).

Market research by the network found that while loyal viewers understood ABC Family's focus on Millennials, those who did not watch regularly associated the network with the terms "wholesome" and "family friendly" (Walker 2016). According to current Freeform president Tom Ascheim, these terms were not representative of the network (Walker 2016) and caused a "roadblock" for some viewers (Holloway 2015). The name change was intended to help close this "perception gap" between what people thought the network was and what it actually offered, bringing the network's brand image in line with its programming (Malone 2016, 19). Additionally, the network chose to disconnect its name from the well-known ABC brand. Ascheim explained,

> We are occupying a space at the Disney company that is between kids and family on the Disney side and the strength with real grownups on ABC and ESPN on the other side. We are a bridge, we believe, between those two zones. But to be a strong brand that speaks so specifically and vividly to our audience the same way the other great brands do, we thought it needed to stand on its own.
>
> (Holloway 2015)

The desire for an independent brand speaks to the image that Freeform is trying to create: one that allows "becomers" to create identities that are independent of the adults in their lives (such as parents) who may watch ABC and separate from their younger selves who watched Disney Channel.

The network's interest in moving away from the "family friendly" image reflected a forward-looking approach as Millennials aged and the teens and young adults of

Generation Z (those born since the early 2000s) become the new desirable audience. Although ABC Family promoted the idea that it targeted a Millennial niche, the network also acknowledged, "today, nearly 70% of 12–34 year olds are Millennials, but in five years, Millennials will be less than half of the target" (ABC Family 2015a). The need to consider Generation Z, as well as future generations, in the brand planning led to a rethinking of the strength of the "family" connection. As Levit (2015) explains, members of Generation Z "don't wait for their parents to teach them things or tell them how to make decisions." Industry insiders perceived these young adults as more independent than Millennials and their relationships with their families as more tenuous. "Family," as a brand value, was falling out of favor with the age demographic sought by the network, encouraging ABC Family to rethink its strategy.

Arriving at ABC Family in 2013 with a mandate to create a clear brand for the network, Ascheim reports finding that there was no contractual issue that required the word "family" to remain in the network's name (Barnes 2015). The new name, "Freeform," was chosen from thousands of options (Malone 2016, 19), Ascheim explains, for three reasons. First, it refers to a targeted audience of "becomers" (discussed later in this chapter) perceived to be "in formation freely" (Walker 2016). Second, the name suggests the way that the targeted viewers use media: freely and without regard to platform (2016). Not just consumers of content, Freeform viewers participate in the creation of media connected to their favorite networks and shows (Wagmeister 2015). When announcing the name, the network urged viewers to send in pictures and videos that expressed their own "freeform" or "what fuels passion for them" (Wagmeister 2015), immediately promoting viewer participation and involvement with the brand in ways designed to make them feel "free" to voice their ideas. Finally, Freeform "evokes a mood, a sense of spontaneity, creativity" (Walker 2016). Before the name change took effect, ABC Family released a series of short videos that answered questions about the new name. In the video titled "What Is Freeform?," Vanessa Marano of the popular series *Switched at Birth* (2011–2017) explains that Freeform means "no boundaries" (she quickly clarifies that she means "the good kind of no boundaries"), "that you can make up your own rules," and that "anything is possible" (ABC Family 2015b). In another video, Isaiah Mustafa of the much-anticipated show *Shadowhunters* (2016–), which at the time had yet to air, describes Freeform viewers as "inquisitive"—they "ask questions" (ABC Family 2015c). Freeform aimed to connect with certain values, feelings, and ideas to form a new brand image, none of which centered on family.

ABC Family's becomers joined the ranks of other made-up demographic groups for cable networks. As Buckman (2015) pointed out, Spike targets "the driven," Pop TV seeks "modern grownups," and Bravo's audience is composed of "affluencers." Like these other groups, the idea of "becomers" combines psychographics (they are optimistic, idealistic, and value hustle) and demographics (ages 14–34) to create a brand identity (Baysinger 2015, 19). Announcing the new name, the ABC Family press release explained:

> The name Freeform speaks to the mindset and attitude of what the channel has defined as Becomers. Traditionally, Becomers are in high school, college and the

FIGURE 21.1 *As the network disconnected from its ABC parent and the family audience, the ABC Family logo with the tagline "A Different Kind of Family" changed to the Freeform logo, using bold graphic design to appeal to "becomers."*

decade that follows and are navigating the wonderful, fun, exciting, and scary time in life when you experience the most firsts—first car, first apartment, first job, first love, first heartbreak—all the firsts that exist between who they are and who they want to become. Becomers represent a life stage rather than a generation.

(ABC Family 2015a)

The strength of Freeform's brand and name needed to speak, then, to the becomers of all generations. Some commentators doubted whether the new name helped the network's branding problem. Jacqui Shine's college class—presumably comprised of becomers—expressed confusion about the name observing that it "could mean pretty much anything" (2015). Columnist Adam Buckman referred to the network's description of its new name and target audience as "gobbledygook," writing, "when I hear the word 'freeform' I imagine something more freewheeling—i.e. something that is self-consciously disorganized, you might say—than a cable TV network owned by a media conglomerate" (2015). Furthermore, a year after the name change, viewers still tweeted about their dislike of the new name. However, although these viewers may have expressed dislike of the new name, they were still excited about much of the programming on Freeform. They tweeted not only about the popular prime-time shows (such as *Pretty Little Liars* and *The Fosters* [2013–]) but also about the continued screenings of the Harry Potter movies,[3] Disney movies, and the late-night airings of old Disney Channel shows such as *Hannah Montana* (2006–2011) and *That's So Raven* (2003–2007). Freeform, then, continues to repurpose Disney material in order to appeal to the nostalgic bent displayed by becomers. Stars of Freeform shows also promote Disney content, for example, posting videos about their favorite Disney characters. The airing of more innocent Disney content, however, continues to connect the network to the idea of family entertainment, creating uncertainty for viewers.[4]

Freeform's use of repurposed Disney content along with the numerous promotional videos for Disney and ABC content on the network's Facebook page and YouTube channel demonstrate that the pressures of fragmentation and conglomeration have not subsided, nor has confusion about the "family" appeal of the network. The seeming disconnect between new programming created for the becomer audience (such as *Shadowhunters* and *Beyond*) and the family content that remains popular, creates potential confusion about the cohesiveness and authenticity of the new network. In its attempt to break free of brand values that do not work for all cohorts of becomers, Freeform successfully maneuvered away from its overt "family" name; but it will be interesting to see how the network navigates the potential contradictions that emerge from the continued desire to reap the benefits of, and meet its responsibilities as, part of a corporate family.

NOTES

1 Although not a term directly used by the network, Gillan discusses the Disney Channel target audience as "in betweeners" who "occupy a life stage between articulating and achieving their aspirations" (2014, 160).

2 For a history of the network, see Mullen (2003) and Murphy (2014).

3 These screenings will end in 2018, when NBC Universal gains the rights to air the *Harry Potter* movies.

4 The airing of Disney movies and children's shows led to some complaints on the network's Facebook page. Parents criticized the network for showing ads that were inappropriate for children during these movies. These parents failed to recognize that these movies and shows are not attempting to attract young audiences, but to continue to appeal to becomers who appreciate opportunities to revisit their childhood memories.

REFERENCES

ABC Family. 2015a. "ABC Family Becomes Freeform in January 2016." *Futoncritic.com*, October 6. Accessed May 26, 2016. www.thefutoncritic.com/news/2015/10/06/abc-family-becomes-freeform-in-january-2016-706311/20151006abcfamily01/.

ABC Family. 2015b. "What Is Freeform?" *YouTube*, December 21. Accessed May 27, 2016. www. youtube.com/watch?v=J8cnAyN9-ic.

ABC Family. 2015c. "Why Is ABC Family Becoming Freeform?" *YouTube*, December 21. Accessed May 27, 2016. www.youtube.com/watch?v=KYOK__YHqew.

"ABC Family, MTV Miss Their Targets." 2015. *RatingsIntel*, July 22. Accessed May 26, 2016. www. ratingsintel.com/abc-family-mtv-miss-their-targets/.

Allen, Robert C. 1999. "Home Alone Together: Hollywood and the 'Family Film.'" In *Identifying Hollywood's Audiences: Cultural Identity and the Movies*, edited by Melvyn Stokes and Richard Maltby, 109–31. London: British Film Institute.

Andreasen, Margaret. 2000. "Evolution in the Family's Use of Television: An Overview." In *Television and the American Family*, 2nd edition, edited by Jennings Bryant and J. Allison Bryant, 3–30. Hillsdale: L. Erlbaum Associates.

Ayres, Chris. 2001. "Eisner Hopes for a Fairytale Ending at His Magic Kingdom." *The Times*, London, September 26.

Barnes, Brooks. 2015. "Disney's Family Channel Aims Younger than Millennials with New Name." *New York Times*, October 6. Accessed May 26, 2016. www.nytimes.com/2015/10/07/business/media/disneys-family-channel-aims-beyond-millennials-with-new-name.html.

Baysinger, Tim. 2015. "Good-Bye, Millennials . . . Hello, Generation Z." *Broadcasting and Cable*, April 27.

Brown, Barry and Louise Barkhuus. 2011. "Changing Practices of Family Television Watching." In *The Connected Home: The Future of Domestic Life*, edited by Richard Harper, 93–110. London: Springer-Verlag.

Buckman, Adam. 2015. "Anatomy of a Name Change: ABC Family Goes 'Freeform.'" *Television News Daily*, October 14. Accessed May 26, 2016. www.mediapost.com/publications/article/260040/anatomy-of-a-name-change-abc-family-goes-freefor.html.

Carter, Bill. 2001. "Disney Discusses Strategy Behind Buying Fox Family." *New York Times*, July 24. Accessed May 26, 2016. www.nytimes.com/2001/07/24/business/disney-discusses-strategy-behind-buying-fox-family.html.

Crupi, Anthony. 2010. "Demo Darling." *Mediaweek*, March 29.

"Disney Buys Fox Family for $3B—July 23, 2001." 2001. *CNNMoney.com*, July 23. Accessed May 26, 2016. http://cnnfn.cnn.com/2001/07/23/deals/fox_disney/.

Fabes, Richard A., Patricia Wilson and F. Scott Christopher. 1989. "A Time to Reexamine the Role of Television in Family Life." *Family Relations* 38 (3): 337–41. Accessed May 26, 2016. doi:10.2307/585062.

Giges, Nancy. 2008. "TV Makeovers." *Advertising Age*, April 25. Cable Guide edition.

Gillan, Jennifer. 2014. *Television Brandcasting: The Return of the Content-Promotion Hybrid*. New York: Routledge.

Holloway, Daniel. 2015. "Inside ABC Family's Dramatic Name-Change Decision." *TheWrap*, October 6. Accessed May 26, 2016. www.thewrap.com/inside-abc-family-freeform-name-change-decision/.

Howe, Neil and William Strauss. 2000. *Millennials Rising: The Next Great Generation*. New York: Vintage Books.

Keeling, Sarah. 2003. "Advising the Millennial Generation." *NACADA Journal* 23 (1–2): 30–6. doi:10.12930/0271-9517-23.1-2.30.

Lee, Dave. 2013. "Living Room TV Is 'Making a Comeback', Says Ofcom." *BBC News*, August 1. Accessed December 29, 2016. www.bbc.co.uk/news/technology-23521277.

Levit, Alexandra. 2015. "Make Way for Generation Z." *New York Times*, March 28. Accessed December 29, 2016. www.nytimes.com/2015/03/29/jobs/make-way-for-generation-z.html.

Livingstone, Sonia. 2007. "From Family Television to Bedroom Culture: Young People's Media at Home." In *Media Studies: Key Issues and Debates*, edited by Eoin Devereux, 302–21. London: Sage.

Malone, Michael. 2016. "ABC Family's New Name? Go Ask Alice." *Broadcasting and Cable*, January 11.

Mullen, Megan. 2003. *The Rise of Cable Programming in the United States: Revolution or Evolution?* Austin: University of Texas Press.

Murphy, Caryn. 2014. "Gender and Generation in the ABC Family Brand." In *The Millennials on Film and Television: Essays on the Politics of Popular Culture*, edited by Betty Kaklamanidou and Margaret Tally, 15–30. Jefferson: McFarland and Company.

Schneider, Michael. 2008. "Part of the Family." *Variety*, February 25.

Selznick, Barbara. 2009. "Branding the Future: Syfy in the Post-Network Era." *Science Fiction Film & Television* 2 (2): 177–204. doi:10.1353/sff.0.0070.

Serazio, Michael. 2013. "Selling (Digital) Millennials: The Social Construction and Technological Bias of a Consumer Generation." *Television & New Media* 16 (7): 599–615. Accessed May 26, 2016. doi:10.1177/1527476413491015.

Shine, Jacqui. 2015. "The Long, Strange History of ABC Family." *New Republic*, October 8. Accessed May 26, 2016. https://newrepublic.com/article/123067/long-strange-history-abc-family.

Sutherland, Anne and Beth Thompson. 2003. *Kidfluence: The Marketer's Guide to Understanding and Reaching Generation Y—Kids, Tweens, and Teens.* New York: McGraw-Hill.

Tapscott, Don. 2009. *Grown Up Digital: How the Net Generation Is Changing Your World.* New York: McGraw-Hill.

Umstead, R. Thomas. 2009. "ABC Family Rides High." *Multichannel News*, April 6.

Vukanovic, Zvezdan. 2009. "Global Paradigm Shift: Strategic Management of New and Digital Media in New and Digital Economics." *The International Journal on Media Management* 11: 81–90. Accessed May 26, 2016. doi:101.1080/14241270902844249.

Wagmeister, Elizabeth. 2015. "ABC Family to Rebrand Network 'Freeform' in January." *Variety*, October 6. Accessed May 26, 2016. http://variety.com/2015/tv/news/abc-family-freeform-rebranding-network-1201610697/.

Walker, Dave. 2016. "ABC Family to Freeform: Six Things to Know about the New Name of the 'Pretty Little Liars' Network." *Forbes*, January 11. Accessed May 26, 2016. www.forbes.com/sites/davewalker/2016/01/11/abc-family-to-freeform-six-things-to-know-about-the-new-name-of-the-pretty-little-liars-network/.

Weprin, Alex. 2008. "Next-Gen Adventures in Audience-Building." *Broadcasting and Cable*, March 10.

 # El Rey

Latino Indie Auteur as Channel Identity

Alisa Perren

In 2011, as part of a commitment made to gain approval from the FCC and to generate public support for its acquisition of a majority stake in media conglomerate NBC Universal ("Comcast" 2012), America's largest multiple system operator, Comcast, resolved to support new minority owned, independently operated channels. Early the following year, after reviewing roughly 100 applications, Comcast identified the first four of ten new independently owned cable channels to be carried on their cable systems.[1] Two of these channels, Aspire and REVOLT, planned to target African American viewers, while the other two, BabyFirst Americas and El Rey, would pursue Hispanic viewers.[2] In addition to favoring "well-thought-out, well-planned, well-financed, and well-programmed" proposals (Umstead 2011b), Comcast leaned heavily on celebrities in choosing which channels to carry. Three of the four channels were affiliated with well-known names: Aspire with NBA star Magic Johnson, REVOLT with music mogul P. Diddy, and El Rey with indie film auteur Robert Rodriguez (known for the *El Mariachi* trilogy and the *From Dusk Till Dawn*, *Sin City*, and *Spy Kids* franchises).

Upon hearing of Comcast's interest in launching at least one new Hispanic owned-and-operated channel, the heads of media incubator FactoryMade (and former William Morris Entertainment talent agents) John Fogelman and Cristina Patwa approached Rodriguez about developing his own "auteur television channel" (Wong 2014). The channel that Rodriguez proposed, the English-language El Rey, was certainly the most idiosyncratic of these new Comcast-supported channels. While writer-producer-director (and frequent Quentin Tarantino collaborator) Rodriguez had been in the public eye for close to two decades, generating a strong following among certain genre film fans, his cultural profile and level of fame was not quite on par with P. Diddy, Magic Johnson, or the other major cable celebrity entrepreneur, Oprah Winfrey (OWN). When asked how he had procured his own cable channel, Rodriguez replied, "There was very little competition for this network. Only about 100 people applied for the slot. And how many of those had a solid business plan like ours? Probably only five" (Wilson 2014, 44–6). More than speaking to the strength of his proposal, such a statement suggests the paucity of high-profile Latino celebrities willing and able to lend their name to ambitious cable ventures targeting English-speaking Hispanic audiences.

Yet Rodriguez loaned far more than his name to El Rey's marketing and promotional materials. By 2017, Rodriguez claimed that for El Rey he did "everything but turn on the TV for you" (Dominguez 2014). Indeed, Rodriguez's roles for El Rey included CEO, programmer, producer, editor, director (of multiple television series, network promos, and branded entertainment segments), and more. As El Rey Vice Chair Scott Sassa aptly noted, "El Rey is different than almost all networks because our founder Robert Rodriguez is a creative with a distinctive brand" (Prudom 2014). Rodriguez's celebrity identity and auteur status became interchangeable with El Rey's brand identity and audience appeals. Through the figure of Rodriguez, El Rey aimed to consolidate viewer interest on the basis of specific identity and taste formations. At the outset, El Rey sought to balance appeals to two distinct audiences: 18-to-49-year-old Hispanic Millennial men and genre fans (primarily males but also "kick-ass females") ("El Rey" 2012; Fretts 2015). When it launched in December 2013, El Rey envisioned its viewer as someone who either identified with Rodriguez's personal experience as a Mexican American DIY multihyphenate filmmaker or appreciated the types of films Rodriguez made and enjoyed watching (low-budget, high-action, genre-oriented content of the science fiction, horror, and exploitation varieties) (Block 2013). As Carina Chocano (2014) of *Texas Monthly* observed shortly after its launch:

> El Rey occupies the section of the Venn diagram where Latinos, non-Latinos, and people who like vampire shows and flamboyant sports intersect—the world of Robert Rodriguez. It's the sensibility manifested as a network, a televised compendium of personal taste. Arguably the first Hispanic-skewed network not to strictly target Hispanics, it doesn't so much fill a niche as explode one.

As illustrated below, such a channel became possible due to a specific set of industrial, economic, and cultural conditions that came into place in the early 2010s. However, El Rey's status as an independent network (one not owned by one of the major media conglomerates such as Comcast, Time Warner, or Disney) as well as its delicate efforts to balance appeals to particular identity and taste formations led it to struggle to find both distribution and an audience. During its first five years in business, the industrial conditions facing niche-oriented linear cable channels—especially channels lacking a conglomerate parent's support—became increasingly fraught. El Rey's efforts to unite Hispanic audiences and genre fans under Rodriguez's "indie cool" auteur identity may have been a viable marketing angle when the channel launched. However, the cultural cachet associated with indie culture (Newman 2009) could not compensate for the structural disadvantages faced by independent distributors such as El Rey.

PAVING THE WAY FOR EL REY

Comcast's decision to support several minority-owned channels may have been driven primarily by regulatory pressure and campaigning by advocacy groups. However, in the early 2010s, investing in Hispanic-targeted outlets was also a smart business decision. Although the media industries had imagined, constructed, and targeted the Hispanic market for several decades (Dávila 2012), the television industry—and especially cable television—paid increasing attention following the 2010 Census report, which identified a 43% jump in Hispanics from 2000 (Piñon and Rojas 2011; Polakoff 2013). Not only did Hispanics constitute 16.3% of the total population (50.5 million people), they also represented 23% of American youth (Levin 2012, 3D). Yet only 4% of advertising dollars were directed toward targeting the Hispanic population (Thielman 2012). Furthermore, while advertising aimed at Hispanic audiences in the US was estimated at $6.1 billion, only $215 million was directed at cable outlets due to a lack of channels featuring programming of interest to this demographic group (Swiatecki 2015). Most advertising dollars went to Spanish-language broadcasters Univision and Telemundo and their affiliated stations. While cable channels such as Telemundo's mun2 (launched in 2001) and MTV's 3 (launched in 2006) programmed for a bilingual viewership, and SiTV (launched in 2004) targeted English-language Hispanics, several companies believed the market continued to be underexploited (Chávez 2013; Rojas and Piñon 2014; Puente 2014). As Rodriguez joked at the time of El Rey's launch, Latinos would make up one third of the US population by 2050, yet a dog channel had been launched before one targeted to the English-language Hispanic market had premiered (Odam 2012, D1).

From this new attention, a flurry of investments and announcements took place between 2011 and 2013. The new Spanish-language ventures included Univision's TlNovelas and Univision Deportes; National Geographic's NatGeoMundo, and News Corp's MundoFox. Most notable on the English-language side were the rebranding of SiTV as NuvoTV (including new collaboration with actress-musician Jennifer Lopez), joint investment in Fusion between Univision and Disney (James 2016), and the launch of El Rey. All three of these English-language channels explicitly sought a Millennial audience, though they varied in the types of programs used to reach viewers.

Significantly, the expansion of outlets targeting Hispanics accompanied a more general boom period in new cable channels as well as a wave of cable rebranding efforts. FXX, Pivot, Al Jazeera Network, and Fox Sports 1 were among the many channels to launch between 2011 and 2013. A variety of factors fueled the rush by major conglomerates and independents alike to launch new networks or rebrand old ones. First, multichannel video programming distributors (MVPDs) such as Comcast, DirecTV, and Verizon FiOS sought to further diversify their channel offerings in the interest of expanding their subscriber base (Lafayette 2013; Littleton 2013).[3] Second, newly launched channels or even "brand refreshes" promised channel owners the possibility of gaining new advertisers or raising advertising rates, while also gaining greater leverage with MVPDs. For example, Univision bundled larger packages of channels (UniMás, Univision Noticias, Fusion, etc.) together when it renewed carriage agreements with MVPDs (Wilson 2014). Through such bundling practices, companies like Univision, Disney, and News Corp. sought to increase the subscriber base of their niche-oriented outlets and also to seek more money from MVPDs for the entire package of channels they provided. In turn, MVPDs sold demographically targeted bundles; for example, many offered consumers the option of subscribing to a "Latino bundle."

It was within this vibrant but competitive environment that El Rey appeared. Though Comcast had anointed El Rey one of its chosen minority-owned channels, by no means did this guarantee that this new venture would be successful. In fact, Comcast did not carry El Rey on all of its cable systems ("5 Questions" 2015).[4] As a means of overcoming its disadvantage in the market as a relatively small-scale operation, FactoryMade wisely sold a 5% ownership stake in El Rey to Univision prior to its launch. As part of this arrangement, Univision agreed to handle El Rey's advertising sales and distribution (Baysinger 2013, 16). Univision's involvement (and estimated $100 million investment) proved vital to an independent outlet such as El Rey (Block 2013). By 2014, in part due to being bundled with other Univision channels, El Rey had secured carriage in roughly 40 million of the approximately 100 million households served by MVPDs (Federal Communications Commission 2016; Moss 2014).

Even as El Rey benefited from Univision's support, the channel's emerging brand identity also enhanced Univision's investment portfolio. Like most broadcasters, Univision's audience was steadily aging; its stakes in both Fusion and El Rey represented efforts to find younger viewers ("ABC" 2013). Furthermore, El Rey's strategic decision to aim mainly for young men with "high-octane" and "cinematic action-packed content" such as the *From Dusk Till Dawn* television series (2014–2016), *Matador* (2014), and *Lucha Underground* (2014-) provided a means of differentiating it from the Spanish-language networks that skewed toward women with their emphasis on telenovelas (Chocano 2014; Littleton 2012; "Univision" 2013).

The choice of the name El Rey—Spanish for "the king"—cued potential viewers to the channel's masculine orientation.[5] The name meant more than that, however: as impressed upon Chocano (2014) by Rodriguez, El Rey would be "a feeling, a mind-set, a way of being in the world. He also liked that El Rey is a common brand name in Mexico—sort of like Acme—a generic catchall that's at once humble and proud, mythical and commonplace." This emphasis on El Rey as a "mind-set" became applicable not only to the channel's name but to its brand positioning more generally. As it launched, Rodriguez and other El Rey executives struggled to articulate El Rey's specific audience appeals. In particular, they faced the challenge of indicating how El Rey was for Latina/os but also for *more* than just Latina/os. El Rey executives felt compelled to aim more widely because that audience—or at least, the English-language viewing Hispanic audience they were targeting—was seen as a particularly challenging one to reach. In a revealing statement, Rodriguez explained:

> If you target to just Hispanics, then they won't watch. They don't want to feel like they have this one little channel in the corner; you want to feel like the whole culture—you

want people to be excited about your show. You want everybody to be interested and watch *From Dusk Till Dawn*—[the audience] doesn't think of it as Hispanic.

(Umstead 2014)

For channels such as Univision and Telemundo, viewers of diverse regional, national, and cultural backgrounds were collectively hailed primarily through their shared Spanish language. El Rey, along with other English-language channels such as Fusion and NuvoTV that targeted Hispanic markets, had to find other mechanisms through which to build an audience large enough to ensure sufficient distribution and advertiser support. In attempting to "dispel the notion that language is the badge of culture" (Umstead 2012), El Rey's "solution" involved awkwardly marrying appeals to Hispanic and youth markets with discourses of "coolness." As Rodriguez stated at one point, "The key is to make [El Rey] universal; I want viewers to watch it because it's cool, not Latino" (de la Fuente 2012).

El Rey sought to move beyond only targeting a Hispanic market to instead pursuing a more generalized, young, male, multicultural viewership that embraced visions of diversity as well as visions of "mayhem, gore, and badassery" ("We Couldn't" n.d.) depicted in genre fare. The channel's marketers employed a strategy of shifting between discourses of universality and cultural specificity, using the figure of Rodriguez—as assimilated Mexican American indie auteur synthesizing myriad cultural and generic influences—to connect these appeals.

EL REY IS RODRIGUEZ, RODRIGUEZ IS EL REY

Throughout its marketing materials and programming schedule, El Rey sought to convey the centrality of Rodriguez's creative sensibility and guiding vision for the channel. "Mi Network es Su Network," Rodriguez declared in one interview, clarifying that "I'm the person who's starting the network. . . . But it's not the Robert Rodriguez Network. It's called El Rey because it's bigger than me" (Moore 2014). Promotional and journalistic discourses regularly emphasized how Rodriguez's own identity—as an outsider to Hollywood, as a DIY filmmaker with a strong business sense, as a fifth-generation Mexican American, as a superfan of kitschy action fare—were built into El Rey's DNA. El Rey appeared as a profoundly personal venture, a means by which Rodriguez could attract "a wider audience whose interests align with his eclectic tastes, which encompass everything from cult films to Mexican wrestling" (Rodman 2014). Rodriguez regularly spoke of himself as curator of the channel's content, sharing with a wider audience the movies and TV shows stored on his own hard drive at home (Wilson 2014). It did not hurt that much of this content was relatively inexpensive to license—including evergreen syndicated fare like *Starsky and Hutch* (1975–1979), *Freddy's Nightmares* (1988–1990), *The X-Files* (1993–2002), and *Dark Angel* (2000–2002), as well as obscure kung fu (*Five Fingers of Death*, 1973), grindhouse (*Switchblade Sisters*, 1975), and horror films (*Fright Night*, 1985).

From the outset, El Rey's channel identity traded on Rodriguez's personal identity as an assimilated Latino and an indie genre auteur with a strong following by young, male genre fans of all races. The low-budget, high-thrill, visceral nature of much of El Rey's programming perfectly meshed with Rodriguez's indie outsider aesthetic. Early in his career, Rodriguez had emerged as a challenger to the excesses of the conglomerate Hollywood system. He initially established his reputation making *El Mariachi* (1992) on a $7,000 budget the summer after his freshman year at the University of Texas at Austin.[6] In a widely reported, oft-repeated tale, Rodriguez decided to make a movie for the Spanish-language home video market, procuring financing in large part by volunteering for drug trials, keeping costs low, and working with a shoestring crew. As would become his practice, Rodriguez served as writer, producer, director, editor, and cinematographer. He managed to show the film to a talent agent, who in turn passed it to executives at Columbia Pictures. Initially planning to remake the movie, Columbia decided to release the original version after it won the Sundance Film Festival Audience Award. The film earned over $2 million at the North American box office, and Rodriguez gained notoriety for making "the least expensive film ever released by a major studio" (Chocano 2014).

Rodriguez cultivated this reputation as an outsider for years to come, publishing a book, *Rebel Without a Crew: Or How a 23-Year-Old Filmmaker With $7,000 Became a Hollywood Player* (1995), and promoting his ability to make Hollywood-quality movies at independent-level prices. He founded his own production company (Los Hooligans) and studio (Troublemaker) in Austin, and shot most of his productions in central Texas. With the exception of partnerships with Columbia Pictures for *El Mariachi* and its bigger-budget sequel, *Desperado* (1995), Rodriguez subsequently worked almost exclusively with indie producer-distributor Miramax. Along with directors such as Quentin Tarantino and Kevin Smith, Rodriguez helped Miramax define a "cinema of cool" that characterized many high-profile indie films during the 1990s and early 2000s (Perren 2012).

With El Rey, Rodriguez continued to trade on what had proven successful for him in the film business. Indeed, as he noted at the time of El Rey's launch, "The network seemed like a way to do in TV what I had been doing for the last 20 years in movies. It felt like a natural evolution but also a revolution" (Fretts 2015). Though some staff was based in New York and Los Angeles, El Rey publicized Austin as its primary home, with much of its original content shot at Troublemaker Studios (Jurgensen 2014). Rodriguez presented a fantasy image of El Rey as a network that worked without reliance on "the suits," wholly dependent on his creative impulses and business instincts (Moore 2014). At El Rey, he not only fulfilled all the creative positions he had previously in his film projects, but now he also served as the face of the network at Univision's upfronts and TCA appearances; he supervised "video vignettes" for sponsors such as Heineken and GM; and he interviewed friends, mentors, and creative influences such as directors John Carpenter, Guillermo del Toro, and Luis Valdez for his talk show, *The Director's Chair* (2014–2015) (Steinberg 2013, 2014).

Notably, the first original series to premiere on El Rey, *From Dusk Till Dawn*, was adapted from one of the early projects that Rodriguez made for Miramax's genre division, Dimension Films. The crime-horror film was an early product of Rodriguez's

FIGURE 22.1 *Promotion for El Rey talk show,* The Director's Chair *(2014–2015), foregrounds series host, producer, director, and channel founder Robert Rodriguez with his signature guitar in Austin, Texas.*

long-standing relationship with Quentin Tarantino (who starred in the film and wrote its screenplay). Speaking frankly about his decision to launch El Rey with *From Dusk Till Dawn*, Rodriguez observed, "We made it the premier title for El Rey because viewers would recognize it and it would help draw them. Rather than create a new show no one's heard of on a network no one's heard of, we needed something to carry people over here" (Fretts 2015). From *Dusk Till Dawn* was not just any pre-sold property, however; its brand catered to two key constituencies most desired by El Rey: young, male genre fans—labeled the "ComicCon audience" by El Rey Vice Chair Scott Sassa—and Hispanic Millennials (Block 2013).

From Dusk Till Dawn's approach to building a Hispanic viewership mirrored El Rey's wider strategy. First, it cultivated Hispanic voices both on-screen and behind-the-scenes. According to Rodriguez, whereas 2% of Hollywood directors and producers were Hispanic, 60% of El Rey directors were Hispanic (of course, Rodriguez directed many of these episodes himself) (Umstead 2014). Second, it appealed to the wider base of young, male action-horror fans not only through its content but also through the talent it featured, including genre favorites Danny Trejo, Don Johnson, Robert Patrick, Tom Savini, Jake Busey, and more. Unfortunately, El Rey's strategy of using Rodriguez as the unifying force of fusing appeals to Hispanic Millennial men and genre fans 18-to-49 met with only mixed success at best.

BECOMING A NETWORK FOR "STRIVERS"

By 2016, Rodriguez became less visible in El Rey's marketing, content, and press coverage. This diminishing presence came in the wake of reports that the channel was hemorrhaging money. In January 2016, Univision reported a $118 million loss from its investment in El Rey (Primack 2016). Meanwhile, El Rey had canceled scripted series *Matador* (2014) after one season, with the fate of *From Dusk Till Dawn* remaining uncertain after three seasons. The channel's most successful venture thus far, the unscripted Mexican wrestling series *Lucha Libre* (2014–), featured only marginal involvement from Rodriguez.

Furthermore, the conditions facing niche-oriented channels had grown increasingly hostile since El Rey's 2012 launch. The rise of over-the-top (OTT) streaming services such as Netflix, Amazon, and Hulu had led many MVPD subscribers to cut the cord. MVPDs responded by developing skinny bundles that featured only the most popular channels. Concurrently, multicultural programming had become increasingly mainstream; a growing number of broadcast, cable, and streaming services began targeting diverse audiences by placing Latina/os in starring roles in series like *Jane the Virgin* (CW, 2014–), *Superstore* (NBC, 2015–), *Shades of Blue* (NBC, 2016–), and *One Day at*

FIGURE 22.2 *Visitors to the webpage for dramatic series* Matador *(2014) following the show's cancellation are redirected to other content that conveys El Rey's aesthetic sensibility.*

a Time (Netflix, 2017–). Within this context, the value proposition of niche-oriented multicultural channels, especially those targeted to English-speaking Hispanics, further diminished (Umstead 2016a, 10). By 2016, NuvoTV had shuttered and Disney sold its stake in Fusion to Univision (Primack 2016). Fusion subsequently pursued a more generalized, non-Hispanic audience (Baysinger 2016).

Consequently, El Rey executives reassessed their marketing and programming strategies, reconsidering their initial pursuit of English-speaking Hispanics and Millennial males. The arrival of new President and General Manager, Daniel Tibbets, in mid-2016 further accelerated changes in El Rey's business practices (Prudom 2016). Tibbets's background as Chief Content Officer for digital programming company Machinima intersected with El Rey's shift to a "multiplatform content distribution strategy" (Anderson 2016). This involved promoting itself more aggressively as "The People's Network" and soliciting fan-produced content and engagement. El Rey planned to focus less on developing costly scripted originals and more on unscripted lifestyle and personality programming such as *Man at Arms: Art of War* (2017–), a series about forging and using weapons, and *Rite of Passage* (2017–) a series about individuals transitioning into manhood in different cultures (N'Duka 2017).

Tibbets announced El Rey's new focus on a group it identified as "strivers"—"working and middle-class male viewers [aged 18 to 63] who defy typical age and race metrics to represent more of a sociographic class" (Umstead 2016b, 12). According to the channel's new president, strivers "hold strong core beliefs about the importance of family, independence, hard work, craftsmanship, and legacy" (Evans 2017). Notably, this newly defined target audience was seen as building on the *existing* El Rey viewership, estimated to be 20% Hispanic, 20% African American, 10% Asian, and 50% white (Moylan 2015).

Ultimately, El Rey did not gain sufficient viewership by exploiting Rodriguez's identity as Latino indie auteur. Close alignment with the Rodriguez brand had not substantively grown the number of Hispanics working in television, nor had it enabled El Rey to attain the widespread support of the English-speaking Hispanics it had so aggressively pursued. FactoryMade and Univision took a chance on marketing Rodriguez-as-auteur to articulate a distinctive blend of audience formations and tastes. Yet indie cachet could not compensate for the structural disadvantages faced by a small, independent channel competing against outlets with far greater scale, reach, and support from the media industries. As industrial conditions and viewer behaviors shifted, El Rey executives altered its programming and marketing strategies accordingly. Although the channel's programming continued to draw from Rodriguez's aesthetic sensibility to some extent, its marketers no longer leaned heavily on exploiting his auteur reputation.

NOTES

1 Comcast pledged that Hispanics or African Americans would maintain majority ownership over eight of the ten channels. The conglomerate planned to solicit applications for these ten channels in a series of phases (Umstead 2011a, 2011b).

2 Both Hispanic and Latino are contested terms. However, Hispanic is the dominant term used by the media industries and the US Census, and as such, is the term used in most instances here (Chávez 2013; Passel and Taylor 2009).

3 According to the FCC, an MVPD is "a cable operator, a multichannel multipoint distribution service, a direct-broadcast satellite service, or a television receive-only satellite program distributor, who makes available for purchase, by subscribers or customers, multiple channels of video programming" (Eggerton 2012).

4 Most notably, El Rey had been unable to gain distribution on Comcast's systems throughout the northeastern United States.

5 Rodriguez spoke of the possibility of a female-branded channel, "La Reina," in the future (Wilson 2014).

6 Reported production costs for *El Mariachi* are somewhat misleading, as they do not include additional postproduction costs required to make the film presentable for theatrical distribution. For more on independent film definitions and economics, see Perren 2004.

REFERENCES

"5 Questions: Talking Fun, Distribution & Kung Fu with El Rey." 2015. *Cablefax*, March 2. www.cablefax.com/programming/5-questions-talking-fun-distribution-kung-fu-el-rey.

"ABC, Univision Launch Fusion for Millennial Hispanics." 2013. *MediaPost*, October 21. www.mediapost.com/publications/article/211711/abc-univision-launch-fusion-for-millennial-hispan.html.

Anderson, Will. 2016. "4 Questions with El Rey Network's New GM." *Austin Business Journal*, May 4. www.bizjournals.com/austin/news/2016/05/04/4-questions-with-el-rey-networks-new-gm.html.

Baysinger, Tim. 2013. "El Plan for El Rey: Hook Next-Gen Viewers." *Broadcasting & Cable*, December 9.

Baysinger, Tim. 2016. "How the Onion Is Helping Univision Grow Beyond the Spanish-Language Market." *Adweek*, April 22. www.adweek.com/tv-video/how-onion-helping-univision-grow-beyond-spanish-language-market-171014/.

Block, Alex Ben. 2013. "Filling a 'Void.' How TV Is Taking Aim at Young Hispanics." *Hollywood Reporter*, October 28. www.hollywoodreporter.com/news/fusion-taking-aim-at-young-651124.

Chávez, Christopher A. 2013. "Building a 'New Latino' in the Post-Network Era: mun2 and the Reconfiguration of the U.S. Latino Audience." *International Journal of Communication* 7: 1026–45.

Chocano, Carina. 2014. "King of Dreams." *Texas Monthly*, April. Accessed May 31, 2017. www.texasmonthly.com/articles/king-of-dreams/.

"Comcast Announces Agreements with Four New Minority-Owned Independent Networks." 2012. *Comcast*, February 21. http://corporate.comcast.com/news-information/news-feed/comcast-announces-agreements-with-four-new-minority-owned-independent-networks.

Dávila, Arlene. 2012. *Latinos, Inc.: The Marketing and Making of a People*, Updated edition. Berkeley: University of California Press.

de la Fuente, Anna Marie. 2012. "Networks Target Fast-Growing Hispanic Aud." *Variety*, March 23. http://variety.com/2012/tv/news/networks-target-fast-growing-hispanic-aud-1118051828/.

Dominguez, Robert. 2014. "Robert Rodriguez Launches TV Network El Rey." *New York Daily News*, March 7. www.nydailynews.com/entertainment/tv-movies/robert-rodriguez-launches-tv-network-el-rey-article-1.1714039.

Eggerton, John. 2012. "What Is an MVPD Exactly? Cable Ops Weigh In." *Broadcasting & Cable*, May 21.

"El Rey Network Announces Antoinette Alfonso Zel as CEO." 2012. *PR Newswire*, August 6. www.prnewswire.com/news-releases/el-rey-network-announces-antoinette-alfonso-zel-as-ceo-165182656.html.

Evans, Greg. 2017. "El Rey Network Taps Brand Strategist Alma Derricks as Chief Marketing Officer." *Deadline Hollywood*, April 19. http://deadline.com/2017/04/el-rey-network-hires-alma-derricks-chief-marketing-officer-1202072570/.

Federal Communications Commission. 2016. *Annual Assessment of the Status of Competition in the Market for the Delivery of Programming*. Washington, DC: FCC.

Fretts, Bruce. 2015. "Robert Rodriguez, Film Director and El Rey Founder, on Creating a Hispanic Network." *New York Times*, September 1. https://artsbeat.blogs.nytimes.com/2015/09/01/robert-rodriguez-film-director-and-el-rey-founder-on-creating-a-hispanic-network/.

James, Meg. 2016. "Walt Disney Co.'s ABC Sells Its Stake to Univision, Exits Joint Venture." *Los Angeles Times*, April 21. www.latimes.com/entertainment/envelope/cotown/la-et-ct-disney-abc-ends-fusion-univision-20160421-story.html.

Jurgensen, John. 2014. "A Channel of One's Own—with Vampires." *Wall Street Journal*, March 6. www.wsj.com/articles/a-channel-of-ones-ownwith-vampires-1394149345.

Lafayette, Jon. 2013. "Leverage Is Key Ingredient for Cable Network Startups." *Broadcasting & Cable*, October 14.

Levin, Gary. 2012. "Cable Goes After Latino Audience." *USA Today*, February 23.

Littleton, Cynthia. 2012. "Rodriguez, FactoryMade Launch Pistoleros Banner." *Variety*, February 21. http://variety.com/2012/tv/news/rodriguez-factorymade-launch-pistoleros-banner-1118050536/.

Littleton, Cynthia. 2013. "Congloms Firing Up New Cable Channels as Climate Improves." *Variety*, September 13. http://variety.com/2013/tv/news/congloms-firing-up-new-cable-channels-as-climate-improves-1200609613/.

Moore, Frazier. 2014. "Rodriguez Gives It to Viewers Straight with El Rey." *San Diego Union Tribune*, March 10. www.sandiegouniontribune.com/sdut-rodriguez-gives-it-to-viewers-straight-with-el-rey-2014mar10-story.html.

Moss, Linda. 2014. "Survival Tips from Unaffiliated Networks." *Multichannel News*, July 28. www.multichannel.com/news/distribution/survival-tips-unaffiliated-networks/382754.

Moylan, Brian. 2015. "US Television Wakes Up to Growing Latino Audience with New Options." *The Guardian*, October 8. www.theguardian.com/tv-and-radio/2015/oct/08/latino-viewers-new-options-us-television-el-rey-fusion.

N'Duka, Amanda. 2017. "El Rey Network to Boost Original Content by 50%." *Deadline Hollywood*, January 13. http://deadline.com/2017/01/el-rey-network-new-series-from-dusk-till-dawn-status-1201885462/.

Newman, Michael Z. 2009. "Indie Culture: In Pursuit of the Authentic Autonomous Alternative." *Cinema Journal* 48 (3): 13–34.

Odam, Matthew. 2012. "Filmmaker Lays Out Vision for Latino Cable Channel." *Austin American-Statesman*, May 11.

Passel, Jeffrey S. and Paul Taylor. 2009. "Who's Hispanic?" *Pew Research Center*, May 28. www.pewhispanic.org/2009/05/28/whos-hispanic/.

Perren, Alisa. 2004. "A Big Fat Indie Success Story? Press Discourses on the Making and Marketing of a 'Hollywood' Movie." *Journal of Film and Video* 56 (2): 18–31.

Perren, Alisa. 2012. *Indie, Inc.: Miramax and the Transformation of Hollywood in the 1990s*. Austin: University of Texas Press.

Piñon, Juan and Viviana Rojas. 2011. "Language and Cultural Identity in the New Configuration of the US Latino TV Industry. *Global Media and Communication* 7 (2): 129–47.

Polakoff, Jonathan. 2013. "Latino Channels' Accent on English: Mun2, NuvoTV Craft Content with Eye on Younger Viewers." *Los Angeles Business Journal*, August 5.

Primack, Dan. 2016. "Here's How Much Disney and Univision Have Lost on Fusion." *Fortune*, January 21. http://fortune.com/2015/12/24/heres-how-much-disney-and-univision-have-lost-on-fusion/.

Prudom, Laura. 2014. "El Rey Ups Chad Blankenship to SVP of Marketing and Communications, Hires Katie Lanegran as PR VP." *Variety*, August 4. http://variety.com/2014/biz/news/el-rey-network-chad-blankenship-svp-marketing-comm-katie-lanegran-pr-vp-1201274903/.

Prudom, Laura. 2016. "Daniel Tibbets Named President of Robert Rodriguez's El Rey Network." *Variety*, May 3. http://variety.com/2016/tv/news/el-rey-network-daniel-tibbets-president-robert-rodriguez-1201765350/.

Puente, Henry. 2014. "NuvoTV: Will It Withstand the Competition?" In *Contemporary Latina/o Media: Production, Circulation, Politics*, edited by Arlene Dávila and Yeidy M. Rivero, 62–81. New York: New York University Press.

Rodman, Sarah. 2014. "Minority-Owned Cable Networks Hope to Blaze a Trail." *Boston Globe*, January 25. www.bostonglobe.com/arts/television/2014/01/25/new-minority-owned-networks-hope-blaze-trail/X4EMY3zvOR314XOqZFrg0K/story.html.

Rojas, Viviana and Juan Piñon. 2014. "Spanish, English, or Spanglish? Media Strategies and Corporate Struggles to Reach Second or Later Generations of Latinos." *International Journal of Hispanic Media* 7 (August): 1–15.

Steinberg, Brian. 2013. "Robert Rodriguez' El Rey Network Lures General Motors in Ad Pact." *Variety*, December 17. http://variety.com/2013/tv/news/robert-rodriguez-el-rey-network-lures-general-motors-in-ad-pact-1200968689/.

Steinberg, Brian. 2014. "El Rey Sets Debut for Orci/Kurtzman Series 'Matador' As March to Upfront Begins." *Variety*, February 26. http://variety.com/2014/tv/news/el-rey-sets-debut-for-orcikurtzman-series-matador-as-march-to-upfront-begins-1201121542/.

Swiatecki, Chad. 2015. "How Robert Rodriguez Plans to Become the King of Cable." *Austin Business Journal*, June 26. www.bizjournals.com/austin/print-edition/2015/06/26/how-robert-rodriguez-plans-to-become-the-king-of.html.

Thielman, Sam. 2012. "TV Bebé Boom." *Adweek*, March 13.

Umstead, R. Thomas. 2011a. "100 Bids for New Network Launches." *Multichannel News*, June 28. www.multichannel.com/news/news/comcast-100-bids-new-network-launches/377265.

Umstead, R. Thomas. 2011b. "Comcast's Network Gatekeeper." *Multichannel News*, April 18. www.multichannel.com/news/content/comcasts-network-gatekeeper/362045.

Umstead, R. Thomas. 2012. "Speaking to Latinos in English." *Multichannel News*, September 10. www.multichannel.com/news/multicultural/speaking-latinos-english/305874.

Umstead, R. Thomas. 2014. "El Rey's Rodriguez Champions Diversity." *Multichannel News*, September 29. www.multichannel.com/news/content/el-rey-s-rodriguez-champions-diversity/384226.

Umstead, R. Thomas. 2016a. "Indies Aren't Catching the Diversity Wave." *Multichannel News*, April 18.

Umstead, R. Thomas. 2016b. "El Rey Network Takes Aim at 'Strivers.'" *Multichannel News*, December 5.

"Univision Communications and El Rey Network Announce Strategic Partnership." 2013. *Business Wire*, May 14.

"We Couldn't Find that Page, But Why Miss Out on All the Mayhem, Gore, and Badassery?" n.d. *El Rey Network*. Accessed May 31, 2017. www.elreynetwork.com/originals/matador/.

Wilson, Stacey. 2014. "Robert Rodriguez." *Hollywood Reporter*, August 29.

Wong, Tony. 2014. "TCA 2014: P. Diddy, Robert Rodriguez Join Celebrity TV Channel Trend." *Toronto Star*, January 13.

Streaming
Channels

AwesomenessTV

Talent Management and Merchandising on Multi-channel Networks

Avi Santo

AwesomenessTV (ATV) is not really a television channel or network in the traditional sense; it is not even a digital platform claiming to be producing and distributing "television," as Netflix, Hulu, and Amazon increasingly insist they are doing. Rather, ATV is a multi-channel network (MCN) consisting of over 92,000 distinct yet interwoven YouTube channels that collectively feature more than two billion videos that have been viewed over eight billion times by 112 million subscribers (Cioletti 2015; Hamedy 2015). Through its talent management division, Big Frame, Awesomeness works to identify emerging YouTube influencers, helps them to monetize their channels, and then leverages their popularity across a range of short-format web series—and more recently direct-to-download feature films, digitally distributed music, and exclusive mobile content. In turn, this content supports converging consumer product extensions with and retail endorsements for companies like Kohl's, Old Navy, Royal Caribbean, and Verizon. Jim Fielding, global head of consumer products for Awesomeness, summed up the company's strategy as follows: "the great news about our creator talent is that they are extremely diverse and interested in a wide array of subjects, so you really can match them to every product category" (Cioletti 2015). Or, as Amanda Cioletti, writing for *Global License!* explains,

> talent is truly the pillar upon which ATV and its supporting product division stand. . . . Because of the fluidity and flexibility of the ATV platform and the talent, many of these stars are not just one thing—not solely an actor, singer, beauty guru or comic. The stars intersect and evolve, often appearing on various different channels simultaneously in all sorts of capacities. . . . And these stars, in whichever capacity they appear, receive ATV support.
>
> (2015)

ATV's consulting firm, Wildness, has claimed that zero out of ten media consumers in Awesomeness' primary demographic of "Generation Z" post-Millennials would choose traditional television if given the option of using only one device ("AwesomenessTV" 2015). Despite this claim of capturing an audience uninterested in television, ATV is very much an outgrowth of the long history of blurred distinctions on radio and television between content and advertising, even as the company's approach intensifies the relationship between branded entertainment and celebrity self-branding for a post-television era. Moreover, even if Generation Z may be uninterested in television, ATV is. Indeed, rhetorical emphasis on the television credentials of many of its top executives frequently validates the company's success and its understanding of what advertisers and audiences want. One need only look to the partnerships ATV built with Nickelodeon, E!, Hulu, and Netflix to see how television offers important leverage for extending Awesomeness' brand reach beyond YouTube. In less than five years since the 2012 launch of its YouTube channel, ATV has grown from a MCN to a multiplatform media company that increasingly treats YouTube as an incubation space for talent and formats as well as an aggregator for mobilizing influencer fan bases to exploit across multiple distribution channels. ATV brand expansion strategies rely upon the rhetorical invocation "TV" and what it might mean in the digital age even as its approach to leveraging talent and subscribers offers potential insights into how television channels might evolve.

Following a brief summary of the company's expansion, this chapter focuses on the career of Lia Marie Johnson, one of Awesomeness' most prolific YouTube celebrities, to demonstrate how the network leveraged her following across genres, formats, platforms, and licensing partnerships to extend both her and Awesomeness' brand into new markets. In particular, I explore Johnson's appearances in three web series: *Terry the Tomboy* (2012–2014), *Life Is So R.A.D.* (2014), and *T@gged* (2016–). I argue that Johnson's work for Awesomeness epitomizes how the network has packaged its channel aggregation capacity, talent management, and merchandising prowess to create what Fielding calls "a new definition of television" for Generation Z consumers looking to access a "content marketplace" that treat them as "culture collaborators" rather than mere shoppers. Her work also captures ATV's strategy of exploiting the social networks cultivated by/around its talent to grow its own brand beyond YouTube.

AWESOME BEGINNINGS

ATV launched its channel on June 12, 2012, as part of YouTube's Original Channel Initiative, which saw Google invest $100 million in original content production to entice advertisers to spend a portion of their television budgets on YouTube. This initiative funded the creation of 100 YouTube channels, which each received monetary advances against ad sales (Szalai 2012). Among the new channels were Jay-Z's Life & Times, Machinima Prime, and the Nerdist, along with channels by Madonna, Ashton Kutcher, Amy Poehler, Rainn Wilson, and other Hollywood celebrities. Given YouTube's attempt to syphon ad dollars away from television, many of the channels Google invested in were unsurprisingly launched by people with close ties to the television industry, among them Brian Robbins and Joe Davola's ATV.

Robbins and Davola had both served as executive producers on a range of television series targeting teen and tween audiences, including the sketch comedy series *All That* (Nickelodeon, 1994–2005), the sitcom *Kenan & Kel* (Nickelodeon, 1996–2000), and dramas *Smallville* (WB/CW, 2000–2011) and *One Tree Hill* (WB/CW, 2002–2012). ATV's initial programming drew from these familiar genres. *Runaways* (2012–2013) was a drama about a teenage couple who disappear following the murder of one of their parents, leading to endless conflict, rumors, and prep school flashbacks. ATV promoted the series asking potential viewers, "do you love *One Tree Hill, Smallville, Gossip Girl*, the *OC, Pretty Little Liars*, and other teen tv dramas? then check out *RUNAWAYS*" ("Runaways" 2012). *IMO* (2012–2013) was billed as the YouTube equivalent of *The View* (ABC, 1997–) featuring teenaged social media celebrities. Jeffrey Katzenberg, former CEO of DreamWorks Animation (DWA), which would acquire ATV in 2013, lauded Robbins's "extraordinary track record in creating family content both for traditional and new platforms and his expertise in the TV arena will be invaluable as we grow our presence in that space" (Szalai 2013).

Even as Robbins and Davola leaned on their TV backgrounds, ATV embraced conventions more common to online content like short format video. *Runaways'* 18 episodes add up to a total running time of 87 minutes, or an average of 4 minutes and 56 seconds per episode. Robbins reasoned that short-form content was more in line with tween and teen viewing habits (Guider 2013). ATV also recognized the value of casting YouTube influencers—teens and tweens with significant online followings—in these new series because these performers were already adept at self-promotion and would be able to bring viewers, comments, and shares to ATV programming. More than mere casting decisions, however, ATV looked to fold performers into its network by including their channels under the Awesomeness umbrella.

Simply put, while performers on the ATV network already have sizable online followings, ATV acts as an intermediary that can help them translate that social capital into greater economic gain through the increased exposure its network brand offers. ATV shares with its talent a small percentage of the ad share revenue from commercials that appear before performers' videos; while YouTube takes 45% upfront, ATV takes around 30% beyond that, leaving some performers with a 25% share despite doing most of the work in producing and promoting their videos (Patel 2016; "Help" n.d.) ATV stresses, however, that their MCN cannot "guarantee that your views and subscribers will skyrocket as a result of joining, but if you are willing to put in the time and effort into making your channel excellent, we will be there to help you every step of the way!" ("Help" n.d.). Even as ATV profits both from its cut of the ad revenue and from talent working largely for free to increase its subscriber and viewership numbers, the MCN does offer its performers opportunities to broaden their appeal by casting them in a range of videos that cut across genres and potentially amplify their own channel followings, which in turn might increase the rates that they receive on ads—though ATV is vague on how those rates are determined, instead claiming that these decisions are made by YouTube and its advertisers. The vagueness surrounding payment rates validates ATV's intermediary role by "simplifying" creator roles and placing responsibility for success upon their ability to follow the network's instructions. In answer to the question, "How do I make money on YouTube?" ATV explains: "1. Create an interesting, original video,

2. Upload it to YouTube, 3. Make sure to turn monetization on!" ("Help" n.d.). ATV also offers these performers opportunities to expand their brand beyond YouTube through multiplatform distribution and merchandising opportunities. Big Frame President Larry Shapiro suggests that the company seeks talent with "true voice and . . . the ability to create IP that will transcend and move across platforms" (Jarvey 2014).

While presenting an opportunity for YouTube personalities to strike it rich and achieve celebrity status, ATV's approach operates within neoliberal ideologies that increasingly stress the constant marketization of self as key to success. Within this framework, YouTube personalities are encouraged to see their creations and interactions—particularly those that produce "authentic" disclosures about their lives—as self-branding opportunities promising career advancement and monetary gain (Banet-Weiser 2012). Of course, this is often contingent on these same personalities—many of whom are between the ages of 12 and 17—contributing a significant amount of (largely free) "affective" labor (Banet-Weiser 2012, 8) that not only promotes their personalities but also ATV and sponsors' brands as well. When YouTube personalities fail to significantly cash in on their social networks compared to the amount of time dedicated to uploading and promoting content, ATV typically attributes this to a lack of personal desire rather than the intense competitiveness, relentless pace, and dehumanizing aspects of self-branding (though never a lack of talent, which would imply ATV somehow erred in signing them). Responding to a question about helping ATV personalities cope with burnout, Fielding (2016) surmised,

> we try to help brand their image and try to brand their logo, and their colors, and the quality of their content, and the lighting, and their production values. But again, it still has to be them. Some of them, you know, don't want to keep doing it.

Beyond this search for talent, ATV identifies its core audience as members of "Generation Z": post-Millennials who do not watch much live television and prefer short-form video, who significantly are brand loyal yet platform agnostic when it comes to content consumption. This particular construction of its audience allows ATV to leverage its MCN and in-house talent management firm to position YouTube personalities for omni-platform co-branding extension, moving across traditional television as well as mobile, retail and product merchandizing. Tracing ATV star Lia Marie Johnson's career offers a close-up glimpse as to how Awesomeness operates.

A TALENT FOR BRANDING

Lia Marie Johnson first emerged as a YouTube personality through her appearances at age 13 on the Fine Brothers' *Kids React* (2010), a web series that featured precocious children and tweens reacting to a range of social, political, and popular culture occurrences (Gallagher 2012). Her popularity on the series bolstered views of her personal YouTube channel, which had launched under her parent's supervision in 2007 (Johnson 2012). By 2012, her channel, which mostly featured short personal vlog posts, sketch comedy, and song performances, had received nearly 16 million views (Gallagher 2012).

While Johnson would continue to work with the Fine Brothers on *Teens React* (2011–) and then *YouTubers React* (2014–), her growing popularity caught ATV's attention and in 2012 she joined her channel to its MCN. Big Frame already represented Johnson when ATV acquired the company. Under ATV's umbrella, Johnson has regularly been cast in a series of high profile projects, which in turn has increased the size of her personal following and lead to other roles in new ATV series. In 2014, *Ad Week* profiled Johnson as one of YouTube's "ten biggest young stars" (Stanley 2014). By 2017, Johnson's channel has reached 1.779 million followers and 85 million views ("About" 2017).

ATV's investment in Johnson and its strategic deployment of her brand reveal the network's cross-platform trajectory and its savvy approach to marketing the Awesomeness brand by ways of its talent. Almost immediately after joining Awesomeness' MCN Johnson was cast in the sketch comedy series *Terry the Tomboy* (2012–2014). The short sketches typically featured Johnson as Terry talking directly to the camera offering farcical advice on fashion, makeup, and dating. Significantly, *Terry the Tomboy* was also featured as a regular segment on ATV's *AwesomenessTV* (2013–2014) series on Nickelodeon, which compiled a handful of ATV's YouTube productions into a weekly 30-minute sketch comedy show. ATV regularly aggregates and packages short form content for secondary viewing on television in this way, striking a similar deal with the E! Network to air a compiled version of the musical dramedy web series *Side Effects* (2013) as a 39-minute TV special only weeks before the second season premiered online. While *AwesomenessTV* offered alternate distribution and ancillary revenue for ATV that allowed it to be less reliant on YouTube's ad share structure, it is worth noting that the deal with Nickelodeon also exposed TV viewers to ATV's network of celebrities and was intended to draw Generation Z viewers away from traditional cable as much as extend ATV's reach onto television. In this regard, ATV treated the *AwesomenessTV* series as a form of branded entertainment intended to build interest for other iterations of its brand.

Amanda Lotz (2007) has argued that branded entertainment represents an emerging strategy designed to offset declining television viewership for traditional advertising. Rather than purchasing an ad package during the television upfronts (where the networks preview their fall lineups), some advertisers have chosen instead to invest in producing "event" programming that showcases their brands/products and brings viewers to them rather than placing ads in between programs they hope their demographic is watching. Jim Fielding's identification of ATV content as "activations" that support the company's brand extension, licensing, and merchandising businesses demonstrates the company's embrace of this approach (Cioletti 2015).

If *AwesomenessTV* serves as an example of how ATV is willing to use television to promote its brand, the company also understands the value its stars possess as brand endorsers (Guider 2013). ATV creator Robbins plainly stated, "the next Martha Stewart or Rachel Ray is coming from this world" (Lisanti 2014). Meanwhile, Fielding enabled ATV to become a third party licensing agency for its performers, helping talent serve as "brand ambassadors" for a range of products and services while profiting from facilitating these partnerships (Lisanti 2014). As of 2014, Fielding had signed 11 performers in ATV's "talent portfolio" to this kind of representation, including Amanda Steele, a then 15-year-old whose YouTube channel, makeupbymandy24, had over 1.8 million subscribers and 115 million views for her makeup tutorials (Lisanti 2014).

ATV paired Steele and Johnson in *Life Is So R.A.D.*, a series produced in partnership with Kohl's to promote the retailer's exclusive new line of juvenile clothing. The first episode debuted on September 19, 2014, three days before the line became available for purchase at Kohl's (Votta 2014). Kohl's covered production costs for the web series and agreed to buy ads on the MCN, sold on the power of ATV's influencers to make the retailer "part of an organic conversation that's already happening in this influential online space" as well as "engage viewers in an authentic social conversation using #sorad on twitter" (Bohannon 2014). More than just an endorsement deal, however, the So R.A.D. line was also based on insights provided by ATV about tween fashion trends, entitling the company to a royalty for every item stocked by Kohl's (Shields 2014). As Fielding explained, "we developed the brand first, found the perfect partner to execute in Kohl's and then created an original series that positions Kohl's as a style destination in a cool way" ("Kohl's" 2014).

To see *Life Is So R.A.D.* as merely a revenue and sales generator for ATV and Kohl's misunderstands the former's focus on brand extension through merchandising and its ability to leverage talent to promote its label. Referring to the emergence of 'Scenes@ AwesomenessTV' pop-up shops in Los Angeles and New York City, Fielding proclaimed,

> Just as short-form content has captivated Gen Z online, we believe that short-form or pop-up retailing will resonate with them offline. . . . Our goal is to create a physical touchpoint to deepen the relationship with our customers . . . I don't want it to be just a

FIGURE 23.1 *ATV's IMO hosts model the MCN's branded merchandise available for purchase at pop-up shop Scenes@AwesomenessTV (screengrab from* Tubefilter *article published October 9, 2014).*

store, but a teen hangout where entertainment, YouTube creators and product all come together.

(Lisanti 2014)

Open for only a handful of weeks, Scenes@AwesomenessTV features merchandise branded with ATV logos alongside products endorsed by its biggest stars. The pop-up shops typically rotate merchandise stock to coincide with stars' in-person appearances while maintaining an array of ATV-branded products. Touting the potential to use the space as a "laboratory" to experiment with different product configurations while collecting data on consumer engagement, Fielding notes the network's goal of identifying merchandisable subbrands that will outlast the talent working to popularize it: "The power of AwesomenessTV as a brand is important because that helps give us longevity, while content and talent that cycles under the network may change and grow" (Lisanti 2014).

Significantly, while Will Setliff, executive vice president of marketing for Kohl's touted Johnson and Steele's creative contributions to its retail line, neither were given the opportunity to develop their own fashion lines independent of ATV through the deal (Bohannon 2014). Instead, the series, which casts Johnson and Steele as themselves, is described as "an imaginative depiction of their involvement" with the fashion line. While the series offers supposedly authentic and intimate glimpses into the two stars' private lives as they show off their wardrobes, shop at vintage clothing stores, and meet with So R.A.D. clothing designers (all suggesting the influence of their personal styles on the collection), Fielding confirms that the line actually "represents an overall AwesomenessTV aesthetic, capturing themes like 'girl creativity' and 'anything is

FIGURE 23.2 *Scenes@AwesomenessTV pop-up shop display, which emphasizes ATV's curatorial role in shaping audience taste cultures (screengrab from* Tubefilter *article published November 18, 2014).*

possible' rather than building the line around one star or style" (Shields 2014). Johnson and Steele's popularity and marketing for the network on their own channels allowed ATV to use them as surrogates for merchandising its own brand. Neither Johnson nor Steele received any royalties from So R.A.D. sales. Indeed, ATV's strategy for the series was to cast two new influencers for each of the three seasons Kohl's was committed to producing. For season two, Johnson and Steele were replaced by two new ATV MCN personalities, Meghan Rienks and Teala Dunn.

If *Terry the Tomboy*, *AwesomenessTV*, and *Life Is So R.A.D.* gave ATV the opportunity to leverage talent like Johnson's to promote its brand beyond YouTube, *T@gged* offers a culminating example of ATV's development from an MCN to a multiplatform network. In 2015, ATV began producing content featuring its talent exclusively for other platforms beyond YouTube, while promoting these series heavily through its YouTube MCN. Taking advantage of parent company DWA's deal with Netflix to develop and distribute content based its properties, ATV produced *Richie Rich* (2015–). Similarly, ATV partnered with toy manufacturer MGA Entertainment to develop *Project MC²* for Netflix while pushing the STEM-inspired brand on the ATV MCN through videos on how to make homemade skin care products (hosted by Amanda Steele) and behind-the-scenes videos of the cast describing their favorite outfits (which were also available for sale). Meanwhile, series like *Freakish* (2016) and *Foursome* (2016) were developed exclusively for Hulu and YouTube Red. These strategies indicate a shift in ATV's imagining of its function as an MCN from coordinating content and moving subscribers and talent across multiple YouTube channels to channeling its brand outward toward multiple platforms, each rhetorically invested in the concept of "television," but not necessarily looking to traditional TV channels and networks as a supplier of content. Of course, for ATV this shift is a matter of degree not emphasis, as from the outset, it has leveraged its members' channels to generate new outlets for promoting the ATV brand.

T@gged represents the first series developed by ATV as "Mobile-first video product" (Scott 2015). Created for Verizon's ad-supported Internet TV service, go90, *T@gged* is the most-viewed and fastest-growing original scripted drama on the platform (which as of 2016 offered more than 250 hours of original content, including other ATV-produced series *Guidance* and *Top Five*). Evidencing ATV's knack for branded entertainment, the series focuses on a trio of teen girls, Johnson among them, who are repeatedly tagged in grisly photos sent by an unknown killer to their prominently displayed and narratively integrated Verizon phones. Hungry for content for its network, Verizon both funds the ATV production and purchased a stake in the company in 2016; yet *T@gged* has allowed Awesomeness to move not just beyond YouTube, but also importantly onto the mobile platform that most coincides with the viewing habits of its sought-after demographic. According to Robbins, in the four years since ATV launched there has been a dramatic increase in the number of Generation Z viewers using mobile to access its content, from 40% to 80% (Villarreal 2016). Despite Generation Z's supposed platform agnosticism, this significant uptick provided an opening for a partnership with Verizon that might lure ATV viewers away from YouTube toward go90 (and incentivize subscription to Verizon over its mobile competitors). Notably, where *AwesomenessTV* recycled content first made available on YouTube, *T@gged* inverts the process, making content available on YouTube only after it has been released on Verizon's go90.

Though not produced for conventional television, *T@gged* is also without doubt ATV's most high-production value and televisual production. Still short of the 22- to 24-minutes typical of "half-hour" television episodes, its 18-minute episodes are significantly longer than the 4- to 7-minute videos ATV otherwise produces; meanwhile, the series uses cinematography, lighting, and editing techniques commonly found in other prime-time dramas. In other words, as ATV seeks to extend its brand beyond YouTube, its programming has begun to resemble the types of television that the network initially claimed Generation Z ignored. To some extent, this trajectory is expressed by Robbins's assertion, "I think in order for us to be successful at Awesomeness, we have to act like a media company" (Villarreal 2016).

As ATV's content becomes more like traditional television—especially programs created for other platforms seeking original, exclusive content—the company's ascent from MCN to "media company" troubles long held understandings of what constitute TV channels and networks. ATV has always approached its MCN as a vehicle for channeling the ATV brand as much as a method for cross-promoting multiple channels. In this regard, it has born a resemblance to traditional TV networks like ABC, CBS, and NBC that similarly extend their brand identities through their affiliate networks. Of course, ATV doesn't supply its channels with content as television networks do, but rather it moves affiliated content and talent across its network (and across platforms); it also relies upon its affiliates to promote ATV content in conjunction with their own self-brands. In some ways, ATV's approach adheres to a distributed peer-to-peer network model more commonly found online than on commercial television networks, wherein each link in the chain is both a spoke and a hub generating more spokes for extending the ATV brand. In turn, this frees ATV to pursue a cross-platform strategy to channel its brand. Without a centralized service, however, ATV may face over time challenges in managing how its brand travels across these many paths.

Johnson's casting in these three series has always been strategic, as ATV has looked to leverage her brand and her fan base to grow and move its own across platforms. The maturation of ATV's productions featuring Johnson—from faux-amateur sketch comedy vlog to faux-unscripted lifestyle branded entertainment to scripted suspense drama—also mirrors Johnson's growing social capital on and off YouTube as well as her preparation to make the leap from YouTube personality to entertainment-industry professional. In September 2016, Johnson uploaded a video to her YouTube channel teasing the release of her new single, "DNA," and excitedly announced that she thought Columbia Records would soon sign her to their label. The potential leap from YouTube to a major record label is presented as a culminating experience that validates everything Johnson has worked to accomplish via her channel, her self-branding, and her partnership with Awesomeness (Johnson 2016). Similarly, ATV's trajectory from multi-channel to multiplatform network is presented as a natural evolution of its popularity and intrinsic understanding of its audience rather than a carefully devised strategy of harnessing talent and promotional partnerships to establish Awesomeness as far more than a YouTube channel. An accompanying claim might also be made about the extension of television channels and networks into online spaces. ATV's relationship to television is far more opaque than its brand name, MCN and YouTube channel designations imply. Though television clearly has influenced many aspects of its operations, ATV also invites a rethinking of how TV networks channel their brands.

REFERENCES

"About." 2017. *Lia Marie Johnson YouTube Channel.* Accessed April 30, 2017.

"AwesomenessTV Launches Consulting Firm." 2015. *Global License!* September 30.

Banet-Weiser, Sarah. 2012. *Authentic™: The Politics of Ambivalence in a Brand Culture.* New York: New York University Press.

Bohannon, Caitlyn. 2014. "Kohl's Showcases Junior Fashion Line in YouTube Series." *Mobile Marketer*, September 4.

Cioletti, Amanda. 2015. "AwesomenessTV Boots Up." *Global License!* June 1.

Fielding, Jim. 2016. Interview with author.

Gallagher, Michael Aaron. 2012. "Lia Marie Johnson Always Wears Her Sunshine." *StayFamous. net*, July 10.

Guider, Elizabeth. 2013. "MIPJUNIOR: AwesomenessTV's Brian Robbins Says Teen Tastes Disrupting Media Landscape." *Hollywood Reporter*, October 6.

Hamedy, Saba. 2015. "Verizon Orders Original Programming from AwesomenessTV, DreamWorksTV." *Los Angeles Times*, March 11.

"Help Center." n.d. *AwesomenessTV.* https://awesomenesstv.zendesk.com/hc/en-us.

Jarvey, Natalie. 2014. "Big Frame Signs YouTube Talent Arden Rose, Aspyn Ovard and More." *Hollywood Reporter*, November 14.

Johnson, Lia Marie. 2012. "YouTube Cutie Lia Marie Johnson Talks Past, Present, & Future." *Fanlala*, August 22. (video).

Johnson, Lia Marie. 2016. "I Can't Believe It . . ." *YouTube*, September 28. (video).

"Kohl's Department Stores Partners with AwesomenessTV on Breakthrough New Fashion Line and Original YouTube Series." 2014. *Business Wire*, September 3.

Lisanti, Tony. 2014. "AwesomenessTV: The New Vibe." *Global License!* December 1.

Lotz, Amanda. 2007. *The Television Will Be Revolutionized.* New York: New York University Press.

Patel, Sahil. 2016. "Why YouTube Networks Are No Longer Hot." *Digiday*, February 23. http://digiday.com/publishers/mcn-not-so-hot/.

"Runaways Episode 1, Season 1." 2012. *YouTube*, August 31. (video description).

Scott, Rob. 2015. "Ad-Sponsored Data to Be Part of Verizon's Internet TV Service." *ET Centric*, June 26.

Shields, Mike. 2014. "Video Series on YouTube to Highlight New Clothing Line for Teen Girls." *Wall Street Journal*, September 3.

Stanley, T. L. 2014. "Meet 12 of the Biggest Young Stars on YouTube." *Adweek*. March 9.

Szalai, Georg. 2012. "YouTube to Cut Less Successful Original Content Channels." *Hollywood Reporter*, August 27.

Szalai, Georg. 2013. "DreamWorks Animation to Acquire Online Teen Network AwesomenessTV." *Hollywood Reporter*, May 1.

Villarreal, Yvonne. 2016. "Verizon to Acquire 24.5% Stake in AwesomenessTV and Launch Premium Mobile Video Brand." *Los Angeles Times*, April 6.

Votta, Rae. 2014. "AwesomenessTV Partners with Kohl's for Clothing Line and New Series." *The Daily Dot*, September 3.

 **ISAtv**

YouTube and the Branding of Asian America

Lori Kido Lopez

Although it is still hotly debated whether or not YouTube should be considered "television," one framework that draws together the online video repository and conventional television is that both are structured through the logic of the channel. Since its inception, YouTube has organized its offerings through discrete collections tied to a single source, whether that source is an individual, a corporation, or a collective. Although many YouTube channels blatantly rip and repurpose videos from a variety of sources, there is still a sense of "ownership" over the content distributed via individual channels, and it is channels that compete with one another for subscribers. Within the realm of television, networks benefit from what Catherine Johnson calls tele-branding, as "the branding of television networks enables them to compete effectively in an increasingly crowded marketplace by creating strong, distinctive and loyal relationships with viewers" (Johnson 2007, 7). The same is true for the channels on YouTube, which similarly must distinguish themselves among their competitors in order to remain marketable and relevant. This is particularly the case because the acquisition of loyal viewers or "subscribers" to YouTube channels is among one of the most valued metrics, as this data is used to determine the rate at which the channel's owner can earn ad revenue. Yet in contrast to the professional industry of marketers who shape branding efforts within the television industry, many YouTube channels become popular and distinctive simply due to the unique appeal of the individuals who are featured within them.

This has certainly been the case for many Asian American YouTubers who have risen to popularity within YouTube's ranks, including Ryan Higa of NigaHiga, Kevin Wu of Kevjumba, Michelle Phan, and Phil Wang from Wong Fu Productions. Each of these stars has worked to independently develop their own self-brand, broadcast through individual channels. With channels devoted to comic skits, makeup lessons, musical performances, and dramatic storytelling, they have earned millions of views and subscribers. The success of these YouTubers stands in contrast to the stark invisibility of

Asian Americans within the mainstream media landscape, where there are few opportunities for young Asian Americans to become stars. Alongside these wildly popular individual YouTube channels, we can additionally note the existence of an Asian American group channel that aggregates the works of these individuals and create a collective space for disseminating Asian American content—ISAtv. Although all YouTube channels are similar to television channels in some ways, this group channel more closely mimics the format of television and can help to reveal how YouTube channels function as part of the history of visibility for Asian Americans on TV.

Since 2012, ISAtv has served as a platform for over a dozen Asian American YouTubers to come together and create new programming. Through this case study, we can see how YouTube channels such as this one are utilizing the structure and frameworks of television channels in new ways, as well as what it means to remediate television into this online platform. At the same time, the case of ISAtv also helps point to the ways in which the grassroots, guerilla media style that is common among YouTubers significantly departs from traditional notions of the channel—in particular, revealing innovations that can more effectively support the minority communities that are often rendered invisible within corporate media. For Asian Americans, YouTube channels have provided a way to create mutually beneficial relationships among producers who might otherwise operate in isolation, all in an effort to collectively raise the profile of Asian American media stars in a new media environment. I argue that such efforts reveal the ways in which Asian American YouTube channels like ISAtv must be understood as moving beyond telebranding to engage in branding Asian America—an undertaking that inherently critiques the absence of Asian Americans within mainstream television and film production.

THE RISE OF DIGITAL TELEVISION

In an increasingly digital media landscape, we must continue to ask what has changed and what remains the same as the distribution of televisual content moves from terrestrial broadcasts and cable delivery to digital platforms such as YouTube. We can first note that entertainment entrepreneurs have been creating serialized narrative content for online distribution since the early days of the Internet, modeling many of their business practices and genres after television (Christian 2012). Yet William Uricchio (2009) argues that we must consider the way that YouTube differs from television in lacking the qualities of liveness, flow, and the aggregation of publics. Rather than viewing a steady and curated stream of content accessed via their television sets, users of YouTube pick and choose content from a database archive of endlessly accumulating options. Moreover, in the early days of YouTube, the site was primarily used to distribute what we might call "clips"—short videos shot on cell phones or webcams, or snippets stolen from mainstream movies, television, and websites. Such content does not seem to reflect the sensibilities of television in any way, reminding us that not all examples of audiovisual content available to mass audiences should be considered "television."

But we started to see a shift in 2012, when Google and YouTube partnered to create the YouTube Original Channel Initiative—a $100 million program designed to encourage the production of more television-like original content created exclusively for YouTube (Bond and Szalai 2011). This initiative was somewhat seen as a failure when they later dropped 60% of their original channels for failing to recoup their initial investments, even after Google spent an additional $200 million in marketing (Blagdon 2012). YouTube has nevertheless continued to pursue original programming, and in 2016 they introduced yet another new initiative focused on original programming called YouTube Red. This subscription service charges subscribers $10/month to gain access to movies and television shows created by some of their most popular personalities (Spangler 2016). Together, these initiatives clearly mark an effort to shift the programming on YouTube toward the familiar formats of television—encouraging the creation of recurring shows (whether fictional/narrative or nonfiction/reality-themed) composed of episodes that are released regularly and organized into a coherent season. Such initiatives seem designed to directly compete with television offerings that reach audiences both through traditional broadcasts and alternative distribution methods such as Hulu, Roku, HBO Go, Amazon Prime, or Netflix.

This resilience in outlasting upheavals in technology and format is consistent with the long history of television. The object that we call television has survived the transition from broadcast to cable and satellite, the rise of time-shifting devices such as the VCR and the DVR, and now the delivery of massive amounts of content via digital or online sources to a multiplicity of screens (Green 2008). Yet these conversations about how the content on YouTube is funded reminds us that there are ways in which the industrial structure of YouTube remains distinct from any of the online distribution venues for television content mentioned here—in particular, that the vast majority of channels are *not* being funded by YouTube or Google, but are simply created and maintained by everyday users. It is perhaps unfair to call these channels "amateur," as this implies that their creators are not experienced, trained, or paid. The reality is that these distinctions are rarely clear-cut, given the wide variety of participants within the YouTube arena; as Burgess and Green state, "YouTube's popular videos are contributed by a range of professional, semiprofessional, amateur and pro-amateur participants, some of whom produce content that is an uncomfortable fit with the available categories" (2009, 92). In examining the specific case of an Asian American YouTube channel that creates serialized and episodic televisual content yet remains independent from corporations and major media conglomerates, we can consider how the commercial imperatives of self-branding in the digital arena offer new political opportunities for minority media producers.

ORGANIZING ISATV AS A CHANNEL

Founded by the videographers from Wong Fu Productions and the musicians of Far East Movement, the International Secret Agents (ISA) started as an Asian American concert tour in 2008. At the time, YouTube was just starting to gain them followers, so their focus remained on live shows that were selling out in cities like Los Angeles, San Francisco, and New York. Following their last concert in 2011, they decided to turn their energies fully to the digital sphere. With the motto "Asian Pacific American Culture + Entertainment Elevated," ISAtv's YouTube channel is organized much like a traditional television channel in that it is populated with serial programs hosted by well-known Asian American personalities (see Figure 24.1).

The shows are not released on a dependable schedule, but new content is made available one episode at a time over the period of a few months. Over time they began to organize their content into seasons, with series such as *ISA! Variety Game Show, ISA Weekly Rewind*, and *Angry Asian America* being "renewed" for second seasons.

The mimicking of the language and format of a television channel is clearly helpful in serving to organize the various offerings of the ISAtv channel. This style of organization contrasts with the channels of individual users, whose lifetime archives of videos are frequently organized by simple chronology with no thematic similarity. Yet one of the significant differences between the way that television channels and YouTube channels operate is through their branding efforts, or the work of distinguishing their own content from that of their competitors. Television channels often differentiate themselves by connecting their identity to that of a celebrity or popular host who then becomes synonymous with their brand. For instance, when we want to see the Kardashians, we turn to E!; Anderson Cooper and Wolf Blitzer can only be found on CNN; Andy Cohen and all of the women from The Real Housewives franchise have become the calling card for Bravo TV. The branding of a television network is then strengthened through audiences association of the network with both specific shows and the celebrities who are connected to them (Lis and Post 2013).

Yet what we see on ISAtv is that individual celebrities such as Linda Dong, Gina Darling, and Joanna Sotomura make little effort to distinguish their participation in ISAtv

Series Title	Description
2 Girls, 1 Lab	Linda Dong and Gina Darling test out some of the weirdest Asian trends.
Asian-ish*	DANakaDAN experiences the "Asian" things he missed out on when he was growing up in an adopted household.
Kawaii for Men	Rekstizzy, a New York based rapper, explores NYC to find the true meaning of "kawaii."
Angry Asian Man	A talk show discussing current events in the Asian American community with Phil Yu and Jenny Yang.
It's...Complicated	Joanna Sotomura is joined by special guests to discuss relationships and dating.
Step by Step	Philip Wang relives his dance crew glory days and gets taught a routine by a special celebrity guest choreographer.

FIGURE 24.1 *A sampling of the series on ISAtv, each helmed by well-known Asian American host.*

from the branding of their own personal channels. Within YouTube, where individual YouTube users are each owners of their own channels, ISAtv is directly in competition with the individual channels of each of its performers. This is certainly not the case for individual celebrities or talent on television, who may star in competing programming but do not in themselves represent channels. As Sarah Banet-Weiser (2012) has theorized, YouTube epitomizes the prevalent discourse on "self-branding," where individuals structure the narratives of their own lives in ways that align with cultural and economic values in order to accrue positive feedback. Yet as we have seen here, this positive feedback can also become monetized if a user's channel becomes popular enough; at a certain threshold of views and subscribers, individuals can turn their self-brands into financial profit through the YouTube Partner Program. This logic is a distinctive feature of the way that YouTube channels are organized, but in looking at the way that ISAtv structures its offerings, we can start to see the way that YouTubers are responding to these differences by sharing the wealth rather than competing with one another.

While television networks like NBC, CBS, and ABC seek to outperform one another in the ratings on a daily basis, this form of "competition" between channels does not seem to surface within ISAtv or its participants. In the parlance of television, we might say that there is no attempt to stop viewers from changing the channel—on the contrary, when individual stars are featured on ISAtv's programs, viewers are encouraged to check out and support their channels. For instance, the show *2 Girls 1 Lab* (see Figure 24.2) on ISAtv features the talent of Dong and Darling, who "test out weird Asian trends." On the descriptions of each individual episode, there are links to the Internet addresses for each performer with clear directives such as "SUPPORT LINDA DONG," followed by links to Dong's personal YouTube, Twitter, and Instagram handles. Moreover, the home page for the ISAtv YouTube channel features a right-hand sidebar titled,

FIGURE 24.2 *On the ISAtv show "2 Girls 1 Lab," co-hosts Linda Dong and Gina Darling try out unique and sometimes bizarre trends that are popular in Asia.*

"They Inspire Us" with links to 17 other channels owned by Asian American YouTubers. Although some of these channels are run by the co-owners of ISAtv (Wong Fu Productions, Far East Movement, and DANakaDAN), others are just the channels of Asian Americans they seek to promote—each of which carries an array of content that is outside the realm of ISAtv, and thus would be seen as promoting the competition with the traditional logic of TV channels.

While the language of television provides a useful structure for channels like ISAtv to organize their content, some of this language takes on a different meaning in this context given that nearly all of the staff and performers on these programs are volunteering their labor. When a television network decides to renew a program and produce a new season, this language indicates the negotiation of a financial contract, or a monetary relationship without which the program could not exist. The talent featured within ISAtv operate within what they casually deem "YouTube style," which indicates a grassroots, guerilla form of production premised on the idea that they value the work outside of monetary compensation. Moreover, participants are always free to produce their own content and share it on their own YouTube channel in the absence of support from ISAtv—and indeed, even while producing programming for ISAtv, individual YouTubers continue to develop programming for their own channels. This is most clear in the case of Wong Fu Productions, who play a guiding role at ISAtv but are consistently developing content for their own channel as well, including their own web series, as well as comic and dramatic short films that are indistinguishable from the material that they post on ISAtv.

This sense that the content on ISAtv is indistinguishable from the content on the channels of its individual YouTubers can in some ways be seen as a failure to effectively create a brand. It would be difficult to say what sets ISAtv apart from any of its competitors within the world of Asian American YouTube, and a distinctive identity is difficult to isolate in interviews with the production team. Yet this "failure" points to the success of ISAtv's actual stated goal, which is to "elevate Asian Pacific American culture and entertainment." As mentioned earlier, Asian Americans are well aware of the fact that they are conspicuously absent from mainstream media, facing a systemic lack of recognition and support for their projects. In this case, it seems that the failure of branding for ISAtv is in part due to a larger desire to participate in branding Asian America, or collectively raising the valuation of Asian American bodies, stories, and media. When considering this larger goal, we can more accurately assess the way that YouTube channels participate in a cultural economy that may operate on a different set of values than television.

CHANNELING ASIAN AMERICA

Given the pervasiveness of branding within contemporary society and identity, it seems natural to extend the notion of brand cultures toward racial groups. We can start from the idea that all identities have been segmented into markets, and thus become commodified. For media industries whose economic structure depends upon audiences becoming the product that is being sold to advertisers, this means that racialized audiences have already been conceived of as a commodified entity. Media studies scholars have examined the way that African American media like Black Entertainment Television (BET) or the ads produced by Latino advertising agencies work to commodify blackness and Latinidad because these racial groups are the target audience for their media (Davila 2001; Smith-Shomade 2007). Although race is not a product or service that can be bought, it is clearly a signifier that possesses cultural value within society and thus plays a part in financial transactions. As we see here, media industries play an important role in creating race through processes of marketing and commodification. This perspective on the value of race is commensurate with theories of race as an ideological construction (Omi and Winant 1994), or something that cannot be understood outside of culture and is upheld through both individuals and social institutions.

This focus on the value of race and racial identities helps us to better understand how YouTube channels like ISAtv seek to benefit from the work of creating and shaping understandings of Asian America, rather than merely the value of their own channel or its contributors individual channels. We often theorize race using deficit thinking—reasoning that race is important to acknowledge only because of the ways that it systemically oppresses racial minorities. Particularly with regard to Asian Americans, the idea that Asians have very little in common with one another demands that unity can only be accomplished as a political protest against being seen and improperly treated as a collective (Espiritu 1992). Similarly, post-racial ideologies denying the continued salience of race and racial critiques have been roundly condemned because they fail to take the realities of discrimination and suffering into consideration. In response, it is asserted that the reason race still exists and continues to matter is because racial minorities continue to suffer inequalities due to overt racism (Bonilla-Silva 2009).

Yet the work of media producers in fighting for control of their own images moves beyond this kind of thinking to further posit that there is something to be gained from shaping a distinct racial identity outside the mainstream. In this case, YouTubers are working together to create and reify an Asian American consumer audience that will view and respond to their online content. This move toward thinking about race as a brand is mirrored within the work of Comaroff and Comaroff (2009) in their examination of the branding of ethnicity. They argue that "ethnic incorporation," or turning ethnicity into a corporation, is an increasingly popular economic strategy for ethnic minorities. They worry that this move can lead to homogenization and abstraction despite internal differences, which is indeed problematic. Yet they also concede that taking ethnicity to the marketplace is perhaps the only way for certain ethnic groups to survive. By commercializing identity, communities who had been formerly dispossessed of their past can participate in a process of reflection, self-construction, and authentic identity production.

One concern about using the logic of branding to understand racial identities is that branding is sometimes assumed to impart a kind of unity and simplification, where brands stand in as shorthand for a complex reality. Racial groups like Asian Americans are diverse, encompassing millions of individuals who hail from diverse countries of origin, who speak dozens of different languages, who participate in specific cultural practices that often have nothing in common with those from other Asian backgrounds. Given this diversity, it would seem counterproductive to reduce the group to a fixed set of attributes. Yet this way of thinking fundamentally misrepresents how the branding of something like a television channel actually works. Although branding may seem like a process for simplifying meaning, it is actually itself a complex process that is co-created by competing parties and resists stability. It is a continual process of shaping ideas wherein the interplay between different contexts and participants contributes to multiple meanings. Although brand managers and corporations may seek to control their brand, the reality is that they are merely one party who participates in the process of competing for their desired brand identity. In the same way, race and identity mean different things to different people invested in them, and there are many different voices competing to shape the way that racial groups are commonly understood through branding processes.

For ISAtv, this means that processes of branding take place through the voices of the hosts and performers, but also the viewers who participate in commenting, upvoting and downvoting, linking to videos, and promoting the talent of its hosts. As a deeply interactive platform, YouTube provides a rich space for discussing and sharing content—in this case, giving participants the opportunity to speak up about an image immediately after it has been posted, and for the creators to immediately respond. In doing so, both content creators and consumers collectively become invested in the project of shaping what it means to be Asian American. By focusing on the way that ISAtv is creating, promoting, and shaping the image of Asian America, we can better understand the way that channels on YouTube can build upon but also differ from the market logics of mainstream television. When the work of ISAtv succeeds, viewers are drawn toward more than simply ISAtv's own videos, but also toward the benefits of associating with Asian American media more broadly. Together, this YouTube channel helps to communicate to others what it means to be Asian American, rather than letting outsiders continue to see race as an assemblage of negative stereotypes and disadvantages. But more importantly, such brand valuation can spread outside of this individual channel and its particular content in order to collectively raise the profile of other Asian American performers and content producers on YouTube and beyond.

REFERENCES

Banet-Weiser, Sarah. 2012. *Authentic TM: The Politics of Ambivalence in a Brand Culture*. New York: New York University Press.

Blagdon, Jeff. 2012. "YouTube to Cull Poorly-Performing Original Channels, 60 Percent Not Getting Renewed." *The Verge*, November 11. www.theverge.com/2012/11/11/3633464/youtube-original-channel-cancel-60-percent.

Bond, Paul and Georg Szalai. 2011. "YouTube Announces TV Initiative with 100 Niche Channels." *The Hollywood Reporter*, October 28. www.hollywoodreporter.com/news/youtube-tv-channels-kutcher-poehler-254370.

Bonilla-Silva, Eduardo. 2009. *Racism Without Racists: Color-Blind Racism and the Persistence of Racial Inequality in America*. New York: Rowman and Littlefield.

Burgess, Jean and Joshua Green. 2009. "The Entrepreneurial Vlogger: Participatory Culture Beyond the Professional-Amateur Divide." In *The YouTube Reader*, edited by Pelle Snickars and Patrick Vonderau, 89–107. Stockholm: National Library of Sweden.

Christian, Aymar Jean. 2012. "The Web as Television Reimagined? Online Networks and the Pursuit of Legacy Media." *Journal of Communication Inquiry* 36 (4): 340–56.

Comaroff, John and Jean Comaroff. 2009. *Ethnicity, Inc.* Chicago: University of Chicago Press.

Davila, Arlene. 2001. *Latinos, Inc.: The Marketing and Making of a People*. Berkeley: University of California Press.

Espiritu, Yen Le. 1992. *Asian American Panethnicity: Bridging Institutions and Identities*. Philadelphia: Temple University Press.

Green, Joshua. 2008. "Why Do They Call It Television When It's Not on the Box? 'New' Television Services and Old Television Functions." *Media International Australia* 126: 95–105.

Johnson, Catherine. 2007. "Tele-Branding in TVIII: The Network as Brand and the Programme as Brand." *New Review of Film and Television Studies* 5 (1): 5–24.

Lis, Bettina and Martin Post. 2013. "What's on TV? The Impact of Brand Image and Celebrity Credibility on Television Consumption from an Ingredient Branding Perspective." *The International Journal on Media Management* 15 (4): 229–44.

Omi, Michael and Howard Winant. 1994. *Racial Formation in the United States: From the 1960s to the 1990s*. New York: Routledge.

Smith-Shomade, Beretta. 2007. "Target Market Black: BET and the Branding of African America." In *Cable Visions: Television Beyond Broadcasting*, edited by Sarah Banet-Weiser, Cynthia Chris and Anthony Freitas, 177–93. New York: New York University Press.

Spangler, Todd. 2016. "YouTube Set to Premiere First Original Movies, PewDiePie Series." *Variety*, February 3. http://variety.com/2016/digital/news/youtube-first-original-movies-pewdiepie-show-1201695813/.

Uricchio, William. 2009. "The Future of a Medium Once Known as Television." In *The YouTube Reader*, edited by Pelle Snickars and Patrick Vonderau, 24–39. Stockholm: National Library of Sweden.

East India Comedy

Channeling the Public Sphere in Online Satire

Subin Paul

After the inauguration of Donald Trump as the 45th president of the United States, a group of young stand-up comedians thousands of miles away in India—going by the name "East India Comedy"—uploaded a musical parody on their YouTube channel. Titled "The Donald Trump Song," the parody altered the lyrics of a popular American song to add references to gun control and heightened sexism in the US, as the comedians sang: "We have no gun control, so you men can enjoy. Just don't make out with any boys" (East India Comedy 2017a). Within a few weeks, the two-minute video had more than a million views. Such playful engagement with politics is a growing trend among the English-speaking, middle- and upper-class population living in the metropolitan cities of India, and such YouTube channels are enabling them to participate in a global "political public sphere" (Habermas 2012) not confined to national boundaries.

In fact, several comedy collectives in addition to East India Comedy such as All India Bakchod and The Viral Fever have recently launched YouTube channels to cater to a thriving online audience with political satire. The popularity of these channels comes at a time of declining credibility for traditional news media in India because of growing interference from corporate and government institutions (Punathambekar 2015). Traditional media certainly persist in India, with more than 100 million print newspapers sold every day (Biswas 2012). Television outlets, too, remain plentiful; from only one television channel prior to the early 1980s, India now has more than 700 television channels ("Give" 2015). However, Internet penetration is 35% ("Internet" 2016), and by 2020 India is estimated to overtake the US in terms of the absolute number of online users (PTI 2016). It is in spaces like YouTube, therefore, that we might look to see this transformation from traditional media institutions to emerging forms of cultural production unfold, where the "channel" structures of existing media adapt and evolve to serve new media logics. This is a question not only of industry, but also of politics, as this transformation enables cultural genres such as comedy to support public dialogue, deliberation, and debate in ways that the channels of previous media institutions could not. Yet the phenomenal prospects of the Internet to expand the public sphere, and specifically the accompanying potential of YouTube channels to foster democratic dialogue and political critique, remain little explored in academic literature.

One of the functions of a channel is to differentiate one industry player from others and create loyalty among the audience in an increasingly competitive market. A channel, in a sense, depends on boundaries that define what their interior contents will be, and perhaps more importantly, what they will not be, demarcating that content from that of other content creators in the market (at least in principle). Channels seek to maximize what Faye Woods (2014) in the context of British television called the "distinguishing difference" in order to develop and grow their niche audiences. In this chapter, thus, I seek to interrogate how and why the distinguishing difference of YouTube channels has become instrumental in contributing to the public sphere in a multi-channel environment. In other words, how have digital entrepreneurs and audiences leveraged these new channels as a way to distinguish themselves from each other as well as to critically discuss politics and culture in contemporary India? In what follows, I will briefly review the historical development of video channels in India, from the sole, state-owned "DD National" to myriad private channels, and then demonstrate how the emergence of digital channels has created new possibilities for the public sphere with a case study of East India Comedy's (EIC) YouTube channel.

FROM ALL INDIA "SERIALS" TO EAST INDIA COMEDY

The shift from a single television channel, DD National, to multiple television and Internet-based channels is one of the most significant developments in the media industry since India's independence in 1947. The government-owned Doordarshan launched India's first television channel, DD National or DD1, in 1959. Broadly, the emergence and development of the national television channel can be traced in three distinct yet interconnected phases (Kumar 2006). The first phase began with the establishment of a preliminary broadcasting center in New Delhi and consisted largely of experimentation with educational programming as well as the technical evaluation of the broadcast equipment. In this phase, television played a subordinate role to radio, which was the preferred medium for mass communication to foster national identity in the newly independent country.

The demands of a developing nation made agriculture, animal husbandry, poultry farming, education, literacy, and family welfare prime agendas for television programming. With the goals of national development clearly taking precedence on Indian television, there was little impetus to promote Doordarshan (DD) either as a commercial medium for entertainment or as a public enterprise free from government control. In 1982, however, India's decision to host the Asian Games and the growing popularity of color television encouraged a realignment of goals. After two years, DD launched another channel, DD2 (or DD Metro) in Delhi and was later telecast to other metropolitan cities of India. Thus, the second phase of television development spawned an era of entertainment programing in India. This phase also saw a marked increase in the reach of television as the potential coverage of DD grew from 23% to 70% of the population (Kumar 2006).

The telecast of family serials, including *Hum Log, Buniyad* and *Nukkad*, on DD National provided a fillip to commercialization of television as private advertisers entered into sponsorship agreements with DD. At the same time, to sustain the political agenda of transcending the diversities of language, religion, region, ethnicity, class, caste, and gender in the modern nation-state, the political elites became so preoccupied with the genre of national programing—family serials telecast across the country showcasing a unified, "Indian" culture—that they overlooked the increasing commercialization of what was heralded as a public medium at its inception. Because the prime goal of the state-owned DD was to create a shared sense of Indian nationality, the two television channels rarely became spaces for political criticism. On the contrary, by the late 1980s, with the production of two prime-time Hindu epics, *Ramayana* and *Mahabharata*, Hinduism started to exert a greater push both in television content and ideology—which has only become more prominent in contemporary India, leading to an aggressive form of religious nationalism that to some extent has curtailed media freedom, as will be explained later.

In 1991, however, the state-owned media monopoly came to an end with the liberalization of the economy. The government opened the media market to private corporations including foreign players. This third phase, which continues to this day, saw the rise of Rupert Murdoch–owned Star TV and Indian-owned Zee TV satellite services. The national satellite reach once monopolized by DD and dedicated to the building of national unity through its channels, DD1 and DD2, now allowed channels in "regional" languages from outside the Hindi belt of states in the northwest to be delivered throughout the nation (Sinclair and Harrison 2004). DD's financial status, moreover, slowly started to worsen. With these initial ruptures in the hegemonic dominance of state-sponsored broadcaster DD, Indian audiences went from a single-channel environment to a world of numerous choices.

Starting in the early 2000s, there was also a marked increase in the penetration of the Internet and mobile phones (Jeffrey and Doron 2013). Within five years of the dot-com boom and bust, which played out from 1998 to 2004 in the Indian context, the digital media economy was integrated into the rest of advertising, marketing, and media industries across the country (Punathambekar 2015). Digital entrepreneurs, ranging from independent artists to formal groups of commercial content creators, started channels on YouTube. Most notable among these was The Viral Fever (TVF), launched in 2010. Labeled as an "online digital entertainment channel," TVF sought to reach out to the "young generation" that seldom watched television ("About TVFPlay" n.d.). Three years later, another collective called the All India Bakchod (AIB) began its YouTube channel, and in a short time, it became one of the most popular digital channels in India ("About Us" n.d.). With more than one billion users visiting YouTube globally every month ("Video" 2015), YouTube channels have also become central to digital comedy production and marketing.

EIC entered this landscape in 2012 as a two-person stand-up act on YouTube (later expanded to seven members) providing various type of comedy, including stand-up acts, workshops, corporate events, as well as television and movie scripting. Asserting the significance of the YouTube channel to EIC's operations, its co-founder, Kunal Rao, explained in an email message to the author on April 19, 2017:

> It is the era of digital content, and people consume content online quite voraciously. So for a bunch of stand-up comedians, it is easier to reach people in different cities and countries through the internet, than to travel and perform shows for them to let them know we exist. So YouTube has helped EIC get popular quicker than if we did not have a channel.

Speaking to that desire for popularity, EIC claims to be India's "busiest" comedy company ("What We Do" n.d.). Its YouTube oeuvre largely targets young, urban Indians with live comedy videos and theme-based shows. The latter include *Comedy News Network* (satirical commentary on 24/7 news and traditional news media), *EIC vs. Bollywood* (commentary on Bollywood controversies and spoofs), *Men Are From Bars* (a show on romantic relationships), *Backbenchers* (comedic commentary on college life), *The Illiterates* (stand-up acts on literary culture in India), *Pant on Fire* (co-founder Sorabh Pant's stand-up acts), *It's Not Okay* (co-founder Kunal Rao's comedic sketches on Indian society and culture), and *Cometh the Hour* (Azeem Banatwalla's stand-up comedy). In addition, EIC hosts an annual award show called "Ghanta Awards," which showcases the "worst" actors and movies of Bollywood in a given year. EIC also produces musical comedies and sketches that explicitly engage with politics—a role that requires us to consider the YouTube channel's role in supporting public dialogue and debate beyond that which traditional news media currently permit.

PLAYFUL POLITICS AND THE ONLINE PUBLIC SPHERE

Aside from growing interest in online platforms more generally, one reason why YouTube channels such as EIC have become popular among the Indian population is because of increasing censorship in news media. The votaries of the government enact this censorship both directly and indirectly. While the Bharatiya Janata Party (BJP), which assumed power in 2014 through a landslide electoral victory (Chakravartty and Roy 2015), has come under scrutiny for its crackdown on journalists who are critical of its policies, Internet trolls following the right-wing Hindutva ideology have been quick to attack any online commentary critical of the BJP or Prime Minister Narendra Modi (Mohan 2015). In addition, as Arvind Rajagopal (2009) notes, traditional media negotiate new, more informal forms of censorship and control via the mechanisms of business practice, including judgments about audience taste that use ratings, and the need to advance advertising revenues as the sole justification for the presentation of programing.

Given these constraints, online channels for comedic satire can support, at least to some extent, criticism of the ruling government and talk about politics in the constructive and adversarial way required of citizens in a democracy but increasingly prohibited by traditional media institutions. In this way, satirical YouTube channels, such as

EIC, have allowed the Indian public sphere to persist as well as expand despite forces working to limit it. This notion of a public sphere typically refers to a common space, in principle accessible to all, which anyone could enter with views on the common good realized wholly or partially. As Rajeev Bhargava (2005) noted, such public spaces could include the *maidan* ("playground"), the coffeehouse, the exhibition hall, the roadside *paan* ("tobacco") shop, or the sweetshop in the neighborhood, as well as the discursive and representational space available in newspapers, magazines, radio, and television. In contemporary times, the Internet has emerged as a public space where the critical dialogue and debate integral to a democratic society is carried out (Papacharissi 2010), and satirical YouTube channels, I argue, are important sites in this process.

With more than half a million subscribers, EIC's YouTube channel is a prime venue to cultivate an audience. According to EIC's co-founder, Sorabh Pant (2014), the You-Tube channel is central to any comedian's success: "One of the first steps for a comedian today has to be setting up a YouTube channel—the 10,000 people who follow you there would also be your audience offline." Yet in marshaling audiences for groups like EIC, these digital channels might also be said to produce publics. Although bounded and differentiated from one another, channels nevertheless support communication between online content creators and the audiences whose opinions, as recorded through surveys and YouTube comment boards, are occasionally incorporated while producing new digital content. In supporting the formation of a specific audience, the channel that distinguishes EIC in a multi-channel environment also relates to the function of comedy in the public sphere. For example, EIC occasionally invites members from the audience to be a part of its stand-up acts, which makes the public performance and, by extension, the public sphere a little more inclusive. This drive for "distinguishing difference" thus helps EIC's YouTube comedy channel make the public sphere function in a more participatory manner as compared to AIB and TVF channels, which have only studio-produced and studio-edited shows.

To illustrate the support for this political public sphere provided by EIC's YouTube channel, I turn to a live musical parody that the group uploaded on YouTube after the Modi-led Indian government undertook banknote demonetization in November 2016. One of the purported goals of the demonetization process, which annulled old 500 and 1000 rupee currency notes, was to crack down on illicit cash used to fund terrorism and illegal activities. Given the sudden—and rather unplanned—implementation of demonetization, countless Indians faced hardships as they stood in front of vending machines for hours, sometimes days, to obtain new currency notes. In the music parody titled "The Modi Song," the seven members of EIC satirized Modi's demonetization decision (East India Comedy 2017b). The video clip received about 1.2 million views and 1,673 comments on the YouTube message board. Without directly referencing Modi in the song (thus leaving things open to interpretation), the EIC comedians critically commented on the effect of demonetization on the public.

Borrowing a tune from a popular 1990s Bollywood song and code-switching to English in between, the EIC members sang: "*ATM hai sab khali. Sab de rahe hain gali. Sutta khareedne ke liye. Maine cheque diya*" ("Vending machines are empty. Everyone is swearing. In order to buy cigarettes. I gave a check") (East India Comedy 2017b). They complained that they had to use a check to buy cigarettes—juxtaposing a mundane act with a serious issue and thus imparting humor (Paul 2017). Further, they accused that although the idea behind demonetization was good, the process was not planned meticulously, and they suggested that the government recall the former governor of the Reserve Bank of India, Raghu Ram Rajan, under whom the Indian economy had ostensibly prospered. Later in the video, the comedians resented, *"Mere bank account pe nasbandi kiya"* ("My bank account was sterilized"), connecting the present to the authoritarian times of the mid-1970s, when Prime Minister Indira Gandhi imposed a National Emergency under which millions of Indians were forcibly sterilized and freedom of expression was curbed. Moreover, demonetization duped the common man as represented by the voices of the EIC comedians: *"Aur ham sabka kat gaya chutiyaaa"* ("And we all were fooled"); yet millionaire businessman Vijay Mallya, who amassed a lot of illegal money, escaped the country scot-free. Thus, through this "personalization of politics" (Highfield 2016), the EIC collective not only generated humor, but also vividly portrayed the plight of citizens in light of demonetization.

Beyond the ability of these performative techniques to produce political humor, what is notable here is the manner in which such videos contribute to the online public sphere in the context of their YouTube channel. Just as playgrounds, shops, and news media have the public sphere potential, a YouTube channel, too, is an important site where public sphere energy is circulated and supported. Through this two-minute video hosted on EIC's persistent channel space, the comedians were able to spawn debates and discussion on demonetization among the Internet public. The video as well as its YouTube message board produced a discursive space where class, caste, and religious nationalism were foregrounded and placed in critical tension with each other. For example, in a comment posted to YouTube, one YouTube user noted that "Indian GDP grew at 7 percent" during the quarter in which demonetization was undertaken. In response to this comment, another user pointed to the fact that the standard of living in the country remained poor, inequality between rich and poor had increased, and the growth figures "hardly had any effect on a layman's life."

As Gray, Jones, and Thompson (2009) have suggested, parody and satire work especially well during periods of social and political "rupture" and offer sharp critiques of established political orders. Furthermore, it can be argued that satire, as shown in the demonetization video, can help us estrange and distance ourselves from the ongoing political moment in order to reflect on and reconnect with historic episodes when government actions had an adverse effect on the lives of the public. Such critiques of the establishment are becoming less common in other, more traditional media outlets, as EIC's co-founder Kunal Rao commented: "Growing censorship on TV channels is a key reason why they [comedians] are moving to the online platform for satire and commentary" (Rathore and Khosla 2014). In other words, because EIC's channel allows the comedians to engage in a critical, political commentary without the fear of censorship, the YouTube channel creates a "distinguishing difference" vis-à-vis television channels.

YouTube channels, such as that of EIC, seem to maintain the formality of a television channel, yet at the same time they are less moderated than their television counterparts, making the former a secure and increasingly popular venue to engage in playful politics.

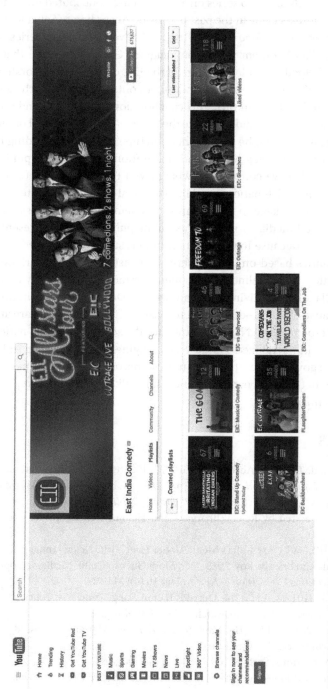

FIGURE 25.1 *On YouTube, East India Comedy presents a channel for public sphere participation.*

In fact, several channels and web series on YouTube have contributed immensely to You-Tube India's revenue, especially in the past two years. According to Satya Raghavan, head of content operations at YouTube India, 2016 was the "year of the web series," and so they created "an umbrella of content under the Laughter Games" initiative that year (John 2016). This move helped multiple members of the EIC collective collaborate with adver-tisers, subscribers, YouTube India staff, and other content partners such as Only Much Louder and Culture Machine. In turn, this collaboration enabled EIC and other comedy collectives to create, promote, and monetize their videos on YouTube and other platforms.

In the final analysis, it can be argued that YouTube channels, including that of EIC, have contributed to the development and maturation of the online public sphere in India. These channels have constructed what Aswin Punathambekar (2015) called an "intertextual field," in which national and international politics are contested and delib-erated through direct linkage to the common problems of the citizenry and their par-ticipation with digital media. However, this online public sphere at present is far from inclusive in practice. Because Internet penetration is still low compared to other coun-tries, and inequalities based on gender, class, and caste further exacerbate this digital divide, participation in the online public sphere is stratified and mainly limited to mid-dle- and upper-class Indians living in urban regions. Despite these limitations—or per-haps in part because of them—digital and television channels in India are at crossroads today: while state-owned DD National aimed for decades to unify the nation based on Bollywood music and serialized Hindu epics (engineering a singular Indian identity reinvented by the government), there are now numerous smaller channels emerging in the digital space that develop niche audiences and talk back to those in power through playful, comedic melodies.

REFERENCES

"About TVFPlay." n.d. *TVFPlay*. Accessed April 22, 2017. https://tvfplay.com/about.

"About Us." n.d. *All India Bakchod*. Accessed April 22, 2017. http://allindiabakchod.in/about-us/.

Bhargava, Rajeev. 2005. "Introduction." In *Civil Society, Public Sphere and Citizenship: Dialogues and Perceptions*, edited by Rajeev Bhargava and Helmut Reifeld, 13–55. New Delhi: Sage Publications.

Biswas, Soutik. 2012. "Why Are India's Media Under Fire?" *BBC News*, January 12.

Chakravartty, Paula and Srirupa Roy. 2015. "Mr. Modi Goes to Delhi: Mediated Populism and the 2014 Indian Elections." *Television & New Media* 16 (4): 311–22.

East India Comedy. 2017a. "EIC: The Donald Trump Song." *YouTube*, February 16. Accessed April 22, 2017. www.youtube.com/watch?v=SF4vL8RN0Kg.

East India Comedy. 2017b. "EIC: The Modi Song." *YouTube*, March 2. Accessed April 22, 2017. www.youtube.com/watch?v=JtpzLsIdIsE.

"Give Facts and Perceptions, Scribes Told." 2015. *Hindu*, March 23.

Gray, Jonathan, Jeffrey P. Jones, and Ethan Thompson. 2009. *Satire TV: Politics and Comedy in the Post-Network Era*. New York: New York University Press.

Habermas, Jürgen. 2012. "The Public Sphere: An Encyclopedia Article." In *Media and Cultural Studies: Keyworks*, edited by Meenakshi Gigi Durham and Douglas M. Kellner, 75–9. West Sussex: Wiley-Blackwell.

Highfield, Tim. 2016. *Social Media and Everyday Politics*. Cambridge: Polity Press.

"Internet Users by Country." 2016. *Internet Live Stats*. Accessed April 22, 2017. www.inter netlivestats.com/internet-users-by-country/.

Jeffrey, Robin and Assa Doron. 2013. *Cell Phone Nation: How Mobile Phones Have Revolutionized Business, Politics and Ordinary Life in India*. Gurgaon: Hachette India.

John, Jessu. 2016. "Comedy, Web Series Combination Strengthening YouTube Viewership." *Hindu Business Line*, August 5.

Kumar, Shanti. 2006. *Gandhi Meets Primetime: Globalization and Nationalism in Indian Television*. Urbana: University of Illinois Press.

Mohan, Sriram. 2015. "Locating the 'Internet Hindu' Political Speech and Performance in Indian Cyberspace." *Television & New Media* 16 (4): 339–45.

Pant, Sorabh. 2014. "Comedy's Long Road." *Economic Times*, February 23.

Papacharissi, Zizi. 2010. *A Private Sphere: Democracy in a Digital Age*. Cambridge: Polity Press.

Paul, Subin. 2017. "A New Public Sphere? English-Language Stand-Up Comedy in India." *Contemporary South Asia* 25 (2): 121–35.

PTI. 2016. "India's Internet Users to Double to 730 Million by 2020 Leaving US Far Behind." *Economic Times*, August 17.

Punathambekar, Aswin. 2015. "Satire, Elections, and Democratic Politics in Digital India." *Television & New Media* 16 (4): 394–400.

Rajagopal, Arvind. 2009. *The Indian Public Sphere: Readings in Media History*. New Delhi: Oxford University Press.

Rathore, Vijaya and Varuni Khosla. 2014. "Social Media Sites Like Facebook, Twitter in Grip of Viral Videos." *Economic Times*, August 16.

Sinclair, John and Mark Harrison. 2004. "Globalization, Nation, and Television in Asia: The Cases of India and China." *Television & New Media* 5 (1): 41–54.

"Video Marketing and Analytics Startup Vidooly Partners with Subhash Ghai's Whistling Woods Film School." 2015. *EFYtimes.com*, November 21.

"What We Do." n.d. *East India Comedy*. Accessed April 22, 2017. http://eastindiacomedy.com/category/what-we-do/.

Woods, Faye. 2014. "Classed Femininity, Performativity, and Camp in British Structured Reality Programming." *Television & New Media* 15 (3): 197–214.

 **Twitter**

Channels in the Stream

James Bennett and Niki Strange

On October 27, 2016, *International Business Times* and other global news outlets reported that Twitter was "killing off the Vine six-second-long video loop mobile app" as part of a cost-cutting exercise (Russon 2016). Just days earlier, Twitter had announced its first non-US deal to secure the live streaming coverage rights to a sports event: Australia's preeminent horse race, the Melbourne Cup. Coming on the back of a range of agreements Twitter has made for coverage of live events—including a global deal for the NFL's Thursday night package of games and the US presidential debates—Twitter's culling of Vine and investment in live streaming suggest how the future of the platform might be as a television "channel." Twitter's move into live streaming has not only exploited ancillary digital rights sold by event owners, but also required acquisition of rights traditionally auctioned *as*, and competed *for*, as "broadcast" rights. In the process, Twitter's repositioning of itself asks us to reconceptualize the notion of a television channel in a digital television age of streaming. This chapter sets out how we might understand television channels in the logics of social media platforms such as Twitter. As such, it challenges us to consider digital media *as television*, suggesting how the future of one media form might be found in the past of another.

The argument that follows does not suggest that the whole of Twitter—now an ecosystem of interrelated services and applications, including Vine, Periscope, and Snappy TV—should be understood as a channel. But a significant proportion of what the platform does, how content is produced, and Twitter's mutual affinity with the television industry all suggest how positioning it as a channel is productive for our understanding of digital television as a "non-site specific, hybrid cultural and technological form that spreads across multiple platforms" (Bennett 2011, 2). Indeed, it is the partnership between the platform and the television industry itself that allows us to understand Twitter as a channel most productively. In 2015, *Guardian Technology* writer Stuart Dredge described both Twitter and Facebook as "love-bombing" the TV industry in the hope of driving more conversation on their platforms. But as Dredge's report recognized, this was only part of the story: "Twitter has become a broadcaster of sorts itself: its 316 million active users currently watch 370 years' worth of video every day on the service" (2015).

As a senior UK broadcasting executive told us, "both Twitter and Facebook want to develop that area. So they are very, very generous with their time," while other industry figures noted the distribution of new applications and additional support for broadcasters and television production companies to try new approaches. With such a huge appetite for video, as well as emerging competition for eyeballs between the social media platform giants, it is perhaps little wonder that Twitter is considering the lessons of television's past to secure its future. This partnership with television is especially important as Twitter moves from an emphasis on user-generated *feeds* to professionally generated content *channels* of video *streams*. At the same time, Twitter's feeds also increasingly draw upon television tactics and partnerships to garner and retain viewer attention. Twitter's gamble on at least partially reimagining the platform as channel speaks to the wider industrial context in which it found itself in late 2015: the *Financial Times* reported its share price had "languished [having] fallen almost 50 per cent in the past year," leading to the return of Jack Dorsey as chief executive to reignite growth of the platform (Kuchler and Foley 2015). A widely circulated press release less than a year later positioned "Twitter [as] increasingly a place where people can find live streaming video" (Slefo 2016). But as we will argue, Twitter's repositioning as channel in partnership with the TV industry is more significant than simply live streaming video. Drawing on 38 interviews from the UK television and digital media industries, including Twitter's director of broadcast partnerships (now director of strategic innovation), we argue that emergent practices on Twitter recycle television production heritage, including practices of live transmission, scheduling and counter-scheduling, content production modes and advertising. These interviews are triangulated with trade press and newspaper coverage as well as ethnographic observation over the two-year period 2015–2016.[1] As such, we position the UK's production cultures in the context of global industrial strategy to suggest how the future of Twitter's social media platform might lie in television's broadcast past.

OF CHANNELS, PLATFORMS, AND STREAMS

> *Twitter [is] the world's biggest sofa.*
> —Dan Biddle, Director of Broadcast Partnerships, Twitter (interview 01/03/2016)

Biddle's metaphorical reference to Twitter's status as a sofa replays a common tactic in the histories of media technologies: the familiarization of a new technology by reference to an older one. However, as it calls our attention to the platform's increasingly intimate relationship with television, it is also suggestive of how metaphors emphasize particular aspects of a media form and downplay others (Gripsrud 1998). Most regularly, as Derek Johnson sets out in the introduction to this volume, television and its channels have made metaphorical allusions to water, often via the notion of "flow." By contrast, most work on Twitter has considered it—explicitly or implicitly—as a platform, upon which a user community develops. Tarleton Gillespie's work (2010) teases out how the term "platform," and its operationalization by companies such as YouTube, subsumes within it four different "semantic territories"—the computational, the architectural, the figurative, and the political. In so doing, the term functions as a powerful and persuasive metaphor that enables platform operators to elide potential tensions between serving all users equally at the same time as delivering audiences to advertisers and commercial partners. Simultaneously the platform is positioned as neutral and passive in terms of legal liability for content housed on the platform. Concluding his analysis, Gillespie persuasively suggests that despite the promises of a different system to traditional media (like television), "platforms are more like traditional media than they care to admit," going on to note that just as with broadcasting, platforms choose what can appear as well as how it is organized and monetized. However, the connection between television channel and platform does not end there for Twitter, with the relationship between the TV industry and social media operator returning us to both an emphasis on liveness and forms of flow that characterize a channel.

Indeed, prior to the series of "broadcast" deals for live streaming of sporting events announced in 2016, academic work on the relationship between Twitter and television focused on its reinvigoration of live TV: either as strategic collaboration (Sørensen 2016) or understanding audience practices (Evans 2014) or audience measurement and tracking (Highfield, Harrington, and Bruns 2013). As Sørensen argues, television channels "are using television's traditional traits—reach and live events—in a bid to dominate the mediascape and exert its power over who wins viewers across platforms and devices" (2016, 14). However, much as digital media is increasingly akin to television, it would be wrong to suggest that this is simply a domination of the mediascape by television in which broadcasters conceptualize "these types of viewing experiences as specifically televisual" (14). Instead, live television events also act as a space of collaboration and experimentation for Twitter as a channel: enabling Twitter, TV industry, rights holders, and sponsors alike to reach and engage audiences in mutually beneficial ways. Such collaborations arguably pave the way for Twitter's move into live streaming events. Here the language of content provision based in channeling or "streaming" returns us to the metaphorical allusions to water.

Before exploring the term stream, it is first important to note that the adoption of streaming by Twitter represents a shift from the Twitter "feed" to Twitter streams: both of which may be interacted with by the act of tweeting. Whereas feed suggests something to be acted upon, or to be consumed, stream returns us to notions of "flow." While feeds remain important, streams are embedded within these and, as we discuss below, usage of video (live or otherwise) is increasingly prominent in Twitter feeds— indeed, leading to greater emphasis on streaming. Our link back to flow and channels is complete when we consider the development of the computing noun "stream" in 1993: "A continuous flow of data. . . . Also, a channel for such data" ("Stream" n.d.). Streaming, as with channeling, suggests that at once there is an active sender at the same time as it posits the audience as a comparatively more passive receiver of the "flow," which washes them along. While the Twitter user, as with so many digital media forms, is figured as (inter)active, selective, and participative, the close relationship between channel, platform, and stream traced here suggests how Biddle's metaphor of the sofa is not simply a clever pun or attempt to familiarize a new technology via reference to an old. Rather it reveals how the strategic ploy of the platform returns us to old media practices of television: from live-relaying events to scheduling, counter-scheduling, advertising, and more that we explore below. Of course, as television scholars have long demonstrated, the audience is never entirely active or passive—even when wrapped up in the "flow": digital media studies would do equally well to learn from such discoveries, or risk finding that the active users of Twitter—and other platforms—are just as likely to be sofa slobs as were television's couch potatoes likely to be interactive participants.

TWITTER AND LIVE TELEVISION PRODUCTION

Twitter's growing emphasis on both embedding video in Twitter feeds and live video streaming is at once competitive and collaborative, with both the television industry and Twitter co-opting and adapting tactics from one another. The result has been the convergence of different approaches to, and meanings of, liveness in the formation of Twitter as channel.

Initially television professionals regarded Twitter, as with any new media form that competes for audience attention, as competition. Our previous work on multiplatform production in UK television suggested how TV producers often viewed digital plat-forms as either sites of peripheral experimentation; insignificantly small in audience size; feared; shunned; or adopted in strategic statements but rarely backed in reality (Bennett et al. 2012). As one senior executive opined, the strategy at his broadcaster had been "basically [to treat] our social feed as the TV guide" for a long time. How-ever, while disjunctures and barriers still remain between television, digital produc-tion teams, and platform operators, the growing ubiquity of smart phones has made television producers more conversant in social media. As one producer described, its become increasingly commonplace because "it's more of a state of mind than part of their contract," or something they are forced to do. Some working in the UK industry noted the viral spread of Susan Boyle's *Britain's Got Talent* clip in 2009 as a pivotal moment in the adoption of Twitter, and social media more widely, by the industry:

> it went from TV producers being reticent to trying anything around digital/social (didn't see value, thought it would destroy brand equity) to them going to the other extreme and wanting to try everything! "let's do it all!" "we don't need to measure it!"

Such adoption has been aided by Twitter's courting of the industry, with a signifi-cant point of collaboration between TV industry and platform coming in the form of SnappyTV.

Acquired by Twitter in 2014, Snappy TV (2014) describes itself as a "cloud-based, live video platform that makes TV and live web streams social, mobile and viral." It enables video producers, especially television, to clip, edit, and share moments from live broad-casts in near real time and has become a significant point of collaboration between television industry and Twitter, even at the same time as it points to competition and co-optation. SnappyTV is pivotal to the blurring of boundaries between Twitter feeds and streams, playing an important part in what Dan Biddle calls the "Tweet Spot," a tactic which has allayed broadcasters' fears of losing audience attention:

> Instead of fearing split attention, think of double attention—TV producers need to find "the tweet spot": OMG moments that everyone will react to and then providing the right clip/gif etc to *own* that moment. Great content mirrored on both screens . . . if you can get that content out to the audience at the time it's happening they will re-tweet that and comment around that and share it and spread it even further.

Similarly, Twitter's UK Managing Director Dara Nasr argued, "When there's great programming it drives a peak of tweets, and when there are a lot of tweets about programming, it drives greater viewing on TV—there's a real reciprocal relationship" (Bell 2016).

The ability of producers to use SnappyTV to hit the Tweet Spot and extend television's liveness into Twitter's feeds is not simply about the viewing experience, but also how production cultures adapt and respond to the integration of social media into their existing processes. Thus the executive digital producer on *The Voice UK* described her team's work in terms similar to those used to explain live television production: "it is chaotic and crazy and kooky and it is a split second. . . . I have a great team and it's a smooth as silk and we know what we're doing." Here the language mimics that of her TV counterparts, "chaotic" and time-sensitive, but a trade allegory of team-building and over-coming all odds makes sense of the difficulties of production. SnappyTV, and similar services, have become an important bridge between television and Twitter: enabling shared understandings and tools to emerge. As another digital producer we interviewed explained, SnappyTV is loved by those working in television because it is "integrated and native to Twitter," enabling them to bypass clunky content management systems. As he put it, this enabled him to "drop LoL bombs" throughout a range of shows quickly and easily, increasing viewer enjoyment and engagement with the show. At one major UK broadcaster, this had led an approach to using SnappyTV that, while ultimately stopping short of "put[ting] the whole show out there in little chunks," allowed producers to do as they liked because it all drove increased attention towards program brands. This senior executive argued television had learnt some of the lessons from social about the importance of giving content and extras away freely and promoting an attitude of generosity around brands, rather than proprietary control.

However, SnappyTV is not simply a point of collaboration between TV and Twitter. It also represents an important strategic tool for Twitter in developing streams: adopting and adapting television's liveness into its own channel. The story Dan Biddle tells of the evolution of the Tweet Spot, a service called Amplify, and the first uses of SnappyTV points to the way in which Twitter's initial co-operation with television was quickly seized as an opportunity to reinvent the platform, channeling both the live video stream and profits in-house rather than collaborating with television.

> college football . . . were the first people to use [SnappyTV] with Amplify . . . going out into Twitter at the peak point of the conversation i.e. the Tweet Spot, [because] . . . any

time that there was some kind of situation or a contested play . . . they bring over an iPad and the referee looks. . . . And it's like "well hang on, if the referee is looking at it we can tweet this out and see what the ref is [seeing]" and then everyone can share this and go "foul," "no way was that a penalty," whatever it might be.

The Amplify service then allowed Twitter to add a short pre-roll commercial to such clips, using the same sponsor as the television broadcast, to reach and extend their audience in a new way. As Biddle explains, liveness remains paramount: the audience "will re-tweet that and comment around that and share it and spread it even further." This "triangle of virtue," led to increased experimentations in collaboration with the television industry via SnappyTV and third party apps like Grabyo. As a result, an increasing amount of near live footage was shared through Twitter's platform enabling it to test transmission/bandwidth incrementally so that it eventually made more sense to stream content themselves. Thus while Twitter may posture as "TV partner, not predator," the story of SnappyTV suggests how the platform might increasingly be positioned as a competitor channel.

Moreover, this strategy indicates Twitter has learnt the lessons of television's past in its reconceptualization. Twitter's focus on live sporting events echoes Rupert Murdoch's strategy in the global television market of using sports as a "battering ram" to enter new markets and drive consumers to new television platforms—such as satellite and digital (Millar 1998, 3). The move by Twitter into partnerships with existing television players such as Bloomberg and new online players such as Buzzfeed in its live streaming of the 2016 US election debates, further asks us to reconceptualize Twitter as akin to a broadcast channel. Twitter's strategy of developing live events coverage mimics Raymond Williams's description of the evolution of television broadcasting as technological and cultural form, whereby content developed "parasitically" via state occasions, public sporting events, and more (2003, 18). Just like early television, Twitter has adopted its purportedly neutral platform to act as a mere relayer of live events—a "channel through which information passes" ("Stream" n.d.) The following section explores how such a move has extended television production practices to Twitter in order to provide the platform with compelling content and TV-like experiences.

TWITTER AND TELEVISION CHANNEL TACTICS: SCHEDULING LIVENESS

Since the network era, television channels have rarely presented us with "live" events. Yet the medium is suffused with the ideology of liveness perpetuated by its continual call to the present: its ability to unite large viewing audiences in the same experience at any one time, stitched together by the carefully curated schedule that responds (and shapes) the routines of daily life to build a powerful sense of copresence. As John Ellis (2000) has argued, scheduling is one of television's most powerful and creative tools, both in terms of organizing the industrial production and reception of programming as well as defining the experience and identity of a channel. Television's collaboration with

Twitter has seen the importance of scheduling extended, ranging from prescripted, pre-scheduled tweets to tactics of tent-poling, counter-scheduling, and stunting.

One of the most prominent examples of scheduling on Twitter is around "live" tele-vision. Interviewees working to produce social media for live programs all discussed the importance of prescripting and scheduling the release of tweets, with format points being particularly useful for preplanning Twitter feeds. As one digital producer explained, the digital team will watch numerous rehearsals for a live show and "script [up to 50%] of the content [so] we can then craft it around acts that we know are going to have an impact." The social media writer discussed this as "writ[ing] a script of tweets . . . and image ideas for GIFs and Vines," which are then time-coded for release, using a tool such as HootSuite or TweetDeck. However, as both explained, the excite-ment was in leaving the "space" to react to live events and audiences that enhances the feeling of copresence, a view widely echoed in the industry. That said, Twitter feeds were rarely simply "live," in the sense of tweeting along to a program on the fly. Even releasing clips or images from the program into its related Twitter feed—the Tweet Spot—was not simply a case of ensuring synchronicity between broadcast and Twitter channel, but rather a carefully configured and debated form of scheduling. Thus one digital producer explained how a compelling piece of content was scheduled around *The Great British Bake Off*:

> We have a picture of a hamster *Bake Off* scene, which was on *Extra Slice* (a spin off TV show at 9/9.30pm). [My colleagues] was on that evening and he messaged me saying "I really think we should put this up," and I said "yes, I'll definitely put it up tomorrow after 6.30." He thought we should strike while the iron was hot and put it up then and now, but my feeling was post it around 6 o'clock as that's when you're going to have people looking at their feeds. Timing matters . . . and that post then did really well.

However, scheduling in a medium that is ostensibly live is not without its dangers, some-thing that was laid bare in *The Sydney Morning Herald*'s coverage of the Melbourne Cup Twitter stream: releasing a prescripted, and perhaps even prescheduled, tweet in a bid to announce the winner first but without updating the information to include the win-ning horse's names. As a result, they announced "XXXX" had won the Melbourne Cup and were widely ridiculed for their error by other Australian news outlets—especially as XXXX is also a well-known Australian beer of questionable quality ("Tweet" 2016).

Despite such risks, tactics that mirrored those of television scheduling were to be widely found in the collaborations between television industry and Twitter. As with the discussion of SnappyTV above, early experimentations and collaborations between Twitter and TV industry have also led to co-optation by the platform. The practice of tent-poling, whereby earlier content in a schedule is simply a teaser or filler to keep audiences tuned in for the "main event" of a high value program at prime-time, is a common strategy of channels in television's network era (Caldwell 1995). Initial exper-imentations by television talent—such as the popular UK duo Ant and Dec or the pre-senters of *Have I Got News for You*—in the use of Periscope to stream backstage access

FIGURE 26.1 *The dangers of prescheduling tweets.*

to a show for viewers prior to the scheduled start of a "live" television program can be understood simply in terms of the promotional role of Twitter for television. But they also clearly function in terms similar to tent-poling: during the ethnographic work on *The Voice (UK)* we saw similar use of backstage Q&A with the judges Periscoped on Twitter before the live semifinal to build audiences for the "main event." The importance of such strategies as a way to build an audience that "stays tuned," rather than simply as a form of promotion, has seen it adopted into the contractual arrangements for Twitter's NFL deal. Significantly, therefore, Twitter's rights include "pre-game Periscope broadcasts from players and teams, giving fans an immersive experience before, during and after games" (Stelter 2016).

But the use of Periscope has also taken a form of counter-scheduling against television to attract users to the Twitter stream. For example, in the US Chris Rock provided viewers of his Twitter feed access to backstage areas of the 2016 Oscars via a Periscope stream during the broadcast commercial breaks. In the UK Rob Delaney "*Goggle Box*-ed" his own series *Catastrophe* by providing a Periscope-streamed commentary on the show during the adverts as a kind of "counter-scheduling" offer. Such techniques point to the tensions between competition and collaboration. For example, some of our interviewees discussed "cross-over" points between the end of a broadcast show and its transmedia extension on to other platforms, such as Twitter, ensuring that they "some of your [sic] strongest bits last" to encourage post-TX engagement. While television producers, and their digital teams, continue to view Twitter as ancillary, the platform has muscled in on traditional television tactics, production modes, aesthetics and experiences. Twitter's current use of live streaming represents the most obvious form of this competition, but it also draws upon historical television practices such as stunting. Michael Saenz's (n.d.) notes that stunting is often used "when a network, station, or program is in special trouble," noting that it will often involve huge levels of promotion of one show or the appearance of stars on another program. Twitter's NFL deal, coming at a time of declining valuation and user-growth, similarly operated to regain audience attention with NFL stars appeared across non-competing programs or affiliated services, such as Periscope. A senior YouTube executive linked Twitter's live streaming stunting to the immature medium of early television:

> Other platforms [are] much more prepared to shove a live stream that happens to be going on . . . they're at an earlier stage in their thinking of where live sits in their overall eco system.

While this interviewee may have strategic reasons for positioning Twitter as "immature," the growth in live streaming emphasizes the growing convergence between Twitter as social media platform and Twitter as channel. Indeed the adoption, and adaption, of television's production strategies and techniques looks only set to continue as Twitter's platform becomes ever more crowded with video, either embedded or live streamed. Echoing Caldwell's description of the development of videographic televisuality's style of "acute hyperactivity and obsession with effects" in the late 1980s and 1990s (1995, 13), one interviewee stated that social media producers' video needed "as much color as possible . . . [you're] actually competing for screen real estate and people's attention. Color grades make things look really super-vibrant." The lines between platform and channel, television and wider forms of digital media are likely to increasingly blur in the foreseeable future.

CONCLUSION

This chapter has suggested we might understand Twitter not simply as a platform but also, and increasingly, as a channel. As we have argued, this is not a case of simple competition, collaboration or co-optation between TV and Twitter, broadcast and social. Rather, this is an evolution of television channels for the digital era that responds to the ubiquity of both social media and television, whereby neither is contained on one device or platform: neither the box in the corner nor the smartphone in the hand. The convergence of these forms is wider than simply Twitter and TV, with Facebook Live and YouTube's streaming of live broadcast TV channels, among other developments, suggesting this a productive moment to consider the meaning of a "channel." As Facebook's Patrick Walker (director of media partnerships, Europe, the Middle East, and Africa) remarked, their increased emphasis on video reflects "a massive sea change," estimating "that 50% of all mobile traffic now is video—in five years it will be about 75% (Bell 2016). Video is clearly a key part of social media platforms' futures, with much of the experimentation of how to curate and monetize it likely to draw on television's past. For Twitter, as its feeds move away from simple chronological or "live" to ones that are algorithmic and directive, the potential to drive more viewers to its increasing range of video content has some fascinating potential implications for its future, where it may find itself acting as a (television) guide to "what's on" its channels.

If Twitter has its way, the future of television might also be one where a channel is coming to a Twitter stream near you. As the competition, co-option and collaboration between broadcast television and social media platforms continues, however, we can equally expect to find Twitter coming to a channel near you. One way or another, we would do well to observe the ways in which the future of digital media is television.

NOTE

1 This study is undertaken as part of ADAPT, a European Research Council–funded project (www.adapttvhistory.org.uk).

REFERENCES

Bell, Matthew. 2016. "Social Media Muscles in on TV." *Royal Television Society*. https://rts.org.uk/article/event-report-social-media-muscles-tv.

Bennett, James. 2011. "Introduction: Television as Digital Media." In *Television as Digital Media*, edited by James Bennett and Niki Strange, 1–30. Duke University Press.

Bennett, James, Niki Strange, Paul Kerr and Andrea Medrado. 2012. *Multiplatforming Public Service Broadcasting: The Economic and Cultural Role of UK Digital and TV Independents*. London: Arts and Humanities Research Council/Royal Holloway/University of London.

Caldwell, John Thornton. 1995. *Televisuality: Style, Crisis, and Authority in American Television*. New Brunswick: Rutgers University Press.

Dredge, Stuart. 2015. "Twitter's TV Strategy: Timelines, Periscope and Troll-Taming Talent." *The Guardian*, October 10. www.theguardian.com/technology/2015/oct/12/twitters-tv-strategy-timelines-periscope-and-troll-taming-talent.

Ellis, John. 2000. *Seeing Things: Television in the Age of Uncertainty*. London: IB Tauris.

Evans, Elizabeth. 2014. "Tweeting on the BBC: Audience and Brand Management via Third Party Websites." In *Making Media Work: Cultures of Management in the Entertainment Industries*, edited by Derek Johnson, Derek Kompare and Avi Santo, 235–53. New York: New York University Press.

Gillespie, Tarleton. 2010. "The Politics of 'Platforms.'" *New Media & Society* 12 (3): 347–64.

Gripsrud, Jostein. 1998. "Television, Broadcasting, Flow: Key Metaphors in Television Theory." In *The Television Studies Book*, edited by Christine Geraghty and David Lusted, 17–32. London: Arnold Publishers.

Highfield, Tim, Stephen Harrington and Axel Bruns. 2013. "Twitter as a Technology for Audiencing and Fandom: The #Eurovision Phenomenon." *Information, Communication & Society* 16 (3): 315–39.

Kuchler, Hannah and Stephen Foley. 2015. "Twitter Rallies as Jack Dorsey Returns in CEO Role." *Financial Times*, October 5.

Millar, Stuart. 1998. "Courtship Ends as Soccer and TV are United." *The Guardian*, September 7.

Russon, Mary-Ann. 2016. "Vine Is Dead—Twitter Kills Social Video Amid Global Workforce Cuts." *International Business Times*, October 27. Accessed February 20, 2017. www.ibtimes.co.uk/vine-dead-twitter-kills-social-video-platform-amid-global-workforce-cuts-1588654.

Saenz, Michael. n.d. "Programming." *The Museum of Broadcast Communications*. www.museum.tv/eotv/programming.htm.

Slefo, George. 2016. "Twitter Pursues 10 More Live Streaming Deals, Sports to Politics." *Advertising Age*, July 6. http://adage.com/article/media/twitter-debuts-live-stream-wimbledon-plans-10-new-deals/304845/.

"Snappy TV." 2014. www.snappytv.com.

Sørensen, Inge Ejbye. 2016. "The Revival of Live TV: Liveness in a Multiplatform Context." *Media, Culture & Society* 38 (3): 381–99.

Stelter, Brian. 2016. "Twitter to Live Stream Thursday Night Football Games." *CNN*, April 5. Accessed February 20, 2017. http://money.cnn.com/2016/04/05/media/twitter-nfl-thursday-night-football/?iid=EL.

"Stream." n.d. *Oxford English Dictionary* Online. Accessed February 20, 2017. www.oed.com/view/Entry/191400?rskey=dVFwcC&result=1&isAdvanced=false#eid.

"Tweet from Sydney Morning Herald Announces XXXX as Winner of Melbourne Cup." 2016. *Herald Sun*, October 31. www.heraldsun.com.au/sport/superracing/melbourne-cup-2013/tweet-from-sydney-morning-herald-announces-xxxx-as-winner-of-melbourne-cup/news-story/b7304e1c94e06be1b4bf82bd57812e5f.

Williams, Raymond. 2003. *Television: Technology and Cultural Form*. London: Routledge.

Twitch.tv

Tele-visualizing the Arcade

Matthew Thomas Payne

Professional video gamer Phillip "Phizzurp" Klemenov died from injuries sustained in a car accident on October 2, 2016 in Aurora, Colorado. He was 23 years old. A week later, about 9,000 people watched a live stream of his funeral services on Twitch.tv (or Twitch), the most popular video platform for video games and gaming culture (Plunkett 2016). This content was atypical fare for the video service. The overwhelming majority of Twitch's live feeds and its archived videos involve gameplay: competitions between professional e-Sports teams, "Let's Play" or walk-through videos featuring voice-over commentaries, and "speed-runs" where gamers compete for record times and scores. The streaming service embraces analog game content as well, including broadcasting poker competitions and board game reviews. The most peripheral content is found on the site's "creative" channel with subchannels for illustration, game programming, food, music, among other interests (where specific ties to the gaming community may be pretty tenuous).

Klemenov was a professional *Call of Duty* player, a member of the London-based e-Sports team H2k-gaming, and he was a regular live-streamer himself. As of October 2016, his Twitch account had over 63,000 followers, and his page contained 610 videos—with some clips being no more than a few seconds in length and others, such as tournament videos, lasting several hours. Klemenov's final video (the one that appears before the three posthumously posted funeral service videos) was a four-plus-hour friendly *Call of Duty: Black Ops III* competition.[1] That day, the gamer posted to Twitter: "Good vibes today, tournaments are just not fun anymore. Chilling and playing wagers with your friends is the move for me till [I win]" (Klemenov 2016). Less than 24 hours later, he would die in a Colorado hospital room as a result of his auto injuries.

Twitch is an oddity when viewed next to the other channels explored in this collection. It does not have the broadcasting legacy of ABC. It lacks the cultural clout of PBS. It is not an extension of an existing property like Disney Junior, Playboy, or the WWE. Its closest relative in this anthology is arguably Twitter because, like that micro-blogging phenomenon, Twitch, too, is the product of user-generated content. But that is not all that sets it apart.

Human play and computer-mediated gameplay are ephemeral things. Play is conceptually difficult to pin down because of its inherent and experiential liminality. This state of being caught between worlds is known as entering the "magic circle" which distinguishes play from other mundane activities (Huizinga 1950). Gameplay—be it analog or digital, face-to-face, or networked—is no less wily. Yet through streaming and sharing, and by recording and archiving play sessions, Twitch does not eliminate play's messiness so much as it creates communicative frameworks around magic circles of video gameplay.

The site utilizes a variety of broadcasting conventions to lend a televisual "shape" to its thousands of gameplay streams. In particular, by foregrounding players' voices and their colorful personalities, facilitating interactions between streamers and viewers (both social and financial), and by establishing an interface similar to cable TV as well as subgenres for navigating content, Twitch applies a televisual framework to its continuous flow of gaming streams with the goal of making game spectatorship a more accessible and, of course, a more profitable activity.

How then can we understand Twitch.tv's affordances as a channel? One way to proceed is by dissecting the name itself: Twitch-dot-tv. First, "twitch"-style gameplay is a kind of reflex needed to best games demanding manual agility and fast reaction times; think of the skills needed to do well in racing, fighting, or shooting games. Most Twitch.tv footage consists of live and recorded gameplay, with a good deal of it featuring a webcam insert of the player's real-time reactions to the on-screen action. Understanding the role of competitive performance in gaming is of central concern to understanding Twitch's overall appeal. Second, the "dot" that separates the site's domain name (Twitch) from its top-level domain (tv) signals that this channel is a URL. As a website and as a streaming platform, this video service contains interactive features absent from more traditional tv channels; features that make it an aggregator of user-created content, material that is generated by the streamer and the participatory audience. Finally, the "tv" in its name simultaneously gestures a desire to exist alongside that medium, highlighting its inherent hybridity. The platform's primary organizational function is to manage its content into thematic subchannels and subgenres. These three components—users and their play (the "twitch"), the site's interactive features (the "dot"), and the platform's televisual fare (the "tv")—offer an organizational roadmap for examining how this channel handles the unruly nature of games and the folks who play them, as well as how it successfully accommodates such disparate fare (including live-streaming the memorial service of a former community member).

TWITCH

In the cultural imaginary there exists the stereotypical image of the gamer: a white, solitary, misanthropic basement-dwelling teenaged boy, who, due to crippling awkwardness has turned to games as a means of escape. Instead of forging bonds with others, he lives multiple lives in virtual realms. Here, he is in control; here, he is the star, the hero.

This tired archetype came into being and it still persists for a host of cultural and commercial reasons. It is owed partly to the foreignness of video games for older generations who did not grow up alongside the game industry's commercial emergence in the 1970s. Additionally, the manner in which blockbuster games have long been marketed to young, male audiences, and their desire for competitive play, likewise make them inaccessible to some. The content, too, is often exclusionary in nature; especially in popular genres like militaristic first-person shooters, fantasy role-playing games, and action-adventure titles. These genres commonly possess graphically violent narratives that trade in racist or sexist tropes—exclusionary elements that are echoed in online toxic gaming subcultures.[2] Other forms of popular entertainment have been complicit in propagating this fairly narrow image of the video gamer as a young, white man.[3] Finally, considerable financial resources and technological literacy are required to successfully access and navigate these complex virtual worlds.

The desire to compete against others in virtual realms, and to witness superlative and masterful play, sees its origins in the electronic amusement halls and video game arcades of the 1970s. These pre-Internet spaces would often host ad hoc "tournaments" that would later give rise to competitions with more codified rules and structures (Kocurek 2015). With the proliferation of personal computing and digital recording devices in the 1990s, and as arcades began to vanish from the American landscape, competitive gamers—still wanting to create and share evidence of gaming excellence—turned to VHS tapes and data files to record their accomplishments. Later, the digital recording of gameplay allowed ingenious gamers to repurpose and reedit footage to create novel stories. From this machinima (a portmanteau of the words "machine" and "cinema") was born, and with it one more practice pointing to a vibrant play community wanting to speak with and through gaming culture. The emergence of machinima coincided with "Let's Play" videos that would populate sites like YouTube and spawn new media celebrities like Felix Arvid Ulf Kjellberg (better known as PewDiePie). Tournaments, machinima, and Let's Play videos all gestured to a vibrant subculture interested in watching superlative gameplay performances be it in heated competition or through everyday play.

Gaming has always been a social event among its participants and—critically for Twitch.tv—for audiences *outside* its immediate magic circle of play. It is hard to imagine the Roman Coliseum's bloody gladiatorial battles without thinking of its thousands of cheering fans. Likewise, any discussion of the Super Bowl, the Olympics, or the World Cup as global media spectacles must account for the billions watching on television and online. The same holds for watching others play video games. In its own peculiar way, Twitch.tv's variety of live-streamed content and its eclectic hosts may help dispel notions of the solo gamer and his monolithic gaming culture. Yet, interestingly, Twitch did not begin its marketplace dominance by broadcasting gaming spectacle but with videos of everyday life.

DOT

In 2007, Justin Kan and Emmett Shear created Justin.tv, a website that allowed users to broadcast all manner of live, user-generated content. Justin.tv featured a wide variety of categories for its tens of thousands of "lifecasters"—those who recorded and shared everyday moments for the world to see. Of the site's numerous categories (including "animals," "entertainment," and "music and radio"), "gaming" was by far the most popular. Its success led Kan and Shear to launch the standalone Twitch.tv in 2011, which quickly cemented its place as the Internet's go-to destination for live-streamed gaming content.

In many ways 2014 was a breakout year for Twitch. Not only did Justin.tv, Inc. officially become Twitch Interactive in 2014—with the former site being completely shuttered (Truong 2014)—but it also attracted the attention of major Internet firms. Google was initially in negotiations to acquire Twitch. However, due to their ownership of YouTube, lingering antitrust concerns caused them to pass on the deal (Mac 2014). Amazon quickly stepped in and purchased Twitch for $970 million in cash. With Twitch accounting for nearly 2% of *all* Internet traffic (making it the fourth largest player after Netflix, Google, and Apple) and more than "43% of all live video streaming traffic by volume," it is little wonder why Amazon wanted to add it to its Web Services division (Eadicicco 2014; Markman 2016). The service is now a part of Amazon's subscription offerings as "Twitch Prime."

As a channel of channels, Twitch has successfully transformed the spectatorship of another's gameplay into an interactive and communal event. As of 2016, the site boasts of over 2 million regular video streamers, with 17,000+ of these accounts being "partners" ("Twitch Partner FAQ" n.d.). The Twitch Partner Program enables its elite streamers to profit from their online labor. Viewers can support streamers at three different levels of investment. First, they are encouraged to "follow" them on the site; a financially free action that contributes to the site's community-building efforts and to the streamer's cultural capital as someone worthy of being watched. Second, for $4.99 a month, viewers can "subscribe" to a streamer's feed; this is akin to a monthly subscription to a cable channel. A subscription grants viewers access to private chats and unique emoticons for use in the chat rooms. This money is then split between the streamer and Twitch (sometimes 50/50, sometimes 60/40, depending on the deal) (Greco 2016). And, finally, viewers can support their favorite streamers by cheering "bits," Twitch's own micro-currency (Conditt 2017), or with direct monetary donations. Viewers' follows, subscriptions, and donations populate the Twitch partner's live stream for all to see, usually acknowledged by the appreciative host.[4]

Twitch payments are not the only way that Twitch streamers make money. PC companies and e-Sports leagues sponsor elite gamers who command large audiences. Advertising is another source of revenue with ads appearing as linear videos and/ or as rotating images overlaid on the stream itself. For instance, the product slideshow appearing on Ninja's stream on Thanksgiving morning 2016 included Monster, SteelSeries, SanDisk, Xfinity Internet, AMD, and NeedforSeat.[5] Video content rarely goes unused or underused for full-time streamers, with repurposed material appearing on their personal sites, social media, and other video platforms like YouTube (where those views are monetized with Google AdSense). Popular streamers also hawk their own merchandise and collectibles. The most successful full-time streamers earn over $100,000 a year in subscription fees alone; a healthy income that is supplemented with these other sales and marketing techniques (Egger 2015).

No less remarkable are the community's collective achievements. The site's spirit of collaborative play is probably best epitomized by the "Twitch Plays *Pokémon*"

FIGURE 27.1 *Professional gamer Tyler "Ninja" Blevins (@Ninja_TB) streams gameplay of PlayerUnknown's Battlegrounds.*

phenomenon, which has since evolved into its own subgenre, having been applied to other titles. This experiment in social gaming began with the crowd-sourced play of *Pokémon Red* in which participants could determine game actions by typing commands into the chat box. According to a Twitch press release, the game took nearly 16 days and 8 hours to complete, with over 1.1 million users issuing over 122 million individual commands (Chase 2014). The "Twitch Plays" format has since been applied to other *Pokémon* titles, as well as infamously difficult games like *Dark Souls* (completed in 43 days) (Frank 2015). The Twitch community even defeated a British chess grandmaster in a match.[6] Charity events are popular too, attracting both viewers and dollars. In fact, the streaming site advertised that it helped 55 different charitable groups raise $17.4 million in 2015 alone (Conditt 2016). Of course, Twitch is wise to highlight its community's goodwill so as to help offset reports of live-streaming's darker elements.

As with most online communities, Twitch isn't immune from the Internet's more vile behaviors. Female streamers' chat rooms are routinely dominated by objectifying language concerning their bodies (whereas discussion in their male counterparts' streams tends to focus on in-game performance and achievements) (D'Anastasio 2016). Furthermore, some of the most heinous acts transpire when harassment moves from chat room into the physical world. For example, the act of "swatting"—where the harasser gets a SWAT or police team to raid a streamer's home while they are broadcasting—has become a real issue for Twitch and for other live video sites.[7] The practice is so well known within the community, that a Twitch streamer was banned from the service after he faked his own swatting (LeJacq 2015). There are likewise continuing fears that streaming services will inadvertently broadcast suicide attempts similar to the one that aired on Twitch's predecessor Justin.tv in 2008 (Kravets 2016).

TV

Twitch.tv reimagined what it means to televise gaming, improving upon previous attempts to broadcast prerecorded gaming competitions by creating a stronger, more immediate sense of community through televisual liveness. The emergence of large-scale gaming tournaments (annual events like Evolution Championship Series or Major League Gaming, which both began in 2002) as well as fan-focused conventions like QuakeCon, immediately inspired technology and media firms to partner with or produce their own e-Sports shows for mass consumption. The history of broadcasting e-Sporting events in the 2000s is marked by a series of false starts, with firms like DirecTV and British Sky Broadcasting coordinating the broadcast of the *Championship Gaming Series* (2007–2008), sports giant ESPN producing the short-lived *Madden Nation* (2005–2008), and technology firms like Microsoft and Samsung sponsoring the *World Cyber Games* (2000–2014), parts of which aired on the cable channel Syfy as *WCG Ultimate Gamer* (2009–2010).[8] These firms were not mistaken in their belief in a market for televised e-Sports—there was and there remains a *real* interest in watching elite players compete. However, the right pieces simply were not yet in place to create sustainable and compelling programming. Twitch succeeded not simply by putting video games on TV—or on one's browser—but by applying a distinctly televisual framework to its live gaming streams.

A closer look at Twitch's primary interface—its home page and the template for streamers' pages—showcases the site's attempts at balancing its "programming" strategies with its community-building efforts. This is a dramatic difference from previous attempts at broadcasting e-Sports to a mass audience. Instead, Twitch's home page, which foregrounds a rotating carousel of featured live streams, functions as a dynamic "TV Guide" of gaming—one that shows what is playing, and—as importantly—what is being watched by its community. Located below these six rotating live streams are additional content areas organized by titles and by platforms. The "Featured Games" section highlights the titles with the largest viewership numbers (as of December 2016 these games were frequently *Hearthstone, Counter-Strike, League of Legends*, and *Overwatch*).

Individual Twitch pages utilize a three-column blog format. The left column contains menu and navigation options. The center column features the live stream, with a customizable space below it where streamers typically post a description of their page, list their streaming schedule, and include links to merchandise and donation opportunities. Finally, the right column is the chat box/room where viewers engage the streamer and one another with text and colorful emojis—graphic features that have quickly evolved into a subcultural language.

These emojis are often anything but obvious. For example, images of people's faces—including streamers, Twitch developers, and celebrities—and images pulled from games populate the chat rooms. For instance, the "Kappa" emote, featuring the face of a former Justin.tv employee, is used to indicate snark or sarcasm, while a crying face called "BibleThump" from the independent game *The Binding of Isaac* is used to communicate sadness. These symbols, which cascade with terrific ferocity in popular streamers' chat boxes, are a means of demonstrating one's gaming cultural capital—as someone who is in the know and who belongs on the site. Twitch partners create their own glyphs that help establish their personal brand, while users deploy these symbols to create a sense of belonging and connection.[9] This combination of navigational tools and interactive features infuses intimacy and liveness into the gameplay streams—elements largely absent from the one-way broadcasting of e-Sport tournaments.

CONCLUSION

The story of Twitch.tv is the story of media convergence; its name—quite literally—says as much. And just as television has helped shaped Twitch's design, Twitch is now reshaping TV with the service appearing on mobile devices (e.g., iPhone, Android) as well as on living room over-the-top boxes and game consoles (e.g., Chromecast, Fire TV, Roku, Xbox One, PlayStation 4, Xbox 360). Twitch's adoption by streaming devices is critical as it battles with Google's YouTube Gaming channel for the global gaming audience. With Twitch viewers watching more video content per month than YouTube users—421.6 to 291 minutes, respectively—it is clear that Twitch's value to Amazon will likely increase (Perez 2016). Yet despite these impressive figures, and despite Twitch's dominance of live content, the channel is nevertheless playing catch-up with YouTube's specialization in recorded online video. Twitch has responded by rolling out new clip recording and video uploading functionality (Gaudiosi 2016). It is also competing with Google by courting advertisers with ads that cannot be blocked or skipped by anti-ad software (Spangler 2016).

Twitch is working to strengthen its brand by doubling down on what it is known for while expanding into new terrain. For instance, it is demonstrating its commitment to e-Sports by signing partnership deals with clubs Team SoloMid and Cloud9 (the latter of which won "Best e-Sports Team" of The Game Awards 2016) (Osborn 2016; Susan 2016). Amazon is also developing games with Twitch in mind—titles that will allow players to interact in the same virtual world as their favorite streamers (Gurwin 2016). The service is also producing non-gaming fare, including *ChefShock*, which will be streamed live, differentiating it from prerecorded cooking shows (Cooper 2016).

Custom emojis, a live cooking show, e-Sports tournaments: the themes of competition, liveness, and community figure as prominently in Twitch's future plans as they did in its prehistory. Twitch's ability to host and archive recorded gameplay is, on the one hand, an obvious response to YouTube's Gaming channel. However, this development is more consequential for the site as a community. Unlike arcades and local LAN meetups of yesteryear, Twitch is a communal play (and now replay) space with a record of its gameplay and its chat logs. These streaming archives offer more than televisual copies or episodic reruns of gaming fare. These are records of collective play. The videos of Klemenov's memorial service exist as a record of his life and place his within the larger Twitch community. His page is a virtual memorial site, a place that this community can return to when they want a to see and to hear him play again. Viewers can listen to Klemenov joke with his friends, witness his gaming prowess, and take joy in him sharing gameplay with others. As a channel, Twitch successfully applies a televisual structure to organize eclectic gaming fare. Yet the recorded videos and live streams of that televisuality also serve as a record of the value we accord to playing against and with one another, and why it is that gamers have never really ever played alone.

NOTES

1 Klemenov's videos are still hosted on www.twitch.tv/phizzurp.

2 For more on this production history, see Kline, Dyer-Witheford, and de Peuter (2003).

3 Consider how films of the 1980s represented the gamer as a technically savvy boy or young man facing considerable odds: be it losing oneself to a spy fantasy in *Cloak & Dagger* (1984); getting lost in an electronic world in *TRON* (1982); demonstrating one's aptitude for space piloting on an arcade game in *The Last Starfighter* (1984); competing for a cash prizes in a gaming competition in *The Wizard* (1989); or saving the world from nuclear horrors in *WarGames* (1983). Again and again, these films offered narratives of boys and men achieving great things through exemplary gameplay.

4 There are numerous video montages of streamers' emotional reactions at receiving large donations.

5 "Ninja" is a professional gamer whose stream had 3,000+ viewers that morning; his account had 20+ million lifetime views. His site is at www.twitch.tv/ninja.

6 To be fair, the audience at home had access to computer chess aids unavailable to the grandmaster. See Parfitt (2016).

7 For a truly troubling piece on a serial offender, see Fagone (2015).

8 Attempts at e-Sports broadcasting via basic cable continue to this day with ESPN2 and ESPN3, and with TBS broadcasting ELEAGUE, a professional league focused on *Counter-Strike: Global Offensive*, launched in summer 2016.

9 One example of this is the "ZombiKindly" emote of *Minecraft* streamer Natalie Cassanoa (an image of her with middle finger up), which is used by viewers in response to trolling. See Magdaleno (2014).

REFERENCES

Chase. 2014. "TPP Victory! The Thundershock Heard Around the World." *Twitch*, March. https://blog.twitch.tv/tpp-victory-the-thundershock-heard-around-the-world-3128a5b1cdf5#.ovje9srp6.

Conditt, Jessica. 2016. "Twitch Streamers Raised $17.4 Million for Charity in 2015." *Engadget*, February 11. www.engadget.com/2016/02/11/twitch-streamers-raised-17-4-million-for-charities-in-2015/.

Conditt, Jessica. 2017. "Twitch's In-Chap Tipping Program Generated $6 Million in 2016." *Engadget*, February 15. www.engadget.com/2017/02/15/twitch-streamers-bits-6-million-year-in-review-2016/.

Cooper, Daniel. 2016. "Twitch Picks Up 'ChefShock,' a Daily Live Cooking Show." *Engadget*, October 25. www.engadget.com/2016/10/25/twitch-picks-up-chefshock-a-daily-live-cooking-show/.

D'Anastasio, Cecilia. 2016. "Study Shows Twitch Chat Is Very Different When Women Are Streaming." *Kotaku*, November 23. http://kotaku.com/study-shows-twitch-chat-is-very-different-when-women-a-1789302281.

Eadicicco, Lisa. 2014. "10 Facts about Twitch, the Company that Amazon Is buying, that Will Blow Your Mind." *Business Insider*, August 25. www.businessinsider.com/statistics-about-twitch-2014-8.

Egger, Jay. 2015. "How Exactly Do Twitch Streamers Make a Living? Destiny Breaks It Down." *Dot Esports*, April 25. https://dotesports.com/how-exactly-do-twitch-streamers-make-a-living-destiny-breaks-it-down-1f5de0971b74#.9s43r6xzv.

Fagone, Jason. 2015. "The Serial Swatter." *New York Times Magazine*, November 24. www.nytimes.com/2015/11/29/magazine/the-serial-swatter.html.

Frank, Allegra. 2015. "Twitch Plays Has Beaten Dark Souls." *Polygon*, September 28. www.polygon.com/2015/9/28/9409795/twitch-plays-dark-souls-beaten.

Gaudiosi, John. 2016. "Twitch Ups Its Game to Compete with YouTube Gaming." *Fortune*, February 26. http://fortune.com/2016/02/26/twitch-ups-its-game-to-compete-with-youtube-gaming/.

Greco, Matt. 2016. "Watch Me Play Video Games! Amazon's Twitch Platform Draws Users and Dollars." *CNBC*, May 14. www.cnbc.com/2016/05/13/amazons-twitch-streamers-can-make-big-bucks.html.

Gurwin, Gabe. 2016. "Amazon Unveils Three Streaming-Friendly Games Built with Twitch in Mind." *Digital Trends*, September 30. www.digitaltrends.com/gaming/amazon-breakway-twitch-in-mind/.

Huizinga, Johan. 1950. *Homo Ludens: A Study of the Play Element in Culture*. Boston: Beacon.

Klemenov, Phillip. 2016. "Good Vibes Today..." *Twitter*, October 1. https://twitter.com/phizzurp/status/782425932963336192?lang=en.

Kline, Stephen, Nick Dyer-Witheford and Greig de Peuter (eds.). 2003. *Digital Play: The Interaction of Technology, Culture, and Marketing*. Montreal: McGill-Queen's University Press.

Kocurek, Carly. 2015. *Coin-Operated Americans: Rebooting Boyhood at the Video Game Arcade*. Minneapolis: University of Minnesota Press.

Kravets, David. 2016. "Woman Broadcasts Herself on Periscope Committing Suicide." *Ars Technica*, May 11. http://arstechnica.com/tech-policy/2016/05/woman-broadcasts-herself-on-periscope-committing-suicide/.

LeJacq, Yannick. 2015. "Twitch Streamer Fakes His Own Joke Swatting, Gets Banned." *Kotaku*, August, 3. http://kotaku.com/twitch-streamer-fakes-his-own-joke-swatting-gets-banne-1721863481.

Mac, Ryan. 2014. "Amazon Pounces on Twitch after Google Balks Due to Antitrust Concerns." *Forbes*, August 25. www.forbes.com/sites/ryanmac/2014/08/25/amazon-pounces-on-twitch-after-google-balks-due-to-antitrust-concerns/#1e1059dd1fd3.

Magdaleno, Alex. 2014. "'Twitch-speak': A Guide to the Secret Emoji Language of Gamers." *Mashable*, August 8. http://mashable.com/2014/08/08/twitch-emoticons/#32KXjApUqkqS.

Markman, Jon. 2016. "Facebook Loves E-Sports." *Forbes*, November 15. www.forbes.com/sites/jonmarkman/2016/11/15/facebook-loves-e-sports/#2f2a577a7874.

Osborn, Alex. 2016. "The Game Awards 2016 Winners Announced." *IGN*, December 1. www.ign.com/articles/2016/12/02/the-game-awards-2016-winners-announced.

Parfitt, Ben. 2016. "Twitch Plays Chess Beats a Grandmaster." *MCV*, September 16. www.mcvuk.com/news/read/twitch-plays-chess-beats-a-grandmaster/0172545.

Perez, Sarah. 2016. "Twitch's Users Watch More Video in a Month, on Average, than Typical YouTube." *TechCrunch*, February 11. https://techcrunch.com/2016/02/11/twitchs-users-watch-more-video-in-a-month-than-youtube-users-do/.

Plunkett, Luke. 2016. "9000 Fans Mourn Pro Gamer in Live Twitch Video." *Kotaku*, October 10. http://kotaku.com/9000-fans-mourn-pro-gamer-in-live-twitch-funeral-1787598767.

Spangler, Todd. 2016. "Twitch Starts Running Its Own Blocker-Proof Ads in Users' Live Games." *Variety*, November 2. http://variety.com/2016/digital/news/twitch-ads-live-game-broadcasts-1201907055/.

Susan. 2016. "Twitch Partners with TSM and Cloud9." *Elotalk*, November 19. http://elotalk.com/gaming/twitch-partners-tsm-cloud9/.

Truong, Alice. 2014. "As Twitch Grows, Justin.tv, Inc. Is Renamed Twitch Interactive." *Fast Company*, February 10. www.fastcompany.com/3026207/fast-feed/as-twitch-grows-justintv-inc-is-renamed-twitch-interactive.

"Twitch Partner FAQ." n.d. *Twitch*. Accessed November 26, 2016. www.twitch.tv/p/partnerfaq.

BBC Three

Youth Television and Platform Neutral Public Service Broadcasting

Faye Woods

In the post-midnight hours of Tuesday, February 16, 2016, the British Broadcasting Corporation's youth-focused digital channel BBC Three went off the air for the last time.[1] Its final evening showcased some of the channel's biggest hits, from factual entertainment show *Don't Tell the Bride* (BBC Three/BBC One/Sky One, 2007–) to family sitcom *Gavin & Stacey* (BBC Three/BBC Two/BBC1 2007–2010). The next day BBC Three was reborn as an online-only channel delivered primarily through BBC iPlayer, the corporation's streaming on-demand platform. "Channel" could seem an inappropriate descriptor for this new BBC Three, as rather than a linear flow delivered over the air it now exists as a navigational database of on-demand streaming content (Bennett 2011, 1). With a fifth of its £30 million programming budget allocated to digital and short-form content, the online-only BBC Three spreads beyond the boundaries of iPlayer, across the BBC website, and onto global social media platforms as a "platform neutral" youth brand (Gannagé-Stewart 2016e). The reorientation of BBC Three as an online-only channel illustrates television's current transitional moment, as it spans linear and on-demand delivery systems and works through the continuities and change presented by the digital media sphere. Moreover, BBC Three's status as a British, youth-focused, public-owned channel highlights the role of nation and public service broadcasting (PSB) within the global, commercial flows of digital media. Its move online extended preexisting tensions at the heart of BBC Three's brand, between British youth television's PSB function and its value as commercial product. As BBC Three becomes a multiplatform youth brand, its challenge is to balance an embrace of powerful international media platforms with the retention of its British PSB identity.

BBC Three's transition to a wholly on-demand channel drew on its role as a vanguard for several of the BBC's strategic developments in digital delivery, as well as its foundational status in British youth television. As I argue elsewhere, British youth television is built on tensions between the national and international, drawing on US teen TV but also pushing against it, offering nationally specific voices and storytelling (Woods 2016). BBC Three drew on these qualities in its online transition, offering a reworked channel identity that asserted its PSB value through prestige markers and nationally distinct youth voices, all supported by digital media's spreadability and storytelling possibilities.

Since its launch in 2003, BBC Three has held a unique status among the UK's niche, youth-focused television channels due to the position of the BBC in the national television market. The BBC is publicly owned and independent from the government, although successive governments have attempted to exert control and influence over the corporation.

It is a public service broadcaster funded by the license fee, which citizens must pay in order to watch and record live television (£145.50 a year per household in 2017). In 2016 the license fee was extended to cover both live and on-demand viewing on iPlayer. The license fee funds not only traditional television content and the infrastructure that carries it, but also covers a broad range of channels, radio stations, services, and technologies, including the BBC's streaming video on demand platform iPlayer. The latter is the UK's most widely used streaming video on demand (SVOD) platform, with 31% of adults having accessed the service in 2015 (Farber 2015). iPlayer would play a central role in delivering the online-only BBC Three.

BBC Three's status as a publicly owned and license-fee funded youth channel distinguishes it from its primary competitors, the free-to-air digital youth channels ITV2 and E4. The former is the sister channel of the UK's largest commercial broadcaster ITV, and the latter the sister channel of the UK's other public service broadcaster Channel 4. Like the BBC, Channel 4 is publicly owned, but it is funded by advertising, and its public service remit pertains only to the main channel, not to E4. As I have argued elsewhere (Woods 2016), over the first decades of the twenty-first century, British digital youth channels and BBC Three in particular have been spaces that have foregrounded tensions surrounding the role and value of PSB. This is in part because the provision of programming for young audiences is asserted as a key component of PSB ("Public Purposes" 2015; "Communications" 2003); yet the 16-to-34 demographic is also the most prized demographic across the commercial television market. As a result, British youth television embodies ideological tensions between television as a public service and as a commercial product.

BBC Three's public service status has meant it has long struggled with a taint of responsibility at odds with its youth address, suggesting that "a channel emblazoned with the BBC logo—however it is animated—will never quite be cool" (Rushton 2009). The channel's institutional identity exists in tension with a need to present itself as an authentic, risk-taking partner to its youth audience; the paternalistic connotations of the BBC's history as the UK's oldest and largest broadcaster is at odds with the rebellious older sibling role a youth channel plays for its audience. The edgy humor and anarchic identity central to youth appeal is easily accessible for commercially funded broadcasters such as E4, cable channel MTV UK, or media company Vice. However, at the BBC this is tempered by fears of censure and scandal, under the watch of a hypervigilant British press ever eager to attack the corporation. The battles fought by its parent institution against criticism from commercial competitors and an aggressive political discourse (Born 2011) become laser-focused around BBC Three.

The channel's niche focus on a youth demographic has seen its value constantly questioned by political and broadcasting figures outside of its target demographic (Rushton 2010). Here a classed ideological construction of "appropriate" public service broadcasting conflicts with the noise and potential controversy required of youth entertainment. These tensions lay at the heart of BBC Three. Former BBC Three channel head Danny Cohen described such attacks as "a kind of chauvinism around young people, a belief that they are less deserving of licence-fee money than anyone else" (Rushton 2010). BBC Three has long been caught between the need to demonstrate its public value by producing popular programming that draws youth audiences, and the need to prove its distinctiveness by providing public service content—news, documentary and the arts—not offered by the commercial market due to their tendency to draw lower ratings. Across its life the channel has been attacked for a perceived reliance on audience-drawing celebrity and lifestyle programming, and by extension their class-informed low cultural status ("BBC3 Criticised" 2004; "BBC Defies" 2005; Rushton 2010).

Since the late 2000s the channel has sought to rectify such assumptions, commissioning a breadth of documentary programming and a string of successful dramas (before budget cuts hampered the genre) (Woods 2016, 50–1). Yet despite critical acclaim and awards attention, BBC Three still pushed against public perceptions that it harbored cheeky lifestyle programming, low-brow sitcom and imports of bawdy US animated series like *Family Guy* (Fox, 1999–2003, 2005–) and *American Dad* (Fox/TBS 2005–). The move online would see BBC Three respond to a huge budget cut by narrowing its focus to comedy and documentary (with a small drama budget), as well as cutting away entertainment programming and imported US animation. This refocusing drew on the channel's legacy in developing new voices and as a source of "original British content" (Gannagé-Stewart 2016a), emphasizing its public service value and national distinction. These were also genres that could readily be deployed across digital spaces through short-form video as the channel increased its investment in digital content.

INNOVATION OR COST-CUTTING?

BBC Three's move online pairs the BBC's PSB responsibilities for both digital innovation and youth reach. The corporation has a remit-required role in leading digital media developments in the UK (Evans 2011, 34) and broadcasting policy positions public service broadcasters as responsible for reaching older children and youth audiences ("Communications" 2003). BBC Three's move online continued its role as a vanguard of the BBC's innovations in streaming video on demand. It was the first British channel to stream live in 2008, and since 2013 has debuted an array of comedy content on iPlayer before linear broadcast. These strategies served as precursors for the BBC's embrace of channel and sport live streams, along with its development of iPlayer streaming originals and early premieres (Deans and Conlan 2014).

The corporation positioned its decision to move BBC Three online as a test case for how the BBC and the British television industry as a whole could reposition itself in the streaming age and a potential non-linear future (Kanter 2014). It also claimed that the shift reflected changes in the viewing behavior of BBC Three's target audience (Kavanagh 2015a). Live viewing fell to just over one third (36%) of 16- to 24-year-olds' total viewing in 2015; however, the reach of broadcast TV among 16- to 35-year-olds stayed stable at 82% due to streaming on demand services, most prominently the BBC's iPlayer and Channel 4's All4 (Farber 2016). The move built on strong viewing figures for BBC Three programming on iPlayer, particularly school sitcom *Bad Education* (2012–2014) and award-winning factual drama *Murdered by My Boyfriend* (2014) (Price 2014; Chapman 2014). Yet most of BBC Three's factual output saw markedly lower viewing figures (Chapman 2014), illustrating the tricky task of drawing BBC Three's audience to the challenging content that was central to its PSB remit, outside of a linear flow.

BBC Three's move online was touted as an innovative decision, but the 2014 announcement came years ahead of schedule, arguably hastened by the corporation's need to implement cost-saving measures in the face of a 26% reduction in its license fee–funded budget (£1.5 billion by 2017) (Kanter 2015). The channel's "reinvention" was accompanied by a £50 million reduction in its programming budget (from £80 million to £30 million), severely hampering its ability to deliver a breadth of content and compete with other channels and platforms. The BBC sought to counter criticism by asserting strong youth viewing of its mainstream channels BBC One and Two (Kanter 2015). Yet arguably, when it came to representing the specificity of British youth experience, the niche focus of BBC Three offered that which broad-appeal family viewing could not. The budget cuts, perhaps even more than the move online, endangered the channel's role in building relationships with the BBC license-fee payers of the future.

The move online required the BBC to discursively reposition BBC Three in the minds of the public and press, with the latter eagerly reporting a drop in the BBC's youth audience following BBC Three's closure as a linear channel (Gannagé-Stewart 2016a). The corporation countered that BBC Three was now "a youth brand on TV, online and social media," that was "not consumed like a traditional TV channel" (2016a). Spread across iPlayer, YouTube, the BBC website, and a range of social media spaces, this multi-platform youth brand faces increased challenges in drawing audiences and asserting its brand identity. It must now define itself within the strong overarching brand of iPlayer, and attempt to cut through the "noisy highway" (Grainge and Johnson 2015, 33) of the online content ecosystem. Here it competes for attention with a range of freely available digital content across social media platforms, including video content from powerful US media brands Vice and Buzzfeed. Alongside this looms the powerful pull of international SVOD platforms Amazon and Netflix, each with a global reach of over 200 countries. These companies' library catalogues and range of new, largely US-produced programming benefit from financial reserves well beyond that of the BBC, with the corporation's PSB remit stretched across a breadth of media, technologies, and social responsibilities (including the World Service, rural broadband, and free TV licenses for old age pensioners).

BBC Three's increased investment in original short-form and digital content (£6 million, or a fifth of its budget) facilitated its spread across the channel's branded spaces on YouTube, Facebook, and Twitter. Long-form programming familiar from linear BBC

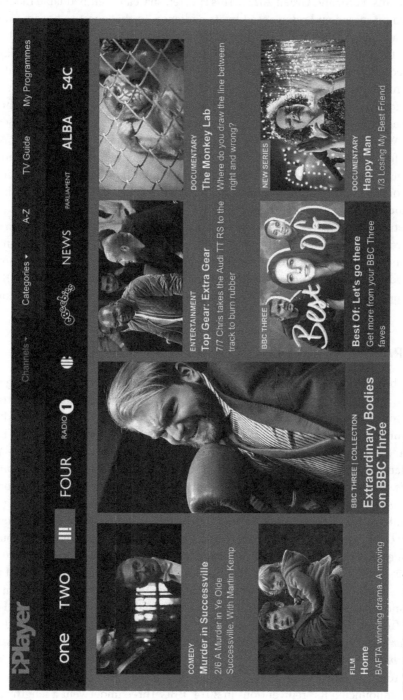

FIGURE 28.1 *BBC Three as it appears in the iPlayer interface.*

Three remained within the boundaries of iPlayer, but short-form was more "spread-able" (Jenkins, Ford, and Green 2013). This shorter, shareable, embeddable media con-tent could be spread and repurposed by its audience. In this quest to become nimble, reactive, and spreadable, BBC Three uses the social media platforms of global media giants to fulfil its PSB remit to reach those youth audiences not drawn to iPlayer or linear media. However, the challenge here is to balance the embrace of powerful inter-national media platforms with the retention of BBC Three's British PSB identity; inde-pendent industry regulator Ofcom's 2015 review of PSB raised questions over how far "young people distinguish public service content from other content" ("Public Service" 2015, 3). Would a spreadable BBC Three risk diluting its connection to the BBC? Across its short-form videos, BBC Three's authorship is signaled by a brief opening ident, and the channel's brand frames each YouTube thumbnail. But the challenge is in retaining a connection between this programming on YouTube and the ideologies and social con-tract embedded in license fee–funded PSB.

The "streamlined" BBC Three sought to maintain this connection through an asser-tion of prestige, youth voice, and national distinction. Breadth had long been central to the channel's PSB remit, yet the transition online and a greatly reduced programming budget led to a narrower programming focus. Here BBC Three asserted its PSB value by drawing on its preexisting critical and awards successes and its remit to develop new voices.

PROGRAMMING: REFINING, DEFINING, AND LEGITIMATING

Since its birth in 2003, BBC Three had been a mixed-genre channel, combining enter-tainment, drama, comedy, documentary, and news. This distinguished it from its entertainment-focused competitors ITV2 and E4, where US imports, comedy, and reality dominate schedules, alongside limited original British youth drama on E4. On BBC Three brash entertainment programming such as *Snog Marry Avoid* (2008–2013), where flamboyant or excessive femininities were given 'make-unders', and *Don't Tell the Bride*, where hapless bridegrooms secretly planned their weddings, sat alongside BAFTA-winning telefantasy dramas *In the Flesh* (2013–2014) and *The Fades* (2011). New comic voices offered a range of perspectives on the world, from sketch show gro-tesquery *Little Britain* (BBC One/BBC Three, 2002–2007) to the surreal world-building of *The Mighty Boosh* (2004–2007) and pirate radio mockumentary *People Just Do Noth-ing* (2012–). BBC Three's wealth of documentary content chronicled the lives of young people at home and across the world, helping to distinguish the channel from ITV2 and E4 and to strongly assert its PSB credentials. Factual programming explored topics ranging from the Middle East conflicts (*Our War* [2011–2014]), to male suicide rates (*Professor Green: Suicide and Me* [2015]), to child labor (*Stacey Dooley Investigates: Child Labour* [2009]), and gun violence in the US (*Reggie Yates: Life and Death in Chi-cago* [2016]).

After announcing its "reinvention" in 2014, BBC Three underwent a lengthy period of development ahead of its 2016 transition. In 2015 the new head of channel Damian

FIGURE 28.2 *BBC Three's presence as a YouTube channel.*

Kavanagh sought to clarify the revised channel brand, in response to an industry campaign against the channel's "closure":

> I want to make it very clear we will always make ground-breaking drama like *Murdered by My Boyfriend* and *In the Flesh*. We will still give you comedy of the calibre of the *Mighty Boosh* and *Gavin & Stacey* and we will still make documentaries like *Our War* and *Life and Death Row*. We will still champion new talent like Georgina Campbell and James Corden. That is what we do now and what we will always do.
>
> (Kavanagh 2015b)

This statement attempted to articulate to viewers, regulators and the industry at large that the "new BBC Three" would be a legitimated space. The programs it highlighted included the small-audience, skewed-perspective cult comedy that had long been the channel's forte, along with risk-taking drama and documentary, and nearly all were BAFTA-winning and critically acclaimed. Notably absent were the channel's high-rating programs from low-status genres that were frequently referenced in critiques or press reports on the channel ("BBC3 Defies" 2005; Rushton 2010; Beaumont-Thomas 2014). Kavanagh's reframing of BBC Three offered up the channel as a model of prestige British youth television: award-winning, nationally distinct, niche targeted, and appropriately PSB. However the further reduction of its already depleted drama budget (a costly genre for a cash-strapped channel, with comedy and documentary notably cheaper to produce), along with the loss of popular but "lowbrow" factual entertainment, panel shows, and imported animation risked shrinking BBC Three's cultural footprint. Could this new "streamlined" BBC Three assert its voice in a crowded online marketplace, where competition increased beyond its traditional linear national foes?

BBC Three was rebranded around the twin themes of "make you laugh" and "make you think," with comedy and documentary each receiving a third (£10 million) of the programming budget. In emphasizing areas where British youth voice could be strongly articulated, the move highlighted the channel's desired balance of PSB remit and youth reach. This asserted its national distinction as a purveyor of "original British content" (Gannagé-Stewart 2016a), a legitimated service worthy of the license fee. In the process it signaled its support for the British independent production sector that had opposed the budget cut and move online.

BBC Three had some notable programming successes with female protagonists and writers in the year following its online transition, previously a rarity on the channel. Along with a 2017 short-form season produced and curated by British actor and producer Idris Elba that showcased British BAME youth,[2] these successes indicate BBC Three as a potential flagship for the corporation's on-going mission to increase its representational and creative diversity. Dark comedy *Fleabag*, written by and starring Phoebe Waller-Bridge, debuted in the summer of 2016 to significant critical acclaim, word-of-mouth success, and BAFTA nominations. This was BBC Three's first international co-production with Amazon Prime Video (as co-productions are increasingly the norm in British fiction programming, to meet the budgetary expectations of home audiences and to facilitate export). As with most co-productions, Amazon's involvement was little heralded in the UK broadcast, lest it trouble BBC Three's assertion of national distinction, but its international reach and critical success conferred additional prestige on the new BBC Three brand. Earlier in 2016, Marnie Dickens's *Thirteen* was the first BBC Three drama to debut as online-only and earned notable critical and ratings success. The thriller benefited from heavy promotion in the last few weeks of linear BBC Three, across all BBC's channels and in the channel's branded social media spaces. Its significant cross-platform promotion indicated the tactics needed to facilitate discovery in SVOD (Grainge and Johnson 2015, 33), and by August it was the most-requested show to feature on iPlayer that year (Gannagé-Stewart 2016b).

DEVELOPING AND MAINTAINING IDENTITIES ONLINE

By mid-2016, the top 20 most-requested shows on iPlayer included seven BBC Three shows, and a strategic focus on YouTube as an additional platform for all short-form video saw the channel doubling its subscribers and trebling its viewing time on the platform (Gannagé-Stewart 2016b). All of BBC Three's factual content up to 30 minutes in length is posted to YouTube as well as iPlayer, and the move online saw an increase in the production of documentaries ranging from 5 to 30 minutes. Where hour-long documentary had been a centerpiece of linear BBC Three (with a prime 9 p.m. timeslot), these shorter running times increased the genre's spreadability.

As a streaming-only service, BBC Three currently faces challenges in promoting and leading its niche audience to its content within the expanse of iPlayer (which holds programming from seven different television channels). At present, iPlayer lacks the personalization algorithms of other SVOD platforms (although individual logins will be introduced in late 2017), and with weekly episode debuts for its long-form programming BBC Three can struggle to draw back a demographic who increasingly expect to "binge" view (Gannagé-Stewart 2016c, 2016d). However, viewers *did* follow BBC Three to iPlayer, and by mid-2016 boosted the channel's monthly views on the platform to 30 million, with requests of its programming rising by 6% to account for 10% of all iPlayer viewing (Gannagé-Stewart 2016b).

In the absence of the "shop window" of the linear channel, the relaunched BBC Three website was positioned as the home of BBC Three, supported by the channel's branded Twitter, Facebook, and Tumblr feeds. These digital spaces sought to retain the cheeky, comic, gossipy BBC Three "voice" that had previously been constructed through the interstitial elements of continuity announcers, idents, and adverts. In shifting from linear to digital spaces, BBC Three spreads out into its audiences' digital everyday, embedding itself into their social media feeds, its programming just a swipe away on ever-present mobile devices. The channel's Twitter identity shifted from the live-tweeting and promotional role that accompanied the linear channel to become a primary facilitator for the channel's online spread. Its Twitter and Facebook feeds took the place of the televisual linear flow, constantly linking to the BBC Three website, iPlayer, and YouTube, as well as hosting short-form content themselves. In sharing new and recent programs, short-form video, and promotional content, these social media spaces keep the relatively static database of on-demand programs "live" and articulate the channel's nationally specific voice in a global media swirl.

As an easily embeddable and spreadable form, short-form content plays a key role in BBC Three's assertion of itself as a "platform neutral" brand. Long-form programming remains within the boundaries of iPlayer, but short-form digital content has a greater freedom of movement. This allows BBC Three to embed PSB content into the digital spaces frequented by its target audience, yet these spaces are already dominated by multinational commercial competitors such as Vice, Buzzfeed, and Fusion. BBC Three leads innovation in short-form among its British youth television competitors; however, in these international digital spaces it comes up against companies that built their brands as digital native media. Here documentary and new comic voices now no longer offer the distinction they did in the linear market of British youth television.

This pulls at the tensions at the heart of BBC Three as a license fee–funded national broadcaster—between British youth television as PSB and as commercial product. As a digital immigrant rather than a native, the channel continues to negotiate its place in the online ecosystem. BBC Three may be small, but its success here plays a key role in the future of nearly a century of British PSB and the social contract at the heart of the license fee. Its audiences will become the license fee payers of the future, and BBC Three must assert its distinctiveness across their digital habitats to convince them of its value in this crowded marketplace, and the necessity of the BBC that birthed it.

NOTES

1 All free-to-air channels in the UK are now delivered digitally since the switchover in 2012.
2 This is a demographic term used across British industry and politics, referring to black, Asian, and minority ethnic.

REFERENCES

"BBC3 Criticised by Governors." 2004. *Broadcast*, May 13. www.broadcastnow.co.uk/bbc3-criti cised-by-governors/1093111.article.

"BBC3 Defies Its Critics." 2005. *Broadcast*, June 30. www.broadcastnow.co.uk/bbc3-defies-its-critics/1026584.article.

Beaumont-Thomas, Ben. 2014. "BBC3—the Shows We'll Miss." *The Guardian*, March 5. www. theguardian.com/tv-and-radio/tvandradioblog/2014/mar/05/bbc3-gavin-stacey-torchwood-summer-heights-high.

Bennett, James. 2011. "Introduction: Television as Digital Media." In *Television as Digital Media*, edited by James Bennett and Niki Strange, 1–27. Durham: Duke University Press.

Born, Georgina. 2011. *Uncertain Vision: Birt, Dyke and the Reinvention of the BBC*. London: Random House.

Chapman, Alexandra. 2014. "BBC3 Eyes Factual Dramas." *Broadcast*, August 21. www.broadcast now.co.uk/news/commissioning/bbc3-eyes-factual-dramas/5076431.article.

"Communications Act 2003." 2003. www.legislation.gov.uk/ukpga/2003/21/contents.

Deans, Jason and Tara Conlan. 2014. "BBC iPlayer: Major Upgrade to Include Exclusive Content from Boyle and Curtis." *The Guardian*, March 11. www.theguardian.com/media/2014/mar/11/bbc-iplayer-revamped-adam-curtis.

Evans, Elizabeth. 2011. *Transmedia Television: Audiences, New Media, and Daily Life*. Abingdon: Routledge.

Farber, Alex. 2015. "Amazon Reverses Declines as Netflix Extends Lead." *Broadcast*, August 13. www.broadcastnow.co.uk/news/amazon-reverses-declines-as-netflix-extends-lead/5091576. article.

Farber, Alex. 2016. "Live TV Loses Young Viewers." *Broadcast*. July 14. www.broadcastnow.co.uk/ live-tv-loses-young-viewers/5106719.article.

Gannagé-Stewart, Hannah. 2016a. "BBC Youth Viewing Drops 18% after BBC3 Closure." *Broadcast*, August 22. www.broadcastnow.co.uk/news/bbc-youth-viewing-drops-18-after-bbc3-closure/5108618.article.

Gannagé-Stewart, Hannah. 2016b. "BBC3 iPlayer Requests Jump after Online Launch." *Broadcast*, August 23. www.broadcastnow.co.uk/news/bbc3-iplayer-requests-jump-after-online-launch/5108645.article.

Gannagé-Stewart, Hannah. 2016c. "Damian Kavanagh: BBC3 Hobbled by Content Discovery." *Broadcast*, August 30. www.broadcastnow.co.uk/news/damian-kavanagh-bbc3-hob bled-by-content-discovery/5108879.article.

Gannagé-Stewart, Hannah. 2016d. "iPlayer to Require Log-in from 2017." *Broadcast*, August 27. www.broadcastnow.co.uk/news/iplayer-to-require-log-in-from-2017/5109809.article.

Gannagé-Stewart, Hannah. 2016e. "TV Rejects Millennial Malaise." *Broadcast*, September 1. www.broadcastnow.co.uk/news/tv-rejects-millennial-malaise/5108930.article.

Grainge, Paul and Catherine Johnson. 2015. *Promotional Screen Industries*. Abingdon: Routledge.

Jenkins, Henry, Sam Ford and Joshua Green. 2013. *Spreadable Media: Creating Value and Meaning in a Networked Culture*. London: NYU Press.

Kanter, Jake. 2014. "BBC Eyes Online-Only Future for BBC3." *Broadcast*, March 5. www.broad castnow.co.uk/bbc-eyes-online-only-future-for-bbc3/5068278.article.

Kanter, Jake. 2015. "Danny Cohen Defends BBC3 Plans." *Broadcast*, June 11. www.broadcastnow. co.uk/news/danny-cohen-defends-bbc3-plans/5089263.article.

Kavanagh, Damian. 2015a. "BBC Three: Where We Are." *About the BBC*, June 26. www.bbc. co.uk/blogs/aboutthebbc/entries/c9a425fb-df7b-454e-b83b-34a139acc4e2.

Kavanagh, Damian. 2015b. "BBC Three: What We've Been Up To." *About the BBC*, August 12. www.bbc.co.uk/blogs/aboutthebbc/entries/aff22c20-b7cd-4e1f-ac92-363fdd1037ed.

Price, Stephen. 2014. "Has BBC3 Fulfilled Its Remit? | In-Depth | Broadcast." *Broadcast*, April 24. www.broadcastnow.co.uk/features/has-bbc3-fulfilled-its-remit/5070914.article.

"Public Purposes." 2015. *BBC—Inside the BBC*. www.bbc.co.uk/aboutthebbc/insidethebbc/who weare/publicpurposes/.

"Public Service Broadcasting in the Internet Age." 2015. *Ofcom*. http://stakeholders.ofcom.org. uk/consultations/psb-review-3/.

Rushton, Katherine. 2009. "BBC3: Search for the Secret of Youth." *Broadcast*, June 18. www. broadcastnow.co.uk/bbc3-search-for-the-secret-of-youth/5002614.article.

Rushton, Katherine. 2010. "Danny Cohen, BBC3." *Broadcast*, February 25. www.broadcastnow. co.uk/features/interviews/danny-cohen-bbc3/5011235.article.

Woods, Faye. 2016. *British Youth Television: Transnational Teens, Industry, Genre*. New York: Palgrave Macmillan.

Open TV

The Development Process
Aymar Jean Christian

TV is more open than at any other time in its history. US television has transitioned from the network era to the "networked" era, characterized by the shift from linear distribution with limited options for producing, financing, and releasing television to decentralized distribution with multiple, converging models for developing programs (Christian 2018). Development begins with the process of pitching; continues through the production of the pilot (a first episode made on spec) or the licensing of a season; and extends to the marketing of the released series. Just as importantly, development is also the process of valuing series. Executives must decide if a story is worthy of investment in production and of the network's brand in marketing its release. The legacy development practices that arose in the network era involved the selection and licensing of original series across specific program types: comedy, drama, reality, and TV movies, historically. Legacy TV channels including broadcasters like ABC and later cable entrants like MTV and HBO dominated the network era and still hold considerable power to create value through development in the early years of the networked era.

Yet development has expanded in the open TV market, offering new opportunities and methods for creating value. Independent producers no longer have to meet with legacy TV network executives to produce and release their shows. Innovative comedians like Issa Rae (*The Misadventures of Awkward Black Girl*), Abbi Jacobson and Ilana Glazer (*Broad City*), Felicia Day (*The Guild, Geek & Sundry*), Franchesca Ramsey (*The Nightly Show*), and Grace Helbig (*Not Too Deep, @midnight*), as well as more dramatic writers like Bernie Su (*The Lizzie Bennet Diaries*) and Katja Blichfeld and Ben Sinclair (*High Maintenance*) produce their own shows using digital technologies and release them directly to fans on open-upload sites like YouTube and Vimeo. This brings innovation to television by expanding the number and styles of stories, the diversity of storytellers, and strategies for marketing them online and through mobile platforms. Independent producers circumvent legacy intermediaries and create value by creating for each other as well as specific fan communities and brands (Christian 2018). This expansion in distribution demands that we reinvent the study of television, pushing our knowledge of how development works beyond canonic case studies focused on corporate intermediaries at major networks and cable channels (Gitlin 1983; Meehan and Byars 2000; Banet-Weiser, Chris, and Freitas 2007).

Yet if we look at the open TV market, a number of challenges persist for the power of legacy channels. Distribution is key. Attempts by entrepreneurs to create indie networks that curate and license programs—a way of creating a real market outside the legacy system—have floundered. Most successful networked distributors operate at the same scale as the legacy networks and similarly privilege exclusive contracts and Hollywood producers; for example, Netflix spends billions licensing blockbuster TV, while Amazon uses TV to bolster its vast consumer marketplace. Only in rare cases can indie channels create sustainable audiences, as was the case in Dennis Dortch and Numa Perrier's Black & Sexy TV, a kind of "black Netflix" for romantic comedies and dramas, as well as Seed & Spark, which combines a crowdfunding platform for indie producers with a subscription TV service. Most importantly, like legacy channels, few indie channels develop consistently intersectional programming, focusing instead on single identities (black LGBTQ, lesbian, etc.) or easily commodified target markets (geeks, gamers, etc.). While open TV markets expand the production and distribution of representations broadly, they have not yet sufficiently valued intersectionality.

To advance theories of value in representation on networked TV I started a platform, Open TV[beta], to develop queer or intersectional networked television in Chicago. I wanted to see what open TV development looked like when it privileged the art of telling sincere stories about sexuality across race, gender, class, disability, religion, citizenship, and so forth. Developing television as research offers deep insights and rich data on the entire process of making and valuing television programs, including production, financing, licensing, marketing and exhibition both online and locally. It has allowed me to see connections between television and various other arts (performance, spoken word, dance, poetry, theatre, and film) across a range of organizations (galleries, universities, museums, festivals, magazines, artist-run/community spaces, and social media). The project uses programming to assess the value and limits of legacy development processes on a smaller scale with communities who have historically not had access to them. *Open TV Presents*, a series of pilots about artists exploring alternative relationships, tests the value of piloting; *Open TV Originals*, wholly produced original series, tests series licensing; *Open TV Re-Presents*, rereleasing existing web series, tests syndication; and *Open TV Community*, documentation of Chicago cultural life, tests reality television and the ways in which the genre can engage communities of artists and fans. The entire project offers new insight into the value and limits of small-scale, local television development.

Here I present a preliminary discussion of small-scale queer production gleaned from running the platform for two programming cycles. In general, queer development allows us to see value created from people and in places historically undervalued by legacy TV channels. It is limited by the same factors that limit intersectional development in the legacy industry, primarily low investment in intersectional artists and producers.

Without pathways to institutions (channels, venture capital, studios, unions) willing to support emerging artists who have been excluded from the industry—and therefore remain not "ready" for Hollywood—most of this work is undercompensated and time-consuming with little guaranteed payoff. Workers have to take on multiple roles: actors market their series, production assistants become extras, producers cook food for crew, and so forth. These constraints and pressures on production in the industry increasingly extend beyond individuals marginalized by their race, gender, sexuality, and so forth, as union labor too is threatened by reality TV and runaway production. Thus, intersectional development forms a critique of the industry as it creates value within it: it spotlights areas of under-investment and the resulting consequences. It shows the limits of a legacy system dominated by a small number of conglomerates while experimenting with paths to reform.

THE PITCH

In Hollywood, a project's readiness is only one of many factors in its development. Often times projects need powerful producers or studios attached, fully employed departments for all elements of production (casting, costumes, makeup, visual effects, etc.), a built-in audience (franchises), the "right" audience (a desirable demographic), and a story that is acceptable to LA executives, advertisers, and/or the press, all of which are brokered by agents, managers, lawyers and unions. There are many more pitches than funds for production, which are high-value and in demand. For Open TV, during the second cycle, 60 projects reached "pitch" stage, meaning an idea or treatment exists but not resources to start preproduction; of those, 33 projects were eventually produced and released. By contrast, broadcast TV networks alone can receive 2,000 pitches each season for only several dozen opportunities for full series licensing (Chozik 2011). Thus, executives are tasked with valuing a few pitches over others, relying on history, norms, and relationships with exclusionary organizations (Gitlin 1983; Bielby and Bielby 1994). The executives making these decisions also do not reflect the range of diversity in US communities along lines of race, gender, class, sexuality, thus inhibiting representations before projects can enter production.

Open TV^{beta} projects enter development after I've met with the artist and we've agreed to work towards collaborating on a project. Many projects come to Open TV already produced or in preproduction; when creators are merely looking for a distributor, projects move through development faster. Most of the projects released during the second cycle were not produced by me and did not need direct production support. Otherwise, projects in development need funding and a production team before we can enter preproduction. For me, a project starts in development and never leaves development. In other words, once we start development with you, we will always be developing your work, even after it is released. This is a necessity when access to capital is low. In order for the platform to function, I need many more projects in development than are ready to release so I can pursue different forms of financing at different levels of production—in the first cycle budgets could reach $30,000—as they arise. Funding sources at this level come from a variety of sources (non-profit grants, crowdfunding, sponsors, and investors), so it helps to have a variety of programs to develop. Still, I aim to help every pitch I receive, even if it is not exactly right for the platform, in order to support a community of producers whom I may need for their assistance or work on future projects. This help typically involves referrals to individuals who can assist in production, distribution, or exhibition and suggestions on how to achieve funding. Yet most pitches work in line with the goals of Open TV, with the big exception of pitches from outside Chicago.

PREPRODUCTION

Projects in preproduction have secured funding and a team to start filming. This is the planning stage. Producers hire the crew, find locations, organize the shoot, and trouble-shoot the whole process. The hiring of actors, writers and crew in Hollywood relies on systems that historically exclude women, queer people, and people of color, including agents and managers, unions, and social networks predicated on structural segregation based on race, gender, class, and education. In either case, having a creator and producer from an underrepresented group improves representation behind the camera, but in indie contexts, producers have more freedom to hire (and fire). In the case of *Brown Girls*, among our most intersectional series at the time and the product of two women—poet Fatimah Asghar, who is South Asian American, and director Sam Bailey, a black cis-woman—most of the crew were women, people of color, and queer people, while many actors representing non-white races were cast in the series. Meanwhile, representation behind the camera in both broadcast, cable, and networked television continues to lag behind the US population distribution (Hunt 2016; Smith, Choueiti, and Pieper 2016). One *Variety* study found broadcast network showrunners were 90% white and 78% male (Ryan 2016). In 2016, Martha Lauzen found women constitute only 27% of creators, directors, writers, producers, executive producers, editors, and directors of photography on broadcast networks, with no progress in a decade; that same study found that series with women behind the camera were more likely to have diverse casts (Lauzen 2016).

Preproduction in small-scale development leverages community and social networks online and locally to get the show done. Often, friends of the creator or the crew perform certain roles on a volunteer basis or at below-market rates in trade for skill-building or assistance on their own projects down the line. Rates are often more negotiable, with production companies and local vendors offering "family" or "community" rates to productions that align with their politics, promote their talent or wares artistically, or have the possibility on getting developed by a larger institution that could later pay higher rates. At times, traditional methods for organizing production are used, including storyboards, call-sheets, tax credit and insurance applications, and work-for-hire agreements or union contracts (several guilds offer "new media" contracts that allow producers to pay below minimums). Yet in the case of very small-scale shoots, such as our three-person crew for *Let Go and Let God* or the single-producer docu-series *Been T/Here*, these norms are less necessary. Most indie series are the result of a single or very small team of writers and producers, so the process of staffing series with several writers is far less common in indie TV than legacy television. Casting is expensive and time-consuming, so most series creators work with actors they already know before entering preproduction, and often write scripts with those performers in mind. In all, the flexible and community-centered nature of preproduction in indie contexts can mitigate some of the persistent problems with diversity that deepen in legacy contexts.

PRODUCTION

Projects enter production when they start capturing the footage they need to complete the story. Here, and in post-production, a legacy network's influence historically wanes as studios like Warner Bros. or Universal control this labor. Nevertheless, in selecting programs to license from studios, networks still get to decide who will run production and supply most of the funding for program development. Scripted comedy and drama series have historically enjoyed high enough licensing fees from the network as well as subsequent syndication revenues to hire union labor both "above-the-line" (writers, producers, directors) and "below-the-line" (the crew who execute creators' visions). However a competitive, networked media environment has forced conglomerate-owned distributors to manage costs more rigorously. Pressure on workers in legacy TV is increasing as legacy networks order reality television to circumvent union protections and profit from syndication and program ownership more directly; reality TV programs are often funded at cost plus profit for the production company in exchange for network ownership of the intellectual property—meaning that the network, not the producer, controls future sales of the program (Caldwell 2008; Mayer 2011; Vanderhoef 2013). Writing opportunities, long the bastion of sustainable union employment in television, also face threat as cable and corporate networked distributors order series from auteurs with small writing staffs, or genres that require no staff at all (on reality TV, editors "write" the show).

The intimate scale and low-budgets of queer production puts their own pressures on workers, often causing stress; for instance, licensing fees for most Open TV projects cannot cover a majority of production costs. Yet lower resources engender innovation out of need to wring as much value out of every participant's time, thus showcasing their talent and potentially serving as evidence for greater investment from larger institutions, communities, or crowdfunding. Open TV shoots last anywhere from a single day (*Let Go and Let God* was shot in one day, *Nupita Obama* in two) to two weeks (for *You're So Talented* season two and *Brown Girls* season one) to several months (primarily docu-series like *Futurewomen*, which shot through all of 2015). Productions need at least one person to capture the image, typically a photographer or cinematographer, and often but not always someone to capture sound on location. As I have noted elsewhere (Christian 2018), small-scale productions have crews that take on multiple roles to get projects completed, often crossing the above/below-the-line divide. I wrote and directed *Nupita Obama* but also provided craft services, served as an extra, and hired some crew; in *Brujos*, writer Ricardo Gamboa also starred, co-directed, and helped cast the series; *Lipstick City* creator-writer-star Jaren Merrell (Shea Couleé) also cast the film, whereas art director Dan Polyak also edited it. In all cases, above- and below-the-line crew additionally helped to market the project in Chicago and online. In open TV contexts, production both problematically and generatively supports the whole development process.

POST-PRODUCTION

Post-production involves the editing of a project, compiling the images and sounds, as well as adding any elements that cannot be or need not be captured in production. This sometimes includes the creation of a score or licensing of music, transcribing (for documentary), dubbing or subtitling, and assembling the story. Editing for scripted series can be planned for in preproduction, whereas documentary has no script. Legacy distributors nevertheless invest heavily in documentary through reality television, but to avoid spiraling costs in post-production they hire robust crews to capture as much footage as possible and large editing teams to craft the story (avoiding unions in both cases; reality TV editors are writers without Writers Guild representation). Moreover, artificially inflating and constructing drama through manipulating copious footage prevents production companies from having to watch lives unfold naturally. The marketing value of reality TV to its participants also incentivizes them to construct drama so their storylines are not prematurely cut. Here we see how network imperatives to profit at low cost shapes post-production by putting pressure on labor.

Editing is costly in indie contexts, though I have had support from my university to train and hire students in editing. Many indie productions underestimate the cost of post-production. I have done this myself in the past, and not planning for post can delay a project for years. Post-production is most difficult to estimate for documentaries, where the story must be crafted in post. Post-production consistently delayed series' release during Open TV's first cycle and artists consistently cited stress in trying to finish editing, so for the second cycle I cut licensing costs for documentary and instead advised producers on how to seek outside sources for financing that would be sufficient to support post-production. As a research and community-based project, Open TV development must consider inequality across all these stages of development and production, adjusting to mitigate it.

EXHIBITION AND MARKETING

After we reach a final cut, it's time to plan release. Corporate distributors can leverage scale to market programs, including stronger brand recognition from releasing hundreds of hours of programming, often over decades; robust marketing budgets for individual series and the network's brand; and large staffs designed to produce content for and track reception across mobile and web platforms. Legacy networks like CBS and HBO, both of which inaugurated over-the-top (or IP-delivered) TV platforms around the time Open TV emerged, have had decades to build trust among viewers and develop coherent brands, giving them an edge in the networked environment. New distributors secured large subscriber bases by matching original programming with access to large libraries of information and entertainment: Netflix and Hulu spend billions to license movies and series from Hollywood studios, and Amazon links television to the wide range of goods it delivers to customers. Without similarly robust funds for licensing, marketing, and branding, indie TV distributors must work to establish trust with their respective communities by consistently releasing sincere and compelling programs and actively engaging them on social media. To do this effectively, they need to target specific communities and speak to them in ways that relate to the cultural, social, political, economic conditions in which they live.

For this reason, all Open TV projects screen locally in Chicago before going online to build on a show's most specific and targeted audience. This requires that we plan events, which can range in size. The first cycle of programming, where one new video or episode premiered every month from March 2015 to August 2016, drew modest audiences in a broad range of venues, from social service offices, artist- and community-run space, galleries, and museums. The premiere for *Southern for Pussy* at TransTech Social Enterprises, a company tasked with employing trans people in tech, attracted around 20 people, whereas the second season premiere of *You're So Talented* drew over 100 people and a line out the door of The Whistler, a popular bar in Logan Square. Yet the second cycle drew much larger crowds, indicating clear growth in local community-building. The second cycle debuted at the Museum of Contemporary Art Chicago in January 2017 and drew around 200 people for the first episode premieres of *Brujos*, *Brown Girls*, and *Afternoon Snatch*. Subsequent premieres for the first seasons of those shows in February at Chicago Art Department and the Chicago Cultural Center, drew around 200 on average—although *Brown Girls* attracted 250–300 people, many of whom were turned away due to the space's capacity. These events include performance, panels and talkbacks, and messages from community members as a way to put television in conversation with arts and communities. The *Brown Girls* premiere showcased

FIGURE 29.1 *Open TV^beta "branding" with an emphasis on community in contrast to legacy network strategies.*

artistry by women of color in song, dance (Bollywood and burlesque), and stand-up comedy. Panel discussions examine the complex dynamics of race, gender, sexuality, religion, disability, and class, including discussions of the police state, white supremacy, empathy, self-care, undertaught histories, trauma, and processes for artistic production.

Events are also key research sites for Open TV, where my graduate students collect feedback from attendees, either through one-on-one interviews, or recording the conversation or Q&A. I conduct Google surveys for demographic and qualitative feedback; this is useful because data from corporate social media platforms like Facebook is limited. Most corporate platforms report audiences along the gender binary (Bivens 2016), but Open TV surveys allow for gender non-conforming, masculine- and feminine-spectrum attendees to identify themselves. Screenings tend to attract majorities of people who identify with the lead characters along lines of race, sexuality, and class, but none are homogenous. Still, a minority of Open TV's audience identifies as cis-male and straight; majorities identify as queer and college-educated with incomes under $50,000.

When a program is ready to release online, Open TV's head of marketing designs a website for the project and a social media campaign across Facebook, Twitter, Instagram, and Tumblr. Videos are uploaded to Vimeo. Navigating marketing on social media requires staff, which most creators cannot afford; Open TV assists creators not only by publicizing Chicago events on Facebook and our newsletter but also populating social media with dedicated hashtags, interviews with the creators, video recaps of events, and relevant press. Across both cycles, Facebook was our most active platform, as it is the platform best amenable to exhibiting video; yet Tumblr proved relevant in the first cycle by driving some traffic to *You're So Talented*. In the second cycle, therefore, we created our own Tumblr. This helped drive traffic to *Brujos* specifically, where around 2,000 notes were generated, through which Tumblr users recommended the show to others and endorsed its Latinx representation.

We also gauge the effectiveness of various publications (news sites and blogs) who cover the shows to see which drive traffic. For both *Brown Girls* and *Brujos*, smaller blogs that had less national name recognition but had built loyalty from intersectional queer communities proved more effective at driving viewership than mainstream sites like *TIME*, the *Guardian*, and *W Magazine*. Sites like *Autostraddle* (covering culture for queer/femme people), *Remezcla* (covering Latinx culture), and *NewNowNext* (covering LGBTQ people) contributed a plurality of views on both shows.

Still, indie distributors face limits in their use of corporate social media platforms, whose business models are primarily based on discriminatory practices. For one, while Facebook is good at driving viewership and better than most social networks, the site clearly discriminates against videos from other players like Vimeo and YouTube, privileging its own videos as it seeks to disrupt the video/television market. While Open TV retains Vimeo as a player because of its active filmmaker community and commitment to not censoring videos, we will occasionally upload promotional content like trailers and recaps directly to Facebook, which does censor videos. We were unable to take out ads on two programs, *Open TV Presents: Southern for Pussy* and *Bronx Cunt Tour*, because Facebook flagged their titles as pornographic (in content, each features nudity though not in overtly sexualized contexts), even as both explorations of the complexities of gender identity have shown in prominent galleries and in partnership with major museums. Lastly, as an artist-driven project Open TV allows actors to create and maintain their own platforms for their projects, and indeed some projects, particularly *You're So Talented* and *Brown Girls*, had larger social media followings than Open TV because users are accustomed to following productions specifically and not distributors.

If Open TV can consistently develop innovative, artistic, and intersectional programming over the course of many years, we could grow an audience large enough to guarantee minimum viewership and possibly solicit small subscriptions or memberships. The project is primarily designed to develop and incubate new programs as data through constant experimentation supported by research funds. Yet the most interesting outcome could be the development of a wholly independent networked distributor developing television supported sustainably by the communities represented in its programs.

REFERENCES

Banet-Weiser, Sarah, Cynthia Chris, and Anthony Freitas (eds.). 2007. *Cable Visions: Television Beyond Broadcasting*. New York: New York University Press.

Bielby, William T. and Denise D. Bielby. 1994. "'All Hits Are Flukes': Institutionalized Decision Making and the Rhetoric of Network Prime-Time Program Development." *American Journal of Sociology* 99: 1287–313.

Bivens, Rena. 2016. "Programming Violence: Under a Progressive Surface, Facebook's Software Misgenders Users." *Cultural Digitally*, January 27. Accessed February 16, 2017. http://culture digitally.org/2016/01/programming-violence-under-a-progressive-surface-facebooks-soft ware-misgenders-users.

Caldwell, John T. 2008. *Production Culture: Industrial Reflexivity and Critical Practice in Film and Television*. Durham: Duke University Press.

Chozik, Amy. 2011. "The Math of a Hit TV Show." *The Wall Street Journal*, May 12. http://online. wsj.com/news/articles/SB10001424052748703864204576315240324571266.

Christian, Aymar Jean. 2018. *Open TV: Innovation Beyond Hollywood and the Rise of Web Television*. New York: New York University Press.

Gitlin, Todd. 1983. *Inside Prime Time*. Los Angeles: University of California Press.

Hunt, Darnell. 2016. "The 2016 Hollywood Writers Report: Renaissance in Reverse?" *Writers Guild of America West*, March. www.wga.org/uploadedFiles/who_we_are/HWR16.pdf.

Lauzen, Martha. 2016. "Boxed in 2015–16: Women on Screen and Behind-the-Scenes in Television." *Center for the Study of Women in Television & Film, San Diego State University*, September. http://womenintvfilm.sdsu.edu/files/2015-16-Boxed-In-Report.pdf.

Mayer, Vicki. 2011. *Below the Line: Producers and Production Studies in the New Television Economy*. Durham: Duke University Press.

Meehan, Eileen R. and Jackie Byars. 2000. "Telefeminism: How Lifetime Got Its Groove, 1984–1997." *Television & New Media* 1: 33–51.

Ryan, Maureen. 2016. "Showrunners for New TV Season Remain Mostly White and Male." *Variety*, June 8. http://variety.com/2016/tv/features/diversity-television-white-male-show runners-stats-fox-nbc-abc-cbs-cw-study-1201789639.

Smith, Stacy, Marc Choueiti, and Katherine Pieper. 2016. *Inclusion or Invisibility? Comprehensive Annenberg Report on Diversity in Entertainment.* Los Angeles: USC Annenberg School for Communication and Journalism.

Vanderhoef, John. 2013. "Guilds Struggle to Organize Reality TV." *Carsey-Wolf Center: Media Industries Project*, December 2. www.carseywolf.ucsb.edu/mip/article/guilds-struggle-organize-reality-tv-labor.

Premium
Television

Netflix

Streaming Channel Brands as Global Meaning Systems

Timothy Havens

Netflix's disruption of conventional television viewing and producing practices have led many observers to argue that Netflix is a new form of entertainment, the evolution of television from an era of programmed scarcity to one of user-driven abundance (Malone 2016). Program schedules, Nielsen ratings, advertising, marketing, and television channels, they argue, are obsolete. While the discourses of techno-utopia correctly identify some of the main differences between Netflix and conventional television channels, in their over-reliance on technological definitions, they gloss over many of the continuities between them. Ultimately, what makes television channels useful, as a concept, is their capacity to brand program content at the broadest possible level, a level of generality beyond those offered by directors or genres or even production houses.

The recognition that brands have multiple levels of meaning—what is often called the brand hierarchy—proves central to understanding how Netflix functions as a channel. Much like its broadcast-era forerunners, Netflix crafts a corporate identity that can encompass the wide diversity of programming it has to offer in order to compete with other subscription streaming services. At the same time, it must make use of more precise forms of branded differentiation in order to allow viewers to navigate the wider range of content available to them. What is more, Netflix's recent global expansion has led the company to introduce new complexities to the channel brand hierarchy in an effort to promote both itself and its programming in unfamiliar territories.

DEFINING NETFLIX

Netflix and its observers often claim that the service has no brand. Ted Sarandos, the chief content officer at Netflix, explains, "Our brand is personalization. . . . We didn't want any show to define Netflix" (Sepinwall 2016). However, what Sarandos seems to be saying more precisely is that he does not want Netflix to be associated with any particular brand *of programming*. The Netflix service, he says, does have a brand identity: personalization. This distinction between having a program-based brand and a service-based brand is important in understanding the transformation of channel branding in the era of non-linear streaming television (Johnson 2011).

Netflix is a subscription streaming service, generating revenue mainly from subscription fees, while other streaming services derive revenue from advertising, or a combination of ads and subscriptions. All of these services seek to construct service brands for their companies in order to compete, but services that charge a subscription fee build their brands around both the general service they offer and the content they provide, despite Sarandos's disavowal.

In what follows, we shall encounter several examples of Netflix's efforts to brand itself as a subscription streaming service. However, to make the broader point that this is a *general* branding strategy for subscription streaming channels, I want to offer as a point of comparison Hulu's "Come TV With Us" campaign. The ads for this campaign emphasize the flexibility of watching anytime, anywhere and the sheer abundance of content available on the service with clips from specific, but widely available television series and films ("Home" n.d.). Thus, much as Johnson (2011) observed about Hulu's branding efforts several years ago, the service primarily sells an *experience* of watching television that is distinct from broadcasting and cable (56). The same can be said of Netflix and some of its branding campaigns. At the same time, however, Netflix continues to employ a good deal of branding related to its individual programming offerings. This dual branding strategy likely arises from the need to compete with conventional subscription channels like HBO while maintaining its distinction from non-professional video streaming services like YouTube and Vimeo.

CHANNELS AND BRAND HIERARCHIES

Several observers have suggested that channel branding became crucial as a way for cable television channels in the 1990s and 2000s to distinguish themselves in an increasingly crowded market for attention (Johnson 2011; Lotz 2014; Selznick 2009). However, channels have always carried brands, even though those brands have served different functions as an overall meaning system at different points in television history.

Brand analysts distinguish between different levels of a brand hierarchy, which includes a corporate brand at the highest level, and subsequent levels of family brand, individual brands, and brand modifiers. Importantly, these four levels are not rigid nor are they all-inclusive, but the approach has the benefit of identifying various levels of generality and specificity in branding practices. The idea of the brand hierarchy recognizes that brands inhabit an entire symbolic ecosystem designed to give products and services emotional and intellectual meanings for consumers. Brand identities at the top of the hierarchy are quite general, allowing a wide range of new and old products to benefit from those corporate associations. At the lowest level of the hierarchy, brand modifiers describe small differences among otherwise identical products (Keller 2000).

An example from the automobile industry can be helpful in understanding the levels of the brand hierarchy (see Figure 30.1). At the level of the corporate brand, the

Brand Hierarchy in Automobile Branding

Corporate Brand	Toyota
Family Brand	Camry
Individual Brand	LE
Modifier	X

FIGURE 30.1 *Brand hierarchy in automobile branding.*

car company itself gives coherent meaning to all of the models its produces, even as that corporate brand may be less well-defined than brand identities at the lower levels. Hence, Ford, Volkswagen, and Toyota each possess unique brand identities, even though those differences may be small for most consumers. Automobile models make up the second level of the hierarchy, the family brand. Each car company tends to brand certain types of cars with the same family name—Camry, for example—that indicates the size and type of car, whether it is a luxury or budget brand, and so forth. Within each family brand, car companies distinguish between similar types of cars with different features through the use of individual brands. So, the Toyota Camry SE has a more powerful engine and sportier body than the Toyota Camry LE. Finally, companies often use "modifier brands" to identify specific product attributes, such as the leather seats and wood-grain interiors of the Toyota (corporate) Camry (family) X (modifier) LE (individual).

Most histories of television branding treat channel branding during the broadcast era as minimalistic, even crude, as compared with the later strategies of cable channels (Johnson 2011; Lotz 2014; Rogers, Epstein, and Reeves 2002). However, careful examination of broadcast channel branding demonstrates concerted efforts to create brand identity at the highest level of the hierarchy, the corporate brand. For most of the history of broadcasting, the networks used corporate logos, graphics, mascots, and slogans to provide general attitudes and sensibilities for their broad lineups of daytime and evening entertainment programming, news, and sports. CBS was the "Tiffany network," a place for upscale programming and audiences; NBC was "proud as a peacock" beginning in 1979, a logo that presented the channel as brash and young (Jue-Steuck 2003). Within broadcast channel branding, moreover, different dayparts tended to function as family brands, identifying a predictable and related set of genres, pleasures, and ideal audiences that distinguished them from other dayparts. Since the 1990s, the broadcast networks have sometimes sought to brand particular evenings of programming, such as ABC's "TGIF" lineup or NBC's "Must See TV" schedule. A 1989 ABC promotional piece for ABC's Saturday morning children's programming offers a clear case of this strategy of family branding. The visuals in the promo alternate between clips of animated Saturday morning programs and a group of children in a playroom with several adults in animal costumes. The audio track includes the children saying the letters "ABC" and a take-off on the Isley Brothers song "Shout" to tout ABC as a source of Saturday morning fun (Retrostatic 2016). More than a mere listing of individual programs, then, this promo seeks to identify the daypart with a particular genre (animation), demographic (children), and sensibility (fun).

Programs provide the specificity of product brands in the channel brand hierarchy. While Johnson (2011) has argued that programs became brands in an era of media convergence, where stories and characters frequently get reworked, elaborated, and extended across multiple media platforms, the origins of program branding lie in broadcasting. American broadcast television was filled with branded franchises like *Law & Order* and *Star Trek*, each a meaningful product in its own right that could then be modified as a brand through successive spin-offs. Moreover, a number of television program titles serve as brand umbrellas for one-off programming, including news magazines like *60 Minutes* and anthology series like *ABC's Movie of the Week*. Indeed, an argument can be made that all episodic television series are similar to convergent program brands, in that they offer a general but meaningful and recognizable roster of characters, sets, and storylines that nevertheless change and extend as the seasons go on.

Because most cable channels embrace narrower, often demographic-specific identities and target markets, they do not have to construct general entertainment brands as broadly as do the broadcast networks, leaving them free to construct somewhat more well-defined and coherent brands carefully tuned to meanings and values attractive to their desired audiences. Thus, the brands of individual cable channels (see Figure 30.2) can often function more like a family brand than a corporate brand, similar to how dayparts could serve as family brands for broadcasters by constructing unities of theme, genre, or taste. The exceptions are general entertainment cable channels, such as AMC, TNT, and TBS, which exhibit branding strategies more similar to broadcasters (Jaramillo 2013).

As the cable channel brand shifts to the family level, the corporate owners of the channels and the multichannel video programming distributors (MVPDs) delivering

Brand Hierarchies for Broadcast, Cable, and Streaming Television Channels

	Broadcast	Cable	Streaming
Corporate Brand	ABC	Fox	Netflix
Family Brand	Dayparts	FX	Categories/genres
Individual Brand	Programs	Program	Programs
Modifier	Franchise/spinoff	Franchise/Spinoff	Franchise/spinoff

FIGURE 30.2 *Brand hierarchies for broadcast, cable, and streaming television channels.*

the channels take on the role of corporate brand. As Johnson (2011) notes, cable channels operate in a dual-product market, selling themselves to cable companies, while also selling their audiences to advertisers. For cable companies looking to carry channels, the corporate owner, who typically owns several channels, is the most immediate corporate brand. Companies like Time Warner and Viacom sell their cable channels in packages to cable operators, and these corporate owners have distinct brands that they promote to cable operators. Much like the network brand during broadcasting, these corporate brands provide only a vague ethos to their channels. At the same time, cable *operators* like Comcast or Spectrum function as corporate brands for most viewers, promoting the channels they carry within their overall service identity. Regardless of the complexity at this level, however, a basic branding hierarchy remains in place for both broadcasting and cable channels.

BRANDING NETFLIX

Netflix's rise as a global television power over the past two years provides the most elaborated case to date of a streaming television service, and an examination of its branding strategies provides valuable insight into the strategies by which subscription streaming services continue to construct brands in meaningful, systematic, and hierarchical ways. Returning to Figure 30.2, we see that like its broadcast and cable predecessors, Netflix too plays the corporate role in its branding hierarchy, combining both product branding and service branding in its messaging. Instead of by linear dayparts or narrowcast demographics, the level of the family brand for Netflix is fulfilled by the categories subscribers see when they launch the application, such as "Popular on Netflix," "Trending Now," "New Releases," and even quirkier categories generated by the service's proprietary algorithms. While general enough to encompass multiple program products, these categories provide levels of specificity designed to allow the viewer to navigate through the service's vast library. Finally, individual brands and modifiers remain similar to what we see on broadcast television.

At the same time, Netflix seeks to compete in multiple different countries, where existing channels may have quite different brands and branding strategies, where cultural codes are distinct, and where television viewing itself may mean something quite different. This leads to the development of another level of brand hierarchy, one that perhaps exists somewhere between the individual brand and the family brand, whose function is to indigenize Netflix's original service and program offerings. We might call this the "translational level" of the global television brand.

Netflix as Service Brand

Obviously, Netflix's most unique characteristic at the level of the corporate brand is its streaming, on-demand subscription service, which promises a cornucopia of films and TV shows from around the world for a nominal monthly fee. Netflix leverages, in particular, its identity as a tech company, as opposed to a media company, in order to articulate a brand identity built around disruption. More specifically, the company champions a disruption of scheduled television viewing, imagining that disruption as both individualist and youthful. This is its primary service brand.

In his address to the Consumer Electronics Show in 2016, when Netflix announced its expansion into 130 countries worldwide, CEO Reed Hastings explained the service's fundamental distinction from other forms of television by narrating a history of disruption, beginning with broadcast television and ending with Netflix. He identified the limitations of broadcast television as the lack of programming choice, and credited cable with giving viewers "hundreds of networks to scroll through. But what consumer really wanted," he continued, "was to be able to choose *when* to watch" (Netflix 2016).

This immediacy of delivery—the erasure between desire for media content and the satisfaction of that desire—takes center stage in Netflix's articulation of a "disruptive" brand. Reinforcing the centrality of immediacy in its brand, Netflix actually began streaming for the first time in dozens of countries *during* Hastings announcement. Netflix's motto launched in 2015, "See What's Next," also points to the immediate availability of whatever we may want to watch, while instructing us to keep watching.

We can see the centrality of immediacy and disruption to Netflix's brand by considering how it introduces itself in new markets around the world. When Netflix launched in both Germany and India, it created quite distinct ad campaigns; yet both emphasized the service itself, rather than any particular programming, positioning immediacy of delivery and satisfaction of desire as disruptive. Moreover, both campaigns emphasized this disruption as *youthful*, helping distinguish itself from cable and broadcasting, while also signaling its identity as a tech company.

One early Netflix television commercial introducing the service to German consumers featured a man in his thirties in his apartment, looking at his watch. He quickly picks up his phone and calls his mother, only to find out that the movie she had been planning to watch on television has just started. As he looks knowingly at the camera, he apologizes for calling at a bad time and hangs up, explaining to the viewer that while he loves his mother, he does not like talking to her for long periods on the phone; we assume, therefore, he waited until the moment his mother's film was linearly scheduled to begin on her "old" television setup before calling her. The man then grabs his television remote and calls up Netflix (Netflix Deutschland 2014). Quite clearly, this commercial directly links Netflix's immediacy, youthfulness, and the disruption of conventional television viewing as well as conventional relationship patterns.

The similarities between this commercial and one introducing Netflix in India are striking. The ad takes place at a dinner table in a modern apartment, where a heterosexual couple sits with a female friend. Each member of the couple is complaining about how the other is "cheating," leaving the female friend aghast, until it becomes clear through flashbacks that "cheating" means individually watching ahead on episodes of a shared television series (Netflix India 2017b). As with the German example, the Indian commercial for Netflix emphasizes simultaneity of viewer satisfaction and its disruption of conventional ways of watching television, as well as personal relationships.

Importantly, Netflix's portrayal of individual gratification disrupting personal relationships in these promotional ads comes off as ironic, with exaggerated acting and situations. As such, it further reinforces the playfulness and youthfulness of its corporate brand identity. This youthful and playful dimension of Netflix's brand, as well as its disruption of traditional patterns, reinforces other efforts to construct its identity as a tech company, rather than strictly a media company.

As part of these efforts, Hastings himself plays the role of the quintessential tech CEO, fond of giving stirring presentations filled with drama and showmanship at industry conferences, à la Apple's Steve Jobs. When the company announced its global expansions in 2016, it chose to make that announcement at the Consumer Electronics Show rather than a conventional television industry event like the National Association of Broadcasters or the network advertising upfronts. In the social media marketing campaign announcing its global expansion, #netflixeverywhere, Netflix identifies itself as "Revolutionary. Disruptive. Fearless," again drawing on commonplace perceptions of the tech industry. Finally, Netflix is given to the hyperbole of tech companies in describing itself: in an interview with *USA Today*, Hastings explained that the company's main competitor is sleep, suggesting that if people never went to bed, they would never stop watching Netflix (Snider 2017).

Netflix uses this tech company identity to address both subscribers and investors. For subscribers, this tech identity projects an image of being youthful, tech savvy, and modern. Meanwhile, for investors, Netflix can maintain high levels of capital investment and investor satisfaction despite small short-term profits in the hopes of massive future revenues—a venture capital tech industry model—whereas investors hold traditional mature legacy media companies to much higher and more immediate profit expectation (LaKosh 2017).

Netflix, therefore, draws on a number of associations related to its *service*, rather than its programming, to brand itself as disruptive, youthful, individualistic, techy, and capable of satisfying immediate viewer desire. All of these elements operate at the level of the corporate brand, emphasizing the experience of streaming television over any particular content. Significantly, Netflix uses the same themes of disruption, youth, and individuality around the world, suggesting it imagines its primary audience as one that shares a generational sensibility.

Netflix and Program Branding

Despite the early ads in India and Germany introducing the service to potential subscribers in those nations, recent Netflix ads in both countries have emphasized specific program offerings, complicating the company's initial emphasis on service branding. The YouTube channels for both Netflix Deutschland, Österreich, und Schweiz, and Netflix India, for example, are devoted exclusively to promotional ads for the service. Out of the hundreds of commercials available online as of 2017, only the oldest ones exclusively sold the service experience. All others foregrounded specific programming in their pitches.

The reliance on programming rather than its service alone to create a brand identity is reflected in a broader rebranding strategy for Netflix that began in 2014. Developed with the design company Gretel NY, Netflix's global branding strategy featured what it called the "stack" (see Figure 30.3), a visual representation of the company's extensive

FIGURE 30.3 *Netflix's "stack" branding technique emphasizes the specific programming available to subscribers.*

program offerings as well as a promotional rendering of its interface screen. As Gretel puts it, this branding strategy "implies both the infinite, ever-changing catalogue and the custom-curated selections that make up the core of the Netflix service." The "stack" is a set of "cards" featuring promotional images, popular stars and characters, and branded Netflix materials. Each card is stacked or alternated with other cards. When animated, the cards shift and move, reinforcing the ever-changing nature of Netflix's offerings while mimicking the experience of browsing its offerings. The stack branding strategy looks remarkably similar to conventional broadcast channel promotions, which often featured collages of popular series and characters interspersed with new ones, as well as branded channel logos, slogans, songs, and so forth. This practice of emphasizing both the range of programming, as well as the mixture of new and old has been commonplace at broadcast channels since the 1950s. We see this practice reprised in Netflix's branding campaign because it allows the positive associations of both the programming brand to permeate the service brand and vice-versa.

Global Netflix and the Translational Brand

One of the more curious elements of Netflix's global branding strategy are what I have called "translational" elements of the brand, which are paratexts (Gray 2010) designed to market Netflix's original television series abroad, but which focus on efforts to translate those programs to local subscribers' frames of reference. These practices are particularly developed on Netflix India, which features a number of short vignettes where well-known Indian actors discuss an original Netflix series, act out scenes, or recreate moods similar to those in the series. One such vignette stars well-known actor Alok Nath and up-and-coming comedian Biswa Kalyan Rath as a father-son duo. Rath explains to his father what happens in *House of Cards* over multiple seasons, as his father fantasizes about employing the techniques used by protagonist Frank Underwood to undermine everyone in his firm and become CEO. The five-minute vignette features only a few short clips of the actual series, focusing instead on the father and son (Netflix India 2017a).

Developed as part of an effort to use the 2017 season of *House of Cards* to drive Netflix subscriptions in India ("Netflix Looks" 2017), this short vignette is similar to localized promotional campaigns for imported American television series around the world, which often use local talent, local references, and local channel brands to help indigenize imported program content (Bernabo 2017). What is unique, however, is that the channel uses these vignettes to promote broader awareness of the parent brand as well, not merely the individual brand of the series. Much like Netflix's service brand, these vignettes are youthful, playful, and often disruptive of cultural differences. While international subscription cable channels like HBO International use these same practices, these channels also frequently license their most acclaimed series to local broadcasters (Havens 2006). Netflix, by contrast, has begun guarding and maintaining its rights to prestigious and expensive programming in every market it can in an effort to build its brand and subscription base abroad (Littleton 2017). Consequently, Netflix must see these translational branded elements as playing an important role in constructing the meaning system of Netflix's brand in many markets abroad, putting its service and program elements in dialogue.

CONCLUSION: BRANDING THE STREAM

As a corporate brand, Netflix foregrounds its service-specific elements, highlighting the distinctive experience of using a streaming service instead of a broadcast schedule. This is a clear attempt to distinguish Netflix from traditional television channels. Over time and across global markets, however, this strategy seemed to disappear in favor of brand identities inflected by the exclusive programming that Netflix provides, often a combination of new acquisitions and old standards. While the strategy of service branding is distinctive to the streaming environment, these programming-based strategies harken back to the broadcast channel and their refinement in cable branding campaigns of the 1980s and 1990s aimed at creating valuable identities for channels largely independent of the particular programs on offer.

How do we explain this return to older practices of channel branding? Analysis of the hierarchical relationships between corporate, family, and individual television brands helps us to see that the branding *strategies* of television services did not change substantially, but rather that the position of the cable channel within the overall brand hierarchy merely shifted from the corporate to the family level. With Netflix, the channel brand returns to the level of the corporate brand identity. In part, this reflects the channel's ambitions of becoming the dominant provider of a broad range of film and video content for a wide subscriber base, while also sourcing and delivering that content around the globe.

Ultimately, what Netflix has in common with broadcast channels is its pursuit of a general entertainment audience, as opposed to the narrower niche orientation of cable channels. Moreover, Netflix seeks to produce an audience not only of service subscribers, but also fans of their original content, which in many ways is the most truly distinctive product Netflix has to offer. Consequently, it must create a service identity broad enough to incorporate all of the programming in its library, much as broadcast channels needed to create corporate brands encompassing diverse slates of programming. At the same time, and also much like its broadcasting forebears, it must rely on high-wattage programming to distinguish itself.

In competitive environments, general entertainment services like broadcasting or streaming need to create coherent corporate brands in order to stand out in comparison to similar providers. Despite Hastings's claim that Netflix's primary competitor is sleep, Netflix must in fact compete strenuously with other international and local streaming services in order to attract and maintain subscribers. In India, for example, Netflix and Amazon's standalone Prime video service are locked in a pitched battle for market dominance. A robust brand hierarchy is crucial to the competition for subscribers, for both Netflix and viewers, for whom branding helps construct a roadmap to relevant media content in a world of ever more abundant television.

REFERENCES

Bernabo, Laurena E. 2017. "Glee-talia: Adapting Glee for an Italian Audience." *Critical Studies in Media Communication* 34 (2): 168–76.

Gray, Jonathan. 2010. *Show Sold Separately: Promos, Spoilers, and Other Media Paratexts*. New York: New York University Press.

Havens, Timothy. 2006. *Global Television Marketplace*. London: Palgrave.

"Home." n.d. *Hulu*. Accessed July 13, 2017. www.youtube.com/user/huluDotCom.

Jaramillo, Deborah. 2013. "AMC: Stumbling toward a New Television Canon." *Television & New Media* 14: 167–83.

Johnson, Catherine. 2011. *Branding Television*. London: Routledge.

Jue-Steuck, Jennifer. 2003. "John J. Graham: Behind the Peacock's Plumage." *Design Issues* 18 (4): 91–6.

Keller, Kevin Lane. 2000. "Building and Managing Corporate Brand Equity." In *The Expressive Organization: Linking Identity, Reputation, and the Corporate Brand*, edited by Majken Schultz, Mart Jo Hatch and Mogens Holten Larsen, 115–37. Oxford and New York: Oxford University Press.

LaKosh, Jeremy. 2017. "Netflix Earnings: Beyond Subscriber Growth." *Seeking Alpha*, April 19. https://seekingalpha.com/article/4063452-netflix-earnings-beyond-subscriber-growth.

Littleton, Cynthia. 2017. "New Platforms, New Profits." *Variety Premier*, March 23.

Lotz, Amanda D. 2014. *The Television Will Be Revolutionized*, 2nd edition. New York: New York University Press.

Malone, Michael. 2016. "The Labor Pains of Peak TV." *Broadcasting & Cable* 146 (16): 10–12. Accessed June 28, 2017. Proquest.

Netflix, 2016. "Netflix CES 2016 Keynote." *YouTube*, June 16. www.youtube.com/watch?v=n-FFfzhtZhg&t=135s.

Netflix Deutschland, Österreich und Schweiz. 2014. "Netflix—Mama Ad Official [HD]Setpo." *YouTube*, September 15. www.youtube.com/watch?v=7XT8SQKU_TY.

Netflix India. 2017a. "House of Cards Feat: Alok Nath and Biswa Kalyan Rath." *YouTube*, May 17. www.youtube.com/watch?v=4MG8KmQhtpA&t=151s.

Netflix India. 2017b. "Serial Cheaters Feat Sumeet & Nidhi." *YouTube*, February 13. www.youtube.com/watch?v=ioXXEm7_mmY.

"Netflix Looks for Icebreaker, Aggressively Promotes *House of Cards* Season 5 Only for Indian Audience." 2017. *exchange4media News Service*, May 31. www.exchange4media.com/digital/netflix-looks-for-icebreaker-aggressively-promotes-house-of-cards-season-5-only-for-indian-audience_69033.html.

Retrostatic. 2016. "ABC Fall Saturday Morning Cartoon Promo (1989)." *YouTube*, May 19. www.youtube.com/watch?v=YPqtKIfguxY.

Rogers, Mark C., Michael Epstein and Jimmie L. Reeves. 2002. "The Sopranos as HBO Brand Equity: The Art of Commerce in the Age of Digital Reproduction." In *This Thing of Ours: Investigating the Sopranos*, edited by David Lavery, 42–59. New York: Columbia University Press.

Selznick, Barbara. 2009. "Branding the Future: Syfy in the Post-Network Era." *Science Fiction Film and Television* 2 (2): 177–204.

Sepinwall, Alan. 2016. "Why Matt Weiner 'Would Lose' If He Wanted to Make a Weekly Netflix Show." *Uproxx*, January 26. http://uproxx.com/sepinwall/ted-talk-state-of-the-netflix-union-discussion-with-chief-content-officer-ted-sarandos/.

Snider, Mike. 2017. "Netflix's Biggest Competition? Sleep, CEO Says." *USA Today*, April 18. www.usatoday.com/story/tech/talkingtech/2017/04/18/netflixs-biggest-competition-sleep-ceo-says/100585788/.

Hulu

Geoblocking National TV in an On-Demand Era

Evan Elkins

In 2016, streaming video platform Hulu released an advertisement entitled "Don't Just Watch TV, Make It Yours," which perfectly captures on-demand television's tension between mass-scale content distribution and individualization. Over many shots portraying a diverse group of viewers watching television on a variety of digital devices while undertaking everyday activities (lazing on the couch, exercising, commuting), a narrator explains that Hulu will allow you, the viewer, to watch television "your way." There is much to say about how this ad defines television at the end of the 2010s—its emphasis on personal customization, promotion of an ethnically and economically diverse audience base, and suggestion that technological convergence has become banal, to name just a few. But particularly notable is how strongly it emphasizes Hulu as a *television* service (a branding strategy reflected in the platform's other recent slogan, "For the Love of TV"). It even goes so far as to suggest, "Movies? They're TV, too!" Through Hulu, television programs, films, and short video clips are all subsumed into the broader category of television, rather than any kind of undifferentiated "online video."

Indeed, of all the major online video on demand (VOD) services in the United States, Hulu is the one that most self-consciously presents itself as television. In doing so, it exemplifies many of the possibilities and problems that come with TV's migration to Internet delivery. On one hand, the platform seems to present itself as part of the vanguard of new entertainment and media industry practices. On the other hand, it is beholden to the American television industry's traditional methods of monetizing, promoting, and distributing its programs. Whereas HBO Go is wrapped in HBO's elevated "not TV" brand, and Amazon Video, YouTube, and Netflix are best understood as Silicon Valley-based ventures that have since become intertwined with Hollywood (with the latter also bearing the cinematic weight of its "-flix" suffix), Hulu grew out of the heart of the American TV industry. Presently, the platform is a joint venture among the conglomerates that own three of the four major broadcast networks (NBC, Fox, and

ABC), with Time Warner also owning a 10% stake in the company. Thus, the conditions of its ownership already mark it as the platform most closely aligned with many of the biggest players in American TV. Yet Hulu is particularly televisual for other reasons, too: its self-promotional rhetoric, approaches to content aggregation and audience construction, newly launched live TV service, and limited geographic reach represent fairly standard post-network era practices.

Regarding this last point, I want to focus on Hulu's distinctly *national* character in particular—something that tends to get lost amid the platform's hybrid program offerings and placeless brand—and consider what it reveals about not only Hulu itself, but also how we define contemporary television and its cultural geography more broadly. It remains easy to get lost amid the "TV everywhere" hype and presume that the seemingly easy availability of VOD platforms translates to a kind of global ubiquity. However, Hulu is only available in two countries, the United States and Japan, with each country's platform containing different content libraries and even ownership structures. These borders of availability are affirmed through geoblocking, a digital rights management mechanism that blocks viewers in prohibited countries from connecting to the platform. As a nationally bound VOD service, Hulu crystallizes a tension between two conditions in streaming television. The first is the idea that online delivery is, or could be, fundamentally global, and the second is the continued importance of the nation to how television operates both functionally and discursively. This tension exists even during a time when, as Graeme Turner (2009) has argued, the relationships between television and the nation-state are increasingly contingent.

FOR THE LOVE OF TV

Before diving into business models and program offerings, we can observe immediately that Hulu's paratexts, interstitials, and branding strategies mark it as more televisual than most other VOD services. This is apparent in an early ad campaign where TV stars like Alec Baldwin, Eliza Dushku, and Will Arnett play extraterrestrials who reveal that Hulu is an alien plot to turn human brains into mush. While clearly meant to be humorous and tongue-in-cheek, the notion that Hulu is a world domination strategy taken straight out of the tropes of science fiction presents the platform in futurist terms as something all-encompassing and inescapable. In doing so, these ads invoke the long-promised dream of the celestial jukebox—a cornucopia of ubiquitous and unceasing content delivery. At the same time, they are quick to frame this in the context of television in particular, with Baldwin explaining that the platform "beams TV directly to your portable computing devices," and Arnett at one point entering Hulu's secret, underground lair through a trapdoor in Milton Berle's Hollywood Walk of Fame star. Exploiting the *Texaco Star Theatre* host's close associations with the medium, the ad positions Hulu as part of a lineage that reaches all the way back to Mr. Television himself. The advertisements also draw ironically on dominant, pejorative cultural assumptions—namely, that TV will rot your brain—which are fairly specific to the medium.

Hulu's self-construction as television is also evident in the platform's reminders of American TV's network structure. Logos and interstitials emphasize the networks and channels on which its programs originally air as well as the time of their broadcast airing. This is different than what we see on VOD platforms like Netflix and Amazon Video, which generally elide their programs' provenance. Hulu's ownership by the major American broadcasters explains its use of channel branding, as its corporate holders have a vested interest in drawing viewers not just to the platform itself but also back to the broadcast and cable environment. Hulu's on-screen remediation of TV networks also bears markers of American broadcasting's particular geographic shape. When a Hulu user watches a program from one of the major broadcast networks, a bug promoting the viewer's local network affiliate appears on-screen—just as it would if she were to watch on broadcast TV. This occurs through IP-address detection mechanisms that can pinpoint a user's geographic location. While these geolocative technologies are often used to collect data and/or help users customize their own experiences on a platform, here they are also used to align Hulu with local broadcast affiliate stations. This alignment takes place both on the user end, with viewers reminded of the local/national structure of American broadcasting, and on the industry end, with the bugs appearing due to agreements between the networks and their affiliates (Weprin 2010). Plugging the affiliates in this way serves to resolve another issue in streaming television: the eroding importance of the local amid distribution infrastructures that increasingly cut out affiliates as well as in viewers' experiences of TV as a nominally placeless, à la carte service.

As these emblems of American broadcasting might suggest, we can also consider Hulu a television service due to its particular industrial composition. This is not to ignore the many ways that the platform as a business, technology, and media delivery

FIGURE 31.1 *Hulu remediates American television's local affiliate/national network structure.*

system differs from television as we have traditionally understood it. Still, Hulu reinforces the idea that television as a cultural practice remains important even as the technologies of its delivery and its modes of engagement shift (Lotz 2014, 3). After all, Hulu is a nationally bound commercial media enterprise that offers television programming. Other scholars have pointed to ways that Hulu reflects some of television's longstanding business models. Derek Kompare (2014) aligns the free, ad-supported version of Hulu with a broadcast model and the subscription version, Hulu Plus, with cable. Catherine Johnson (2012, 56) argues that Hulu constructs itself as a "service brand," which is built around offering a service to consumers. Although she argues that Hulu's particular service brand is geared toward selling a specific, interactive televisual experience, Johnson points out that the platform's ad-supported nature marks it as similar to the broadcast networks that make their money by selling viewer attention to advertisers. Indeed, at its founding in 2007 as a joint venture between NBC Universal and News Corporation, Hulu aimed to draw viewers away from pirate activities like torrenting as well as the practice of watching unauthorized clips on YouTube by building an over-the-top (OTT) service that offered a more clearly official and authorized online television experience ("NBC Universal" 2007). Although the platform has enjoyed various partnerships with Silicon Valley–based tech companies over the years, it has remained the streaming platform most entrenched within the traditional television industries (even in spite of a failed attempt by its owners to sell the platform in 2013).

HULU AS AMERICAN TELEVISION

While Hulu presents itself as more closely aligned with television than many of its competitors, we can see when we dig a bit deeper how the platform remediates *American* television in particular and recreates many of the country's dominant TV practices. After all, like mainstream American television, Hulu is a commercial enterprise built on syndication that offers a combination of free, ad-supported, and subscription programming. Beyond this, it was started by two of the four major networks to serve as an online clearing-house for their broadcast content, and indeed its ownership by four major American entertainment conglomerates characterizes the consolidated, oligopolistic structure of the American TV industries. We might compare and contrast this with a service like the BBC's iPlayer. Both platforms serve as online extensions of their respective countries' major television institutions, but only the iPlayer reflects the BBC's centralized, public nature in its nation-bound distribution of BBC content to UK-based users who pay the national television license fee. Netflix offers another useful contrast, as its Silicon Valley origins and eventual entrée into original program production has positioned the platform as alternately competitive and collaborative with American TV's traditional powers rather than direct extensions of them.

Of course, one might point out that the characterization of Hulu as a distinctly American television service is undercut by the fact that the platform is also available in Japan. While Hulu does indeed have a Japanese outpost that it launched in 2011, I would consider this a separate platform—one that shares a name and brand with the US version of Hulu but otherwise exists on its own. Hulu Japan has its own library of content, its own URL, and it even operates as its own company, Hulu Japan, LLC, which has been a subsidiary of Nippon Television since Hulu sold the platform to the Japanese commercial broadcaster in 2014 (James 2014). The ad-free, subscription-based Hulu Japan carries a wealth of Japanese content—both from Nippon TV and elsewhere, including original productions—as well as international fare like Korean drama and American film and television. Because Hulu Japan is no longer owned by the American broadcasters and instead represents a distinct international distribution window, its American TV library is notably different than that of Hulu US. This is most apparent in the Japanese platform's exclusive arrangement with HBO to stream the premium cable channel's programming. This is all to say that it makes sense to consider Hulu US and Hulu Japan two distinct national platforms, rather than one platform made available in two countries.

This nationally confined reach is shored up technologically through geoblocking, which is part of a broader cluster of digital rights management practices called regional lockout. Regional lockout refers to any technological mechanism installed on digital hardware and/or software that attempts to control media's geographic distribution by prohibiting users in certain regions from accessing a platform or content—for example, DVD and video game region codes and chips (Elkins 2016; Lobato and Meese 2016). Geoblocking operates via geolocation technologies that block a user's access based on her IP address—the same principle that enables the Hulu platform to promote local affiliates and advertisements to viewers. Because IP addresses indicate a user's geographic location, platforms use IP address databases and detection software to block access to users in locations where the platform has not been introduced or to offer different prices and libraries to different countries. On Hulu, when one attempts to watch a video when connecting from a prohibited territory (i.e., anywhere that isn't the US), the site displays a message: "We're sorry, currently our video library can only be streamed within the United States." Because geoblocking can impose borders on the nominally global Internet, it affirms the continued importance of national boundaries in contemporary TV, even amid industry talk of globalization and the move to online delivery. This is because television distribution licensing agreements are still often arranged territory by territory. Historically, television distributors have syndicated programs internationally by selling them into various windows, defined by Timothy Havens (2006, 13) as "distinct markets separated by either geography or time, where buyers receive differential access and variable prices." Because digital technologies threatened to erode the borders separating these windows, geoblocking serves to retain nation-based distribution practices. Indeed, the platform's help site contains an explanation of Hulu's geoblocking practices—pointing to the ways licensing deals are still territorial in nature:

> While one of our long-term goals is to make Hulu's growing content lineup available worldwide, we don't have a timetable or any news regarding expansion beyond Hulu Japan at this time. Expansion requires working with content owners to clear the rights for each show or film in each specific region, and those agreements can take a while to be established.
>
> ("Why Can't I" 2016)

As a public explanation, this message is somewhat vague, but it also points to some of the problems that arise when television's territorialized distribution practices meet technologies that would seem oppositional to them.

While Hulu touts its plans to develop globally, it's hard to tell how much the platform actually *wants* to expand by negotiating global distribution deals or to what degree this is merely an excuse to deflect blame onto content owners. We can contrast this with Netflix, which recently made waves with its announcement that it would be launching in almost every country in the world (Steel 2016). Hulu's rhetoric is much more tempered, with its suggestion that there's no "timetable" for global expansion. Indeed, many observers saw the selling off of Hulu Japan as a moment when the company gave up on its plans for international expansion and instead turned all its attention onto the American version of the platform—something affirmed by its owners investing money back into the platform after its failed sale in 2013. As *TechCrunch* wrote in 2014, "With $1 billion in revenue in 2013 and no signs of slowing down, Hulu's not going anywhere in the US. It just might not be going anywhere internationally, either" (Lawler 2014). The platform's promise to go global has been long promised but always deferred.

Geoblocking exemplifies a fundamental truth about television—that in spite of the McLuhanesque discourses of unfettered globalization we've seen emerge again and again throughout its history, the medium usually has a limited spatial reach. As a structural component of contemporary transnational viewing, geoblocking evokes and manages long-standing anxieties about media's transgression across political and geographical borders (Hilmes 1997, 15). Thus, the possibility for broadcasting signals to splay outward in all directions, or what media historian Thomas Streeter has called their "omnidirectionality" (1996, 61), combined with the industrial imperative for powerful stakeholders to control this condition, find contemporary analogs in geoblocking. Through the possibilities of IP address detection, Hulu attempts to ensure that its national windows remain intact even as users regularly find ways of circumventing digital geoblocks. Most popularly, viewers will connect to prohibited platforms using proxy servers or virtual private networks (VPNs), which fool a platform into thinking that they are connecting from a different country. Many companies sell access to proxy and VPN services, and in response Hulu has begun to block IP addresses associated with these commercial services (Ernesto 2014). Even as viewers find workarounds, Hulu is committed to remaining a national platform.

This is a cultural issue as much as an industrial or political-economic one. Geoblocking sets conditions for who around the world can participate in viewing, sharing, and talking about global television, and which countries the media industries perceive as most valuable—and not simply in economic terms. On the viewer end, encounters with geoblocked platforms can remind us of where we exist within these global hierarchies, and they lay bare the continued salience of geographic borders in digital culture. As Ira Wagman and Peter Urquhart have recently argued about geoblocking in Canada, confrontations with geoblocked technologies remind Canadians of the "power of place" even while the rhetoric of the borderless Internet surrounds VOD (2014, 125). Indeed, Hulu's unavailability in that country is often particularly frustrating to Canadians, due to the demand for American television north of the border and the cultural proximity between the two nations (Hertz 2014). All this is to say that geoblocking is not merely a way to coldly draw geographical borders around a particular platform. It serves to align Hulu with American television as a cultural-geographic enterprise.

HULU'S INTER/NATIONAL PROGRAMMING

Ironically, while Hulu's distribution practices and technological makeup indicate its composition as a national platform, it likely does not strike its average user as obviously and apparently American. Rather, it elides its nationality in two major ways. The first is through the promotion of the Hulu brand as not having any identifiable national ties—as always *potentially* global. It does not incorporate the aesthetics of nationalism, or the nation, as part of its brand. Instead, it brands itself as perceptibly but vaguely global—a strategy exemplified by the aforementioned alien-takeover ad campaign's slogan that the platform is "an evil plot to destroy the world." Hulu's "globalness" generally is not presented in Benneton-style, corporate multicultural terms as much as it evokes a sense of blank placelessness in its antiseptic, clean tech-sheen. This glossy aesthetic is part of a broader design practice shared by streaming platforms to mask their infrastructural complexity behind simple, user-friendly interfaces (Vonderau 2015, 719). More deeply, however, it ensures that the platform remains devoid of any identifiable "cultural odor" (Iwabuchi 2002). Thus, Hulu often trades on familiar discourses of utopian ubiquity that are actually at odds with its limited geographic accessibility.

At the same time, the platform also presents itself as global (or at least transnational) through its slate of what it calls "international" programming. This mainly comprises Korean dramas, Anime, British TV, telenovelas and other Spanish-language series, and some Canadian programs. This content is designed to reach two broad, heterogeneous, and occasionally overlapping audience groups: (1) mediaphiles who self-identify as, for instance, Anglophiles, anime fans, Korean drama fans, or general cosmopolitans, and (2) diasporic viewers interested in material to which they have some kind of cultural proximity. We can see this, for example, in the platform's deal to stream programs from Univision, the US-based Spanish language television network with whom Hulu made a non-exclusive distribution deal in 2011 (Stelter 2011), as well as its partnership with DramaFever, the Korean drama streaming platform that provides content to Hulu ("DramaFever" 2010). Even still, the platform's international library is in line with the corporate practice of targeting diaspora groups as niche, narrowcast market segments within American media culture. So, although Hulu promotes this programming (and its audience) as international to some degree, it simultaneously characterizes this audience as national by incorporating cosmopolitan and diasporic viewers into national television structures. Furthermore, even if Hulu does not outwardly present its audience or its programming in obviously national terms, its hybrid offerings are promoted to an audience defined nationally through the geographic limitations made possible by geoblocking. The strategy of offering a wide variety of American and foreign programming on one platform—a practice that Kompare (2014) aptly characterizes as seemingly "scattershot in an era of increasing cultural niches"—in fact makes sense if we consider Hulu as something akin to a traditional American cable provider. Like a cable provider,

Hulu serves a rather distinct geographic market (though in this case defined as national rather than local or regional), while at the same time attempting to reach as many consumers as possible by offering a diverse menu of options. If, as Michael Newman argues, one of television's "traditional" identities is as a local or national medium and one of its "emergent" identities is as a globalized and cosmopolitan one (2012, 468), Hulu shows how the traditional and the emergent comingle in contemporary on-demand television.

FROM CABLE TO HULU... TO CABLE

Hulu's existence as a national television platform first and foremost is underscored by its recently launched live television service. The service costs $39.99 a month and offers a "skinny bundle" that includes livestreams of programming from various properties run by Hulu's owners: ESPN, The Disney Channel, FX, Cartoon Network, and many others along with NBC, ABC, and Fox (Dent 2016). The platform's live service is often compared to cable in the trades, and indeed many point to it as a major reason for Time Warner buying into the platform. As the telecom conglomerate contends with viewers ditching their cable subscriptions in favor of various combinations of streaming services, its deal with Hulu ensures that the platform's live service will get much of the conglomerate's content out to viewers even if they cut the cord. So, while we tend to talk about streaming television platforms in terms of fragmentation, individualization, time-shifting, and a la carte viewing, Hulu's future could look pretty familiar: a nation-bound platform offering a variety of programs and channels to different niche audiences tuning in live. Ultimately, then, rather than exemplifying a forward march toward a new future of televisual ubiquity, unrestrained access, and radically new ways of selling and viewing television, Hulu shows how online TV blends emergent technologies and cultural practices with rather traditional understandings of television as a nationally defined exhibitor of TV programs.

REFERENCES

Dent, Steve. 2016. "Hulu Will Host All Turner Networks on Its New Live Service." *Engadget*, August 3. www.engadget.com/2016/08/03/hulu-will-host-all-turner-networks-on-its-new-live-service.

"DramaFever Brings Asia's Top TV Hits to Hulu." 2010. *DramaFever*, May 18. www.dramafever.com/news/dramafever-partners-with-hulu.

Elkins, Evan. 2016. "The DVD Region Code System: Standardizing Home Video's Disjunctive Global Flows." *International Journal of Cultural Studies* 19: 225–40.

Ernesto. 2014. "Hulu Blocks VPN Users over Piracy Concerns." *TorrentFreak*, April 25. https://torrentfreak.com/hulu-blocks-vpn-users-over-piracy-concerns-140425.

Havens, Timothy. 2006. *Global Television Marketplace*. London: British Film Institute.

Hertz, Barry. 2014. "Hulu Takes Aim at Netflix, Leaving Canadians Sidelined." *Maclean's*, January 8. www.macleans.ca/culture/hulu-takes-aim-at-netflix-leaving-canadians-on-the-sidelines.

Hilmes, Michele. 1997. *Radio Voices: American Broadcasting, 1922–1952*. Minneapolis: University of Minnesota Press.

Iwabuchi, Koichi. 2002. *Recentering Globalization: Popular Culture and Japanese Transnationalism*. Durham: Duke University Press.

James, Meg. 2014. "Hulu to Sell Its Japan Service to Nippon TV." *Los Angeles Times*, February 27. http://articles.latimes.com/2014/feb/27/entertainment/la-et-ct-hulu-japan-service-sold-to-nippon-tv-20140227.

Johnson, Catherine. 2012. *Branding Television*. New York: Routledge.

Kompare, Derek. 2014. "Adverstreaming: Hulu Plus." *Flow* 19. htttp://www.flowjournal.org/2014/02/adverstreaming-hulu-plus.

Lawler, Ryan. 2014. "Hulu Says Sayonara, Sells Off Japanese Unit to Nippon TV." *TechCrunch*, February 27. https://techcrunch.com/2014/02/27/hulu-says-sayonara-sells-off-japanese-unit-to-nippon-tv.

Lobato, Ramon and James Meese (eds.). 2016. *Geoblocking and Global Video Culture*. Amsterdam: Institute of Network Cultures.

Lotz, Amanda D. 2014. *The Television Will Be Revolutionized*, 2nd edition. New York: New York University Press.

"NBC Universal, GE Call Online Video Venture 'Hulu.'" 2007. *Wall Street Journal*, August 30.

Newman, Michael Z. 2012. "Free TV: File-Sharing and the Value of Television." *Television & New Media* 13: 463–79.

Steel, Emily. 2016. "At CES, Netflix Adds over 130 Countries to Streaming Service." *New York Times*, January 6. www.nytimes.com/2016/01/07/business/media/netflix-expands-its-streaming-service-worldwide.html?_r=0.

Stelter, Brian. 2011. "Hulu to Stream Spanish-Language Shows." *New York Times*, October 5. http://mediadecoder.blogs.nytimes.com/2011/10/05/hulu-to-stream-univision-shows/?_r=0.

Streeter, Thomas. 1996. *Selling the Air: A Critique of the Policy of Commercial Broadcasting in the United States*. Chicago: University of Chicago Press.

Turner, Graeme. 2009. "Television and the Nation: Does This Matter Anymore?" In *Television Studies after TV: Understanding Television in the Post-Broadcast Era*, edited by Graeme Turner and Jinna Tay, 54–64. London: Routledge.

Vonderau, Patrick. 2015. "The Politics of Content Aggregation." *Television & New Media* 16: 717–32.

Wagman, Ira and Urquhart, Peter. 2014. "'This Content Is Not Available in Your Region': Geoblocking Culture in Canada." In *Dynamic Fair Dealing: Creating Canadian Culture Online*, edited by Rosemary J. Coombe, Darren Wershler and Martin Zellinger, 124–32. Toronto: University of Toronto Press.

Weprin, Alex. 2010. "ABC Affils Get Plugged on Hulu." *Broadcasting and Cable*, April 12. www.broadcastingcable.com/news/programming/abc-affils-get-plugged-hulu/36307.

"Why Can't I Use Hulu Internationally? (Outside USA)." 2016. *Hulu Help Center*, April 27. https://help.hulu.com/articles/171122.

iQiyi

China's Internet Tigers Take Television
Michael Curtin and Yongli Li

iQiyi is the leading video streaming service in the People's Republic of China (PRC). Its surging popularity reflects significant changes in TV production and distribution. It also marks a transformation of the cultural experience of television in mainland China, allowing audiences to interact among themselves and with producers. Companies like iQiyi are furthermore building out services that forge innovative connections between the online and offline worlds, affecting a growing number of social activities and experiences. Whereas television once served as a proprietary instrument of the Communist Party, the medium has to a large extent passed into the hands of commercial enterprises such as Baidu, Alibaba, and Tencent, commonly referred to as "Internet Tigers." Although the Party maintains powerful influence over the medium, popular video streaming services like iQiyi have fueled a diversification of content and a dramatic transformation in the status and meaning of television.

China initially had a highly centralized network television system, but today it would be more appropriate to say that television in the PRC is part of a sprawling ensemble of media services, marking a distinctive and increasingly substantial break with the past. Some critics say we have moved into a post-network era, but the term fails to convey the shift from a broadcast era of centralized institutions, technologies, and social relations to a television environment that is far more malleable and dynamic than its predecessor. This is why online and mobile (O&M) media channels in China have much to teach us about the breathtaking changes currently taking place in East Asia and their implications for media systems worldwide.

The founding of the People's Republic of China in 1949 followed a half century of social strife engendered by a failing imperial dynasty, competing regional warlords, Japanese military invasion, and fierce civil war between Communist and Nationalist political factions. After the Communists took power, they found their ability to rule was challenged by the sheer size of the country as well as the cultural and linguistic diversity of its population. The new government therefore made a priority of speaking to its citizens with a single voice, using a highly centralized radio broadcasting system to serve as a "bridge" between the Communist Party and the people.

Television, however, did not begin to flourish until the 1980s, and like radio, it was initially managed from above. China Central Television (CCTV) operated as the flagship national service that was complemented by provincial, county, and municipal stations, all of them owned and overseen by bureaucrats and party officials. As satellite and cable television emerged during the 1990s, viewers enjoyed a growing selection of channels because it became possible to access the satellite signals of provincial channels from other parts of the country, with some stations becoming quite popular because they offered innovative or distinctive programming. Competition for audiences and advertisers began to grow, so that CCTV, despite its unchallenged leadership, began to roll out new specialty channels of its own, featuring news, movies, sports, and children's programming. Although new services mushroomed, government censorship and CCTV's favored status proved to be constraints on the range and creativity of programming. It was not until the rise of digital technologies that Chinese media started to become more prolific and freewheeling (Zhao 2008; Zhu 2012). iQiyi is therefore emblematic of a new era in Chinese television, but as we shall see, its success is based not only on technological innovation but also on its ability to mediate between audience aspirations, commercial imperatives, and the enduring power of the Communist state.

FROM ON AIR TO ONLINE

As in many other parts of the world, young people in China have been digital innovators, often developing services specifically for their peers rather than commercial or government purposes. As Internet services improved, the circulation of audiovisual content moved online and by 2005 the Chinese Internet was teaming with P2P sites that offered high quality film and television programs, many of them subtitled by volunteer teams of translators and fans. Urban, well-educated, and wealthy Chinese were early adopters of Internet services and many of them initially went online via computers they used at school, at work, and some cases at home (Yang 2011). Many other Chinese gained access at Internet cafes where they paid to log on, mainly to watch videos and play games (Qiu 2009). But the biggest surge in online use came with the popularization of smartphones, allowing personal and ongoing access to a burgeoning variety of resources where again, video proved to be one of the most popular (Keane 2015).

Between 2006 and 2016, the number of netizens in China skyrocketed from 137 million to 656 million, most of them smartphone users. China's telecommunications infrastructure also grew dramatically during this period, as did the number of O&M services, many of them commercial enterprises. Today, the leading companies in China's Internet economy are involved in most aspects of daily life, from news to shopping to socializing. These companies have also brought transformative change to Chinese entertainment with online video services that provide a far greater range of popular content than government-owned television channels (Zhao 2014; Zhao and Keane 2013).

This is not to say, however, that the government has been sidelined or disempowered. Around 2005, Communist Party officials began to express concern about the growth of unregulated video services, in part because the PRC was being pressured by foreign governments (especially the United States) to enforce intellectual property laws regarding the piracy of, for example, Hollywood movies. Officials were also concerned about the migration of many young Chinese away from state television to unregulated, and sometimes unruly, uses of the Internet. They therefore began to impose rules that required video sites to register with the government and to observe a set of standards that ultimately favored a few big companies. Most significantly, in 2008, the State Administration of Radio, Film, and Television (SARFT) implemented Document 56, which over the next few years reduced the number of streaming and download sites from over 250 to fewer than 10. Officials believed, quite correctly, that this would to some extent make it easier for the government to oversee the content and practices of online video channels. In the wake of this shakeout, iQiyi emerged as one of the leading providers of streaming video for the world's largest television market.

THE COMMERCIALIZATION OF ONLINE VIDEO

iQiyi is owned by Baidu, the company that runs China's largest search engine, which garners more than 80% of all searches in the PRC and more than 90% of search-related advertising. Worldwide, it is second only to Google in the very prosperous online search industry. Co-founder Robin Yanhong Li leads the company, which was listed on the NASDAQ stock exchange in 2005, giving the company access to global financing to support the development of a broad range of services that include information, navigation, social media, and e-commerce. Over all, the company generates more than $10 billion in annual revenue and is considered one of the top three Internet companies in China. Baidu began to move into video streaming in 2010 when it helped Tim Gong Yu, an experienced O&M media executive, establish iQiyi. Initially the company operated as an independent enterprise, but at the end of the following year it was folded into Baidu.

During the early years of video streaming in China, most sites provided user-generated content (UGC) or unlicensed videos from abroad. Under Gong Yu's leadership, however, iQiyi focused on the delivery of licensed content, including feature films, TV series, and variety shows. By the end of 2012, iQiyi was the second most successful streaming service (Baidu 2012, 45). The following year, Baidu acquired PPStream, a company that mainly provided P2P services, and merged it with iQiyi. By the end of 2013, iQiyi had become the leading online video platform in China, serving most of its users via mobile devices (Baidu 2014, 46). Although iQiyi acquired most of its content from professional producers, it also began to produce some of its own programming and build out a social media component to facilitate user communication and interaction. User recommendations, reviews, and commentary have proven to be powerful forms of promotion, especially because a substantial amount of iQiyi's content comes from foreign producers that do not have the capacity for conducting promotional campaigns in China.

iQiyi's rapid rise to leadership has nevertheless been accompanied by fierce competition from other providers, such as Youku Tudou, Tencent Video, and Sohu Video. Each of these services is backed by deep-pocketed corporations that believe online video will someday be both a profitable and indispensable element of leading Internet-based conglomerates. So far, however, their ongoing profitability remains unproven. This is partly due to the fact that audiences have been reluctant to pay for subscriptions, forcing the companies to rely on advertising revenue to support their expensive operational costs. Just as significantly, the cost of programming has skyrocketed as channels compete with each other for premium content and especially for exclusive rights to popular films and television programs. This requires providers to cover the shortfall with funds from other divisions of the conglomerate.

iQiyi PROGRAMMING

In June 2016, China had 514 million online video viewers with 37% between the ages of 20 and 29 and another 24% between the ages of 30 and 39. Thus, more than 60% of the audience for online video is in the demographic group that is most desirable to advertisers. These viewers are also considered the most likely purchasers of subscription video on demand (SVOD) channels. Another 18% are students, who are less likely to subscribe during their school years, but are considered good candidates for future enrollment (CNSA, CINIC 2016).

Currently, the vast majority of iQiyi viewers opt for free streaming content that is accompanied by copious amounts of advertising; but for less than $3 per month, iQiyi also offers a premium service with no advertising, supplementary content, and superior functionality. Indeed, the quality of the premium service surpasses its counterparts in Western countries. For a relatively low price iQiyi provides a very broad range of content, social media enhancements, and an extensive array of supplementary information and ancillary products. By the end of 2016, iQiyi claimed to have 481 million active monthly users, although only 20 million of them subscribed to the premium channel (Frater 2016). The company is aiming to triple the number of subscribers by 2020 (Jewel 2016).

Like all streaming services in China, iQiyi's main objective is to grow the number of paying subscribers, and therefore its main target audience is the youth demographic described above, which means it has a programming philosophy that is very different from the government-owned television channels. The latter must please party officials while also aiming for a broad mass audience. By comparison, iQiyi focuses on young viewers looking for shows that are unlikely candidates for inclusion on broadcast TV. This audience is also distinguished by the fact that it views most programs on mobile devices at work or in transit. Commuting time in major Chinese cities averages 90 minutes a day, mostly on public transport. iQiyi's parent company, Baidu, is especially well positioned to understand and respond to the behaviors and tastes of these viewers, as suggested by the periodic online surveys it conducts of millions of commuters in major cities across the country (Nelson 2015).

The breadth of iQiyi's services are truly expansive, offering licensed content on 30 channels that feature domestic and foreign TV series, blockbuster commercial films,

FIGURE 32.1 *iQiyi offers a wide range of domestic and foreign content, including* Descendants of the Sun, *the most popular Korean TV drama of 2016, which this ad promotes as exclusive content on the iQiyi VIP subscription service.*

and art house independent movies from countries like US, UK, France, Korea, and Japan. It also caters to audiences for animation, sports, and news. Initially most of its content was licensed from abroad and over the years, iQiyi has bargained with foreign distributors for shorter release windows, so that titles that used to take months to clear now appear within weeks of their overseas premier. Foreign programming has been crucial to the company's success because, until recently, government-run film and television institutions controlled most domestic content production, leaving relatively little room for commercial services. Audiences were likewise constrained, but many adventurous young viewers nevertheless turned to pirated videodiscs and online web servers where they developed a taste for foreign programming. As this audience mushroomed, iQiyi seized the opportunity to develop a commercial service with licensed content that responded both audience aspirations and official policy guidance.

Interestingly, iQiyi's distinctive leadership niche grew out its ability to tap the astounding popularity of trendy "youth idol" TV dramas from South Korea. The term "youth idol" actually originated in Japan during the 1970s when talent agents began to systematically recruit, train, and manage young talent across a range of media. Managers cultivated the musical, acting, and promotional talents of young and unproven performers, signing them to long-term contracts and then engineering their rise to stardom. The few that succeeded became heartthrobs for passionate young fans, and some even became popular with audiences overseas. Given this success, the strategy spread overseas and was adapted to media in other parts of East Asia, including Korea where during the 1990s, a surge of feature films, TV shows, and musical performaces that contributed to what became known regionally as Hallyu—the "Korean Wave" of exported pop culture. Although the quality of Korean content has waxed and waned for 20 years, recent TV series have proven extraordinarily popular with iQiyi's target audience in China. iQiyi has therefore spent lavishly on Korean television imports.

The first big uptick came in 2013 when iQiyi showcased *My Love From the Star*, a romantic fantasy about an alien from a distant solar system stranded on earth four centuries ago during the Joseon dynasty. Because he does not age at the same rate as humans, he appears eternally youthful, handsome, and athletic, but this also proves to be a curse, as he must change his identity periodically in order to avoid detection. For centuries he lives a solitary existence while awaiting a rescue mission that will take him back home. With only three years left until the mission's arrival, he works as a college professor in modern-day Seoul when unexpectedly he falls in love with his next-door neighbor—who turns out to be a famous Hallyu actress.

Crisp scripts, special effects, and glamorous youth idols helped to make *My Love From the Star* a huge success in South Korea. Clever product placement also resulted in a surge of fashion and cosmetics sales, turning the show into a trendsetter among young viewers. This wave of enthusiasm spread to the mainland as Chinese celebrities began to post praise for the program on social media. iQiyi paid a record-setting $735,000 for exclusive rights to 21 episodes, which were reportedly streamed more than 14 billion times during the show's initial run (Kang 2016; Lin 2014; "Chinese" 2016).

iQiyi consequently became a regular customer of Korean producers and established a dedicated subchannel for Korean dramas, licensing top shows and furthermore weighing in as an investor during the production phase in order to secure advance streaming rights for mainland China. In 2016 it scored another spectacular hit with *Descendants of the Sun*, a romantic medical-military drama that cost almost $11 million to produce. iQiyi reportedly provided more than 40% of the total production cost up front, paying $250,000 to stream each episode on the same day and date of the South Korean broadcast. This represented a staggering sevenfold increase over what iQiyi paid only three years earlier for *My Love From the Star*, providing a stark indication of the intense and growing competition for Korean shows.

To some extent, the investment in *Descendants* paid off. As with *My Love From the Star*, the show drew billions of views and according to Korea's Yonhap News Agency, iQiyi's subscriber base grew by 50% during the run of the series, generating about $30 million in additional revenue. But the show also attracted the attention of Chinese government officials. In fact, the Ministry of Public Security posted a warning on its Weibo social media account that "watching Korean dramas could be dangerous, and even lead to legal troubles" (Tan 2016). Officials also began to express unease about other popular foreign shows on streaming media, both publicly and in conversations with company executives. Perhaps most dramatically, in 2014 government bureaucrats snatched several of the most popular foreign shows off the Internet and licensed them exclusively to government-run broadcasting channels. *The Big Bang Theory* was, for example, rerouted to CCTV, which was put in charge of editing and translating a "healthy" version for the Chinese mass audience (Mikinen and Flint 2014). These political developments, along with the rising cost and limited availability of popular foreign shows have encouraged iQiyi to escalate its commitment to domestic content, not simply acquiring rights but also producing shows of its own.

iQiyi PICTURES

In July 2014, three months after the *Big Bang*, Baidu founded iQiyi Pictures to develop and produce original feature films and television programs, making it the second major streaming service to take the plunge. In 2015, it co-produced 14 movies and TV series and 18 the following year, ranging from commercial feature film blockbusters like *The Monkey King 2* to art house films like *Kaili Blues*. CEO Gong Yu contends that iQiyi is an attractive co-production partner, because in addition to financing and distribution clout, it can also offer marketing support on Baidu's platform and online ticketing for theatrically released titles. Perhaps most importantly, iQiyi can use Baidu's vast compendium of data on the viewing preferences of Chinese netizens. Given its commanding position in the search business, Baidu enjoys privileged access to data about popular topics, tastes, and preferences, which iQiyi producers can turn to their advantage.

It therefore is not surprising that one of iQiyi Picture's early successes proved to be *The Lost Tomb*, a TV adaptation of Kennedy Lei Xu's series of Internet novels. In China, Internet novels enjoy special popularity with young readers because they are not subjected to the same level of official vetting as printed books. Lei Xu, sometimes referred to as the "Chinese Stephen King," became renowned for stories that mix adventure and history with supernatural elements, the latter of which is a sensitive subject with government censors. Although iQiyi was intimately involved in financing and development, *The Lost Tomb* video series was helmed by H&R Century Pictures, a subsidiary of Beijing Enlight Media, an experienced producer and distributor of many feature films and TV shows that have scored well with young audiences. The first episodes launched in June 2015 and enjoyed rapid success, becoming the most popular Chinese web drama of the year.

The Lost Tomb recounts the adventures of a young antique shop owner who comes from a family of tomb raiders. His investigations and discoveries not only yield insights about the Warring States period more than 2,000 years ago but also offer clues to a tragic massacre that took the lives of some of his ancestors. Reportedly, the series drew more than five million new subscribers as well as billions of streams (Yan 2016).

Building on this success, iQiyi Pictures then developed another series based on Xu's work, this one set in the 1930s and featuring a hunt for clues that would eventually unravel a sinister plot by Japanese military occupation forces. *Old Nine Gates* was budgeted lavishly at more than $500,000 per episode, so iQiyi collaborated with Dragon TV, the government-owned municipal channel in Shanghai, which also distributes its signal nationally via satellite. The series premiered in June 2016, with iQiyi releasing each episode to its paid subscribers at 10 p.m. on Mondays and Tuesdays, the same time as the Dragon TV broadcasts (Tang 2016). Two hours later, iQiyi's remaining audience could stream the show. Impressively, this strategy paid off for both partners as the show attracted more than four billion online views and drew a solid broadcast audience as well.

Other important iQiyi genres include reality and variety shows, which feature far greater experimentation than their broadcasting counterparts on government-owned stations. For example, *U Can U BiBi* is a weekly talk show competition anchored by a panel of celebrity judges that give two competing teams a hot topic to discuss, such as "Should we shield our parents from social media?" or "Should we urge a friend to repay a loan?" Judges evaluate team members on both the content of their argument and the style of presentation. Indeed, style and affect are key elements of the show as indicated by the title, *U Can U BiBi*, which is saucy Internet slang that translates as: if you think you can say it better, then just stand up and say it.

Usually *U Can* topics aim to raise controversial issues while skirting the boundaries of censorship, but during the second season government officials intervened to ban a single episode without comment. The topic: "Should homosexual marriage be legalized?" This episode was especially contentious due to the fact that one of the judges was a famous transgender dancer and another was an openly gay and very popular Taiwanese TV host. Moreover, two of the contestants were out of the closet, contributing to a highly personalized exploration of the topic. Even though the episode was banned, news of the government's action spread, generating a tremendous amount of online commentary about the topic (Quingyun 2015).

In this context, each episode of *U Can U BiBi* draws more than 15 million views. Although those numbers are far smaller than popular dramas, the show contributes to a wide-ranging universe of variety shows where experimentation and controversy are often rewarded by passionate audience engagement. The success of such shows stems partly from a more relaxed censorship environment as well as lower production costs. Furthermore, and quite importantly, the O&M distribution platform allows new shows to evolve without having to compete for broadcast airtime. Unlike linear television, a new show does not have to displace an older one. At the 2016 China Internet Audio-Video Industry Forum, iQiyi vice president Chen Wei claimed that some 90 web variety shows in 2015 generated $145 million in revenue, a figure that is projected to grow to $825 million by 2020. Thus, variety shows are becoming an increasingly important component of iQiyi's programming mix.

iQiyi's variety/reality shows also allow movie, music, and broadcast TV stars the opportunity to exploit and expand their popularity with a core fan base. In many cases, iQiyi purchases exclusive streaming rights to popular reality shows from provincial satellite TV channels that feature major entertainment personalities. For example, *Running Man* features actors, singers, and comedians that compete as teams to complete a series of missions as part of a season-long race. The show was originally developed by a South Korean TV station, which then licensed the format to the provincial Zhejiang TV station, based in Hangzhou. The teams are mostly comprised of young performers who appreciate the national exposure they get via satellite broadcasts. At the same time, however, their core fan base aligns with iQiyi's demographic of 13- to 39-year-old viewers, most of whom follow the show on smartphones and tablets. Therefore iQiyi is able to share production costs on the series, but just as importantly, both the partners (and performers) benefit from cross-fertilization across media.

Just as film and television stars can benefit from Internet variety/reality shows, the reverse is also true: "wang hong" (Internet celebrities) can develop a fan base online that can pave the way to guest appearances in film and television, all the while driving more traffic to streaming platforms like iQiyi in which they already thrive (Flemming 2016;

FIGURE 32.2 U Can U Bibi *has generated online buzz about controversial topics, creating a sizable fan base for the show. Internet celebrities ("wang hong") often appear as guest stars and are prominently promoted in ads like this.*

Tsoi 2016). Streaming services can also serve as a testing ground to innovative programs with small audiences that ultimately become transmedia phenomena, spinning off branded counterparts in broadcasting, cinema, or gaming.

CONCLUSION

In China, the very concept of television and of a television channel has undergone dramatic changes since the 1980s. Initially, government-controlled CCTV served as the only channel between the Communist Party and the Chinese people. Satellite, cable, and home video then expanded the range of offerings during the 1990s, followed by the rise of online and mobile media that have engendered a wide diversity of channels, genres, and content. These services offer far greater variety than their counterparts abroad and they provide sophisticated interfaces, functionality, and interactive features.

At the center of this transformation are services like iQiyi, one of the leading innovators in the digital media universe. Party and government leaders therefore hail it as a national champion and as a counterweight to the daunting global influence of companies like Time Warner, Fox, Google, and Facebook. Yet the government is also leery of O&M media, perhaps realizing that its former monopoly over television has swiftly and unexpectedly slipped from its hands. The Party has therefore sought numerous ways to assert its influence over the content and structure of these new channels in both formal and informal ways. Companies like iQiyi have largely been cooperative and deferential, but at the same time they are aware that they must cater to the needs and desires of their preferred customers lest they drift away to competitors or to pirated content from abroad. Streaming services are especially concerned about young viewers given their spending power and demonstrated desire for access to a diverse range of programming content. iQiyi also has to be responsive to investors on Wall Street where the company is subject to ongoing scrutiny by the investment community. Its commercial success is therefore measured by very different metrics than those embraced and promoted by government officials and Communist Party leaders.

Consequently, the development of television in China is being shaped by multiple and sometimes conflicting forces that so far have fostered the proliferation of many new and innovative channels that nevertheless must operate under the enduring pressures and constraints exerted by the Communist Party. The growing power of iQiyi therefore represents a significant shift for Chinese television, which in the 1980s served largely as a national medium with a singular voice, but today supports hundreds of channels—across broadcast, satellite, cable, online, and mobile—that envision their audiences along various axes defined by age, gender, taste, and locality.

REFERENCES

Baidu, Inc. 2012. "2012 Annual Report." December 31. http://media.corporate-ir.net/media_files/IROL/18/188488/BaiduAR2012.pdf

Baidu, Inc. 2014. "2014 Annual Report." December 31. http://media.corporate-ir.net/media_files/IROL/18/188488/2016/2014%20Baidu%20Annual%20Report.pdf

China Netcasting Services Association, Chinese Internet Network Information Center. 2016. "Research Report on Internet Audio-Video Industry Development in China in 2016." www.dvbcn.com/2016/12/07-135580.html.

"Chinese Love for Descendants of the Sun Hits 2.3 Billion Views in Latest Episode." 2016. *AsiaOne*, April 11. http://news.asiaone.com/news/showbiz/chinese-love-descendants-sun-hits-22-billion-views-latest-episode.

Flemming, Sam. 2016. "The State of Chinese Social Media in 2016: What You Need to Know." *Advertising Age*, August 10. http://adage.com/article/viewpoint/state-chinese-social-media-2016/305392/.

Frater, Patrick. 2016. "China Video Platform iQiyi Reaches 20 Million Subscribers." *Variety*, June 14. http://variety.com/2016/digital/asia/iqiyi-reaches-20-million-subscribers-1201795179/.

Hong, Yu. 2017. *Networking China: The Digital Transformation of the Chinese Economy*. Urbana: University of Illinois Press.

Jewel, Catherine. 2016. "iQiyi on China's Booming Online Film Market." *WIPO Magazine*, May. www.wipo.int/wipo_magazine/en/2016/05/article_0007.html.

Kang, John. 2016. "Korean Drama 'Descendants of the Sun' Breaks Records Thanks to Chinese Investments." *Forbes*, April 5. www.forbes.com/sites/johnkang/2016/04/05/korean-drama-descendants-of-the-sun-breaks-records-thanks-to-chinese-investments/.

Keane, Michael. 2015. *The Chinese Television Industry*. London: Palgrave Macmillan.

Lin, Lilian. 2014. "Korean TV Show Sparks Chicken and Beer Craze in China." *Wall Street Journal*, February 26. http://blogs.wsj.com/chinarealtime/2014/02/26/korean-tv-show-sparks-chicken-and-beer-craze-in-china/.

Mikinen, Julie and Joe Flint. 2014. "'Big Bang Theory,' Other U.S. Shows Vanish from Chinese Internet." *Los Angeles Times*, April 28. www.latimes.com/entertainment/envelope/cotown/la-et-ct-china-blackout-20140429-story.html.

Nelson, Katie. 2015. "Beijing's Commutes Worst in China, Followed by Shanghai's." *Shanghaiist*, January 28. Accessed February 26, 2017. http://shanghaiist.com/2015/01/28/commuters_in_beijing_have_it.php.

Qiu, Jack Linchuan. 2009. *Working-Class Network Society: Communication Technology and the Information Have-Less in Urban China*. Cambridge: MIT Press.

Quingyun. 2015. "In China, Government Still Holds a Conservative Attitude toward Same-Sex Relationships." *Ball State Daily*, September 25. www.ballstatedaily.com//blog/the-494/2015/09/the-494-news-chinese-government-coservative-view.

Tan, Huileng. 2016. "Beijing's New Worry: A TV Drama That's Just Too Hot." *CNBC*, March 16. www.cnbc.com/2016/03/16/descendants-of-the-sun-smash-hit-prompts-beijing-to-warn-on-south-korean-dramas.html.

Tang, Ping. 2016. "Zhang Yixing Takes the *Hua Dan* Role 'Old Nine Gates': The Investment of the Show Has Exceeded 169 Million RMB." *People's Daily*, June 7. http://ent.people.com.cn/n1/2016/0607/c1012-28418770.html.

Tsoi, Grace. 2016. "Wang Hong: China's Online Stars Making Real Cash." *BBC News*, August 1. www.bbc.com/news/world-asia-china-36802769.

Yan, Pengfei. 2016. "'The Descendants of the Sun' Goes Viral, iQiyi Makes at Least 190 Million RMB." *The Paper*, March 27. www.thepaper.cn/newsDetail_forward_1449154.

Yang, Guobin. 2011. *The Power of the Internet in China: Citizen Activism Online*. New York: Columbia University Press.

Zhao, Elaine Jing. 2014. "The Micro-Movie Wave in a Globalising China: Adaptation, Formalisation and Commercialisation." *International Journal of Cultural Studies* 17 (5): 453–67.

Zhao, Elaine Jing and Michael Keane. 2013. "Between Formal and Informal: The Shakeout in China's Online Video Industry." *Media, Culture & Society* 35 (6): 724–41.

Zhao, Yuezhi. 2008. *Communication in China: Political Economy, Power, and Conflict*. Lanham: Rowman & Littlefield Publishers.

Zhu, Ying. 2012. *Two Billion Eyes: The Story of China Central Television*. New York: The New Press.

Amazon Prime Video

Where Information Is Entertainment

Karen Petruska

After a disappointing debut with shows like *Alpha House* (2013–) and *Betas* (2013), Amazon Prime Video has more recently gained acclaim as an online television network for its original programming, winning Emmys for *Transparent* (2014–) and a Golden Globe for *Mozart in the Jungle* (2014–). Yet while Amazon invests in content, its programming serves significantly different functions than comparable content at more traditional broadcast and cable networks as well as subscription streaming media services like Netflix and HBO Now. Sure enough, all of these services seek to develop prestigious content that encourages audiences to be dedicated to their subscriptions; but as former head of production arm Amazon Studios Roy Price explained, Amazon doesn't want the show that is sort of liked by everyone—instead, it wants the quirky show really liked by a small but passionate group (Jarvey 2014). Beyond this interest in smaller niches, Amazon's programming also needs to fulfill another rather different job than mere entertainment; instead, content attracts customers to the Amazon website to initiate, extend, and solidify a relationship between that customer and all of Amazon's retail and service lines.

In 2013, David Carr reflected on the significance of Amazon's first attempt at original television programming, *Alpha House*, a program that has yet to be officially cancelled (de Moraes 2016) but has not aired an episode since completing its second season in 2014. While comparing the program to Netflix's *House of Cards*, Carr distinguished Amazon's TV content strategy by referring to the "flywheel effect." The flywheel is a business concept that says an established commercial enterprise can keep its proverbial wheel spinning (or momentum increasing) with small additions to that core business (Carr 2013). According to Carr's article, *Alpha House* helped sustain Amazon's growth objectives as an online retail company, and the flywheel has continued to resonate as a metaphor for the role of television within the company. Amazon founder Jeffrey Bezos himself described the company's original television content this way in his 2015 annual report letter to stockholders. After describing *The Man in the High Castle* as their "most-viewed show," Bezos writes, "these shows are great for customers, and they feed the Prime flywheel," by encouraging Prime members to renew their annual subscriptions (Bezos 2016). As part of the flywheel effect, Amazon's television content must be considered within the broader context of Amazon's larger goals and consumer product divisions. While key competitors in streaming television like Netflix, HBO, and Hulu all focus on television content, Amazon sells a wide-range of products and services, including books, home and garden products, electronics, video games, clothing, accessories and beauty products, and others. Television, for Amazon, is merely one part of a much larger and complex enterprise.[1]

Analysts and journalists trying to understand Amazon's remarkable growth have pointed towards its devotion to exceptional customer service and its technological innovations (including its "one-click" purchase option, Kindle device, and the cloud storage business "Amazon Web Services"). In terms of television, however, it is Amazon's Prime shipping service that most distinguishes its approach to video content. Having already offered free shipping for purchases over $25, Amazon created the Prime subscription program in 2005, promising the benefit of free, two-day shipping to those willing to pay for a year's membership up front, at the rate of $79 per year.[2] Amazon's Prime approach was risky, with the company spending more than it took in from subscription fees to attract and retain users. Since then, Amazon has intensified its determination to add value to Prime, adding streaming video in 2011 as a free benefit to subscribers, with an initial library of around 5,000 programs. Prime also now includes discounts on diapers and other benefits for "Amazon Moms," access to a streaming music service, freebies for Kindle users and gamers, and unlimited photo storage. As one journalist described the company's approach to innovation, "Spend money. Spend more money. See what happens" (Sternbergh 2015). The relationship between Prime and Amazon's television content most distinguishes the company when compared with Netflix, Hulu, HBO, and other terrestrial and digital networks.

Despite these significant differences between Amazon and the competition at Netflix, Hulu, and HBO, all these companies streaming television content online share a common struggle to adapt their business models to an online environment that has weakened the mandate for consumers to pay for content (Lobato and Thomas 2015). As Chris Anderson explores in *Free: The Future of a Radical Price*, digital distribution innovations have pushed down prices online, resulting in a variety of experiments to fund the production and sale of media distributed through the Internet (2009). In a landmark year for streaming, 2011 marked a moment when the technology had advanced and the costs had lessened to make streaming viable, both financially and functionally (Seymour 2012). Since then, subscription video on demand (SVOD) has emerged as a crucial piece of the overall financing strategy for online content, with Netflix's direct-to-consumer subscription model one prominent example of a shift within the media industries (Tryon 2015). Although Netflix generates the most attention in popular press discourses for its programming, its global expansion efforts, and its pricing, Amazon, as a company once built on selling print media, has diversified dramatically. Accordingly, the way Amazon has incorporated online video access into its business model prompts a reconsideration of how we should incorporate streaming media entities into the frameworks of television and media industry studies.

To help develop these new frameworks, we can consider the ways Amazon reinforces long-standing business practices within the media industries while also defying expectations for how those practices should operate or generate revenue. Amazon is indicative of a larger debate within television and media industry studies about whether distribution or content demands more attention (Knee 2011; Perren 2013; Steemers 2014). These debates, while impossible to resolve, open up larger questions about content value and quality, the importance of infrastructure for the media business, and the intermediaries who sometimes go unnoticed behind the glamour of the content and its stars. Amazon's own investments in television content evoke similar questions, ultimately suggesting that television studies today must account for the logics of retail geared toward creating and maintaining markets for consumer product. However, the dynamics of scale and commercialism—deployed in pursuit of measurable sales across a field of retail products and services—simultaneously hint at the persistence of long established television industry frameworks. Even as Amazon may actively work to distance its video content from the idea of television, it nevertheless begs us to consider the continued relevance of television to the emerging content and infrastructure strategies of the tech-based retail sector.

SCALE AND THE COMMERCIAL LURE

The importance of Amazon's relationship with consumers cannot be overstated, particularly in understanding the investment it makes in Prime Video. Amazon is willing to lose money on services such as this because its primary goal is customer relationship maintenance (Tuttle 2013). In naming named Amazon its 1999 "Marketer of the Year," *Advertising Age* quoted the head of a marketing consultancy to observe: "What [Mr. Bezos] has done with Amazon.com [shows] he understands they are in the business of manufacturing consumer relations, not selling goods" (Williamson 1999). This quote highlights something significant when comparing Amazon's television business to its competitors—while Amazon makes its money selling a range of products, its true business is customer maintenance. To support this objective, Amazon Prime Video (like Prime more broadly) operates as a loss leader. Whether figured as the discovery vehicle that brings new visitors into the web of products and services sold by Amazon, or the value added that sustains the patronage of longtime customers, the television services of Amazon Prime Video function as marketing, as a brand builder, and as a reward for loyalty. For Amazon, content and distribution are interdependent, with television programming, retail product, and other service lines creating multiple points of engagement for Prime members, increasing their own dependence upon Amazon as a vendor. In fact, it is not unusual for Amazon executives to conflate its media content with other products for sale on the site. Bezos described this well in 2015: "You can have the best technology, you can have the best business model, but if the storytelling isn't amazing, it won't matter. . . . Nobody will watch. And then you won't sell more shoes" (Jarvey 2015).

All of Amazon's Prime benefits serve one end: to situate customers within its corporate ecosystem more fully, firmly, and inescapably. Discussing Prime's growth upon its ten-year anniversary, Vice President of Amazon Prime Global Greg Greeley addressed the company's motivation to add more benefits to the same Prime subscription: "Over the long term, we'll want to be able to unlock benefits across the whole ecosystem." As Greeley notes, Prime is a loyalty vehicle because all subscribers, no matter what part of Amazon's business attracted them, will have a reason to maintain their subscription (Tsukayama 2015). According to *Time* business journalists, Prime's real effect upon the marketplace is that it centralizes purchasing for members with Amazon: "The net result of Prime membership—and the thing that has to scare the bejesus out of Amazon's competition—is that it tends to cause subscribers to stop shopping anywhere else" (Tuttle 2013).

One continuity with traditional television practices, however, is Amazon's embrace of the strategy of scale; indeed, Amazon depends mightily upon achieving scale to underwrite the costs of Prime. Scale is a strategy for businesses with high upfront costs, particularly those like media production and distribution that require infrastructural investments. These large up-front costs are amortized, or spread out, across a broad customer (or viewer) base. Amazon's free and discounted shipping models, too, revolve around questions of scale. The creation of the Amazon Prime membership program in 2005 made investors nervous because the company was losing hundreds of millions on discounted shipping already (Birchall 2005; "Sales" 2005), but the company's leadership had confidence the economics would eventually work out if they achieved sufficient scale. The Prime subscription model, therefore, extends scale logics common to media industries, but with the added elegance and sophistication of offering entry into a wide-range of Amazon's consumer product lines.

As legendary cable executive Barry Diller commented, the foundations of Amazon Prime in a free shipping benefit makes its television subscription service something "no one has ever heard of" (Gruenwedel 2015a). That said, the link between Amazon's television business and the sale of consumer goods and services establishes clear continuities with the past. For decades television's financial success has depended upon sponsors underwriting the costs of developing and airing programs in order to attract viewers to advertising spots positioned within and between TV content. The fact that Amazon's content is supported through subscriptions rather than advertising sets it apart from traditional television alongside Netflix and HBO; upon closer inspection, the economics of Amazon reproduces some of the familiar structures and logics of advertising-supported television industries—but with a twist. Now, instead of television content serving as bait to lure the viewer to advertisements (Meyers 2009), Amazon's television content inspires Prime subscriptions and subsequent purchases meant to take advantage of that membership. Even though Amazon does not include spot ads as interstitials, the sale of consumer goods remains an a priori priority that undergirds its streaming business.

Among the many criticisms Amazon has faced as the "Walmart of the Web" for driving down prices, creating uncompetitive markets, relying upon exploitative labor practices, and extending from a cutthroat corporate culture (Kantor and Streitfeld 2015;

FIGURE 33.1 *Amazon Prime packaging reflects the company's linkage of shipping and video service.*

Kelly 2016; "Walmart" 2011), its use of media as a lure for consumer purchases extends potential critical suspicion about the commercialization of culture. In an article in the *New Yorker*, George Packer complained, "due to bargain basement prices, the book is no longer a thing of value—it is instead a widget" (Packer 2014). As part of the Amazon Prime package, TV content, too, functions as a widget—a small item whose purpose may be unclear in the wider range of products and consumer experiences forwarded by the company. To some extent, this is not new. Television has always been part of a bait and switch—come for the "free" entertainment program but "pay" by watching the ads. As a result, Amazon's treatment of TV content as a widget merely seems a perfection of the logic undergirding the advertiser-supported model.

PRIME DATA

All these consumer actions generate an incredible amount of consumer data, all proprietary, that allows Amazon to service customers across their points of contact with the company. Here, too, the importance of consumer data demonstrates continuity with the past of the television industries. The elusive "holy grail" of consumer product advertising has long been proof that traditional television advertisements generate subsequent purchases (Barr 2014). Amazon, in fact, has gathered data that suggests the relationship consumers have with and through Prime Video does indeed encourage consumption of further products. Like Netflix, Amazon has eschewed Nielsen ratings as a measure for success,[3] instead assessing Prime Video through metrics related to the Prime subscription package and consumer behavior within it. While Amazon does not reveal exact membership numbers for Prime (stating in its 2013 annual report that worldwide membership runs in the tens of millions), outside studies have reported two significant findings that confirm the value Amazon sees in the service: (1) Prime subscribers spend more than non-Prime members (maybe even two or three times as much, depending on the study) (Sternbergh 2015); and (2) Prime members who stream video content are more likely to renew their subscription (Gruenwedel 2015b). According to these findings, then, Prime Video encourages members to renew their subscription, which encourages them to spend much more money on Amazon.

Amazon's data is not just proof of the power of television to drive consumption of product, but also a means to enhance and support consumer relationships with the company. Because streaming technologies capture customer behavior with increasing reliability and specificity, data has become the currency of online economics. As early as 1999, *Advertising Age* noted that loyalty programs at commerce companies like Amazon were generating more specific and actionable consumer data for marketing purposes than that available to traditional media companies (Gilbert 1999). *Newsweek* observed that on Amazon, "information is entertainment," attracting and holding its customers through a variety of resources provided to empower them as buyers (Levy 1999). In other words, Amazon doesn't merely sell products—it sells information about products, and it sells unique mechanisms for interacting with those products. Early in its history in 1997, Amazon founder Jeff Bezos described Amazon's investment in collecting information as a boon to customers, who need to be informed, and as a boon for their product manufacturers, who need customers ("River" 1997). Yet as Amazon's reach across product and service lines has spread, its control over vast quantities of consumer data has transformed the company into what Bezos later described as an "artificial intelligence company," employing technology that allows the company to understand not only products but also individual customers and their needs (Spector 2000). In a 2016 letter to shareholders, Bezos lauded the company's "machine-learning tools," available to all their Amazon Web Services clients, which enable companies to track consumers more easily. As the *Atlantic* noted, Amazon Web Services is "the backbone of the commercial web," which means the data that drives Amazon also supports the business models of many other companies who use Amazon's software and tools (Lafrance 2017).

THE AMAZON STUDIOS DIFFERENCE

With these differences in market outlook and emphasis on ecosystems of consumer relationships, Amazon's content production and acquisition operations also put established television production cultures in tension with the worlds of tech-based retail. Reporters often contrast the culture at Amazon Studios with Hollywood's, describing the former as penny-pinching and unpredictable. Before his dismissal from Amazon Studios following allegations of sexual misconduct in 2017, Roy Price aligned the company's culture more with Silicon Valley as well, saying he was more likely to text than call, and you might have found him brown bagging it at his desk—except that Price was so hip he did not have a desk (Tate 2012). Yet the differences between Amazon and its competitors in television extend far beyond corporate culture. Traditional television players want Amazon to play by their rules—to release ratings, to support the syndication model where producers make the most money, to strive for the same forms of success as legacy companies, among others (Winslow 2012). A critical write-up of Amazon's TV business in the *Wall Street Journal* suggested morale was low in 2017 after Hulu and Netflix managed to win Emmy Awards while Amazon remained empty-handed. But these critiques fail to account for fundamental differences between streaming companies that focus exclusively on video content and Amazon where TV production is one of many, many ventures (Fritz and Flint 2017). Amazon maintains a distinct approach to television knowing that its content serves other, larger ends—its focus on customer relations—and that its efforts may not be best measured by the same notions of "quality" to which other television companies are dedicated.

In an article exploring Amazon's pilot process and its intersection with discourses of quality television, Cory Barker (2016) describes how the company works to distance its television content from traditional television. Efforts to promote programs like *Transparent* as more akin to film than television participates in a long tradition of equating quality with the "cinematic" and defining value in television programming as that which aspires to emulate more legitimate media (Newman and Levine 2012). This insistence of fundamental distinction between Amazon's programming and that of "television" resonates with the business practices that seek to make television newly operative in the creation and maintenance of customers for Amazon's online retail empire. Despite these distinctions in programming and economic practice, however, traditional television industry frameworks from scale to commercial lures to the disavowal of television in claims to quality all persist in the Amazon Prime Video model—despite the fact that digital code makes television content online as equivalent and interchangeable as zeroes and ones as the shoes Amazon also sells. In other words, even as Amazon treats television as a means to its end of building and maintaining consumer relationships largely based in retail, the logics that have long supported the business of television continue.

Even as the transformation of television viewers into product consumers intensifies and extends across a wide range of business, our understanding of television as a domestic medium tied to consumerism remains critically relevant. While I have compared Amazon to other companies that produce and distribute television content, future research may consider Amazon alongside its tech company competitors, including Apple, Google, Microsoft, and others who not only oversee hardware-software empires but also dabble in the television business as well. In each of these cases, we might expect the frameworks with which we understand television to give us some productive insight into how culture and content is being used at scale to move consumer products.

CONCLUSION

The point is not that Amazon Prime Video has advanced the death of television or Netflix or any other particular segment of the television industries. Despite countless articles predicting the death of this or that industry, "old media" forms persist, and competitive new media forms often align with those interests. For example, Comcast Corporation has partnered with Netflix to deliver its content through their Xfinity service (Swisher 2016). Amazon itself has been busy opening brick-and-mortar stores, including bookstores and a drive-through grocery store (Alter and Wingfield 2016). New media companies also continue to alter their own practices in response to market pressures, as Amazon has done in offering Prime Video as a separate, and monthly, subscription offer more reminiscent of cable (Soper 2016). Subscription as a business model may also evolve, as we are seeing with skinny bundles ("Cutting" 2016) and with reports of special offers that will create separate price points and unique deals based on consumer behavior (McNea 2017). Recent studies also predict a ceiling to how many subscriptions consumers will be willing to purchase, so one can safely assume not all will survive (Albiniak 2016). Television today is a fluid, evolving industry, hard to pin down.

In terms of television, though, Amazon's future seems fairly secure because while it built its brand on media (books), its business today is known more for its overall customer service and convenience than any one product line or any benefit. The company is somewhat immune from the normal risks of TV production because failures can be covered by any of its many alternate revenue streams. Amazon also does not suffer for licensed content because—for now, at least—it stands as a rival to larger perceived competitors, like Netflix, which allows it to benefit from blockbuster distribution deals and partnerships with PBS, HBO, Showtime, and Starz. The larger lesson of Amazon, however, may be that their emphasis upon technological innovation and maintenance of consumer relationships demands analysis based in the intersection of new media and retail with the television industries.

NOTES

1 It is worth noting that Amazon has long sold television and movies in hard copy, as DVDs and Blu-ray discs, and in digital formats, through electronic sell-through. These businesses

continue, even as Amazon is expanding its investment in original content production. For example, you can buy through Amazon DVDs of Netflix originals *House of Cards* and *Orange is the New Black*. Amazon originals *Transparent, Mozart in the Jungle*, and *Man in the High Castle* are not available in a DVD format through the Amazon site, however, suggesting that the company sees value in their exclusivity to the streaming service.

2 Amazon raised the price of Prime subscriptions from $79 to $99 in 2013.

3 Despite not being dependent upon advertiser support, HBO reports ratings data, and has worked with Nielsen to generate data for its SVOD service since 2007.

REFERENCES

Albiniak, Paige. 2016. "Netflix Raises the Ante for Hollywood." *Broadcasting & Cable*, March 28.

Alter, Alexandra and Nick Wingfield. 2016. "A Trip Through Amazon's First Physical Store." *New York Times*, March 10. Accessed February 15, 2017. www.nytimes.com/2016/03/12/business/media/a-virtual-trip-through-amazons-physical-store.html?_r=0.

Anderson, Chris. 2009. *Free: The Future of a Radical Price*. New York: Hyperion.

Barker, Cory. 2016. "'Great Shows, Thanks to You': From Participatory Culture to 'Quality TV' in Amazon's Pilot Season." *Television & New Media*. https://doi.org/10.1177/1527476416667817.

Barr, Alistair. 2014. "Google Tests a Way to Follow You to the Mall." *Wall Street Journal*, April 11. Accessed January 20, 2017. www.wsj.com/news/articles/SB10001424052702303847804579479672289163220?mod=WSJ_hp_RightTopStories&mg=reno64-wsj.

Bezos, Jeffrey B. 2016. *2015 Letter to Shareholders*. Seattle: Amazon.com.

Birchall, Jonathan. 2005. "Wall Street Skeptical on Amazon Delivery Pledge." *Financial Times*, May 19.

Carr, David. 2013. "Amazon Makes a Claim for the Living Room and Beyond." *New York Times*, November 4.

"Cutting the Cord: The Future of Television." 2006. *The Economist*, July 16.

de Moraes, Lisa. 2016. "*Alpha House* Is Shuttered, or Not, Amazon Exec Tells Frustrated TV Critics: TCA." *Deadline Hollywood*, August 7. Accessed April 5, 2017. http://deadline.com/2016/08/amazon-alpha-house-canceled-interestings-not-ordered-roy-price-tca-1201799950/.

Fritz, Ben and Joe Flint. 2017. "Where Amazon Is Failing to Dominate: Hollywood." *Wall Street Journal*, October 6. Accessed October 6, 2017. www.wsj.com/articles/where-amazon-is-failing-to-dominate-hollywood-1507282205.

Gilbert, Jennifer. 1999. "Commerce Strategies Drive Web Sites." *Advertising Age*, March 8.

Gruenwedel, Erik. 2015a. "Amazon Is Going to the Movies." *Home Media Magazine*, January 26.

Gruenwedel, Erik. 2015b. "Amazon Primes Its SVOD Biz with $1.3B." *Home Media Magazine*, February 9.

Jarvey, Natalie. 2014. "Amazon Studios Head Roy Price on Competing with Netflix, Xbox Studios' Demise (Q&A)." *Hollywood Reporter*, July 30.

Jarvey, Natalie. 2015. "The Secrets Inside Amazon's Shopping Cart." *The Hollywood Reporter*, July 24.

Kantor, Jodi and David Streitfeld. 2015. "Inside Amazon: Wrestling Big Ideas in a Bruising Workplace." *New York Times*, August 15. Accessed November 15, 2016. www.nytimes.com/2015/08/16/technology/inside-amazon-wrestling-big-ideas-in-a-bruising-workplace.html?_r=0.

Kelly, Lorraine. 2016. "Amazombies: Seven Seconds to Find an Item, Every Move Filmed and Blistering 12-hours Shifts with Timed Toilet Breaks. . . . What YOUR Christmas Order Does to Your 'Worker Elves!'" *Daily Mail*, December 3. Accessed January 8, 2017. www.dailymail.co.uk/news/article-3997864/Amazombies-Seven-seconds-item-filmed-blistering-12-hours-shifts-timed-toilet-breaks-Christmas-order-does-worker-elves.html.

Knee, Jonathan. 2011. "Why Content Isn't King." *Atlantic Monthly* 308 (1): 34, 36–38.

Lafrance, Adrienne. 2017. "Amazon Is Making It Easier for Companies to Track You." *The Atlantic*, April 14. Accessed April 14, 2017. www.theatlantic.com/technology/archive/2017/04/amazon-is-making-it-easier-for-companies-to-track-you/522999/.

Levy, Steven. 1999. "Wired for the Bottom Line." *Newsweek*, September 20.

Lobato, Ramon and Julian Thomas. 2015. *The Informal Media Economy*. Cambridge: Polity Press.

McNea, Blair. 2017. "How the Subscription Economy Will Change the Price We Pay." *Advertising Age*, February 17.

Meyers, Cynthia B. 2009. "From Sponsorship to Spots: Advertising and the Development of Electronic Media." In *Media Industries: History, Theory, and Method*, edited by Jennifer Holt and Alisa Perren, 69–80. Malden: Wiley-Blackwell.

Newman, Michael Z. and Elana Levine. 2012. *Legitimating Television*. New York: Routledge.

Packer, George. 2014. "Cheap Words." *New Yorker*, February 17.

Perren, Alisa. 2013. "Rethinking Distribution for the Future of Media Industry Studies." *Cinema Journal* 52 (3): 165–71.

"A River Runs Through It." 1997. *The Economist*, May 10.

"Sales, Frustrations Build at Amazon." 2005. *Publishers Weekly*, February 7.

Seymour, Chris. 2012. "Building a Sustainable Streaming Media Model." *EContent* 35 (9): 14–18.

Soper, Taylor. 2016. "Jeff Bezos Gets Lots of Hollywood Love as Amazon's 'Transparent' Wins More Emmy Awards." *Geekwire*, September 18. www.geekwire.com/2016/jeff-bezos-gets-lots-hollywood-love-amazons-transparent-wins-emmy-awards/.

Spector, Robert. 2000. "The Customer Is King: How Amazon.com Turned Browsers into Buyers by Obsessing over Customer Service." *Profit*, June 1.

Steemers, Jeanette. 2014. "Selling Television: Addressing Transformations in the International Distribution of Television Content." *Media Industries* 1 (1). www.mediaindustriesjournal.org/index.php/mij/article/view/16.

Sternbergh, Adam. 2015. "The 'Moneyball' Network: Amazon Has Turned Last-Dibs Status into a Competitive Advantage." *New York*, May 4.

Swisher, Kara. 2016. "Comcast Will Let Customers Get Netflix on Its Set-Top Box (Which Is a Very Big Deal)." *Recode*, July 5. Accessed February 27, 2017. www.recode.net/2016/7/5/12096380/comcast-to-let-netflix-onto-its-x1-platform-which-is-a-very-big-deal.

Tate, Ryan. 2012. "Why He Ditched Posh Hollywood Perks: 10 Questions with Amazon Studios Chief Roy Price." *Wired*, November 12. Accessed May 19, 2017. www.wired.com/2012/11/amazon-studios-roy-price/.

Tryon, Chuck. 2015. "TV Got Better: Netflix's Original Programming Strategies and Binge Viewing." *Media Industries* 2 (2): 104–16.

Tsukayama, Hayley. 2015. "What Amazon's Learned from a Decade of Prime." *Washington Post*, February 3.

Tuttle, Brad. 2013. "Amazon Prime: Bigger, More Powerful, More Profitable than Anyone Imagined." *Time*, March 18. http://business.time.com/2013/03/18/amazon-prime-bigger-more-powerful-more-profitable-than-anyone-imagined/.

"The Walmart of the Web: Amazon." 2011. *The Economist*, October 1.

Williamson, Debra Aho. 1999. "Marketer of the Year: Amazon.com." *Advertising Age*, December 13.

Winslow, George. 2012. "A Divide that's Not as Deep as You Think." *Broadcasting & Cable*, September 17.

Playboy TV

Contradictions, Confusion, and Post-network Pornography

Peter Alilunas

Given this book's television guide–style structure, it is fitting that this chapter appears near the end. My cable service, Comcast, puts Playboy TV's subscription service at number 994 of 1000, buried past more than 50 music channels, six "local insert" channels, and an on-demand jobs channel. This part of the channel guide probably remains rarely seen by many viewers, and not seen at all by those who have activated the "Safe Browse" option blocking adult channels. Playboy TV maintains roughly 70 series on its subscription channel and a corresponding On Demand service, as well as on Play-boytv.com for an additional fee, thus adhering to Amanda Lotz's post-network era description, in which "viewers now increasingly select what, when, and where to view from abundant options" beyond linear and time-fixed conventional systems (2007, 15). Given its often hidden status in this post-network environment, pornography resides in a strange (but familiar) liminal position, simultaneously desirable and dangerous (Kendrick 1987), and presenting an especially confusing question for television industry. What role can channels for sexually explicit adult content play on subscription television in an era when online pornography is ubiquitous and frequently free?

Playboy was founded in 1953 by Hugh Hefner as a men's magazine, but it has also been, from the beginning, interested in selling itself as a fantasy lifestyle.[1] Elizabeth Fraterrigo describes this effort as a carefully constructed set of discourses that "allowed readers to envision an upscale, masculine identity based on tasteful consumption and sexual pleasure" (2009, 3). Hefner made that identity abundantly clear in the very first issue: "If you're a man between the ages of 18 and 80, *Playboy* is meant for you. . . . If you're somebody's sister, wife, or mother-in-law and picked us up by mistake, please pass us along to the man in your life and get back to your *Ladies Home Companion*" (Hefner 1953, 3). This was, of course, as images of nude women simultaneously made up the company's most desirable and profitable content, alienating many women and galvanizing the growing feminist movement (Bronstein 2011). As Playboy grew, sought investors, went public, and answered to shareholders, Hefner's deliberate dismissal of half the world's consumers wasn't economically viable. The company needed women as subscribers in order to continuing growing. Hefner's exclusionary philosophy became increasingly difficult to sustain. The resulting contradiction—trying to appeal to women while also alienating them—has defined the myriad tensions around the company and its brand ever since.[2] This is nowhere more visible than in Playboy's television operations.

Currently, Playboy's interest in a variety of media, including television, works primarily to support licensing opportunities, which bring in the majority of the company's revenue (Fickenscher and Kelly 2016). Nevertheless, the magazine remains at the center of the brand identity—even with the numerous instances of "refreshing" over seven decades aimed at appealing to new (and younger) audiences. For example, in 2002, as the British-born "lad magazine" *Maxim* ate into *Playboy*'s circulation, Hefner not only decided to imitate the rival, but also hired away its editor to make graphic design changes and create a new editorial tone; Hefner even flirted briefly at that time with eliminating nudity from the magazine (Allen 2004, 20, 120; Offman 2002, 11, 84). That previously dismissed option became a reality in November 2015 as part of an effort to reach younger readers, but the stunt was scrapped in February 2017 when the magazine again embraced nudity as part of its core content (Somaiya 2015, A1; Ember 2017, B2). The core website also moved to a no-nudity format in summer 2014 in an effort to boost traffic and advertisers, and to soothe anxious potential licensing partners, even as the subscription-based Playboyplus.com continues to feature nudity (Hagey 2013). Such moves have all been part of a much larger effort to streamline the company and focus on licensing the brand and logo. Playboy-branded products now sell in 180 countries, with a third of overall recent licensing revenues originating in China, despite *Playboy* magazine having no sales presence there (Yan 2015).

Playboy first ventured into television in 1959 with *Playboy's Penthouse*, a 32-episode variety show hosted by Hefner at the WBKB studios in Chicago (Horowitz 1960, 27, 54). Billed as a sophisticated cocktail party at Hefner's swanky apartment, the show featured celebrities such as comedian Lenny Bruce and musical performances from Ella Fitzgerald and many others. Nudity was not part of the show, nor was sexual content beyond slight innuendo. Hefner returned in 1969 as host of the 52-episode syndicated series *Playboy After Dark*, this time from a soundstage in Los Angeles but with the same variety show conceit. Occasional television specials followed, such as *Playboy's Roller Disco and Pajama Party*, airing in November 1979 on ABC.

At the beginning of the 1980s, Playboy, beset by dropping magazine circulation, began searching for ways to maintain cultural relevance. Christie Hefner, the founder's daughter, became CEO in April 1982 and began emphasizing "electronic communications," especially television and home video content that could be repackaged and reused ("Playboy's New Prez" 1982, 144, 146). Her strategy centered on the "cable boom": by 1982, more than 20 million homes were wired for cable, with another 40 million expected within ten years (Clark 1982, 58; Zacks 1982, 36, 38). It was the beginning of what Lotz calls the multi-channel transition: new technologies, less control by broadcast networks, and new subscription options free from conventional advertising (2007,

12). Playboy was also obviously aware of the growing economy of adult film distribution in various exhibition contexts: in traditional theaters, on home video, and, finally, in edited form on cable television (Alilunas 2016; Heffernan 2015).

By late 1977, a small number of cable operators offered softcore adult films as pay-per-view (PPV) options, and the Private Screenings subscription service debuted in December 1980 (Bedell 1977, 18–20; Preston 1981, B1; Schwartz 1981, 44).[3] "Plenty of sex but no X," boasted Private Screenings to reassure nervous operators. The films, according to founder Mark Brenard, featured "no penetration, no oral-genital contact . . . nothing extremely perverse" (Preston 1981, B6). By 1981, a small group of distributors offered adult content to approximately 200 local channels around the country, and the field was growing (B6). Predictable regulatory efforts came, too—but often just created free publicity that led to even more subscribers (Waters and Gelman 1981, 48). As Luke Stadel argues, adult content on television, as well as its regulation, led to new cultural understandings of television as a sexual technology rather than simply a delivery device, placing it both inside and outside conventional conceptions and histories of television. Playboy, as he notes, had a significant hand in that process (2014, 52–75).

Escapade, the most successful of the early adult cable services with 100,000 subscribers across 45 systems, offered programming from 5 p.m. to 2 a.m., seven days per week (Schwartz 1981, C23). Seeking to link itself to that success, Playboy made a partnership deal with Rainbow Programming Services, Escapade's parent company: Playboy would provide five hours of branded content per month, before eventually boosting its contribution and taking over as the Playboy Channel ("Cable TV" 1981, 22, 23). The first program, *Video Playboy Magazine*, predictably attempted to translate the magazine to television. Hugh Hefner oversaw the project, and gave producers Bob and Anne Shanks a clear set of directives: no explicit sex, no erections, no penetration, and no violence ("Playboy Channel" 1982, 18). Debuting in January 1982, it featured an interview with John and Bo Derek, a celebrity news segment, a musical performance by Blondie, and a "video centerfold" featuring Playmate Shannon Tweed ("Cable Review" 1982, 64, 71). Reviews were mixed at best. "So soft as to be barely erotic," panned one ("Playboy Channel" 1982, 18).

In the spring of 1982, Playboy Productions President Russ Barry was forced to admit the channel was struggling to grow its subscriber base—mostly because it was failing to appeal to women. He announced a group of new series: one about psychological problems and relationships; a sitcom, *Four Play*, about infidelity, produced by Madeline David, former head of daytime programming at NBC; and *Women on Sex*, a talk show produced in a studio without men in the audience or crew that would later be described as "generally no more explicit than . . . Oprah Winfrey" ("Playboy Wants a Partner" 1982, 126, "Programming Potpourri" 1983, 8; "No Males Allowed" 1983, 90; Verrengia 1987, 18). These were the first of many such attempts, all of which promised adherence to the company's core brand while also trying to attract women and nervous cable operators (Salmans 1983, D1, D8). Yet, those attempts were rooted in deeply stereotypical beliefs about women's desires that often emphasized everything but sex and pleasure as a way to not go "too far" or be "too dirty." Over time, these discourses increasingly became what Timothy Havens calls "industry lore," the kinds of "organizational common sense" that turn industrial beliefs into representational practices and guide programming strategies and marketing decisions (2014, 40). Yet even as the company was constructing lore about how to appeal to women, it was simultaneously churning out Playmate-based content such as the ubiquitous "video centerfolds" that would become a programming staple (McCullaugh 1986, 55).

Playboy's television operation was stagnant at the end of the 1980s, with subscriptions stuck at less than 500,000 ("Deadline Coming Fast" 1989, 56). While some consumers appeared to prefer short trials and quick cancellation of Playboy's service, upstart rival channel Spice had nevertheless found greater success. The reason was simple: Spice offered edited versions of hardcore adult movies, which Playboy refused to offer in its steadfast belief that women would not purchase pornography. By mid-1995, the fully rebranded Playboy TV had lost almost half its remaining subscribers—but also averaged 900,000 PPV orders per month (Brown 1995b, 30). That growth was spurred by the introduction of remote control instead of telephone-based ordering, which eliminated potential customer embarrassment, further challenging the company's perception of the limited market for explicit content (as well as perhaps the interest of women in ordering it). To capitalize (and compete with Spice), Playboy launched AdultVision, a PPV channel offering more explicit content, slowly moving away from its long-standing programming policy (Brown 1995a, 78, 82). Playboy thus employed simultaneous strategies: on Playboy TV, it produced original programming aimed at women, such as *Night Calls* (1995–2007), a live call-in show about sexual fantasies; or erotic programming originally aired elsewhere, such as *Red Shoe Diaries* (1992–1997), and *Women: Stories of Passion* (1996–1999), both from Showtime. At the same time, the company raked in profits from the more explicit content on AdultVision, thus preserving the illusion that company didn't trade in pornography or go "too far."

In 1999, Playboy expanded this strategy by acquiring the Spice networks—but did not keep Spice Hot, which had then been playing the most explicit material on cable to date (Schlosser 1999, 38–9). The company sold that channel for $25 million to Bill Asher, a former Playboy executive who had moved to Vivid Video, a preeminent adult film production company. Asher rebranded the venture as Hot Network and predicted that PPV revenue across the industry would grow to $500 million annually. He based that on the audience desire for explicit content—which on Hot Network now included everything but anal penetration and visible ejaculation, two boundaries which continue to remain in place on adult television (Dempsey 1998).[4] The effect on Playboy was immediate: its channels, with their far tamer content, quickly fell behind, and the company was forced to admit that its efforts to avoid explicit content were leading to economic failure. In a spectacularly profitable move, Asher and Vivid sold Hot Network (along with two new channels, Vivid TV and Hot Zone) back to Playboy for $73 million in 2001 (O'Connor 2004, A1).

Despite the buyback, Playboy TV revenues continued to drop in the next decade as online pornography continued to grow. A 2009 internal focus group concluded a new Playboy programming strategy was necessary—but there was ultimately nothing new about the company's latest "reinvention." The reality was that Playboy TV continued to operate from a belief that women would not subscribe to explicit sexual images. "The channel is too tame to compete with sex-related video on demand services—or even certain HBO shows—yet too raunchy to appeal strongly to women, who typically control the household cable bill, according to industry research," described the *New York Times*, deftly capturing the industry lore that had long preoccupied Playboy's television operations (Barnes 2010, C1, C6). The resulting lineup, called TV for 2, placed increased emphasis on what Playboy called "intimacy and learning as a couple," and was designed to attract women who would subscribe to something between "tame" and "raunchy." Announced in fall 2010, the slate was anchored by programming focused, predictably, on couples and relationship problems, adding plot and narrative to "justify" the sexual content (Alilunas 2016, 15–20). *Brooklyn Kinda Love* was the centerpiece, following four real-life couples as they navigated various emotional situations. The effort also represented more industrial confusion, given the much more explicit (and successful) content on Playboy's PPV channels—not to mention the competing plethora of pornography available widely, and often free, online.

In the late 2000s, much of that online pornography emanated from a single company, called Manwin. Founded by German software engineer Fabian Thylmann, Manwin was built on a network of free "tube" sites, modeled on YouTube, featuring user-uploaded content, and, eventually, material produced by Manwin. Ultimately, Manwin's vertical integration created a monopoly (Wallace 2011). The result, for the traditional adult industry, has been devastating, given that Manwin's tube sites are epicenters of pirated content. By the mid-2010s, global adult content revenues had cratered, with Thylmann himself estimating that there had been a drop of at least three-quarters ("Naked Capitalism," 2015).

The impact of Manwin's success rippled into cable television, which had been riding on PPV's profitable wave. On August 5, 2011, the *Wall Street Journal* detailed the looming crisis, with Glenn Britt, CEO of Time Warner, stating the obvious: "There's been a fairly steady trend over some time period now for adult [PPV] to go down largely because there's that kind of material available on the Internet for free" (Schechner and Vascellaro 2011). That same day, Playboy announced it had partnered with none other than Manwin, putting that company in charge of programming on its channels and websites (Briel 2011). It was a significant—and ironic—decision to put an Internet company in charge of Playboy's television programming, given that the dissemination of pornography online had all but destroyed Playboy's television operation over the previous decade.

Manwin, sold by Thylmann and rebranded as Mindgeek in 2013, now supplies hardcore content that appears in minimally edited form on Playboy TV (Pardon 2013). Current programming fits into what I would describe as five primary, often overlapping classifications: scripted, reality, omnibus, Playmate-related, and sex shorts. Costly to produce and frequently serialized, scripted shows are the least prevalent type. *Canoga Park* (2007–2008), a sitcom about an adult film production company, and *7 Lives Xposed* (2013), which follows a voyeuristic apartment owner who manipulates her tenants, have been among the few recent examples.

Reality shows makes up roughly half of the channel's programming, and, in recent years, the focus of most of its marketing. Often obviously scripted, these shows are inexpensive and quick to produce. Examples range all over a generic map. First: "sexy" versions of mainstream reality trends, such as *Sex Court* (1998–2002), *Sextreme*

Makeover (2010), and *Cougar Club LA* (2016), which add nudity and softcore sex to familiar types of television content, or *Swing* (2011–2015), in which monogamous couples stay (and play) in a mansion full of experienced swingers. Second: competition shows, such as *Jenna's American Sex Star* (2005), in which young women compete in various pornography-related challenges in front of celebrity judges for an adult film contract. Third: loose excuses to show nude women or sex-related content with little to no structuring conceit, such as *Hot Yoga* (2013) or *Foursome* (2016), which offer little to no plot and consist almost entirely of sex scenes.

The omnibus shows present lists, countdowns, and short pieces. The show *69 Sexy Things 2 Do Before You Die* (2008) is essentially a travelogue, and *Arcade* (2016) offers a mix of comedy, animation, and vintage trailers. *The Stash* (2011–2016) copies mainstream comedy clip shows such as *The Soup* (E!, 2004–2015) but with pornography-related material. Playmate programming has long been a staple too, offering what are essentially video centerfold shoots with extremely loose narratives; *Dream Dates*, *Playboy Amateurs*, and *Playmate Playback*, among many others, fit this type.

The final classification, sex shorts, did not exist before the Mindgeek partnership and for the first time represents an actual programming policy change for Playboy. These shows mimic online-based pornography, often representing Mindgeek's online content as a television program, with a visual interface akin to someone browsing an online tube site (see Figure 34.1). For example, *Naughty Amateur Home Videos*, which has been on the channel in various iterations and formats since 2000, offers Mindgeek-produced videos from Mindgeek-operated tube sites. *Dare Dorm*, *Money Talks*, and *Hardcore Partying* (all originally produced for unedited online distribution) all adhere to this model; all would previously have been unthinkable on Playboy TV. Such programming raises a question about Playboy TV's post-network structure: why would someone pay for a subscription to the channel or purchase PPV content to access the same Mindgeek material that can be found unedited and free (or at lower cost) online?

Despite the presence of Mindgeek's hardcore programming, Playboy TV continues to market and circulate familiar, and regressive, discourses about its own programming

FIGURE 34.1 *Mindgeek's programming for Playboy TV mimics the aesthetics of online pornography browsing.*

strategies that are rooted in the belief that women do not want—or will not pay for—explicit sexual images that go "too far." In a June 2016 promotional video posted to You-Tube, "Bryce Finkelman, Vice President of Programming" seeks show ideas from the public. Tongue-in-cheek, the advertisement eventually reveals Finkelman to be an actor pretending to be an executive, but the solicitation is real—and specific: "At Playboy TV, we're not interested in anything obvious, derivative, offensive, judgmental, objectifying of women, or stupid. There's a lot of other networks for that. We want sexy, smart, surprising programs" (Playboy TV 2016). He goes on to cite examples from the current programming slate, exclusively from the reality classification, including *Swing* and *Cougar Club LA*, that fit squarely into the company's long-time strategy of trying to appeal to women through familiar, minimally explicit narratives and content, reinforcing the company's industry lore on those topics. Pointedly, there is no mention whatsoever of Mindgeek's content.

In its contemporary incarnation, then, Playboy clearly wants to preserve the narrative that its original, branded content falls squarely between "tame" and "raunchy," even as it simultaneously offers Mindgeek's hardcore material. Thus, the tension that has long complicated Playboy's desire for growth continues to serve as its one of its defining characteristics, perhaps more than ever as it moves into a post-network era in which the lines between online and television continue to blur. The decision to partner with Mindgeek has ultimately amplified the confusion within the Playboy brand, given that the familiar, stereotyped appeals to women now reside alongside the kinds of hardcore content Playboy long deliberately avoided for fear of alienating those same women. One thing is certain: pornography will never disappear, from television or its many evolving post-network iterations, even after Playboy TV eventually goes dark and something else takes its place. After all, pornography's staying power is well established, even as it sits at the very end of the cable guide.

NOTES

1 For more on the history of Playboy, see Russell Miller, *Bunny: The Real Story of Playboy* (New York: Henry Holt, 1984).

2 For more on feminist analyses of Playboy: Carrie Piztulo, *Bachelors and Bunnies: The Sexual Politics of Playboy* (Chicago: University of Chicago Press, 2011); Fraterrigo, *Playboy and the Making of the Good Life in Modern America*, 167–204.

3 For a discussion of softcore: David Andrews, *Soft in the Middle: The Contemporary Softcore Feature in Its Contexts* (Columbus: Ohio State University Press, 2006): 23–44.

4 For legal histories of adult cable content: Stadel, "Cable, Pornography, and the Reinvention of Television"; Elana Levine, *Wallowing in Sex: The New Sexual Culture of 1970s American Television* (Durham, NC: Duke University Press, 2007); John E. Samanche, *Censoring Sex: A Historical Journey Through American Media* (New York: Rowman & Littlefield, 2007).

REFERENCES

Alilunas, Peter. 2016. *Smutty Little Movies: The Creation and Regulation of Adult Video*. Berkeley: University of California Press.

Allen, Ted. 2004. "Nip and Tuck." *Print*, July/August.

Barnes, Brooks. 2010. "Courting Women, Playboy TV Puts Emphasis on Intimacy." *New York Times*, November 16.

Bedell, Sally. 1977. "Too Hot to Handle." *TV Guide*, October 8.

Briel, Robert. 2011. "Manwin Takes over Playboy TV Operations." *Broadband TV News*, October 31. Accessed September 11, 2016. www.broadbandtvnews.com/2011/10/31/manwin-takes-over-playboy-tv-operations/.

Bronstein, Carolyn. 2011. *Battling Pornography: The American Feminist Anti-Pornography Movement, 1976–1986*. New York: Cambridge University Press.

Brown, Rich 1995a. "Playboy Pay Per View Is Hopping." *Broadcasting & Cable*, November 13.

Brown, Rich 1995b. "PPV Outlook: Partly Sunny." *Broadcasting*, April 3.

"Cable Review." 1982. *Variety*, January 27.

"Cable TV 'Skin' Competition Gets Hot." 1981. *Broadcasting*, August 24.

Clark, Kenneth. 1982. "Turning on Television." *American Film*, March.

"Deadline Coming Fast for Playboy Night Life Channel Investment Deal." 1989. *Variety*, June 14.

Dempsey, John. 1998. "Playboy Backs Away from Spice Hot Net." *Variety*, September 30. Accessed September 6, 2016. http://variety.com/1998/tv/news/playboy-backs-away-from-spice-hot-net-1117480935/.

Ember, Sidney. 2017. "Playboy, Shedding a Policy Change, Brings Back Nudes." *New York Times*, February 14.

Fickenscher, Lisa and Keith J. Kelly. 2016. "Playboy's Licensing Deals Give Slim Hope for $500m Sale." *New York Post*, March 27. Accessed August 9, 2016. http://nypost.com/2016/03/27/playboys-licensing-deals-give-slim-hopes-for-500m-sale/.

Fraterrigo, Elizabeth. 2009. *Playboy and the Making of the Good Life in Modern America*. New York: Oxford University Press.

Hagey, Keach. 2013. "Rebuilding Playboy: Less Smut, More Money." *Wall Street Journal*, February 20. Accessed August 4, 2016. www.wsj.com/articles/SB100014241278873244320045783041020041831988.

Havens, Timothy. 2014. "Towards a Structuration Theory of Media Intermediaries." In *Making Media Work: Cultures of Management in the Entertainment Industries*, edited by Derek Johnson, Derek Kompare, and Avi Santo, 39–62. New York: New York University Press.

Heffernan, Kevin. 2015. "Seen as a Business: Adult Film's Historical Framework and Foundations." In *New Views on Pornography: Sexuality, Politics, and the Law*, edited by Lynn Comella and Shira Tarrant, 37–56. Santa Barbara: Praeger.

Hefner, Hugh. 1953. "Untitled Editorial." *Playboy*, December.

Horowitz, Murray. 1960. "Range of Syndie Shows Widening." *Variety*, October 5.

Kendrick, Walter. 1987. *The Secret Museum: Pornography in Modern Culture*. Berkeley: University of California Press.

Lotz, Amanda. 2007. *The Television Will Be Revolutionized*. New York: New York University Press.

McCullaugh, Jim 1986. "Playboy Makes Inroads with Video Projects." *Billboard*, August 2.

"Naked Capitalism." 2015. *The Economist*, September 26. Accessed August 6, 2016. www.economist.com/news/international/21666114-internet-blew-porn-industrys-business-model-apart-its-response-holds-lessons?zid=319&ah=17af09b0281b01505c226b1e574f5cc1.

"No Males Allowed." 1983. *Variety*, August 31.

O'Connor, Clint. 2004. "Cleveland's X-Rated Connection." *The Plain Dealer* (Cleveland, OH), January 4.

Offman, Craig. 2002. "Bunny Bunch Looks to Reverse Tailspin." *Variety*, October 21.

Pardon, Rhett. 2013. "Manwin Changes Name to Mindgeek." *Xbiz.com*, October 28. Accessed September 11, 2016. www.xbiz.com/news/170554.

"Playboy Channel in US Is 'Good Housekeeping' of Sexuality." 1982. *Screen International*, March 20.

Playboy TV. 2016. "Playboy TV Wants You to Be a Glamorous Big Time Producer!" *YouTube*, June 25. www.youtube.com/watch?v=K1k7cEXJFY8&t=3s.

"Playboy Wants a Partner for New Pay-TV Venture." 1982. *Variety*, May 5.

"Playboy's New Prez Maps Out TV, Homevid Expansion Course." 1982. *Variety*, May 5.

Preston, Marilynn. 1981. "Adult Cable Ties Owners in Knots." *Chicago Tribune*, June 4.

"Programming Potpurri." 1983. *Broadcasting*, April 18.

Salmans, Sandra. 1983. "Playboy's Hopes in Cable TV." *New York Times*, March 15.

Schechner, Sam and Jessica E. Vascellaro. 2011. "TV Porn Doesn't Sell Like It Used To." *Wall Street Journal*, August 5. Accessed August 10, 2016. www.wsj.com/articles/SB1000142405311 19038856045764885404473540 36.

Schlosser, Joe. 1999. "Adult Channels Mate." *Broadcasting & Cable*, March 15.

Schwartz, Tony. 1981. "The TV Pornography Boom." *New York Times*, September 13.

Somaiya, Ravi. 2015. "Nudes Are Old News at Playboy." *New York Times*, October 12.

Stadel, Luke. 2014. "Cable, Pornography, and the Reinvention of Television." *Cinema Journal* (Spring): 52–75.

Verrengia, Joseph B. 1987. "Playboy Channel Goes on Road to Ask Questions about Sex and AIDS." *The Telegraph* (Nashua, New Hampshire), July 13.

Wallace, Benjamin. 2011. "The Geek Kings of Smut." *New York*, January 30. Accessed August 4, 2016. www.nymag.com/news/features/70985/index3.html.

Waters, Harry F. and Eric Gelman. 1981. "Cable's Blues in the Night." *Newsweek*, August 24.

Yan, Sophia. 2015. "Playboy Is Betting on China Expansion." *CNN.com*, May 6. Accessed August 15, 2016. http://money.cnn.com/2015/05/06/media/playboy-china/.

Zacks, Richard. 1982. "The Cable Boom." *Film Comment*, May/June.

Starz

Distinction, Value, and Fandom in Non-linear Premium TV

Myles McNutt

In March 2016, premium cable service Starz announced its latest rebranding, which came with a new tagline: "Obsessable." This rebranding came at a crucial time for Starz, which had initially entered the premium cable ecosystem in 1994 as a "third wheel" alongside the already established HBO and Showtime. With hit original series like *Power*, critically acclaimed series like *Survivor's Remorse*, cult appeals like *Ash vs. Evil Dead*, and high-profile adaptations like *Outlander*, 2016 saw Starz with its most robust lineup of original series since its inception. The "Obsessable" branding was designed to communicate the depth of this programming lineup to would-be subscribers. Jeffrey Hirsch, Starz's president of Global Marketing and Product Planning, argued at the time that "as an insurgent in the original programming landscape, Starz has made a point of serving the fan first, while staying true to the creators and the powerful stories they tell" (Maglio 2016). By suggesting that Starz provides its viewers "fan-centric experiences," Hirsch worked to articulate the two primary goals crucial for any premium cable brand to consider: creating a sense of distinction from its competitors, and articulating a sense of value for both its consumers and its shareholders.

Historically, these questions of distinction and value have been understood and generated in relative juxtaposition to traditional broadcast television, most famously through HBO's "It's not TV, it's HBO" slogan that emerged in the mid-1990s, and the highly successful and critically acclaimed series that became associated with it. However, while HBO was distinguishing itself with shows like *The Sopranos* and *Sex and the City* that spoke to its value added on top of a traditional cable subscription package, "insurgent" Starz was—based on its late entry into the landscape—forced to approach these goals from a different direction. Its efforts to establish distinction and value through original programming came into conflict with increased competition and the uncertainty surrounding new forms of distribution, an evolutionary path that led Starz to construct premium audiences specifically as fan audiences. The result is a brand that challenges preconceived notions of how premium cable channels distinguish themselves, and showcases how new forms of distribution force changes in how cable's "elite" services understand their audiences.

"YOU'RE NOT DREAMING—YOU'RE JUST SEEING STARZ!"

When Starz—or, as it was known at the time, Starz!—launched in 1994, it was marketed using simple logic: "More of what you want . . . for less!" In an extended advertisement that played ahead of the launch of the channel, a group of actors portray individuals unsatisfied with their cable service. Some complain they have nothing to watch, even though they have 40 channels; others complain "everything is so expensive." The mob of viewers, each placed in a television screen as part of a giant wall, eventually settle on a mantra: they want more movies for less money. They chant this demand until actor Christopher Reeve, serving as the celebrity spokesman, says he's found a solution: Starz!, packaged with sister channel Encore, all for just $4.95 a month (compared to HBO's $10 a month).

From a programming perspective, Starz did not deviate from established premium cable business model with its launch. While live sports and original content were emerging as key elements of HBO and Showtime's brand identities at the time, premium cable's primary appeal was through exclusive licensed content, specifically in the form of big-budget films from Hollywood studios. Whereas HBO and Showtime had shouldered the burden of educating audiences on why premium cable was a worthwhile investment, Starz arrived at a time when premium cable was an already established part of the television landscape: in 1994, HBO had 18 million subscribers, with Showtime garnering close to 12 million (Hornaday 1994). Starz did not necessarily need to supplant HBO or Showtime in terms of subscribers: they simply needed to distinguish themselves enough to be perceived as a viable third alternative, and create a value proposition that supported such an investment on the part of cable subscribers.

After utilizing a competitive price and exclusive content to establish a place within the cable landscape, Starz looked to the programming strategy of multiplexing to address both distinction and value. Multiplexing refers to the presentation of multiple channels within a given service, providing separate feeds which can provide subscribers more choice within a given timeslot while also allowing each individual channel to create a programming flow targeted at specific viewers. For example, in 1997 Starz partnered with BET on "BET Movies: Starz!," a channel focused on movies targeted to African American audiences. While BET would leave the venture in 2001, the channel remains part of the Starz lineup as "Starz in Black," and Starz is the only premium cable service with a channel explicitly targeting this demographic. This joined more routine efforts to differentiate multiplexed channels in the resulting Starz package by taste culture (indie-focused "Starz Cinema"), genre ("Starz Comedy"), and age group (younger-skewing "Starz Edge," family-focused "Starz Kids and Family"). All channels are offered as part of a single Starz subscription, but the differentiation offers clearer "service" to its subscribers by matching them with appealing content categories.

Multiplexing showcases the breadth of content being provided by Starz, and allowed it to articulate its specific appeals and emerge as a third premium cable option throughout the 1990s and 2000s.

ORIGINAL CONTENT: *CRASH* LANDING

When Starz launched in 1994, HBO had only aired a handful of original series, and Showtime had only recently begun making a significant push into made-for-TV films. There was, at the time, no significant expectation that a premium cable channel would offer original scripted content in addition to exclusive film rights, meaning that most channels accrued distinction and value through the library of film titles available and how those titles were scheduled and branded for audiences through multiplexing strategies.

However, this changed rapidly over the course of the next decade, with HBO and then Showtime shifting their focus toward developing original series. For consumers, original content provided clear and obvious forms of distinction and value: content not simply exclusive to the channel in a secondary window of distribution, but only available to its subscribers. When *The Sopranos* launched in 1999, it gave HBO programming that was not available anywhere else (although this would change slightly with the advent of TV on DVD in the early 2000s), creating greater pressure on competitors like Showtime and Starz to compete on the same grounds. As critic Tim Goodman wrote in 2008, "who cares about theatrical movies you've either seen already, [or] skipped in the first place because they looked terrible . . .? There's nothing remotely cool about that."

Because original content reshaped the concept of "value" in the context of premium cable services, Starz faced new challenges in remaining competitive. The financial dynamics of Starz when it began were comparatively straightforward: the money Starz invested in licensing pay cable rights to feature films would be deemed a productive investment if it generated enough money from subscription fees to result in a profit. However, competitors like HBO now embraced deficit financing models to fund original programming: while premium cable channels bought licenses to distribute films, they would need to invest significantly more upfront money to produce original content (or license it from other producers). If they chose to produce the shows themselves, as HBO would do with *The Sopranos*, then it would need to recoup those costs through secondary markets, which is difficult when your channel is already perceived in some sense as a secondary market. Original programming thus created substantially more risk than licensing existing content, and Starz was ill-suited to make this kind of investment based on both its smaller subscription base and its lack of conglomerate backing (remaining independent of a larger corporation until its 2016 acquisition by Lionsgate).

Accordingly, it took 14 years for Starz to create its first full-length original series. January 2008 saw the launch of three: comedies *Head Case* and *Hollywood Residential*, as well as the drama *Crash*, based on the Academy Award-winning film.[1] However, *Crash* was dismissed by critics as a poor imitation of prestige programming on HBO and Showtime, and suffered due to the expansion of original drama production across both premium and basic cable in the preceding years. Goodman, in a scathing *San Francisco Chronicle* review of *Crash*, writes that

> original programming is not easy. There's a big pool. So many choices for consumers creates diminished demand. If you want in, you'd better have patience. And you'd better offer quality goods: Viewers are discerning in a way now that they weren't even a mere five years ago.
>
> (2008)

Comparing *Crash* to shows like Showtime's *Dexter*, AMC's *Mad Men* and *Breaking Bad*, and FX's *Sons of Anarchy*, Goodman's critique points to the inability for Starz to distinguish itself as easily as HBO had in the mid-1990s given the huge influx in original series production within both premium and basic cable since. Accordingly, the two comedies were quickly canceled, and *Crash* lasted only two seasons.

Starz's initial efforts to use original content to distinguish itself among consumers ultimately failed: while comedy *Party Down* would give the service its first critically acclaimed series in 2009, the series drew miniscule ratings, suggesting that actual subscribers to the channel did not consume the original content the service provided. While Starz attempted to emulate HBO's move into original programming, the television landscape had changed in ways that now made such duplication infeasible. The financial risk of producing original programming amplified in a crowded space where basic cable channels as well as HBO and Showtime all invested in original series, resulting in a costly false start for Starz.

NOW THEY'RE STREAMING STARZ: VALUE IN AN AGE OF NON-LINEAR DISTRIBUTION

While Starz was struggling to support a move into original scripted content, the television landscape continued to change in additional ways that altered the market for distinction among premium cable services and their programming. Beginning in 2008, premium cable began to embrace streaming video as an alternate form of distribution, and as the insurgent third party competitor Starz was quick—perhaps too quick—to embrace this new frontier and all it represented as a means of generating new kinds of value.

In the wake of its original series launches earlier in the year, Starz introduced in May 2008 "StarzPlay," a streaming video service that allowed users to watch and download content from Starz on their computers.[2] In addition to providing a new revenue stream, the service gave Starz an opportunity to promote its original series; the press release announcing the service touted access to *Crash*, *Head Case*, and *Hollywood Residential* alongside hit films like *Spider-Man 3* and *Ratatouille*. In a more significant move, October 2008 also saw Starz make a landmark deal with Netflix, agreeing to make their licensed content—both films and television series—available on Netflix's nascent Watch Instantly service that had been added to its DVD mailing service the previous year.

The deal represented a win for both Netflix and Starz at that moment. It dramatically expanded Netflix's library of recently released, high-profile Hollywood films, which had previously been denied of the service due to the oligopoly of the premium cable channels and their stranglehold on post-theatrical streaming rights. For Starz, it was another way to assure value for its content: the licensing fee paid by Netflix was an additional source of revenue, allowing them to make more money from films they licensed and potentially offset the production deficits for original series production by taking advantage of a new secondary market. Starz also negotiated to have Starz Play branding on the content it made available to Netflix, with the *New York Times* specifically emphasizing the promotion of *Crash* as part of the terms of the deal; the goal, ultimately, was for Netflix subscribers to watch this content on their computers, see the Starz branding, and then add the service to their cable subscription in order to see movies and more on their televisions (Stone 2008). Bill Myers, president of Starz at the time, told the *Times* "we clearly don't expect to see people leaving their big television and big screens to watch Starz Play. This is a complimentary service."

Starz Play's launch, and the deal with Netflix, positioned Starz at the forefront of an industry seeking to maximize the value of its content amid the rise of streaming media. Faced with criticism from cable operators worried about the implications, Starz CEO Bob Clasen defended the Netflix deal in 2009 by noting how it asserted the value of Starz content in this new space: observing that HBO and Showtime had given away HD and On Demand for free to cable operators as part of their distribution agreements, he argued "we think those valuable products should have been worth money. We think the IP rights are worth money. Our deal with Netflix got everyone's attention that there was value for this product" (Farrell 2009).

However, the deal with Netflix hinged on a belief that streaming would not serve as a direct competitor to traditional TV distribution, failing to foresee the rise of set-top boxes (Roku, Apple TV), Blu-ray players, game consoles, and smart TVs able to utilize streaming applications to watch Netflix and other streaming services on television sets. Cable operators' concern about Starz's deal with Netflix came to fruition as Netflix positioned itself as a competitor to premium cable, leading Starz—under new leadership in the form of former HBO Chairman Chris Albrecht—to refuse to renegotiate the deal in the fall of 2011. Starz's content departed Netflix in early 2012.

While Albrecht cited the decision to license content to Netflix as a "terrible" one in 2014, at the time the deal spoke to the challenges of articulating value for an "insurgent" channel such as Starz in the space of premium cable (Littleton 2014). Without a base of original series to provide clearer distinction from HBO and Showtime, Starz was susceptible to the immediacy of Netflix's offer, without fully understanding the ramifications of that deal for its ability to grow within the non-linear marketplace.

"SERVING THE FAN FIRST": PROGRAMMING IN THE AGE OF STREAMING

Although the rise of streaming video proved disadvantageous to Starz in the context of its deal with Netflix, it also provided the foundation for a new form of premium cable distinction. Albrecht, who took over as Starz's CEO in 2010 and gained the title of president in 2016, was hired to replicate his work at HBO, where he had been a key architect of their original series as both president of original programming (1995–2002) and eventually chairman (2002–2007). However, rather than turning Starz into another HBO, Albrecht developed original programming strategies that matched the evolving television marketplace, responding to and preparing for shifts in the premium cable landscape.

Albrecht's tenure began with two primary original drama series tracks.[3] The first offered more traditional premium cable content, represented by 2011 political drama *Boss* (starring Kelsey Grammer) and 2012 mob period drama *Magic City*. Albrecht put both into development and renewed them for second seasons before their premieres, based on their creative pedigrees and their sales in overseas markets. The second track of programming, meanwhile, included 2010's *Spartacus*, a blood-and-sandals epic too pulpy to register as prestige TV, but still appropriate to generate an "edge" (Curtin 1996) that would make a strong appeal to a specific, intensely interested audience. The *Los Angeles Times* described *Spartacus* as "part *300*, part Harlequin bodice-ripper and part soft-core porn" (Martin and Flint 2010). *Spartacus*, like *Boss* and *Magic City*, received a second season order before its first premiered, although it entered development before Albrecht was hired. However, of the three shows, only *Spartacus* lasted more than two seasons, as it was the only show to generate and maintain an audience across its four-season run.

Reflecting on *Boss'* failure, Albrecht told the *Hollywood Reporter*, "there was a time when you could keep a show on just because you liked it—I certainly really liked *Boss*—but it didn't resonate enough with the two constituents that are important to us: our subscribers and our distributors" (Goldberg 2013b). Although *Boss* earned Starz's strongest critical reviews for a drama series (earning a 78 out of 100 on review aggregate site Metacritic), and *Spartacus* was the most poorly reviewed of the three series (earning only a 52), Albrecht canceled *Boss* and *Magic City*, and instead embraced a brand distinguished by a very different type of programming from its competitors. After Spartacus debuted with strong ratings, Albrecht told the *Los Angeles Times* that its performance "made me think about a lot of stuff. I thought, 'Wow, we could do a whole network like this, and it would be different.' It's not a bad place to start in terms of restarting the brand." Following this instinct, Albrecht built on *Spartacus* with 2013 period thriller *Da Vinci's Demons* and 2014 pirate drama *Black Sails*; while neither series drew critical praise on the level that supported HBO's claims of quality distinction during the early 2000s, the series connected with audiences, and with the global distributors whose licensing revenues helped make the programs economically feasible for Starz.

Although some critics would eventually reclaim *Spartacus*, the drama is significant for separating premium cable distinction from the prestige economies traditionally associated with HBO and Showtime. While those channels measure their worth based on critical acclaim and Emmy nominations, Starz focused its attention on creating programming that generated fanbases, regardless of the prestige attached to them. *Black Sails*, like *Spartacus*, earned a second season before its first premiered; but while executives framed *Spartacus'* early pickup as a "vote of confidence" for the "most ambitious original project we've ever undertaken," the early pickup of *Black Sails* came instead "based on the strong fan response to the preview screening at last week's Comic-Con," where the show had a presence on the floor six months before its premiere (Gold-berg 2013a). Starz's aforementioned "Obsessable" branding was thus born out of this shift wherein an economy of affect replaced an economy of prestige, as large crowds at Comic-Con or a strong presence on social media can affirm programming value with or without an Emmy nomination.

This strategy is well-suited to the increasingly direct relationship that premium cable services have with their subscribers amid the rise of streaming platforms. Starz joined Showtime in 2015 in offering itself as an "add-on" to Amazon Prime, allowing existing subscribers to Amazon's video services to pay an extra $9 per month in order to access Starz's original series and licensed movies. In April 2016, Starz followed HBO and Showtime's lead in offering a standalone, over-the-top streaming service, also $9 per month, which users could subscribe to independent of a larger cable package.[4] These moves broadened their potential subscription base to those without a traditional cable subscription, resulting in over one million subscriptions to the standalone streaming service in its first six months (Littleton 2016). And while Starz's acquired films and its library of original series are crucial to the value of the service, these standalone offerings benefit most from active fanbases who have generated a significant cultural footprint for Starz online and in fan-focused spaces like Comic-Con, and can choose to invest specifically in these services even if they have "cut the cord" of cable delivery.

Streaming platforms have altered the logics of premium cable narrowcasting: while previously figuring the value of their programming as an add-on for viewers already subscribing to cable, premium cable channels can now reach any viewer with access to a cell phone, tablet, computer, or streaming device. Its "Obsessable" branding is notable not only for its focus on audience affect rather than critical prestige, but also because

FIGURE 35.1 *Screenshot from Starz's YouTube tour of the booth for its original series* American Gods *at the 2016 San Diego Comic-Con (Starz 2016).*

it allows for a wide range of "obsessive" audiences, whether romance fans (time-travel drama *Outlander*), cult horror fans (spin-off *Ash vs. Evil Dead*), or the same black audiences originally targeted by Starz's multiplexing (crime drama *Power* and basketball comedy *Survivor's Remorse*). The result is an increasingly open, flexible definition of distinction that allows for multiple coexisting conceptions of value, preparing Starz for an increasingly non-linear future.

CONCLUSION

While HBO is the most widely regarded example of a successful programming model in the space of premium cable, and Showtime has effectively positioned itself as its closest rival, Starz represents the most compelling case study for the evolution of premium cable in a contemporary, convergent television landscape. Although the service faced a number of setbacks and missteps in its move toward original programming, over time it embraced a collection of populist genre series and reshaped the rules of distinction and value in premium cable. The result was a more diverse development slate that matched shifts in distribution and placed increased value on service to television fans, distinguishing Starz from HBO and Showtime and helping grow the service's subscriber base. For a brief period in 2015, Starz passed Showtime in subscribers for the first time, an achievement that spoke to the success of its continuing "insurgency" over the previous two decades.

However, the clearest evidence of Starz's success might be that the channel it once tried to duplicate now aspires toward the Starz business model. HBO has some history with affect-based programming, with 2008 fan-favorite *True Blood* holding multiple Comic-Con panels and offering a populist alternative to critically acclaimed and award winning shows like *The Wire* and *Boardwalk Empire* airing concurrently. More recently, though, the breakout success of genre shows beginning with fantasy adaptation *Game of Thrones* in 2011 and continuing with science fiction western *Westworld* in 2016 has merged these two paths. Although these series are still relying on critical acclaim and awards recognition to articulate prestige, HBO has more actively embraced spaces like Comic-Con in articulating its distinction, embracing the affect of fandom as a centerpiece of its brand as opposed to an ancillary audience. This expansion of the service's branding comes as the channel puts more focus on their standalone HBO Now service, embracing the link between non-linear distribution and affect-based branding strategies that Starz began cultivating years earlier. If Starz found its success from reshaping the goal of premium cable from "laudable" to "obsessable," HBO is aiming for the union of both, following Starz in much the way that Starz once followed HBO.

Starz continues to aspire to be like HBO, too: shows like *Outlander* and its 2017 religious fantasy drama adaptation *American Gods* straddle the line between prestige drama and high-concept genre fare, creating a balance of prestige and affect not dissimilar to that which HBO has struck with *Game of Thrones*. While Starz may not build its brand around Emmy nominations, it still actively campaigns for them, holding "For Your Consideration" events for *Outlander, Survivor's Remorse,* and *Power* in 2016.

When none of his shows were nominated in major categories, Albrecht told reporters that "it's all silly," and that "it's not a level playing field," but his investment in these campaigns points to the channel's aspirational origins (O'Connell 2016). While once an "insurgent," Starz is now an established part of the premium cable landscape, where its "obsessable" programming focus has helped to introduce affect-focused branding into an increasingly non-linear marketplace.

NOTES

1 Head Case originally launched as a short-form series, with 12-minute episodes, in 2007.
2 The service was based on VONGO, a previous video on demand service launched by Starz's parent company Liberty Media Group.
3 After *Party Down* and paired comedy *Gravity* were canceled in 2010, Albrecht halted comedy development at Starz, until *Survivor's Remorse* debuted four years later.
4 Notably, over two decades later, Starz continues to undercut its competitors on price: in 2017, Showtime's stand-alone streaming option cost $10.99, while HBO NOW charges $15.

REFERENCES

Curtin, Michael. 1996. "On Edge: Culture Industries in the Neo-Network Era." In *Making and Selling Culture*, edited by Richard Ohmann, 181–201. Hanover: Wesleyan University Press.

Farrell, Mike. 2009. "Starz Entertainment's Clasen Dishes on Netflix Pact." *Multichannel News*, November 19. www.multichannel.com/news/internet-video/starz-entertainments-clasen-dishes-netflix-pact/298697.

Goldberg, Lesley. 2013a. "Michael Bay's 'Black Sails' Gets Early Second-Season Renewal at Starz." *The Hollywood Reporter*, July 26. www.hollywoodreporter.com/live-feed/michael-bays-black-sails-gets-594102.

Goldberg, Lesley. 2013b. "TCA: Starz Chief Talks 'Boss' Failure, Reveals Movie Is in Creator's Hands." *The Hollywood Reporter*, January 5. www.hollywoodreporter.com/live-feed/tca-starz-chief-talks-boss-408890.

Goodman, Tim. 2008. "TV Review: 'Crash' Wrecks the Small Screen." *The San Francisco Chronicle*, October 16. www.sfgate.com/news/article/TV-review-Crash-wrecks-the-small-screen-3190174.php.

Hornaday, Ann. 1994. "The Media Business: Channel Executive Seeks to Build Showtime's Slate of Original Fare." *New York Times*, August 29. www.nytimes.com/1994/08/29/business/media-business-channel-executive-seeks-build-showtime-s-slate-original-fare.html

Littleton, Cynthia. 2014. "Starz CEO: 'Shortsighted' to Sell Hot Shows to Netflix." *Variety*, December 9. https://variety.com/2014/tv/news/starz-ceo-shortsighted-of-networks-to-sell-hot-shows-to-netflix-1201374752/.

Littleton, Cynthia. 2016. "Starz's Standalone Broadband Service Draws Nearly 1 Million Subscribers." *Variety*, October 27. http://variety.com/2016/tv/news/starz-outlander-streaming-deal-earnings-q3-1201902755/.

Maglio, Tony. 2016. "Starz Brings Encore Under Umbrella, Unveils Rebrand." *The Wrap*, March 28. www.thewrap.com/starz-encore-rebrand-obsessable/.

Martin, Denise and Joe Flint. 2010. "Spicy 'Spartacus Slays' em for Starz." *Los Angeles Times*, March 23. http://articles.latimes.com/2010/mar/23/business/la-fi-ct-spartacus23-2010mar23.

O'Connell, Michael. 2016. "Starz Chief Chris Albrecht Shrugs Off Emmy Snubs: 'It's Not a Level Playing Field.'" *Hollywood Reporter*, August 1. www.hollywoodreporter.com/live-feed/starz-chief-chris-albrecht-shrugs-916165.

Starz. "American Gods | 2016 San Diego Comic Con Booth Tour | Starz." 2016. *YouTube*, July 24. www.youtube.com/watch?v=OHwvMoVTjEU.

Stone, Brad. 2008. "Starz Gives Netflix Fans a Reason to Stream." *The New York Times*, October 1. http://bits.blogs.nytimes.com/2008/10/01/starz-gives-netflix-fans-a-reason-to-stream/?_r=1.

WWE Network

The Disruption of Over-the-Top Distribution
Cory Barker and Andrew Zolides

On February 24, 2014, World Wrestling Entertainment (WWE) launched the WWE Network, an over-the-top (OTT) Internet-only channel that provides a continuous stream of programming as well as on-demand content. While at this point other streaming video services like Netflix and Hulu offered original programming, the network established new ground by delivering live coverage alongside on-demand content, crucial for broadcasts of major spectacles like *WrestleMania*. The network was initially marketed as a one-stop shop for fans of WWE programming, mixing access to classic archival material amassed over decades with new, original programming only available through the service. This—combined with cheaper, easier access to live pay-per-view (PPV) specials—made the pitch to fans as to why they needed the network.

With the network, WWE positioned itself as a pioneering disruptor looking toward the future of digital media. Yet, the network also created several disruptions *for* WWE—including how it produces and distributes content and how it tells stories and engages with fans. As with most media companies, WWE's business is deeply interconnected with other culture industries. The culture industries are nothing if not a complex arrangement of institutions collaborating, compromising, and clashing over how media is produced, distributed, and regulated. The shift to the web has complicated those preexisting relationships in a multitude of ways, impacting not just consumers, but producers and institutions as well.

This chapter explores the effects of disruption, the modern catch-all buzzword for strategic change within the technology and media industries. It demonstrates that leaders in specialized markets like WWE must constantly innovate to capture the attention of both audiences and more influential forces within the culture industries. Still, we argue that despite the hopeful rhetoric that streaming video will open the doors for new, diverse sources of content creation, the particulars of the system still privilege those corporations powerful enough to afford the risks. As other chapters in this collection can attest, OTT streaming services are only growing in number and reach. All these shifts require us to readjust our understanding of television in the age of the Internet to attune for these new forms of distribution and the impact they have on industrial relationships and creative practices.

DISRUPTING INDUSTRIAL RELATIONSHIPS

WWE traveled a long and complicated road to launch the network, highlighting industrial anxieties surrounding OTT distribution models in the early 2010s. Plans for the network date back to 2011, with WWE pursuing the creation of a premium cable channel featuring repeats of past content, new original programs, and monthly PPV specials. With a launch date in place for 2012, WWE began production on early network exclusives, including the *Big Brother*-esque reality series, *Legends' House*. However, by mid-2012 WWE missed its target launch and quietly dropped any future discussion of the channel. Two years later, at the 2014 Consumer Electronics Show (CES), WWE reintroduced the network, this time emphasizing an OTT model, with references to the service overtly playing on "over-the-top" as both another industry buzzword and a description of the spectacular programming for which the company is known.

Initial coverage of the network focused on this distinctive delivery system that married an Internet-only live streaming channel with on-demand content. WWE's corporate website touted the service as "the first-ever 24/7 direct-to-consumer premium network." There is a historical parallel here, as professional wrestling companies have regularly been at the forefront of new television distribution systems. In the 1980s, for instance, Vincent K. McMahon broke from the regional territory system of wrestling's past by launching a national company bolstered by rise of cable distribution (Beekman 2006). Since that time WWE has partnered with both broadcast networks (NBC, UPN, and The CW) and cable channels (MTV, USA Network, TNN/Spike TV) while simultaneously leveraging PPV distribution through deals with cable and satellite companies. Thus critics like Seth Berkman (2014) labeled the network as the next step in the evolution of television distribution. Indeed, WWE's chief revenue and marketing officer Michelle D. Wilson pitched the move as forward-thinking when she stated to *Time*,

> Digital over-the-top offerings represent the future, and given that our passionate fans consume five times more online video content than non-WWE viewers and over-index for purchasing online subscriptions such as Netflix and Hulu Plus, we believe the time is now for a WWE Network.
>
> (Luckerson 2014)

WWE's desire to develop its own distribution channel was fueled by many factors, all of which relate to improving its bottom line. As a publicly traded company since 1999, WWE cannot simply rest on its laurels as the only major wrestling promotion in the United States (and the most successful internationally). Growth is necessary, and the network can thus be understood as a way to expand the audience for its product (both domestically and worldwide), enable new revenue streams by cutting out intermediaries, and utilize a library with over 150,000 hours of content that was inconsistently dispersed among the home video market and WWE Classics (an on-demand subscription add-on for cable customers). With DVD sales plummeting and streaming video subscriptions on the rise, WWE would seek a more direct path to profit from its content; yet the network required new programming and a restructuring of its productions in order to improve upon the on-demand subscription model of WWE Classics.

Despite its continued embrace of new forms of distribution, WWE is still best understood as a media production company, staging and filming live performances while touring around the world. In fact, every week WWE currently produces roughly six hours of wrestling programming for cable or syndication, not including E! reality series *Total Divas* and *Total Bellas*, network originals, and films through WWE Studios. This programming appears on multiple networks and channels in over 180 countries. What makes the network such a departure for the company, and therefore any producer interested in this direct-to-consumer mode of delivery, is the shift to digital distribution.[1] Cutting out the middlemen—cable and satellite providers as well as channels like USA Network—grants WWE more control over its content and the path content takes to reach fans. However, WWE must also contend with the challenges of entering a media sector with which it was unfamiliar and where it was reliant on those partners.

By opening up a new distribution channel for its product, WWE upset its relationships with traditional media providers who were previously the only outlet for its content. The biggest shift came in the form of the PPV market, a significant part of WWE's creative and industrial strategies for decades. WWE was one of the earliest proponents of PPV, cooperating with cable and satellite companies to sell the first *WrestleMania* in 1985. PPV was more than just a key revenue stream for the company; indeed, the entire creative structure of WWE was built around PPVs acting as a narrative climax for weeks of storytelling. However, the demands of the changing industry and launching the network meant shifting away from the PPV structure.

In the new era of WWE Network, monthly specials are still presented as significant events; indeed, in promotional material, WWE emphasizes that these events are now free with a subscription instead of $45–$60 on PPV via cable and satellite providers. This price point positions the network as a fantastic value, but also lessens the import of those specials and frustrates the providers that previously made a substantial profit selling them to customers each month. Although WWE specials are still offered as PPVs, the network makes such a purchase through cable or satellite companies virtually redundant for its new subscribers. In reformulating its approach to special events, WWE risked ruining its relationship with cable and satellite companies. It is then no surprise that these companies reacted negatively to the announcement of the network in 2014. DirecTV immediately released a statement noting, "Clearly we need to quickly re-evaluate the economics and viability of their business with us, as it now appears the WWE feels they do not need their PPV distributors" (Graser 2014). Dish went a step further, refusing to carry the first PPV after the announcement, *Elimination Chamber*, claiming, "WWE is not willing to adjust their PPV costs to satellite and cable companies, which is unfair to their customers. We need to re-focus our efforts to support partners that better serve Dish customers" (Graser 2014).

Ultimately these proved to be empty threats. Providers have continued to offer WWE events despite a massive drop in monthly sales, primarily because such revenue comes in with minimal investment on their part. For WWE, PPV revenue has predictably declined following the launch of the network; total revenue during quarters one and two—the company's peak *Wrestlemania* season—has dipped from $37.3 million in 2014 to $12.5 million in 2015 to $8.0 million in 2016 (Caldwell 2016a). PPV interest in WWE events has decreased enough that in May 2016, WWE announced it would no longer report buy rates in its public business statements (Caldwell 2016b). Network subscription income helps bear the brunt of the PPV revenue decrease, yet in shifting to OTT and ceasing its reporting of PPV financials, WWE has signaled to cable and satellite providers that it no longer prioritizes those partnerships.

The network has also disrupted the relationship between WWE and its primary distributor in traditional subscription cable, USA Network, and parent company NBCUniversal. Prior to the creation of the network, WWE and its distributor agreed to a streaming deal with Hulu for the exclusive day-after rights of *Raw* and *Smackdown*, where NBCU is a primary investor and where all parties benefit from advertising revenue. While USA Network and NBCU have never publicly expressed concern with WWE's push toward the OTT future, they have forced WWE to uphold the preexisting Hulu deal—meaning network subscribers cannot access most recent episodes of WWE's primary product. Likewise, in the lead-up to its licensing renegotiations with NBCU in 2014, WWE publicly stated that the appeal of its live programming in the world of DVRs would be worth "at least double" the previous $90 million annual fee, but the two sides ultimately settled on a $150 million deal, sending WWE's stock into a free fall (Flint 2014). Though the relationship with NBCU continues, WWE has discovered the limitations of its position within the larger television industry. WWE needs audiences to watch the weekly television programs—and thus needs partnerships with USA and NBCU—as it is there where the company sells them on the importance of the monthly special events, and now, the importance of the network.

The network's launch teaches many lessons about the shift from traditional television distribution models brought on by the rise of Internet-streaming services and subscription-based payment models. One of the primary sources for both excitement and consternation about OTT models is the rearrangement of the relationship between audiences and media content creators. This is positively presented as a closer connection brought on by the Internet, allowing content producers to find new avenues for reaching audiences or, in WWE's case, creating its own platform that cuts out middlemen at the level of delivery. Content providers are able to build their own streaming channels, enabling consumers more access to the personalized, on-demand services that have flourished online. Simply put, the rise of digital and Internet distribution means that content producers are heavily invested in finding new methods to reach consumers—methods that, increasingly, eschew traditional media outlets.

At first glance it might seem odd that WWE would launch the first OTT streaming channel of its kind. Its programming is not particularly varied in genre or style, and it has been considered somewhat outside the mainstream since the early 2000s. Nevertheless, this desire by a nominal production company to enter the lucrative arena of television

FIGURE 36.1 *The WWE Network interface emphasizes its strategic balance between weekly series, pay-per-view events, and library programming.*

distribution, utilizing new technologies, makes sense. With Netflix, Hulu, and others proving that consumers are happy to get their content directly via the Internet without preestablished channels to guide them, WWE saw the opportunity to reach—and hopefully expand—its target audience where they were: online. WWE's embrace of digital distribution has simultaneously fueled creative decisions that are perhaps better suited for this new delivery system while also establishing new challenges for the company's production processes.

DISRUPTING PRODUCTION PRACTICES

The network has been even more disruptive to WWE's role as a content producer. While the company runs over 300 live events every year, the majority of those are non-televised "house shows" intended only for local audiences and not part of the official canon of storylines. On television, however, WWE functions much like any long-running serialized drama: episodes of *Raw* and *Smackdown* weave characters and storylines into a never-ending drama that builds to weekly and monthly climaxes before beginning anew in the next televised episode. In recent years, WWE has begun to supplement its television product with in-house documentaries, the *Total Divas* reality series, and backstage clips and social content posted to YouTube, Facebook, and Twitter. This flood of ancillary content has expanded the boundaries of the WWE Universe, but never taken away from the primary programming on USA.

With the introduction of the network, however, WWE must navigate the seemingly unlimited potential of OTT streaming and its established agreements with cable partners. WWE has increased its production slate to include network-exclusive events like 2016's *Cruiserweight Classic* and 2017's *United Kingdom Championship Tournament*, as well as an array of inexpensive reality shows following performers outside of the ring. It has also utilized the 24/7 streaming capabilities of the network to deploy breaking news coverage, ESPN-style pre- and post-shows, and live recordings of a popular podcast hosted by former star "Stone Cold" Steve Austin. On one hand, WWE shows how OTT and cable television can work in concert, as it regularly promotes the network through televisual "flow" (Williams 2003, 86), using the platform of USA to drive viewers to the new streaming content directly after *Raw* or *Smackdown*. On the other hand, WWE can only show *so much*; network content is promoted, but outside of the monthly supercard events, it is never elevated above *Raw* or *Smackdown*, nor are many of the network exclusives deemed relevant to storylines playing out on USA's prime-time schedule.

WWE has attempted to have it both ways, to mixed results. In 2016, the company encountered even more problems with its integration of smaller "cruiserweight" performers across the network and cable television. After garnering rave reviews for the network-only *Cruiserweight Classic*, WWE gave the group its own streaming series, *205 Live* (in reference to the weight limit). To promote this new endeavor, WWE began integrating cruiserweight performers into *Raw*, complete with separate branding and color schemes. Yet, while the *Cruiserweight Classic* had the benefit of full attention during its production at WWE's Florida studios, *205 Live* and the *Raw* segments are tacked onto the middle of the television presentation where the set changes prove distracting and the smaller performers do not deliver their usual acrobatic feats. In this instance, WWE's crafts an awkward flow between its live shows, cable product, and network exclusives.

The network has also complicated WWE's storyline design. In promotional materials, WWE makes it clear: the key selling point for the network is not the library or the new exclusive content; instead, the value lies in the monthly supercard events like *WrestleMania* that were previously available on PPV. The storytelling has always followed a similar pattern: plots that develop on *Raw* and *Smackdown* were intended to build to a payoff at that month's PPV event (the narrative importance of which was reaffirmed by its high access cost). In the network era, WWE has kept the promotional push for special events the same, but increased production of and around them. The number of supercards has jumped from 13 to more than 20, bolstered by new pre-shows complete with analysts, interviews, and video packages promoting upcoming matches. While the in-ring product during these events is identical to what WWE would do in the PPV era or on cable, the storylines have grown increasingly less worthy of the incessant promotion. With nearly two network specials per month and a weekly cable TV output of five hours, WWE rarely allows stories to climax at special events. Instead, matches and interviews set up *additional* matches and segments for *Raw* and *Smackdown*, and the cycle begins again. Likewise, the supplemental material surrounding these specials does not divulge from WWE's production style; it does, however, add *more* content to an already exhaustive output.

Through years of conditioning the audience to this demanding cycle, WWE has stretched its core storytelling mechanisms quite thin. The introduction of the network did not create this issue but did exacerbate it. Industry reporters and fans have been wondering aloud if the network has forced WWE to produce too much content (Durant 2016). Here then, we can see another challenge for OTT services. Now that fans can access specials for $9.99 on the network instead of $45–$60 on PPV, WWE only has to produce one show that is good enough to keep them subscribed for another 30 days. Yet, like other subscription services, WWE has instead chosen to release as much new content as possible to increase the likelihood that the network offers at least one appealing product to fans with disparate interests. In doing so, the network has equally demonstrated the obstacles facing independent companies hoping to launch an OTT streaming service—chief among them the allocation of creative resources across a greater number of productions.

The reality is that, despite its over-the-top disruption of traditional television markets, WWE is still a niche product with a limited fan base and responsibilities to its partners on cable. Network promotion often centers on the library not just because it is inherently great; it also costs WWE next to nothing to stream. WWE lacks the financial resources—and time—to produce and distribute high-end content for the network. Production staff and talent travel to five different cities a week, putting a strain on potential network offerings. WWE's repurposing of its archives and utilization of reality shows, interview segments, and younger, cheaper talent mirrors the strategy of a niche cable channel rather than an enormous streaming platform like Netflix. Meanwhile, the higher production value live drama continues to play out on USA.

DISRUPTING AUDIENCE SEGMENTATION

WWE would prefer all of the nearly three million live viewers of *Raw* and *Smackdown* subscribe to the network; however, the subscriber base has never topped the two million mark, signaling that a significant portion of the audience consumes WWE product too casually to be motivated to sign up for the service. Therefore, WWE has been confronted with a clear segmentation of casual and diehard viewers. On USA, WWE employs its sports entertainment approach, filling programming with endless recaps, comedic backstage segments, and cross-promotions. The focus is often on big moments intended to go viral on social media, and events happening on-screen are presented as real. In contrast, on the network, WWE underlines programs tailored for fans invested in the larger world of professional wrestling and its history. The platform offers over 30 years of library content repackaged through WWE's self-mythologizing. Documentary series like *The Monday Night Wars*, *WrestleMania Rewind*, and *Rivalries* skim the surface of wrestling history by maneuvering in and out of "kayfabe," the industry's scripted reality (Shoemaker 2014). These projects are not inaccessible to the non-initiated, but generally remind WWE's core audience of events they have already experienced with an additional air of historical import. Meanwhile, special events like the UK tournament spotlight wrestling's footprint abroad and documentary series like *Ride Along* or *Table for 3* follow the performers in their "real" lives.

Wrestling fans have long been obsessed with how performers maintain characters *outside* the ring, but the expansion of wrestling discussion online has grown this obsession tenfold. WWE has smartly embraced this interest, bringing legitimate biographic details into storylines and, now with the network, giving fans more access to wreslers than ever before. *Table for 3* and *Ride Along* spotlight WWE talent in their everyday lives: in rental cars traveling from town to town, at dinner with friends on the roster, and playing pranks on one another backstage. Superstars play themselves and give dedicated viewers reasons to support them as people, not simply as characters. As an informal chat show, *Table for 3* highlights the camaraderie of performers who battle every week on USA, or who worked together in smaller companies long before WWE. Although these "real" versions of the talent are still performative, they perpetuate a level of authenticity that viewers of WWE programming on cable rarely see.

An optimistic view of the network would suggest that WWE is constructing an immersive "transmedia" experience (Jenkins 2006, 93) where fans can follow performers in and out of the ring and grow more invested in them as real people. Indeed, establishing this kind of fan investment has always been key to WWE's production model. However, the way the network remixes wrestling's conventional notions of authenticity to appeal to a devoted fan base cannot be underestimated—even when it creates confusion with the cable output. In mid-2016, WWE encouraged fans to watch the network documentary detailing Seth Rollins's recovery from knee surgery, constructing a sympathetic portrait of a performer who first made his name outside of WWE. Yet, when Rollins returned to storylines on USA, he was positioned as a villain, despite the audience's desperation to cheer him as a hero. The disconnect between Seth Rollins's authentic self on the network and his character on USA is yet another example that demonstrates WWE's difficulties merging network content into *Raw* and *Smackdown*. While more companies are exploring streaming options, the network reminds us that, at its core, changes in distribution have further segmented an already fracturing audience, leading to services that cater specifically to *fans* not just a broad consumer base.

WWE's treatment of the network is full of contradictions. The network is an exemplar of audience segmentation, and a WWE superfan's dream—an on-demand platform targeted almost exclusively at those who already consume all things professional wrestling. Yet, WWE's inconsistent integration of network content into its programming on cable and its rigorous production schedule have created a platform with an excess of content that *only* those most dedicated to wrestling can manage. Ultimately then, the network illustrates that streaming video enables content producers to foster intense loyalty among consumers like never before, but also that shifts to digital distribution are rarely seamless, particularly for independent companies with a multitude of partnerships elsewhere in the industry. Disruption goes both ways; once a company pushes itself to the front of innovation, it must immediately navigate all the counter-disruptions that innovation has inspired.

NOTE

1 WWE did previously operate its own home video distribution subsidiaries, Coliseum Home Video, later called WWE Home Video. This was closed in December 2014 when Warner Home Video took over following the launch of the WWE Network earlier that year.

REFERENCES

Beekman, Scott. 2006. *Ringside: A History of Professional Wrestling in America*. Westport: Praeger.

Berkman, Seth. 2014. "WWE Network Is Loud Introduction to the Video Streaming Ring." *New York Times*, March 30. Accessed April 28, 2016. www.nytimes.com/2014/03/31/business/media/the-body-slam-is-buffering.html.

Caldwell, James. 2016a. "WWE Q1 2016—PPV Revenue Near Extinction." *PW Torch*, May 10. Accessed February 25, 2017. www.pwtorch.com/site/2016/05/10/wwe-q1-2016-ppv-revenue-nearing-extinction/.

Caldwell, James. 2016b. "WWE Q1 2016— WWE Makes Big Reporting Shift, Eliminates PPV Buys and Monthly Biz Reports." *PW Torch*, May 10. Accessed February 25, 2017. www.pwtorch.com/site/2016/05/10/wwe-q1-2016-wwe-makes-big-reporting-shift-eliminates-ppv-buys-monthly-biz-reports/.

Durant, Toby. 2016. "Is WWE Putting on Too Much Wrestling?" *RealSport101.com*, October 26. Accessed April 12, 2017. https://realsport101.com/news/sports/wwe/is-wwe-putting-on-too-much-wrestling.

Flint, Joe. 2014. "WWE Stock Gets Smacked Down after New TV Deals Are Unveiled." *Los Angeles Times*. May 16. Accessed April 12, 2017. www.latimes.com/entertainment/envelope/cotown/la-et-ct-wwe-stock-falls-tv-deals-20140516-story.html

Graser, Marc. 2014. "Dish Stops Offering WWE's PPVs Before New Network Launch." *Variety*, February 19. Accessed April 28, 2016. http://variety.com/2014/biz/news/dish-stops-offering-wwes-ppvs-before-new-network-launch-1201113177/.

Jenkins, Henry. 2006. *Convergence Culture: Where Old and New Media Collide*. New York: New York University Press.

Luckerson, Victor. 2014. "Holds Barred: Why the WWE Isn't Going to Cable." *Time*, January 10. Accessed April 28, 2016. http://business.time.com/2014/01/10/holds-barred-why-the-wwe-isnt-going-to-cable/.

Shoemaker, David. 2014. "Grantland Dictionary: Pro Wrestling Edition." *Grantland*, August 13. Accessed June 5, 2016. http://grantland.com/features/grantland-dictionary-pro-wrestling-edition/.

Williams, Raymond. 2003. *Television: Technology and Cultural Form*. London: Routledge.

CBS All Access

To Boldly Franchise Where No One Has Subscribed Before

Derek Johnson

In January 1995, a 15-year-old television viewer in Rockford, Illinois struggled with a problem of channel access. Although local broadcast station WQRF-Channel 39 had long carried first-run episodes of *Star Trek: The Next Generation* (1987–1994) and *Star Trek: Deep Space Nine* (1993–1999), it would not air the next spin-off in the long-running space exploration franchise. While Paramount Television had previously syndicated these series to local stations on an individual basis, *Star Trek: Voyager* (1995–2001) would only be available to stations that became affiliates of the brand new United Paramount Network (UPN) by adopting its network identity and entire programming schedule. The new network and series would launch as one. Unfortunately, Rockford had lost its last non-affiliated broadcaster when WQRF signed with the Fox network in 1989. Although dual affiliations were possible (typically requiring one network's programming to air in off-peak hours), no Rockford station opted to join UPN. Consequently, *Voyager* would not launch in that market.

A glance at *TV Guide*, however, showed this viewer that stations in nearby broadcast markets had affiliated with UPN: Chicago's WPWR-Channel 50 and Madison's WISC-Channel 3. Although his family had accessed local broadcast channels through cable provider Cablevision for several years, a rotating aerial antenna remained mounted to the roof of their house. Reconnecting the control dial, he spent hours before the Monday, January 16 premiere fine-tuning to maximize reception of these distant over-the-air signals. On launch night, however, reception from Chicago failed. The next night, he turned the antenna toward Madison, where WISC, as a dual UPN/CBS affiliate, held the premiere until Tuesday; but again, brief moments of clarity gave way to static. This viewer simply lacked access to the channel that could provide continued access to the franchise.

This story of thwarted viewing in a bygone broadcast era seems far removed from streaming video on demand and plentiful access to television content. Yet its emphasis on the efforts (some) viewers will make to access desirable content makes a perfect entrée for considering how emerging over-the-top services like CBS All Access use familiar franchises to incentivize viewer embrace of online delivery and its accompanying costs. Named to valorize the access it provides, the CBS streaming service launched in October 2014, adapting advertising-supported, domestic broadcast network economies to subscription-based online distribution. CBS All Access subscribers paid $5.99 monthly to stream the kind of programs that CBS, since forming as a radio network in 1927 and moving into television in 1941, had elsewhere provided viewers for free (or rather, in exchange for exposure to advertising). The service included live streams of the local broadcast feeds CBS affiliates continued to deliver over-the-air, as well as a library of historical television programs to which CBS Studios owned the rights, from *I Love Lucy* to *CSI*. While All Access introduced a $9.99 subscription option for ad-free on-demand content in 2017, the service remained embedded in broadcast economies through the persistence of advertising in the standard package as well as in all affiliate live streams. The service did not, therefore, fully extract CBS or its audiences from older broadcast models.

Yet CBS did need to motivate subscription to this new means of accessing its network, and the practice of using highly desired content to encourage viewers to gain access—or as often, to maintain it—remained central to efforts to support the service. CBS All Access promised a year after launch it would "accelerate" growth by investing in renewed production of the *Star Trek* franchise—in this case, *Star Trek: Discovery*, envisioned as the service's "first original series" ("New" 2015). Just as UPN had

Exclusive Access to Originals

Enjoy subscriber-only CBS All Access Originals like *The Good Fight* and *Big Brother: Over the Top* – with more exciting original shows on the way, including *Star Trek: Discovery*.

Learn more

Stream Live TV 24/7

Stream your local live broadcast – including *NFL on CBS*! Just sign in to watch news, sports, special events and the shows you love. (NFL games are not available via CBS All Access on mobile phones.)

Check availability

FIGURE 37.1 *CBS All Access promoted its streaming service through appeals to exclusive premium content and continued access to broadcast feeds.*

previously wagered, CBS All Access exploited exclusive claim to new franchise product to compel consumers to gain access—this time, not by fumbling with antennas, but by paying subscription fees.

By considering how CBS All Access used established broadcast television franchises to motivate subscription to its streaming business, we can learn much about the persistent power of content in disaggregated, unbundled industrial environments. While proliferating streaming channels compete as standalone, over-the-top services actively chosen by viewers (not included by default in cable bundles), content franchises offer built-in appeal to support demand for access. Beyond this, CBS All Access franchising strategies reveal the industrial challenges of building bridges between broadcasting and streaming. While exclusive original content like *Discovery* facilitated CBS' adaptation to premium streaming economies, this strategy simultaneously evoked the broadcast origins of both network and franchise as well as their continued articulations to that industrial model—prompting consumer questions about the value of streaming compared to broadcast. To explore these ideas, we can first contextualize this franchise strategy within the initial priorities of CBS All Access between 2015 and 2017. Second, we can address the specific value *Star Trek* brings as an anchor or flagship for a newly launched channel. Finally, we can trace the limits of this strategy by considering the responses of would-be subscribers when presented with new access barriers to franchises previously available through broadcast channels. While CBS All Access relied upon legacy franchise power to lead audiences to a premium subscription economy, it simultaneously confronted the challenges of adapting broadcast legacies to that streaming environment.

ACCESS GRANTED

Whereas upstart broadcast networks like UPN suffered from poor affiliate coverage and resulting lack of audience access, CBS All Access promised easy content access to anyone with a broadband connection and the monthly fee. At launch, the service provided over 5,000 episodes of programming, including full runs of *Cheers*, *MacGyver*, and, of course, *Star Trek* (Ellingson 2014). That programming library grew as CBS Studios produced more television content; because long-term exploitation rights typically belong to studios producing programming, anything CBS Studios made (aired on the CBS broadcast network or not) could eventually augment this library. CBS did often license its library programs in parallel to competing streaming services like Netflix, Amazon Prime Video, or Hulu. Yet these agreements typically extended temporary, non-exclusive streaming rights to individual programs and did not represent a wholesale commitment to making all CBS Studios content available on competing services. In other words, the comparative value of All Access came at least in part from full access to the larger library CBS controlled.

In this context, exclusive programming like *Discovery* not intended to be shared with these competitors served as "premium" content—or, as CBS CEO Les Moonves puts it, "content to die for" (Pascale 2017b). The idea that audiences might be led to specific channels by desirable content recalls long-standing industry discourses about the power of programming, often expressed in the adage "content is king" (Dumenco 2014; Lafayette 2016; Neff 2011). The primacy of content is by no means accepted fact; in the age of streaming, especially, many experts believe the distributional and infrastructural control enjoyed by tech companies like Google, Netflix, or Facebook provides more competitive edge than control over any specific content (Knee 2011; Raddon 2016). In this debate over content versus distributional hegemony, CBS hedged its bets with All Access. CBS could retain control and internalize the value of its content library while developing a new online distribution channel of its own (no longer at the mercy of other companies' streaming pipelines). Nevertheless, the centrality of media franchising to CBS All Access programming strategy demonstrates that the reproduction of recognizable content with proven audience demand remained a crucial means of supporting television services given the abundance of choice among different channels and services.

Media franchising is the logic through which industries reuse proven intellectual properties (like a successful television show) to generate more content across different sites, moments, and contexts of production; this supports both multiplication of cultural production and processes of reproduction that facilitate exchange of creative resources across different institutions, moments, creative communities, and industry sectors (Johnson 2013, 3–4). In television development, this production logic most commonly manifests in "spin-off" practices that use already successful characters, settings, or brands to support new creative endeavors (2013, 67; Gitlin 2000, 64). Spun-off from a familiar franchise formula, *Discovery* poses less risk than a more original concept. However, the CBS All Access franchising strategy went beyond defraying development risks to additionally enhance the value of the existing library. The original production strategy publicly championed by All Access between 2015 and 2017 revolved around creating new iterations of existing CBS franchises; beyond *Discovery*, CBS promised spin-offs of *The Good Wife* (a legal melodrama that aired on CBS from 2009 to 2016) and *Big Brother* (the ongoing reality television format launched by CBS in 2000, which had already supported experimentations with subscriptions for exclusive online content). Although CBS intended *Discovery* as the first original All Access series, repeated production delays meant that *Good Wife* spin-off *The Good Fight* launched first in 2017. CBS promotional material explicitly noted the added value this spin-off would bring to older *Good Wife* episodes in the All Access library. "Remember that every episode of *The Good Wife* is available on demand with CBS All Access," one press release noted. "Looking to catch up on this series? Check out *The Good Wife* Binge-Watch Guide which highlights key episodes and important moments you need to know" ("Good" 2016). A franchise strategy thus increases the value of library access to the parent series for viewers following a spin-off into the streaming environment.

In this way, the CBS All Access strategy paralleled efforts of other studios to "revive" production of library series, where the creation of valuable new television content also enhanced the value of older episodes. On the basis of the increased "leverage" and visibility afforded by renewed production of *The X-Files* (FOX, 1993–2002), for example, 20th Century Fox could ask higher license fees from Netflix for older episodes (Barr 2015). With *Discovery* in the pipeline, CBS could similarly demand higher license fees from Netflix or Amazon for the previous *Star Trek* series; but it had even more leverage

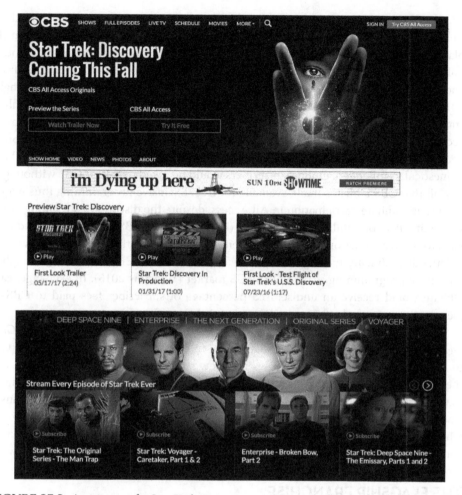

FIGURE 37.2 *Anticipation for* Star Trek: Discovery *in 2017 offered leverage to bring new value to the entire library of franchise series.*

because it could always retain exclusive rights and enjoy their value on All Access. As analyst Cynthia Littleton argues, the worth of programming in development in this context is determined "by how much it will contribute to the intrinsic value of its commissioning network or digital platform as part of a library of shows available en masse for years to come" (2017, 2).

These franchising practices also provided some leverage in encouraging traditional broadcast affiliates to participate in the new online network economy of CBS All Access. Reflecting its domestic market emphasis, CBS promised to air the first *Discovery* episode on its broadcast network (as it did for *Good Fight*) ("New" 2015) and signed a deal that ceded international distribution to Netflix ("Netflix" 2016). Yet following the premiere of the new series on September 24, 2017, CBS reserved all subsequent episodes exclusively for All Access within the US. This effectively blocked legacy CBS affiliates from participation in the program beyond episode one—unless they chose to contribute to the new online domestic service. Syncbak software embedded in the platform allowed CBS All Access to detect subscribers' geographic locations and potentially match them to local affiliate programming feeds that offered local programming and syndicated fare in non-network hours outside the prime-time schedule (Spangler 2015). Yet CBS required additional contractual permission from individual affiliate stations to stream those local feeds. Without affiliates, CBS All Access could provide access to the CBS Studios library and emulate the CBS prime-time experience, but it could not duplicate the local character of broadcasting in which CBS had long been domestically embedded. Online subscribers would be asked to pay for CBS without getting all that CBS affiliates made available for free. Exclusive programming thus helped incentivize affiliate participation in All Access, despite the disruption streaming posed to existing network-affiliate relationships (because online CBS no longer needed affiliates to deliver its national network content to viewers). By the end of 2015, over 100 independent affiliates had signed carriage agreements with CBS All Access, enough to offer local programming to 75% of the US market (Winslow 2015). In exchange, each affiliate would receive an undisclosed percentage of subscriber fees paid to CBS—a piece of the action to be driven by *Discovery* and other franchises.

The continuity offered across broadcast and streaming by *Discovery* and *The Good Fight* encouraged audiences and affiliates alike to continue their relationship with CBS to maintain access to those franchises in a new streaming economy. Put another way, these franchises represented not just exclusive content, but an exclusivization of content to which audiences and affiliates previously enjoyed broadcast access. With that exclusivization in mind, we can consider how the specific broadcast legacy of *Star Trek* supported CBS efforts to carve out space in the crowded over-the-top market while also creating confusion about what it meant to be a streaming service compared to a broadcast network.

THE FLAGSHIP FRANCHISE

Echoing the ways UPN used the *Star Trek* franchise as support for launching a new channel, CBS executives too highlighted the value of *Discovery* as a flagship for its growing service. Since acquiring the television rights to *Star Trek* in its merger and later separation with Viacom/Paramount, CBS executives have called the franchise the "family jewel/s" (Goldberg 2015; Pascale 2017b) or the "crown jewel" (Bond 2016) of its library holdings. Through this special value, the *Star Trek* franchise is often framed as uniquely able to deliver upon corporate goals. By February 2017, the CBS All Access subscriber base had grown to almost 1.5 million, up 50% over seven months (Spangler 2017a). Yet Les Moonves nominated *Star Trek* as a vehicle by which the service would aim for eight million by 2020; *Discovery* was the "big kahuna" that would attract even bigger and younger audiences for All Access (which already averaged 20 years younger than the CBS broadcast network) (Pascale 2017a). CBS cagily withheld actual subscriber numbers, yet claimed that the premiere of *Discovery* drove a "record" number of subscriber sign ups for a single day as well as a 64% increase in downloads of the All Access mobile app compared to the previous two weeks (Spangler 2017b).

Similarly, CBS placed unique faith in *Star Trek* to appeal to global buyers and, in doing so, guarantee its own domestic profitability on All Access. Recognizing the success of previous *Star Trek* series on Netflix, Moonves remarked that "Star Trek [Discovery] could have sold anywhere"; and yet he "felt it was odd taking our content, which is the family jewels, and putting it in an organization with our competitors" (Pascale 2017b). Instead, Moonves claimed this franchise power should be brought under the umbrella of CBS' proprietary US streaming platform. Moonves also noted that the "action-adventure" spectacle—only affordable in this emerging market thanks to lucrative international licensing fees from Netflix—would make the series "travel" better (2017b). Indeed, *Variety's* Cynthia Littleton reported that the "marquee" status of the *Star Trek* franchise "commanded immediate interest from global buyers," leading Netflix to sign an $80 million contract for international rights to the new series as well as the five library series (some 727 episodes) (2017, 7). This arrangement would exceed *Discovery's* first season production budget of $6–$7 million per episode.

In relying upon *Discovery* as its flagship, CBS All Access participated in an historical valuation of the *Star Trek* franchise (though some might say overvaluation) as a viable support for new television services. In fact, the 1995 launch of *Voyager* as UPN flagship was not the first time television industries sought to launch a new channel on the back of the franchise. As a studio supplier of programming, Paramount Pictures had long sought its own network to gain greater control over distribution, even investing in the

FIGURE 37.3 *A scanned advertisement for the 1995* Star Trek: Voyager *premiere highlights use of the ongoing franchise as support to launch the new UPN network.*

DuMont Network, a failed attempt to sustain a fourth national television network, in the 1950s (Hilmes 1991, 72–4). By 1977, continued efforts led to plans for the Paramount Television Service, a new network that would initially offer its 58 signed affiliates a single night of programming combining original television movies with a new *Star Trek* series ("New" 1977). This spin-off, *Star Trek: Phase II*, would feature the return of William Shatner as Captain Kirk, capitalizing on the continuing success of the original 1966–1969 series in second-run syndication. Because its affiliate network reached only 57% of US households, however, Paramount could not command the same advertising rates as other networks. Disappointing revenue projections led to delay and eventual cancellation of the network's launch (Pearson and Messenger-Davies 2014, 51–2). In the fallout, Paramount redirected plans for *Phase II* into the first *Star Trek* feature film in 1978.

Successful or not, these broadcast era efforts to launch new television services relied upon franchising logic, using revival of successful library product to drive demand from audiences, affiliates, and advertisers alike. To support its own launch of a fourth US network a decade later, FOX too sought the rights to spin-off *Star Trek: The Next Generation* (Gendel 1986). At the time, however, Paramount aimed to use the growing market for syndicated programming to sell that new series directly to broadcast stations without the need for a network in first-run. Presaging Les Moonves's comments about *Discovery*, Paramount Television President Mel Harris explained: "since it is one of our family jewels, it made no sense to put it into somebody else's hands for distribution when we had the capability to give it the best possible shot ourselves" (Weinstein 1988). The later reliance of UPN and now CBS All Access on *Star Trek* extended an established broadcast framework for using the franchise to anchor new forms of television distribution.

BROADCAST TELEVISION AS PAY TELEVISION

This deep history accompanying CBS and this use of the *Star Trek* franchise, however, also calls into some question the value of such broadcast legacies in the streaming subscription realm. In a 2017 interview, CBS Interactive's Marc DeBevoise grappled with skepticism about All Access' transformation of a free broadcast service into a subscription purchase. "We totally hear you. We've seen the comments," he acknowledged of criticisms that CBS should put its best programming on its broadcast network rather than using exclusivity to prop up All Access. Yet he countered that "there are only so many slots and programs," as well as broadcast limitations on "the way the story is told and language and things like that" (Adalian 2017). Although *Discovery* promised to turn legions of fans into subscribers—in order to "super-serve those superfans," as DeBevoise puts it—many of these potential viewers resisted the notion that a *Trek* series might newly sit behind a paywall as "premium" content. As both CBS-branded product and a franchise embedded in the histories of broadcast delivery, *Trek* sometimes chafed against its new subscription premise.

Some fan reactions to the initial *Discovery* announcement challenged the exclusivization of the franchise. "First, let's talk about the giant Sehlat in the room," began an article on major fan portal *TrekMovie.com* days after CBS announced the series, highlighting disjuncture between the subscription model and the franchise's broadcast history. "The notion that it would cost money to see the new show upset a lot of people, who resent having to cough up more quatloos in order to watch something they should get over the broadcast airwaves or through their cable subscriptions," authors Brian Drew and Kayla Iacovino (2015) claimed.[1] Here the program's "cost" operated in relative rather than absolute terms: the authors believed US fans would have been "jumping up and down" had the series been announced for Netflix—assuming many already subscribed to that dominant streaming service—whereas the cost of subscribing to CBS All Access specifically for *Discovery* would likely be a new, additional cost. Cable was not free, but it generally included the local CBS channel, making the need to add All Access streaming an increase to an already burdensome cost. Meanwhile, cord cutters who abandoned cable would slowly see overall costs increase if forced to pay for individual subscriptions for all the services carrying desirable but exclusive franchises. Drew and Iacovino also suggested subscription barriers to access could hurt the series' ability to find an audience. Older *Star Trek* fans may not embrace streaming television, they posited, while casual viewers might have reduced chance of exposure to the series if not already subscribed to All Access for another reason.

While Drew and Iacovino glossed over a vast fan discourse, more than 1,000 comments other potential viewers made in response to their analysis, as well to the first *TrekMovie* article relaying CBS' announcement of the series (Drew 2015), fed these debates over the effective value of All Access as a means of accessing *Discovery*. "The problem for me is that CBS All-Access is, by its very nature, limited," wrote one commenter. "I will not pay $6/mo just to watch ONE episode of a show every week." Questioning whether fan viewership would be large enough to support the venture, and citing the mediocre ratings of the UPN series, another offered, "Don't they remember that nobody watched the last couple of series when it was on tv for free?" In this view, the broadcast history of the franchise made its ability to command premium subscriptions uncertain. Indeed, the status of *Discovery* as a product of the legacy broadcast institution CBS, rather than a premium cable outlet like HBO, created additional skepticism. One fan opined, "if you have CBS as part of a paid cable or satellite package . . . CBS All Access should be free similar to apps and other streaming services like HBO GO." The streaming service HBO Go was not, of course, "free" in its own right—but it was included at no extra cost for subscribers to the traditional HBO cable package. By that logic, some believed *Discovery* should be accessible to any viewers served by the original CBS network. A second comparison to HBO centered on the notion of quality, opposing CBS' broadcast legacy to HBO's premium reputation. *Discovery* "would only achieve its full potential if it was on HBO. Instead we have CBS." Skeptical that CBS could convince viewers to pay "for something they used to get for free," another devalued the service by reference to the traditional broadcast genres in which the network had traded: "Who really wants to watch the crappy sitcoms that CBS streams?" The broadcast context from which both CBS and *Star Trek* hailed encouraged many to question whether franchise content could sustain the value of broadcast institutions within the online subscription environment.

No consensus emerged here; even as some thought CBS was "taking for granted" fan willingness to pay, just as many reported eagerness to part with their money.

Nevertheless, these debates pointed to the tensions and challenges accompanying CBS use of franchise content to build bridges between legacy broadcast economies and streaming television. As potential viewers confronted those tensions, they worked through the value of these different forms of television delivery, evaluating not just economic costs, but just as crucially the continued accessibility of franchised television content to an existing viewership. On that point, debates about the merits of All Access often considered differentials in access that some viewers faced. As one fan noted, "there's the percentage of the population that doesn't have access to high speed internet." Viewers in rural locations watching via their cell phone faced excess provider data charges in addition to the All Access subscription fee, added several others.

Of course, as the case of UPN shows, broadcast models did not guarantee accessibility. Moreover, CBS occasionally disavowed the franchise's broadcast pedigree when deploying it to support the premium All Access model. CBS Interactive's Jim Lanzone, for example, argued that broadcast television has not often nurtured the more niche science fiction genre: while broadcast television supported a few cult hits, he stated, "historically, a show like 'Star Trek' wouldn't necessarily be a broadcast show, at this point" (Johnson 2016). Lanzone added that while CBS could have matched *Discovery* to the more niche CW network or Showtime premium cable service (both CBS-owned), the franchise "just fit" better with the digital space of All Access. Some commentators scoffed at this, recuperating the broadcast legacy that perennially sustained the franchise—"the place it has been for hundreds of years" (Trendacosta 2016). Yet the question of what is truly the best "fit" for the franchise seems less important than the way in which CBS' use of *Trek* to move into new industry territory made the franchise a site of struggle over the comparative virtues of broadcasting and streaming, free and paid television—all centered on considerations of maintaining access.

CONCLUSION

Television franchising has long supported attempts to launch new channels. As this process continues into the future, the case of CBS All Access may provide further insight into the franchise strategies of competitors seeking to build their own over-the-top subscription television services in turn. After announcing in 2017 plans to launch its own proprietary streaming service, for example, Disney claimed it would soon withhold online distribution rights for film franchises like *Star Wars* and the Marvel Cinematic Universe from former close partner Netflix (Lopez 2017). As potential flagships for the premium over-the-top service envisioned, these franchises had been targeted for exclusivization. Within these ongoing industry efforts, however, access to new channel spaces has sometimes become a source of consternation for those trying to follow familiar content across different channel boundaries. The movement across channel spaces that franchising can encourage requires consumers and industries alike to negotiate significant geographic, technological, economic, and cultural barriers to access along the way. In the case of CBS All Access, where a legacy television provider adapted its networking models to online subscription economies, reliance on franchises like *Star Trek* provided broadcast continuity amid the transformation to over-the-top streaming—while also situating those efforts in a longer historical tradition of managing industry changes via content appeals.

The central, ongoing challenge for CBS All Access lies in building a distinct, differentiable, and desired service that offers sufficient value for viewers to actively choose to subscribe. Franchising offers one logic whereby that value might be constructed and communicated. As Les Moonves stated in 2015, "There's about a billion channels out there and because of *Star Trek*, people will know what All Access is about" (Goldberg 2015). Franchise programs like *The Good Fight* and *Big Brother* play similar roles here, too—establishing what makes CBS different as a delivery service by providing more of the content to which CBS has exclusive control. The exclusivization of that content behind a paywall, however, foregrounds the considerations of access built into the name and premise of the service. CBS hopes viewers will make new efforts to access legacy products as it moves them into a streaming environment; viewers, for their part, must consider the value such access offers, as well as the barriers in the way of maintaining access. Whether in relation to *Star Trek*, or other library product, all seem to be asking: how much is access to this franchise worth?

NOTE

1 Sehlats are fictional Vulcan fauna. Quatloos are an alien currency from the *Star Trek* episode "The Gamesters of Triskelion."

REFERENCES

Adalian, Josef. 2017. "How CBS All Access Aims to Be a Streaming Player with *the Good Fight*, *Star Trek*, and More." *Vulture*, April 14. Accessed June 1, 2017. www.vulture.com/2017/04/cbs-all-access-good-fight-star-trek.html.

Barr, Merrill. 2015. "The 'X-Files' Revival Isn't about Fans or Closure, It's about Netflix." *Forbes*, March 24. Accessed May 31, 2017. www.forbes.com/sites/merrillbarr/2015/03/24/x-files-reboot/#f9287757c150.

Bond, Paul. 2016. "Leslie Moonves: Five CBS Freshman Shows Will Likely Be Renewed. *Hollywood Reporter*, March 8. Accessed June 1, 2017. www.hollywoodreporter.com/news/leslie-moonves-five-cbs-freshman-873429.

Drew, Brian. 2015. "CBS Announces New *Star Trek* Series to Premiere in January 2017." *TrekMovie*, November 2. Accessed June 1, 2017. http://trekmovie.com/2015/11/02/cbs-announces-new-star-trek-series-to-premiere-in-january-2017/.

Drew, Brian and Kayla Iacovino. 2015. "What *Star Trek's* Move to CBS All Access Means for the Franchise." *TrekMovie*, November 16. Accessed June 1, 2017. http://trekmovie.com/2015/11/16/what-star-treks-move-to-cbs-all-access-means-for-the-franchise/.

Dumenco, Simon. 2014. "What We Talk about When We Talk about 'Content.'" *Advertising Age*, October 13. Accessed May 31, 2017. Proquest.

Ellingson, Annlee. 2014. "Hulu Holdout CBS Launches On-Demand and Live Streaming." *LA Biz*, October 16. Accessed May 26, 2017. www.bizjournals.com/losangeles/news/2014/10/16/hulu-holdout-cbs-launches-on-demand-and-live.html.

Gendel, Morgan. 1986. "New 'Trek' Is on the Launch Pad." *Los Angeles Times*, October 11. Accessed June 1, 2017. Proquest Historical Newspapers.

Gitlin, Todd. 2000. *Inside Prime Time*. Berkeley: University of California Press.

Goldberg, Lesley. 2015. "Leslie Moonves Explains Why 'Star Trek' Went to CBS All Access." *Hollywood Reporter*, November 3. Accessed June 1, 2017. www.hollywoodreporter.com/live-feed/why-star-trek-went-cbs-836710.

Hilmes, Michele. 1991. *Hollywood and Broadcasting: From Radio to Cable*. Urbana: University of Illinois Press.

Johnson, Derek. 2013. *Media Franchising: Creative License and Collaboration in the Culture Industries*. New York: New York University Press.

Johnson, Eric. 2016. "Next Year's 'Star Trek' Reboot May Have Naked Aliens and Swearing, CBS Digital Chief Says." *Recode*, November 10. Accessed June 1, 2017. www.recode.net/2016/11/10/13557358/star-trek-reboot-naked-aliens-swearing-cbs-digital-chief-jim-lanzone-podcast.

Knee, Jonathan. 2011. "Why Content Isn't King." *The Atlantic*, July/August. Accessed May 31, 2017. www.theatlantic.com/magazine/archive/2011/07/why-content-isnt-king/308551/.

Lafayette, Jon. 2016. "TV Feels Its Oats." *Broadcasting & Cable*, May 23. Accessed May 31, 2017. Proquest.

Littleton, Cynthia. 2017. "New Platforms, New Profits." *Variety Premier*, March 23.

Lopez, Ricardo. 2017. " 'Star Wars,' Marvel Films Moving from Netflix to Disney Streaming Service." *Variety*, September 7. Accessed October 8, 2017. http://variety.com/2017/biz/news/star-wars-marvel-movies-disney-streaming-service-1202549993/.

Neff, Jack. 2011. "As Devices and Distribution Compete, Content Enjoys a Renaissance." *Advertising Age*, October 3. Accessed May 31, 2017. Proquest.

"Netflix to Beam New CBS 'Star Trek' Television Series to 188 Countries Around the World." 2016. *Netflix Media Center*, July 18. Accessed May 32, 2017. https://media.netflix.com/en/press-releases/netflix-to-beam-new-cbs-star-trek-television-series-in-188-countries-around-the-world.

"New *Star Trek* Debut Postponed." 1977. *Los Angeles Times*, November 9. Proquest Historical Newspapers.

"New *Star Trek* Series Coming to CBS All Access." 2015. *CBS.com*, November 2. Accessed May 26, 2017. www.cbs.com/shows/star-trek-series/.

Pascale, Anthony. 2017a. "Moonves: Couple of Star Trek Discovery Episodes 'In the Can'—Expects Younger Demo." *TrekMovie*, May 3. Accessed June 1, 2017. http://trekmovie.com/2017/05/05/moonves-couple-of-star-trek-discovery-episodes-in-the-can-expects-younger-demo/.

Pascale, Anthony. 2017b. "*Star Trek Discovery* Back on for Fall; CBS CEO Talks Netflix Importance." *TrekMovie*, May 3. Accessed June 1, 2017. http://trekmovie.com/2017/05/03/star-trek-discovery-back-on-for-fall-cbs-ceo-talks-netflix-importance/.

Pearson, Roberta and Márie Messenger Davis. 2014. Star Trek *and American Television*. Berkeley: University of California Press.

Raddon, Rich. 2016. "In 2017, Media Companies Will Finally Realize They Are Being Disrupted by the Very Platforms that Distribute Their Content." *Recode*, December 13. Accessed June 1, 2017. www.recode.net/2016/12/13/13913184/2017-platform-disrupts-network-content.

Spangler, Todd. 2015. "CBS Expands 'All Access' Live Local TV Streaming to Two-Thirds of U.S." *Variety*, May 14. Accessed May 26, 2017. http://variety.com/2015/digital/news/cbs-expands-all-access-live-local-tv-streaming-to-two-thirds-of-u-s-1201495915/.

Spangler, Todd. 2017a. "Showtime Hits 1.5 Million Streaming Subscribers, CBS All Access Nears Same." *Variety*, February 13. Accessed May 26, 2017. http://variety.com/2017/digital/news/showtime-cbs-all-access-streaming-1-5-million-subscribers-1201986844/.

Spangler, Todd. 2017b. "'Star Trek: Discovery' Drives CBS Mobile App Downloads Up by 64%." *Variety*, September 26. Accessed October 9, 2017. http://variety.com/2017/digital/news/star-trek-discovery-drives-cbs-mobile-app-downloads-up-by-64-study-1202573634/.

"*The Good Wife* Spinoff to Star Christine Baranski and Cush Jumbo." 2016. *CBS.com*, May 18. Accessed May 26, 2017. www.cbs.com/shows/the_good_wife/news/1005235/the-good-wife-spinoff-to-star-christine-baranski-and-cush-jumbo/.

Trendacosta, Katharine. 2016. "Despite Current Glut of Successful Scifi Shows, CBS Executive Says New *Star Trek* Wouldn't Work on TV." *io9*, November 11. Accessed June 1, 2017. http://io9.gizmodo.com/despite-current-glut-of-successful-scifi-shows-cbs-exe-1788962348.

Weinstein, Steve. 1988. "Newest 'Star Trek' Zooms at Warp Speed." *Los Angeles Times*, May 3. Accessed June 1, 2017. http://articles.latimes.com/1988-05-03/entertainment/ca-2130_1_star-trek.

Winslow, George. 2015. "CBS All Access Expands Access." *Broadcasting & Cable*, July 16. Accessed May 26, 2017. www.broadcastingcable.com/news/next-tv/cbs-all-access-expands-access/142623.

Contributors

Peter Alilunas is an assistant professor of Media Studies at the University of Oregon. He is the author of *Smutty Little Movies: The Creation and Regulation of Adult Video*.

Cory Barker is a Ph.D. candidate in the Department of Communication & Culture at Indiana University. He researches the intersections between television and social media, particularly how contemporary television networks use social media to reaffirm core industry strategies. His work appears in *Television & New Media, The Popular Culture Studies Journal*, and *The Projector: A Journal on Film, Media, and Culture*.

Christine Becker is an associate professor in the Department of Film, Television, and Theatre at the University of Notre Dame specializing in film and television history and critical analysis. Her book *It's the Pictures That Got Small: Hollywood Film Stars on 1950s Television* won the 2011 IAMHIST Michael Nelson Prize for a Work in Media and History. She is currently working on a research project exploring contemporary American and British television and issues of cultural taste.

James Bennett is Professor of Television and Digital Culture at Royal Holloway, University of London. He is co-director of the Centre for the History of Television Culture & Production.

Courtney Brannon Donoghue is an assistant professor in Cinema Studies at Oakland University in Rochester, Michigan. Her first book, *Localising Hollywood*, explores Hollywood's localized operations across Europe and Latin America since the 1990s. Her work has appeared in *Cinema Journal, Media, Culture & Society*, and *Quarterly Review of Film & Video*.

Hanne Bruun is an associate professor and head of the Media, Communication and Society research program at the Department of Media and Journalism Studies, Aarhus University (AU), Denmark. She is the founder and head of the Centre for Media Production Studies at AU, and her research areas are production studies, the aesthetics and genres of television, and media industry studies. She is the author of seven books, including *Danish Television Satire*.

Christopher Chávez is an associate professor at the University of Oregon and his research lies at the intersection of globalization, media, and culture. He is author of *Reinventing the Latino Television Viewer: Language Ideology and Practice* and co-editor of *Identity: Beyond Tradition and McWorld Neoliberalism*. His work has appeared in peer-reviewed journals including *Television and New Media, International Journal of Communication*, and *Critical Studies in Media Communication*.

Aymar Jean Christian is an assistant professor of Communication Studies at Northwestern University and a Fellow at the Peabody Media Center. His first book, *Open TV: Innovation Beyond Hollywood and the Rise of Web Television*, argues that the web brought innovation to television by opening development to independent producers. He leads Open TV (beta), a research project and platform for television by queer, trans, and cis-women and artists of color.

David Craig is a media and entertainment professor, scholar, producer, and activist. As a Clinical Assistant Professor at USC's Annenberg School for Communications and Journalism, he manages the Media and Entertainment track in the Masters in Communications Management Program. He is engaged in a global, multiyear research initiative mapping the dimensions of social media entertainment.

Michael Curtin is the Duncan and Suzanne Mellichamp Professor in the Department of Film and Media Studies at the University of California, Santa Barbara. He is also director of the 21st Century Global Dynamics Initiative and executive editor of *global-e*.

Evan Elkins is an assistant professor of Media and Visual Culture in the Department of Communication Studies at Colorado State University, where he researches and teaches on various issues regarding media industries, film and television, digital culture, and globalization.

Jonathan Gray is Professor of Media and Cultural Studies at University of Wisconsin-Madison. He is author of four books including *Watching with The Simpsons: Television, Parody, and Intertextuality* and *Television Entertainment*, and co-editor of seven collections including *Keywords in Media Studies* and *The Companion to Media Authorship*.

Timothy Havens is a professor of Communication Studies, African American Studies, and International Studies at the University of Iowa, where he also serves as chair of the Department of Communication Studies. He is the author of *Black Television Travels: African American Media Around the Globe* and *Global Television Marketplace*; co-author of *Understanding Media Industries*; and co-editor of *Popular Television in Eastern Europe Before and Since Socialism*. He is also a former Senior Fulbright Scholar to Hungary.

Michele Hilmes is Professor Emerita at the University of Wisconsin–Madison. Her many books include *Radio Voices: American Broadcasting 1922–1952, Network*

Nations: A Transnational History of British and American Broadcasting, and *Only Connect: A Cultural History of Broadcasting in the United States*. In 2017 she received the Distinguished Career Achievement Award from the Society for Cinema and Media Studies.

Kyra Hunting is an assistant professor of Media Arts and Studies at the University of Kentucky. Her work has appeared in *Quarterly Review of Film and Video, Transformative Works and Culture, Communication Review, Cinema Journal, Spectator*, and *Journal of Popular Culture*.

Deborah L. Jaramillo is an associate professor of Film and Television Studies at Boston University. Her first book, *Ugly War Pretty Package: How CNN and Fox News Made the Invasion of Iraq High Concept*, analyzes how cable news narrativized, stylized, and marketed the 2003 invasion of Iraq. Her current book project examines the circumstances leading to the National Association of Radio and Television Broadcasters' adoption of the 1952 Television Code.

Derek Kompare is an associate professor of Film and Media Arts in the Meadows School of the Arts at Southern Methodist University. He is the author of *Rerun Nation: How Repeats Invented American Television, CSI*, and several journal articles and anthology chapters on television history and form. He is also the co-editor of *Making Media Work: Cultures of Management in the Entertainment Industries*.

Jon Kraszewski is an associate professor and program coordinator of Visual and Sound Media at Seton Hall University. He is author of the books *Reality TV* and *The New Entrepreneurs: An Institutional History of Television Anthology Writers*.

Yongli Li is a Ph.D. candidate in the Department of East Asian Languages and Cultural Studies at the University of California, Santa Barbara. Her research interests include Chinese film and media, media industries, and urban studies.

Lori Kido Lopez is an associate professor of Media and Cultural Studies in the Communication Arts Department at the University of Wisconsin–Madison. She is the author of *Asian American Media Activism: Fighting for Cultural Citizenship* and co-editor of *The Routledge Companion to Asian American Media*.

Amanda D. Lotz is Professor in the Department of Communication Studies at the University of Michigan and Fellow at the Peabody Media Center. She is the author, co-author, or editor of eight books that explore television and media industries including *The Television Will Be Revolutionized* and *Portals: A Treatise on Internet-Distributed Television*.

Nick Marx is an assistant professor of Media Studies at Colorado State University. He is the author of a forthcoming book about television sketch comedy, and he is co-editor of the book *Saturday Night Live and American TV*.

Myles McNutt is an assistant professor of Communication at Old Dominion University, researching the media industries with a focus on contemporary television. His work can be found in *Television & New Media, Media Industries Journal*, and *The Velvet Light Trap*, as well as online at *The A.V. Club, Slate*, and his personal blog, *Cultural Learnings*.

Caryn Murphy is an associate professor of Radio-TV-Film at the University of Wisconsin Oshkosh. Her research on television has appeared in the *Historical Journal of Film, Radio and Television, Journal of Screenwriting*, and several edited volumes.

Laurie Ouellette is Professor of Media and Cultural Studies at the University of Minnesota. She is author of *Lifestyle TV* and co-editor of *Keywords for Media Studies*, among other books.

Subin Paul is a doctoral candidate in the School of Journalism and Mass Communication at the University of Iowa. His research articles have appeared in *Journalism, Contemporary South Asia, Journalism History, Journalism Practice*, and *Newspaper Research Journal*. He was awarded the Columbia University Taraknath Das Foundation Fellowship for the year 2017.

Matthew Thomas Payne is an assistant professor in the Department of Film, Television, & Theatre at the University of Notre Dame. He is author of *Playing War: Military Video Games after 9/11* as well as co-editor of the anthologies *Flow TV: Television in the Age of Media Convergence* and *Joystick Soldiers: The Politics of Play in Military Video Games*.

Allison Perlman is an associate professor in the Department of Film and Media Studies and Department of History at the University of California, Irvine. She is the author of *Public Interests: Media Advocacy and Struggles Over US Television* and co-editor of *Flow TV: Television in the Age of Media Convergence*. She also is the faculty director of The Public Media Research Project.

Alisa Perren is an associate professor and associate Chair in the Department of Radio-TV-Film at The University of Texas at Austin. She is co-editor of *Media Industries: History, Theory, and Method* and author of *Indie, Inc.: Miramax and the Transformation of Hollywood in the 1990s*. She is also co-founder, editorial collective member, and former co-managing editor for the journal *Media Industries*. Her current co-authored book project is *The American Comic Book Industry and Hollywood*.

Karen Petruska is an assistant professor of Communication Studies at Gonzaga University. A graduate of Georgia State University, she has published in *Creative Industries, Spectator, Popular Communication, The Velvet Light Trap, In Media Res, Flow, Antenna*, and *MIP Research*, as well as three edited volumes.

Avi Santo is an associate professor in the Department of Communications at Old Dominion University and Director of the Institute for the Humanities at ODU. He is the author of *Selling the Silver Bullet: The Lone Ranger and Transmedia Brand Licensing* and co-editor of *Making Media Work: Cultures of Management in the Entertainment Industries*. His research focuses on consumer products, licensing, merchandising, and retail practices within the media industries.

Barbara Selznick is an associate professor in the School of Theatre, Film, and Television at the University of Arizona. She is the author of *Sure Seaters: The Emergence of Art House Cinema* and *Global Television: Co-Producing Culture*. Her work has appeared in *Science Fiction Film and Television, Film History, Quarterly Review of Film and Television, Spectator*, and *Global Media Journal*.

Erin Copple Smith is an assistant professor in Media Studies at Austin College in Sherman, Texas. Her work has been published in *Beyond Prime Time: TV Formats in the Post-Network Era* and *Popular Communication*. Her primary areas of interest are in media conglomerates and the relationship between ownership and content, television and film's advertising and promotional strategies, as well as conglomerate-based overlaps among the broadcasting, film and music industries.

Niki Strange is currently a post-doctoral researcher for the ADAPT Social Media Project at Royal Holloway, University of London. She is also an innovation and business strategist for creative media companies.

Travis Vogan is an associate professor in the School of Journalism & Mass Communication and the Department of American Studies at the University of Iowa. He is the author of *Keepers of the Flame: NFL Films and the Rise of Sports Media* and *ESPN: The Making of a Sports Media Empire*.

Kristen J. Warner is an associate professor in the Department of Journalism and Creative Media at The University of Alabama. She is the author *The Cultural Politics of Colorblind TV Casting*. Her research interests explore televisual racial representation and its place within the media industries, particularly within the practice of casting and other kinds of creative labor. Her work can be found in academic journals and a host of anthologies and online websites such as the *Los Angeles Review of Books, Antenna, Flow*, and *In Media Res*.

Faye Woods is a lecturer in Film and Television at the University of Reading and author of the monograph *British Youth Television*. Her work has also appeared in the journals *Television & New Media, Critical Studies in Television, Cinema Journal*, and *Journal of British Cinema and Television*, as well as the edited collections *Television Aesthetics and Style, Shane Meadows: Critical Essays*, and *Multiplicities: Cycles, Sequels, Remakes and Reboots in Film & Television*.

Melissa Zimdars is an assistant professor in Communication and Media at Merrimack College. She earned her Ph.D. from the University of Iowa, and her book, *Watching Our Weights: Televising Fatness in the "Obesity Epidemic,"* is forthcoming.

Andrew Zolides is a visiting assistant professor at Xavier University. He researches the influence economy, a framework for understanding the strategies celebrities and brands use on social media to create audiences with significant value. His work appears in *Persona Studies, Childhood & Celebrity, Horror Studies,* and *Antenna.*

Index

Page numbers in *italic* indicate a figure on the corresponding page.